the
deliberate
dumbing
down
of america

the deliberate dumbing down of america

A Chronological Paper Trail
Revised and Abridged Edition

by Charlotte Thomson Iserbyt

CONSCIENCE PRESS

Copyright 1999, 2011 by Conscience Press. All rights reserved.
First Edition 1999
Revised and Abridged Edition 2011

Printed in the United States of America.
Acid-free paper. Archival quality.

Library of Congress Catalog Card Number: 98–89726
ISBN: 978-0-9667071-1-3

Conscience Press • P.O. Box 564 • Parkman, Ohio • 44080–0564

Printed by The Athens Printing Company, Athens, Georgia
Graphic design by Colin Leslie
Cover design by 3–D Research Company
Cartoons created by Joel Pett, Herald Leader of Lexington, Kentucky

---

IN MEMORIAM

This book is a small tribute to the late Honorable John M.
Ashbrook, 17th Congressional District of Ohio, whose work
in Congress during the 1960s and 1970s exposed the treasonous plans which ultimately led to the internationalization
and deliberate dumbing down of American education.

TABLE OF CONTENTS

A WORD

from the editor

Welcome to the "little edition" of the "big book"—*the deliberate dumbing down of america: A Chronological Paper Trail*. Since the original publication of the 743-page, 8½" x 11" tome, readers have requested a smaller, lighter version. In answer to those many requests, this revised and abridged version is now available.

The author, Charlotte Thomson Iserbyt, in the intervening decade since the original publication, obligingly posted the book as a free download at the Internet address deliberatedumbingdown.com. This accommodating access makes the revised and abridged version an interactive treat. Because of this arrangement, the purchaser of the new version has not only the advantage of a smaller book format, an additional chapter to update the content from 1999 to 2011, but the extra feature of being able to read any and all of the material in the original edition as well!

The afterword, glossary, resources, appendices and index have all been removed from the 2011 version, but are all available at your fingertips for further examination on the website. Entries within the book that have been abridged or removed in the 2011 edition are marked with the symbol **[ddd]**, and references to appendices, etc., are noted so the reader can examine them at the download site on the Internet at the point they were introduced in the original. All instances where there are references like "Ed. Note" or "ed." within an inserted comment are the expressions of the author. Except for the new Update, the rest of the book is in its original form regarding dates of events.

We hope we have met your needs and requests with this new version. For those who are reading the book for the first time, enjoy!—and as the cover note says, "This book will change *forever* the way you look at your child's education."

CYNTHIA WEATHERLY

The human brain should be used for processing, not storage.

—Thomas A. Kelly, Ph.D.
The Effective School Report

FOREWORD

Charlotte Iserbyt is to be greatly commended for having put together the most formidable and practical compilation of documentation describing the "deliberate dumbing down" of American children by their education system. Anyone interested in the truth will be shocked by the way American social engineers have systematically gone about destroying the intellect of millions of American children for the purpose of leading the American people into a socialist world government controlled by behavioral and social scientists.

Mrs. Iserbyt has also documented the gradual transformation of our once academically successful education system into one devoted to training children to become compliant human resources to be used by government and industry for their own purposes. This is how fascist-socialist societies train their children to become servants of their government masters. The successful implementation of this new philosophy of education will spell the end of the American dream of individual freedom and opportunity. The government will plan your life for you, and unless you comply with government restrictions and regulations your ability to pursue a career of your own choice will be severely limited.

What is so mind boggling is that all of this is being financed by the American people themselves through their own taxes. In other words, the American people are underwriting the destruction of their own freedom and way of life by lavishly financing through federal grants the very social scientists who are undermining our national sovereignty and preparing our children to become the dumbed-down vassals of the new world order. It reminds one of how the Nazis charged their victims train fare to their own doom.

One of the interesting insights revealed by these documents is how the social engineers use a deliberately created education "crisis" to move their agenda forward by offering radical reforms that are sold to the public as fixing the crisis—which they never do. The new reforms simply set the stage for the next crisis, which provides the pretext for the next move forward. This is the dialectical process at work, a process our behavioral engineers have learned to use very effectively. Its success depends on the ability of the "change agents" to continually deceive the public which tends to believe anything the experts tell them.

And so, our children continue to be at risk in America's schools. They are at risk academically because of such programs as whole language, mastery learning, direct instruction, Skinnerian operant conditioning, all of which have created huge learning problems that inevitably lead to what is commonly known as Attention Deficit Disorder and the drugging of four million children with the powerful drug Ritalin. Mrs. Iserbyt has dealt extensively with the root causes of immorality in our society and the role of the public schools in the teaching of moral relativism (no right/no wrong ethics). She raises a red flag regarding the current efforts of left-wing liberals and right-wing conservatives (radical center) to come up with a new kid on the block—"common ground" character education—which will, under the microscope, turn out to be the same warmed-over values education alert parent groups have resisted for over fifty years. This is a perfect example of the Hegelian Dialectic at work.

The reader will find in this book a plethora of information that will leave no doubt in the mind of the serious researcher exactly where the American education system is headed. If we wish to stop this juggernaut toward a socialist-fascist system, then we must restore educational freedom to America. Americans forget that the present government education system started as a Prussian import in the 1840's–'50's. It was a system built on Hegel's belief that the state was "God" walking on earth. The only way to restore educational freedom, and put education back into the hands of parents where it belongs, is to get the federal government, with its coercive policies, out of education. The billions of dollars being spent by the federal government to destroy educational freedom must be halted, and that can only be done by getting American legislators to understand that the American people want to remain a free people, in charge of their own lives and the education of their children.

SAMUEL L. BLUMENFELD

PREFACE

Coexistence on this tightly knit earth should be viewed as an existence not only without wars... but also without [the government] telling us how to live, what to say, what to think, what to know, and what not to know.
—Aleksandr Solzhenitsyn, from a speech given September 11, 1973[1]

Educated men are as much superior to uneducated men as the living are to the dead.
—Aristotle, 384–322 B.C.[2]

[ddd]

The United States is engaged in a war. People write important books about war: books documenting the battles fought, the names of the generals involved, the names of those who fired the first shot. This book is simply a history book about another kind of war:

- one fought using psychological methods;
- a one-hundred-year war;
- a different, more deadly war than any in which our country has ever been involved;
- a war about which the average American hasn't the foggiest idea.

The reason Americans do not understand this war is because it has been fought in secret—in the schools of our nation, targeting our children who are captive in classrooms. The wagers of this war are using very sophisticated and effective tools:

- Hegelian Dialectic (common ground, consensus and compromise)

- Gradualism (two steps forward; one step backward)
- Semantic deception (redefining terms to get agreement without understanding).

The Hegelian Dialectic[3] is a process formulated by the German philosopher Georg Wilhelm Friedrich Hegel (1770–1831) and used by Karl Marx in codifying revolutionary Communism as dialectical materialism. As Sam Blumenfeld pointed out, Hegel believed that the state was "God" walking on earth, the evidence of which can be found in his dialectic. This process can be illustrated as:

Thesis   Antithesis

Synthesis
(consensus)

The "Thesis" represents either an established practice or point of view which is pitted against the "Antithesis"—usually a crisis of opposition fabricated or created by change agents—causing the "Thesis" to compromise itself, incorporating some part of the "Antithesis" to produce the "Synthesis"—sometimes called consensus. This is the primary tool in the bag of tricks used by change agents who are trained to direct this process all over the country; much like the in-service training I received. A good example of this concept was voiced by T.H. Bell when he was U.S. Secretary of Education: "[We] need to create a crisis to get consensus in order to bring about change." (The reader might be reminded that it was under T.H. Bell's direction that the U.S. Department of Education implemented the changes "suggested" by *A Nation at Risk*—the alarm that was sounded in the early 1980s to announce the "crisis" in education.)

Since we have been, as a nation, so relentlessly exposed to this Hegelian dialectical process (which is essential to the smooth operation of the "system") under the guise of "reaching consensus" in our involvement in parent-teacher organizations, on school boards, in legislatures, and even in goal setting in community service organizations and groups—including our churches—I want to explain clearly how it works in a practical application. A good example with which most of us can identify involves property taxes for local schools. Let us consider an example from Michigan—

The internationalist change agents must abolish local control (the "Thesis") in order to restructure our schools from academics to global workforce training (the "Synthesis"). Funding of education with the property tax allows local control, but it also enables the change agents and teachers' unions to create higher and higher school budgets paid for with higher taxes, thus infuriating homeowners. Eventually, property owners accept the change agents' radical proposal (the "Anti– thesis") to reduce their property taxes by transferring education funding from the local property tax to the state income tax. Thus, the change agents accomplish their ultimate goal: the transfer of funding of education from the local level to the state level. When this transfer occurs it increases state/federal control and funding, leading to the federal/internationalist goal of implementing global workforce training through the schools (the "Synthesis").[4]

Regarding the power of "gradualism," remember the story of the frog and how he didn't save himself because he didn't realize what was happening to him? He was thrown into cold water which, in turn, was gradually heated up until finally it reached the boiling point and he was dead. This is how "gradualism" works through a series of "created crises" which utilize Hegel's dialectical process, leading us to more radical change than we would ever otherwise accept.

In the instance of "semantic deception"—do you remember your kindly principal telling you that the new decision-making program would help your child make better decisions? What good parent wouldn't want his or her child to learn how to make "good" decisions? Did you know that the decision-making program is the same controversial values clarification program recently rejected by your school board and against which you may have given repeated testimony? As I've said before, the wagers of this intellectual social war have employed very effective weapons to implement their changes.

This war has, in fact, become the war to end all wars. If citizens on this planet can be brainwashed or robotized, using dumbed-down Pavlovian/Skinnerian education, to accept what those in control want, there will be no more wars. If there are no rights or wrongs, there will be no one wanting to "right" a "wrong." Robots have no conscience. The only permissible conscience will be the United Nations or a global conscience. Whether an action is good or bad will be decided by a "Global Government's Global Conscience," as recommended by Dr. Brock Chisholm, executive secretary of the World Health Organization, Interim Commission, in 1947—and later in 1996 by current United States Secretary of State Madeline Albright. (See quotes in entry under 1947.)

You may protest, "But, no one has died in this war." Is that the only criteria we have with which to measure whether war is war? Didn't Aristotle say it well when he said, "Educated men are as much superior to uneducated men as the living are to the dead"? To withhold the tools of education can kill a person's spirit just as surely as a bullet his body. The tragedy is that many Americans have died in other wars to protect the freedoms being taken away in this one. This war which produces the death of intellect and freedom is not waged by a foreign enemy but by the silent enemy in the ivory towers, in our own government, and in tax-exempt foundations—the enemy whose every move I have tried to document in this book, usually in his/her/its own words.

For over a twenty-five-year period the research used in this chronology has been collected from many sources: the United States Department of Education; international agencies; state agencies; the media; concerned educators; parents; legislators, and talented researchers with whom I have worked. In the process of gathering this information two beliefs that most Americans hold in common became clear:

1) If a child can read, write and compute at a reasonably proficient level, he will be able to do just about anything he wishes, enabling him to control his destiny to the extent that God allows (remain free);

2) Providing such basic educational proficiencies is not and should not be an expensive proposition.

Since most Americans believe the second premise—that providing basic educational proficiencies is not and should not be an expensive proposition—it becomes obvious that it is only a radical agenda, the purpose of which is to change values and attitudes (brainwash), that is the costly agenda. In other words, brainwashing by our schools and universities is what is bankrupting our nation and our children's minds.

This book, or collection of research in book form, was put together primarily to satisfy my own need to see the various components which led to the dumbing down of the United States of America assembled in chronological order—in writing. Even I, who had observed these weird activities taking place at all levels of government, was reluctant to accept a malicious intent behind each individual, chronological activity or innovation, unless I could connect it with other, similar activities taking place at other times. This book, which makes such connections, has provided for me a much-needed sense of closure.

the deliberate dumbing down of america is also a book for my children, grandchildren, and great-grandchildren. I want them to know that there were thousands of Americans who may not have died or been shot at in overseas wars, but were shot at in small-town "wars" at school board meetings, at state legislative hearings on education, and, most importantly, in the media. I want my progeny to know that whatever intellectual and spiritual freedoms to which they may still lay claim were fought for—are a result of—the courageous work of incredible people who dared to tell the truth against all odds.

I want them to know that there will always be hope for freedom if they follow in these people's footsteps; if they cherish the concept of "free will"; if they believe that human beings are special, not animals, and that they have intellects, souls, and consciences. I want them to know that if the government schools are allowed to teach children K–12 using Pavlovian/Skinnerian animal training methods—which provide tangible rewards only for correct answers—there can be no freedom.

Why? People "trained"—not educated—by such educational techniques will be fearful of taking principled, sometimes controversial, stands when called for because these people will have been programmed to speak up only if a positive reward or response is forthcoming. The price of freedom has often been paid with pain and loneliness

Just as Barbara Tuchman or another historian would do in writing the history of the other kinds of wars, I have identified chronologically the major battles, players, dates and places. I know that researchers and writers with far more talent than I will feel that I have neglected some key events in this war. I stand guilty on all counts, even before their well-researched charges are submitted. Yes, much of importance has been left out, due to space limitations, but the overview of the battlefields and maneuvers will give the reader an opportunity to glimpse the immensity of this conflict.

In order to win a battle one must know who the "real" enemy is. Otherwise, one is shooting in the dark and often hitting those not the least bit responsible for the mayhem. This book, hopefully, identifies the "real" enemy and provides Americans involved in this war—be they plain, ordinary citizens, elected officials, or traditional teachers—with the ammunition to fight to obtain victory.

[ddd]

Endnotes:

1 Noted Soviet dissident, slave labor camp intern, and author of *The Gulag Archipelago* and numerous other books.

2 *The Basic Works of Aristotle*, Richard McKeon, Ed., from *Familiar Quotations* by John Bartlett, 14th ed. (Little, Brown & Co.: Boston, Toronto, 1968).

3 Dean Gotcher, author of *The Dialectic & Praxis: Diaprax and the End of the Ages* and other materials dealing with dialectical consensus building and human relations training, has done some excellent work in this area of research. For more detailed information on this process, please write to: Dean Gotcher, Box 233, Herndon, KS 67739; or contact him by email at deangotcher@gmail.com. You may access his website at: http://www.authorityresearch.com.

4 See the Internet version for Appendix XXII for an article by Tim Clem which explains this process in much more detail.

ACKNOWLEDGMENTS

In particular I want to thank a handful of government officials who provided me with important documents. They must remain anonymous for obvious reasons.

I would also like to mention several incredibly fine Americans who are unfortunately no longer with us, who provided me with the priceless research and necessary resources to write this book. They are: Jo-Ann Abrigg, O. Jerome (Jed) Brown, Erica Carle, Shirley Correll, Rexford Daniels, Norman Dodd, Ruth Feld, Ann Frazier, Peggy Grimes, Rosalind Haley, Maureen Heaton, Mary Jo Heiland, Mary Larkin, Gene Malone, Judge Robert Morris, Walter Crocker Pew, LuAnne Robson, Mary Royer, Elisabeth Russinoff, and Georgianna Warner.

Very special thanks go to the following education researchers and writers with whom I have worked and who have contributed to and made this book possible (in alphabetical order): Mary Adams, Polly Anglin, Virginia Birt Baker, Marilyn Boyer, Peggy and Dennis Cuddy, Bettina Dobbs, Janet Egan, Melanie Fields, Betty Freauf, Jeannie Georges, Peggy and Robert Goldsborough, Karen Hayes, Tracey Hayes, Ann Herzer, Anita Hoge, Berit Kjos, Betsy Kraus, Jacqueline and Malcolm Lawrence, Mina Legg, Bettye and Kirk Lewis, Joanne Lisac, Billie Lyon, Joan Masters, Nancy Maze, Judith McLemore, Janelle Moon, Opal Moore, Barbara Morris, Kelleigh Nelson, Debbie Niwa, Cris Shardelman, Chey Simonton, Debbie Stevens, Rose Stewart, Mary Thompson, Elisabeth Trotto, Geri Wenta, and Jil Wilson. Thanks are also extended to their respective spouses who made their contributions possible.

Obviously, the job of editing this book was monumental! Cynthia Weatherly, who is one of the nation's finest education researchers and talented writers and with whom I have worked for twenty years, took my rough manuscript and turned it into a mammoth historical presentation. Her incredible work on this book represents a true labor of love for this nation and for our children and grandchildren. I will forever be grateful to Cindi and her husband, Neal, who extended a gracious welcome to me each time I descended upon them, including a four-month stay one winter!

In addition, my deepest thanks go to the Leslie family of Conscience Press—Sarah, Lynn and Colin, and Sarah's parents, Paul and Jean Huling, each of whom contributed in his own vital way to the publication of this book in such a professional manner. How this family published this book and managed at the same time to make three moves in and out of different houses during this one-year period is beyond belief. There are no words to express this writer's gratitude for this one family's contribution to the preservation of liberty for all Americans.

Of course, the book would never have seen the light of day without the very professional job delivered by Tim and Janet Field of The Athens Printing Company of Athens, Georgia. Tim's unbelievable patience with interminable delays was beyond the call of duty. Additionally, thanks to Tim and Janet's son, Chan Field, who has taken up the mantel at Athens Printing and produced the "Revised and Abridged" version of *the deliberate dumbing down of america*.

And last, but not least, thanks to the folks at the reference desk of the University of Georgia Library, who cheerfully and professionally assisted the writer and editor with critical documentation, and to Air Tran, whose extremely reasonable airfare from Boston to Atlanta allowed Cindi and me to collaborate on the most important stages of this book's production.

Deepest apologies to whomever I have neglected to mention. You will find a special place in Heaven.

INTRODUCTION

In the fall of 1972 a small group of students in an introduction to educational psychology class at a midwestern university saved every single soul in the lifeboat.

The professor became agitated. "No! Go back and do the exercise again. Follow the instructions."

The students, products of the radical 1960s culture, expected this to be a small group assignment in creativity and ingenuity. They had worked out an intricate plan whereby everyone in the lifeboat could survive. When the professor persisted, the students resisted—and ultimately refused to do the exercise. Chalk up a victory to the human spirit.

However, it was a short-lived victory. This overloaded "lifeboat in crisis" represented a dramatic shift in education. The exercise—in which students were compelled to choose which humans were expendable and, therefore, should be cast off into the water—became a mainstay in classrooms across the country. Creative solutions? Not allowed. Instructions? Strictly adhered to. In truth, there is to be only one correct answer to the lifeboat drama: death.

[ddd]

Publication of *the deliberate dumbing down of america* is certain to add fuel to the fire in this nation's phonics wars. Ever since publication of her first work (*Back to Basics Reform or OBE Skinnerian International Curriculum*, 1985), Iserbyt has been trumpeting the fact that the Skinnerian method applied in the Exemplary Center for Reading Instruction (ECRI) is the very same method applied in Siegfried Engelmann's DISTAR (Direct Instruction System for Teaching and Remediation, now known as Reading Mastery). In her latest work, Iserbyt provides exhaustive documentation that Direct

Instruction (a.k.a. systematic, intensive phonics)—which is being institutionalized nationally under the guise of "traditional" phonics thanks to the passage of *The Reading Excellence Act of 1998*—relies on the Skinnerian method to teach reading.

Charlotte Iserbyt is the consummate whistle-blower. The writer describes her own personal experiences as a school board director and as senior policy advisor in the U.S. Department of Education's Office of Educational Research and Improvement—from which emanated most of the dumbing down programs described in this book. There are no sacred cows in Iserbyt's reporting of the chronological history of education reform. With little fanfare, the agendas and methods of key reform leaders (conservative and liberal) are allowed to unmask themselves in their own words and by their own actions. Of particular interest is Iserbyt's material on the issue of school "choice"—abundant evidence from both sides of the political spectrum. The reader will learn that private, Christian and home schools are all neatly tied into the reform web via computer technology, databanking, assessment testing and, ultimately, the intention to use rewards and penalties to enforce compliance to the "transformed" system of education in this country.

The careful researcher will appreciate the fact that the book is heavily documented but user-friendly. Citations are designed for the average reader, not just the academician. The chronological format of the book allows one to read forward or backward in time, or one entry at a time, according to personal preference. The accompanying appendices provide a source of in-depth topical material, which frees up the chronological text from becoming bogged down in details. The index and glossary are such valuable research tools that they are worth the price of the book.

Iserbyt does very little hand-holding throughout the book. Commentary is sparse; readers can make their own connections and insert their own personal experiences. Iserbyt has strategically laid down key pieces to a giant jigsaw puzzle. The overall picture is purposefully arranged to portray one point of view. However, readers will be hard-pressed to come up with an alternative view. Just when it seems that one piece of the puzzle is an isolated, insignificant event, suddenly one comes across a stunning new entry that puts the pieces tightly together to form a vivid picture of the overall plan. Try as one might, the reader cannot escape the consistent, deliberate, 100-year plan to dumb down the populace.

Amidst all of the policy documents and historical data in the book, one can easily identify the heart of the writer. Iserbyt gently reminds the reader that the real issue at hand is the child. It is America's children who are experiencing the full brunt of the new methods, new curricula and new agendas in the classroom. Many readers will experience the "light bulb" turning on as they fully come to understand how the innovations which have occurred in education during the last century affected their parents, themselves, their children and grandchildren.

Teachers may find the contents of this book particularly enlightening and refreshing. Iserbyt takes the reader behind the scenes to reveal the true nature of many popular classroom curricula. The truth will be comforting to those who have utilized certain programs or methods, and perhaps were troubled by them, but didn't know the full scope or plan behind them. Iserbyt does not ignore or soft-peddle the ethical issues, but encourages the reader to take the high moral ground.

[ddd]

S<small>ARAH</small> L<small>ESLIE</small>

the
deliberate
dumbing
down
of america

UPDATE:

from the noxious nineties
through the terrible twos

(You know it's true when it happens to you!)

Since the 1999 publication of *the deliberate dumbing down of america: A Chronological Paper Trail*, we have ushered in a new decade and millennium. The long-awaited 2000s are with us—"the terrible twos." Some legislative initiatives aimed at the year 2000 have had to be renamed or reformulated (*America 2000, Goals 2000*) because they did not meet their target goal of being in effect by the year 2000. We can thank the good Lord and strong-hearted Americans who saw through these proposals for what they were and rejected them out of hand.

During the "terrible twos" we have elected for two four-year terms another George Bush, former Texas governor who ushered in the school-to-work agenda for Texas schools. We have lived through 9/11, the first terrorist attack to take place on American soil. This decade has seen America at war in two different Middle Eastern countries—Iraq and Afghanistan. For the first time in our history we have experienced an effort to federalize the activities of "faith-based" organizations and their charities (communitarianism[1]). All of this has taken place in the midst of the federal establishment of educational outcomes. Education in these nebulous, unacademic outcomes has left our young people unable to cope with the ever-present global social upheaval.

In addition to the above, we have, for the first time in our history also, elected our first black President—Barack Obama, a self-professed community organizer who has been taught all of the methods used to move groups of citizens from one position to another. Thus far, during his administration he has attempted to lift the U.S. out of the financial hole this country

1

found itself in in 2008, allowed the military to find and assassinate Osama Bin Laden for planning and financing the attack on 9/11, and appointed a secretary of education from the failed Chicago school administration, Arne Duncan, who called for paying students for good grades.

Now you know why I have named this Update "from the noxious nineties to the terrible twos"!

For those who wonder if the education change agents have introduced any new programs, methods or ideas during this last decade, the answer is "No." While we have a new title—*No Child Left Behind*—it is in fact the carefully planned agenda that was spelled out in a small book published by The American Historical Association. This book entitled *Report of the Commission on the Social Studies: Conclusions and Recommendations of the Commission* (Charles Scribner's Sons: N.Y., 1934) was funded by the Trustees of the Carnegie Corporation. Harold Laski, a professor of British Socialism, said of this *Report*: "At bottom and stripped of its carefully neutral phrases, the *Report* is an educational program for a socialist America."[2]

The call for a socialist America, of course, requires that the schools abandon traditional academic "teaching" and substitute "workforce training" or "techademics" to accommodate the needs of a planned economy. The following two quotes pertain to the dangers inherent in such an abandonment of traditional education:

> "If education is beaten by training, civilization dies," he (C.S. Lewis) writes, for the "lesson of history" is that "civilization is a rarity, attained with difficulty and easily lost." It is the liberal arts, not vocational training, that preserves civilization by producing reasonable men and responsible citizens.
> —Gregory Dunn, "C.S. Lewis on Liberal Arts Education," *On Principle*, Vol. 7, No. 2, April, 1999.

> In the communist ideology the function of universal education is clear and easily understood. Universal education fits neatly into the authoritarian state. Education is tied directly to jobs—control of the job being the critical control point in an authoritarian state. Level of education, and consequently the level of employment, is determined first by the level of achievement in school. *They do not educate people for jobs that do not exist.* No such direct, controlled relationship between education and jobs exists in democratic countries. [emphasis added]
> —Eugene Maxwell Boyce, Professor of Educational Administration, College of Education, University of Georgia, *The Coming Revolution in Education: Basic Education and the New Theory of Schooling* (University Press of America, Inc.: Baton Rouge, 1983).

For those of you who may not have read the original *deliberate dumbing down of america* and for those of you who may have missed the importance of the following entry, in 1984 *The Washington Post* (May 14) published an article entitled "Industrial Policy Urged for GOP." Some quotes from this article will explain why the quotes from C.S. Lewis and Eugene Boyce are so important:

SAN FRANCISCO (UPI)—A conservative study group founded by supporters of President Reagan is about to issue a report that advocates Republicans shed some of their deep-rooted antipathy to a planned economy.

An industrial policy accepted by both political parties and by business and labor is essential to revitalize America's dwindling clout in the world economy, according to the study's editor, Professor Chalmers Johnson of the University of California.

"The Industrial Policy Debate" is to be issued today by the Institute for Contemporary Studies, a think-tank founded by presidential counselor Edwin Meese, Secretary of Defense Caspar Weinberger and other Reagan supporters.

...."Americans must come to grips with economic policy or go the way of England. We have probably got a decade before it becomes irreversible. ...many Republicans are painting themselves into a corner by attacking the very concept of industrial policy—arguing that it violates the sacred principles of private enterprise and free trade."

He [Johnson] cited as valid and successful national economic policy "the kind of government-business relationship" that has made Japan a leading economic force in the world. "A government-business relationship is needed in a competitive capitalist economy," he said.

"Reaganomics without an accompanying industrial policy to guide it, has been costly," Johnson said.

In 1992 President George H.W. Bush signed the *North American Free Trade Agreement* along with the President of Mexico and the Prime Minister of Canada. Our "industrial policy" was now in place. In 1993 the Heritage Foundation of Washington, DC, home of many policy-making neo-conservatives, celebrated their twentieth year of operation by publishing an annual report that featured a congratulatory story about Richard Allen, a Heritage policy analyst. An excerpt reads:

> The idea of the North American Free Trade Agreement (NAFTA) origi-
> nated with Heritage Fellow Richard Allen and has long been advocated by
> Heritage policy analysts.... The idea of creating a North American free trade
> zone from the Yukon to the Yucatan was first proposed by Heritage Distin-
> guished Fellow Richard Allen in the late 1970s, refined by then Presidential
> candidate Ronald Reagan, and further developed in a major 1986 Heritage
> Foundation study. (p. 4)

From 1994 forward, industry has vacated much of the United States, leaving the job market bereft of entry level jobs for many Americans. In the meantime, the educational establishment has continued to convert itself into a workforce training mode, even though there were going to be no jobs available. Since the schools have converted themselves into workforce train-ing centers, some industries are beginning to make their way back to the United States. They will be happy to have the prepared workers join their and other countries' industries that have built facilities here, since benefit packages have been reduced to bare bones and workers are completely trained for the jobs. There is no question that the "deliberate dumbing down" has been successful.

The agenda, initiated by Carnegie Corporation in the early thirties and facilitated by the United Nations Educational, Scientific, and Cultural Orga-nization (UNESCO), the Office of Economic Cooperation and Development

(OECD), numerous tax-exempt foundations, the U.S. Department of Education, the U.S. Chamber of Commerce and other governmental agencies, has been implemented over the years to the tune of hundreds of billions of taxpayers' dollars. The first ten years of this century have seen full-speed implementation of the above Carnegie Corporation's totalitarian/socialist world government agenda.

A press release dated October 14, 2011, issued by the Department of Housing and Urban Development,[3] relates to the finalization of the world government agenda through the use of sustainable development, primary weapon to destroy our republic through unconstitutional regional government. Proof that regional government is Communism was made very clear in an article by Morris Zeitlin, a sociology professor at the University of California at Los Angeles (UCLA), in an article he wrote for *The Communist Daily World*, November 1976, entitled "Planning Is Socialism's Trademark." Pertinent excerpts follow:

> In socialist countries, metropolitan regions enjoy metropolitan regional government and comprehensive planning, Of the many regions on the vast territory of the Soviet Union, the Moscow Region commands special attention, for it has been, since the 1917 Revolution, the country's economic and political center.
>
> The economic and functional efficiencies and the social benefits that comprehensive national, regional, and city planning make possible in socialist society explain the Soviet Union's enormous and rapid economic and social progress. Conversely, our profit-oriented ruling capitalist class makes comprehensive social and economic planning impossible, causing waste and chaos and dragging the entire nation into misery and suffering as its rule deteriorates and declines.

Zeitlin should be delighted with the HUD action mentioned above. His concerns, back in 1976, regarding the United States refusing to adopt this communist system of central planning seem, in retrospect, to have been unwarranted. We have accepted Communism (state planning and all its attendant evils) hook, line and sinker. The aforementioned press release from HUD's Brian Sullivan follows:

> HUD Awards Nearly $100 Million in new Grants to Promote Smarter and Sustainable Planning for Jobs and Economic Growth
>
> WASHINGTON: For the first time ever, the US Department of Housing and Urban Development (HUD) is awarding nearly $100 million in new grants to support more livable and sustainable communities across the country. HUD Secretary Shaun Donovan today announced that 45 regional areas will receive funding through a new initiative intended to build economic competitiveness by connecting housing with good jobs, quality schools and transportation.
>
> HUD's new *Sustainable Communities Regional Planning Grant Program* will support State, local, and tribal governments, as well as metropolitan planning organizations, in the development and execution of regional plans that integrate affordable housing with neighboring retail and business development. Many of the grants will leverage existing infrastructure and all reward local collaboration and innovation.

"Regions that embrace sustainable communities will have a built-in competitive edge in attracting jobs and private investment," said Donovan. "Planning our communities smarter means parents will spend less time driving and more time with their children; more families will live in safe, stable communities near good schools and jobs; and more businesses will have access to the capital and talent they need to grow and prosper. In awarding these grants we were committed to using insight and innovation from our stakeholders and local partners to develop a 'bottom-up' approach to changing federal policy as opposed to 'top-down.' Rather than sticking to the old Washington playbook of dictating how communities can invest their grants, HUD's application process encouraged creative thinking."

These grants are part of the Obama Administration's Partnership for Sustainable Communities, which brings HUD, the US Department of Transportation, and the US Environmental Protection Agency together to ensure that the agencies' policies, programs and funding consider affordable housing, transportation, and environmental protection together. The interagency collaboration gets better results for communities and uses taxpayer money more efficiently. Coordinating federal investments in infrastructure, facilities and services meets multiple economic, environmental, and community objectives with each dollar spent. The Partnership is helping communities across the country to create more housing choices, make transportation more efficient and reliable, reinforce existing investments and support vibrant and healthy neighborhoods that attract business. At a time when every dollar the federal government invests in jumpstarting the economy is critical, the President's plan ensures that all these agencies are coordinating efforts and targeting resources with precision. Reflecting this new collaboration, these grants were judged by a multidisciplinary review team, drawn from eight federal agencies and partners in philanthropy.

HUD's inaugural grants under this program will support metropolitan and multi-jurisdictional planning efforts that incorporate housing, land use, economic development, transportation and infrastructure. This holistic planning approach will benefit diverse areas across the US, including $25.6 million split evenly between regions with populations less than 500,000 and rural places (fewer than 200,000 people). HUD is reserving $2 million to help all of these areas build the needed capacity to execute their plans [in education, capacity building has meant computerization, ed].

The grants are awarded through one of two categories. One category of grants will assist regional planning for sustainable development where such plans do not currently exist. A second category of funding will support the implementation of existing sustainability plans.

Shelley Poticha, the director of HUD's new Office of Sustainable Housing and Communities, said, "The response to this program is huge. We were inundated with applications from every state and two territories—from central cities to rural areas and tribal governments. This program was designed by people from local government, and incorporated local input at every stage."

The use of small grant monies to implement the process of causing local, state and regional planning to meet federal standards is reminiscent of the use of federal education dollars to cause changes in curriculum and adopting of standards and "assessments"—the tail wagging the dog. This process was not successful in the days of the 1970s "Community Development Block Grants" nor in the improvement of public education.

Within the last ten years or so, many new tax exempt foundations have copied the Carnegie model. The Bill & Melinda Gates Foundation is one of the largest that is devoted almost exclusively to education and is a strong proponent of technology in education. They are joined by The Gund Foundation, The William and Flora Hewlett Foundation, The Broad Foundation, Hoover Institute, The Joyce Foundation, The Spencer Foundation, The John Templeton Foundation, and the Walton Family Foundation. In addition to tax exempt entities, education has attracted the attention of other high profile individuals who plan to profit from the coming emphasis on technology and individualization in education. None other than Rupert Murdoch, "the man who owns the news," has entered the education market. Murdoch's organization already owns Wireless Generation and has been in receipt of many contracts in the New York City region. Murdoch's empire is the second largest media corporation in the world—and could have, in the coming decades, a substantial impact on what technology and curriculum are available to schools.

Another such foundation is the Foundation for Excellence in Education, whose chairman is former Florida governor Jeb Bush—a third member of the George H.W. Bush family. An article by Kathryn Baron appeared on the Silicon Valley Education Foundation blogspot "Thoughts on Public Education"[4] that describes a meeting recently held (October 14–15, 2011) in San Francisco and featured many of those who are presently involved in education reform supported by most of the foundations mentioned in the previous paragraph. Excerpts from the article follow:

> Jeb Bush's ed reform show in San Francisco
> Former Fla. Gov's summit seeks choice, tests and tech
>
> You could say that the only folks missing from the National Summit on Education Reform at San Francisco's Palace Hotel were teachers, but that would be wrong, on a technicality; they were outside protesting. Teachers might have a vested interest, or even an interesting viewpoint, in the issues raised during the two-day conference. Stuff like tenure, seniority, testing, Common Core standards, and using technology in education.
>
> But, no, they weren't invited into the inner sanctum of power brokers, policy makers, and politicians brought together for two days of learning and lobbying by former Florida governor Jeb Bush's Foundation for Excellence in Education.[5] It might have been awkward for them to be in the room when Idaho's schools chief praised his state legislature for eliminating teacher tenure,...
>
> Still, anyone expecting a strict conservative ideology would have been confused. Don't get me wrong; the only *bona fide* liberal in sight was Ben Austin, director of Parent Revolution,[6] the Los Angeles-based nonprofit behind the parent empowerment movement. And even Austin is having a hard time maintaining his pedigree these days, at least with the teachers' unions. Still, he was on the inside with other players who also can't be pinned down other than to say they're all "reformers."
>
> For example, Checker [Chester] Finn, voice of the conservative Thomas

B. Fordham Institute, moderated a panel with Anne Bryant, director of the National Association of School Boards—who playfully quipped that she and Checker disagree about 100 percent of the time—at one end of the dais, and Joel Klein, the former New York City schools chancellor and current Vice President and COO of News Corp's Education Division, on the other end....

But last night, the keynoter was Melinda Gates, and earlier Thursday attendees heard from Sal Khan, the unassuming Silicon Valley genius behind Khan Academy,[7] the nonprofit developer of thousands of high-quality online lessons available *free of charge*, who joked that he used to think YouTube was for cats playing pianos, not for serious mathematics....

"My personal belief is there is no one single thing that needs to get done," said Bush during his opening remarks.[8] What it will require, he said, is a combination of school choice (vouchers), Common Core standards, rigorous assessments, consequences for anything less than excellence, and using technology to transform education....

Mary Thompson, respected education researcher and writer, wrote an article in 1972 (See June 11, 1972 entry in this version of *the deliberate dumbing down of america.*) opposing the national piloting of Planning Programming and Budgeting System (PPBS, systems management/TQM, etc.) in the California public schools. There was significant opposition amongst public school teachers who understood that the system represented total control over what and how they taught. Americans are fortunate indeed that Mary is still around and able to submit her comments regarding the implementation of the system she opposed so long ago. Mary's remarks regarding the Jeb Bush article follow:

Difficult to know where to begin with this one with all the information, documentation and validation of what some have been saying for a long time about who is orchestrating the "brave new schools" and moving rapidly to Distance Learning. It is a well oiled and orchestrated partnership between neocons, old line bureaucrats and the old line foundations (Chester Finn, Fordham Foundation, etc.) who have been steering the deliberate dumbing down of America for decades, and the "newbies" on the street such as Gates Foundation, venture capitalists, tech oligarchs, and Alinsky organizer such as Ben Austin with the Parent Trigger agenda. Quite a nest of change agents in high places all together in one place to plot the final "refreezing" of the system since the "unfreezing" has been successfully accomplished. Thank you, RAND corporation, for the descriptive terminology: the planned process. The "refreezing" is to be modeled as a system of global Distance Learning. The warning bears repeating that teachers had better leave their concentration on the minutia of each maneuver in the process being carried out by all of the above and others, to concentrate on the big picture of plans afoot for the function of teachers being planned and programmed for extinction or demotion to becoming tutors, monitors, or overseers to keep students on task in front of their computer screens with "direct instruction" being imparted from anywhere in the world. I repeat, wake up teachers, your jobs are about to be "offshored" just as manufacturing, engineering and other professions have been. Your unions won't be able to counteract it any more than industry unions were able to do for the unemployed of empty factories and lost professional positions. Students will be phased into "programmed" curricula designed to produce worker bees for global economies. The authority of those selected to represent the voters and taxpayers is already being undermined as charter schools, with their unelected boards, are being used as a transmission belt to the final objective of Distance Learning.

As schools increasingly substitute computer learning for traditional textbook learning, as illustrated in the article regarding Florida's former governor Jeb Bush's Foundation for Excellence in Education meeting in San Francisco and Mary Thompson's reactions, the following quote from Dustin Heuston of Utah's World Institute for Computer-Assisted Teaching (WICAT) from "Discussion: Developing the Potential of an Amazing Tool" in *Schooling and Technology* (Vol. 3, Planning for the Future: A Collaborative Model, an Interpretive Report on Creative Partnerships in Technology—An Open Forum, Southeastern Regional Council for Educational Improvement: Research Triangle Park, North Carolina, 1984) becomes more and more relevant—if not plain scary:

> We've been absolutely staggered by realizing that the computer has the capability to act as if it were ten of the top psychologists working with one student... you've seen the tip of the iceberg. Won't it be wonderful when the child in the smallest county in the most distant area or in the most confused urban setting can have the equivalent of the finest school in the world on that terminal and no one can get between that child and that curriculum? We have great moments coming in the history of education.

The following quote from an article in the *New York Times*, October 12, 2011, written by Matt Ritchtel of Los Altos, California entitled "A Silicon Valley School that Doesn't Compute" is a classic example of how an elite, over the past one hundred years (See Rockefeller-Gates entry in 1913.), has wanted one thing for their children and something entirely different for the children of the underprivileged and the middle class in our nation:

> The chief technology officer of eBay sends his children to a nine-classroom school here. So do employees of Silicon Valley giants like Google, Apple, Yahoo and Hewlett-Packard.
> But the school's chief teaching tools are anything but high-tech: pens and paper, knitting needles, and, occasionally, mud. Not a computer to be found. No screens at all. They are not allowed in the classroom, and the school even frowns on their use at home.
> Schools nationwide have rushed to supply their classrooms with computers, and many policy makers say it is foolish to do otherwise. But the contrarian point of view can be found at the epicenter of the tech economy, where some parents and educators have a message: computers and schools don't mix.
> This is the Waldorf School of peninsula [sic], one of around 160 Waldorf schools in the country that subscribe to a teaching philosophy focused on physical activity and learning through creative, hands-on tasks. Those who endorse this approach say computers inhibit creative thinking, movement, human interaction and attention spans.

In my own state of Maine, which has been used for national piloting of radical education and social change programs for half a century, we have recently implemented the Reinventing Schools Coalition (RISC) which states in one of its publications that

> The RISC Approach to Schooling is a revolutionary approach to education that represents a dramatic shift in the educational process. The RISC approach is the first comprehensive school reform framework set up as a performance-based system [outcomes-based/results-based/Skinnerian mastery learning/direct instruction, ed.] rather than a Carnegie unit or time-based system....

TRADITIONAL VS. RISC PHILOSOPHY

20th Century Classroom	RISC 21st Century Classroom
Movement based on time	Movement based on performance
Students sitting in rows	Controlled chaos
Driven by textbooks	Driven by a shared vision
Commercial bulletin boards	Student boards
Teacher-controlled class	Students are navigators
10% student engagement	100% student engagement
3R's	Global curriculum
Teacher is the judge	Self, peers, business leaders, and teachers judge students' work

An April 16, 2002 *Washington Post* article by David Broder entitled "Remote school district lights path to success" discussed Richard DeLorenzo's revolutionary education agenda. Broder's article states in part:

> Last week, the Chugach (Alaska) superintendent, Richard DeLorenzo, stood before a ballroom full of high-powered executives, explaining how little Chugach (Alaska) had won the Malcolm Baldridge National Quality Award, an honor that in the past has gone to companies such as Cadillac and Ritz-Carlton as a signal of their success in providing customer satisfaction....

Broder also reveals that with the RISC plan, K–12 academics will change from the traditional competitive, academic, content-driven curriculum to a non-competitive, individualized, non-graded, take as long as is necessary to graduate at 14 or at 21[!], computerized workforce and values re-training agenda. This is a good description of the communist system of education/workforce training referred to earlier by Professor Boyce.

Implementation of this radical, socialist agenda has been relatively smooth due to the accomplishment of values destruction and dumbing down which took place between passage of the *Elementary and Secondary Education Act of 1965* and 1999, the date of publication of *the deliberate dumbing down of america*. How our schools, and in turn our nation, including corporations, have been restructured using Total Quality Management—and other large organizational management techniques popularized by Peter Drucker and others—for a socialist future without the American people rising up in rightful indignation, can be attributed to a combination of factors that I refer to as "The Devil's Seven-Pronged Fork":

1. **Gradualism:** implementing world government agenda gradually, over many years (two steps forward, one step back) so that succeeding

generations are unaware of what has happened in the past and unable to question or apply reason to current events or future events (heating up the water gradually until the frog is cooked). Or, in the words of Florida's former Associate Commissioner of Education Cecil Golden, "...like those assembling an atom bomb, very few of them understand exactly what they're building, and won't until we put all the parts together" [PPBS, ed.]. You'll know it's true when it happens to you!

2. **Hegelian Dialectic:** in order to get what change agents want it is necessary first for them to create the problem—such as high taxes. When citizens resist, suggest a solution. Example: move education funding and control to the state level, a solution citizens would never have accepted had problem with high taxes not been deliberately created. This can be called reaching common ground, coming to consensus and compromise.

3. **Semantic deception:** redefining terms to get agreement without understanding. Example: use of words that mean one thing to parents and another thing to change agents. Parents define "basics" in education as reading, writing, mathematics, history, science, etc. The education change agents' definition of "basics" is: education stressing the fact that the U.S. Constitution is outdated; education stressing the need for non-judgmental/non-absolutist attitudes and values; education stressing an environmental/sustainable development agenda, including the need for land use regulations, etc.; and workforce training.

4. **100% conservative and liberal media control:** the importance of *the deliberate dumbing down of america* can best be measured by its across-the-board censorship since its publication in 1999, not just by the usual culprits (establishment media), but by respected old line conservative media as well.

5. **Endless supply of money:** Federal Reserve, non-profit foundations, grant funding, and partnering with industry.

6. **Brainwashing in the schools and our communities, using psychological techniques:** Pavlov, Lewin, Skinner, Bloom, Chisholm, and others.

7. **Keeping the public unaware that both political parties (Republican and Democrat) espouse the same values:** these underly the international socialist/world government agenda. Most disheartening is that researchers have added to this unsavory alliance many Christian churches and organizations who formerly could be counted on to go up against the secular humanists and globalists and their values-destroying programs. These groups have been infiltrated by members of the corporatist/globalist leadership, and can no longer be counted on to support the free enterprise system, the U.S. Constitution, or religious principles which place God above man.

One example of the tragic falling away of the Christian community is highlighted by researcher Sarah Leslie in a blurb she wrote concerning Peter Drucker:

> Peter Drucker first came on my radar screen when I was researching Rick Warren, the popular evangelical pastor who authored the bestselling book, *The Purpose Driven Life.* I learned that Drucker, known widely as a business "guru," had mentored Rick Warren. I discovered that Drucker invented the term "knowledge capital" to refer to human value ("human capital"), an assessment of economic worth based on one's education and training. Drucker promoted a futuristic vision for society based on German mysticism (his parents were a part of the Vienna Circle), which included community, society and family performance-based standards and outcomes. I was shocked to realize that Rick Warren's term "purpose driven" meant "outcome-based"! No wonder there was virtually no opposition from evangelical Right leaders to OBE! Thousands of evangelical pastors were trained by Drucker through an organization known as Leadership Network during the decades of the 1980s and 1990s, and were perfectly on board for education reform when it came to full fruition in *No Child Left Behind.*[9]

An understanding of "The Devil's Seven-Pronged Fork" is helpful in combatting the cognitive dissonance all of us are experiencing at this point in time—the inability to sort out facts and alien values which are 100% in conflict with our former way of life and thinking in America. Although basically all components of the agenda were either planned or implemented in the last century, there are some components within the agenda which may seem new to the public and even to some education researchers. They are: the above co-opting of the Christian community; school choice; and Marxist curriculum (Paulo Freire, International Baccalaureate, etc.).

School choice (charter schools, vouchers, etc.) has been initiated and supported primarily by corporations and the neoconservative movement and is necessary for socialist workforce training in the planned economy. Conservative support for this unconstitutional school choice agenda brings to mind the following advice from Francis Bacon, British statesman and philosopher (1561–1626): "A false friend is more dangerous than an open enemy."

The public schools were deliberately dumbed down so that people would accept "any" substitute, no matter how lethal (the dialectic at work). Charter schools are NOT private schools since they are federally and state funded. They must administer the federal National Assessment of Educational Progress (NAEP), of which at least 50% of the questions deal with attitudes and values. Chester Finn, Jr., former assistant secretary of education, U.S. Department of Education, presently president of the Thomas B. Fordham Institute, is a strong supporter of school choice proposals and charter schools. Finn was very clear about the dangers involved in public funding of private education when he stated in an article entitled "Public Support for Private Education" published in *American Education*, May, 1982:

> Short of scattering money in the streets or handing it out to everyone who wants some, the funding agency must define eligible recipients....

This means, in a word, "regulation," the inevitable concomitant of public financial support.

The other side of the coin, Finn says, is "the obligation of private schools to recognize certain limits to their differentness and certain ways they must conform to the norms and expectations of a society that values and supports them."

Charter schools are unconstitutional and certainly violate traditional government practices since they do not have locally *elected* school boards. The Georgia Supreme Court recently ruled that only local school boards have the power to create charter schools, striking down a law that created Georgia's Charter Schools Commission. An article in *The Atlanta Journal/Constitution* on May 16, 2011 stated that

> The Supreme Court of Georgia ruled 4-to-3 to strike down as unconstitutional a 2008 Act that authorized creation of a new kind of state charter school called "commission charter schools." The high court decided that the charter schools did not fit the definition of "special schools" as envisioned in the state Constitution. The landmark case is the first to rule on the constitutionality of an alternate authorizer of charter schools that has already opened campuses that are educating students.

> Under the current Constitution, which voters approved in 1983, local school boards have the exclusive authority to create and maintain K–12 public education, Chief Justice Carol Hunstein writes for the majority. The Constitution only allows the state government to create "special schools." [schools for the deaf, blind, etc., ed.] Yet in the 2008 Act, the State authorized the "Georgia Charter Schools Commission," whose members are appointed by state officials, to approve petitions for a new type of general K–12 public school known as a "commission charter school."

Flying in the face of the Georgia Supreme Court's ruling, at an October 22, 2011 Roundtable at Stanford University in California entitled "Education Nation 2.0: Redefining Education before It Redefines Us,"[10] Reed Hastings, CEO of Netflix and former president of the California State Board of Education, stated the following:

> Technology and Charter schools—two big change vectors. Technology will allow us to go around and through the system. It will allow software-based individualized tutoring.... hugely transformative in the next twenty years. Charter schools are non-profit public schools.... Problem is not with people. There are great people.... If corporations had elected boards, they would operate as mediocre as most school districts. Problem is the elected school board. The solution is getting into non-profits, like Stanford.

Most dangerous of all is the possibility that if Americans accept the legitimacy of charter schools, they will be going down a very slippery slope which may well lead to the unraveling of our representative, constitutional form of government. This is called "taxation without representation." We can be sure that the highly-trained socialist change agents in our state capitols—who have been so successful in pushing regionalism (a pillar of communist government structure) on our local communities, will be working night and day to get Americans to accept unelected councils (soviets) to run government at all levels! The deliberate dumbing down has been so complete that it is very likely Americans will say, "If our public schools can be run by appointed councils, why not appoint our local Board of Select-men (Commissioners), why not appoint citizens to town councils, to the Legislature, to Congress, to the White House?"

Education researcher Debbie Niwa of Arizona shared the following with the author:

> "School choice" furthers the reforms envisioned a century ago by peddlers of progressive education. Through school choice—or more accurately "con-trolled choice"—progressive reforms are cleverly marketed as special pro-grams to targeted groups. Programs can be implemented as magnet themes, smaller learning communities, and charter schools, to name a few.
>
> On the surface, the programs may appear to differ, but internally they share similar non-academic (affective) goals and Marxist education theory and praxis. Specifically, a focus on values, attitudes, and feelings—is catego-rized under the "affective domain." These non-academic issues are referred to today by a host of labels: workplace skills, soft skills, skills for the 21st century, or profile of a global citizen among others.
>
> School choice options that have gained promotional traction claim to deliver a global or multicultural dimension to education (with a socialist twist!). UNESCO-connected[11] International Baccalaureate (IB) programs are a popular venue; likewise various culture-oriented "studies" based on ethnicity, gender, sexual orientation, etc.
>
> The 1985 booklet entitled *Back to Basics... or OBE Skinnerian Interna-tional Curriculum*[12] describes the central goals of global/international/multi-cultural (socialist) education. Today, most, if not all the issues covered in *Back to Basics Reform* are concentrated in International Baccalaureate programs.
>
> As of August 2011, nearly 3,300 IB programs are authorized globally with more than 1,300 in use in the United States where the vast majority exist in public schools. Thus, taxpayers at the local, state, and federal level are paying for the many extra costs incurred by IB. Yet, in general there is very little public notification.[13]
>
> In the globalist paradigm, there must be deconstruction of the apprecia-tion for national heritage, allegiance, governance and traditional social norms. Various forms of Marxist "critical theory"—delivered under the guise of "criti-cal thinking"—are increasingly used in the classroom to achieve these ends.

Given that so many of the troublesome and destructive education pro-grams that parents and teachers have resisted have as their origin "human relations" training and all of its cohorts, we should probably explore some of the origins of these programs Niwa has referenced. In 1946 *Time* magazine (November 16) published an article about a man named Col. H. Edmund Bullis who was conducting a "new program in preventive psychiatry" in classrooms in Delaware. These programs were sponsored by the Delaware State Society for Mental Hygiene. Col. Bullis called them "human relations in the classroom." In 1949 Col. H. Edmund Bullis wrote a paper that was presented at a Joint Session of the American School Health Association and the Maternal and Child Health, Public Health Nursing, and School Health

Sections of the American Public Health Association at the 75th Annual Meeting in New York (October 27, 1949). The paper was published in the *American Journal of Public Health,* September 1950 (pp. 1113–1117). Some important excerpts follow:

> If our Human Relations Class project continues to be as successful as our experience to date indicates, we hope that from their better understanding of their own emotional strengths and weaknesses, most of these boys and girls completing three years of weekly Human Relations Classes may progress toward emotional maturity.
>
> The theory on which these Human Relations Classes are operating is that little can be learned about personality problems except through emotional experiences and that ordinary teaching or lecturing or giving advice fall far short in providing the kind of insights that come out of life encounters with emotional problems. While it is impossible to furnish children in classrooms with real life situations to discuss, to learn, and to understand, our efforts and techniques are to endeavor to create as nearly as possible these actual "life situations."
>
> Our weekly class generally starts with the teacher reading a stimulus story which features emotional problems. The students are then encouraged to discuss freely the emotional problems presented in the stimulus story, to give an appraisal of the solutions effected in the story, to speculate on the motivations lying back of the behavior of the individuals in the story. In this retelling of emotional experiences—often bringing out in to the open problems they have never discussed before—a better understanding of their actions often results. The students also gain insights by listening to their classmates tell freely of how they met certain emotional problems.
>
> We have been pleased to find out that the instructions given in our lesson plans are practical enough so that teachers who have never witnessed one of our demonstration classes have no difficulty in successfully conducting our Human Relations Classes.

Col. Bullis's book *Human Relations in the Classroom—Course I* (Harold Edmund Bulllis, Emily E. O'Malley, Delaware State Society for Mental Hygiene, 1947), contained the following excerpts in the preface:

> In 1932 the President of the Carnegie Foundation for the Advancement of Teaching said to Dr. C.M. Hincks, distinguished Canadian psychiatrist and to me, "You in the mental hygiene field are making little real progress with educators with your philosophical lectures, pamphlets and books. Our teachers need something to help them meet the every day pupil adjustment problems of their classrooms. They need simple mental hygiene manuals and practical lesson plans to help their students to gain insights regarding their emotional problems."
>
> In 1940 I resigned as Executive Officer, the National Committee for Mental Hygiene, to endeavor to work out practical means of introducing the teaching of positive mental hygiene principles to normal children in public schools. I wished to develop and try out positive mental hygiene lesson plans, which from the beginning I called Human Relations Lesson Plans.
>
> At this time, Dr. M.A. Tarumianz, outstanding psychiatric leader of Delaware, invited me to come to Delaware to start this experimental work under the auspices of the Delaware State Society for Mental Hygiene. Shortly after,

the Committee on Research in Dementia Praecox (financed by the Supreme Council, Scottish Rite Masons, Northern Jurisdiction) and Mrs. Henry Ittleson of New York City also made grants to my work. This combined financial support made it possible for my capable teaching assistant, Emily E. O'Malley, and I to carry on our experimental work in a number of schools in the State of Delaware, in Nassau County, New York, and in Brooklyn, New York. We had enthusiastic cooperation from the Delaware State Department of Public Instruction, the New York City Board of Education, Hofstra College, the University of Delaware and the superintendents, principals and teachers of the schools in which we were trying out our Human Relations classes....

Present indications lead us to believe that starting in September of 1947, a large percentage of the sixth grade classes in the public schools throughout the state of Delaware will have weekly Human Relations Classes based on the lesson plans in this book. During the coming year we expect to develop and try out Human Relations in the Classroom—Course II, for those classes which have had Course I. In addition, we hope to experiment with Human Relations Classes in primary grades, in youth organizations and in religious education.

Obviously, Col. Bullis and his fellow Mental Hygiene Society members have been very successful. Some of the "Human Relations Lesson Plans" bear a strong resemblance to teaching strategies contained in federally-funded and developed Curriculum for Meeting Modern Problems (*The New Model Me*) and other controversial National Diffusion Network programs resisted by parents in the 1970s to the present. These programs were so damaging and outrageous that the U.S. Senate passed unanimously the *Protection of Pupil Rights Amendment* and subsequent regulations for enforcement which—due to change agent chicanery and opposition—were never enforced at the local level.

For over sixty years those who have wanted to experiment with our children in classrooms all over the country have had tools produced with support from tax-exempt foundations, the government, and, at least once, a Masonic organization. Did we know? Did we inadvertently support experimentation with our children and their emotional health in public school classrooms, youth organizations and in our churches?

In closing this chapter, I would like to share with you some thoughts from our Librarian of Congress James Billington. In chapter 4 of Billington's book, *Fire in the Minds of Men: Origins of the Revolutionary Faith* (Basic Books, Inc.: New York, 1980), he explains some of the problems we have had:

The story of the secret societies can never be fully reconstructed, but it has been badly neglected—even avoided, one suspects—because the evidence that is available repeatedly leads us into territory equally uncongenial to modern historians in the East and the West.... In what follows I will attempt to show that modern revolutionary tradition as it came to be internationalized under Napoleon and the Restoration grew out of occult Freemasonry; that the early organizational ideas originated more from Pythagorean mysticism than from practical experience; and that the real innovators were not so much political activists as literary intellectuals, on whom German romantic thought in general—and Bavarian Illuminism in particular—exerted great influence....

This author is concerned that many of the problems we have encountered in education in this country may have many of the same roots.

As this book goes to press, our nation is experiencing demonstrations and protests by "student-led" groups angry over "capitalist oppression." These demonstrations, which are spilling into the streets of foreign cities as well, call to mind James Billington's *Fire in the Minds of Men* and his earlier remarks related to the origins of revolutionary movements. As we stated in the preface to *the deliberate dumbing down of america*, "The United States is engaged in war... it has been fought in secret—in the schools of our nation, targeting our children who are captive in classrooms." We may be seeing, in these demonstrations, the results of this war against our children's consciences and intellects. As Edward Hunter, the man who coined the term "brainwashing" and wrote *Brainwashing: The Men Who Defied It*, said of this war, and in regard to finally standing on principle and actively going up against evil: "There is no 'behind the lines' any longer."

Endnotes:

1   In *Webster's New World Dictionary* (1976) a communitarian is "a member or an advocate of a communistic community." [See the first entry under 1997 which contains information on the National Commission on Civic Renewal for the quote "Communitarianism is the social philosophy of the Skinnerian Walden II experimental commune at Los Horcones, Mexico," ed.]

2   This important book can be accessed at: http://www.americandeception.com.

3   To access the US Department of Housing and Urban Development website, please go to http://portal.hud.gov/hudportal/HUD?src = /press/press_releases_media_advisories/2010/HUDNo.10-233.

4   This article can be found on the Internet at: http://toped.svefoundation.org/2011/10/14/jeb-bushs-ed-reform-show-in-san-francisco/.

5   The website for Jeb Bush's Foundation for Excellence can be found at: http://www.exce-lined.org/.

6   The Parent Revolution website can be found at: http://parentrevolution.org/.

7   The Khan Academy can be accessed at: http://www.khanacademy.org/.

8   Jeb Bush's entire speech at the opening of the conference can be accessed at: http://toped. svefoundation.org/wp-content/uploads/2011/10/Speech-by-Jeb-Bush-National-Summit-on-Education-Reform.pdf.

9   Please access a monograph written by Lynn D. and Sarah H. Leslie, and Susan J. Conway entitled *The Pied Pipers of Purpose: Part 1: Human Capital System and Church Performance* (Conscience Press, 2004) at: http://www.discernmentministries.org/Purpose Driven.pdf.

10 Please access the Stanford Roundtable discussion at: http://news.stanford.edu/news/2011/october/2011-roundtable-education-102211.html.

11 Important information regarding the original directors of UNESCO follows: Out of a total of fifteen directors, fourteen were communist officials from the Soviet Union, Hungary and Poland, and one was from France. This information was published in the mid-nineteen sixties by "Project Each Reach One," (P.O. Box 494, Redondo Beach, California).

12 Please access deliberatedumbingdown.com for the pdf booklet *Back to Basics... or OBE Skinnerian International Curricuum*.

13 See *International Baccalaureate (IB) Unraveled* by Debra K. Niwa, September 2009 (updated March 2010), pp. 5–7 at: http://www.freedomadvocates.org/images/pdf/IB%20Unrav-eled%203.28.10Niwa.pdf.

1

THE SOWING OF THE SEEDS:
late eighteenth and
nineteenth centuries

"The Sowing of the Seeds: late eighteenth and nineteenth centuries" is the shortest chapter of *the deliberate dumbing down of america*. Undoubtedly, this chapter may be one of the most important since the philosophies of Jean-Jacques Rousseau, Wilhelm Wundt, and John Dewey et al., reflect a total departure from the traditional definition of education like the one given in *The New Century Dictionary of the English Language* (Appleton, Century, Crofts: New York, 1927):

> The drawing out of a person's innate talents and abilities by imparting the knowledge of languages, scientific reasoning, history, literature, rhetoric, etc.—the channels through which those abilities would flourish and serve.[1]

A quantum leap was taken from the above definition to the new, dehumanizing definition used by the experimental psychologists found in *An Outline of Educational Psychology* (Barnes & Noble: New York, 1934, rev. ed.) by Rudolph Pintner et al. That truly revolutionary definition claims that

> learning is the result of modifiability in the paths of neural conduction. Explanations of even such forms of learning as abstraction and generalization demand of the neurones only growth, excitability, conductivity, and modifiability. The mind is the connection-system of man; and learning is the process of connecting. The situation-reponse formula is adequate to cover learning

17

of any sort, and the really influential factors in learning are readiness of the neurones, sequence in time, belongingness, and satisfying consequences.[2]

An in-depth understanding of the deplorable situation found in our nation's schools today is impossible without an understanding of the redefinition in the above statements. Education in the twenty-first century will, for the majority of youth, be workforce training. Thus, the need for Pavlovian/Skinnerian methodology based on operant conditioning which, in essence, is at the heart of the above dehumanizing definition of education. This "sowing of the seeds" through redefinition will reap the death of traditional, liberal arts education through the advent of mastery learning, outcome-based education, and direct instruction—all of which will be performance-based and behaviorist.

1762

EMILE BY JEAN-JACQUES ROUSSEAU (CHEZ JEAN NEAULME DUCHESNE: A. Amsterdam [Paris], 1762) was published. Rousseau's "Social Contract" presented in *Emile* influenced the French Revolution. In this book Rousseau promoted child-centered "permissive education" in which a teacher "should avoid strict discipline and tiresome lessons." Both Rousseau (1712–1788) and Swiss educator Johann Heinrich Pestalozzi (1746–1827) believed that the "whole child" should be educated by "doing," and that religion should not be a guiding principle in education, a theme we shall see repeated over the next 238 years.

1832

WILHELM WUNDT, FOUNDER OF EXPERIMENTAL PSYCHOLOGY AND THE FORCE behind its dissemination throughout the Western world, was born in 1832 in Neckarau, southern Germany. The following excerpts concerning Wundt's contribution to modern education are taken from *The Leipzig Connection: The Systematic Destruction of American Education* by Paolo Lionni and Lance J. Klass[3] (Heron Books: Portland, Ore., 1980):

> To Wundt, a thing made sense and was worth pursuing if it could be measured, quantified, and scientifically demonstrated. Seeing no way to do this with the human soul, he proposed that psychology concern itself solely with experience. As Wundt put it... Karl Marx injected Hegel's theories with economics and sociology, developing a "philosophy of dialectical materialism."... (p. 8)
>
> From Wundt's work it was only a short step to the later redefinition of education. Originally, education meant drawing out of a person's innate talents and abilities by imparting the knowledge of languages, scientific reasoning, history, literature, rhetoric, etc.—the channels through which those abilities would flourish and serve. To the experimental psychologist, however, education became the process of exposing the student to "meaningful" experiences so as to ensure desired reactions:

[L]earning is the result of modifiability in the paths of neural conduction. Explanations of even such forms of learning as abstraction and generalization demand of the neurones only growth, excitability, conductivity, and modifiability. The mind is the connection-system of man; and learning is the process of connecting. The situation-response formula is adequate to cover learning of any sort, and the really influential factors in learning are readiness of the neurones, sequence in time, belongingness, and satisfying consequences.[4]

If one assumes (as did Wundt) that there is nothing there to begin with but a body, a brain, a nervous system, then one must try to educate by inducing sensations in that nervous system. Through these experiences, the individual will learn to respond to any given stimulus, with the "correct" response. The child is not, for example, thought capable of volitional control over his actions, or of deciding whether he will act or not act in a certain way; his actions are thought to be preconditioned and beyond his control, he is a stimulus-response mechanism. According to this thinking, he is his reactions. Wundt's thesis laid the philosophical basis for the principles of conditioning later developed by Pavlov (who studied physiology in Leipzig in 1884, five years after Wundt had inaugurated his laboratory there) and American behavioral psychologists such as Watson and Skinner; for laboratories and electroconvulsive therapy; for schools oriented more toward socialization of the child than toward the development of intellect; and for the emergence of a society more and more blatantly devoted to the gratification of sensory desire at the expense of responsibility and achievement. (pp. 14–15)

[Ed. Note: The reader should purchase *The Leipzig Connection: The Systematic Destruction of American Education*, a slim paperback book which, in this writer's opinion, is the most useful and important book available regarding the method used to change children's behavior/values and to "dumb down" an entire society. The authors, Lionni and Klass, have made an outstanding contribution to the history of American education and to the understanding of why and how America, which up until the 1930s had the finest education system in the world, ended up with one of the worst education systems in the industrialized world in a short period of fifty years.

Another commentary on the importance of Wundt's theories comes from Dennis L. Cuddy, Ph.D., in an excellent article entitled "The Conditioning of America" (*The Christian News*, New Haven, Mo., December 11, 1989).[5] An excerpt follows:

The conditioning of modern American society began with John Dewey, a psychologist, a Fabian Socialist and the "Father of Progressive Education." Dewey used the psychology developed in Leipzig by Wilhelm Wundt, and believed that through a stimulus-response approach (like Pavlov) students could be conditioned for a new social order.]

1862

THE FIRST EXPERIMENT WITH "OUTCOME-BASED EDUCATION" (OBE) WAS conducted in England in 1862. Teacher opposition resulted in abandonment of the experiment. Don Martin of University of Pittsburgh, George E. Over-holt and Wayne J. Urban of Georgia State University wrote *Accountability in American Education: A Critique* (Princeton Book Company: Princeton, N.J., 1976) containing a section entitled "Payment for Results" which chronicles the English experiment. The following excerpt outlines the experiment:

> The call for "sound and cheap" elementary instruction was answered by legislation, passed by Parliament during 1862, known as The Revised Code. This was the legislation that produced payment [for] results, the nineteenth century English accountability system.... The opposition to the English payment-[for]-results system which arose at the time of its introduction was particularly interesting. Teachers provided the bulk of the resistance, and they based their objections on both educational and economic grounds.... They abhorred the narrowness and mechanical character the system imposed on the educational process. They also objected to the economic burden forced upon them by basing their pay on student performance.

[Ed. Note: "Payment for Results" and Outcome-Based Education are based on teacher accountability and require teaching to the test, the results of which are to be "measured" for accountability purposes. Both methods of teaching result in a narrow, mechanistic system of education similar to Mastery Learning. Teachers in the United States in 1999, as were teachers involved in the experiment in England, will be judged and paid according to students' test scores; i.e., how well the teachers teach to the test. Proponents of Mastery Learning believe that almost all children can learn if given enough time, adequate resources geared to the individual learning style of the student, and a curriculum aligned to test items (teach to the test). Mastery Learning uses Skinnerian methodology (operant conditioning) in order to obtain "predictable" results. Benjamin Bloom, the father of Mastery Learning, says that "the purpose of education is to change the thoughts, actions and feelings of students." Mastery Learning (ML) and its fraternal twin Direct Instruction (DI) are key components of Outcome-Based Education (OBE) and Effective Schools Research (ESR).[*] The one common thread running through this book relates to these terms and their importance in the implementation of workforce training and attitude and value change.]

1874

Edward Lee Thorndike was born August 31, 1874 in Williamsburg, Massachusetts. Thorndike was trained in the new psychology by the first generation of Wilhelm Wundt's protegés. He graduated from Wesleyan University in 1895 after having studied with Wundtians Andrew C. Armstrong and Charles Judd. He went to graduate school at Harvard and studied under psychologist William James. While at Harvard, Thorndike surprised James by doing research with chickens, testing their behavior, and pioneering what later became known as "animal psychology." As briefly stated by Thorndike himself, psychology was the "science of the intellect, character, and behavior

---

[*]   Please access the Internet version for definitions in the Glossary.

of animals, including man."[6] To further excerpt *The Leipzig Connection*'s excellent treatment of Thorndike's background:

> Thorndike applied for a fellowship at Columbia, was accepted by Cattell, and moved with his two most intelligent chickens to New York, where he continued his research and earned his Ph.D. in 1893. Thorndike's specialty was the "puzzle box," into which he would put various animals (chickens, rats, cats) and let them find their way out by themselves. His doctoral dissertation on cats has become part of the classical literature of psychology. After receiving his doctorate, he spent a year as a teacher at Western Reserve University, and it wasn't long before Cattell advised Dean [James Earl] Russell to visit Thorndike's first classroom at Western Reserve: "Although the Dean found him 'dealing with the investigations of mice and monkeys,' he came away satisfied that he was worth trying out on humans."
>
> Russell offered Thorndike a job at Teachers College, where the experimenter remained for the next thirty years. Thorndike was the first psychologist to study animal behavior in an experimental psychology laboratory and (following Cattell's suggestion) apply the same techniques to children and youth; as one result, in 1903, he published the book *Educational Psychology*. In the following years he published a total of 507 books, monographs, and articles.
>
> Thorndike's primary assumption was the same as Wundt's: that man is an animal, that his actions are actually always reactions, and that he can be studied in the laboratory in much the same way as an animal might be studied. Thorndike equated children with the rats, monkeys, fish, cats, and chickens upon which he experimented in his laboratory and was prepared to apply what he found there to learning in the classroom. He extrapolated "laws" from his research into animal behavior which he then applied to the training of teachers, who took what they had learned to every corner of the United States and ran their classrooms, curricula, and schools, on the basis of this new "educational" psychology.
>
> In *The Principles of Teaching Based on Psychology* (1906), Thorndike proposed making "the study of teaching scientific and practical." Thorndike's definition of the art of teaching is

> > the art of giving and withholding stimuli with the result of producing or preventing certain responses. In this definition the term stimulus is used widely for any event which influences a person—for a word spoken to him, a look, a sentence which he reads, the air he breathes, etc., etc. The term response is used for any reaction made by him—a new thought, a feeling of interest, a bodily act, any mental or bodily condition resulting from the stimulus. The aim of the teacher is to produce desirable and prevent undesirable changes in human beings by producing and preventing certain responses. The means at the disposal of the teacher are the stimuli which can be brought to bear upon the pupil—the teacher's words, gestures, and appearance, the condition and appliances of the school room, the books to be used and objects to be seen, and so on through a long list of the things and events which the teacher can control.

1896

PSYCHOLOGY BY JOHN DEWEY, THE FATHER OF "PROGRESSIVE EDUCATION," was published (University of Chicago Press: Chicago, 1896). This was the first American textbook on the "revised" subject of education. *Psychology* would become the most widely-read and quoted textbook used in schools of education in this country. Just prior to the publication of his landmark book, Dewey had joined the faculty of the Rockefeller-endowed University of Chicago as head of the combined departments of philosophy, psychology and pedagogy (teaching). In that same year, 1895, the university allocated $1,000 to establish a laboratory in which Dewey could apply psychological principles and experimental techniques to the study of learning. The laboratory opened in January 1896 as the Dewey School, later to become known as The University of Chicago Laboratory School.[7] Dewey thought of the school as a place

> where his theories of education could be put into practice, tested, and scientifically evaluated....
>
> ...Dewey... sought to apply the doctrines of experience and experiment to everyday life and, hence, to education... seeking via this model institution to pave the way for the "schools of the future." There he had put into actual practice three of the revolutionary beliefs he had culled from the new psychology: that to put the child in possession of his fullest talents, education should be active rather than passive; that to prepare the child for a democratic society, the school should be social rather than individualist; and that to enable the child to think creatively, experimentation rather than imitation should be encouraged.[8]

Samuel Blumenfeld in his book, *The Whole Language/OBE Fraud* (Paradigm Co.: Boise, Idaho, 1996), further explains Dewey's perspective:

> What kind of curriculum would fit the school that was a mini-cooperative society? Dewey's recommendation was indeed radical: build the curriculum not around academic subjects but around occupational activities which provided maximum opportunities for peer interaction and socialization. Since the beginning of Western civilization, the school curriculum was centered around the development of academic skills, the intellectual faculties, and high literacy. Dewey wanted to change all of that. Why? Because high literacy produced that abominable form of independent intelligence which was basically, as Dewey believed, anti-social.
>
> Thus, from Dewey's point of view, the school's primary commitment to literacy was indeed the key to the whole problem. In 1898, Dewey wrote an essay, "The Primary-Education Fetish," in which he explained exactly what he meant:
>
>> There is... a false education god whose idolators are legion, and whose cult influences the entire educational system. This is language study—the study not of foreign language, but of English; not in higher, but in primary education. It is almost an unquestioned assumption, of educational theory and practice both, that the first three years of a child's school life shall be mainly taken up with learning to read and write his own language. If we add to this the learning of a certain amount of numerical combinations, we have the pivot about which primary education swings.... It does not follow, however, that conditions—social, industrial and intellectual— have undergone such a radical change, that the time has come for a thoroughgoing examination of the emphasis put upon linguistic work in elementary instruction.... The plea for the predominance of learning

to read in early school life because of the great importance attaching to literature seems to me a perversion.

Endnotes:

1 Paolo Lionni and Lance J. Klass. *The Leipzig Connection: The Systematic Destruction of American Education* (Heron Books: Portland, Ore., 1980).

2 Ibid.

3 *The Leipzig Connection* may be obtained by sending a check for $11.45 to: Heron Books, P.O. Box 503, Sheridan, OR, or by calling 1–503–843–3834.

4 Rudolph Pintner et al. *An Outline of Educational Psychology*, Revised (Barnes & Noble: New York, 1934), p. 79.

5 Dr. Cuddy's important publications on the history of American education, from which this writer has frequently quoted, can be obtained by writing: Dr. Stanley Monteith, 199 Outlook Ridge, Soquel, California 95073; or by calling 831–475–6651; or by email to DoctorStanRadio@aol.com. Cuddy's newly revised edition of *Chronology of Education with Quotable Quotes* and *Secret Records Revealed: The Men, the Money and the Methods Behind the New World Order* should be in the library of every serious education researcher.

6 *The Leipzig Connection*, pp. 36–39.

7 Ibid.

8 These quotes taken from Ida B. DePencier's book, *The History of the Laboratory Schools: The University of Chicago, 1896–1965* (Quadrangle Books: Chicago, 1967) and *A History of Teachers College: Columbia University* by Lawrence A. Cremin, David A. Shannon, and Mary Evelyn Townsend (Columbia University Press: New York, 1934), as cited in *The Leipzig Connection*.

2

THE TURNING OF THE TIDES*:
early twentieth century

For a nation that had been able to point with pride to extraordinary advances in all areas of endeavor carried out by *individuals*, with no assistance whatsoever from the government, the early years of the twentieth century surely reflected a "turning of the tides." An alien collectivist (socialist) philosophy, much of which came from Europe, crashed onto the shores of our nation, bringing with it radical changes in economics, politics, and education, funded—surprisingly enough—by several wealthy American families and their tax-exempt foundations.

The goal of these wealthy families and their foundations—a seamless non-competitive global system for commerce and trade—when stripped of flowery expressions of concern for minorities, the less fortunate, etc., represented the initial stage of what this author now refers to as "the deliberate dumbing down of america."

Seventy years later, the carefully laid plans to change America from a sovereign, constitutional republic with a free enterprise economic base to just one of many nations in an international socialist (collectivist) system (New World Order) are apparent. Only a dumbed down population, with no memory of

---

* "The Turning of the Tides" is the title of a report submitted to Congress by Hon. Paul W. Shafer (Mich.) and John Howland Snow. The original text was delivered in the U.S. House of Representatives on March 21, 1952.

America's roots as a prideful nation, could be expected to willingly succumb to the global workforce training planned by the Carnegie Corporation and the John D. Rockefellers, I and II, in the early twentieth century which is being implemented by the United States Congress in the year 1999.

1902

THE GENERAL EDUCATION BOARD (GEB) WAS INCORPORATED BY AN ACT OF the United States Congress. Approved January 12, 1902, the General Education Board was endowed by Mr. John D. Rockefeller, Sr., for the purpose of establishing an educational laboratory to experiment with early innovations in education.

1905

[ddd]

THE CARNEGIE FOUNDATION FOR THE ADVANCEMENT OF TEACHING WAS founded in 1905. Henry S. Pritchett served as the foundation's first president. Pritchett was the author of *What Is Religion and Other Student Questions* (Houghton Mifflin Company: Boston, 1906), *Relations of Denominations to Colleges* (1908), and *A Woman's Opportunities in Christian Industry and Business* (1907).

[ddd]

1913

JOHN D. ROCKEFELLER, JR.'S DIRECTOR OF CHARITY FOR THE ROCKEFELLER Foundation, Frederick T. Gates, set up the Southern Education Board (SEB), which was later incorporated into the General Education Board (GEB) in 1913, setting in motion "the deliberate dumbing down of America." *The Country School of Tomorrow: Occasional Papers No. 1* (General Education Board: New York, 1913) written by Frederick T. Gates contained a section entitled "A Vision of the Remedy" in which he wrote the following:

> Is there aught of remedy for this neglect of rural life? Let us, at least, yield ourselves to the gratifications of a beautiful dream that there is. In our dream, we have limitless resources, and the people yield themselves with perfect docility to our molding hand. The present educational conventions fade from our minds; and, unhampered by tradition, we work our own good will upon a grateful and responsive rural folk. We shall not try to make these people or any of their children into philosophers or men of learning or of science. We are not to raise up from among them authors, orators, poets, or men of letters. We shall not search for embryo great artists, painters, musicians. Nor will we cherish even the humbler ambition to raise up from among them

lawyers, doctors, preachers, politicians, statesmen, of whom we now have ample supply.

1914

A RESOLUTION WAS PASSED BY THE NORMAL SCHOOL SECTION OF THE NA-tional Education Association at its annual meeting in St. Paul, Minnesota in the year 1914. An excerpt follows:

> We view with alarm the activity of the Carnegie and Rockefeller Founda-tions—agencies not in any way responsible to the people—in their efforts to control the policies of our State educational institutions, to fashion after their conception and to standardize our courses of study, and to surround the institutions with conditions which menace true academic freedom and defeat the primary purpose of democracy as heretofore preserved inviolate in our common schools, normal schools, and universities.

[ddd]

1918

IN THE JANUARY 13, 1918 ISSUE OF *NEW YORK WORLD* WILLIAM BOYCE Thompson, Federal Reserve Bank director and founding member of the Council on Foreign Relations, stated that

> Russia is pointing the way to great and sweeping world changes. It is not in Russia alone that the old order is passing. There is a lot of the old order in America, and that is going, too.... I'm glad it is so. When I sat and watched those democratic conclaves in Russia, I felt I would welcome a similar scene in the United States.

[Ed. Note: M. Maxine Tremaine of Massachusetts, recognized for her careful research related to international affairs, made the following statements re-garding Willian Boyce Thompson before the National Convention of Women for Constitutional Government in a July 1983 speech entitled "Russia Is the Model Country of International Bankers and Industrialists Administered by the United Nations Headquarters in Geneva, Switzerland": "William Boyce Thompson personally contributed $1 million to the Russian Revolution. He also arranged for the transfer of money from the United States to (the Com-munist revolutionaries)."]

[ddd]

1919

THE INSTITUTE OF INTERNATIONAL EDUCATION (IIE) WAS FOUNDED IN 1919 through a grant from the Carnegie Endowment for International Peace. The Institute's purpose was to operate a student exchange program. This process of "exchanges" grew in concept and practice with the IIE administering visitor exchange programs for the U.S. Information Agency (USIA) in the 1990s. The U.S.-Soviet Education Agreements were negotiated by the Carnegie Endowment's parent organization, the Carnegie Corporation, fostering exchanges of curriculum, pedagogy and materials as well as students.

THE PROGRESSIVE EDUCATION ASSOCIATION (P.E.A.) WAS FOUNDED IN 1919 and organized by John Dewey, even though he would not become a member in its early years. P.E.A.'s goals and aims were projected for the last half of this century at a board meeting held November 15–17, 1943 in Chicago, Illinois. Attendees included: Harold Rugg, Marion Carswell, Arthur Gould, Theodore Brameld, Prudence Bosterick, and Carson Ryan. Speaking of their plans for the period following World War II, the board published a statement in its journal *Progressive Education* (December 1943, Vol. XX, No. 8) which included the following excerpt:

> This is a global war, and the peace now in the making will determine what our national life will be for the next century. It will demonstrate the degree of our national morality. We are writing now the credo by which our children must live....
>
> Your Board unanimously proposes a broadening of the interests and program of this Association to include the communities in which our children live. To this end, they propose additions to the governing body to include representatives of welfare services, health, industry, labor and the professions. In short, a cross-section body to give scope to our program....
>
> Yes, something happened around a table in Chicago. An organization which might have become mellowed with the years to futility, in three short days again drew a blueprint for children of the world.

[Ed. Note: For what "our national life will be for the rest of this century" and perhaps on into the next, see the 1946 *Montgomery County Blueprint* and 1999 *Gwinnett Daily* entries.]

1921

IN 1921 THE LEAGUE FOR INDUSTRIAL DEMOCRACY CHANGED ITS NAME FROM the Intercollegiate Socialist Society (ISS) and stated its purpose as: "Education for a new social order based on production and not for profit" ("A Chronology of Education," Dorothy Dawson, 1978).

HAROLD RUGG, WRITER OF SOCIAL STUDIES TEXTBOOK SERIES ENTITLED *THE Frontier Thinkers* which was published by the Progressive Education Association, in 1921 became president of the National Association of Directors of Education Research which would later become known as the American Educational Research Association.

THE COUNCIL ON FOREIGN RELATIONS WAS ESTABLISHED IN 1921 THROUGH the efforts of Col. Edwin Mandell House, *confidant extraordinaire* to President Woodrow Wilson and about whom Wilson said, "Mr. House is my second personality... His thoughts and mine are one." House was the initiator of the effort to establish this American branch of the English Royal Institute of International Affairs. Prior to 1921, House's group, "the Inquiry," called the CFR the "Institute of International Affairs." In 1912 House had authored *Philip Dru: Administrator* which promoted "socialism as dreamed of by Karl Marx" about which book Wilson's Secretary of the Interior Franklin Lane wrote to a personal friend: "All that book has said should be, comes about. The President comes to Philip Dru in the end."

Walter Lippmann, member of the Fabian Society and Intercollegiate Socialist Society, was a founding member of the CFR. Whitney Shepardson was a director of the CFR from 1921 until 1966. Shepardson had been an assistant to Col. House in the 1918 peace conference following World War I and served as secretary of the League of Nations committee. Shepardson later became a director of the Carnegie Corporation British and Colonies fund. Other early CFR members included: Charles E. (Chip) Bohlen, first secretary to the American embassy in Moscow during World War II and President Franklin Roosevelt's interpreter for his meeting with Josef Stalin at the Teheran conference; Frank Aydelotte, a trustee of the Carnegie Foundation, president of Swarthmore College, American secretary to the (Cecil) Rhodes Trustees (of the Rhodes Scholarship Fund), and director of the Institute for Advanced Study at Princeton; Secretary of War Henry Stimson, who initiated George Bush into "Skull and Bones" and whose special consultant Bernadotte Schmitt had also been a special advisor to Alger Hiss when he had served as secretary-general of the United Nations Conference on International Organization in San Francisco in 1945; and William Paley, founder of the Columbia Broadcasting System (CBS) whose chief advisor was Edward Bernays, Sigmund Freud's nephew who wrote *Propaganda*, in which Bernays reveals:

> Those who manipulate the organized habits and opinions of the masses constitute an invisible government which is the true ruling power of the country.... It remains a fact in almost every act of our daily lives, whether in the sphere of politics or business, in our social conduct or our ethical thinking, we are dominated by this relatively small number of persons.... As civilization has become more complex, and as the need for invisible government has been increasingly demonstrated, the technical means have been invented and developed by which opinion may be regimented.

The late Professor Carroll Quigley of Georgetown University described the CFR as "a front for J.P Morgan and Company in association with the very small American Round Table Group." Quigley further commented:

> The board of the CFR have carried ever since the marks of their origin.... There grew up in the 20th century a power structure between London and New York which penetrated deeply into university life, the press, and the practice of foreign policy.... The American branch of this "English Establishment" exerted much of its influence through five American newspapers (*New York Times, New York Herald Tribune, Christian Science Monitor, Washington Post*, and the late lamented *Boston Evening Transcript*).[1]

Arthur Schlesinger, Jr., penned a tome entitled *A Thousand Days* in 1965 in which he wrote that

> the New York financial and legal community was the heart of the American establishment.... Its front organizations [were] the Rockefeller, Ford and Carnegie foundations and the Council on Foreign Relations.

[ddd]

1925

IN 1925 TENNESSEE VS. JOHN THOMAS SCOPES, OR THE SCOPES "MONKEY trial," took place in Dayton, Tennessee. This trial was an important educational milestone regarding the teaching of the theory of evolution in public schools. *Scopes* pitted two famous barristers of the day—William Jennings Bryan and Clarence Darrow—against each other. The basic argument of the American Civil Liberties Union (ACLU) and the evolutionists was that evolutionary theory should not be censored from the public schools. After this trial, Fabian Socialist and first head of UNESCO Sir Julian Huxley claimed that humanism's "keynote, the central concept to which all its details are related, is evolution."

[Ed. Note: Huxley could have continued by predicting that educational and training methods in the future would be based on the theory of evolution—that man is an animal to be trained as Pavlov, Thorndike and Skinner trained animals, as with outcome-based education, mastery learning and direct instruction.]

[ddd]

1928

A DELIBERATE MATH "DUMB DOWN" WAS SERIOUSLY DISCUSSED IN 1928. A teacher named O.A. Nelson, John Dewey, Edward Thorndike (who conducted early behavioral psychology experiments with chickens), and other Council on Foreign Relations members attended a Progressive Education Association meeting in 1928 at which O.A. Nelson was informed that the purpose of "new math" was to dumb down students. Nelson revealed in a later interview with Young Parents Alert that the Progressive Education Association was a Communist front. According to the *National Educator* (July, 1979):

> Mr. O.A. Nelson, retired educator, has supplied the vitally important documentation needed to support the link-up between the textbooks and the Council on Foreign Relations. His letter was first printed in "Young Parents Alert" (Lake Elmo, Minnesota). His story is self-explanatory.
>
> I know from personal experience what I am talking about. In December 1928, I was asked to talk to the American Association for the Advancement of Science. On December 27th, naïve and inexperienced,

I agreed. I had done some special work in teaching functional physics in high school. That was to be my topic. The next day, the 28th, a Dr. Ziegler asked me if I would attend a special educational meeting in his room after the AAAS meeting. We met from 10 o'clock [p.m.] until after 2:30 a.m.

We were 13 at the meeting. Two things caused Dr. Ziegler, who was Chairman of the Educational Committee of the Council on Foreign Relations, to ask me to attend... my talk on the teaching of functional physics in high school, and the fact that I was a member of a group known as the Progressive Educators of America, which was nothing but a Communist front. I thought the word "progressive" meant progress for better schools. Eleven of those attending the meeting were leaders in education. Drs. John Dewey and Edward Thorndike, from Columbia University, were there, and the others were of equal rank. I checked later and found that ALL were paid members of the Communist Party of Russia. I was classified as a member of the Party, but I did not know it at the time.

The sole work of the group was to destroy our schools! We spent one hour and forty-five minutes discussing the so-called "Modern Math." At one point I objected because there was too much memory work, and math is reasoning; not memory. Dr. Ziegler turned to me and said, "Nelson, wake up! That is what we want... a math that the pupils cannot apply to life situations when they get out of school!" That math was not introduced until much later, as those present thought it was too radical a change. A milder course by Dr. Breckner was substituted but it was also worthless, as far as understanding math was concerned. The radical change was introduced in 1952. It was the one we are using now. So, if pupils come out of high school now, not knowing any math, don't blame them. The results are supposed to be worthless.

[Ed. Note: Mr. Nelson was formerly assistant principal at Wilson High School, Minneapolis, Minnesota, as well as Johnson High School in St. Paul. This writer was fortunate enough to verify the above story by calling a teacher colleague of the late Mr. Nelson. Also, members of the "Young Parents Alert" in Lake Elmo, Minnesota provided the writer with an audiocasette of the speech he gave at a Young Parents Alert education conference on April 28, 1979.]

Endnotes:

1 Much of the information in the entry concerning the formation of the Council on Foreign Relations, including Prof. Quigley's quote, is taken from the recently updated edition of Dr. Dennis Laurence Cuddy's *Secret Records Revealed: The Men, the Money, and the Methods Behind the New World Order* (Hearthstone Publishing, Ltd.: Oklahoma City, 1999).

3

THE TROUBLING THIRTIES

"And the builder of this new world must be education....
Plainly, the first step in the case of each country is to train an elite to think,
feel, and act internationally." The preceding words of Paul Mantoux of Paris,
France are taken from the foreword to *International Understanding* by John
Eugene Harley, published by the Stanford University Press in 1931.

A flock of individuals of collectivist persuasion jumped on Monsieur
Mantoux's bandwagon in "the troubling thirties." Aldous Huxley brought
along his *Brave New World*; Professor George Counts contributed his *Dare the
School Build a New Social Order?*; William Z. Foster (national chairman of the
Communist Party of the United States of America) wrote his *Toward a Soviet
America*; John Dewey co-authored *The Humanist Manifesto I*; the Carnegie
Corporation added its *Conclusions and Recommendations for the Social Studies*
and its Eight-Year Study (which was in the 1990s referred to by the Education
Commission of the States as the model for Outcome-Based Education); and
surprisingly, Herbert Hoover proposed a Research Committee on Recent Social
Trends to Implement the Planned Society.

The thirties were indeed troubling. Unfortunately, the average American
was unaware of the important steps being taken to collectivize (socialize) this
nation, particularly that of utilizing the schools as the vehicle through which
Mantoux's "new world" could be brought into being.

33

1931

INTERNATIONAL UNDERSTANDING BY JOHN EUGENE HARLEY (STANFORD University Press: Stanford, Calif., 1931) was published. Excerpts from the foreword by Paul Mantoux of Paris, France follows:

> And the builder of this new world must be education. Education alone can lay the foundation on which the building is to rest. On this point a kind of consensus has been reached by those who trust the future of international cooperation and those who refuse to believe in it. When the latter go about repeating that to succeed in such a task one would have to change human nature, they do but exaggerate the acknowledged need for a gradual and patient reshaping of the public mind.... How can a well-prepared elite be raised throughout the world to spread its influence over the masses, who can then support them in their turn?... Here we encounter the real problem, and it is essentially a problem of education.... During the last decade of the nineteenth century, in England, a group of men devoted to the study of economic problems endeavored to prepare the public mind for broad changes which, in their view, must be effected if social peace is to be preserved. To this end they founded the London School of Economics and Political Science, which today ranks among the most famous institutions of education. In our day, the problem has become more far-reaching still. Brutal events have supplied evidence of a truth that had been slowly gaining ground, namely, the interdependence of nations and the need for establishing in the world an order and harmony hitherto lacking.
>
> Some [undertakings] have specialized in one branch of knowledge, like the Institute of Pacific Relations; others cover the whole field of political science, like the Ecole des Sciences Politiques, the London School of Economics, and the Deutsche Hochschule fur Politik. Some are debating or research centers, widely differing in character from one another according as their tendency is scientific rather than political; such are the Royal Institute of International Affairs, the Council on Foreign Relations, the Social Science Research Council, and the American Academy of Political and Social Science.... the World Education Association and the International Bureau of Education are endeavoring to compare education in civilized countries and to bridge differences by a process of mutual borrowing of methods.... Plainly, the first step in the case of each country is to train an elite to think, feel, and act internationally.

1932

BRAVE NEW WORLD (DOUBLEDAY, DOTAN: GARDEN CITY, N.Y., 1932) BY Aldous Huxley, the renowned English novelist and essayist, was published. In this famous work Huxley satirized the mechanical world of the future in which technology replaced much of the everyday activities of humans.

PROFESSOR GEORGE COUNTS OF COLUMBIA UNIVERSITY TEACHERS COLLEGE wrote *Dare the School Build a New Social Order?* (John Day Company: New York, 1932). He and many other American educators traveling back and forth to Russia became completely convinced that the Soviet Communist system was the ultimate system. Counts was deeply involved in, and a member of, the Carnegie Foundation-financed Commission on the Social Studies which produced the American Historical Association's *Conclusions and Recommendations: Report of the Commission on the Social Studies* in 1934. He was also the author of *The American Road to Culture* series (Quinn and Broden, Co., Inc.: Rahway, N.J., 1930–1934) and *The Soviet Challenge to America* (John Day Co.: New York, 1931). Excerpts from this entry's major focus, Counts's *Dare the School Build a New Social Order?* follow:

> If property rights are to be diffused in industrial society, natural resources and all important forms of capital will have to be collectively owned.... This clearly means that, if democracy is to survive in the United States, it must abandon its individualistic affiliations in the sphere of economics.... Within these limits, as I see it, our democratic tradition must of necessity evolve and gradually assume an essentially collectivistic pattern.
>
> The important point is that fundamental changes in the economic system are imperative. Whatever services historic capitalism may have rendered in the past, and they have been many, its days are numbered. With its dedication [to] the principle of selfishness, its exaltation of the profit motive, its reliance upon the forces of competition, and its placing of property above human rights, it will either have to be displaced altogether or changed so radically in form and spirit that its identity will be completely lost.

Toward a Soviet America (Elgin Enterprises, Inc.: Los Angeles, 1932) by William Z. Foster, national chairman of the Communist Party of the United States, was published. Foster died in 1961 in Moscow and was given a state funeral in the Kremlin. His book called for

> a U.S. Department of Education; implementation of a scientific materialist philosophy; studies revolutionized, being cleansed of religious, patriotic and other features of the bourgeois ideology; students taught on the basis of Marxian dialectical materialism, internationalism and general ethics of a new socialist society; present obsolete methods of teaching will be superseded by a scientific pedagogy. The whole basis and organization of capitalist science will be revolutionized. Science will become materialistic, hence truly scientific. God will be banished from the laboratories as well as from the schools.

[Ed. Note: Everything called for by Foster has taken place. "Scientific pedagogy" is OBE/mastery learning/direct instruction (Pavlov/Skinner).]

President Herbert Hoover appointed a research committee on recent social trends to implement the planned society in 1932. (In 1919 Franklin Roosevelt had told a friend that he personally would like to see Hoover in the White House.) The Research Committee was not approved nor funded by Congress; it became an Executive Action and was underwritten by the Rockefeller Foundation. No report was made to Congress or to the people during the time it functioned. The work of that committee has been called "a monumental achievement by the largest community of social scientists ever assembled to assess the social condition of a nation."[1]

THE NATIONAL EDUCATION ASSOCIATION CREATED THE EDUCATIONAL POLI-
cies Commission (EPC) in 1932 for the purpose of changing the Goals for
American Education. In 1944 the EPC prepared a volume of extreme importance entitled *Education for All American Youth*. This highly promoted
document told, in fictional format and as though it were a *fait accompli*,
how the "Planners" would solve all the problems; not just of youth, but
of two imaginary communities—a village and a city—through involving
citizens in cooperation for the goals of the planners. The following goals
are laid out in this book:

- federal programs for health, education and welfare combined in one
  giant bureau
- Head Start programs
- getting pre-school children into the system
- teacher participation in curriculum decisions
- federal funds without federal control
- youth services through a "poverty program"
- removal of local control of political and educational matters "without
  seeming to do so"
- sex education

[Ed. Note: The involvement of "citizens in cooperation for the goals of the
planners" is "participatory democracy," unheard of publicly until twenty
years later.[2]]

THE EIGHT-YEAR STUDY WAS INITIATED BY THE COMMISSION ON RELATION
of School and College of the Progressive Education Association in 1932.
Chairman of the Commission and author of *The Story of the Eight-Year Study*
(Harper & Brothers: New York, 1942) Wilford M. Aikin chronicled the study's
beginnings and purposes. Recounting the proceedings at the 1930 annual
meeting of the Progressive Education Association, Aikin wrote:

> In the course of... discussion many proposals for improvement of the
> work of our secondary schools were made and generally approved. But almost
> every suggestion was met with the statement, "Yes, that should be done in
> our high schools, but it can't be done without risking students' chances of
> being admitted to college. If the student doesn't follow the pattern of sub-
> jects and units prescribed by the colleges, he probably will not be accepted."
> ...[S]omeone with courage and vision proposed that the Progressive Education
> Association should be asked to establish a Commission on the Relation of
> School and College to explore possibilities of better co-ordination of school
> and college work and to seek an agreement which would provide freedom
> for secondary schools to attempt fundamental reconstruction.... All members
> agreed that secondary education in the United States needed experimental
> study and comprehensive re-examination in the light of fuller knowledge of
> the learning process and the needs of young people in our society.... (p. 2)
> It has been assumed that physical and emotional reactions are not in-
> volved in the learning process, but if they are, they are not very important.
> The newer concept of learning holds that a human being develops through

doing those things which have meaning to him; that the doing involves the whole person in all aspects of his being; and that growth takes place as each experience leads to greater understanding and more intelligent reaction to new situations.

Holding this view, the participating schools believed that the school should become a place in which young people work together at tasks which are clearly related to their purposes.... The school should stimulate his whole being. It should provide opportunities for the full exercise of his physical, intellectual, emotional and spiritual powers as he strives to achieve recognition and a place of usefulness and honor in adult society. (p. 17)

Beginning in 1933 and continuing through 1941, the Eight-Year Study laid the groundwork for many of the education "reforms" and innovations we are encountering today. Most of the funding for the study came from the Carnegie Corporation of New York and the General Education Board. Commission and working committee members of note who participated in the study are: Wilford Aikin, Bruno Bettelheim, Burton P. Fowler, Frances Knapp, Louis Raths, Harold Rugg, Ralph Tyler, Hilda Taba, and Goodwin Watson.

Over the eight years of the study five volumes were published: *The Story of the Eight-Year Study* by Wilford Aikin; *Exploring the Curriculum: The Work of the Thirty Schools from the Viewpoint of Curriculum Consultants* by H.H. Giles, S.P. McCutcheon, and A.N. Zechiel; *Appraising and Recording Student Progress: Evaluation Records and Reports in the Thirty Schools* by Eugene R. Smith, Ralph W. Tyler and the evaluation staff; *Did They Succeed in College?: The Follow-up Study of the Graduates of the Thirty Schools* by Neal E. Drought and William E. Scott with preface by Max McConn; and *Thirty Schools Tell Their Story: Each School Writes of Its Participation in the Eight-Year Study*.

[Ed. Note: As will be seen in later entries in this book, the Eight-Year Study was foundational to outcome-based education and proposals to remove the Carnegie Unit. The Carnegie Unit has traditionally been the measure of participation; a certain number of units—hours in each class—in various disciplines have been required of the student in order to graduate or be accepted at a college. The Carnegie Unit measure is representative of the educational philosophy reflected in most state constitutions—that the state is responsible to provide and make available educational opportunities to all its citizens. The removal of this unit has been a central feature of current OBE/ML reform plans which reflect the philosophy that the state must guarantee that all citizens receive and achieve an educational outcome determined by the state. A change from "inputs" to "outputs."]

1933

HUMANIST MANIFESTO I WAS ORIGINALLY PUBLISHED IN 1933 IN THE *NEW Humanist* (Vol. VI, #3, 1933: Yellow Springs, Ohio), the main publication of the American Humanist Association. Co-author John Dewey, the noted philosopher and educator, called for a synthesizing of all religions and a "socialized and cooperative economic order." The following are excerpts taken from *Secular Humanism and the Schools: The Issue Whose Time Has*

Come by Onalee McGraw, Ph.D. (Critical Issues, Series 2, The Heritage Foundation (1979–1981): Washington, D.C., 1976):

> The basis of humanist belief is that there is no Almighty God, the Creator and Sustainer of life. Humanists believe that man is his own god. They believe that moral values are relative, devised according to the needs of particular people, and that ethics are likewise situational.
>
> Humanists reject Judeo-Christian moral and ethical laws, such as those contained in the Ten Commandments, calling them "dogmatic," "outmoded," "authoritarian," and a hindrance to human progress. In humanism, self-fulfillment, happiness, love, and justice are found by each man individually, without reference to any divine source. In the Judeo-Christian ethic, there is and can be no real self-fulfillment, happiness, love, or justice on earth that can be found which does not ultimately issue from Almighty God, the Creator and Sustainer.
>
> Several main differences between the humanist ethic and the Judeo-Christian ethic become clear upon reading the Humanist Manifestos I and II (1933 and 1973) and comparing them to the tenets of the Judeo-Christian ethic contained in the Old and New Testaments.... At issue is the basic concept concerning the nature of man and the "rules" by which men govern themselves individually, in society, and in government. In the Judeo-Christian ethic, man's ultimate deliverance and salvation—his finding a means of living together on this planet, in peace, harmony, justice, and love—is through God's given "rules."
>
> For the humanist, man's greatness, his coming of age, his total fulfillment is found when he no longer needs the idea of God. Man gets rid of God, not just to do what he wills but to regain possession of human greatness.
>
> Is Humanistic Education unconstitutional? Inasmuch as humanistic curriculum programs and "values clarification" and "moral education" teaching strategies are based upon materialistic values found only in man's nature itself, they reject the spiritual and moral tradition of theistic faith and religion. Thus, many parents who subscribe to Judeo-Christian belief oppose humanistic education in the tax-supported schools on grounds that such programs promote and advocate the religion of secular humanism in violation of the First Amendment to the *United States Constitution.*
>
> The U.S. Supreme Court cited Secular Humanism as a religion in the 1961 case of *Torcaso v. Watkins* (367 U.S. 488). Roy Torcaso, the appellant, a practicing Humanist in Maryland, had refused to declare his belief in Almighty God, as then required by State law in order for him to be commissioned as a notary public. The Court held that the requirement for such an oath "invades appellant's freedom of belief and religion." The Court declared in *Torcaso* that the "no establishment" clause of the First Amendment reached far more than churches of theistic faiths, that it is not the business of government or its agents to probe beliefs, and that therefore its inquiry is concluded by the fact of the profession of belief.
>
> The Court stated: "We repeat and again reaffirm that neither a State nor the Federal Government can constitutionally force a person to profess a belief or disbelief in any religion. Neither can constitutionally pass laws or impose requirements which aid all religions as against non-believers, and neither can aid those religions based on a belief in the existence of God as against those religions founded on different beliefs."
>
> The Court has also stated "Among religions in this country which do

not teach what would generally be considered a belief in the existence of God are Buddhism, Taoism, Ethical Culture, Secular Humanism and others." The *Torcaso* and *Abington* cases defined secular humanism as a religion and prohibited the government from establishing a religion of secularism by affirmatively opposing hostility to theistic religion, values, and beliefs.[3]

IN 1933 DR. PAUL MORT, CHAIRMAN OF THE PROGRESSIVE EDUCATION Association's Committee on the Emergency in Education and one of the foremost authorities in the U.S. on school finance, wrote an article entitled "National Support for Our Public Schools," which was published in the December issue of *Progressive Education* (The Progressive Education Association: Washington, D.C., 1933). An excerpt follows:

> At a time when schools should be particularly alert in helping to meet new conditions [Depression era], far too many of the individuals equipped to help in meeting these conditions have been removed from the payrolls, and in a vast number of communities schools have been reduced to the task of dishing out traditional subject matter.

[Ed. Note: Read this quote at the next school budget meeting when taxpayers are being manipulated into paying more and more taxes to pay for controversial programs that have nothing to do with "traditional subject matter." You might point out that children were compelled to receive a better academic (traditional subject matter) education during the Depression due to hard times (less money). See the 1946 entry dealing with *Community-Centered Schools: The Blueprint* for another quote by Paul Mort regarding how long it takes to implement "change."]

DR. GEORGE HARTMANN, PROFESSOR OF EDUCATIONAL PSYCHOLOGY AT Pennsylvania State College, wrote "A New Definition of the Educated Man" for the December 1933 issue of *Progressive Education*. Hartmann was active in the League for Independent Political Action, the Farmer-Laborer Political Federation, and the Socialist Party. He was co-author of *Readings in Industrial Psychology* (Appleton) and a frequent contributor to psychological journals. Excerpts from "A New Definition of the Educated Man" follow:

> Some may at once protest, "What? Is education to have as one of its symptoms the acceptance of radical views?" The answer is "Yes," if "radicalism" means any serious endeavor to alter our social arrangements for the better. We must consciously adopt and foster the position that it is the prime business of education to remake our institutions and our traditions—and learn to recognize the possession of this spirit as one of the main earmarks of the educated man.... The principal obstacle to the acceptance of this outcome is the persistence of a set of "inert" ideas (to use Whitehead's phrase) which lingers to afflict our civilization. One of the most subtle and pernicious of these inherited and unexamined postulates is the view that the aim of education (or life, for that matter) is the development of the individual's personality as such....
> ...For good or for ill, we must cease training people for what they are going to do, and point out instead what they *should* do. It will probably fall

to our generation to resurrect the word "ought" to its rightful status in the affairs of men—for what else are values if not areas of experience with an imperious push or pull emanating from them? [Emphasis added.]

There are some purists who will be frightened by the indoctrination which must inevitably follow if this recommendation is effective.... Such an objection is silly, for since indoctrination of attitudes occurs anyhow, our sole concern must be to ensure that the right ones are established....

How any one with the least pretensions to higher education can fail to be thrilled by the ultimate prospects of a single world government, the abolition of war and poverty, the enhancement of beauty in daily life, and the enlightened practice of eugenics and euthenics, is a riddle which can be explained only by a blind, exclusive regard for the immediately practicable.... What nobler and more enlightened aim for education in this century can possibly be proposed than that it enlists the enthusiasms of youth for the attainment of more rational forms of group living.

1934

CONCLUSIONS AND RECOMMENDATIONS FOR THE SOCIAL STUDIES (CHAS. Scribner's Sons: New York, 1934) compiled by the American Historical Association was published. This book was the result of a project funded to the tune of $340,000 by the Carnegie Corporation of New York called "Investigation of the Social Studies in the Schools," and was carried out by the American Historical Association. Professor Harold Laski, a philosopher of British socialism, said of this report: "At bottom, and stripped of its carefully neutral phrases, the report is an educational program for a Socialist America."[4] Important excerpts from *Conclusions* follow:

[Preface] The Commission is under special obligation to its sponsor, the American Historical Association. Above all, it recognizes its indebtedness to the Trustees of the Carnegie Corporation, whose financial aid made possible the whole five-year investigation of social science instruction in the schools, eventuating in the following *Conclusions and Recommendations*.

The Commission could not limit itself to a survey of textbooks, curricula, methods of instruction, and schemes of examination, but was impelled to consider the condition and prospects of the American people as a part of Western Civilization merging into a world order. (p. 1)

Of utmost importance is the following admission of the planners' goals to change our free enterprise/representative republic:

The Commission was also driven to this broader conception of its task by the obvious fact that American civilization, in common with Western civilization, is passing through one of the great critical ages of history, is modifying its traditional faith in economic individualism, and is embarking upon vast experiments in social planning and control which call for large-scale cooperation on the part of the people.... (pp. 1–2)

Cumulative evidence supports the conclusion that in the United States as in other countries, the age of *laissez faire* in economy and government is closing and a new age of collectivism is emerging.... (p. 16)

The implications for education are clear and imperative: (a) the efficient functioning of the emerging economy and the full utilization of its potentialities require profound changes in the attitudes and outlook of the American people, especially the rising generation—a complete and frank recognition that the old order is passing, that the new order is emerging.... (pp. 34–35)

Organized public education in the United States, much more than ever before, is now compelled, if it is to fulfill its social obligations, to adjust its objectives, its curriculum, its methods of instruction, and its administrative procedures to the requirements of the emerging integrated order.

If the school is to justify its maintenance and assume its responsibilities, it must recognize the new order and proceed to equip the rising generation to cooperate effectively in the increasingly interdependent society and to live rationally and well within its limitations and possibilities.... Signed: A.C. Krey, Chairman; Charles A. Beard; Isaiah Bowman (signed with reservations printed as Appendix C); Ada Comstock; George S. Counts; Avery O. Craven; Guy Stanton Ford; Carlton J.H. Hayes; Henry Johnson; A.C. Krey; Leon C. Marshall; Jesse H. Newton; Jesse F. Steiner. (Frank A. Ballou, Edmund E. Day, Ernest Hom, and Charles E. Merriam declined to sign these *Conclusions*.) (p. 35)

1939

MEIN KAMPF BY ADOLPH HITLER (STACKPOLE SONS PUBLISHERS: GERMANY, 1939) was published. Excerpts follow:

Academic school training, which today is the be-all and end-all of the State's entire educational work, can be taken over by the populist state with but slight changes. These changes are in three fields....

In the first place, the childish brain must in general not be burdened with things ninety-five per cent of which it does not need, and which it therefore forgets [emphasis in original]. The curriculum of primary and grammar schools, in particular, is a hybrid affair. In many of the individual subjects the material to be learned has increased to such an extent that only a fraction of it sticks in the individual's head, and only a fraction of this abundance can be used, while on the other hand it is not enough for the purpose of a man working and his living in a certain field. Take for instance the ordinary civil servant who has graduated from secondary school or from the upper *realschule*, when he is thirty-five or forty; and test the school learning which he once so painfully acquired. How little of all the stuff that was then drummed into him still remains! One will, indeed, be answered: "Yes, but the object of the amount that was learned was not simply to put a man in possession of a great deal of information later, but to train his power of intellectual absorption, and the thinking power, particularly the power of observation of the brain." This is true in part. But still there is danger that the youthful brain may be drowned in a flood of impressions which it is very seldom able to master, and whose individual elements it can neither sift nor judge according to their greater or less importance; and on top of that, it is usually not the inessential but the essential which is forgotten and sacrificed. Thus the main object of learning so much is lost; for after all it cannot consist in making the brain able to learn by unmeasured piling-up of instruction, but in creating for later life a fund of knowledge which the individual needs, and which through him once more benefits society....

Summing up: the populist state will have to put general scholastic instruction into a shortened form, including the very essentials. Outside of that, opportunity must be offered for thorough, specialized scholarly training. It is enough if the individual person is given a store of general knowledge in broad outline, receiving a thorough detailed and specialized training only in the field which will be his in later life.... The shortening of the schedule and of the number of classes thus attained would be used for the benefit of the development of the body, the character, of will and resolution....

There should be a sharp distinction between general and specialized knowledge. As the latter threatens, especially today, to sink more and more into service of Mammon, general cultivation, at least so far as its more idealistic approach is concerned, must be preserved as a counter-weight. Here too the principle must be incessantly pounded in that industry and technology, trade and commerce can flourish only so long as an idealistically-minded national community provides the necessary conditions. These conditions are founded not on materialistic egoism, but on self-denying readiness for sacrifice.

[Ed. Note: This author has quoted extensively from *Mein Kampf*'s chapter on education in order that the reader may see the similarity between Hitler's views on education and workforce training and those of American government officials implementing OBE and school-to-work programs in the 1990s. The above quotations also bear a striking resemblance to Theodore Sizer's Coalition of Essential Schools' philosophy of "less is more" and to the 1988 Association for Supervision and Curriculum Development's Robert Muller *World Core Curriculum* in use in Eugene, Oregon and elsewhere.]

[ddd]

Endnotes:

1   This material has been excerpted from *The Impossible Dream* by K.M. Heaton (Hart Publications: Bellingham, Wash., 1990). The Hon. John R. Rarick, former member of Congress, says of Mrs. Heaton's *The Impossible Dream*: "This is a dynamic volume of must reading for every American who loves this country and our system of government. Her in-depth writing arouses an awareness of the greatness this nation has achieved, a fear as to where we are heading, and of how far we must fall before it will all come to a halt.... There is an obvious, concerted program to irrevocably change our USA, yet many go on day after day, taking for granted what they didn't earn, and presuming the USA will go on forever. The change of our system from one of individual rights and freedoms to a one-world collective is taking place right before our very eyes." This book can be downloaded from the americandeception.com website.

2   Ibid, p. 215.

3   See 1988 entry for Supreme Court Justice Clarence Thomas's ruling on protection in the workplace from "abusive and intrusive" training, rendered when Thomas served as chairman of the Equal Employment Opportunity Commission (EEOC).

4   "A New Education for a New America"(*The New Republic*, July 29, 1936) carried quote by Prof. Harold Laski.

4

THE FOMENTATION
of the forties and fifties

Most *Webster*'s dictionaries define the word "fomentation" as follows: "to stir up trouble, instigate; incite (as to foment a riot)." The forties and fifties will be remembered for the radical, un-American activities and views of some Americans and their paid staffs who, having risen to the highest levels in the tax-exempt foundations and government, were unfortunately accepted by the man on the street as having the best interests of this nation at heart.

Had these individuals been dressed in dirty, ragged clothes, worn old shoes and funny felt hats, they would likely have been accused of "fomenting" or instigating trouble—planning the transformation of our nation from a sovereign, free constitutional republic to only one of many socialist democracies subservient to an internationalist world government. However, the fact that many of these gentlemen and their paid staffs were associated with Ivy League colleges, major industries, and prestigious civic and religious institutions, wore Brooks Brothers suits and button-down-collared shirts, and many had served with distinction in World War II worked to obscure the fact that their goals were alien to those of the average Main Street American—for that matter, alien to the *Constitution of the United States of America* and its *Bill of Rights*.

United States membership in the United Nations Educational, Scientific and Cultural Organization (UNESCO) in 1946 set in motion the destabilization of our society through the rejection of absolute morals and values, Judeo-Christian

tradition, and Roman law. Legislation authorizing United States membership
in UNESCO marked the end of United States autonomy in a very crucial area:
that of education. From this time on UNESCO would dictate education policy
to our government and others. This legislation was accompanied by President
Harry Truman's remarkable statement: "Education must establish the moral
unity of mankind." Truman's recommendation was bolstered by General
Brock Chisholm, a Canadian psychiatrist and friend of Soviet agent Alger Hiss.
Chisholm redefined health to include "mental" health, and presented a paper
entitled "The Psychiatry of Enduring Peace and Social Progress" to the United
Nations World Health Organization (WHO) in 1946 which "reinterpreted"
(eradicated) the word "morality." Chisholm asserted that

> The reinterpretation and eventually eradication of the concept of right
> and wrong... these are the belated objectives of practically all effective
> psychotherapy.

Brock Chisholm went on to recommend that teachers all over the world
be trained in "no right/no wrong" psychotherapeutic techniques found in the
schools today. The use of these techniques has resulted in (1) a high percentage
of the populace (60% if the polls taken during the summer of 1998 related to
the public's approval of President William Jefferson Clinton are to be believed)
responding that lying under oath is not sufficient reason for a president's removal from office, and (2) incredibly immoral/amoral and violent behavior
of American youth.

Has the reader ever seen a more exquisite illustration of the dialectic at
work? Create the chaos; people naturally call for help. The next step is to
impose the totalitarian solution. The "New World Disorder" (chaos), evident
on the nightly news, will ultimately require the same totalitarian control described so well by George Orwell in his novel *1984*. Orwell said, "If you want
a picture of the future, imagine a boot stamping on the human face—forever...
and remember, that is forever."

If one believes, as does this writer, that the well-being of mankind and the
stability of this world and its institutions depend on the rule of law, then the
1940s and 1950s will be remembered as the commencement of the unraveling
of civic order in the United States of America and throughout the world. The
rule of law is usually based on concepts of right and wrong, grounded in some
very widely accepted values that have been laid down since earliest times, and
even spelled out in Roman law. Since the end of World War II, instead of the
concept of law nations have been basing their actions on the United Nations'
humanistic (non-absolutist) situational ethics philosophy set forth in the state-

ments of General Brock Chisholm and President Harry Truman.

In 1948, shortly after General Chisholm made his recommendation to banish the concept of right and wrong, Professors B.F. Skinner and Alfred C. Kinsey published their books, *Walden Two* and *Sexual Behavior in the Human Male*, respectively. Skinner's novel, *Walden Two*, recommended—amongst other radical things—that "children be reared by the state, to be trained from birth to demonstrate only desirable characteristics and behavior." Kinsey, as a taxonomic scientist, wrested human sexuality from the constraints of love and marriage in order to advance the grand scheme to move America and the world toward the eugenic future envisioned by the elite scientists of the "New Biology," a shift which would affect the legal and medical professions.[1]

In 1953 Professor Skinner published *Science and Human Behavior* in which he said, "Operant conditioning shapes behavior as a sculptor shapes a lump of clay."[2] Also, in 1953, as if commissioned by Skinner and Kinsey to come up with a system to facilitate the necessary "changes" in behavior through operant conditioning and restructuring of the human personality (taxonomizing it), Professor Benjamin Bloom with the assistance of Professor David Krathwohl completed *Taxonomy of Educational Objectives*—a classification of learning behavior encompassing the cognitive, affective and psychomotor "domains" of learning.[3] *Webster's Dictionary* defines "taxonomy" as follows: "the study of the general principles of scientific classification: systematics." It should be noted that "scientific classification" related to education of a human being involves breaking behavior down into categories—to be measured and observed—behavior (actions) which can be isolated from the human personality with its important spiritual dimension.

Bloom said in *Taxonomy* that "the philosopher, as well as the behavioral scientist must find ways of determining what changes (values) are desirable and perhaps what changes are necessary." He stated that for the schools to attempt to change values is a virtual "Pandora's Box," but that

> [O]ur "box" must be opened if we are to face reality and take action, and that it is in this "box" that the most influential controls are to be found. The affective domain contains the forces that determine the nature of an individual's life and ultimately the life of an entire people.

Kinsey and Bloom, as scientists, were involved in the breaking down of man (taxonomizing) into units of behavior which Skinner, as a behaviorist, could identify, measure and change. This breaking down or "deconstructing of Man" was intended to separate man from his God-given, freedom-providing identity. This opened the door to the study of methods to control man and society: enter

Skinner, representing the Behaviorist School of the non-science "science" of psychology. Bloom changed the focus of education from a general, liberal arts education which benefited man as a whole to a narrow training which would be based on the behavioral psychologists' determination of what changes in "thoughts, feelings, and actions" would be desirable and, perhaps, necessary for the benefit of society as a whole.[4] Bloom's Taxonomy provided the finishing and crucial touch to the foundation laid by Dewey and others of the bedrock of today's education and teacher training.

The work of Bloom, Kinsey and Skinner provided the ingredients for future moral chaos with which we are struggling today at the national and international levels. *People Weekly*'s cover story for the week of June 23, 1997, "Heartbreaking Crimes: Kids without a Conscience? Rape, murder, a baby dead at a prom: A look at young lives that seem to have gone very, very wrong," offers vivid examples of incredibly immoral/amoral and violent behavior. Melissa Drexler, 18—baby was found dead at the prom; Daphne Abdela, 15— accused of a Central Park murder; Jeremy Strohmeyer, 18—accused of killing a 7-year-old; Corey Arthur, 19—accused of murdering Jonathan Levin; and Amy Grossberg, 18—accused of killing her newborn. In addition, the past few years have provided Americans with news of tragedy after tragedy involving young people shooting their peers and teachers at schools across the country in Arkansas, Kentucky, Oregon, Washington state, Georgia, and with the most tragic of all because of the numbers involved, in Littleton, Colorado where twelve students and one teacher were murdered, two perpetrators committed suicide, and many others were critically injured.

President Dwight D. Eisenhower signed the first agreements with the Soviet Union in 1958, including an education agreement—something that would not come as a surprise to those familiar with the White House-directed plan to merge the United States and the Soviet Union explained to Norman Dodd in 1953 by Rowan Gaither, president of the Ford Foundation. Similar agreements have been signed from that time forward. The most important education agreements negotiated between the Carnegie Corporation and the Soviet Academy of Science, and those signed by presidents Reagan and Gorbachev in 1985, remain in effect to this day.

The forties and fifties set all the essential ingredients in place for implementation in the sixties of a system of education geared to behavior and values change.

1941

EDUCATION FOR DESTRUCTION WAS WRITTEN BY DR. B.R. BURCHETT AND published by her in Philadelphia, Pennsylvania in 1941. The promotional flyer for Dr. Burchett's book read as follows:

Arresting... Disturbing... Exciting

NOW for the First Time—the AMAZING STORY OF COMMUNISTS' INIQUI-TOUS CORRUPTION OF AMERICA'S SCHOOL CHILDREN

HOW does the small Sovieteer minority control loyal teachers in our schools and colleges?
HOW are anti-American, anti-religious, anti-Christ textbooks forced upon teachers and students?
WHY are Washington and Jefferson ridiculed, while Marx and Lenin are canonized in the schools?
WHY are boys and girls of 13 taught free love, sexual promiscuity, and other degrading subjects?

WHAT'S GOING ON IN OUR AMERICAN SCHOOLS ANYWAY?

The answers to these and other dismaying questions are all found in *Education for Destruction*

[A]n eyewitness account by Dr. B.R. Burchett, former Head of Department of Latin in the Philadelphia public school system. It is a fearless and devastating exposé of Communism in America's schools, its concealed objectives, hidden motives, serpent-like power, and its vicious demoralization of children and adolescents. EVERY parent... EVERY educator... EVERY clergyman should read this book! [emphasis in original]

Dr. Burchett has included, opposite the title page of her book, a photograph of one of the classrooms in the school in which she taught. Under the photo are the words "No communism in the public schools?" accompanied by the following comments:

An observer, seeing that the largest poster in sight bears the letters U.S.S.R., might think that this is a picture of a school room in Russia. It is a picture of a room in a public school in Philadelphia. Did Superintendent Broome know about this? Did the Board of Education know about it? The picture is taken from Dr. Broome's Annual Report to the Board of Education, for the year ended June 30, 1936....
There had been a branch of the Young Communist League meeting in the South Philadelphia High School. According to the papers Miss Wanger made a great virtue of having disbanded it. Strangely, there was no "investigation" as to how it came to be meeting here in the first place, with a regularly assigned room and with a teacher as sponsor.
In spite of the facts presented in Mr. Allen's circular, and in spite of such an amazing thing as the meeting of the Young Communist League in the school, Dr. Broome, Superintendent of Schools, according to the *Philadelphia Record* of May 7, 1936, said: "I don't propose to investigate any general statement; if she (myself, Burchett) has anything specific to say I will be glad to hear her and investigate."... Recently, a special committee was appointed to consider the attacks on the "books of Harold O. Rugg and others on the

ground of subversive teaching." Dr. Edwin C. Broome was a member of that Committee. It is not surprising, therefore, that the Rugg books were white-washed in the Committee report of February 26, 1941.

According to the above quotes, Dr. Edwin Broome, under whom Dr. Burchett worked, was deeply involved in curriculum changes favorable to indoctrination of the students in communism. Of special interest is the fact that Dr. Edwin Broome is the same Dr. Edwin Broome about whom Dorothy Dawson wrote in her article entitled "The Blueprint: Community-Centered Schools" for the Montgomery County, Maryland *Advertiser*, April 11, 1973. Mrs. Dawson personally typed the original *Blueprint for Montgomery County Schools* for Dr. Broome to present to the board of education in 1946. An additional excerpt from Mrs. Dawson's article follows:

> In 1946 Dr. Edwin W. Broome was Superintendent of Schools.... From the *Maryland Teacher*, May 1953: "Dr. Edwin W. Broome announces retire-ment from Superintendency" by Mrs. Florence Massey Black, BCC High School. "Edwin W. Broome, the philosopher who took John Dewey out of his writings and put him to work in the classrooms of Montgomery County, is being honored upon his retirement this year by various groups in the State of Maryland and in his own county. He has served thirty-six years as superintendent of schools and forty-nine years in the county system. Greatly influenced by the late John Dewey, Edwin W. Broome set to work to show by analogy, specific example, and curriculum development, how each teacher could bring that philosophy into his work. And so it was that John Dewey came into the classrooms of Montgomery County."

[Ed. Note: Additionally, the *Maryland Teacher* did not mention that Dr. Broome had also served a controversial term as superintendent in the Philadelphia, Pennsylvania public school system. One might add that John Dewey not only came into the classrooms of Montgomery County, but also into all the classrooms of the United States, since the Montgomery County Plan was a pilot for the nation. This writer, when serving on her school's Philosophy Committee in 1973, had an updated copy of the "Montgomery County Philosophy" given to her by her Harvard-educated, change-agent superintendent. He recommended it as one philosophy statement to which our committee might wish to refer as we drew up a new philosophy for our school district. (See the Internet version for access to Appendix I for further excerpts from the *Blueprint for Montgomery County Schools*.)]

1942

IN 1942 *TIME* MAGAZINE (MARCH 16, 1942) RAN AN EXTENSIVE ARTICLE in its Religion section dealing with a proposal by Protestant groups in the United States for a plan of action toward "a just and durable peace" for the years following the end of World War II. Excerpts from *Time*'s "American Malvern" follow:

> These are the high spots of organized U.S. Protestantism's super-protes-tant new program for a just and durable peace after World War II:

- Ultimately, "a world government of delegated powers."
- Complete abandonment of U.S. isolationism.
- Strong immediate limitations on national sovereignty.
- International control of all armies and navies.
- A universal system of money... so planned as to prevent inflation and deflation.
- Worldwide freedom of immigration.
- Progressive elimination of all tariff and quota restrictions on world trade.
- "Autonomy for all subject and colonial peoples" (with much better treatment for Negroes in the U.S.).
- "No punitive reparations, no humiliating decrees of war guilt, no arbitrary dismemberment of nations."
- A "democratically controlled" international bank "to make development capital available in all parts of the world without the predatory and imperialistic aftermath so characteristic of large-scale private and governmental loans."

This program was adopted last week by 375 appointed representatives of 30-odd denominations called together at Ohio Wesleyan University by the Federal Council of Churches. Every local Protestant church in the country will now be urged to get behind the program. "As Christian citizens," its sponsors affirmed, "we must seek to translate our beliefs into practical realities and to create a public opinion which will insure that the United States shall play its full and essential part in the creation of a moral way of international living."...

The meeting showed its temper early by passing a set of 13 "requisite principles for peace" submitted by Chairman John Foster Dulles and his inter-church Commission to Study the Basis of a Just and Durable Peace. These principles, far from putting all the onus on Germany or Japan, bade the U.S. give thought to the short-sightedness of its own policies after World War I, declared that the U.S. would have to turn over a new leaf if the world is to enjoy lasting peace....

Some of the conference's economic opinions were almost as sensational as the extreme internationalism of its political program. It held that "a new order of economic life is both imminent and imperative"—a new order that is sure to come either "through voluntary cooperation within the framework of democracy or through explosive political revolution." Without condemning the profit motive as such, it denounced various defects in the profit system for breeding war, demagogues and dictators, "mass unemployment, widespread dispossession from homes and farms, destitution, lack of opportunity for youth and of security for old age." Instead, "the church must demand economic arrangements measured by human welfare... must appeal to the Christian motive of human service as paramount to personal gain or governmental coercion."

"Collectivism is coming, whether we like it or not," the delegates were told by no less a churchman than England's Dr. William Paton, co-secretary of the World Council of Churches, but the conference did not veer as far to the left as its definitely pinko British counterpart, the now famous Malvern Conference (*Time*, Jan. 20, 1941). It did, however, back up Labor's demand for an increasing share in industrial management. It echoed Labor's shibboleth that the denial of collective bargaining "reduces labor to a commodity." It urged taxation designed "to the end that our wealth may be more equitably distributed." It urged experimentation with government and cooperative ownership....

The ultimate goal: "a duly constituted world government of delegated powers: an international legislative body, an international court with adequate jurisdiction, international administrative bodies with necessary powers, and adequate international police forces and provision for enforcing its worldwide economic authority." (pp. 44, 46–47)

1943

THE AMERICAN FEDERATION OF TEACHERS (AFT) PUBLISHED THE BOOK *America, Russia and the Communist Party in the Postwar World* by John L. Childs and George S. Counts (The John Day Co., New York). (The reader will recall previous entries in this book relating to George S. Counts's role in the promotion of collectivism in the early part of this century and a similar agenda mapped out by the Federal Council of Churches referenced earlier.)

Prior to reading excerpts from this remarkably naïve book, the reader is reminded that it was written after Stalin's mass terror of the 1930s, which included purges, trials, self-denunciations, disappearances, imprisonments and executions. Excerpts taken from the book's jacket follow:

> This book is the first in a series projected for publication by The Commission on Education and the Postwar World of the American Federation of Teachers.... It demonstrates beyond all argument that if this war is to be followed by a just and lasting peace, America and Russia must find a way to get along together. For the United Nations, including America and Russia, is the only agency that can establish such a peace. Russia's stupendous achievements, and her vast area, population, and resources, make her a world power second to none. We are blind if we think we can continue half grateful ally, half suspicious rival, of Russia. What then, stands in the way of good relations between America and Russia? It is not differences in social systems and ideologies, for these *can* [emphasis in original] exist side by side.... It is a twenty-five year legacy of mutual suspicion, fear, and active hostility. The removal of this legacy requires concessions on both sides.

The preface states in part:

> Among the subjects already chosen (by the Commission) for study are the problems of American youth, education for world-citizenship, and the kind of educational program required to meet the demands of our technological society.

Excerpts from chapter X, "Bases of Collaboration," are revealing:

> 6. The United States, on her side, will have to make profound readjustments in her historical policy with regard to the rest of the world in general and with regard to the Soviet Union in particular.... The following constitute the bare minima of readjustments required of our country:
>
>> a. She must abandon the notion that she can enjoy security and maintain her democratic way of life by adhering to her historic policy of no "entangling alliances." She cannot have peace if she continues to

disregard the fact of world-wide interdependence—economic, political, military, and cultural. (p. 80)

   c. She must enter unreservedly into the partnership of the United Nations....

   e. She must revise her estimate of the enduring character of a collectivist state. She must banish from her mind the naïve doctrine, which controlled her relations with the Soviet Union in the early years of the Russian Revolution, that a collectivist state, being contrary to the laws of human nature, economics, and morality, must sooner or later collapse. (p. 81)...

   g. She must repudiate her earlier policy toward the Soviet Union. She must convince the Russian people she will have no part whatsoever in any effort to isolate, to encircle, and to destroy their collectivist state.... She must show by word, deed, and spirit that she is prepared to collaborate with nations of different traditions, different ideologies, and different economic and political systems in the organization of the world for peace and progress.... All of this means that those privileged groups in our own society which are fearful of any change in our property relations [free enterprise system] and which were primarily responsible for the shaping of the earlier policy must not be permitted to determine our postwar relations with Russia. (p. 82)

   h. She must, finally, have a vivid consciousness of the weaknesses in her own domestic economy. She must realize that, in spite of the very real advances made in recent years, we have only begun to face the problem of rebuilding the economic foundations of our democracy. In the process of rebuilding perhaps we may be able to learn something from the experiences of the Russian people. (p. 83)

1945

[ddd]

UNITED NATIONS CHARTER BECAME EFFECTIVE ON OCTOBER 24, 1945. Playing an important role in the creation of the United Nations was the United States Chamber of Commerce. In 1999 when parents find their local Chamber of Commerce deeply involved in the highly controversial, socialist/fascist, dumbing-down workforce training—necessary for a planned, global economy—the fact that the U.S. Chamber was a prime mover in establishing the United Nations should not be forgotten. The following information is excerpted from an important research paper by Erica Carle entitled "The Chamber of Commerce: Its Power and Goals" (December, 1983):

    Two slogans were popularized in order to gain backing for Chamber leadership: "World peace through world trade" and "More business in government and less government in business."

    The Chamber sought to commercialize the world under its own direction. To do this it needed to find ways to affect and bypass operating policies of various states and nations. To change national policies, and even laws, required popular support and collective action. A new type of blanket organization was needed, one that could blanket not only governments, but professions, unions, educational institutions, farms, industries, sciences, religions and even families. An organization was sought which could bring about the cooperation and commercialization of all of these. A strong controllable international blanket organization was needed.

By the 1930's plans for the new blanket organization to serve the Chamber's purposes, the United Nations, were already well under way. The Chamber had the cooperation of tax-exempt foundations, some of which, such as the Carnegie Foundation for International Peace and the Rockefeller Foundation, had been set up early in the century. Large banks and trusts could see future profits for themselves if they cooperated with the Chamber; and the cooperation of international corporations was assumed, especially since Thomas J. Watson was President of the International Chamber of Commerce and a Trustee of the Carnegie Foundation for International Peace.

World War II aided... efforts to establish a "rational" international commercial system.... The United Nations organization could be used to gain governments' compliance with the Chamber's plans for a unified, controlled world economy, and also the cooperation of various non-Governmental organizations.

The following are some of the measures the Chamber of Commerce has supported to aid in the transfer of power from individuals and independent governments, groups, businesses and professions to the Chamber-advocated management system:

1. Creation of the United Nations.
2. Creation of the Organization for Economic Cooperation and Development.
3. Regional Government or "New Federalism."
4. Medicare (Commercialization of medical professions).
5. Postal reorganization.
6. Organized Crime Control Act.
7. Contracting for school services with private industry.
8. Voucher system for education.
9. Management and human relations techniques for handling personnel in industry.
10. Health care planning councils.
11. Prepaid medical practice (HMOs).
12. Federal land use planning.
13. Federally-imposed career education.
14. Equal Rights Amendment.
15. Cross-town busing for desegregation.[5]

INDIANA UNIVERSITY ADDED TWO NEW FACULTY MEMBERS TO ITS ROSTER IN 1945. Dr. Burrhus Frederic (B.F.) Skinner became chairman of the Psychology Department and continued work on his forthcoming book, *Walden Two*. Dr. Hermann J. Muller (future Nobel Prize winner), zoologist and private advocate of forced sterilization and selective eugenics, arrived in the Zoology Department to join long-time faculty member Alfred C. Kinsey. A publicly-allied communist, Muller had authored the book *Out of the Night: A Biologist's View of the Future* (The Vanguard Press: New York, 1935), which dealt with selective breeding and the advocacy of cloning of masses of human "resources." (Thirteen years after Muller's death in 1967 a sperm bank was established in California in Muller's honor, the Repository for Germinal Choice, which stores and distributes the sperm of Nobel Prize winners and others of "exceptional" ability.)

1946

"THE PSYCHIATRY OF ENDURING PEACE AND SOCIAL PROGRESS" IN *THE William Alanson White Memorial Lectures by Major General G.B. [Brock] Chisholm, C.B.E., M.D., Deputy Minister of Health, Dept. of National Health and Welfare, Canada* (Vol. 9, No. 1) was published in 1946. The book contained a foreword by Abe Fortas, former U.S. secretary of state. The article "The Psychiatry of Enduring Peace and Social Progress" was re-published in the March 1948 (No. 437) issue of *International Conciliation* published by the World Health Organization and Carnegie Endowment for International Peace. This last version included a preface written by Alger Hiss, former president of the Carnegie Endowment who would later be convicted of spying for the Soviet Union. It is important also to remember that Dr. David Hamburg, former president of the Carnegie Corporation of New York who signed the Carnegie Corporation/Soviet Academy of Science education agreement in 1985, is a psychiatrist. Excerpts from Brock Chisholm's article follow:

> The re-interpretation and eventually eradication of the concept of right and wrong which has been the basis of child training, the substitution of intelligent and rational thinking for faith in the certainties of the old people, these are the belated objectives of practically all effective psychotherapy. Would it not be sensible to stop imposing our local prejudices and faiths on children and give them all sides of every question so that in their own time they may have the ability to size things up, and make their own decisions? ...If the race is to be freed from its crippling burden of good and evil it must be psychiatrists who take the original responsibility.... The people who matter are the teachers, the young mothers and fathers, the parent-teacher associations, youth groups, service clubs, schools and colleges, the churches and Sunday schools—everyone who can be reached and given help toward intellectual freedom and honesty for themselves and for the children whose future depends on them....

> The battle, if it is to be undertaken, will be long and difficult but the truth will prevail—whenever enough people want it to. With luck we have perhaps fifteen or twenty years before the outbreak of the next world war if we remain as we are, twenty years in which to change the dearest certainties of enough of the human race, twenty years in which to root out and destroy the oldest and most flourishing parasitical growth in the world, the tree of the knowledge of good and evil, so that man may learn to preserve his most precious heritage, his innocence and intellectual freedom, twenty years in which to remove the necessity for the perverse satisfactions to be found in warfare.

If the reader is inclined to dismiss the above statements by Brock Chisholm as statements from an individual biased by his psychiatric profession and spoken at a point in time remote from today, please read the following statement by U.S. Ambassador to the United Nations Madeline Albright in

Atlanta, Georgia, September of 1996, as it appeared in *The Congressional Digest* for January 1997:

> Setting Global Standards. The United Nations is one instrument that we use to make this world a little less inhumane, a little less brutal, a little less unfair than it otherwise would be. This brings us to another important, and basic, function of the United Nations. And that is its role in creating a global consensus about what is right and what is wrong. (p. 14)

[ddd]

C.S. LEWIS WROTE *THAT HIDEOUS STRENGTH* (COPYRIGHT BY CLIVE STAPLES Lewis: Macmillan Company: New York, 1946). Lewis's uncanny ability to predict accurately how society would be manipulated into acceptance of totalitarian control was displayed in the following excerpt taken from a conversation Lewis's fictitious Lord Feverstone had with a young man named Mark:

> [Feverstone] "Man has got to take charge of Man. That means, remember, that some men have got to take charge of the rest—which is another reason for cashing in on it as soon as one can. You and I want to be the people who do the taking charge, not the ones who are taken charge of. Quite."
>
> "What sort of thing have you in mind?"
>
> "Quite simple and obvious things, at first—sterilization of the unfit, liquidation of backward races (we don't want any dead weights), selective breeding. Then real education, including pre-natal education. By real education I mean one that has no 'take-it-or-leave-it' nonsense. A real education makes the patient what it wants infallibly: whatever he or his parents try to do about it. Of course, it'll have to be mainly psychological at first. But we'll get on to biochemical conditioning in the end and direct manipulation of the brain...."
>
> "But this is stupendous, Feverstone."
>
> "It's the real thing at last. A new type of man: and it's people like you who've got to begin to make him."
>
> "That's my trouble. Don't think it's false modesty, but I haven't yet seen how I can contribute."
>
> "No, but we have. You are what we need: a trained sociologist with a radically realistic outlook, not afraid of responsibility. Also, a sociologist who can write."
>
> "You don't mean you want me to write up all this?"
>
> "No. We want you to write it down—to camouflage it. Only for the present, of course. Once the thing gets going we shan't have to bother about the great heart of the British public. We'll make the great heart what we want it to be." (p. 42)

[Ed. Note: See Internet version for Appendix XXVI, which contains an example of Brian Rowan's literary fulfillment of Feverstone's request for "a trained sociologist who can write." It is also interesting to note that William Spady, the "father of OBE," is a sociologist as well. The definition by Feverstone of "real education" not being "take-it-or-leave-it nonsense" reflects the 1990s outcome-based education reform call for emphasis on "outputs" rather than on constitutionally supported "inputs" discussed in chapter 1.]

COMMUNITY-CENTERED SCHOOLS: THE BLUEPRINT FOR MONTGOMERY COUNTY *Schools, Maryland,* was proposed by Dr. Nicholaus L. Englehardt and Associates, Consultants, and written by Dr. Walter D. Cocking of New York City on April 1, 1946. This material was provided by the late Dorothy Dawson who was secretary to the superintendent of schools of Montgomery County, Maryland, Dr. Edwin Broome. Mrs. Dawson typed this *Blueprint* for presentation to the Montgomery County Board of Education. (See Internet version for Appendix I.) The Letter of Transmittal that accompanied *The Blueprint* said:

> Dr. Paul Mort and others have accumulated evidence which shows a period of almost fifty years between the establishment of need [needs assessment] and the school programs geared to meet it... if the school as an agency of society is to justify itself for the period ahead of us, it must be accepted that its fundamental function is to serve the people of the entire community, the very young children, the children of middle years, early adolescent youth, older youth and the adults as well.

[ddd]

THE EDUCATIONAL TESTING SERVICE (ETS) OF PRINCETON, NEW JERSEY, was funded with an initial endowment of $750,000 from the Carnegie Corporation in 1946.

[Ed. Note: For further amplification and understanding of the far-reaching implications of the relationship between Educational Testing Service and the Carnegie Corporation, the reader should be sure to read: 1964 entry regarding the National Assessment of Educational Progress (NAEP) which ETS administers; two 1995 entries for articles from *The Bismarck* (North Dakota) *Tribune* dealing with NAEP; and the Internet version for Appendix IV.]

1947

NATIONAL TRAINING LABORATORY (NTL) WAS ESTABLISHED IN **1947.** THE first laboratory session on human relations and group processes was held at Gould Academy in Bethel, Maine. Founders of the National Training Laboratory had important connections with the Office of Strategic Services (OSS)—World War II forerunner to the Central Intelligence Agency (CIA). The NTL would become—with the National Education Association (NEA)—a premiere agency for human relations training (change agent/brainwashing).

A 1962 book published jointly by NTL and the NEA entitled *Five Issues in Training* addressed the process of "unfreezing, changing, and refreezing" attitudes in order to bring about change by stating the following: "The Chinese communists would remove the target person from those situations and social relationships which tended to confirm and reinforce the validity of the old attitudes." (p. 49)

This process is widely used in education, theology, medicine, business, government, etc., by pressuring individuals to participate in "retreats," removing them from familiar surroundings to "unfreeze" their attitudes and values. People have been coming from all over the world to attend these retreats at NTL in Bethel, Maine since its founding. An excerpt from the 1977 issue of *NTL Newsletter* follows:

> From the New Britain workshop dialogues of the founders emerged the notions of "action research laboratory" and "change agent" which were terms coined to denote a very vigorous proactive social change kind of posture, a merging of radical education, deviant behavioral science, and humanistic democracy.

HIGHER EDUCATION FOR AMERICAN DEMOCRACY; V. 3, ORGANIZING HIGHER Education, report of the President's Commission on Higher Education (U.S. Government Printing Office: Washington, D.C., 1947) was circulated. It revealed that

> [t]he role which education will play officially must be conditioned essentially by policies established by the State Department in this country and by ministries of foreign affairs in other countries. Higher education must play a very important part in carrying out in this country the program developed by the United Nations Educational, Scientific, and Cultural Organization and in influencing that program by studies and reports bearing upon international relations.... The United States Office of Education must be prepared to work effectively with the State Department and with the UNESCO. (p. 48)

1948

SEXUAL BEHAVIOR IN THE HUMAN MALE BY ALFRED C. KINSEY WITH Wardell Pomeroy, Clyde Martin and Paul Gebhard (W.B. Saunders: Philadelphia, Pa., 1948) was published. This book and the controversial "research" it represented became a lightning rod around which much social turmoil was generated in this country and abroad.

As Judith Reisman, Ph.D., has described in her book, *Kinsey: Crimes and Consequences*[6] (Institute for Media Education: Arlington, Va., 1998):

> Three books written by leading legal, scholarly, and scientific authorities and assisted by Kinsey, were published in 1948 in tandem with *Kinsey's Sexual Behavior in the Human Male*. All three books called for legal implementation of Kinsey's "grand scheme" to loosen, alter and/or overturn America's laws concerning sexual behavior.

Those books were: (1) *Sexual Habits of American Men: A Symposium on the Kinsey Report*, edited by Albert Deutsch (Prentice Hall: New York, 1948); (2) *American Sexual Behavior and the Kinsey Report* by Morris Ernst and David Loth (W.W. Norton: New York, 1948); and (3) a re-publication of the 1933 book *The Ethics of Sexual Acts* (Alfred A. Knoff: New York, 1948) by René Guyon, French jurist and pedophile noted for having coined the phrase in reference to children: "Sex before eight or it's too late." To further elaborate on the connections of these books and ideas generated by them, Reisman wrote on page 189 of her book:

> Dr. Harry Benjamin, an endocrinologist and international sexologist, and close friend and correspondent of both Kinsey and Guyon, wrote of their collaboration in his Introduction to Guyon's 1948 book:
>
> > Many... sex activities, illegal and immoral, but widely practiced, are recorded by both investigators... Guyon speaking as a philosopher, and Kinsey, judging merely by empirical data... [are] upsetting our most cherished conventions. Unless we want to close our eyes to the truth or imprison 95% of our male population, we must completely revise our legal and moral codes.... It probably comes as a jolt to many, even open-minded people, when they realize that chastity cannot be a virtue because it is not a natural state.

[Ed. Note: The above extraordinary statement revealed the depth of some very perverse thinking in the area of human sexuality—thinking which would become institutionalized to the extent that in 1999 the American Psychological Association (APA) felt comfortable publishing in its *Journal* a study suggesting that pedophilia is harmless and even beneficial if consensual. According to an article in the June 10, 1999 issue of *The Washington Times*, entitled "Psychology Group Regrets Publishing Pedophilia Report: Practice Not Always Harmful, Article Said," the APA was taken by surprise when "its report provoked angry public reaction, including a House of Representatives resolution condemning it. It followed up with an abrupt about-face in an apologetic letter to House Majority Whip Tom DeLay" which expressed regret—not that it supported the idea of acceptable adult-child sex—but that the article had been published in a public journal.]

To prove the march toward sexual revolution had, indeed, reached the courts, Reisman further quotes Manfred S. Guttmacher, M.D., author of *The Role of Psychiatry and Law* (Charles C. Thomas: Springfield, Ill., 1968) and special consultant to the American Law Institute Model Penal Code Committee:

> In 1950 the American Law Institute began the monumental task of writing a Model Penal Code. I am told that a quarter of a century earlier the Institute had approached the Rockefeller Foundation for the funds needed to carry out this project, but at that time, Dr. Alan Gregg, man of great wisdom, counseled the Foundation to wait, that the behavioral sciences were on the threshold of development to the point at which they could be of great assistance. Apparently, the Institute concluded that the time has arrived.

WALDEN TWO, A NOVEL BY B.F. SKINNER (THE MACMILLAN COMPANY: New York, 1948) was published. Skinner recommended in this novel that children be reared by the state; to be trained from birth to demonstrate only desirable characteristics and behavior. He also wrote on page 312 of the paperback edition:

> What was needed was a new conception of man, compatible with our scientific knowledge, which would lead to a philosophy of education bearing

some relation to educational practices. But to achieve this, education would have to abandon the technical limitations which it had imposed upon itself and step forth into a broader sphere of human engineering. Nothing short of a complete revision of a culture would suffice.

The late Professor Skinner died before his ideal school described in *Walden Two* would become somewhat of a reality—a "Model School for the 21st Century." The following excerpts from *Walden Two* contain some restructuring terminology and resemble in many ways what a "restructured" school is supposed to look like in the 1990s:

> A much better education would cost less if society were better organized.
>
> We can arrange things more expeditiously here because we don't need to be constantly re-educating. The ordinary teacher spends a good share of her time changing the cultural and intellectual habits which the child acquires from its family and surrounding culture. Or else the teacher duplicates home training, in a complete waste of time. Here we can almost say that the school *is* the family, and vice versa. [emphasis in original]
>
> ...We don't need "grades." Everyone knows that talents and abilities don't develop at the same rate in different children. A fourth-grade reader may be a sixth-grade mathematician. The grade is an administrative device which does violence to the nature of the developmental process. Here the child advances as rapidly as he likes in any field. No time is wasted in forcing him to participate in, or be bored by, activities he has outgrown. And the backward child can be handled more efficiently too.
>
> We also don't require all our children to develop the same abilities or skills. We don't insist upon a certain set of courses. I don't suppose we have a single child who has had a "secondary school education," whatever that means. But they've all developed as rapidly as advisable, and they're well educated in many useful respects. By the same token, we don't waste time in teaching the unteachable. The fixed education represented by a diploma is a bit of conspicuous waste which has no place in Walden Two. We don't attach an economic or honorific value to education. It has its own value or none at all.
>
> Since our children remain happy, energetic, and curious, we don't need to teach "subjects" at all. We teach only the techniques of learning and thinking. As for geography, literature, the sciences—we give our children opportunity and guidance, and they learn them for themselves. In that way we dispense with half the teachers required under the old system, and the education is incomparably better. Our children aren't neglected, but they're seldom, if ever, *taught* anything. [emphasis in original] (pp. 118–120)

In the United States, 1990s teachers are instructed to act as facilitators and guidance counselors. Computer technology will take care of workforce training and whatever "education" remains. Wisconsin history teacher Gene Malone wrote a short review of *Walden Two*. Some of Malone's excerpts follow:

> *Walden Two* is fiction based on a Utopian community named after Henry David Thoreau's nature-Utopia, Walden Pond. Burris... telling the story of a planned society appears to be B.F. Skinner speaking. Frazier is the planner/manager/founder of the Utopia.... The Utopia/Walden Two is presented in

the United States. Burris and his friends are given a tour of Walden Two and Castle is unimpressed. Burris, at the end, joins Walden Two. Quotes follow from pages:

92—"Community love"
245—"We not only can control human behavior, we MUST."
219—"The new order."
189—"Psychologists are our priests."
188—"Walden Two is not a religious community."
282—"Their behavior is determined, yet they're free."
286—"What is love, except another name for the use of positive reinforcement?"
278—"Let us control the lives of our children and see what we can make of them."
274—"Behave as you ought!"
186—"We can make men adequate for group living.... That was our faith."
134—"Our goal is to have every adult member of Walden Two regard our children as his own, and to have every child think of every adult as his parent."
135—"No sensible person will suppose that love or affection has anything to do with blood."
112—"Education in Walden Two is part of the life of the community.... Our children begin to work at a very early age."
108—"History is honored in Walden Two only as entertainment."
105—"We are always thinking of the whole group."
160—"We are opposed to competition."
139—"The community, as a revised family"

Conclusion: This fictional presentation of Skinner's ideal community is much like the language and laws in use today by the behavioral elite—describing their plans for your children, your schools, your country. It is behavior management by the unchosen.

During the year of 1948, Dr. Skinner moved his family from Indiana University to Cambridge, Massachusetts to join the faculty of Harvard University.

DURING 1948 ALGER HISS, WHO LATER WOULD BE CONVICTED OF SPYING for the Soviet Union, wrote the preface to Gen. Brock Chisholm's lecture, "The Psychiatry of Enduring Peace and Social Progress," which was republished in *International Conciliation* (No. 437, March, 1948, p. 109). Alger Hiss was at that time president of the Carnegie Endowment for International Peace, the publisher of *International Conciliation*. The preface to Chisholm's lecture, which redefined the word "health," follows:

The World Health Organization came into formal existence early in February. For nearly a year and a half its most urgent functions have been performed by an Interim Commission.
The new specialized agency carries on one of the most successful parts of the work of the League of Nations. The Constitution of the World Health Organization, however, has a far wider basis than that established for the League organization, and embodies in its provisions the broadest principles in public health service today. Defining health as a "state of complete physical, mental, and social well-being, and not merely the absence of disease or

infirmity," it includes not only the more conventional fields of activity but also mental health, housing, nutrition, economic or working conditions, and administrative and social techniques affecting public health. In no other field is international cooperation more essential and in no other field has it been more effective and political difference less apparent.

The present issue of *International Conciliation* reviews the history of the Interim Commission through its last meeting in February. The first World Health Assembly will convene in June 1948. A brief introductory article has been prepared by Dr. Brock Chisholm, Executive Secretary, World Health Organization, Interim Commission. Dr. Chisholm is an eminent psychiatrist and served during the war as Director-General of Medical Services of the Canadian Army. The main discussion of the World Health Organization has been contributed by C.E.A. Winslow, Professor Emeritus of the Yale University and Editor of the American Journal of Public Health. Dr. Winslow has been a member of the Board of Scientific Directors of the International Health Division of the Rockefeller Foundation, Medical Director of the League of the Red Cross Societies, and Expert Assessor of the Health Committee of the League of Nations.

> Alger Hiss, President
> New York, New York
> February 21, 1948

1949

BASIC PRINCIPLES OF CURRICULUM AND INSTRUCTION (UNIVERSITY OF CHIcago Press: Chicago, 1949) by Professor Ralph Tyler, chairman of the Department of Education at the University of Chicago, was published. Tyler stated that

> Since the real purpose of education is not to have the instructor perform certain activities but to bring about significant changes in the student's pattern of behavior, it becomes important to recognize that any statement of the objective... should be a statement of changes to take place in the student.

1950

IN 1950 "MAN OUT OF A JOB: PASADENA TRIES TOO LATE TO HOLD ONTO Its School Superintendent" was carried in *Life Magazine* (December 11, 1950). An excerpt follows:

> Last month criticism of [Willard] Goslin took a serious turn. A militant citizens' group accused him of permitting Communistic influences in the schools—because he continued already established classes in sex education and favored the elimination of report cards. Then while Goslin was in New York City on business, the school board sent him a telegram asking him to resign.

1951

"THE GREATEST SUBVERSIVE PLOT IN HISTORY: REPORT TO THE AMERICAN People on UNESCO" from *The Congressional Record, Proceedings and Debates*

of the 82nd Congress, First Session in 1951 included the extended remarks of
Hon. John T. Wood (Idaho) in the U.S. House of Representatives, Thursday,
October 18. Excerpts follow:

> Mr. Speaker, I am herewith appending an article published by the Ameri-
> can Flag Committee... bearing the title "A Report to the American People on
> UNESCO." Just how careless and unthinking can we be that we permit this
> band of spies and traitors to exist another day in this land we all love? Are
> there no limits to our callousness and neglect of palpable and evident treason
> stalking rampant through our land, warping the minds and imaginations of
> even our little children, to the lying propaganda and palpable untruths we
> allow to be fed to them through this monstrous poison?...
>
> UNESCO's scheme to pervert public education appears in a series of
> nine volumes, titled *Toward World Understanding* which presume to instruct
> kindergarten and elementary grade teachers in the fine art of preparing our
> youngsters for the day when their first loyalty will be to a world government,
> of which the United States will form but an administrative part....
>
> The program is quite specific. The teacher is to begin by eliminating any
> and all words, phrases, descriptions, pictures, maps, classroom material or
> teaching methods of a sort causing his pupils to feel or express a particular
> love for, or loyalty to, the United States of America. Children exhibiting such
> prejudice as a result of prior home influence—UNESCO calls it the outgrowth
> of the narrow family spirit—are to be dealt an abundant measure of counter
> propaganda at the earliest possible age. Booklet V, on page 9, advises the
> teacher that:
>
>> The kindergarten or infant school has a significant part to play in
>> the child's education. Not only can it correct many of the errors of home
>> training, but it can also prepare the child for membership, at about the
>> age of seven, in a group of his own age and habits—the first of many
>> such social identifications that he must achieve on his way to member-
>> ship in the world society.

[ddd]

IMPACT OF SCIENCE UPON SOCIETY BY BERTRAND RUSSELL (COLUMBIA UNI-
versity Press: New York, 1951; Simon and Schuster: New York, 1953) was
published. What follows calls to mind the extensive use of behavior modification techniques on students, causing them to question and reject traditional
values, and preparing them to willingly submit to totalitarian controls:

> Education should aim at destroying free will so that after pupils are thus
> schooled they will be incapable throughout the rest of their lives of think-
> ing or acting otherwise than as their school masters would have wished....
> Influences of the home are obstructive; and in order to condition students,
> verses set to music and repeatedly intoned are very effective.... It is for a
> future scientist to make these maxims precise and discover exactly how
> much it costs per head to make children believe that snow is black. When
> the technique has been perfected, every government that has been in charge
> of education for more than one generation will be able to control its subjects
> securely without the need of armies or policemen.

1952

SUBVERSIVE INFLUENCE IN THE EDUCATIONAL PROCESS: HEARINGS BEFORE the Subcommittee to Investigate the Administration of the Internal Security Act and Other Internal Security Laws of the Committee on the Judiciary: United States Senate, Eighty-Second Congress, Second Session on Subversive Influence in the Educational Process was printed for the Committee on the Judiciary (Printing Office: Washington, D.C., Sept. 9, 10, 23, 24, 25 and October 13, 1952). Robert Morris was counsel and Benjamin Mandel was director of research for this project. Excerpts from the testimony of Bella V. Dodd, New York, who was accompanied by her attorney Godfrey P. Schmidt, follow:

> Mr. Morris: Dr. Dodd, how recently have you been associated with the Communist Party?
>
> Mrs. Dodd: June 1949.
>
> Mr. Morris: Do you mean you severed your connection with the Communist Party at that time?
>
> Mrs. Dodd: They severed their connection with me. I had previously tried to find my way out of the Communist Party. In 1949 they formally issued a resolution of expulsion....
>
> Mr. Morris: Dr. Dodd, will you tell us what relationship you bore to the Communist Party organization while you were the legislative representative for the Teachers' Union?
>
> Mrs. Dodd: Well, I soon got to know the majority of the people in the top leadership of the Teachers' Union were Communists, or, at least, were influenced by the Communist organization in the city.
>
> Sen. Homer Ferguson (Mich.): In other words, the steering committee, as I take your testimony, was used for the purpose of steering the teachers along the line that communism desired?
>
> Mrs. Dodd: On political questions, yes.... I would say also on certain educational questions. You take, for instance, the whole question of theory of education, whether it should be progressive education or whether it should be the more formal education. The Communist Party as a whole adopted a line of being for progressive education. And that would be carried on through the steering committee and into the union.[7]

[Ed.Note: Let us look ahead to 1985 to the U.S.-Soviet Education Agreement signed by presidents Reagan and Gorbachev, and the Carnegie-Soviet Education Agreement. It was the same Robert Morris who served as counsel for the Senate Judiciary Committee's investigation who later, in 1989 as the new president of America's Future, Inc., permitted the publication of this writer's pamphlet "Soviets in the Classroom: America's Latest Education Fad"—four years after the agreements were signed. At that time, Mr. Morris—as politically knowledgeable and astute a person as one could hope to meet—was completely unaware of the agreements! The major conservative organizations and media had refused to publicize these treasonous agreements, with the exception of two well-known organizations which gave them "once over lightly" treatment.]

COOPERATIVE PROCEDURES IN LEARNING (COLUMBIA UNIVERSITY PRESS: New York, 1952) by Alice Miel, professor of education at Teachers College of Columbia University, and associates at the Bureau of Publications at Teachers College of Columbia University was published. Excerpts follow:

> [Foreword] As is true of most of the publications of the Horace Mann-Lincoln Institute of School Experimentation, *Cooperative Procedures in Learning* represents the work of many people and emphasizes the experimental approach to curriculum improvement.
>
> Having just completed a unit in social studies, we spent today's class period planning the procedure for a new unit. I started the discussion by pointing out the three methods by which we had studied other units: (1) individual project work, (2) group project work, (3) textbook work. I asked the class to consider these three methods and then to decide which they preferred, or suggest another method for studying our coming work.
>
> It was here that I noticed that most of those who seemed in favor of group projects were students who were well developed socially and had worked well with others in the past, whereas those favoring individual projects were almost entirely the A students who obviously knew they were capable of doing good work on their own and would receive more recognition for it through individual work.

[Ed. Note: The collectivist philosophy that the group is more important than the individual got off the ground in education in the 1950s as a result of the experimental research of educators conducting work similar to that of Alice Miel. By the 1990s egalitarian dumbing-down, outcome-based education—with its cooperative learning, mastery learning, group grades, total quality management, etc.—is the accepted method in the schools of education and in the classroom.]

[ddd]

1953

NORMAN DODD, A YALE GRADUATE, INTELLECTUAL AND NEW YORK CITY investment banker, was chosen to be the research director for the Reece Committee of the U.S. House of Representatives in 1953. The Reece Committee was named for its creator, Rep. Carroll Reece of Tennessee, and was formed to investigate the status of tax-exempt foundations. Dodd sent committee questionnaires to numerous foundations, and as a result of one such request, Joseph E. Johnson, president of the Carnegie Endowment for International Peace, invited Dodd to send a committee staffer to Carnegie headquarters in New York City to examine the minutes of the meetings of the foundation's trustees. These minutes had long since been stored away in a warehouse. Obviously, Johnson, who was a close friend of former Carnegie Endowment's president and Soviet spy Alger Hiss, had no idea what was in them.

The minutes revealed that in 1910 the Carnegie Endowment's trustees asked themselves this question: "Is there any way known to man more effective than war, to so alter the life of an entire people?" For a year the trustees sought an effective "peaceful" method to "alter the life of an entire people." Ultimately, they concluded that war was the most effective way to change people. Consequently, the trustees of the Carnegie Endowment for International Peace next asked themselves: "How do we involve the United States in a war?" And they answered, "We must control the diplomatic machinery of the United States by first gaining control of the State Department." Norman Dodd stated that the trustees' minutes reinforced what the Reece Committee had uncovered elsewhere about the Carnegie Endowment: "It had already become a powerful policy-making force inside the State Department."

During those early years of the Carnegie Endowment, war clouds were already forming over Europe and the opportunity of enactment of their plan was drawing near. History proved that World War I did indeed have an enormous impact on the American people. For the first time in our history, large numbers of wives and mothers had to leave their homes to work in war factories, thus effectively eroding woman's historic role as the "heart" of the family. The sanctity of the family itself was placed in jeopardy. Life in America was so thoroughly changed that, according to Dodd's findings, "[T]he trustees had the brashness to congratulate themselves on the wisdom and validity of their original decision." They sent a confidential message to President Woodrow Wilson, insisting that the war not be ended too quickly.

After the war, the Carnegie Endowment trustees reasoned that if they could get control of education in the United States they would be able to prevent a return to the way of life as it had been prior to the war. They recruited the Rockefeller Foundation to assist in such a monumental task. According to Dodd's Reece Committee report: "They divided the task in parts, giving to the Rockefeller Foundation the responsibility of altering education as it pertains to domestic subjects, but Carnegie retained the task of altering our education in foreign affairs and about international relations."

During a subsequent personal meeting with Mr. Dodd, President Rowan Gaither of the Ford Foundation said, "Mr. Dodd, we invited you to come here because we thought that perhaps, off the record, you would be kind enough to tell us why the Congress is interested in the operations of foundations such as ours?" Gaither answered his own rhetorical question with a startling admission:

> Mr. Dodd, all of us here at the policy making level of the foundation have at one time or another served in the OSS [Office of Strategic Services, CIA forerunner] or the European Economic Administration, operating under directives from the White House. We operate under those same directives.... The substance under which we operate is that we shall use our grant making power to so alter life in the United States that we can be comfortably merged with the Soviet Union.

Stunned, Dodd replied, "Why don't you tell the American people what you just told me and you could save the taxpayers thousands of dollars set aside for this investigation?" Gaither responded, "Mr. Dodd, we wouldn't think of doing that."

In public, of course, Gaither never admitted what he had revealed in private. However, on numerous public occasions Norman Dodd repeated what Gaither had said, and was neither sued by Gaither nor challenged by the Ford Foundation. Dodd was subsequently warned that "If you proceed with the investigation as you have outlined, you will be killed."[8]

The Reece Committee never completely finished its work of investigating and receiving testimony in open hearings involving the representatives of the major tax-exempt foundations. The process was completely disrupted and finally derailed by the deliberately disruptive activity of one of its members, Congressman Wayne Hays of Ohio. According to general counsel for the Reece Committee, Renee A. Wormser's account in *Foundations: Their Power and Influence* (Devin-Adair: New York, 1958, p. 341), "[Hays] was frank enough to tell us that he had been put on the committee by Mr. [Sam] Rayburn, the Democratic Leader in the House, as the equivalent of a watchdog. Just what he was to 'watch' was not made clear until it became apparent that Mr. Hays was making it his business to frustrate the investigation to the greatest extent possible."

[Ed. Note: The Cox Committee, created by Congress as a result of Rep. E.E. Cox of Georgia submitting a resolution to the House of Representatives in the 82nd Congress, was a forerunner of the Reece Committee. The Cox Committee was created to "direct a thorough investigation of foundations." However, just as the Reece Committee which followed, the Cox Committee was unable to get to the bottom of tax-exempt foundation affairs. Again, according to Mr. Wormser, "The Cox Committee did find that there had been a Communist, Moscow-directed plot to infiltrate American foundations and to use their funds for Communist purposes."]

SCIENCE AND HUMAN BEHAVIOR by B.F. SKINNER (MACMILLAN & CO.: NEW York, 1953) was published. To quote Skinner again, "Operant conditioning shapes behavior as a sculptor shapes a lump of clay."

ALFRED C. KINSEY, ALONG WITH WARDELL POMEROY, CLYDE MARTIN, AND Paul Gebhard, published *Sexual Behavior in the Human Female* (W.B. Saunders: Philadelphia, Pa., 1953). According to Professor David Allyn, lecturer in the Department of History at Princeton University, this book, along with Kinsey's *Sexual Behavior in the Human Male*, served to solidify the move which

> changed the way social scientists studied sexuality by breaking from the accepted social hygienic, psychoanalytic, psychiatric and physiological approaches.... [Kinsey's work] played [a] critical role in the mid-century privatization of morality. In the post-WWII era, experts abandoned the concept of "public morals," a concept which had underpinned the social control of American sexuality from the 1870's onward.... In the 1950's and 60's, however, sexual morality was privatized, and the state-controlled, highly regulated moral economy of the past gave way to a new, "deregulated"

moral market.... Kinsey's [work] argued against government interference in private life.

[Ed. Note: The above statement by Allyn was made during a presentation entitled "Private Acts/Public Policy: Alfred Kinsey, the American Law Institute and the Privatization of American Sexual Morality" at the 1995 Chevron Conference on the History of the Behavioral and Social Sciences as part of a special symposium on Alfred Kinsey. Allyn acknowledged the Charles Warren Center at Harvard University and the Rockefeller Archive Center as providing grants which made his research possible.]

DR. LEWIS ALBERT ALESEN PUBLISHED A FASCINATING BOOK ENTITLED *MENtal Robots* (The Caxton Printers, Ltd.: Caldwell, Idaho, 1953). Dr. Alesen, distinguished physician and surgeon, served as president of the California Medical Association from 1952–1953, and also wrote *The Physician's Responsibility as a Leader*. Some excerpts from Dr. Alesen's chapter 7 of *Mental Robots*, "The Tools of Robotry," follow:

> Herbert A. Philbrick [double agent and author of *I Led Three Lives*] has been recently quoted as stressing that Soviet psychiatry is the psychiatry of Pavlov, upon whose original work on dogs the theory of the conditioned reflex is based. This conditioned reflex is the principle underlying all of the procedures employed by the Soviets in their brain-washing and brain-changing techniques. Under its skillful use the human can be, and has been in countless instances, so altered as completely to transform the concepts previously held and to prepare the individual so treated for a docile acceptance of all manner of authoritarian controls. The psychiatrist boasts that he possesses the power to alter human personality, and he has certainly made good his boast in many respects, at least to the extent of being able to force phony confessions out of men like Cardinal Mindszenty, Robert Vogeler, and a host of others who have been subjected to all manner of torture during their period of conditioning.
>
> In a book entitled *Conditioned Reflex Therapy* by Andrew Salte, published in 1949 by the Creative Age Press, individual free will, freedom of choice, and, of course, individual responsibility are categorically denied in these words:
>
>> We are meat in which habits have taken up residence. We are a result of the way other people have acted to us. We are the reactions. Having conditioned reflexes means carrying about pieces of past realities.... We think with our habits, and our emotional training determines our thinking. Where there is a conditioned reflex, there is no will. Our "will power" is dependent on our previously learned reflexes.
>
> Certainly it is true that the Communists, both in Russia, China, and the Iron Curtain countries, have accomplished spectacular changes in the thinking of millions of their citizens. Whether or not this mass changing is altogether sincere or durable is not for the moment as significant as the fact that it has taken place, and that based upon it there has been, apparently, a ready acceptance of revolutionary doctrines radically defying former custom and accepted usage, and transforming the individual under this spell of persuasion or compulsion into an individual possessing entirely different characteristics from those formerly exhibited. And thus, whole new social,

economic, political, and even religious regimes have been accepted in a comparatively short time.

In order to comprehend at all adequately what has been and what is happening to the mental processes and attitudes of the American people during recent years, and in order most particularly to be aware of and alert to the carefully planned goals of the inner and hard-core sponsors of the so-called mental health program, it is pertinent to explore briefly the science and art of cybernetics. Cybernetics, according to Gould's medical dictionary, "The science dealing with communication and communication-control theory as applied to mechanical devices and animals; and including the study of servo-mechanisms, that is, feed-back mechanicisms; Josiah Macy, Jr. Foundation, 565 Park Avenue, N.Y. 21, N.Y., has published a series of symposia on cybernetics 'Circular Causal and Feed-Back Mechanisms in Biology and Social Systems.'"

In a Freedom Forum presentation entitled "Inside U.S. Communism" by Herbert Philbrick, at Harding College, Searcy, Arkansas, April 16, 1954, and distributed by the National Education Program, Mr. Philbrick had this to say about cybernetics:

> The Communists, I have discovered, have a favorite term for their system of influencing people in devious ways. The word they use as an over-all title of this technique is "cybernetics." Cybernetics as a pure science has a very legitimate and worth-while function. It has to do with how to improve conduits and cables, how to make better coaxial cables for television, how to improve telephone service, how to make more efficient electronic brains, etc. It has a very legitimate service as a pure science.
>
> But since a human being, to a Communist, is simply another machine; since human nerve centers have exactly the same function as an electronic circuit; since a human has not a soul—he is only a mechanical apparatus—the Communists have decided that this particular science has a very useful application—not on machines but on humans.
>
> Now we've heard a great deal more recently about brain-washing. Back in 1940 that word wasn't familiar to us, but what was going on inside these Young Communist League cells was a technique of cybernetics, a technique of brain-washing, if you will; the highly developed science of *demolishing the minds and the spirits of men.* [emphasis in original] The Communists brag that theirs is a "technique of Soviet psychiatry." Now Soviet psychiatry is based on the same basic principles as that of our own doctors and psychiatrists except that the Communists have a different purpose in their psychiatry. Our doctors work with unhealthy minds and try to make them healthy and whole again. The Communists have decided that cybernetics provides a very wonderful way to go to work on healthy minds and to destroy them. And of course we are now getting a bit of that picture from our own prisoners of war who were jailed and imprisoned by the North Koreans and the Red Chinese. One of my good friends is Robert Vogeler. We've learned a great deal from Bob Vogeler about the technique of brain-washing. It's a horrifying story.
>
> I would suggest that you folks who are interested in this subject, perhaps some of you students, could adopt for special study this field of cybernetics. It is brand new. I don't know of a single book on the subject in connection with what the Communists are doing with it. As a matter of fact, my own knowledge is very limited because the only facts I have are those few things which we have gathered from inside the Communist Party which indicate that the Reds have been working around the clock

in this study of the scientific manipulation and control of information. It is based on the findings of Pavlov which say that a man, like an animal, conditioned to respond to certain impulses, can be conditioned to respond to words, phrases and symbols. Therefore you pour in the words, phrases and symbols to which he will respond *without thinking* [emphasis in original]. And then you withhold other certain words which will cause him to respond in a way which you may not desire. It is the scientific control of human beings by means of control [of] information.

As the pattern for the international robot of the future, so meticulously drawn to scale by our condescending planners and masters, becomes increasingly clear, it behooves us to study that plan carefully, to determine to just what extent it has already been effectuated, to appraise the multitudinous forces aiding and abetting its adoption, and to determine, finally, whether we as individuals do, in fact, possess characteristics of sufficient value to justify any resistance to this seemingly almost overwhelming juggernaut of collectivism which is rushing headlong upon us. Have we in America, the greatest land upon which God's sun has ever shone, succumbed to the fleshpots of a modern Egypt? Have we become so softened by bellies lined with rich food, wives clad in rich raiment, and housing and appurtenances designed to shield us from every intellectual endeavor that we are no longer interested in making any effort to reclaim and to reinvigorate the one economic, social, and political system which has made all of this possible for us?

[Ed. Note: Please examine the cartoon on the flyleaves of this book!]

1954

ALICE A. BAILEY, AN AMERICAN THEOSOPHIST, WROTE *EDUCATION IN THE New Age* (Lucis Trust: New York and London, 1954).[9] The following information was written in the front of the book: "The publication of this book is financed by the Tibetan Book Fund which is established for the perpetuation of the teachings of the Tibetan and Alice A. Bailey. This fund is controlled by the Lucis Trust, a tax-exempt, religious, educational corporation. It is published in Dutch, French, Spanish, German, Italian and Portugese. Translation into other languages is proceeding." Following are some excerpts from chapter 3, "The Next Step in the Mental Development of Humanity":

The Mental Transition Period

There are three immediate steps ahead of the educational system of the world, and some progress has already been made towards taking them. First: The development of more adequate means of understanding and studying the human being. This will be made possible in three ways:

1. The growth and the development of the Science of Psychology. This is the science of the essential man, and is at this time being more generally recognised as useful to, and consistent with, the right development of the human unit. The various schools of psychology, so numerous and separative, will each eventually contribute its particular and peculiar truth, and thus the real science of the soul will emerge from this synthesis.

2. The growth and the development of the Science of the Seven Rays. This science will throw light upon racial and individual types; it will clearly formulate the nature of individual and racial problems; it will indicate the

forces and energies which are struggling for expression in the individual and in the race; and when the two major rays and the minor rays (which meet in every man) are recognised and studied by the educator in connection with the individual, the result will be right individual and group training, and correct vocational indications.

3. The acceptance of the Teaching anent [about] the Constitution of Man given by the esotericists, with the implied relation of soul and body, the nature of those bodies, their qualities and purpose, and the interrelation existing between the soul and the three vehicles of expression in the three worlds of human endeavors.

In order to bring this about, the best that the East has to offer and the knowledge of the West will have to be made available. The training of the physical body, the control of the emotional body, and the development of right mental apprehension must proceed sequentially, with due attention to the time factor, and also to that period wherein planned coordination of all aspects of the man should be carefully developed. (pp. 69–70)

[Ed. Note: After returning from a stint in the U.S. Department of Education in the early 1980s, this author attended a school board meeting and noticed the change agent superintendent's scrawlings on a blackboard, which had evidently been used as part of some sort of in-service training. He had divided a circle into the following sections: physical, mental, creative, and "spiritual." My reaction was "Hmmm," since it was he with whom I had sparred over the use of values clarification—which destroyed any real Judeo/Christian spirituality—when I served on the board in the late 1970s.]

1955

THE NEW YORK TIMES REPORTED ON AUGUST 6, 1955 THAT PRESIDENT Dwight D. Eisenhower called for the first White House Conference on Education. The announcement follows:

WASHINGTON, D.C.—Reservations have been made in eight hotels here for 2045 rooms to be occupied November 20 through December 1 by participants in the White House Conference on Education. This conference, first of its kind to be called by a President, will be unusual in many ways. The ground rules call for two or more noneducators to each educator in order to stir up the widest possible education support by citizenry in the States.... However, the really unusual part of the conference plan lies in its sharp departure from the conventional, somewhat haphazard way of conducting big conferences. The President's committee has set up six subjects to be discussed; five of them to be thrashed out at the conference, and one to be taken home. Each of the five questions to be gone into here will be discussed in successive all-delegate sessions of 200 tables of 10 persons plus a discussion leader. The five questions under mass consideration will be:

1. What should our schools accomplish?

2. In what ways can we organize our school system more effectively and economically?

3. What are our school building needs?

4. How can we get good teachers—and keep them?

5. How can we finance our schools—build and operate them?

The question to be taken home is: How can we obtain a continuing interest in education?

At the close of each all-delegate session a stenographic pool will be on hand to compile the consensus at each table and to jot down the dissents. The 200 discussion leaders will convene around 20 tables in a smaller room, further refine the results and give their "consensus" and "dissents" to a second flight of stenographers. The mass of delegates then proceed to another question. The leaders of the 20 tables subsequently move to two tables. Their findings, set down by stenographers, will be forwarded to the conference committee for incorporation in the final report.

[Ed. Note: This conference was probably one of the first national conferences to use the manipulative and non-representative group dynamics/ Delphi Technique to orchestrate the participants into reaching consensus on pre-determined goals. Anyone who has participated in local or state goal-setting committees should recognize the drill. This conference provided an excellent example of the dialectical process at work.]

1956

TAXONOMY OF EDUCATIONAL OBJECTIVES: THE CLASSIFICATION OF EDUCA-tional Goals, Handbook II, Affective Domain by David Krathwohl, Benjamin Bloom, and Bertram Massie (Longman: New York/London, 1956) was published. This *Taxonomy* provided the necessary tool for the schools of education to restructure education from academics to values (behavior) change. The swinging door was finally propped open to incorporate attitudes, values and beliefs into the definition of education. It is impossible to overestimate the *Taxonomy*'s importance. An excerpt follows:

> In fact, a large part of what we call "good teaching" is the teacher's ability to attain affective objectives [attitudes, values, beliefs] through challenging the students' fixed beliefs and getting them to discuss issues. (p. 55)

1958

IN 1958 AT THE PEAK OF THE COLD WAR PRESIDENT DWIGHT D. EISEN-hower signed the first United States-Union of Soviet Socialist Republics (U.S.S.R.) agreements. These agreements included education.

NATIONAL DEFENSE EDUCATION ACT WAS PASSED IN 1958 BY THE U.S. Congress as a result of Soviet success in space, demonstrated by the launching of *Sputnik*. This *Act*, which set the stage for incredible federal control of education through heavy financing for behavior modification, science, mathematics, guidance counseling, and testing, etc., involved "modern techniques developed from scientific principles," the full weight of which would be felt at the end of the century. Title I, General Provisions, Findings and Declaration of Policy, Sec. 101 of this *Act* reads:

> The Congress hereby finds and declares that the security of the Nation requires the fullest development of the mental resources and technical skills of

its young men and women. The present emergency demands that additional and more adequate educational opportunities be made available. The defense of this nation depends upon the mastery of modern techniques developed from complex scientific principles. It depends as well upon the discovery and development of new principles, new techniques, and new knowledge.

Endnotes:

1 For a thorough treatment of this subject, please read Dr. Judith A. Reisman's book *Kinsey: Crimes and Consequences—The Red Queen and the Grand Scheme* (The Institute for Media Education, Inc.: Arlington, Va., 1998). To order, call 1–202–591–3292.

2 B.F. Skinner. *Science and Human Behavior* (Macmillan & Co.: New York, 1953).

3 The Taxonomy involves: Cognitive—how a student perceives or judges knowledge or facts; Affective—how a student feels or what he believes about a subject; Psychomotor—what a student does as a result of what he perceives or believes; converting belief to action.

4 See the Internet version for Appendix XIX for an excellent critique of Bloom's *Taxonomy*.

5 This document may be ordered from: Education Service Council, P.O. Box 271, Elm Grove, WI 53122. Erica Carle's latest and very important book, *Why Things Are the Way They Are* (Dorrance Publishing Co.: Pittsburgh, Pa., 1996), can be ordered in hardcover from: Dorrance Publishing Co., 643 Smithfield Street, Pittsburgh, PA 15222.

6 To order Dr. Reisman's book, call 1–202–591–3292.

7 For further information, purchase *School of Darkness: The Record of a Life and of a Conflict between Two Faiths* by Bella V. Dodd (P.J. Kennedy & Sons: New York, 1954. Copyright transferred in 1963 to Bella V. Dodd, Devin-Adair Publishers).

8 This section dealing with the Dodd Report was written by Robert H. Goldsborough and published in his book *Lines of Credit: Ropes of Bondage* (The American Research Foundation, Inc.: Baltimore, 1989). This fascinating book may be accessed on the americandeception.com website.

9 The offices of Lucis Trust (formerly Lucifer Publishing) which were previously located across from the United Nations Building in New York have offered for sale the Robert Muller *World Core Curriculum* (a New Age elementary education curriculum), written by Muller who served as the under secretary of the UN. The *World Core Curriculum* states that it is based on the teachings of Alice Bailey's spirit guide, the Tibetan teacher Djwhal Khul. The present address for Lucis Trust is: 120 Wall St., New York, NY. Muller's curriculum can also be ordered from: Robert Muller School, 6005 Royaloak Dr., Arlington, TX. It should be noted that the Robert Muller School is a member of the UNESCO Associated Schools Project, certified as a United Nations Associated School.

5

THE SICK SIXTIES:
psychology and skills

Presidents Eisenhower, Kennedy and Johnson, while ostensibly concerning themselves with racial injustice, economic inequities, and equal educational opportunities, were, in fact, responsible for installing the lifelong control system—the Planning, Programming, Budgeting Management System (PPBS)—into all departments of government. This was accomplished during what would become "the sick sixties" under the guise of "accountability to the taxpayers," a theme which will be repeated throughout the remainder of this century.

American education would henceforth concern itself with the importance of the group rather than with the importance of the individual. This would be true in spite of the push towards individualized education (mastery learning and computers), leading people to believe that concern for the individual was the driving force behind change.

Like "accountability," another common thread running through "the sick sixties" was the idea that for the first time in America the purpose of education would be to focus on the student's emotional health rather than on his academic learning. In order to change society, it was essential to identify the attitudinal changes needed in each student; then, modify the student's behavior according to the preconceived model approved by government social engineers known as "change agents." This model did not allow for competition or individual

73

thought, belief, etc., but was conceived to standardize (robotize) human be-ings—particularly Americans—so that the entire populace would be in general agreement with government policy and future planning for world government.

Removal of the last semblance of local control would come through the pas-sage of *The Elementary and Secondary Education Act of 1965* (ESEA), the most important piece of legislation to pass during Lyndon Johnson's administration.

Two of the major federal initiatives developed with funding from *The Elementary and Secondary Education Act of 1965* which have contributed to the "deliberate dumbing down" of not only students but teachers as well, are listed below:

1. the 1965–1969 *Behavioral Science Teacher Education Program* (BSTEP), and

2. the 1969 publication by the federal government of *Pacesetters in Innova-tion*, a 584-page catalogue of behavior modification programs to be used by the schools.

Pacesetters provided evidence of a concerted effort to destroy the last vestiges of traditional academic education, replacing it with a behavior and mind control system guaranteed to create the "New Soviet Man" who would be unlikely to challenge totalitarian policies emanating from his local, state or federal/inter-national government. Professor John Goodlad, the nation's premiere change agent who has been receiving federal and tax-exempt foundation grants for at least thirty years, said in 1969:

> The most controversial issues of the twenty-first century will pertain to the ends and means of modifying human behavior and who shall determine them. The first educational question will not be "what knowledge is of the most worth?" but "what kinds of human beings do we wish to produce?" The possibilities virtually defy our imagination.[1]

Behavior change on such a massive scale necessitated the creation of many agencies and policy devices which would oversee the implementation of the necessary innovations. Three agencies were: (1) the National Assessment of Educational Progress (NAEP), which tested students at various grade levels; (2) the Education Commission of the States (ECS), which enabled the states to become unified regarding education and its outreach—one entity suppos-edly controlled by its member states, but in reality controlled by its consensus policy which invariably reflected federal policy; and (3) the National Diffu-sion Network (NDN) which served as the transmission belt and advertising agency for federally funded programs, the majority of which were intended to destroy traditional right/wrong absolutist values through psychotherapeutic and behavioral techniques.[2]

Congressman John M. Ashbrook of Ohio, to whose memory the writer has dedicated this book, expressed his concern over the above-described radical shift in the direction of education before the U.S. House of Representatives on July 18, 1961 in a speech he delivered entitled "The Myth of Federal Aid to Education without Control." With extraordinary foresight, John Ashbrook warned that

> [i]n the report *A Federal Education Agency for the Future* we find the vehicle for Federal domination of our schools. It is a real and present danger.... The battle lines are now being drawn between those who seek control and uniformity of our local schools and those who oppose this further bureaucratic centralization in Washington. It is my sincere hope that the Congress will respond to this challenge and defeat the aid to education bills which will implement the goals incorporated in *A Federal Education Agency for the Future*.

Unfortunately, Congressman Ashbrook's words of wisdom did not convince his fellow colleagues and, therefore, did not influence the burgeoning sentiment of the majority in Congress. Had Ashbrook's views prevailed, the citizens of this great nation would be in a far better position to deal with the problems we face at home and abroad in 1999.

1960

UNITED NATIONS EDUCATIONAL, SCIENTIFIC AND CULTURAL ORGANIZATION'S *Convention Against Discrimination* was signed in Paris, France in 1960. This *Convention* laid the groundwork for control of American education—both public and private—by U.N. agencies and agents.

SOVIET EDUCATION PROGRAMS: FOUNDATIONS, CURRICULUMS, TEACHER *Preparation* by William K. Medlin (specialist in Comparative Education for Eastern Europe, Division of International Education), Clarence B. Lindquist (chief of Natural Sciences and Mathematics, Division of Higher Education), and Marshall L. Schmitt (specialist for Industrial Arts, Division of State and Local School Systems) was published in 1960 under the auspices of U.S. Department of Health, Education and Welfare Secretary Arthur S. Flemming and Office of Education Commissioner Lawrence G. Derthick (OE–14037, Bulletin 1960, No. 17). Americans familiar with the details of American school-to-work restructuring will see that the United States is adopting the Soviet polytechnic system described in the following paper. The "Pavlovian conditioned reflex theory" discussed is the Skinnerian mastery learning/ direct instruction method required in order to implement outcome-based education and school-to-work. Excerpts from this extraordinarily important report follow:

HIGHLIGHTS

In the school classroom and workshop, in the machine building plant, at the countryside, and wherever we went, we felt the pulse of the Soviet Government's drive to educate and train a new generation of technically skilled and scientifically literate citizens. Such is the consensus of the three specialists who are authors of this volume.

The ideas and practices of Soviet education form a philosophy of education in which the authoritarian concept predominates.... With 60 percent of the adult male population illiterate in 1900, a massive educational effort was deemed necessary to transform this situation into one where new skills and scientific inquiry could meet national needs.

The curriculum is unified and is the same for all schools throughout the U.S.S.R. with but slight variations in non-Russian nationality areas.... Principles of Darwinism, which are studied in grade 9 of U.S.S.R. schools, teach children about the origin of life together with the history of evolution in the organic world. The main theme of the course is evolution.

Major efforts of U.S.S.R. schools during the past 30 years have been to train youngsters for the Government's planned economic programs and to inculcate devotion to its political and social system.... Science and mathematics occupy 31.4 percent of the student's time in the complete U.S.S.R. 10-year school.

According to school officials, all work of pupils in these subjects has to be done in pen and ink in order to inculcate habits of neatness and accuracy.

U.S.S.R. plans are to bring all secondary school children into labor education and training experiences through the regular school program. The "school of general education" is now named the "labor-polytechnic school of general education."

Industrial and agricultural sciences and technical developments are causing Soviet educators to be concerned about future needs for readapting the schools to give more appropriate instruction for the coming age of automation, atomic power, and space.... The authors consider the polytechnic program in the Soviet elementary-secondary schools "as an integral part of the Soviet philosophy of education." It is not a subject but in fact a *type* [emphasis in the original] of education, and other subjects... contribute to the polytechnic area.

Soviet patriotism—fidelity to the Soviet land and to the ideas of communism—occupies a leading place in this educational conditioning, and in this sense gives the school a political character as well as a moral one. Employing primarily the conditioned reflex theory as elaborated by Pavlov (1849–1936), Soviet psychologists have worked out a system of didactics which are strict and fixed in their conception and application; one might even use the term "narrow" to distinguish them from the broad scope of methods employed, for example, in most U.S. schools. Soviet psychologists maintain that fundamentally all (except physically disturbed or handicapped) children can learn the standardized subject matter through the teaching methods devised for all schools. By definition, therefore, they exclude from practical consideration many educational techniques.... The curriculum, dominated until now by the so-called "hard" subjects, is designed to give all future citizens an intellectual foundation that is, in form, a traditional European one. This systematic approach to education tends to give Soviet teachers a classroom control that appears complete.

Certain of their psychological research findings in the past are not the only explanation that we observe for this principle, however, and it is well to point out that Soviet psychologists have only recently been in a position to try out new methods in connection with a more diversified curriculum. As one Moscow educator pointed out to us in a discussion on methods, the research- ers are not always successful in getting their results and viewpoints adopted in school programs. Psychologists and other researchers are busily engaged in work on such areas as development of the cognitive activity of pupils in the teaching process (especially in relation to the polytechnic curriculum); simplification in learning reading and arithmetic skills in the lower grades; the formation of character and teaching moral values, including Soviet patriotism; psychological preparation of future teachers; the principles and methods for meeting individual children's needs (such as "self-appreciation"),[3] in terms of handicaps and as regards a child's particular attitudes, peculiarities, and maturity; and understanding the internal, structural integrity of each school subject and its interrelationships with other branches of knowledge. These research activities are carried out under Soviet conditions and exemplify some of the major problems which educators there now face.

Soviet educators define their system as an all-round training whereby youth can participate in creating the conditions for a socialist, and ultimately, Communist society. Such participation can become possible, they hold, only as students cultivate all the basic disciplines and only through a "steady rise in the productivity of labor"... which is linked closely with the educative process. School children and students are engaged in a total educational program which aims to teach all the same basic subjects, morals and habits in order to provide society with future workers and employees whose general education will make them socialist (Communist) citizens and contribute to their productivity upon learning a vocation (profession). (pp. 10–11)

IN 1960 PRESIDENT DWIGHT D. EISENHOWER RECEIVED A FINAL REPORT from his Commission on National Goals entitled *Goals for Americans*. The 372-page volume recommended carrying out an international, socialist agenda for the United States. This report, following on the heels of the 1955 White House Conference on Education's use of the Delphi technique,[4] served to carve in stone the use of dialectic methods in public policy mak- ing through the use of results-based "planning" by consensus, not consent. This also may have marked the beginning of restructuring America from a constitutional republic to a socialist democracy.

Before listing an excerpted version of *Goals for Americans*, the writer would like to point out that although on their face these goals may sound legitimate, they are, in fact, blatantly socialistic. Only those recommendations which lean towards socialism have been included in this entry.

GOALS FOR AMERICANS

II. EQUALITY. Every man and woman must have equal rights before the law, and an equal opportunity to vote and hold office, to be educated, to get a job and to be promoted when qualified, to buy a home, to participate fully in community affairs.

III. THE DEMOCRATIC PROCESS. ...With firm faith in individual Ameri- can responsibility, the Commission answered these questions with a confident and yet measured "yes." While stressing private responsibility, the Commission also forthrightly favors government action at all levels whenever necessary to achieve the national goals.... The Commission adopted as its own his [Professor Wallace S. Sayre of Columbia University] principal recommendations, that "the President be given unequivocal authority and responsibility to develop a true senior civil service," and that the pay of top government employees should be drastically increased.

IV. EDUCATION. Annual Public and Private Expenditure for Education by 1970 Must Be Approximately $40 Billion—Double the 1960 Figure.... There must be more and better teachers, enlarged facilities, and changes in curricula and methods. Above all, schooling should fit the varying capacities of individuals; every student should be stimulated to work to his utmost; authentic concern for excellence is imperative....

Among specific steps, the Commission recommended that:

1. Small and inefficient school districts should be consolidated, reducing the total number from 40,000 to about 10,000.[5]
2. Teachers' salaries at all levels must be improved.
3. Two-year colleges should be within commuting distance of most high school graduates.
4. Adult education should provide a new emphasis on education throughout life....

VI. DISARMAMENT. Disarmament should be our ultimate goal.

VII. LESS DEVELOPED NATIONS. The success of the underdeveloped nations must depend primarily on their own efforts. We should assist by providing education, training, economic and technical assistance, and by increasing the flow of public and private capital.... Doubling their rate of economic growth within five years is a reasonable objective.... The U.S. share of such an effort would require by 1965 an outflow of $5 to $5.5 billion per year of public and private capital, as compared with $3.4 billion per year in the 1956–59 period....

X. THE UNITED NATIONS. A key goal in the pursuit of a vigorous and effective foreign policy is the preservation and strengthening of the United Nations.

At the end of the Commission on National Goals report is the following:

[A]ttributed to American Assembly, founded by Dwight D. Eisenhower in 1950 when he was President of Columbia University.

Attached to the report was a pamphlet entitled "Suggestions for Holding a Local Assembly on National Goals." The process for arriving at "consensus" explained in the pamphlet is actually group dynamics. Consensus is *not* consent! These documents prove there has been a well-formulated and funded plan to change the American system of government through decision-making by unelected task forces, Soviet-style five-year plans, Delphi-type discussion groups, etc. This type of participatory decision making called for by regional government—involving partnerships and unelected councils—is taking place in every state of the nation today. It is rarely challenged since few Americans understand our constitutional form of government, and are, therefore, unable to recognize the important differences between a representative republic and the parliamentary form of government found in socialist democracies.

TEACHING MACHINES AND PROGRAMMED LEARNING: A SOURCE BOOK (DE-partment of Audio-Visual Instruction, National Education Association: Washington, D.C., 1960), edited by A.A. Lumsdaine (program director of the American Institute for Research and professor of education at the University of California in Los Angeles) and Robert Glaser (professor of psychology at the University of Pittsburgh and research advisor at the American Institute for Research) was published. Extensive excerpts from this document can be found in the Internet version in Appendix II. Some interesting selections follow:

> [Chapter entitled] The Science of Learning and the Art of Teaching by B.F. Skinner
>
> Recent improvements in the conditions which control behavior in the field of learning are of two principal sorts. The "law of effect" has been taken seriously; we have made sure that effects do occur and that they occur under conditions which are optimal for producing the changes called learning. Once we have arranged the particular type of consequence called a reinforcement, our techniques permit us to shape the behavior of an organism almost at will. It has become a routine exercise to demonstrate this in classes in elementary psychology by conditioning such an organism as a pigeon. (pp. 99–100)...
>
> In all this work, the species of the organism has made surprisingly little difference. It is true that the organisms studied have all been vertebrates, but they still cover a wide range. Comparable results have been obtained with rats, pigeons, dogs, monkeys, human children, and most recently—by the author in collaboration with Ogden R. Lindsley—with human psychotic subjects. In spite of great phylogenetic differences, all these organisms show amazingly similar properties of the learning process. It should be emphasized that this has been achieved by analyzing the effects of reinforcement and by designing techniques which manipulate reinforcement with considerable precision. Only in this way can the behavior of the individual organism be brought under such precise control. It is also important to note that through a gradual advance to complex interrelations among responses, the same de-gree of rigor is being extended to behavior which would usually be assigned to such fields as perception, thinking, and personality dynamics. (p. 103)

1961

PROGRAMMED LEARNING: EVOLVING PRINCIPLES AND INDUSTRIAL APPLICA-tions (Foundation for Research on Human Behavior: Ann Arbor, Mich., 1961) edited by Jerome P. Lysaught was published. The Internet version Appendix III contains significant material from this book. An excerpt from the introduction by Thomas H. Miller follows:

> To introduce the subject, we would like to have each of you work through the first lesson of Dr. B.F. Skinner's course in psychology. We would hope, incidentally, that a portion of the material is somewhat new to you so that

some learning will actually take place in your encounter with the subject matter. Further, we hope it will demonstrate certain phenomena that will be spoken of repeatedly today, such as effective reinforcement of the learner and progress at the individual rate.

Imagine yourself to be a freshman student at Harvard. You are taking, for the first time, a college course in psychology. This is your first day in that course. Your introduction to the course consists of the presentation of the programmed learning sequence on the next pages.

The directions are simple. You should read the first stimulus item, S-1, consider it, and then construct in your own words the best possible answer. As soon as you have done this, turn the page and compare your answer with the answer listed at R-1, the first response item. Proceed through the program, going on to S-2 on the next page.

Under the section entitled "Principles of Programming," written by Robert Glaser, we find the following excerpts to be revealing:

It is indeed true that this book would never have been conceived without the well-known and perhaps undying work of Professor Skinner.... It is largely through Professor Skinner's work that all this theory and excitement about teaching machines and programmed learning has come about.

The essential task involved is to evoke the specific forms of behavior from the student and through appropriate reinforcement bring them under the control of specific subject matter stimuli. As a student goes through a learning program certain of his responses must be strengthened and shaped from initial unskilled behavior to subject matter competence.... Our present knowledge of the learning process points out that through the process of reinforcement, new forms of behavior can be created with a great degree of subtlety. The central feature of this process is making the reinforcement contingent upon performances of the learner. (Often the word "reward" is used to refer to one class of reinforcing events.)...

The term "programming" refers to the process of constructing sequences of instructional material in a way that maximizes the rate of acquisition and retention and enhances the motivation of the student.... A central process for the acquisition of behavior is reinforcement. Behavior is acquired as a result of a contingent relationship between the response of an organism and a consequent event. In order for these contingencies of reinforcement to be effective, certain conditions must be met. Reinforcement must follow the occurrence of the behavior being taught. If this is not the case, different and perhaps unwarranted behavior will be learned.

ON JULY 18, 1961, CONGRESSMAN JOHN M. ASHBROOK DELIVERED A SPEECH before Congress entitled "The Myth of Federal Aid to Education without Control" (*Congressional Record*: pp. 11868–11880). Excerpts from his very important speech, which documented and exposed the plans for the internationalization and transformation of American education, follow:

That there was any doubt of the Federal bureaucrats' intentions in this matter was laid to rest with the discovery of a Health, Education, and Welfare publication, *A Federal Education Agency for the Future*, which is a report of the Office of Education, dated April 1961.... I feel that its pronouncements

are a blueprint for complete domination and direction of our schools from Washington. The publication was not popularly distributed and there was some difficulty in obtaining a copy.

Fifty-six pages of findings contain recommendations which call for more and more Federal participation and control and repeatedly stress the need for Federal activity in formulating educational policies. It recommends a review of teacher preparation, curriculum and textbooks. It calls for an implementation of international education projects in cooperation with UNESCO in the United Nations, and ministries of education abroad. Of course, it recommends an enlarged office of education and the use of social scientists as key advisers.... It places stress on "implementing international educational projects in the United States and bringing maximum effectiveness to the total international educational effort." Would not the Communists, with their footholds and infiltrations in these organizations, love this? No detail has been overlooked—"curriculum will have to undergo continual reshaping and upgrading; and new techniques and tools of instruction will have to be developed" and "teacher preparation, textbooks, and the curriculum in these subject fields must be improved in the decade ahead." In the report... we find the vehicle for Federal domination of our schools.

...The battle lines are now drawn between those who seek control and uniformity of our local schools and those who oppose this further bureaucratic centralization in Washington. It is my sincere hope that the Congress will respond to this challenge and defeat the aid to education bills which will implement the goals incorporated in *A Federal Education Agency for the Future*.

Ashbrook went on to point out that

[Under] The Mission [as stated in the report]... the basic mission of the Office [of Education] to "promote the cause of education" remains unchanged since its establishment in 1867.

...What is meant when he [Sterling M. McMurrin, Commissioner of Education] says, "I anticipate that much of this activity will take place through normal administrative processes within the Office and the Department"? In the jargon of Washington bureaucracy this means that the report will be largely implemented on the administrative level without Congressional action and approval.

The House Committee on Education and Labor recently voted out H.R. 7904 which would extend the *National Defense Education Act*.... It is evident that the administration has chosen this vehicle for enacting piecemeal the recommendations of *A Federal Education Agency for the Future*.

Ashbrook continued to quote from *Agency for the Future* which he said "laid bare the real nemesis of the Federal bureaucrats—the tradition of local control." The report stated, "The tradition of local control should no longer be permitted to inhibit Office of Education leadership." The Committee on Mission and Organization called for

[An] Office of Educational Research that would administer a separate program of extra-mural contracts and grants for basic and experimental research in disciplines bearing upon the educational situation, and would serve the other parts of the Bureau with advice on research problems.... Since it is presumed that the Centers, oriented to education as it is organized and administered, will deal with educational problems directly confronting schools and colleges, it is believed desirable that extra-mural research be significantly attentive to basic problems of human development, training and teaching, regardless of whether or not they are acknowledged as immediately pressing problems by educators. In short, some research should be conducted precisely because it challenges the assumptions upon which practicing educators are proceeding.

The above is obviously a reference to behavioral sciences research which, until that time, had not found a permanent home at the local school educator level nor was there the need to conduct such research in order to challenge the "assumptions upon which practicing educators are proceeding." Attached to the Committee's report were appendices from which the following excerpts are taken:

Appendix B
The Mission of the Office of Education in the 1960s

The schools of tomorrow must prepare their students for living in a world of continuous and rapid change, presenting them with unprecedented social, economic, and political problems. We must, in fact, give to education a character that will initiate and support a process of lifelong learning if Americans are to keep abreast of the accelerating advent of new knowledge and of the increasing complexity of modern life. These prospective conditions are already suggested in part by the rapidly increasing demand for highly specialized and professional skills. During the coming decade, new means must be developed for identifying and releasing student potential; curriculums will have to undergo continual reshaping and upgrading; and new techniques and tools of instruction will have to be developed....

- Education is basic to effort to bring about an enduringly peaceful world.
- Next decade will bring closer and multiple relationships with Ministries of Education abroad and international organizations, such as UNESCO, the Organization of American States, International Bureau of Education.
- Variations among States and school districts in standards of instruction, facilities, staff, and services expose serious inadequacies. Our progress toward the ideal of equality of educational opportunity is tragically uneven.
- In the area of international educational cooperation, in particular, it must play the major role, since only the Federal Government can enter into agreements with other governments. Along with these responsibilities should be included that of stimulating and participating activity in the process of formulation, examination, and reformulation of the goals of our national society in terms of educational objectives.
- The development of uniform, consistent and compatible statistical data in all States and in all institutions of higher education will call for both technical and financial assistance to these sources from the Office of Education....
- Economists, sociologists, and other social scientists will be needed on the staff to assist in dealing with educational problems in their total context.

National Defense Education Act (NDEA) Amendment of 1961—Additional Views, which accompanied H.R. 7904, included very important testimony regarding the dangers of the NDEA and the recommendations made in the above *Agency for the Future* report. A discussion of the dangers of federal control follows:

> We [the undersigned] reject, furthermore, the philosophy that there can exist Federal aid to any degree without Federal control. We further hold that there should not be Federal aid without Federal control. It is the responsibility of the Federal Government to so supervise and control its allocations that waste and misuse is kept to a minimum. Since we do not desire such federal control in the field of public education, we do not desire Federal aid to education.
>
> We should never permit the American educational system to become the vehicle for experimentation by educational ideologues. A careful analysis of the writings and statements of vocal and influential spokesmen in the governmental and educational fields indicates a desire on the part of some of these individuals to utilize the educational system as a means of transforming the economic and social outlook of the United States.
>
> We point to a statement by Dr. Harold Rugg, for many years professor of education at Teachers College, Columbia University, who declared in *Frontiers of Democracy* on May 15, 1943 (pp. 247–254) concerning the teachers' colleges:
>
>> Let them become powerful national centers for the graduate study of ideas and they will thereby become forces of creative imagination standing at the very vortex of the ideational revolution. Let us make our teacher education institutions into great direction finders for our new society, pointers of the way, dynamic trailblazers of the New Frontiers.
>
> We could supply pages of documentation analyzing the type of new frontier planned. It is indeed a Socialist frontier. It had been hoped that the philosophy of education expressed by Dr. Rugg and his cohorts back in the early forties, had long since been repudiated. However, in April of 1961, the U.S. Department of Health, Education, and Welfare published a booklet entitled *A Federal Education Agency for the Future*. Anyone who doubts that the Federal aid to education bills now before Congress would mean eventual Federal control of education, should carefully read and analyze for himself what the Office of Education is planning for tomorrow's schools. They openly predict their "need" for new powers on the passage of the multimillion-dollar aid legislation now before us. They recommend that their Office of Education be elevated to the status of U.S. Education Agency, "to reflect the more active role of this unit of Government." They envision the new Agency's mission as one of "leadership" (p. 42), "national policymaking" (p. 43), "national planning" (p. 47), "to prepare students to understand the world of tomorrow" (p. 40). The Office of Education writers further say "along with these responsibilities should be included that of stimulating and participating in the process of formulation, examination, and reformulation of the goals of our society in the terms of educational objectives" (p. 43).

[Ed. Note: A careful warning was sounded through the *National Defense Education Act Amendment of 1961—Additional Views* when the Congressmen said, "We reject that there can exist Federal aid to any degree without

Federal control. We further hold that there should not be Federal aid without Federal control." This applies as well to all of the voucher and tax credit proposals before us today (in 1999) flying under the banner of "choice."

The Mission Statement of the Office of Education clearly called for the establishment of the National Center for Education Statistics, the National Assessment of Educational Progress, and the "wholistic" approach to education through the inclusion of social scientists in the education process—a clear departure from academically oriented educational pursuits into intrusive areas totally unrelated to education.

Even taking into account the collectivist direction taken by radical educators in the first half of this century, this movement could not have borne fruit had it not been for President Dwight Eisenhower's Commission on National Goals which produced *Goals for Americans* in 1960. These goals, along with the implementation of PPBS and Bloom's *Taxonomy of Educational Objectives*, seem to have provided the catalyst for the "planned economy" being implemented in the United States in 1999.]

[ddd]

"HARRISON BERGERON," ONE OF THE SEVERAL SHORT STORIES BY KURT VONnegut, Jr., included in his book *Welcome to the Monkey House* (Delacorte Press/Seymour Lawrence: New York, 1961), provided uncanny insight into the nature of America's dumbed-down society in the year 2081. How the elitist "planners, managers" deal with Americans whose intellects and independence create problems for the smooth functioning of a society controlled for the benefit of all is the focus of the story.[6] An excerpt follows:

> The year was 2081, and everybody was equal. They weren't only equal before God and the law. They were equal every which way. Nobody was smarter than anybody else. Nobody was stronger or quicker than anybody else. All this equality was due to the 211th, 212th, and 213th Amendments to the Constitution, and to the unceasing vigilance of agents of the United States Handicapper General.

[Ed. Note: The reader will, later in this book, recall this fictional forecast when encountering outcome-based education, Individual Education Plans (IEP's) for ALL—not just the handicapped—and the *Reading Excellence Act* passed by Congress October 16, 1998, which will provide federal tax support for Skinnerian phonics instruction programs developed and used with special education children for over 25 years. In 1999 House Education and Workforce Committee Chairman William Goodling (PA) will also propose the removal of funding from present titles of the *Elementary and Secondary Act of 1965* (ESEA) in order to completely fund the *Individuals with Disabilities in Education Act* (IDEA). Vonnegut's office of "Handicapper General" may not wait until 2081!]

[ddd]

1963

THE ROLE OF THE COMPUTER IN FUTURE INSTRUCTIONAL SYSTEMS WAS published as the March/April, 1963 supplement of *Audiovisual Communication Review* (Monograph 2 of the Technological Development Project of the National Education Association [Contract #SAE9073], U.S. Office of Education, Dept. of Health, Education and Welfare: Washington, D.C., 1963). James D. Finn of Los Angeles was the principal investigator and Donald P. Ely was the consulting investigator for this project. (Donald Ely also became project director for the U.S. Department of Education's *Project BEST: Basic Educational Skills through Technology*, which will be discussed in a later entry in this book.) Excerpts from a chapter entitled "Effortless Learning, Attitude Changing, and Training in Decision-Making" follow:

> Another area of potential development in computer applications is the attitude changing machine. Dr. Bertram Raven in the Psychology Department at the University of California at Los Angeles is in the process of building a computer-based device for changing attitudes. This device will work on the principle that students' attitudes can be changed effectively by using the Socratic method of asking an appropriate series of leading questions designed to right the balance between appropriate attitudes, and those deemed less acceptable. For instance, after first determining a student's constellation of attitudes through appropriate testing procedures, the machine would calculate which attitudes are "out of phase" and which of these are amenable to change. If the student were opposed to foreign trade, say, and a favorable disposition were sought for, the machine would select an appropriate series of statements and questions organized to right the imbalance in the student's attitudes. The machine, for instance, would have detected that the student liked President Kennedy and was against the spread of Communism; therefore, the student would be shown that JFK favored foreign trade and that foreign trade to underdeveloped countries helped to arrest the Communist infiltration of these governments. If the student's attitudes toward Kennedy and against Communism were sufficiently strong, Dr. Raven would hypothesize that a positive change in attitude toward foreign trade would be effectively brought about by showing the student the inconsistency of his views. There is considerable evidence that such techniques do effectively change attitudes.
>
> Admittedly, training in decision-making skills is a legitimate goal of education in this age of automation, but the problem remains—does the educator know what values to attach to the different outcomes of these decisions?... What about students whose values are out of line with the acceptable values of democratic society? Should they be taught to conform to someone else's accepted judgment of proper values? Training in decision-making is ultimately compounded with training in value judgment and, as such, becomes a controversial subject that needs to be resolved by educators before the tools can be put to use.

UNIVERSITY OF PITTSBURGH'S LEARNING RESEARCH AND DEVELOPMENT Center introduced in 1963 the Individually Prescribed Instruction (IPI) model which would allow for the implementation of continuous progress programs necessary for value change and school-to-work training. A good example of what Individually Prescribed Instruction is designed to do is given in *Planned Change in Education: A Systems Approach*, edited by David S. Bushnell of Project Focus and Donald Rappaport of Price Waterhouse & Co. (Harcourt, Brace and Jovanovich, Inc.: New York, 1971). Excerpts from chapter 7, "Individualizing Instruction" by Robert G. Scanlon, program director for the Individualizing Learning Program of Research for Better Schools, Inc., and Mary V. Brown, assistant program director to the project, are reprinted below:

> IPI is an instructional system that permits the teacher to plan and conduct a program of studies tailored to the needs and characteristics of each student. Its procedures have been designed to enable the school to meet more of the needs of more individual pupils and take a new direction in the continuing search for ways to adapt instruction to individual pupils. The rate of learning, amount of practice, type of materials, and mode of instruction are the parameters of individual differences emphasized in IPI.
>
> During the school year 1963–64, the Learning Research and Development Center and the Baldwin-Whitehall public schools (a suburban Pittsburgh school system) initiated an experimental project to investigate the feasibility of a system of individualized instruction in an entire K–6 school (Oakleaf). This came as a result of a series of exploratory studies begun in 1951–1962 designed to test preliminary notions in a single classroom. The work started with the use of programmed instruction in an intact classroom.
>
> As work proceeded, it became apparent that the significant individualization feature of programmed instruction could not be augmented unless the organization of the classroom was changed to permit a more flexible context. Out of this experience grew the current Individually Prescribed Instruction project in which various combinations of instructional materials, testing procedures, and teacher practices are being used to accommodate individual student differences.
>
> IPI is a system based on a set of specified objectives correlated with diagnostic instruments, curriculum materials, teaching techniques, and management capabilities. The objectives of the system are:
>
> 1. to permit student mastery of instructional content at individual learning rates;
> 2. to ensure active student involvement in the learning process;
> 3. to encourage student involvement in learning through self-directed and self-initiated activities;
> 4. to encourage student evaluation of progress toward mastery and to provide instructional materials and techniques based on individual needs and styles. (pp. 93–95)

[Ed. Note: IPI is necessary to the success of outcome-based education because it does away with norm-referenced testing and the traditional grading system. The Carnegie Unit is also jeopardized by the introduction of IPI. The federally funded laboratory Research for Better Schools, Inc., in Philadelphia, Pennsylvania field-tested IPI, thus setting the stage for Skinnerian mastery learning/direct instruction and the use of Skinner's "box" (the computer) to be incorporated into curriculum. Homeschoolers and Christian educators should be reminded that this project is reflected in many of the curricular and organizational designs advocated for their use.]

IN 1963 A NATIONAL PROJECT WAS INITIATED WHICH WAS THE FORERUNNER of the National Assessment of Educational Progress (NAEP) and became the model for individual state assessments which have created enormous controversy due to their focus on attitudinal and value change. This study was presented in *A Plan for Evaluating the Quality of Educational Programs in Pennsylvania: Highlights of a Report from Educational Testing Service to the State Board of Education of the Commonwealth of Pennsylvania* (Educational Testing Service: Princeton, N.J., June 30, 1965). The combination of the Skinnerian method of training and the assessments' emphasis on change in attitudes, values and beliefs resulted in what the average parent considered a "lethal concoction," absolutely guaranteed to create a "robotized citizen for the New Pagan Age." (See Appendix IV in the Internet version.) The following excerpts provide a fairly clear picture of the *Plan*:

> This Committee on Quality Education sought the advice of experts [including Dr. Urie Bronfenbrenner of the Department of Sociology, Cornell University; Dr. David R. Krathwohl of the College of Education, Michigan State University, a co-author with Benjamin Bloom of *The Taxonomy of Educational Objectives: Affective Domain*; and Dr. Ralph Tyler, director of the Center for Advanced Study in the Behavioral Sciences in Palo Alto, California. These experts constituted a Standing Advisory Committee for the project....

> It [the Committee] concluded that an educational program is to be regarded as adequate only if it can be shown to contribute to the total development of pupils.... The Committee recognizes that many of the desirable qualities that schools should help pupils acquire are difficult to define and even more difficult to measure. It feels, nevertheless, that any evaluation procedure that leaves these qualities out of account is deficient as a basis for determining whether the program of any school district is educationally adequate....

> The first step in judging the quality of educational programs is to decide on the purposes of education. What should children be and do and *know* [emphasis in original] as a consequence of having gone to school? What are the goals of the schools? These questions have been high on the agenda of the Committee on Quality Education. Its members wanted a set of goals that would reflect the problems society faces in the world of today.... Measures of conventional academic achievement, for instance, are at a more advanced stage of development than measures of attitude and values.

> Measures of progress toward the ten goals are unequally developed. Some are more dependable and valid than others. For example, tests of reading comprehension are relatively well developed and reasonably well understood while tests of such qualities as self-understanding and tolerance are less well developed and poorly understood.... Where the available measures are clearly inadequate, intensive research and development should be undertaken immediately to bring them to the point where they can have full effect in the evaluation program.

JAMES CLAVELL WROTE *THE CHILDREN'S STORY* (DELACORTE PRESS/ELEANOR Friede: New York, 1963). In this book Clavell, author of *King Rat, Tai-Pan, Shogun* and *Noble House*, explains most eloquently how little children can have their minds manipulated into believing anything the teacher wants them to believe, even to the point of believing their parents are old-fashioned and should go back to school to unlearn bad thoughts, and that God does not exist. On the dust jacket of the book we learn:

> It was a simple incident in the life of James Clavell—a talk with his young daughter just home from school—that inspired this chilling tale of what could happen in twenty-five quietly devastating minutes. He [Clavell] writes: "*The Children's Story* came into being that day. It was then that I really realized how vulnerable my child's mind was—any mind for that matter—under controlled circumstances."

Some excerpts from the last pages of this remarkable book follow:

> "Sit down, Johnny, and we'll start learning good things and not worry about grown-up bad thoughts. Oh yes," she said when she sat down at her seat again, brimming with happiness. "I have a lovely surprise for you. You're all going to stay overnight with us. We have a lovely room and beds and lots of food, and we'll all tell stories and have such a lovely time."
>
> "Oh, good," the children said.
>
> "Can I stay up till eight o'clock?" Mary asked breathlessly.
>
> "Well, as it's our first new day, we'll all stay up to eight-thirty. But only if you promise to go right to sleep afterward."
>
> The children all promised. They were very happy. Jenny said, "But first we got to say our prayers. Before we go to sleep."
>
> The New Teacher smiled at her. "Of course. Perhaps we should say a prayer now. In some schools that's a custom, too." She thought a moment, and the faces watched her. Then she said, "Let's pray. But let's pray for something very good. What should we pray for?"
>
> "Bless Momma and Daddy," Danny said immediately.
>
> "That's a good idea, Danny. I have one. Let's pray for candy. That's a good idea, isn't it?"
>
> They all nodded happily.
>
> So, following their New Teacher, they all closed their eyes and steepled their hands together, and they prayed with her for candy.
>
> The New Teacher opened her eyes and looked around disappointedly. "But where's our candy? God is all-seeing and is everywhere, and if we pray, He answers our prayers. Isn't that true?"
>
> "I prayed for a puppy of my own lots of times, but I never got one," Danny said.
>
> "Maybe we didn't pray hard enough. Perhaps we should kneel down like it's done in church."
>
> So the New Teacher knelt and all the children knelt and they prayed very, very hard. But there was still no candy.
>
> Because the New Teacher was disappointed, the children were very disappointed. Then she said, "Perhaps we're using the wrong name." She thought a moment and then said, "Instead of saying 'God,' let's say 'Our Leader.' Let's pray to Our Leader for candy. Let's pray very hard and don't open your eyes till I say."
>
> So the children shut their eyes tightly and prayed very hard, and as they prayed, the New Teacher took out some candy from her pocket and quietly

put a piece on each child's desk. She did not notice Johnny—alone of all the children—watching her through his half-closed eyes.

She went softly back to her desk and the prayer ended, and the children opened their eyes and they stared at the candy and they were overjoyed.

"I'm going to pray to Our Leader every time," Mary said excitedly.

"Me, too," Hilda said. "Could we eat Our Leader's candy now, teacher?"

"Oh, let's, please, please, please."

"So Our Leader answered your prayers, didn't he?"

"I saw you put the candy on our desks!" Johnny burst out. "I *saw* you.... I didn't close my eyes, and I saw you. You had 'em in your pocket. We didn't get them with praying. You put them there."

All the children, appalled, stared at him and then at their New Teacher. She stood at the front of the class and looked back at Johnny and then at all of them.

"Yes, Johnny, you're quite right. You're a very, very wise boy. Children, *I* put candy on your desks. So you know that it doesn't matter whom you ask, whom you shut your eyes and 'pray' to—to God or anyone, even Our Leader—no one will give you anything. Only another human being." She looked at Danny. "God didn't give you the puppy you wanted. But if you work hard, I will. Only I or someone like me can *give* you things. Praying to God or anything or anyone for something is a waste of time." [all emphases in original]

1964

AN ARTICLE ENTITLED "ETHICAL EDUCATION" WAS PUBLISHED IN *FREE MIND,* the journal of the American Humanist Association, in its June/July 1964 issue. The following is an excerpt:

At the 1962 Humanist meeting in Los Angeles four women attended a workshop on humanist family services and began to lay the groundwork for the AHA's widespread involvement in ethical education for children.... The purpose of a humanist ethical education program should be to provide the child with tools by which he can make his own decisions.

[Ed. Note: From this time on efforts would be made to develop and implement humanistic (no right/no wrong) values education under many labels, just a few of which were/are: values clarification; decision making; critical thinking; problem solving; and moral, character, citizenship and civic education.]

IN 1964 THE CARNEGIE CORPORATION APPOINTED RALPH TYLER CHAIRMAN of the Committee on Assessing the Progress of Education which continued the project begun in 1963 that would in 1969 become the National Assessment of Educational Progress (NAEP).

[Ed. Note: In 1999 NAEP is funded by the federal government and widely used across the United States. Individual states are passing legislation to use NAEP as a state test and parents and legislators are mistakenly believing that these "tests" (assessments) will give them information about the performance of their children in academic subjects. This is a misconception; NAEP tracks conformity to government-generated goals.]

1965

THE BEHAVIORAL SCIENCE TEACHER EDUCATION PROGRAM (BSTEP), FUNDED
by the U.S. Department of Health, Education and Welfare, was initiated in
1965 at Michigan State University and carried out between the years 1965
and 1969. BSTEP's purpose was to change the teacher from a transmitter of
knowledge/content to a social change agent/facilitator/clinician. Traditional
public school administrators were appalled at this new role for teachers.
(For more extensive reading of the BSTEP proposal, see Appendix V in the
Internet version.)

ELEMENTARY AND SECONDARY EDUCATION ACT OF 1965 (ESEA) WAS PASSED
by Congress. This marked the end of local control and the beginning of
nationalization/internationalization of education in the United States. Use
of goal-setting, Management by Objectives (MBO), Planning, Programming,
Budgeting Systems (PPBS) and systems management for accountability
purposes would be totally funded by and directed from the federal level.
The table of contents for ESEA included:

- Title I—Financial Assistance to local educational agencies for educa-
  tion of children from low-income families
- Title II—School library resources, textbooks, and other instructional
  materials
- Title III—Supplementary educational centers and services, guidance
  counseling, and testing
- Title IV—Libraries, learning resources, educational innovation, and
  support
- Title V—Grants to strengthen State Departments of Education
- Title VI—Vacant
- Title VII—Bilingual education programs
- Title VIII—General provisions
- Title IX—Ethnic heritage program

ESEA targeted low income/minority students for experimentation with
Skinnerian "basic skills" programs; i.e., Follow Through [mastery learning/
direct instruction], Right-to-Read, Exemplary Center for Reading Instruction
(ECRI), Project INSTRUCT, etc. By the end of the 1980s state departments
of education would be receiving between 60–75% of their operating budget
from the U.S. Department of Education—which was not even in existence
at the time of passage of the ESEA!

PRESIDENT LYNDON B. JOHNSON ISSUED AN EXECUTIVE ORDER IN 1965
introducing the Planning, Programming and Budgeting System (PPBS) into
use throughout all departments of the entire federal government.

THE EDUCATION COMMISSION OF THE STATES (ECS) WAS CREATED IN 1965
"in order to bring some degree of order out of this chaos," wrote Harvard

University President James B. Conant in 1964 in reference to education policy making in the United States. ECS was to be made up of dues-paying "members" comprising representatives of each participating state's legislative Education Committees and their governors. The Competency-Based Education (CBE) movement—which evolved into outcome-based education (OBE), both using mastery learning as a base—was orchestrated by ECS. Since ECS served as the resource and coordinator of information flowing to state legislative committees and governors' offices across the land, it is no wonder that all states ended up having the same curriculum.

A very important article, entitled "E.C.S. at 20: The Compact's Potential Is Still To Be Realized" by Thomas Toch which covered the history of ECS, was printed in *Education Week* (October 24, 1984). Excerpts follow:

> "Some degree of order needs to be brought out of this chaos," wrote James B. Conant, the President of Harvard University, in 1964 in reference to education policy making in the nation. "We cannot have a national educational policy," he added in his book *Shaping Educational Policy*, "but we might be able to evolve a nationwide policy." The solution, Mr. Conant concluded, was a "new venture in cooperative federalism," a compact among the states to create an organization to focus national attention on the pressing education issues of the day. The following spring, the Carnegie Corporation and the Ford Foundation awarded a grant to Terry Sanford, who had recently left the governorship of North Carolina, to transform the Conant idea into reality. John W. Gardner was Carnegie's president at the time. A preliminary draft of the compact was completed by July and endorsed by representatives from all 50 states and the territories in September. Within five months, 10 states had ratified the agreement, giving it legal status. Out of the compact was born the Education Commission of the States (E.C.S.)....
>
> "We invented a little device to get the compact approved quickly," Mr. Sanford, now the President of Duke University, said recently. "We didn't need money from the legislatures, we had plenty of foundation funding, so we agreed that the governors could ratify it by executive order."...
>
> But since the establishment under Governor James B. Hunt of the Commission's Task Force on Education for Economic Growth two years ago, ECS's role has begun to change. The task force's report *Action for Excellence* joined *A Nation at Risk* and the Carnegie Foundation for the Advancement of Teaching's *High School* acted as principal voices in the chorus of reform. It gained Gov. Hunt and several other "education governors" who were linked to ECS wide national publicity, and, in making a series of specific reform recommendations, thrust ECS into the policy-making arena.

PSYCHOSYNTHESIS: A MANUAL OF PRINCIPLES AND TECHNIQUES (Psychosynthesis Research Foundation: Crucible imprint of Aquarian Press, Thorsons Publishing Group: Northamptonshire, England, 1965) by Dr. Roberto Assagioli, a practicing psychiatrist in Florence, Italy, was published.

Roberto Assagioli defined "psychosynthesis" as the "formation or reconstruction of a new personality—the transpersonal or 'spiritual Self.'" An excerpt from *Psychosynthesis* explained that

> What distinguishes psychosynthesis from many other attempts at psycho-

logical understanding is the position we take as to the existence of a spiritual Self.… We consider that the spiritual is as basic as the material part of man… essentially we include within the study of psychological facts all those which may be related to the higher urges within man which tends to make him grow towards greater realization of his spiritual essence. Our position affirms that all the superior manifestations of the human psyche, such as creative imagination, intuition, aspiration, genius, are facts which are as real and as important as are the conditioned reflexes, and therefore, are susceptible to research and treatment just as scientifically as conditioned reflexes.

As psychology began to assert itself as an "acceptable science" in the "sick sixties," Assagioli's "psychosynthesis" concept is credited with creating a paradigm that enabled an integration (synthesis) of psychology with spirituality. Assagioli emphasized a holistic worldview, laying the groundwork for the future educational pedagogy of "holistic education" of the 1990s—teaching the "whole child." He was also the originator of a group of exercises for "Spiritual Psychosynthesis" based on what we now call "role playing." These include: "on the *Legend of the Holy Grail*," "on Dante's *Divine Comedy*," and "on the *Blossoming of the Rose*."

Assagioli's view of the human psyche included a progression from lower to higher order "consciousness" (or thinking) which is similar to "New Age" ideas about the evolution of man into a "collective consciousness." These ideas laid the philosophical foundation for character education, values clarification, and consciousness-altering techniques used in the classroom. For example, the "sick sixties" were hallmarked by the emergence of "transpersonal psychology," a designation typified today by the statement, "I'm OK, you're OK." One of its promoters—and a disciple of Roberto Assagioli—was Jack Canfield. Canfield's name appears on many education curricula and training programs utilizing behavior modification for values clarification.

Significantly, Roberto Assagioli's selected appendices in *Psychosynthesis* include an article entitled "Initiated Symbol Projection" (ISP) written by a German psychiatrist named Hanscarl Leurner. According to a note by Assagioli, "Dr. Leurner now prefers to call his method 'Guided Affective Imagery'"—a form of guided imagery widely practiced in elementary and secondary classrooms, business training sessions, counseling sessions, and religious services. A description of what Leurner called his "psycho-diagnostic and psycho-therapeutic technique" is provided:

> The subject is seated in a comfortable chair or on a couch (lying down), asked to close his eyes, and induced to relax…a light hypnoid state has proved valuable. Deep and regular breathing…[t]hen, in a psychological state characterized by diminished consciousness of the outer world, reduced conscious criticism and self-control, the subject is asked to visualize…. In the phenomenology of medical psychology, they are similar to "hypnogic visions."

[Ed. Note: The fact that guided imagery is a psychological technique raises a question regarding its use in the classroom by teachers who are not professional therapists.]

1966

Psychology by Wilbert James McKeachie of the University of Michigan and Charlotte Lackner Doyle of Cornell University (Addison-Wesley Publishing Co., Inc.: New York, 1966) was published. An excerpt from a chapter entitled "What Does a Psychologist Observe?" follows:

> Watson's approach to psychology, with its emphasis on observable behavior, became known as behaviorism. The major problem with this approach was that it excluded from psychology some of its major concerns. No one can directly observe the motives, feelings, perceptions, thoughts, and memories of others. Re-defining thought in terms of muscle movements made thought a measurable event, but ignored some of the properties of thought that make it psychologically interesting. The behaviorists became committed to the study of muscle movements in place of an analysis of thought. (pp. 4–5)

1967

The Computer in American Education edited by Don D. Bushnell and Dwight W. Allen (John Wiley & Sons: New York, 1967) was published. Excerpts follow:

> The technology for controlling others exists and it will be used, given the persistence of power-seeking motives. Furthermore, we will need to use it, since the necessary social changes cannot come about if the affected people do not understand and desire them.... How do we educate "run-of-the-mill" citizens for membership in a democratic society?... How do we teach people to understand their relationship to long range planning?... And how do we teach people to be comfortable with the process of change? Should we educate for this? We shall probably have to. But how?...
>
> The need for educating to embrace change is not limited to youngsters.... Education for tomorrow's world will involve more than programming students by a computer; it will equally involve the ways in which we program... parents to respond to the education... children get for this kind of world. To the extent we succeed with the youngsters but not with the parents, we will have... a very serious consequence: an increasing separation of the young from their parents.... It will have psychological repercussions, probably producing in the children both guilt and hostility (arising from their rejection of their parents' views and values in lifestyles). (p. 7)

Project Follow Through was initiated in 1967, funded under the *Economic Opportunity Act of 1964*, and carried out as a part of President Lyndon Johnson's "War on Poverty." Follow Through was administered by the U.S. Office of Education in the Department of Health, Education and Welfare. One of the models of instruction examined in trial under Follow Through was the Direct Instruction (DI) model developed by W.C. Becker and Siegfried Engelmann. Direct Instruction is based on the work of the late B.F. Skinner of Harvard, Edward Thorndike of Columbia University, and Ivan Pavlov of Russia, even though their works are not directly quoted in the DI literature.

Alice M. Rivlin,[8] a member of the Brookings Institute staff, in a lecture entitled "Systematic Thinking for Social Action" for the institute's H. Rowan Gaither Lectures Series at the University of California at Berkeley (under the sponsorship of the Graduate School of Business Administration and the Center for Research in Management Science, 1970), critically evaluated Project Follow Through and its results. Following are excerpts from Rivlin's speech:

> The Follow Through program is another example of a current attempt to use federal funds to learn how to produce services effectively—in this case, services for young children. Follow Through is a quasi-experiment, with a statistical design far less sophisticated than that of the New Jersey income maintenance experiment. There was evidence that children could move ahead rapidly in a good preschool program, but that when they were dumped back into the same dismal slum school the gains were lost. The objective of Follow Through was to determine whether the gains achieved through Head Start could be maintained through special programs in the early years of elementary school.... The approaches were extremely varied. The Becker-Engelmann program [Direct Instruction], developed at the University of Illinois, emphasized intensive work with small groups of children on the cognitive skills that deprived children often lack—verbal expression, reading, math skills. The methods involve rapid-fire questioning of students by instructors with rewards in the form of praise and stars for the right answers. It is a highly-disciplined approach and has been described as an intellectual "pressure cooker."...
>
> Since Follow Through was not a scientifically designed experiment, there is reason to question whether valid conclusions can be drawn from it about the relative effectiveness of the various approaches.... In any case, there are not enough projects of any type to support definitive statements about what works best with different kinds of populations.

[Ed. Note: Although the evaluation of Follow Through cited some academic and self-esteem gains at some Direct Instruction model sites, it would have been virtually impossible for these gains not to have been made considering the models with which they were compared—the non-academic focus of the "touchy-feely" open classroom. Had the Direct Instruction model been in competition with a traditional phonics program which was not based on animal behavioral psychology ("scientific, research-based"), it is most unlikely it would have been able to point to any gains at all. Unsuspecting parents in the 1990s seeking more structured academic education for their children than can be found in schools experimenting with constructivistic developmental programs (whole language, etc.) are turning to DI, not realizing they are embracing a method based on mastery learning and animal psychology.]

PLANNING, PROGRAMMING, BUDGETING SYSTEM (PPBS) WAS APPLIED TO education in 1967. During Ronald Reagan's tenure as governor of California, PPBS was installed in the California school system. The California Assembly passed AB 61 (1967) which authorized a pilot study of PPBS; ACR 198 (1970) created the Joint Committee on Educational Goals and Evaluation; AAB 2800 (1971) and SB 1526 (1971) set up the essential PPBS subsystems to facilitate federal funding and centralized control of state schools' goals, evaluation and management of all school programs and people; AB 293 (1971), the "Stull Bill," provided for teacher evaluation; the California State Board of Education approved Program Budgeting in a new *California School Accounting Manual* (Phase I of PPBS); and Reagan signed AB 1207 (1973), giving the accounting manual legal mandate in districts throughout the state. PPBS implementation in education (and in other governmental functions) was given considerable impetus by Governor Reagan who "strongly expressed" the intent of his administration to activate PPBS, a management tool of political change through funding, in *Implementing PPB in State, City and County: A Report on the 5-5-5 Project.* (State-Local Finances Project of The George Washington University: Washington, D.C., June, 1969). This entry summarizes this *Report,* published in cooperation with: The Council of State Governments, The International City Managers Association, The National Association of Counties, The National Governors' Conference, The National League of Cities, and The United States Conference of Mayors.

1968

B.F. Skinner: The Man and His Ideas by Richard I. Evans was published (Dutton and Company: New York, 1968). Evans's excellent critique of the totalitarian views of Professor Skinner was funded by the National Science Foundation. (Extensive quotes from this book are included in the Internet version in Appendix XXIV.) A few pertinent excerpts follow:

> "I could make a pigeon a high achiever by reinforcing it on a proper schedule.".... His [Skinner's] concern for what he believes to be the inadequacy of our formal education system led to applying the principles of operant conditioning to a learning system which he called the teaching machine, but Skinner's approach is concerned with more than merely methods and techniques. He challenges the very foundations by which man in our society is shaped and controlled. (p. 10)...
>
> ..."[F]or the purpose of analyzing behavior we have to assume man is a machine. (p. 24) ...You can induce him to behave according to the dictates of society instead of his own selfish interest." (p. 42)...
>
> ..."I should not bother with ordinary learning theory, for example. I would eliminate most sensory psychology and I would give them no cognitive psychology whatsoever [meaning the students, ed.]." (p. 91)" *...It isn't the person who is important, it's the method. If the practice of psychology survives, that's the main objective. It's the same with cultural practices in general: no one survives as a person."* (p. 96) "...It does bother me that thousands of teachers don't understand, because immediate gains are more likely in the classroom than in the clinic. Teachers will eventually know—they must [understand]—and I am more concerned with promoting my theories in education [operant conditioning]." (p. 96) "...I should like to see our government set up a large educational agency in which specialists could be sent to train teachers." (p. 109) [Emphasis added.]

In 1953 Skinner wrote *Science and Human Behavior* (Macmillan & Co.: New York, 1953), within which is found the following quote:

A rather obvious solution is to distribute the control of human behavior among many agencies which have so little in common that they are not likely to join together in a despotic unit. In general this is the argument for democracy against totalitarianism. In a totalitarian state all agencies are brought together under a single super-agency.

[Ed. Note: Obviously, even before the U.S. Department of Education was established and organized teacher in-service training had taken a behaviorist (performance-based) turn, Skinner was advocating these very operant conditioning methods in all phases of education. Beginning in 1965, the federal government implemented several teacher education programs based on performance—performance-based teacher education—which would fulfill Skinner's plan. Skinner was always more concerned with "how" teachers teach than with "what" teachers teach. (The reader should refer to Bettye Lewis's fine summary of the establishment of the *Behavioral Science Teacher Education Program* in Appendix V of the Internet version for descriptions of these programs.)]

THE MAY 1968 ISSUE OF THE EDUCATIONAL JOURNAL *THE INSTRUCTOR* RAN an article by Dr. Paul Brandwein, adjunct professor at University of Pittsburgh, entitled "School System of the Future" which outlined the changes on the horizon relative to the relationship between children, parents and schools. The following quotes will be of interest:

> [Parents] often have little, if any knowledge of the rudiments of the human enterprise we call teaching and learning, or even the elements of the behavioral sciences undergirding child development.... The most formative years are what we call pre-kindergarten years.... Television can be utilized to provide the proper instruction [indoctrination] to the parent... a minimum of an hour a day... continuing over four or five years... aimed at the parent to equip him as "teacher."
>
> Learning is synonymous with environmental behavior change.... Learning... is the modification of behavior through interaction with the environment.... [New school system structure] would maintain continuity over some nineteen years, with three carefully articulated periods of schooling... 1. *Primary*, with the first four or five years in the home with "informed" parents as teachers; 2. *Secondary*, with parents as teacher aides; 3. *Preparatory*, to be used differently for children with varying gifts and destinations.... The student would be able to choose vocational training, studies related to semi-skilled occupation, or collegiate work for the next four years, with one year given over to public service....
>
> [P]rimary education with the parents as teacher has the aim of making the home a healthy and healing environment.... Education must heal. If it does not heal and make strong, it is not education.
>
> Assume with me that education, as profession and enterprise, would join forces with government and industry to support education of the parent in the mode, manner, and morality befitting the early education of children. Teachers and behavioral scientists—psychologists, psychiatrists, sociologists, students of child development—would be called upon. We have common, indeed universal, communication with the home through radio, television,

and printed materials; and soon other aspects of electronic technology will be available.

The Secondary Years, beginning with kindergarten, concern themselves with the concepts and skills required for effective participation in our society.... In *structure* [emphasis in original], the curriculum might well be organized in terms of continuous and progressive experience (synonyms: non-graded curriculum, continuous progress).... Grades (marks, scores) as we know them would not be used, but there would be reports to the parents of child's progress, similar to what some schools are doing now.

Each boy and girl would choose an area of public service coordinated with his gifts and destination. Care of children, care of the aged and infirm, assisting in schools and in hospitals, conserving our natural resources, could well be among such tasks. The major peace-seeking and peace-keeping strategy of society is education. Peace is inevitable.

LEARNING AND INSTRUCTION, A CHICAGO INNER CITY SCHOOLS POSITION Paper presented in June of 1968 to the Chicago Board of Education, was produced by the planning staff in Chicago made up of: Dr. Donald Leu, William Farquhar, Lee Shulman, and the Chicago and Michigan State universities in collaboration. One reference used was *Soviet Preschool Education*, translated by Henry Chauncey (Educational Testing Service, Princeton, N.J.). Excerpts from the Chicago Mastery Learning Project position paper, *Learning and Instruction*, follow:

We view the child with his defined characteristics as input to a school organization which modifies his capabilities toward certain goals and objectives as output. The school organization is an optimal deployment of teachers employing a special subject matter who attempt through instruction, with the aid of selected elements of the community, to achieve specified outputs. The joint participation of the children, school and community leave none of these elements unchanged....

This emphasis should be accomplished within the context of a truly ungraded structure which we shall denote by the terms Continuous Development-Mastery Learning. This approach has the following characteristics: (a) Beginning with Chicago's present concept of Continuous Development, the objectives of the language arts curriculum must be much further differentiated and articulated in the manner currently being conducted by Sophie Bloom [wife of the late Benjamin Bloom, ed.] in Chicago, and Pittsburgh's Individually Prescribed Instruction Project. In the Continuous Development-Mastery Learning approach, a large number of sequentially designated objectives, tied into specific capabilities to be mastered by pupils, are identified. This is done by curriculum development specialists in collaboration with instructional personnel. [References used in this paper were from the late Benjamin Bloom, John Carroll, Robert Gagne, Robert Glaser and Henry Chauncey, ed.]

The following is an excerpt from an article published in *Education Week*, March 6, 1985 entitled "Half of Chicago Students Drop out, Study Finds: Problem Called Enormous Human Tragedy":

Calling the dropout problem in Chicago "a human tragedy of enormous dimensions," a recent study has found that almost half of the 39,500 public school students in the 1980 freshman class failed to graduate, and that only about a third of those who did were able to read at or above the national 12th grade level. "These statistics about the class of 1984 reflect the destruction of tens of thousands of young lives, year in and year out," says the study, released in January by Designs for Change, a nonprofit research and child-advocacy organization in Chicago.... "Most of these young people are permanently locked out of our changing economy and have no hope of continuing their education or getting a permanent job with a future," the authors wrote.

Professor Lee Shulman's involvement in the Chicago Mastery Learning disaster was, however, quickly forgotten or considered unimportant. According to *Education Daily* of May 21, 1987—two years later:

> Shulman, who heads Stanford's Education Policy Institute, last week was awarded $817,000 by Carnegie Corporation to develop over the next 15 months new forms of teacher assessment materials that would be the basis of standards adopted by a national teacher certification board.

The *Education Daily* article further discussed the requirement for teacher critique of the way two textbooks treat photosynthesis and how they (teachers) developed a lesson plan based on each one:

> The teacher then would be directed to use the textbooks to tell the examiners how he or she would teach students with varying religious, cultural and ethnic backgrounds.

Nine years later *Education Week* of October 23, 1996 reported Shulman again leading the outcome-/performance-based teacher education bandwagon of social change agents:

> His successful performance as developer of new forms of teacher assessment materials leads to his being named President of the Carnegie Foundation for the Advancement of Teaching, filling the vacancy created by the death last year of Ernest L. Boyer.

An excerpt from an October 21, 1996 *New York Times* article entitled "Carnegie Foundation Selects a New Leader" emphasized Shulman's importance in the field of behavioral psychology:

> He [Shulman] has been a Guggenheim Fellow, a Fellow of the American Psychological Association and a Fellow of the Center for Advanced Study in the Behavioral Sciences. He is the immediate past president of the National Academy of Education and a former president of the American Education Research Association.

IN A 1968 SPEECH ENTITLED "THE UNITED NATIONS AND ALTERNATIVE Formulations—The Hard Road to World Order," Richard Gardner, former U.S. deputy assistant secretary of state and U.S. ambassador to Italy, provided an accurate forewarning and picture of the environment in which Americans and citizens of other countries live today, explaining how the elitist planners would, through the use of gradualism, succeed in their century-long plan to create a One World Government. In an excerpt from the speech Gardner explains the following:

> In short, we are likely to do better by building our "house of world order" from the bottom up rather than the top down. It will look like a great, "booming, buzzing confusion," to use William James's famous description of reality, but an end run around national sovereignty, eroding it piece by piece, is likely to get us to world order faster than the old-fashioned frontal attack.

ETHNA REID OF THE GRANITE SCHOOL DISTRICT, SALT LAKE CITY, UTAH received $848,536 in federal grants under Title III of the *Elementary and Secondary Education Act of 1965* in 1968 to develop the Exemplary Center for Reading Instruction (ECRI), a Mastery Learning program. This grant far exceeded the legal cap on federal education program funding at that time. In 1982 Reid claimed that her mastery learning program "is undoubtedly one of those in greatest use today in the United States at all grade levels, K–12."[9]

The 120-page teacher pre-service training manual from ECRI was devoted to the training of teachers in stimulus-response-stimulus/operant conditioning techniques (Skinner), and materials on the "adaptation of birds, monitoring forms before and after instruction" (observation data sheet records). *How to Teach Animals* by B.F. Skinner and *How to Teach Animals: A Rat, a Pigeon, a Dog* by Kathleen and Shauna Reid are both listed as teacher and resource materials. The *ECRI Teacher Training Manual* cites the work of Siegfried Engelmann, the developer of DISTAR (Direct Instruction System for Teaching and Remediation)/Reading Mastery, and Direct Instruction in instructing teachers how to use operant conditioning, stimulus-response-stimulus to get desired behaviors. Reviewed by the U.S. Department of Education's Joint Dissemination Review Panel (JDRP) and approved as an exemplary education program in 1974, ECRI was promoted throughout the National Diffusion Network (NDN), the federally funded transmission belt for controversial and mostly non-academic programs.

On May 5, 1984 the officers of the Arizona Federation of Teachers unanimously passed a resolution—spearheaded by Ann Herzer, an Arizona teacher—which stated in part that members of the Arizona affiliate

> oppose such programs as ECRI, Project INSTRUCT and/or any other programs that use operant conditioning under the guise of Mastery Learning, Classroom Management, Precision Teaching, Structured Learning and Discipline, and petition the U.S. Congress for protection against the use of such methods on teachers and students without their prior consent.

The Arizona resolution was supported by Dr. Jeanette Veatch, internationally known expert in the field of reading, who in a July 1980 letter to Ann Herzer called the ECRI program "a more modern version of breaking children to the heel of thought control.... It is so flagrantly dangerous, damaging and destructive I am appalled at its existence." Unfortunately, Albert Shanker, then president of the national American Federation of Teachers (AFT), tabled the Arizona affiliate's resolution at AFT's August, 1984 national convention in Washington, D.C.

With this historical perspective in mind, consider an article which appeared in *Education Week* September 6, 1997 entitled "New AFT President Urges Members to Help Floundering Schools." The late Albert Shanker would be pleased that the AFT continues to support Skinnerian mastery learning/direct instruction, for the article states in part: "Also featured [at AFT's QUEST Conference] was Direct Instruction, a scripted set of lessons used for teaching at-risk students."

JOHN GOODLAD'S ARTICLE, "LEARNING AND TEACHING IN THE FUTURE," was published by the National Education Association's journal *Today's Education* in 1968. Excerpts from Goodlad's article follow:

> The most controversial issues of the twenty-first century will pertain to the ends and means of modifying human behavior and who shall determine them. The first educational question will not be "what knowledge is of the most worth?" but "what kinds of human beings do we wish to produce?" The possibilities virtually defy our imagination.

TECHNOLOGY OF TEACHING BY B.F SKINNER WAS PUBLISHED (PRENTICE Hall: New York, 1968) and became part of the educational lore of the day. An excerpt follows:

> Absolute power in education is not a serious issue today because it seems out of reach. However, a technology of teaching will need to be much more powerful if the race with catastrophe is to be won, and it may then, like any powerful technology, need to be contained. An appropriate counter control will not be generated as a revolt against aversive measures but by a policy designed to maximize the contribution which education can make to the strength of the culture. The issue is important because the government of the future will probably operate mainly through educational techniques. (p. 260)

[Ed. note: Skinner was 100% correct. The government in 1999 "operates mainly through educational techniques." Those individuals and agencies conforming with government policies, criteria, etc., are rewarded, whereas those who do not conform are either ignored or denied special privileges and funding. In the late twentieth century, following the philosophy of B.F. Skinner that the "environment is all," all evil is attributed to the environment and no one is held responsible for his actions.]

"THE FOUNDATION MACHINE" BY EDITH KERMIT ROOSEVELT WAS PUBLISHED in the December 26, 1968 issue of *The Wanderer*. In this important article Mrs. Roosevelt discussed problems that had been created by the Carnegie Corporation's new reading program as follows:

> Even now the Carnegie Corporation is facing protests from parents whose children are exposed to the textbooks financed by the foundation under its "Project Read." This project provides programmed textbooks for schools, particularly in "culturally deprived areas." An estimated five million children

throughout the nation are using the material in the programmed textbooks produced by the Behavioral Research Laboratories, Palo Alto, California. This writer has gone over these textbooks in the "Reading" series financed by the Carnegie Corporation and authored by M.W. Sullivan, a linguist. These foundation-funded books reveal a fire pattern that amounts to an incitement to the sort of arson and guerilla warfare that took place in Watts, Washington, D.C., and elsewhere. On one page in the series we find a torch next to a white porch. The caption reads invitingly, "a torch, a porch." Further along there is a picture of a man smiling while he holds a torch aloft. The caption beneath it reads: "This man has a t_rch in his hand." The children are required as an exercise to insert the missing letter to fill in the word torch. The next picture shows the burning torch touching the porch, with a caption, "a torch on a porch." Thus, the children are led in stages to the final act that suggests itself quite naturally. The picture in the series shows a hand moving the hands of a clock to twenty-five minutes past one, while this same shack is being devoured by flames. The message is plain: an example of a man who deliberately commits the criminal act of setting a home on fire. Tragically, these young children are being indoctrinated with a pattern of anti-social ideas that will completely and violently alienate them from the mainstream of American middle-class values.... Other pictures in the Carnegie-funded supposedly educational texts include a comparison of a flag with a rag, the ransoming of an American soldier in a Chinese prison, a picture that shows people kneeling in a church to say their prayers beside a picture of a horse being taught to kneel in the same way, a reference to a candidate elected to public office as a "ruler," a picture of a boy stealing a girl's purse, and another boy throwing pointed darts at a companion whom he uses as target practice.

Understandably, the Carnegie-financed books are causing concern to local law-enforcement officials, many of whom have to cope with riot or near-riot conditions. Ellen Morphonios, prosecutor for Florida in its attorney's office, and a chief of its Criminal Court Division, said recently: "It's a slap in the face and an insult to every member of the Negro community, saying that the only way to communicate with Negro children is to show a robber or violence. It's like subliminal advertising. If this isn't subversive and deliberately done as part of a master plan.... Only a sick mind could have produced it."

Repeated instances of this type of anti-social activity obviously constitute a strong argument for removing the tax-exempt status of these educational foundations, and for curbing their activities by Federal regulations and Congressional oversight.

[Ed. Note: The programmed textbooks used in Project Read are based on Skinnerian animal psychology. Programmed instruction calls for individualized instruction/self-instruction (programmed books and or teaching machines) and differs from the lecture/discussion method of teaching where the teacher, not the program, is the dispenser of knowledge.]

AGENDA FOR THE NATION, EDITED BY KERMIT GORDON (BROOKINGS INSTI-tution: Washington, D.C., 1968) and funded by the Ford Foundation, was published. Ralph Tyler's article "Investing in Better Schools" (pp. 207–236) was included in the compilation of articles which were written as a contribution to public discussion and debate as a new president and a new Congress assumed their responsibilites. Other contributors included: Stephen K. Bailey, Kenneth B. Clark, Clark Kerr, Henry A. Kissinger, Edwin O. Reischauer, and Charles L. Schultze. The following excerpted recommendations from Tyler's article which refer to the Certificate of Initial Mastery, no more Carnegie Units, the Eight-Year Study and outcome-based education, read like pages out of *Goals 2000: Educate America Act* and reports prepared by Marc Tucker's National Center on Education and the Economy, the Secretary's Commission on Achieving Necessary Skills (SCANS), etc.—all of which are involved in the socialistic restructuring of the nation's schools and economy:

> What is required is a major effort to furnish high school students with significant adult activities—job programs, community service corps experience, work in health centers, apprentice experience in research and development, and in staff studies conducted by public agencies. It will be necessary to redesign the high school in order to open it to the community and to utilize many kinds of persons in education. The school will need to serve a wider range of ages and allow students to vary the amount of time devoted to studies. To supply a substitute for grades and credits as qualification for employment opportunities, a certification system will need to be developed to validate the student's competence in various major areas. This will also tend to reduce the emphasis upon purely formal requirements such as class attendance and the completion of prescribed courses.

1968–1969. *Narrative Report of Project Funded under Title III, Elementary and Secondary Education Act (FY 1969)—Title of Project: OPERATION PEP, a Statewide Project to Prepare Educational Planners for California* (U.S. Office of Education Grant Award No. OEG 3–7–704444410–4439, 7–1–68 to 6–30–69. $299,457 grant to San Mateo County Superintendent of Schools, Redwood City, California, Project Director: Donald R. Miller) was compiled and registered with the U.S. Office of Education in the Department of Health, Education and Welfare. An excerpt from this report follows:

> Major Objectives: The objectives of Operation PEP have been specified with respect for the educational needs of society and the role requirements of professional educators. They include: (1) to plan, develop, validate, and implement an instructional program for educational planners and managers featuring a system approach to educational management; (2) to establish an orderly diffusion process for system approach concepts, principles, and procedures involving key agencies, organizations, and individuals; (3) to provide assurance that the program developed by Operation PEP will be continuously renewed and presented, and (4) to promote the utilization and adoption of a system approach to educational management and educational leaders in California.

[Ed. Note: Mastery learning/direct instruction fits into PPBS systems management, Management by Objectives (MBO) and computer-assisted instruction as a hand fits into a glove. OBE in 1999 is Operation PEP in 1968. California's teachers' union was adamantly opposed to its enabling legislation and to Operation PEP in general.]

1969

PACESETTERS IN INNOVATION: CUMULATIVE ISSUE OF ALL PROJECTS IN OP-
*eration as of February 1969 under Title III, Supplementary Centers and
Services Program, Elementary and Secondary Education Act of 1965* (U.S.
Department of Health, Education and Welfare: Washington, D.C.,1969) was
published. This incredible 584-page catalog of education programs gives
abstracts of innovative programs dealing with humanistic education; i.e.,
values clarification, self-esteem programs, individualized education, open
classroom, etc. Shirley Correll, Ph.D., president of Florida's Pro-Family Forum, wrote "An Evaluation of HEW's Publication *Pacesetters in Innovation*"
which said in part:

> A thorough evaluation of HEW's 584-page publication, *Pacesetters in In-
> novation*, is alarming, even to one accustomed to the thrust of today's public
> schools, and even more interesting when placed in its proper perspective of
> total HEW funding. It is described as a program "to support supplementary
> education centers and services, guidance counseling and testing" on state and
> local levels. These PACE programs (Projects to Advance Creativity in Educa-
> tion) describe "Psychotherapy," "Behavior Modification," "Psychoeducation
> Clinics," "Changed Parent-Student Relationships," "Total Environmental
> Control," "Humanistic Curriculum," "Sensitivity Training," and attitudinal
> measuring devices, ad nauseam. One program discusses "Experimental
> Buses featuring multichannel programming, individual receivers and active
> response opportunities (allowing audio presentations of cognitive and/or
> affective [emotional] instructional materials." Could it be that there's more
> to this busing than integration?
>
> I found that PACE's direction was to "organize the process of change
> to restructure and reorganize the school system." Many different methods
> were used to accomplish this. Teachers are subjected to "Sensitivity Training"
> and "Change Agentry" training (an educational term used to describe the
> role of group leader as that of changing the attitude of students and others),
> not only to condition the teachers to new philosophies, but to "spread their
> influence to others in their own district and throughout the state via various
> visitation programs."
>
> Through the influences of these and various other programs, "structured
> or graded classes are systematically phased out and replaced by ungraded
> individualized instruction" (which ultimately becomes the opposite of in-
> dividualized instruction as all children eventually are fit to a pre-conceived
> mold or norm by computerized assessment).

THE ROLE OF THE SCHOOL IN THE COMMUNITY WAS PUBLISHED (PENDELL
Publishing Co.: Midland, Michigan, 1969). This slim 136-page book, edited
by Dr. Howard W. Hickey, Dr. Curtis Van Voorhees, and associates, was
"written to serve as a much-needed textbook for teachers and students in
Community Education; and to serve as a handbook on Community Education for school officials and community education leaders." The following
excerpts are from *The Role of the School in the Community*:

> Chapter III. An Overview by Jack D. Minzey and Clarence R. Olsen
> As the social forces have sought to bring action to bear on community prob-

lems, the need for a vehicle of action has become apparent. Not all groups have identified the most effective means of implementing their programs structured about community problems, but a number of influential persons and groups are aware of the community education concept and are extremely optimistic about its possibilities as the means by which their goals of social engineering can be accomplished.(p. 40)

Chapter VI. A Developmental Process by Curtis Van Voorhees
When a community school director attempts to identify courses to be included in the questioning process it is important to remember, as previously mentioned, that people are typically unable to identify many of their own problems and needs. While they may sometimes be able to identify what they want in the way of a class, it is unlikely that many people who need assistance in preparing nutritious meals are aware of that fact. And parents who are in need of information about child health practices are unlikely to recognize that they need such help. So it must be remembered that the simple existence of a problem does not guarantee its recognition by the person with the problem. Community school coordinators must, therefore, develop a questioning form which will get at the unidentified problems of people without unduly alarming or offending the respondent; they must seek to solicit information from people which will allow community school coordinators to plan better programs for the people they attempt to serve—programs that will hopefully change, in a positive way, the attitude, behavior and life style of the community residents.

[Ed. Note: The term "community education" is rarely used today due to its socialistic philosophy causing extreme controversy in the 1960s, 1970s and early 1980s. The average American rejected the notion that the community was there to serve his/her needs and that decision-making by unelected councils was acceptable or perhaps preferable to decision-making by elected officials. The change agents wisely dropped the label and now use terms such as "communitarianism," "participatory democracy," "site-based management," "school-based clinics," "year-round schools," Hillary Clinton's *It Takes a Village to Raise a Child* concept, all of which are individually or collectively Community Education. As Anita Hoge, a well-known education researcher, says, "It doesn't take a village to raise a child unless you live in a commune." At a Community Education Conference held in Washington, D.C. in 1976 a community educator from Alaska stated that "community education could be likened to the system in Russia and China."[10]]

MASTER PLAN FOR PUBLIC EDUCATION IN HAWAII—TOWARD A NEW ERA *for Education in Hawaii* was published in 1969 by the State of Hawaii Department of Education, Honolulu, Hawaii. This publication was partially funded under Title V, Sec. 503, P.L. 890–10 (U.S. Office of Education). Excerpts follow from this extraordinarily frank *Master Plan* which would serve as a model for the rest of the nation:

Implications for Education... Second, the computer will enhance learning.... The teacher will operate as a manager.... The teacher will have a ready record of each student's performance and a ready access to the information the student needs during each stage of his progress. (p. 36)

[ddd]

The task of the schools during the past stable, relatively unchanging world was to emphasize fixed habits, memorization of facts, and development of specific skills to meet known needs. But for a future which will include vast changes, the emphasis should be on how to meet new situations, on the skills of research, observation, analysis, logic and communication, on the development of attitudes appropriate to change, and on a commitment to flexibility and reason. (p. 50)

Behavioral sciences subject matter should form a part of our modern curriculum to provide a basis for self knowledge and behavioral concepts.... Study of ethical traditions, concepts and changes in value structure should be emphasized.... Department of Education should experiment with the group therapy, role playing and encounter group approach that are professionally planned and conducted, as a basis for understanding other people, races, cultures and points of view. (pp. 51–52)

From the point of view of the teacher, individualized instruction should provide for opportunities to diagnose the learning styles, and strengths and weaknesses of pupils; direct assistance by skilled counselors, psychologists, social workers and physicians will assist in accurate and meaningful diagnosis.... The Department should adopt team teaching and non-gradedness as the basic approach to classroom instruction. The present system of age and grade classification of students is excessively rigid and not conducive to individualized instruction. A non-graded approach, therefore, on a K–12 basis, is sought as an ultimate goal. (p. 54)

The school system will seek financial support of educational programs on the basis of educational outputs, that is, the improvement, growth and changes that occur in the behavior of the pupil as a result of schooling. (p. 55)

This school system will systematically study the benefits of any promising non-educational input to enhance learning. Recent discoveries from the field of bio-chemistry suggest that there already exists a fairly extensive class of drugs to improve learning such as persistence, attentiveness, immediate memory, and long term memory.... The application of biochemical research findings, heretofore centered in lower forms of animal life, will be a source of conspicuous controversy when children become the objects of such experimentation. Schools will conceivably be swept into a whole new area of collaboration in research with biochemists and psychologists to improve learning. The immediate and long-term impact on teaching as well as on learning and the ethical and moral consequences of extensive use of chemicals to assist in the learning process must be studied extensively.... The Department should initiate a long term, continuing series of discussions with individuals directly associated with these research efforts. Lay persons from our community should be an integral part of these discussions. (p. 56)

The Department should take the initiative to establish a state compact of all agencies with responsibilities in education in this state. The purpose of such a compact will be to coordinate planning and execution of educational programs.... Assuming that the basic period of schooling required for the youth of Hawaii may remain at twelve years, extending the school day and the school year may be the solution to this pressing problem. Some of the benefits which can be anticipated from an extended school year and a school day are: An improvement in economic and professional status of our teachers,... an increased use of facilities and equipment. School facilities will be in use throughout the year.... (p. 62)

That our system of values should change as the conditions in which these values find their expression change is evident in history.... Our past also has shown that society courts trouble when it clings stubbornly to outmoded values after experience has clearly shown that they need to be revised. For example, developments in our society have now cast considerable doubts on the worth of such deep-seated beliefs, still held strongly in some quarters, as extreme and rugged individualism or isolationism in international affairs. While values tend to persist, they are tentative. They provide the directions basic to any conscious and direct attempt to influence pupil behavior.... Some will argue, of course, that direct and purposeful effort at changing value orientations of pupils is no concern of the schools. But from what we know of the pupil and his development, the school is inescapably involved in influencing his moral values and ethical structure. (p. 63)

The roles and responsibilities of teachers will change noticeably in the years ahead. By 1985 it should be more accurate to term a teacher a "learning clinician" for the schools will be "clinics" whose purpose is to provide individualized educational and psychological "services" to the student.[11] (p. 69)

...However, in the spring of 1967, the Department undertook to install a new "System," more commonly referred to as "PPBS." This sophisticated system of budgeting was crystalized in the federal defense agency during the early 1960's, and has, since 1965, been formally adopted by all departments within the federal government.... From a long-range standpoint, PPBS is surely the direction we must move toward if we are to do more than survive in a rapidly approaching computerized world.... However, operationally, there are several reasons why the entire PPBS anatomy cannot be totally... operable at this time. Although some of the problems are due to the system itself, most are due to the present undeveloped state of the educational industry. Some of these factors are: While we accept the PPBS concept, we must constantly be mindful that the system is a tool of management, not an end in itself, not a panacea or solution for all our management problems. Further, it should never be considered a replacement for experienced human judgment, but only an aid in arriving at sound judgments... in the field of education, which deals primarily in human behavior, there is almost no reliable research data on causal relationships. We do not know exactly why or how students learn.... Cost/effectiveness analysis which lies at the heart of PPBS is virtually impossible without this kind of data.... As can readily be seen, the multiplicity and complexity of objectives and the difficulty of quantifying human behavior makes it exceedingly difficult to state our objectives in the manner specified by PPBS.... Another significant problem—this time to do with PPBS—is that it does not formally allow for value consideration. And yet, values—academic, economic, political, social, esthetic—appear to play a crucial role in the decision-making process. But how do we quantify values? How do we negotiate conflicting values? What will be the proper mix of values and how do we factor it into the array of alternatives and the decision-making process? These are vital questions that must be answered if we are to rationalize the decision-making process. (pp. 96–97)

Mount a comprehensive and continuing effort to develop standards and a system of measurement that will permit effective evaluation of student and Department of Education performance. (p. 98)

[Ed. Note: PPBS and MBO are essentially the same as TQM. At a 1992 Total Quality Management (TQM) in Education Conference in St. Paul, Minnesota—sponsored by the National Governors' Association and attended by the writer—a representative from IBM stated that TQM is a more "sophisticated, refined form of PPBS."]

IN 1969 DON DAVIES, FORMER DEPUTY COMMISSIONER OF EDUCATION FOR the U.S. Office of Education and editor of *Communities and Their Schools*, wrote "Changing Conditions in American Schools" as part of the "Elementary Teacher Training Models," a section of the *Behavioral Science Teacher Education Program* (U.S. Office of Education, Department of Health, Education and Welfare [developed at Michigan State University under HEW grant]: Washington, D.C., 1969). The following are excerpts from "Changing Conditions in American Schools":

(1) Moving from a mass approach to an individual approach in education;

(2) Moving from an emphasis on memorizing to an emphasis on the non-cognitive, non-intellectual components of life;

(3) Moving from a concept of a school isolated from the community;

(4) Moving from a fear of technology to using machinery and technology for educational purposes;

(5) Moving from a negative to a positive attitude towards children who are different;

(6) Moving from a provincial perspective of the world in education to a multicultural perspective;

(7) Moving from a system characterized by academic snobbery to one which recognizes and nurtures a wide variety of talents and values; and

(8) Moving from a system based on serving time to one which emphasizes performance.

[Ed. Note: 1, 2, 4, 7, and 8 should be familar to the reader. They represent OBE/ML/DI and technology. Numbers 5 and 6 are global education/values education.]

PROFESSOR DEAN CORRIGAN, IN A 1969 SPEECH BEFORE THE 22ND ANNUAL Teacher Education Conference at the University of Georgia, predicted that "teaching machines will pace a student's progress, diagnose his weaknesses and make certain that he understands a fundamental concept before allowing him to advance to the next lesson."

[Ed. Note: Skinner said "computers are essentially sophisticated versions of the teaching machines of the 1960s... programmed learning." (See "There Has Been a Conspiracy of Silence about Teaching: B.F. Skinner Argues that Pedagogy Is Key to School Reforms" from *Education Week* 8/31/83 in Chapter 7.)]

A Report from the State Committee on Public Education to the California State Board of Education—Citizens for the 21st Century—Long-Range Considerations for California Elementary and Secondary Education (California State Assembly: Sacramento, California, 1969) was prepared by Professor John I. Goodlad. Funded by the *Elementary and Secondary Education Act of 1965*, the Report states

> Experimentation, Innovation, Implementation.
> We have seen that mechanisms are needed for systematically determining the appropriate responsibilities of local, state, and federal education agencies. Similarly, we need mechanisms for systematically determining the kinds of human beings to be developed in our schools. Such mechanisms do not now exist in this state or any state. We need, too, mechanisms for appraising the quality of innovations and for systematically determining how a full range of projects might be put in a single school. (p. 471)

Improving Educational Assessment and an Inventory of Measures of Affective Behavior by Walcott H. Beatty, chairman and editor (Association for Supervision and Curriculum Development Commission on Assessment of Educational Outcomes [NEA Stock No. 611–17804]: Washington, D.C., 1969) was published. A chapter entitled "The Purposes of Assessment" by Ralph Tyler, "the father of educational assessment," was included in this important book. The following excerpts relate primarily to the principle of transfer in learning:

> The function of the school's teaching is to develop young people whose behavior outside the classroom is effective and significant. Therefore, in appraising the relative effectiveness of curriculum materials or programs, one goes beyond a checking of program and purpose to consider whether the learnings are generalizable to life outside the school. The Progressive Education Association's Eight-Year Study, for example, followed a group of high school graduates into college and occupational roles to learn the extent to which they were able to utilize ways of thinking, feeling, and acting that the school had tried to develop....
> We are all familiar with the general principle that any measures of education should be based upon educational objectives—what kind of learning are we seeking? Thirty-eight years ago, when Paul Diederich and I began some of these efforts in the Progressive Education Association, much was said about determining educational objectives. We talked about educational objectives at a level so general that such objectives represented desirable and attainable human outcomes. Now, as the people from conditioning have moved into an interest in learning in the schools, the notions of behavioral objectives have become much more specific....
> As far as I know, one cannot very well teach a pigeon a general principle that he can then apply to a variety of situations. The objectives for persons coming out of the Skinnerian background tend to be highly specific ones. When I listen to Gagne, who is an intelligent and effective conditioner, talk about human learning objectives, I wince a good deal because he sets very specific ones. I know that we can attain levels of generalization of objectives that are higher than that....

As a graduate student at Chicago 42 years ago, I did a study with Judd, who was at that time arguing with Thorndike over the principle of transfer in learning. Thorndike had demonstrated that transfer was not automatic among the formal disciplines; a person could take a course in Latin and not be able to handle other kinds of languages any more effectively. Thorndike reached the conclusion that every objective had to be very specific, like conditioning objectives. His first treatise on the psychology of arithmetic established some 3,000 objectives for elementary school arithmetic. Judd, however, had come out of the social psychology tradition, having studied with Wundt at Leipzig. His view was that generalization was not only possible but was essential in education. The task he assigned me was to check on Thorndike's view that the addition of every one of the 100 pairs of one-digit combinations had to be practiced by the learner before he could add all of the pairs. The design of my study was to take the principles of grouping for addition and help pupils see them. I noted that five and two, and six and one, and zero and seven and three and four all total seven and had the students practice 21 out of the 100, emphasizing that each operation illustrated a general principle. I found that the youngsters in the experimental group who had practiced on only 21 illustrations did just as well on the average over the sample of the total 100 as the pupils who had practiced systematically every one of the 100....

The possibility of generalization is of course not new to the reader of this booklet. In curriculum development we now work on the principle that human beings can generalize, so they do not have to practice every specific. The question is at what level of generalization do we set up objectives. There are overgeneralizations you can immediately see; for example, the use of "you" for both singular and plural forms often confuses students in grammar exercises. The problem of the effective curriculum maker and teacher is to figure out the level of generalization that is possible with a certain child or a certain group, then to establish objectives based on reaching that level of generalization. You will have twenty objectives perhaps, but not more. The conditioning view, based upon specific situations and practices, may involve several hundred objectives for a course because specific practices must be used to accomplish each aspect of the conditioning. (pp. 8–9)

"U.S. PLAN TO 'TAKE OVER' GRADE SCHOOLS INTIMATED" BY JOHN STEIN-bacher was an article which appeared in the *Anaheim Bulletin* (Anaheim, California) in 1969. Excerpts follow:

Is the U.S. Office of Education, a division of the Department of Health, Education and Welfare, poised for a total takeover of every elementary school in the nation?

That was indicated Thursday in a federally funded project at Cal State, Fullerton by Bernard Kravett, a professor at the school who took part last year in a federally funded project at the University of Washington. Known as the Tri-University Project, three universities were involved in a massively funded federal project to restructure the entire higher education system for training teachers, which, in effect, would make local elementary schools only a subsidiary arm of the federal government.... This system, to be called Teacher Preparation Experienced Systematically, is to be instituted at once.... All teacher training institutions will operate jointly with local school districts and teacher organizations to "establish performance criteria which become

behavioral objectives." ...Students in colleges who are studying to be teachers
will be placed in "clinical settings," where there will be a clinical counselor
for each 12 students....

As the teacher trainees progress through the four-year course, they will
be constantly assessed by testing and performance criteria, as well as constantly counseled by the trained psychologists.... At the end of each year,
the teacher trainee will either pass on to the next level or will be recycled
to take additional work in the areas in which he is found deficient.... The
new approach is to stress attitudinal changes on the part of the teachers
and the students....

Built into the system is a strong emphasis on the findings of the behavioral
scientists. Teacher trainees will be counseled into becoming a "good team
member on the faculty," and those who cannot adapt to "teamstanding" will
be washed out of the teacher courses. The teacher is to learn how to "carry
out the order of the team and the team leader." ...The purpose of the so-called
college activities will be to "build on behavioral objectives in order to help
children find out who they are and help the child in his quest for identity.
All education will be built on behavioral tasks rather than on course credits
and grade point averages," he said. Kravett said the federal government had
financed nine universities to come up with "programs" and it is from these
programs, largely developed in behavioral science laboratories, that the new
elementary program will come. California, he said, has a long way to go to
catch up with the rest of the nation in accepting this new program. However,
he said the government was spending "fantastic amounts of money and the
Federal Government is totally behind it, pushing it and providing all the
money you can possibly need." (p. 4)

THE NATIONAL ASSESSMENT OF EDUCATIONAL PROGRESS (NAEP), MANDATED
by the U.S. Congress, was initiated in 1969. NAEP has periodically "assessed"
(monitored the knowledge, skills, and performance of) students aged 9, 13,
and 17, as well as various grade levels. The subject areas assessed have
included: reading, writing, mathematics, science, citizenship, U.S. history,
geography, social studies, art, music, literature, computer competence, and
career and occupational development. NAEP also has collected background
information from students, teachers, and administrators, and has related
these data to student achievement. The Educational Testing Service (ETS)
in 1983 took over the contract to administer the NAEP from the Carnegie
Corporation-spawned Education Commission of the States. This move effectively kept Carnegie in control of educational assessment, since it was the
Carnegie Foundation for the Advancement of Teaching (a subdivision of the
Carnegie Corporation) which had provided the $750,000 initial endowment
(start-up funds) to launch ETS in 1947. Through an agreement between the
American Council on Education, the Carnegie Foundation and the College
Entrance Examination Board, all of whom turned over their testing programs
and a portion of their assets to ETS, the move to establish Educational Test-
ing Service as the primary provider of testing material was accomplished.

In 1988 Congress established the National Assessment Governing Board
(NAGB). The purpose of NAGB was to provide policy guidance for the ex-

ecution of NAEP. The board was composed of nationally and locally elected officials, chief state school officers, classroom teachers, local school board members, and leaders of the business community, among others. Specifically, NAGB has been charged by Congress to perform the following duties: select subject areas to be assessed; identify appropriate achievement goals for each age group; develop assessment objectives; design a methodology of assessment; and produce guidelines and standards for national, regional, and state comparisons.

[ddd]

Endnotes:

1   John Goodlad, "A Report from the State Committee on Public Education to the California State Board of Education—Citizens for the Twenty-first Century—Long Range Considerations for California Elementary and Secondary Education," 1969.

2   The function of the National Diffusion Network has been distributed throughout the U.S. Department of Education's organizational subdivisions. The dissemination process is now carried on by individual offices and their projects. This was done as a result of the "Reorganization of Government according to the Malcolm Baldridge Award criteria" (TQM) under Vice President Al Gore's supervision.

3   This is another term, used in this publication, for today's "self-esteem."

4   The writer recommends that those readers interested in the radical, leftist substance of "Recommendations for Delphi Discussion Groups," read K.M. Heaton's *Road to Revolution* that contains information on this subject. Access *Road to Revolution* at americandeception. com.

5   The reader should turn to the inside cover of this book for the excellent cartoon by Joel Pett which carries the title "Consolidation."

6   "Harrison Bergeron" has been made into a video, available at your local video store.

7   Dan Smoot was a former Harvard professor who served for 9–1/2 years in the Federal Bureau of Investigation.

8   Alice Rivlin later became director of the Congressional Budget Office, and presently serves as the chairman of the Board of Control for the District of Columbia.

9   Ethna Reid was quoted in Dennis Bailey's article "Learning to Read the ECRI Way" for the January 8, 1982 issue of *The Maine Times*.

10 Audio tape of meeting from personal file of researcher who attended conference.

11 In the January 1969 issue *of Today's Education*, journal of the National Education Association, two professors of education at Indiana University refer to schools of the 1970s as "clinics, whose purpose is to provide individualized psychosocial 'treatment' for the student."

6

THE SERIOUS SEVENTIES

"Concerned with grave, important, or complex matters, problems" and "giving cause for concern" are two out of five definitions given in *Webster's Dictionary* for the word "serious" which definitely apply to this chapter, "The Serious Seventies." Unfortunately, since the average American was purposely kept in the dark about what was taking place, being able "to be concerned" was an impossibility. To the change agents roaming the education landscape, "change" was the goal, and the end justified the means, even if it meant misleading through semantic deception the parents and taxpayers who paid the bills and provided the resources—the children and teachers upon whom the change agents would experiment.

"The Serious Seventies" contains excerpts from important government documents, education journal articles, professional papers, and critiques by key educationists regarding the major components of reform planned for the end of the century as a result of federal legislation passed in the 1960s. From a study of the key documents one detects a vigorous tug-of-war taking place at the highest decision-making levels in education. Stringent debate was carried on regarding the pros and cons of the use of systematic planning and technology in an area of human endeavor (education) which until this time had had relatively little interference from political, social and economic planners (social engineers). State commissioners of education, local education agency superintendents, and especially teachers and school boards had been able to make decisions at the state and local level—decisions which they considered to be in the best interest of students and the communities in which they lived and worked. But "change" was the name of this serious new game.

A careful reading of "The Serious Seventies" documents, especially the 1972 Association for Educational Computing and Technology (AECT) report entitled *The Field of Educational Technology: A Statement of Definition* (October, 1972), has convinced this writer that significant resistance to goal setting, systems management, computer-assisted instruction, etc., which existed at the beginning of the 1970s was, unfortunately, overcome. For instance, the above-referenced document contained the following most important warning regarding the use of technology in the classroom; a warning that, evidently, was not heeded in the years to come. The warning read in part:

> It should be clear that the concerned professional does not have to be a "liberal," or a "conservative." The concerned professional must, however, show moral sensitivity to the effect of what he or she does [in the field of technology]. It does not matter what position an individual comes to as long as it is not "I'll do it because it can be done."

The above recommendation relating to the ethical use of technology in the classroom was evidently ignored by the change agents who decided instead that "We'll do it because it can be done."

In 1971 *Phi Delta Kappan* published a paper entitled *Performance-Based Teacher Education* [PBTE]: *What Is the State of the Art?* This paper spelled out the *raison d'etre* for the transition from teacher education based on knowledge of subject matter to teacher education based on the ability to "perform" in the classroom. Skinnerian methods adopted by Madeline Hunter and others would become the foundation for future teacher training and accreditation, and ultimately the method for workforce training. This paper makes it all too clear that the purpose of PBTE was to "lower standards" so that the teaching profession could be more "inclusive"—or so "they" said. However, this writer believes inclusion was more than likely the cover (excuse acceptable to those who believed in equal opportunity) to install the performance-based system necessary for the eventual implementation of the school-to-work polytech system planned in 1934 and activated in the 1990s. From this time forward, the deliberate dumbing down would proceed with a vengeance.

During "the serious seventies" the ship of education set a new course. Navigating these new waters would require a new chart, one entirely different from that used in the past.

1970

A Prohibition against Federal Control of Education, Section 432, *General Education Provisions Act* (GEPA), was enacted in 1970 and reads as follows:

> Sec. 432. No provision of any applicable program shall be construed to authorize any department, agency, officer, or employee of the United States to exercise any direction, supervision, or control over the curriculum, program of instruction, administration, or personnel of any educational institution, school, or school system, or over the selection of library resources, textbooks, or other printed or published instructional materials by any educational institution or school system, or to require the assignment or transportation of students or teachers in order to overcome racial imbalance. (20 U.S.C. 1232a) Enacted April 18, 1970, P.L. 91–230, Title IV, sec. 401(a)(10), 81 Stat.169.

[Ed. Note: The interpretation of the above prohibition lies in the eyes of the beholder. Parents and traditional teachers have held that all curriculum and teaching based on the federally funded Northwest Regional Educational Laboratory Goals Collection, National Diffusion Network Programs, and "scientific research-based" reading programs funded under the *Reading Excellence Act of 1998* should be covered by GEPA and are consequently illegal. Educrats, on the other hand, have held that the only way for a program to be covered by GEPA would be for the secretary of education to sit on the sidewalk outside the U.S. Department of Education, developing curriculum, and passing it out to interested passersby.]

[ddd]

REPORT OF THE STUDY, TITLE III, ESEA by Emery Stoof was produced by the Educational Innovation Advisory Commission and the Bureau of Planning and Development of the California State Department of Education in 1970. Excerpts follow:

> Origin of the Bureau... An Instructional Program Planning and Development Unit was established by State Board action in 1965 and was funded through a Title V, ESEA project. This unit was comprised of persons responsible for the state level administration of Title III, ESEA, and co-ordination of Title V, ESEA. A general conceptual model for effective planned change in education, as well as a management model for the administration of Title III, ESEA, was submitted to the State Board's Federal Aid Committee in 1965, with November 10, 1965 as the first deadline for receiving applications for funds....
>
> Two significant developments early in the state administration of Title III, ESEA, were (1) the project to Prepare Educational Planners (Operation PEP), and (2) the funding of twenty-one regional planning centers. "PEP" sessions trained administrators in systematic planning procedures, systems analysis techniques, "planning, programming and budgeting system" and cost-benefit analysis. PACE (Projects to Advance Creativity in Education) was to encourage school districts to develop imaginative solutions to educational problems, to utilize more effectively research findings, to translate the latest knowledge

about teaching and learning into widespread educational practice, and to create an awareness of new programs. Through the regional centers, the Bureau has endeavored to (1) encourage the development of creative innovations, (2) demonstrate worthwhile innovations in educational practice through exemplary programs, and (3) supplement existing programs and facilities.

[Ed. Note: This is an example of how the Federal government began its takeover of all state and local education agencies, removing any semblance of what could be considered local control. The California report explains exactly what happened in every single state due to our elected officials' inability to resist taking federal money and their trust of education change agents (administrators, principals, superintendents, etc.). How many American children have been severely handicapped academically and morally by experimental, "innovative" programs which had absolutely nothing to do with academics, but everything to do with attitude, value and belief change?]

IN 1970 LEONARD S. KENWORTHY, PROFESSOR OF EDUCATION AT BROOKLYN College of the City of New York, wrote *The International Dimension of Education: Background Paper II Prepared for the World Conference on Education* (Asilomar, California, March 5–14, 1970), edited by Norman V. Overly. The conference was sponsored by the Association for Supervision and Curriculum Development, National Education Association, and the Commission on International Cooperation in Education. Excerpts from the report follow:

III. The International Dimensions of Our Schools: Some Overall Considerations

Here and there teachers have modified individual courses.... Schools have rewritten syllabi or added courses.... But nowhere has there been a rigorous examination of the total experiences of children and/or youth in schools and the development of a continuous, cumulative, comprehensive curriculum to create the new type of people needed for effective living in the latter part of the 20th century....

...All the work we do in developing internationally minded individuals should be directed to improved behavior.

That means that all the efforts in this dimension of education must be predicated on the research in the formation, reinforcement, and change of attitudes and on the development of skills. Knowledge is tremendously important, but we should be clear by now that it must be carefully selected knowledge, discovered by the learners rather than told to them, and organized by them with the help of teachers or professors around concepts, generalizations, or big ideas. Teaching, therefore, becomes the process of helping younger people to probe, discover, analyze, compare, and contrast rather than telling.

There is a rich mine of data now on attitude formation, change, and reinforcement which teachers need to study carefully and apply to this dimension of education as well as to others. For example, we know that most basic attitudes are learned very early but that attitudes can be changed at any age. We know that times of personal and societal crisis are the best times to bring about change. But we also know that people must not be threatened by changes. They must be relatively secure and much of their resistance to change recognized and tolerated as a manifestation of an inner struggle to reject the old and accept the new. Therefore, the acceptance of the old views with equanimity is important, so that the threat to a person is minimal. We know, too, that appeals to pride and self-interest may be helpful in bringing about change. So are the statements and actions of prestige persons. Membership in new groups is often helpful in insulating a person from slipping back into old patterns. We also know that changing a total group is easier and more likely to produce results than trying to change individuals. And it is clear that concentration upon specific areas of change rather than general approaches is usually most effective....

Changed behavior is our goal and it consists in large measure of improved attitudes, improved skills, and carefully selected knowledge—these three—and the greatest of these is attitudes....

The program emphasizes feelings as well as facts. In some parts of the world in the field of education today, the emphasis is upon cognitive learning or intellectual development. This is especially true in the United States.... But in the international dimensions of education, as in other dimensions, the affective domain or emotional development is just as important....

We need to get at the "gut level" in much of our teaching. We need to use music, art, powerful literature, films and other approaches which get at the feeling level of learning. For example, the writer has found tremendously effective a 10-minute film on the United Nations, entitled "Overture." There is no narrative in this film; the pictures are shown against a background of music, with the Vienna Symphony Orchestra playing the *Egmont Overture*. It is a powerful learning device and moves its viewers in a way few other approaches touch them. (pp. 23–39)

1971

EDUCATION: FROM THE ACQUISITION OF KNOWLEDGE TO PROGRAMMED, Conditioned Responses was submitted by Assemblyman Robert H. Burke (70th California Assembly District) to the California Legislature in 1971. An excerpt follows:

INTRODUCTION

Several months ago, my office began accumulating material which had particular significance in the area of Planning, Programming, Budgeting Systems because of its potential use as a tool of fiscal accountability in the field of education. As we searched into the information available on the application of this subject in education, it became increasingly difficult to see any relationship between the proposed programs and fiscal accountability. It was apparent after a study of the methods proposed for use by the schools for accountability purposes that fiscal accountability was being minimized and that techniques were being promoted for achieving behavioral objectives. Other seemingly unrelated organizations, projects, and programs were uncovered because of their influence on the application of accountability methods. They were as parts in a puzzle—analyzed by themselves, each of these projects appeared to be either harmless or an expression of someone's "dream." When linked together with other "harmless" programs, they were no longer formless but could be seen as an entire package of plans outlining methods of implementation, organization structures (including flow-charts), computerization, use of behavioral profile catalogs, and goals and objectives determination.

[ddd]

IN 1971 THE SECRETARIAT OF THE UNITED NATIONS EDUCATIONAL, SCIENtific, and Cultural Organization (UNESCO) called upon George W. Parkyn of New Zealand to outline a possible model for an education system based on the ideal of a continuous education process throughout the lifetime of the learner—a means of bringing an existing national school system into line with lifelong learning. The result of this effort was a book entitled *Towards a Conceptual Model of Life-Long Education*, published in 1973 by UNESCO (English Edition ISBN 92–3–101117–0). The preface of the book contained the following interesting biographical sketch of the little-known Dr. Parkyn:

> The Secretariat called on George W. Parkyn of New Zealand to prepare this first study. Dr. Parkyn has rendered extensive service to education in many parts of the world: in New Zealand, as a teacher in primary and secondary schools, as a senior lecturer at the University of Otago, and as director of the New Zealand Council for Educational Research, 1954–1967; at UNESCO, where he made substantial contributions to the *World Survey of Education*; at Stanford University, California, as a visiting professor; in New Zealand again, as a visiting lecturer in Comparative Education at the University of Auckland; and as Professor of Comparative Education at the University of London, Institute of Education.... Dr. Parkyn was asked to review the available literature in this field and to involve several of his colleagues at Stanford University, California, in discussions on the basic concept. Psychologists, sociologists, and anthropologists, as well as professional educators took part in the conceptual stage, contributing a rich variety of views. Among those who helped the author in the preparation of the study were his research assistants, Mr. Alejandro Toledo and Mr. Hei-tak Wu, and his colleagues, Dr. John C. Bock, Dr. Martin Carnoy, Dr. Henry M. Levin and Dr. Frank J. Moore.

[Ed. Note: The Dr. Henry M. Levin mentioned above is the same Henry Levin whose K–8 Accelerated Schools Project is one of the seventeen reform models that schools may adopt to qualify for their share of nearly $150 million in federal grants, according to the January 20, 1999 edition of *Education Week* (p. 1). The article "Who's In, Who's Out" listed Accelerated Learning as being used in urban schools. It is based on a constructivist philosophy which has echoes of and references to Maria Montessori's and John Dewey's philosophies of education and incorporates the controversial Lozanov method of Superlearning.]

PSYCHOLOGY APPLIED TO TEACHING BY ROBERT F. BIENTER (HOUGHTON Mifflin Co.: Boston, 1971) was published. This popular psychology text was recommended for use in Introduction to Educational Psychology courses in universities in the early 1970s. Chapter 5, under the sub-heading of "S-R Associationism and Programmed Learning," is excerpted here:

Watson [John B.] (who did the most to popularize Pavlovian theory in the United States) based one of his most famous experiments (Watson and Rayner, 1920) on the observation that young children have a "natural" fear of sudden loud sounds. He set up a situation in which a two-year-old boy named Albert was encouraged to play with a white rat. After this preliminary period, Watson suddenly hit a steel bar with a hammer just as Albert reached for the rat, and the noise frightened the child so much that he came to respond to the rat with fear. He had been conditioned to associate the rat with the loud sound. The success of this experiment led Watson to believe that he could control behavior in almost limitless ways, by arranging sequences of conditioned responses. He trumpeted his claim in this famous statement:

> Give me a dozen healthy infants, well formed, and my own special world to bring them up in, and I'll guarantee to take any one at random and train him to become any type of specialist I might select—doctor, lawyer, artist, merchant-chief and yes, even beggarman and thief—regardless of his talents, penchants, tendencies, abilities, vocations, and race of his ancestry. (pp. 152–3)

Later on in the chapter, Skinner's contributions are discussed:

> An even more striking example of Skinner's overwhelming enthusiasm for programmed learning is his claim that mere manipulation of the teaching machine should be "reinforcing enough to keep a pupil at work for suitable periods every day.".... Thus it is apparent that Skinner's enthusiasm has prevented him from seeing some of the deficiencies of programmed instruction. Many critics have been especially dissatisfied with his attempt to refute the charge that programs limit creativity. Clearly when the person composing a program decides in advance what is to be learned and how it is to be learned, a student has no opportunity to develop in his own way. He is limited by what the programmer knows and by how the programmer learned....
>
> It is true that the student might use the material in an original way after he had finished the program, but there is the possibility that programmed instruction interferes with this process. For example, some students who have completed programs report that although they have progressed quickly and satisfactorily and feel that they have learned something, they aren't sure where to go from here. Typically, the next step is to take an exam, usually of the multiple-choice type, which is highly similar to the program in which that stimuli are presented and responses are chosen. But what happens after the exam? If the student cannot respond unless he is stimulated in the same way he was in the program or exam, he will rarely be able to apply what he has learned to real life situations.
>
> What we are dealing with here is the subject of transfer... which is basic to education. Ellis has pointed out that little research has been done on the transferability of programmed learning; in almost all studies the experimenter determines the degree of learning solely on the basis of each child's performance on a test given immediately after the completion of the program. Skinner maintains that the student can be taught to transfer ideas through separate programs designed for this purpose and that a properly written program will wean the student from the machine, but there is little evidence to back up this contention. On logical grounds alone it seems reasonable to question the transfer value of programmed instruction.
>
> Markle notes that in order to ensure that approximately 95 percent of the

answers will be correct, as Skinner suggests, programmers are forced to keep revising programs for the lowest common denominator—the slowest students in the group. This eventually leads to programs which most students can complete fairly easily, but it also leads to programs which are oversimplified and repetitious. (pp. 168–171)

THE INDIVIDUALIZED LEARNING LETTER (T.I.L.L.): ADMINISTRATOR'S GUIDE to Improve Learning; Individualized Instruction Methods; Flexible Scheduling; Behavioral Objectives; Study Units; Self-Directed Learning; Accountability, Vol. I (February 22, 1971: T.I.L.L., Huntington, N.Y.)[1] was published and circulated. Excerpts follow:

Opting to become a greater force in promoting I.I. (Individualized Instruction), The Northeast Association for Individualization of Instruction (Wyandanch, N.Y.) has gone national—by substituting the word "national" for "northeast."…. The enlarged 2-1/2 day convention is geared to give registrants more time to watch I.I. in action in live classrooms. Several of the nation's I.I. leaders already lined up to run workshops include: Dr. Lloyd Bishop, NYU; Dr. Sid Rollins, Rhode Island College; Dr. Robert Scanlon, Research for Better Schools [Research for Better Schools and University of Pittsburgh Learning Research and Development Center (Robert Glaser) were instrumental in development of IPI in the early 1960s, ed.]; Dr. Edward Pino, Superintendent of Cherry Creek Schools (Englewood, CO); Dr. Robert Anderson, Harvard University; Dr. Leon Lessinger, Georgia State University; Dr. Robert Sinclair, University of Massachusetts; Jane Root, Stanford Research Associates; and Dr. Glen Ovard, Brigham Young University. Representatives of USOE, NEA, NY State Department of Education will be present. (The latter supports the conference with an annual grant.)….

QUOTES YOU CAN USE:
DOWN WITH BOOKS. "Textbooks not only encourage learning at the wrong level (imparting facts rather than telling how to gather facts, etc.), they also violate an important new concern in American education—individualized instruction…. Textbooks produce superficially knowledgeable students… who know virtually nothing in depth about anything…. A good start would be to… declare a moratorium on textbook use in all courses." Dwight D. Allen, Dean of Education, University of Massachusetts, writing on "The Decline of Textbooks, Change."[2]

RECOMMENDED BOOKS: *Behavioral Objectives: A Guide for Individualized Learning.* Four-volume set covering more than 4000 objectives representing four years' work of more than 200 teachers. Arranged by subject area. Covers language arts, social studies, math and science. A comprehensive collection. Westinghouse Learning Corp., 100 Park Avenue, New York, N.Y. 10017.

MEETINGS STRESSING INDIVIDUALIZED INSTRUCTION: Ninth National Society for Programmed Instruction Convention, March 31–April 3, 1971. University of Rochester, Rochester, N.Y. Heavy emphasis on applying principles and processes of individualized instruction. Session on redesigning schools of tomorrow. Contact Dr. Robert G. Pierleone, College of Education, University of Rochester, Rochester, N.Y. First Educational Technology Conference. April 5–8, 1971. Americana Hotel, N.Y. City, N.Y. Conference seminars and workshops will cover curriculum design, use of computers, programmed instruction, simulation, innovation theory, etc.

IN FORTHCOMING ISSUES: Update of 46 Case Studies of Individualized Instruction as originally reported by Jack V. Edling, Oregon State System of Higher Education.

[ddd]

PERFORMANCE-BASED TEACHER EDUCATION: WHAT IS THE STATE OF THE *Art?* by Stanley Elam, editor of Phi Delta Kappa Publications (AACTE Committee on Performance-Based Teacher Education, American Association of Colleges for Teacher Education: Washington, D.C., 1971), was published. This paper was originally prepared in 1971 pursuant to a contract with the U.S. Office of Education through the Texas Education Agency, Austin, Texas. Excerpts follow:

> The Association is pleased to offer to the teacher education community the Committee's first state of the art paper.... In performance-based programs... he [the teacher] is held accountable, not for passing grades, but for attaining a given level of competency in performing the essential tasks of teaching.... Acceptance of this basic principle has program implications that are truly revolutionary.
>
> The claim that teacher education programs were not producing people equipped to teach minority group children and youth effectively has pointed directly to the need for reform in teacher education.... Moreover, the claim of minority group youth that there should be alternative routes to professional status has raised serious questions about the suitability of generally recognized teacher education programs.

[Ed. Note: The above paper was one of the first—and perhaps the most influential—professional papers setting the stage for full-blown implementation of Skinnerian outcome-based/performance-based education. The definitions, criteria, assessment, etc., are identical to those found in present professional OBE literature. (See Appendix VII in the Internet version for fuller excerpts from this paper.)]

CONCERN REGARDING THE DELIBERATE DUMBING DOWN OF AMERICA IS NOT confined to this author according to an article entitled "Young People Are Getting Dumber," by David Hawkins, editorial staff writer, in the August 26, 1971 issue of *The Dallas Morning News*. Excerpts from this interesting article, which discusses the importance of acquiring a large vocabulary, follow:

> John Gaston, who bosses the Fort Worth branch of the Human Engineering Laboratory (half his clients are from Dallas), dropped a bomb on me as we discussed aptitude testing.
>
> "Do you know," he said, "that the present generation knows less than its parents?"

"You mean to say that young people aren't smarter than we are—that all we've heard about this generation being the last and best isn't so?"

Gaston nodded solemnly: "Young people know fewer words than their fathers. That makes them know less." He fixed me with a foreboding eye: "Can you imagine what a drop in knowledge of 1 per cent a year for 30 years could do to our civilization?"

The question answered itself. And though I could hardly believe what Gaston was saying, I knew it wasn't instant sociology.

What he says is based on hundreds of thousands of tests given in several parts of the country since 1922 by what is probably the most prestigious non-profit outfit in the field of vocational research. The Human Engineers don't even advertise.

But Gaston wasn't through: "We also believe," he was saying, "that the recent rise in violence correlates with the drop in vocabulary. Long [range] testing has convinced us that crime and violence predominate among people who score low in vocabulary. If they can't express themselves with their tongues, they'll use their fists."

"We test many gifted people who are low in vocabulary and we tell them all—we tell the world—to learn the words. Swallow the dictionary. Brilliant aptitudes aren't worth much without words to give them wings."

Gaston paused and then dropped another bomb. "The one thing successful people have in common isn't high aptitudes—it's high vocabulary, and it's within everybody's reach. Success actually correlates more with vocabulary than with the gifts we're born with."

"Aptitudes will only show them which road to take. Vocabulary will determine how high they climb. Right now, the present generation is headed downwards."

SOME IMPORTANT STATEMENTS BY PROFESSOR JOHN I. GOODLAD, PRESIDENT of Educational Inquiry, Incorporated, appeared in *A Report to the President's Commission on School Finance (Schooling for the Future: Toward Quality and Equality in American Precollegiate Education)* October 15, 1971. Goodlad makes the following comments under "Issue #9—Educational Innovation: What changes in purposes, procedures or institutional arrangements are needed to improve the quality of American elementary and secondary education?":

> The literature on how we socialize or develop normative behavior in our children and the populace in general is fairly dismal.... [T]he majority of our youth still hold the same values as their parents....
>
> In the second paradigm... the suggestion is made that there are different targets for the change agent. For example, in a social system such as a school probably five to fifteen percent of the people are open to change. They are the "early majority" and can be counted on to be supportive. A second group, sixty to ninety percent, are the resisters. They need special attention and careful strategies need to be employed with them. Also, there are the leaders, formal and informal, and their support is critical. In his research, for example, Demeter noted some time ago the special role of the school principal in innovation:
>
>> Building principals are key figures in the (innovation) process. Where they

are both aware of and sympathetic to an innovation, it tends to prosper. Where they are ignorant of its existence, or apathetic if not hostile, it tends to remain outside the bloodstream of the school.

Few people think in these ways today. Rather, as a people, we tend to rely upon common sense or what might be called conventional wisdom as we make significant decisions which, in turn, seriously affect our lives.... More often than not, school board members, parents and the public make important decisions about what should happen in their schools based upon these past experiences or other conventional wisdom.... The use of conventional wisdom as a basis for decision-making is a major impediment to educational improvement....

The child of suburbia is likely to be a materialist and somewhat of a hypocrite. He tends to be a striver in school, a conformist, and above all a believer in being "nice," polite, clean and tidy. He divides Humanity into the black and white, the Jew and the Christian, the rich and the poor, the "smart" and the "dumb." He is often conspicuously self-centered. In all these respects, the suburban child patterns his attitudes after those of his parents.... If we do not alter this pattern, if we do not resocialize ourselves to accept and plan for change, our society may decay. What may be left in the not too distant future is what other formerly great societies have had, reflections on past glories....

In the social interaction model of change, the assumption is made that the change agent is the decision-maker about the innovation. That is, it is assumed that he decides what the adopter will change to. This is a serious problem for two very good reasons. First, as we have shown, people cannot be forced to change until they are psychologically ready. Thus, at every stage, each individual is, in fact, deciding how far he is ready or willing to move, if at all.

[Ed. Note: As a former school board member, this writer can relate to the above quote. Principals who resisted innovation eventually ended up being forced out of the system undergoing radical change. Their trials and tribulations were known only to them, and what they underwent during the change agents' activities in their schools could be described as inhumane treatment.]

THE TRI-COUNTY K–12 COURSE GOAL PROJECT, THE RESULTS OF WHICH were later published by the Northwest Regional Laboratory of the U.S. Department of Education and used extensively throughout the nation as the formulaic sample for "goals setting," was initiated in 1971. In the appendix entitled "Classification System for the School Curriculum" for her *Practitioner's Implementation Handbook [series]: The Outcome-Based Curriculum* (Outcome Associates: Princeton, N.J., 1992), Charlotte Danielson, M.A., a prominent educator and proponent of outcome-based education, said: "The knowledge and inquiry and problem-solving skills sections of this taxonomy were first developed by the Tri-County Goal Development Project, Portland, Oregon."[3] Assistant superintendent Victor W. Doherty, Evaluation Department of the Portland Public Schools in Portland, Oregon, in a November 2, 1981 letter to Mrs. Opal Moore, described this Goal Development Project as follows:

The Tri-County Goal Development Project was initiated by me in 1971 in an effort to develop a resource for arriving at well-defined learning outcome statements for use in curriculum planning and evaluation. At that time the only language available was the behavioral objective, a statement which combined a performance specification with a learning outcome often in such a way as to conceal the real learning that was being sought. By freeing the learning outcome statements from performance specification and by defining learning outcomes of three distinctly different types (information, process skills, and values), we were able to produce outcome statements that served both the planning and evaluation functions. The project was organized to include 55 school districts in Multnomah, Clackamas, and Washington Counties and writing was done initially by teachers whose time was donated to the project by member districts.

[Ed. Note: The writer believes that this very controversial project which provided the goals framework for OBE was illegal—in clear violation of the 1970 GEPA prohibition against federal government involvement in curriculum development.]

1972

THE NEWPORT HARBOR ENSIGN OF CORONA DEL MAR, CALIFORNIA CARRIED an article entitled "Teachers Are Recycled" in its January 20, 1972 issue. The following are excerpts from this important article:

Education in California is finally going to catch up with the "innovative" Newport-Mesa Unified School District. With the passage of the Stull Bill, AB 293, all school districts are mandated to evaluate their classroom teachers and certificated personnel through new guidelines. Another portion of the bill will allow a district to dismiss a teacher with tenure, without going to court.

A teacher will no longer have the prerogative of having his own "style" of teaching, because he will be held "accountable" to uniform expected student progress. His job will depend on how well he can produce "intended" behavioral changes in students.

"School districts just haven't had time to tool up for it," explained Dr. William Cunningham, Executive Director of the Association of California School Administrators (ACSA). Until recently, he was superintendent of the Newport-Mesa district.

The Newport-Mesa district, under the guidance of Dr. Cunningham, accomplished this task years ago. In fact we have warned of this appraisal plan in many of our columns throughout the past 2 years. Its formal name is "staff performance appraisal plan," at least in this district, and was formulated as early as 1967.

In 1968 five elementary schools in our district (California, Mariners, Presidio, Victoria, Monte Vista) and one high school (Estancia) were selected from schools that volunteered for the project. They were accepted on the basis that at least 60% of the teachers were willing to participate in the "in-service training sessions" and to "apply" the assessment processes learned at these sessions in their own classroom situations. A total of 88 teachers participated in all aspects of the pilot study....

FORMAL TRAINING SESSIONS: participants attended two 2–1/2 hour sessions to acquire the prerequisite tools. Evidence was collected to show that by the end of the final training session, 80% of the participants had acquired a minimal level of ability to apply these competencies.

PREREQUISITE TOOLS: Teachers learning how to identify or diagnose strengths and weaknesses, learning to write and use behavioral objectives, learning new teaching techniques and procedures, etc. Teachers learn these through workshops and in-service training, having acquired these skills, teachers had to go through the "appraisal" technique.

APPRAISAL TECHNIQUE: During the observation phase, observation teams composed of teacher colleagues and a resource person from UCLA or the District collected data regarding the execution of the previously planned lessons. The observation team recorded both the verbal behavior of pupils and teacher (e.g., teacher questions and pupil responses) and non-verbal behavior which could be objectively described....

What all this amounts to is "peer group" analysis. Group dynamics would be the term used in other circles. To be more blunt, others would call it sensitivity training in its purest form—role-playing, to say the least....

The teacher must cooperate and learn the new methods of teaching, writing behavioral objectives, playing psychologist.

THE NEW YORK TIMES CARRIED A LENGTHY FRONT PAGE ARTICLE ON APRIL 30, 1972 by William K. Stevens entitled "The Social Studies: A Revolution Is on—New Approach Is Questioning, Skeptical—Students Examine Various Cultures." This article explained the early history of the twenty-six-year controversy which has raged across the United States between those desiring education for a global society versus those desiring education in American History and Western Civilization; i.e., the question of "social studies" versus traditional history, and "process" education versus fact-based education. Excerpts follow:

> When C. Frederick Risinger started teaching American History at Lake Park High School near Chicago, he operated just about as teachers had for generations. He drilled students on names and dates. He talked a lot about kings and presidents. And he worked from a standard text whose patriotic theme held that the United States was "founded on the highest principles that men of good will and common sense have been able to put into practice."
>
> That was ten years ago, but it might as well be 50. For the social studies curriculum at Lake Park has changed almost beyond recognition. The 32-year-old Mr. Risinger, now head of the department, has abandoned the traditional text and set his students to analyzing all revolutions, not just the American, and from all points of view, including the British one that George Washington was both a traitor and an inept general.

AN ARTICLE ENTITLED "PEOPLE CONTROL BLUEPRINT" BY CAROL DENTON was published in the May, 1972 issue (Vol. 3, No. 12) of *The National Educator* (Fullerton, CA). [ddd] Excerpts follow:

> A "Top Secret" paper from the Center for the Study of Democratic Institutions, now in the hands of *The National Educator*, reveals a plan for total control of the people of the United States through behavioral modification

techniques of B.F. Skinner, the controversial behaviorist author of *Beyond Freedom and Dignity*....

According to the "Dialogue Discussion Paper," marked "Top Secret" across the bottom of the cover page, a conference was held at the Center on January 17 through 19, 1972, at which time a discussion on "The Social and Philosophical Implications of Behavior Modification" was held. The paper in question is the one prepared [by] four individuals for presentation at that conference entitled "Controlled Environment for Social Change." The authors are Vitali Rozynko, Kenneth Swift, Josephine Swift and Larney J. Boggs....

The second page of the paper carries the inscription, "To B.F. Skinner and James G. Holland.".... Page 3 of the paper states that the "Top Secret" document was prepared on December 31, 1971....

The authors of this tome are senior staff members of the Operant Behavior Modification Project located at Mendocino State Hospital in California and the project is partially supported by a grant from the National Institute on Alcohol Abuse....

On page 5 of this blueprint for totalitarianism, the authors state that "we are presently concerned with controlling upheavals and anarchic behavior associated with social change and discontent.".... The authors go on to say that they believe an "Orwellian world" is more likely under presently developing society than under the kind of rigorous controls of a society envisioned by Skinner....

On page 6, the authors deplore the growing demands for "law and order," stating that the population is now more apt to support governmental repression than previously, in response to "their own fears.."...

They add that "with the rising population, depletion of natural resources, and the increase of pollution, repressive measures may have to be used to guarantee survival of our species. These measures may take the form of forced sterilization, greatly restricted uses of energy and limits on population movement and living location.".."...

Skinner, on the other hand, they allege—"advocates more sophisticated controls over the population, since punishment (by the government) for the most part works only temporarily and only while the punishing agent is present.".."...

On the other hand, the authors allege, operant conditioning (sensitivity training) and other behavioral techniques can be used to control the population through "positive reinforcement."

MARY THOMPSON, SECRETARY AND MEMBER OF THE SPEAKERS' BUREAU OF the Santa Clara, California Republican Women's Federation, gave a very important speech regarding Planning, Programming, Budgeting Systems (PPBS) on June 11, 1972. Following are key excerpts:

When I was first asked to speak to you about PPBS (Planning, Programming, Budgeting Systems), I inquired whether it was to be addressed to PPBS as applied to education. I shall deal with it at the education level today, however you should remember that PPBS is a tool for implementing the very restructuring of government at all levels in every area of governmental institutions. What is involved is the use of government agencies to accomplish mass behavioral change in every area....

PPBS is a plan being pushed by Federal and State governments to completely change education....

The accountability involved in PPBS means accountability to the state's predetermined education goals....

One leader of education innovation (Shelly Umans—Management of Education) has called it "A systematic design for education revolution."...

In a systems management of the education process, the child himself is the product. Note: the child... his feelings, his values, his behavior, as well as his intellectual development....

PPBS is the culmination of the "people planners" dreams....

Then in 1965 the means for accomplishing the actual restructuring of education was provided in the *Elementary and Secondary Education Act* (ESEA). President Johnson has said that he considered the ESEA the most significant single piece of legislation of his administration. Recall that it was also the same year of 1965 when the presidential order was given to introduce PPBS throughout the entire federal government. 1965 was the year which unleashed the actual restructuring of governmental processes and formally included education as a legitimate Federal government function....

PPBS is the systems management tool made possible by technology of computer hardware to affect the planned change....

In order to make an explanation of PPBS intelligible, you must also know that education itself has been redefined. Simply put, it has become the objective of education to measure and diagnose the child in order to prescribe a program to develop his feelings and emotions, values and loyalties toward predetermined behavioral objectives.... Drawing it right down to basics, we are talking about conditioned responses in human terms. Pavlov experimented on dogs!...

Taking each element of PPBS will show how the process is accomplished. PLANNING—Planning phase (please note that the process involved with a systems approach is always described in terms of "phases") always includes the establishment of goals committees, citizens committees, needs assessment committees.... These are referred to as "community involvement." The committees are always either self appointed or chosen—never elected. They always include guidance from some trained "change agents" who may be administrators, curriculum personnel or local citizens. Questionnaires and surveys are used to gather data on how the community "feels" and to test community attitudes. The ingeniousness of the process is that everybody thinks he is having a voice in the direction of public schools. Not so... for Federal change agencies, specifically regional education centers established by ESEA, influence and essentially determine terminology used in the questionnaires and surveys. The change agents at the district level then function to "identify needs and problems for change" as they have been programmed to identify them at the training sessions sponsored by Federal offices such as our Center for Planning and Evaluation in Santa Clara County. That is why the goals are essentially the same in school districts across the country. It also explains why three years ago every school district was confronted with the Family Life Education issue at the same time....

Unknowing citizens' committees are used by the process to generate acceptance of goals already determined. What they don't realize is that professional change agents are operating in the behaviorist's framework of thought and Mr. or Mrs. Citizen Parent is operating in his traditional education framework of thought. So, the local change agents are able to facilitate a group to a consensus in support of predetermined goals by using familiar, traditional terms which carry the new behaviorist meanings....

Another name for this process is Participatory Democracy, a term by the way, which was coined by Students for a Democratic Society in their *Port Huron Manifesto* to identify the process for citizen participation in destruction of their own political institutions....

Richard Farson of Western Behavioral Sciences Institute made a report to the Office of Education in Sacramento in 1967. He said it this way:

> The application of systems analysis is aided by several phenomena that would be of help in almost any situation of organizational change. First, it is relatively easier to make big changes than to make small ones—and systems changes are almost always big ones. Because they are big, it is difficult for people to mount resistance to them, for they go beyond the ordinary decision-making, policy-making activities of individual members of an organization. It is far easier to muster argument against a $100 expenditure for partitions than against a complete reorganization of the work flow....

Teachers, you have professional organizations to protect your professional interests. Use them to protect your personal privacy and professional integrity. Encourage organizations of teachers to take positions publicly in opposition to PPBS....

We believe the time has come to establish private schools to keep our children from falling victim to the behaviorists while there is still opportunity to do so. BE AWARE OF THE FACT THAT THE VOUCHER SYSTEM IS LURKING IN THE WINGS TO BRING THE PRIVATE SCHOOLS INTO THE NATIONAL CONTROL [emphasis in original].

THE LEDGER OF TALLAHASSEE FLORIDA ON JULY 27, 1972 IN AN ARTICLE entitled "Schools to Try New Program" quoted Florida state education officials as saying that a new program being field-tested in Florida will tell teachers and parents not only why Johnny can't read, but why the school can't teach him and how much it's costing to try. Excerpts follow:

> "We're putting all the various components together now," said Associate Education Commissioner Cecil Golden. "What we're doing should soon become very visible." However, he estimates it will take seven to ten years before the program is completely operational....
>
> Golden says it may sound like a lot of gibberish at this point, but "when we bring it all together" it should produce a more flexible and relevant educational system....
>
> He said many people in the State Department of Education are working independently on various facets and aspects of the program and, like those assembling the atom bomb, "very few of them understand exactly what they are building, and won't until we put all the parts together."

[Ed. Note: This article refers to PPBS/MBO—the early years. *The Atlanta Constitution* published an article entitled "Georgia Schools OK Tracking System" in its July 1, 1998 issue which describes later PPBS implementation and which is included in this book's entry of the same date.]

[ddd]

"THE FIELD OF EDUCATIONAL TECHNOLOGY: A STATEMENT OF DEFINITION" by Donald P. Ely, editor and chairman of the Definition and Terminology Committee of the Association for Educational Computing and Technology (AECT, a spin-off of the National Education Association), was circulated in October, 1972. In this paper leading specialists in the field of educational technology warn of the potential dangers of computers and the need for ethics in programming. One of the participants in the production of this position paper said: "If it is decided the work will bring about negative ends, the concerned professional refuses to perform it." (See Appendix VIII in the Internet version for fuller excerpts.)

DR. CHESTER M. PIERCE, M.D. OF HARVARD UNIVERSITY WROTE AN ARticle entitled "Becoming Planetary Citizens: A Quest for Meaning" which appeared in the November 1972 issue of *Childhood Education*. Excerpts follow which include alarming recommendations for "education":

Creative Altruism
In the past forty years social science experimentation has shown that by age five children already have a lot of political attitudes. Regardless of economic or social background, almost every kindergartner has a tenacious loyalty to his country and its leader. This phenomenon is understandable in the psychological terms of loyalty to a strong father-figure and of the need for security. But a child can enter kindergarten with the same kind of loyalty to the earth as to his homeland....

Systems Analysis
Children can be taught to integrate knowledge of systems in ever-widening circles. I don't know how to tell you to do it, but as professionals you will be challenged to find ways. Just because no one yet knows how doesn't mean it can't be done....

New Views of Parenting
Another essential curricular decision you will have to make is what to teach a young child about his future role as a man or a woman. A lot will depend on what you know and what your philosophy is about parenting.... Already we are hearing about experiments that are challenging our traditional views of monogamous marriage patterns....

Learning to Relinquish
Finally—perhaps most difficult of all—you will have to teach children how to unlearn, how to re-learn and how to give up things....

Public Problem Number One
If we truly accept that today's child must grow [up] to be a cosmopolite and "planetary citizen," we face major problems. How do you get a child to see that the whole world is his province when every day on television he sees people who can't live next door to their neighbors, who argue about things like busing?... Before the horizon I think the major problem to be solved in America if we are to enable people to grow as super-generalists and "planetary citizens" is the elimination of racism. Paradoxically, both the two chief deterrents and the two chief facilitators to this goal are the public school system and the mass media.... Early childhood specialists have a staggering

responsibility but an unrivaled importance in producing "planetary citizens" whose geographic and intellectual provinces are as limitless as their all-embracing humanity.

BRUCE JOYCE AND MARSHA WEIL OF COLUMBIA TEACHERS' COLLEGE WROTE *Models of Teaching* (Prentice Hall, Inc.: Englewood Cliffs, New Jersey, 1972). The book was the product of research funded by the U.S. Office of Education's Bureau of Research under a contract with Teachers' College, Columbia University, in 1968. *Models of Teaching*'s importance lays not only in the fact that the book itself would be used extensively for in-service teacher training in behavior modification, but that the book would serve as the foundation from which Joyce would develop his "Models of Teacher Repertoire Training," which has been used extensively (since the 1970s to the present) in order to change the teacher from a transmitter of knowledge (content) to a facilitator of learning (behavior modifier). Several excerpts from *Models of Teaching* follow:

> Principles of teaching are not conceived as static tenets but as dynamically interactive with social and cognitive purpose, with the learning theory underlying procedures, with available support technology, and with the personal and intellectual characteristics of learning groups. What is emphasized is the wide range of options the teacher may adopt and adapt to his unique situation.

In the preface, which has a subtitle, "We Teach by Creating Environments for Children," Joyce and Weil explain:

> In this book we describe models which represent four different "families" of approaches to teaching. Some of the models focus on the individual and the development of his unique personality. Some focus on the human group and represent ways of teaching which emphasize group energy, interpersonal skills, and social commitment. Others represent ways of teaching concepts, modes of inquiry from the disciplines, and methods for increasing intellectual capacity. Still others apply psychological models of operant conditioning to the teaching-learning process. For the teacher we provide some advice on how to learn the various models based on our experiences in the Preservice Teacher Education Program at Teachers College, Columbia University. For curriculum and materials designers we include chapters on systematic planning using a variety of models of teaching. For both, we present a system for deciding what approaches to teaching are appropriate for what ends and how models can be selected to match the learning styles of children. (pp. xiii–xiv)

Excerpts from the table of contents of *Models of Teaching* include:

> (2) Group Investigation—Democratic Process as a Source. The school is considered as a model of an ideal society. This chapter explores a variety of democratic teaching designed by Herbert Thelen to bring about a new type of social relationship among men....

> (5) The Laboratory Method—The T-Group Model. The National Training Laboratory has developed approaches to train people to cope with change through more effective social relationships. This model is the father of the encounter-group strategies.

(6) Concept Attainment—A Model Developed from a Study of Thinking. This model was developed by the authors from a study of work by Jerome S. Bruner and his associates. [Bruner will be encountered in a later entry as a developer, along with B.F. Skinner, of the humanistic social studies curriculum, *Man: A Course of Study*, ed.]

(7) An Inductive Model—A Model Drawn from Conceptions of Mental Processes and General Theory-Building. The late Hilda Taba developed a series of models to improve the inductive thinking ability of children and adults. Her strategies are presented in this chapter.... [In 1957 a California State Senate investigative committee exposed the work of Hilda Taba as harmful to children, ed.]

(12) Non-Directive Teaching—Rogerian Counseling as a Source. From his studies of counseling and therapy, Carl Rogers has developed a flexible model of teaching emphasizing an environment which encourages students to create their own environments for learning.

(13) Classroom Meeting Model—A Model Drawn from a Stance toward Mental Health. Another therapist, [William] Glasser, has also developed a stance toward teaching—one which emphasized methods easily applicable to the classroom situation.... [In 1971 the Citizens Committee of California, Inc., presented "A Bill of Particulars" for the abolition of Dr. William Glasser's theory from the Orange County Unified School District which stated in part: "Dr. Glasser has developed a method of education which negates a desire to achieve and compete; destroys respect for authority; expounds a 'situational ethics' philosophy; and develops group thinking." William Glasser's philosophy is a component of Outcome-Based Education, ed.]

(15) Awareness Training—A Model to Increase Human Awareness. Gestalt therapists and other humanistic psychologists have focused on strategies for increasing the awareness and sense of possibilities of individuals. A number of models for sensitivity training have been developed by William Schutz.

(16) Operant Conditioning—The pioneering work of B.F. Skinner has been followed by a mass of approaches to teaching and training based on the shaping of learning tasks and use of reinforcement schedules. Several such models are explored here.

(17) A Model for Matching Environments to People—The psychologist David Hunt has generated a "model of models"—an approach to teaching which suggests how we can match teaching styles to learning styles so as to increase growth toward personal flexibility.

(18) The Models Way of Thinking—An Operational Language. The chapter explores the philosophical and practical implications of a stance toward education and includes a spectrum of models which have different uses for different students.

One finds the following information in chapter 16 under the title "Operant Conditioning":

The person most responsible for applying behavioral principles to education is B.F. Skinner, whose Theory of Operant Conditioning provided the basis for programmed instruction.

The Theory of Operant Conditioning represents the process by which human behavior becomes shaped into certain patterns by external forces. The theory assumes that any process or activity has observable manifestations and can be behaviorally defined, that is, defined in terms of observable behavior. Either or both of the theory's two major operations, reinforcement and stimulus-control, are emphasized in the educational applications of operant conditioning theory.

Conditioning refers to the process of increasing the probability of occurrence of existing or new behavior in an individual by means of reinforcement. In operant conditioning the response (behavior) operates upon the environment to generate consequences.

The consequences are contingent upon the emission of a response, and they are reinforcing. For example, the response "Pass the butter" operates upon the environment, another person, to obtain the butter. The response is reinforced by the receipt of the butter. In other words, the probability that a future desire for butter will elicit the same response is increased by its initial success.... The stimulus and reinforcement are independent variables upon which the response is dependent. As Skinner phrases it "the stimulus acting prior to the emission of the response, sets the occasion upon which the response is likely to be reinforced." (1) A stimulus is "any condition, event or change in the environment of an individual which produces a change in behavior." (2) It may be verbal (oral, written) or physical. A response may be defined as a unit of behavior.... According to Skinner, reinforcement must immediately follow a response if it is to be effective. Delayed reinforcement is much less effective in modifying behavior. (pp. 271–273)

An official overview of the "Models of Teacher Repertoire Training" program, made available to the author while working in the U.S. Department of Education, states under "Brief Description of Intervention" the following:

The objective of the intervention is to prepare teachers who can choose from a number of available alternatives the most appropriate strategy to be used with a particular group of students in a particular situation at a particular time. "Most appropriate" refers to the effectiveness of the strategy selected vs. the alternatives in terms of the probability that the students will learn what the teacher has predicted for them. The feasibility of achieving this objective in a clinical, or controlled situation has been long established. This intervention establishes that feasibility in the real world of the elementary and secondary school settings and offers a reliable, cost effective plan to do so.... The models which have been selected for this system are ones for which there is empirical evidence and/or theoretical grounding which supports the probability that students will learn what is predicted from them. Teachers learn to select the models and match them to the objectives they seek.... The families include: (1) Behavior Modification and Cybernetic Models which have evolved from attempts to develop efficient systems for sequencing learning tasks and shaping behavior by manipulating reinforcement.... Clinical analysis guides are useful to provide feedback about performance and to support on-site coaching. In addition to print material there are more than thirty hours of video tapes to support the training system.... The principal criterion of effectiveness rests upon existing empirical evidence that pre-specified changes in teaching behavior will produce predictable changes in pupil performance.

This information suggests that Skinner—and, evidently, Joyce and Weil—believe that man is truly only a response organism with no intrinsic soul or intellect, definitely a product of evolution. During a U.S. Department of Education Joint Dissemination Review Panel meeting at which Bruce Joyce and Jim Stefansen submitted application for funding, some of the participants made the following statements:

> JOYCE: "It has been difficult in the past to bring about curriculum change, behavior change. In California we are establishing a network of 100 school districts. New strategies for teaching and exporting programs."
> COULSON: "Couldn't agree more that what you are doing needs to be done. Maybe we are not ready yet to talk about selective use of repertoire. You must gather data supporting selective use of methods."
> STEFANSEN: "Primary claim is we do know how to train teachers to make ultimate choices so that when those behaviors take place students are affected. Question is, can you train teachers to accept strategies each of which we know are the better of two or more choices?"
> JACKSON: "No question in my mind that Joyce is onto something of great importance. Problem here has to do with claims of effectiveness rather than evidence of effectiveness. Relationship between teacher behavior and student achievement."
> (UNKNOWN PANEL MEMBER) "There are thousands of investigations to support Skinner strategies."

The following excerpt from the "Models of Teacher Repertoire Training"—which includes most of the highly controversial behavior modification methods in existence—is taken from *Models of Teaching* by Joyce and was furnished to this writer by the Maine Facilitator Center in Auburn, Maine in 1985.[4]

(1) Information Processing—how do students acquire and act on information?
Concept Attainment—Jerome Bruner, Goodnow, Austin
Inductive Thinking—Hilda Taba
Direct Instruction—Benjamin Bloom, Madeline Hunter, James Block and Ethna Reid [How interesting that Joyce identifies the four most influential developers and promoters of Skinnerian "Mastery Learning/Teaching" with "Direct Instruction," which is the method attributed to Siegfried Engelmann and called for in the *Reading Excellence Act of 1998*, ed.]

(2) Personal Family—How does each person develop his/her unique possibilities?
Nondirective Teaching—Carl Rogers
Synectics—Thomas Gordon
Classroom Meetings—William Glasser

(3) Social Models—How does the individual relate to society or other people?
Jurisprudential Inquiry—Oliver and Shaver
Role Playing—Shaftel, Chesler and Fox

(4) Behavioral Models—How is visible behavior changed?
Training Model
Stress Reduction—Decker
Assertiveness Training—Wolpe, Lazarus

[Ed. Note: The writer has given extensive coverage to *Models of Teaching* since these teacher behavior modification training programs have been in effect for thirty years and are probably the most inclusive. It includes many, if not all of the controversial methods about which parents complain, if they are lucky enough to find out they are being used. Most parents are unaware of these manipulative methods intended to change their children's behavior. Considering the prevalence of behavior modification in the schools it is a wonder our schools and our children are not in worse shape than they are. There has obviously been immense teacher and student resistance to this type of manipulation.]

PRESIDENT RICHARD NIXON CREATED THE NATIONAL INSTITUTE OF EDUCAtion (NIE) in 1972. Serving as a presidential assistant at that time, Chester Finn (who would later be appointed assistant secretary of education, Office of Educational Research and Improvement under Secretary William Bennett in the Reagan administration) was one of the principal authors of Nixon's proposal for NIE. The December 8, 1982 issue of *Education Week* contained an interesting article on the history and purpose of NIE entitled "Success Eludes 10-Year-Old Agency." An excerpt which pertains to the redefinition of education from academic/content-based to scientific, outcome-/performance-based follows:

> "The purpose of a National Institute of Education," said Daniel P. Moynihan who was the agency's principal advocate in the Nixon Administration, "is to develop the art and science of education to the point that equality of educational opportunity results in a satisfactory equivalence of educational achievement."

For those who have difficulty understanding Daniel Moynihan's education jargon, "develop the art and science of education to the point that equality of educational opportunity results in a satisfactory equivalence of educational achievement" means that education from that time on would be considered a "science." In other words, with education becoming a "science," behavioral psychology (Pavlov/Skinner) would be used in the classrooms of America in order to equalize results which would be predictable and could be scientifically measured. The teacher and student would be judged not on what they know, but on how they perform—like rats and pigeons—facilitating the "redistribution of brains." Professor James Block, a leader in Skinnerian/mastery learning circles, discussed this redistribution of brains in an article published in *Educational Leadership* (November 1979) entitled "Mastery Learning: The Current State of the Craft." Block explained that:

> One of the striking personal features of mastery learning, for example, is the degree to which it encourages cooperative individualism in student learning as opposed to selfish competition. Just how much room is there left in the world for individualists who are more concerned with their own performance than the performance of others? One of the striking societal features of mastery learning is the degree to which it presses for a society based on the excellence of all participants rather than one based on the excellence of

a few. Can any society afford universal excellence, or must all societies make most people incompetent so that a few can be competent?

Reinforcing Harris

"Harris, we're moving you to the
dumbing-down project. You've earned it."

Returning to the *Education Week* article referenced above, the story of NIE continued:

> Among the serious, continuing obstacles to the Institute's attainment of its goals, those interviewed for this article cited the following three: Understanding, Funding, and Leadership.... Under "Understanding" one reads: "Because educational research is a relatively young area of social science, it does not enjoy wide respect among scholars, and its relationship to teaching and learning is poorly understood by many of those who work in the schools."
>
> The first director chosen by the current [Reagan] Administration to head the institute, Edward A. Curran, articulated the conservatives' position in a memorandum to the President last May that called for dismantling the institute. "NIE is based on the premise that education is a science whose progress depends on systematic 'research and development.' As a professional educator, I know that this premise is false," wrote Mr. Curran, who was dismissed from the agency shortly thereafter.

[Ed. Note: Ed Curran was the first "shoe to drop"; he would be followed by some of the nation's finest academic teachers who also held Curran's view that education is not a science.

Of interest to this writer is the extensive influence NIE's research has on local classroom practice considering its rather paltry budget. The reason for this lies in the fact that 90% of all education research is federally funded, thus guaranteeing that NIE controls 90% of the national research product— teaching and learning. When the National Institute of Education was finally abolished none of its functions were eliminated since it was subsumed by the Office of Educational Research and Improvement.

"Equivalence of educational achievement," described by Patrick Moynihan, equals Performance-Based Education (PBE) and Outcome-Based Education (OBE), which in turn equal a deliberate dumbing down of American teachers and youth—necessary in order to implement the performance-based workforce training agenda planned since the early nineteen hundreds.

Good academic- and content-oriented teachers understand that education is not social science. In 1999 efforts are being made to encourage these good teachers to get out of the way so that teachers trained in performance-based Skinnerian teaching and Total Quality Management can be hired to replace them.]

1973

SCHOOLING IN THE UNITED STATES BY JOHN GOODLAD, M. FRANCES KLEIN, and Jerrold M. Novotney (Charles F. Kettering Foundation Program: McGraw-Hill Co., New York, 1973) was published. Excerpts follow:

CONDITIONING OR BEHAVIOR MODIFICATION:

Several experimental preschool programs make extensive use of behaviorist theory (now called "operant conditioning" or "behavior modification") as a means of instruction in both the cognitive and socioemotional realms. [Professor Lawrence] Kohlberg notes:

In general, such a program implies a play for shaping the child's behavior by successive approximation from responses. At every step, immediate feedback or reward is desirable and immediate repetition and elaboration of the correct response is used. A careful detailed programming of learning is required to make sure that (a) each response builds on the preceding, (b) incorrect responses are not made since once made they persist and interfere with correct responses, and (c) feedback and reward are immediate.

The Liverpool Laboratory School at the Research and Development Center in Early Childhood Education at Syracuse University is a program based directly on reinforcement theory.... The school is to determine whether children can learn cognitive skills during the preschool years and to identify techniques which will be successful in bringing about such learning. The program is built around a highly detailed schedule of reinforcement. Skills to be taught are broken down into specific components, each of which is immediately reinforced when it appears correctly. Teachers reinforce in four steps: in the first, raisins or candies are awarded for each correct response; in the second, the candies are replaced by tokens which can be traded for a small prize; the third involves distributing tokens which can be exchanged for more valuable tokens. Two or more of the latter may be traded for a prize. In the fourth step, four valuable tokens are required to receive a prize....

Bereiter and Engelmann [Direct Instruction/DISTAR/Reading Mastery (SRA)] also use operant conditioning in their program. Their reinforcement program contains both verbal and tangible rewards. Weber describes a rapid-fire sequence in language training in which the teacher verbally reinforces each response of the students:

Teacher: What is the same as beautiful?

Children: Pretty.

Teacher: Good. You are so good. If someone is beautiful they are pretty. What is the opposite of pretty?

Children: Ugly.

Teacher: I'll have to shake everyone's hand....

She also speaks of an arithmetic lesson in which the children were given a cracker for each correct response....

Teaching and managing behavior by means of operant conditioning does not appeal to all and raises several moral issues. In the first place, it postulates an image of the learner as passive and receptive and leaves little room for individuality and creative thinking. According to William E. Martin in *Rediscovering the Mind of the Child*:

> A science of behavior emphasizes the importance of environmental manipulation and scheduling and thus the mechanization and routiniza-tion of experience. Similarly, it stresses performance in the individual. Doing something, doing it efficiently, doing it automatically—these are the goals. It is the mechanization of man as well as the mechanization of the environment. The result is the triumph of technology: a push button world with well-trained button-pushers. (pp. 40–43)

[Ed. Note: Surely, if American parents understood this dehumanizing method being implemented in the nation's schools under whatever label—OBE, ML, DI in conjunction with computers—they would see the many dangers to their children. One of those dangers being that after twelve years of rewards for correct answers, will their children ever have the courage or be motivated to do anything on their own—to take a stand when what is left of their "principles" is challenged? If this method is implemented *in all schools of the nation*, and I mean ALL—public, private, religious and home school (in many cases due to the use of computers or "Skinner's box") as is happening right now—our nation will become a nation of robotic drones responding to whomever wishes to control them for whatever purpose.]

RONALD G. HAVELOCK'S *THE CHANGE AGENT'S GUIDE TO INNOVATION IN Education* was published (Educational Technology Publishing: Englewood Cliffs, New Jersey, 1973). This *Guide,* which contains authentic case studies on how to sneak in controversial curricula and teaching strategies, or get them adopted by naïve school boards, is the educator's bible for bringing about change in our children's values. Havelock's *Guide* was funded by the U.S. Office of Education and the Department of Health, Education and Welfare, and has continued to receive funding well into the 1980s. It has been republished in a second edition in 1995 by the same publishers.

[Ed. Note: Why is it that the change agents' plans and their tools to "trans-form" our educational system never change, while parents and teachers are told, repeatedly, that they must be ready and willing to change?]

[ddd]

1974

THE NATIONAL DIFFUSION NETWORK (NDN), THE TRANSMISSION BELT FOR federally funded and developed innovative and/or behavior modification programs, was established in 1974. This network, which bears much of the blame for the dilution of absolute values of those children and parents exposed to NDN programs from the mid-seventies to the present, was created to facilitate the adoption by local schools of innovative programs which had been approved by the Joint Dissemination Review Panel (JDRP), a federal panel of educators.

Most, if not all, states received funding from the U.S. Department of Education to set up Facilitator Centers staffed by educators familiar with NDN programs. These individuals who had contacts in school districts throughout the individual states promoted the programs and arranged for the "developers," or other staff associated with the program, to visit the state to conduct in-service training at schools which had adopted the programs.

Often these programs were described in benign NDN program terms and flew under the banner of "basic skills." Local school boards accepted them since they were subsidized and less expensive to implement than programs developed by private sector textbook companies. The NDN's penetration of the national educational landscape in the early 1980s is exemplified by the fact that Texas alone had approximately seventeen NDN offices which facilitated the adoption of the programs. The State of Maine received some sort of "gold medal" for being the number one state in its number of program adoptions.

There is no question that the National Diffusion Network programs have caused more controversy among parents than any other programs developed with federal funds. The regional hearings held by the U.S. Department of Education in 1984 to take testimony from citizens regarding the need for regulations to enforce the *Protection of Pupil Rights Amendment* (PPRA) consisted of emotional and angry testimony from teachers and parents regarding the value-destroying programs in the NDN. The two most destructive programs developed prior to 1984 were *Curriculum for Meeting Modern Problems*, which contained *The New Model Me* for the high school level, and *Positive Attitude toward Learning*. Both of these curricula employed behavior modification techniques, values clarification, role playing and, specifically, such games as "The Survival Game"—sometimes known as "The Lifeboat Game"—where students were enlisted to decide who is worthy of survival in a shipwreck: the priest, the lawyer, the pregnant mother, angry teenager, etc.—pure humanistic curricula.[5]

[Ed. Note: **[ddd]** As late as 1994 the NDN continued to list *The New Model Me* as an "exemplary program" in its *Educational Programs that Work*, the catalog of the National Diffusion Network.[6] Such blatant continuation of programs designed to destroy children's values, no matter which administration is in office, is shocking.]

A PERFORMANCE ACCOUNTABILITY SYSTEM FOR SCHOOL ADMINISTRATORS (Parker Publishing Co., Inc.: West Nyack, N.Y., 1974) by T.H. Bell, Ph.D., was published. T.H. Bell later served as secretary of education during President Ronald Reagan's first term in office, 1981–1985. Excerpts from Bell's book follow:

USE OF TESTS IN NEEDS ASSESSMENT:

> The economic, sociological, psychological and physical aspects of students must be taken into account as we look at their educational needs and accomplishments, and fortunately there are a number of attitude and inventory scales that can be used to assess these admittedly difficult to measure outcomes. (pp. 33–34)

> Most of these efforts to manage education try to center in one place an information center that receives reports and makes available to all members of the management team various types of information useful to managers. (p. 45)

[Ed. Note: There is no question in this writer's mind that this one man bears much of the responsibility for the deliberate dumbing down of our schools. He set the stage for outcome-based education through his early support for systems management—Management by Objectives and Planning, Programming, Budgeting Systems. These systems later evolved into full-blown Total Quality Management for education, having gone through the initial stage of Professor Benjamin Bloom's Mastery Learning and ending up in 1984 as William Spady's Transformational OBE. Outcome-Based or results/performance/competency-based education requires mastery learning, direct instruction, individualized instruction, systems management and computer technology.

Bell's earlier activities in the 1970s as U.S. Commissioner of Education, including his role in promoting and supporting dumbed-down life role competencies for K–12 (see 1975 Adult Performance Level Study and the 1983 Delker article) and his testimony before the U.S. Congress in favor of a U.S. Department of Education, should have kept his name off of any list of potential nominees presented to President Reagan. Concerns regarding this nomination expressed by Reagan supporters were proved well-founded when: Bell spearheaded the technology initiative in 1981 (see *Project BEST: Better Education Skills Through Technology*); funded in 1984 William Spady's infamous Far West Laboratory (Utah OBE) grant which promised to (and did!) put OBE "in all schools of the nation"; predicted that schools would be bookless by the year 2000; recommended that all students have computers; and fired Edward Curran, the director of the National Institute of Education, when Curran recommended to President Reagan that his office (the NIE) be abolished.

According to a former member of the Utah Education Association who was a close friend of Bell's in the 1970s, had the Senate Committee that confirmed T.H. Bell as secretary of education read Bell's book, *A Performance Accountability System for School Administrators*, it is unlikely he would have been confirmed. (See the Internet version for Appendix IX quotes from Bell's book.)]

"PARENTS FEAR 'BIG BROTHER' ASPECT OF NEW CONCEPT" BY MONICA Lanza was written for the Passaic, New Jersey *The Herald News* on March 20, 1974. Excerpts follow from the first of a two-part series:

> Questioning the purpose of modern educational *goals* by parents has brought to light the possibility that a new curriculum ultimately could force all school children to fit a pre-conceived mold or norm by computerized evaluation [emphasis in original]. And, students who don't could be branded misfits and sent to a school psychologist for therapy. The threat, they say, is in the form of a bill before the state legislature that would take effect July 1, if passed. This bill would provide for two new Educational Improvement Centers in New Jersey, bringing the total of such centers in the state to four. The centers are currently being used by the federal government to reach the grass-roots level through its *Elementary and Secondary Education Act....* Under the stated aim of developing "critical thinking skills" in children, the centers, as agents for the Planning, Programming, Budgeting System (PPBS), have been charged with using behavior modification and sensitivity training to develop those skills....
>
> At the Cedar Knolls center in Morris County, Joseph T. Pascarelli, program developer, recently conducted a workshop which was attended by a number of teachers who reviewed one method of sensitivity training, known as the "Who Shall Survive" game. Participants in the game are given the sexes, backgrounds and capabilities of 15 people in a bomb shelter that supports only seven people, and are asked to decide which seven are the best equipped to re-populate the earth. The answer that none should be put to death is not accepted. This type of training, according to opponents, changes the values of the students who may have been taught at home that murder is wrong under all circumstances.

From the second article in the series, "Teachers Taught to Be 'Agents of Social Change,'" the reader is informed that

> Educational Improvement Centers (EICs) provide training to prepare teachers to become agents for social change....
>
> A publication entitled *Education: From the Acquisition of Knowledge to Programmed Conditioned Response* states: "Teachers who are seemingly impervious to change will be sought out and trained on an individual basis, and forces which block the adoption of new ideas will be identified and ways to overcome these forces will be explored."...
>
> Behavior modification was the theme of a learning center at a workshop at the Northwestern New Jersey EIC recently. A teacher rattled off the three domains of behavior modification as propounded by a Benjamin Bloom, who more than a dozen years ago, redefined the purpose of education as "behavior modification."....
>
> The multitude of programs available is mind-boggling. Programs filter down from entities like the Educational Resource Information Center [ERIC] and are presented to local school systems with a flourish. They are praised by gullible administrators and put into action by unwitting teachers....
>
> One of the reasons for their current success is that the language used in the presentation of new programs is almost unintelligible. There are teachers who will admit to not understanding the jargon, but not publicly—and those who do see underlying dangers say nothing for fear of losing their jobs....

The father of the myriad federally financed programs is "Projects to Advance Creativity in Education" (PACE). The PACE programs are described in a 584–page publication entitled *Pacesetters in Innovation* which lists such "subjects" as psychotherapy, sensitivity training, behavior modification, and humanistic curriculum....

According to the Department of Health, Education and Welfare (HEW) *Catalog of Assistance*, the PACE program reached seven million children during 1971 and 1972 at a cost of $250 million. The Office of Education has more than 100 such programs, and HEW funded 70,000 behavioral research programs—some among prison inmates which were soundly criticized and are being withdrawn from the prison system....

Mr. Thomas Hamill of the EIC Northwest, said that funds for "specific kinds of research and development" are channeled to 16 national laboratories attached to colleges and universities, a dozen national laboratories studying "individually prescribed instruction," and a number of Educational Resource Information Centers, for delivery to the EIC's.

[Ed. Note: Whenever and wherever *individualized education* is mentioned in professional educational literature, parents should realize that Mastery Learning/OBE/DI is the required instructional method. Homegrown individualized instruction, non-programmed kitchen table type instruction, with a parent instructing his/her child using traditional textbooks and tests, is not the same thing as institutionalized individualized instruction with its programmed, computer-assisted instruction or programmed reading from a script, which often provides immediate reinforcement with tokens, candy—rewards. Also of interest is the fact that prison inmates are protected from subjection to behavior modification techniques and workers in government offices are protected from subjection to training programs which are violations of their religious liberties, but prohibition of the use of behavior modification techniques on normal, American school children is non-existent. (See 1988 Clarence Thomas, chairman of the Equal Employment Opportunity Commission and present U.S. Supreme Court Justice, ruling concerning employment protection.)]

IN 1974 *INDIVIDUAL RIGHTS AND THE FEDERAL ROLE IN BEHAVIOR MODIfication: Report of the Subcommittee on Constitutional Rights* from the Committee on the Judiciary, U.S. Senate, Washington, D.C. was prepared under the chairmanship of North Carolina's late Senator Sam Ervin, who, unfortunately, was unable to continue his work on this important issue due to his being called to serve as a member of the Senate Judiciary Committee investigating the Watergate break-in. Ervin stated in the preface to the report:

[T]echnology has begun to develop new methods of behavior control capable of altering not just an individual's actions but his very personality and manner of thinking as well. Because it affects the ability of the individual to think for himself, the behavioral technology being developed in the United States today touches upon the most basic sources of individuality, and the very core of personal freedom. To my mind, the most serious threat posed by the technology of behavior modification is the power this technology gives one man to impose his views and values on another. In our democratic society, values such as political and religious preferences are expressly left to individual choice. If our society is to remain free, one man must not be empowered to change another man's personality and dictate the values, thoughts and feelings of another.

IN 1974 *A CURRICULUM FOR PERSONALIZED EDUCATION* BY ROBERT SCAN-lon, former Pennsylvania Secretary of Education, was published by one of the U.S. Department of Education research laboratories, Research for Better Schools in Philadelphia, Pennsylvania. Predicting the future, Scanlon stated:

> The emphasis in schools in 1985 will be to free the individual from subject matter as bodies of knowledge and provide him or her with higher order skills.... One type is values clarification.

IN A SPEECH GIVEN TO AND RECORDED BY THE ASSOCIATION FOR SUPERVISION and Curriculum Development in 1974,[7] Dr. Leon Lessinger, superintendent of schools in Beverly Hills, California and former associate commissioner of education in the U.S. Office of Education, called for the implementation of Skinnerian behavior modification and discussed environmental influence when he said:

> Would that we had such a system; a system of accountability. Do we have a hog cholera vaccine? Three ingredients of such a vaccine:
>
> 1. Target the experience in terms of outcomes;
> 2. Self-paced learning. We have the technology now. Modules. Small groups working on common learning targets. Free learner from having to be there always in front of teacher. If we know the target, we can do beautifully if we know the target.
> 3. Use of contingency rewards. May make you feel uncomfortable. Does me, but he who shirks this responsibility does a disservice to the children of the United States. Behavior Modification is here. Better for us to master and use wisely. Powerful ... powerful... powerful.
>
> Carolina Inn exists right across from my school. In the restaurant, rug is red; in the bar, rug is orange. I know that because I happen to pass by!... Red in the restaurant—because you feel uncomfortable and it keeps you from dilly-dallying around dinner. Ah, but in the bar, it's [warm, comfortable] orange!

MAN, EDUCATION & SOCIETY IN THE YEAR 2000, WRITTEN BY GRANT VENN, director of the Chief State School Officers Institute and professor of education at Georgia State University, was a report or summary of discussions which took place at the Fifth Annual Chief State School Officers Institute at Jackson Hole, Wyoming, July 25–August 2, 1974. The report of the Institute was sponsored by the U.S. Office of Education in cooperation with the Council of Chief State School Officers, funded by the Office of Education, U.S. Department of Health, Education and Welfare. There is a notation on the back cover which states: "The availability of this report is limited. A single copy may be obtained free on request to the U.S. Office of Education as long as the supply lasts." Dr. Venn's best known publications are *Man, Education and Work* (1963) and *Man, Education and Manpower* (1971). Excerpts from Dr. Venn's introduction to the Summary Report of the Institute follow:

> Seven days of intensive study and discussion with the top leadership of the U.S. Office of Education and specialists invited to speak to the Chiefs reached an apparent consensus regarding issues that are facing Man, Education and Society: The Year 2000....
>
> The seven topics chosen for study by the Executive Committee of the Council of Chief State School Officers, the U.S. Office of Education and the Institute Director... follow:
>
> 1. The Role of the Future in Education—Alvin Toffler
> 2. Education and Human Resource Development—Willard Wirtz
> 3. The International Situation: The Role of Education—Frederick Champion Ward
> 4. Economic Matters: Public Dollar Availability—Allan K.Campbell
> 5. The Shape of Democracy: The Citizen Role—Forbes Bottomly
> 6. The Public and Private Life of the Individual—Harold Shane
> 7. Energy, Natural Resources and Growth—Charles J. Ryan

Excerpts from the body of Dr. Venn's summary follow:

> We have reached a point where society either educates everyone or supports them....
>
> Technological change has, suddenly and dramatically, thrown up a challenge to our nation's political, economic, and education institutions. If it is to be solved, it is going to demand a massive response on the part of American education. Technology has, in effect, created a new relationship between man, his education and his society....
>
> The home, the church, and the school cannot be effective maintainers since the future cannot be predicted....
>
> The clearest overall approach to finding better ways seemed to be a new role for the state departments of education....
>
> From the question of finances to the question of values that should be taught in the schools, the consensus was that leadership and priority changing by state departments was the most important step to be taken....
>
> After all the questions had been asked and all the dialogue ended, it appeared that the most difficult matter would be one of instituting new approaches to education....
>
> Toffler's belief that the schools have been a "maintaining" institution for a static predictable society was not agreed to by all, but there was agreement that education for the future had to end its reliance on the past as predictor of the future....
>
> The traditional cluster of knowledge, skills, values, and concepts will not help our young face the future in their private life, the international situation, their citizen role, their work role, nor in the area of energy, national resources or growth....
>
> ...Individuals need more learning about social process with a greater emphasis on participation in group decision making. Again we come face to face with the fact that many problems of the future must be solved based on values and priorities set by groups. Many of these values will have to be enforced by group action and will need the involvement of many individuals

in order that hard decisions can be implemented. Many of the future problems cannot be solved by individual decision or action. The heavy emphasis on individual achievement and competition may need to include learning about cooperation and group achievement....

As learning becomes more tied to the future, personal and societal change "values" come to the foreground. It is doubtful that we shall ever return to the concept of values in the same way we saw them in the past.... Perhaps there is a need for the clarification of new values needed to solve future problems. They may become clear as we begin a deliberate search for values we wish to teach and provide experiences for our young in using these values in solving real problems....

It would appear that our young have become isolated from the "real work" of society and from the real decision making of society. Decision making [values clarification] may become the subject of the learning process if there are greater opportunities for "action learning" and group learning by teachers and students....

The over emphasis on knowledge, information, and theories have caused our youth to be freed from the testing of their beliefs in a non-controlled environment—the real world....

Conclusions

In addition to the three R's, the basic skills would appear to include group participation, environmental relationships and planning for the future!... Organization, structure, role and purpose, methods, content, financing, relationships among school and society, leadership and time frames must all be evaluated and changed. The greatest danger seems to be that simple improvement rather than basic change might be attempted....

The following conclusions seem to be suggested as approaches which might bring about major change!... The states collectively should establish specific minimal competencies in each of the basic tool skill areas and each state should make them the first priority for funding, staffing and organizing....

Annual state reports should be devised to replace the normative achievement test in the future with competency achievement.... The states should convene a task force to study and report the ways that are being tried and ways that might be used to provide alternatives to earning the high school diploma....

Students achieving minimal credits ought to be encouraged to develop their unique aptitudes and to test these in the community, workforce, and the school systems.... There should be a policy devised in each of the states that ends the long held basic of "time in place" [Carnegie Unit] as the evaluation of learning for credit.

Regulations must be developed which encourage the use of the community, adults, students and other learning sites than the classroom and teachers.... Full-time attendance from grades one through twelve may have become a barrier to learning—what are the alternatives?... Educational credit should be available to students for activities related to their studies in work, volunteer action, community participation, school volunteer programs and other programs contributing to the betterment of the home, school, community and society.... The time traps of learning for the young, earning for the middle-aged and yearning for the retired must be changed to a concept of continuous learning [UNESCO's lifelong learning, ed.].

Greater use of adults and students from other countries and cultures should be emphasized.... It is obvious that the schools alone cannot educate our youth. State Departments should encourage, through policies and financing, the use of other societal agencies and resources to be part of the planned educational program of high school and older youth.... Since the future indicates a smaller share of the public dollar for education, states should develop regulations and policies which use the entire year and the entire society as educational resources....

The fifty states should organize a commission to establish the values that are significant in approaching problems that must be faced in the future.... Since change is so great and problem solving the necessity of the future, the state should establish a study which would define the essential skills, understandings and approaches that our young should learn in order to participate in the social decisions that must be made in the future....

Knowledge and information is not the only basis for solving problems; our schools need to help our youth gain experience in group decision making as a basis for future citizenship....

Each state ought to look at the problem of the role of the school in making the entry job a means rather than an end.... Would a placement function for the schools help motivate youth?... Every high school student ought to devote a portion of their time to the development of a career related to the future and sensible public and private life....

Most research in education has looked at parts and pieces rather than the total relationship of man, education and society. The CCSSO should establish a long-range planning and policy group to look at societal issues and the implications for education. At present, there is no such body looking at this problem. Can the education Chiefs afford to let others do all the directing of the future?

[Ed. Note: The reader cannot help but see that the above highly controversial recommendations made in 1974 have been implemented with hardly a hitch.]

PROFESSOR LAWRENCE KOHLBERG'S MORAL DEVELOPMENT APPROACH curriculum, "Ethical Issues in Decision Making," was developed in the early 1970s and was used extensively in law education courses in public and private schools. In 1974 Kohlberg was still developing his classifications of "Stages of Moral Development" to include a Seventh Stage—that of "Faith." Kohlberg's program was listed in the National Diffusion Network's catalog *Programs that Work* as an exemplary program. Kohlberg's Moral Development Approach includes education in the following "stages of moral development":

Stage 1—"Avoid punishment" orientation: decisions are based on a blind obedience to an external power in an attempt to avoid punishment or seek reward.

Stage 2—"Self-Benefit" orientation: decisions are based on premise of doing something for others if they reciprocate.

Stage 3—"Acceptance by others" orientation: decisions are based on whether or not their behaviors perceived as pleasing to others.

Stage 4—"Maintain the social order" orientation: decisions are based on fixed rules which are "necessary" to perpetuate the order of society as a whole.

Stage 5—"Contract fulfillment" orientation: decisions are based on the individual respecting impartial laws and agreeing to abide by them while society agrees to respect the rights of the individual.

Stage 6—"Ethical principle" orientation: decisions are based on "conscience" and respect for each person's individuality is paramount with the values believed to be valid for all humanity.

After Stage 6, the individual experiences despair. He or she has developed principles of justice, yet is faced with an unjust world. Moral philosophy cannot solve the problem.

Stage 7—"Faith" orientation: decisions are concerned with "what is the ultimate meaning of life?"

This "Faith" orientation stage does not conflict with the principles developed through the first six stages; rather, it integrates those stages and provides a perspective on life's ultimate meaning. In Stage Seven the individual advances from an essentially human to a cosmic point of view. With Stage Seven there is a modification to a wider view of life. Emphasis changes from the individual to the cosmos.

1975

SUPERINTENDENT RAY I. POWELL, PH.D., OF SOUTH ST. PAUL, MINNESOTA public schools spoke out regarding values clarification and sensitivity training in 1975, saying, "It's all brainwashing!" Excerpts follow from a memorandum to "All Administrators from Ray I. Powell" concerning Center Bulletin No. 39: 1974–1975, dated February 26, 1975:

1. Parents have the prime responsibility for the inculcation of those moral and spiritual values desired for their children in the areas of abortion and birth control. Indeed, this is an inherent right of parents and must not be denied....

Effective immediately, the teaching, advising, directing, suggesting, or counseling of students in these two (2) areas cannot be/shall not be the responsibility nor the task of the South St. Paul Public Schools.

Rather, the efforts of the public schools, henceforth, shall be directed towards expanding those complimentary learning experiences in other areas of the total curriculum that will enhance these two (2) parental values, i.e.:

- preservation of the family unit.
- feminine role of the wife, mother, and homemaker.
- masculine role of guide, protector, and provider.
- advocacy of home and family values.
- respect for family structure and authority.
- enhancement of womanhood and femininity.
- restoration of morality.

2. There are more and more concerns and questions being registered today regarding the questionable results and the true intent of SENSITIVITY TRAINING, as well as its germaneness to the goals and objectives of public education, the training of educators, and the learning experiences of students.

Consider these two (2) definitions of SENSITIVITY TRAINING (sources furnished upon request):

Sensitivity training is defined as group meetings, large or small, to discuss publicly intimate and personal matters, and opinions, values or beliefs; and/or to act out emotions and feelings toward one another in the group, using the techniques of self-confession and mutual criticism.

It is also "coercive persuasion in the form of thought reform or brainwashing."

Is the prime concern in education today not to impart knowledge, but to change "attitudes," so that children can/will willingly accept a controlled society? Are the public schools being unwittingly re-shaped to accomplish this and without realizing it?

[Ed. Note: Dr. Powell then lists 54 terms which can all be included under Sensitivity Training, a few of which are: T-Group Training, Operant Conditioning, Management by Objectives, Sex Education, Self-Hypnosis, Role Playing, Values Clarification, Situation Ethics, Alternative Life Styles, etc. Had all our schools had superintendents with Dr. Powell's character and courage, most of the problems facing our children and families today would not exist.]

CONGRESSMAN JOHN CONLAN OF ARIZONA ISSUED A PRESS RELEASE REGARDing the controversial federally funded program for ten-year-old children called *Man: A Course of Study* (*M:ACOS*) (Education Development Center: Cambridge, Massachusetts, 1975). On April 9, 1975 Conlan said that the $7 million National Science Foundation-funded program was designed by a team of experimental psychologists under Jerome S. Bruner's and B.F. Skinner's direction to mold children's social attitudes and beliefs along lines that set them apart and alienated them from the beliefs and moral values of their parents and local communities. As a matter of fact, fifty commercial publishers refused to publish the course because of its objectionable content. The following gory story of cannibalism is excerpted from *M:ACOS* (Vol. 1):

The wife knew that the spirits had said her husband should eat her, but she was so exhausted that it made no impression on her, she did not care. It was only when he began to feel her, when it occurred to him to stick his fingers in her side to feel if there was flesh on her, that she suddenly felt a terrible fear; so she, who had never been afraid of dying, now tried to escape. With her feeble strength she ran for her life, and then it was as if Tuneq saw her only as a quarry that was about to escape him; he ran after her and stabbed her to death. After that, he lived on her, and collected her bones in a heap over by the side of the platform for the purpose of fulfilling the taboo rule required of all who die. (p. 115)

OCTOBER 24, 1975 THE WORLD AFFAIRS COUNCIL OF PHILADELPHIA ISSUED "A Declaration of Interdependence" written by well-known historian and liberal think tank Aspen Institute board member Henry Steele Commager. This alarming document, which called to mind President Kennedy's July 4, 1962 speech calling for a "Declaration of Interdependence," was written as a contribution to our nation's celebration of its 200th birthday, and signed by 125 members of the U.S. House and Senate. Excerpts follow:

WHEN IN THE COURSE OF HISTORY the threat of extinction confronts mankind, it is necessary for the people of The United States to declare their interdependence with the people of all nations and to embrace those principles and build those institutions which will enable mankind to survive and civilization to flourish....

Two centuries ago our forefathers brought forth a new nation; now we must join with others to bring forth a new world order....

WE AFFIRM that the economy of all nations is a seamless web, and that no one nation can any longer effectively maintain its processes of production and monetary systems without recognizing the necessity for collaborative regulation by international authorities.

[Ed. Note: In 1976 the National Education Association produced a social studies curriculum entitled *A Declaration of Interdependence: Education for a Global Community* which Congresswoman Marjorie Holt (R.-MD) described as "an atrocious betrayal of American independence." It wasn't until the 1980s and 1990s that the relationship between "interdependence" or "new world order" and America's education of children became prominent in outcomes in each state. Interdependence is also an undergirding concept in global education.

In 1976 a coterie of internationalists thought their plans would have smooth sailing, not the resistance they encountered at the grassroots level which set them back a good twenty years. What we are experiencing in 1999 (American soldiers being deployed world-wide as part of United Nations "peace-keeping" operations, and UN land confiscation through executive orders, etc.) was delayed by the activism of courageous Americans to whom we all owe an enormous debt of gratitude.]

U.S. COMMISSIONER OF EDUCATION T.H. BELL MADE THE FOLLOWING STATEment in a U.S. Office of Education (HEW) press release on October 29, 1975, dealing with results of the University of Texas Adult Performance Level (APL) Study. The study, headed by Dr. Norvell Northcutt, was funded at approximately $1 million under Sec. 309 of the *Adult Education Act*. T.H. Bell's statement follows:

One out of five American adults lacks the skills and knowledge needed to function effectively in the basic day-to-day struggle to make a living and maintain a home and family, according to a four-year investigation of adult functional competency released today by HEW's Office of Education. Referring to the results of the Adult Performance Level (APL) study as "rather startling," U.S. Commissioner of Education Terrell H. Bell said that they call for some major rethinking of education on several levels. "To begin with," Dr. Bell added, "adult education has to be reshaped so that students receive the kind of information that will make modern life easier for them. I also think that State and local education agencies will want to examine what they are teaching, even at the elementary levels, and perhaps reconsider their requirements for high school graduation." APL research defines functional competency as "the ability to use skills and knowledge needed for meeting the requirements of adult living."

[Ed. Note: Secretary Bell's recommendations were adopted by Oregon and Pennsylvania one year later. In 1976 Pennsylvania commenced implementation of its controversial "Project '81" which, according to its 1976 State Department of Education informational materials, "restructured Pennsylvania's Goals of Quality Education and developed a new program of basic skills and initiated studies designed to help in developing comprehensive programs in general and specialized education." The same informational materials also stated that "Pennsylvania's Contemporary Family Life Competencies were taken from an outline of a course being implemented at Parkrose High School in Oregon which focused on consumer economics competencies and makes use of both school and community resources."

There is no question in this writer's mind that the "pre-determined" results of the Texas APL Study set the stage for all state education agencies to commence dumbed-down continuous progress competency-based education, which is just another label for Benjamin Bloom's and William Spady's outcome- /performance- /results-based, school-to-work "education"—all of which use Skinnerian pigeon-training methods (mastery learning and direct instruction)—and that the initial thrust for this type of "all children can learn/redistribution of brains" lifelong education came straight out of the United Nations.]

[ddd]

PROJECT **INSTRUCT,** ANOTHER MASTERY LEARNING PROGRAM MODELED along the lines of the Exemplary Center for Reading Instruction (ECRI), was approved for dissemination throughout the nation by the U.S. Office of Education's Joint Dissemination Review Panel (JDRP) May 14, 1975. The final evaluation of Project INSTRUCT stated that

> The intent and emphasis in 1970 was on behavioral indices and concrete ways of showing accountability; and the data would suggest that the reading of the students themselves may not have increased, but the impact of Project INSTRUCT in the Lincoln, Nebraska Public Schools seems to be very extensive and influential.

[Ed. Note: According to the final evaluation of Project INSTRUCT, Ronald Brandt, former executive editor of the Association for Supervision and Curriculum Development's publication *Educational Leadership*, was involved in the project.]

1976

CHILDHOOD IN CHINA, A BOOK EDITED BY WILLIAM KESSEN (YALE UNIVERsity Press: New Haven, Connecticut, 1976), was reviewed by Kent Garland Burit of *The Christian Science Monitor*. The following excerpts from Burit's review provide insight into the similarities of education in Communist China in 1973 and Skinnerian Effective School Research used in American restructuring in the 1980s and 1990s:

They were well-behaved, non aggressive with peers....

The immediate yielding to a teacher's request seemed remarkable to the Americans....

The strategies and communication style of the teachers is also described. They initiate, supervise closely, and terminate all activities. They teach by repetition and by formula. Their verbal and nonverbal indications of approval are in a high ratio to indications of disapproval. They discipline through persuasion and moralistic reasoning rather than punishment. They exude a confident expectation of their pupils' compliance and cooperation....

The curriculum is saturated with ideological goals, the team reported. The child is exposed to repeated exhortations to serve the society.

[Ed. Note: The foregoing quote with its behavioral terminology could come from an issue of *The Effective School Report*, from which this writer has repeatedly quoted throughout this book. Education in non-violence, tolerance, peer resolution, cooperative learning, and politically-correct curriculum—all of which will modify the behavior of American children so that they will be like the above Communist Chinese children—is taking place in American schools in 1999. (See April 21, 1982 Spady quote calling for the above "compliance.")]

THE LOS ANGELES TIMES OF MAY 21, 1976 (PART 1–B) CARRIED AN article entitled "Cuban Children Combine Studies, Work" which clearly explained the communist work-study system and the impact of community service, both of which are being implemented in the United States in the 1990s. Important excerpts follow:

HAVANA (AP)—The door to the side room of an old cigar factory had been left ajar, and a small knot of children could be seen preparing boxes of cigars for export. "It's part of our education system," a Cuban tobacco official explained. "They are helping and learning." The children, elementary school pupils about 9 to 11 years old, were examples of the unique Cuban educational system of combining studies with physical work. The system, started in 1967, applies to all schools, including the island's four universities....

The Cubans say the idea is to produce well-rounded citizens capable of manual labor. But the system also provides extra hands for an economy that urgently needs more production.... Says Prime Minister Fidel Castro, "This helps to temper them from early childhood in the habits of creative work, without running the risk of possible deformation through the exclusive exercise of intellectual activity.".

One example of the system is found at Havana's 1,639 pupil U.S.S.R.-Cuba technical school, so named because the Soviet Union equipped the school and trained the instructors. The students, mainly boys 14 to 17, learn how to melt metal and to mold it into machine parts. They are taught how to cast, weld, grind and operate a lathe. Girls work in laboratories, learning to operate testing equipment for metals and machine parts. The parts, produced while learning, are sent to factories that make machinery. The students themselves spend part of their time working inside the factories. The school also teaches language, culture, sports, political philosophy and ordinary school subjects....

Those who study for two years become what are called general workers for the factories, while four-year students become skilled technicians. All are guaranteed factory jobs upon graduation....

At the University of Havana, there are 54,000 students this year. Full-time students study four hours a day, six days a week and work another four hours daily in fields, factories or at jobs related to their future careers.... Many older students fill their work requirement by teaching, to offset the teacher shortage created when hundreds of thousands of Cubans emigrated after Castro's 1959 revolution.... This commitment to working for the good of the country remains after graduation. Graduates must serve anywhere in Cuba for three years, then are allowed to return home to continue their careers.

LAWRENCE C. PIERCE DELIVERED A PAPER IN 1976 ENTITLED "SCHOOL SITE Management" to a meeting of the Aspen Institute for Humanistic Studies in which he referred to site-based management as an "intermediate structure between centralized school management and education vouchers." An excerpt follows:

On January 6, 1976, San Francisco School Superintendent Robert F. Alioto proposed an organizational redesign of the district that included a shift from school district to school site management. He said, in part:

I recommend that we move toward a school site management model that values staff and a community involvement and stresses accountability. We must recognize the principal as the instructional leader of the school. We must expand the budgeting and fiscal control at each school site.... We must establish at each school site one active advisory committee which includes parents, students, and staff representatives of the school's ethnic population....

Further support for proposals to decentralize school management arises from the desire to increase public participation in school governance policies. Local control of the schools, originally instituted to make them responsive to the people, nevertheless proved to be cumbersome, and it frequently obscured the state's responsibility for providing every child with a basic education. In pursuit of greater accountability and higher professional standards, the pendulum of school government, which in the early days of this country swung toward representativeness and local control, later swung back toward greater professional autonomy and stronger executive control....

...School site management is an intermediate structure between central-ized school management and educational vouchers.

[Ed. Note: Read that last statement again. Twenty-one years later the care-fully laid plans of the internationalist Aspen Institute for Humanistic Studies are being implemented under the guise of unaccountable choice/charter schools, funded by the taxpayers. School-site management is an early term for site-based or school-based management promoted by the National Edu-cation Association in the 1980s and 1990s. Of extreme importance is the unambiguous call for the use of (need for) vouchers, which will supplant "choice," essential for the implementation of the international school-to-work agenda. The dollar amount of the voucher will depend on the school council's determination of how much it will cost to train your child to be a janitor (very little) or doctor (a lot).]

Lawrence P. Grayson of the National Institute of Education, U.S. Department of Education, wrote "Education, Technology, and Individual Privacy" (ECTJ, Vol. 28, No. 3, pp. 195–208) in 1976. The following are some excerpts from this important paper which serves as a clear warning regarding the indiscriminate use of behaviorist methods and technology:

> The right to privacy is based on a belief in the essential dignity and worth of the individual. Modern technological devices, along with advances in the behavioral sciences, can threaten the privacy of students. Fortunately, invasions of privacy in education have not been widespread. However, sufficient violations have been noted to warrant specific legislation and to promote a sharp increase in attention to procedures that will ensure protection of individual privacy. Technology that can reveal innermost thoughts and motives or can change basic values and behaviors, must be used judiciously and only by qualified professionals under strictly controlled conditions. Education includes individuals and educational experimentation is human experimentation. The educator must safeguard the privacy of students and their families....
>
> Privacy has been defined as "the right to be let alone" (Cooley, 1888) and as the "right to the immunity of the person—the right to one's personality" (Warren and Brandeis, 1890). Individuals have the right to determine when, how, and to what extent they will share themselves with others. It is their right to be free from unwarranted or undesired revelation of personal information to others, to participate or withdraw as they see fit, and to be free of unwarranted surveillance through physical, psychological, or technological means.
>
> Justice William O. Douglas expressed the concerns of many people when he stated:
>
>> We are rapidly entering the age of no privacy; when everyone is open to surveillance at all times; when there are no secrets from the government.... [There is] an alarming trend whereby the privacy and dignity of our citizens is being whittled away by sometimes imperceptible steps. Taken individually, each step may be of little consequence. But when viewed as a whole, there begins to emerge a society quite unlike any we have seen—a society in which government may intrude into the secret regions of a man's life at will. (*Osborn v. U.S.*, 1966, pp. 341–343)
>
> Behavioral science, which is assuming an increasing role in educational technology, promises to make educational techniques more effective by recognizing individual differences among students and by patterning instruction to meet individual needs. However, behavioral science is more than an unbiased means to an end. It has a basic value position (Skinner, 1971) based on the premise that such "values as freedom and democracy, which imply that the individual ultimately has free will and is responsible for his own actions, are not only cultural inventions, but illusions" (Harman, 1970). This position is contradictory to the basic premise of freedom and is demeaning to the dignity of the individual. Behavioral science inappropriately applied can impinge on individual values without allowing for personal differences and in education can violate the privacy of the student....
>
> Reflecting on the ethical values of our civilization in 1958, Pope Pius XII commented:
>
>> There is a large portion of his inner world which the person discloses to a few confidential friends and shields against the intrusion of oth-

ers. Certain [other] matters are kept secret at any price and in regard to anyone. Finally, there are other matters which the person is unable to consider.... And just as it is illicit to appropriate another's goods or to make an attempt on his bodily integrity without his consent, so it is not permissible to enter into his inner domain against his will, whatever is the technique or method used....

Whatever the motivations of the teacher or researcher, an individual's privacy must take precedence over effective teaching, unless good cause can be shown to do otherwise. Good cause, however, does not relieve the teacher or school administrator from the responsibility of safeguarding the privacy of the student and the family. Yet, many teachers and administrators remain insensitive to the privacy implications of behavioral science and modern technology in education....

Intent on improving education, educators, scientists, and others concerned with the development and application of technology are often insensitive to the issues of privacy raised by the use of their techniques. For example, many psychological and behavioral practices have been introduced on the ground that they will make education more efficient or effective. However, improvements in efficiency through technological applications can reinforce these practices without regard to their effects. What is now being done in education could be wrong, especially if carried out on a massive scale. As the use of technology becomes more widespread, we may reach the point where errors cannot be detected or corrected. This is especially important because technology interacts with society and culture to change established goals and virtues. Propagating an error on a national level could change the original goals to fit the erroneous situation. The error then becomes acceptable by default.

In developing and applying technology to education, potential effects must be analyzed, so that negative possibilities can be identified and overcome before major resources are committed to projects that could produce undesirable long-term social consequences.

In matters affecting privacy it is better to err on the side of the individual, than on that of research or improved educational practice. Violations of privacy can never be fully redressed.

———

Ftnt. No. 14. Privacy is a constitutionally protected right; education is not. The Supreme Court ruled in *Griswold v. Connecticut* (decided in 1965) that the right of privacy is guaranteed by the Constitution. In *Rodriguez v. San Antonio Independent School District* (decided in 1973), the Court ruled that education is not a protected right under the Constitution.

UNITED NATIONS EDUCATIONAL, SCIENTIFIC, AND CULTURAL ORGANIZATION (UNESCO) in Paris, France published *The International Standard Classification of Education* (ISCED–COM.75/WS/27) in 1976. This publication revealed efforts at the highest international level to set up a classification system which will be available for use by planners assigned to the management of the global economy. Some quotes from the introduction to this 396-page document follow:

The International Standard Classification of Education (ISCED) has been designed as an instrument suitable for assembling, compiling, and presenting statistics of education both within individual countries and internationally. It is expected to facilitate international compilation and comparison of education statistics as such, and also their use in conjunction with manpower and other economic statistics....

ISCED should facilitate the use of education statistics in manpower planning and encourage the use of manpower statistics in educational planning. For this purpose, the most closely associated classification system in the manpower field is the *International Standard Classification of Occupations* (ISCO), prepared by the International Labour Office.

CATHERINE BARRETT, PRESIDENT OF THE NATIONAL EDUCATION ASSOCIATION (NEA), gave a speech at the 1976 NEA Annual Conference in which she made the following comments concerning the change in the role of the teacher:

> At this critical moment no one can say with certainty whether we are at the brink of a colossal disaster or whether this is indeed mankind's shining hour. But it is certain that dramatic changes in the way we raise our children in the year 2000 are indicated particularly in terms of schooling, and that these changes will require new ways of thinking. Let me propose three.
>
> First, we will help all of our people understand that school is a concept and not a place. We will not confuse "schooling" with "education." The school will be the community, the community, the school. Students, parents, and teachers will make certain that John Dewey's sound advice about schooling the whole child is not confused with nonsense about the school's providing the child's whole education....
>
> We will need to recognize that the so-called "basic skills," which currently represent nearly the total effort in elementary schools, will be taught in one quarter of the present school day. The remaining time will be devoted to what is truly fundamental and basic—time for academic inquiry, time for students to develop their own interests, time for a dialogue between students and teachers. When this happens—and it is near—the teacher can rise to his true calling. More than a dispenser of information, the teacher will be a conveyor of values, a philosopher. Students will learn to write love letters and lab notes. We will help each child build his own rocket to his own moon....
>
> Finally, if our children are to be human beings who think clearly, feel deeply, and act wisely, we will answer definitely the question "Who should make what decisions?" Teachers no longer will be victims of change; we will be the agents of change.

[Ed. Note: Catherine Barrett's idea of "school is a concept, not a place" is an idea whose time may have come in the 1990s. Many educators, including Lewis Perelman (See 1995 Perelman's book *School's Out*), are of the same opinion. This seems to follow on the heels of the concept of "education as behavior change" instead of the acquisition of knowledge.]

IN THE SEPTEMBER 1976 ISSUE OF *PHI DELTA KAPPAN*, "AMERICA'S NEXT Twenty-Five Years: Some Implications for Education," Harold Shane described his version of the "new and additional basic skills" as follows:

Certainly, cross-cultural understanding and empathy have become fundamental skills, as have the skills of human relations and intercultural rapport... the arts of compromise and reconciliation, of consensus building, and of planning for interdependence become basic.... As young people mature we must help them develop... a service ethic which is geared toward the real world... the global servant concept in which we will educate our young for planetary service and eventually for some form of world citizenship.... Implicit within the "global servant" concept are the moral insights that will help us live with the regulated freedom we must eventually impose upon ourselves.

[Ed. Note: The writer would like to contrast Harold Shane's comments with those of C.S. Lewis as compiled in an article "C.S. Lewis on Liberal Arts Education" by Gregory Dunn which was published in the newsletter *On Principle* from the John M. Ashbrook Center for Public Affairs (April 1999, Vol. VII, No. 2). Excerpts from Dunn's article follow:

The first reason we study the liberal arts has to do with freedom. That freedom is an integral part of the liberal arts is borne out of [C.S.] Lewis's observation that "liberal comes of course from the Latin, liber, and means free."[8] Such an education makes one free, according to Lewis, because it transforms the pupil from "an unregenerate little bundle of appetites" into "the good man and the good citizen."[9] We act most human when we are reasonable, both in thought and deed. Animals, on the other hand, act wholly out of appetite. When hungry, they eat; when tired, they rest. Man is different. Rather than follow our appetites blindly we can be deliberate about what we do and when we do it. The ability to rule ourselves frees us from the tyranny of our appetites, and the liberal arts disciplines this self-rule. In other words, this sort of education teaches us to be most fully human and thereby, to fulfill our human duties, both public and private.

Lewis contrasts liberal arts education with what he calls "vocational training," the sort that prepares one for employment. Such training, he writes, "aims at making not a good man but a good banker, a good electrician... or a good surgeon." Lewis does admit the importance of such training—for we cannot do without bankers and electricians and surgeons—but the danger, as he sees it, is the pursuit of training at the expense of education. "If education is beaten by training, civilization dies," he writes, for the "lesson of history" is that "civilization is a rarity, attained with difficulty and easily lost."[10] It is the liberal arts, not vocational training, that preserves civilization by producing reasonable men and responsible citizens....

A third reason we study the liberal arts is because it is simply our nature and duty. Man has a natural thirst for knowledge of the Good, the True, and the Beautiful, and men and women of the past have made great sacrifices to pursue it in spite of the fact that, as Lewis puts it, "human life has always been lived on the edge of a precipice." In his words, "they propound mathematical theorems in beleaguered cities, conduct metaphysical arguments in condemned cells, make jokes on scaffolds." So, finding in the soul an appetite for such things, and knowing no appetite is made by God in vain, Lewis concludes that the pursuit of the liberal arts is pleasing to God and is possibly, for some, a God-given vocation....[11]

...Truly, we ignore the liberal arts only at our peril. Without them we will find ourselves increasingly unable to preserve a civilized society, to escape from the errors and prejudices of our day, and to struggle in the arena of ideas to the glory of God.]

TODAY'S EDUCATION, THE JOURNAL OF THE NATIONAL EDUCATION ASSOCIA-tion, carried an article in the September–October 1976 edition entitled "The Seven Cardinal Principles Revisited." On page 1 this article stated that:

> In 1972, the NEA established a Bicentennial Committee charged with develop-ing a "living commemoration of the principles of the American Revolution." This 200th anniversary celebration of the *Declaration of Independence* was to focus on the next 100 years of education in an interdependent global community. The initial work of the Committee culminated in the NEA *Bi-centennial Idea Book*. Among its ideas was that of developing a definitive volume to "contain a reframing of the Cardinal Principles of Education and recommendations for a global curriculum." After recognizing the importance of the original Cardinal Principles, which were published in 1918, the Com-mittee made the point that "today, those policy statements about education are obsolete, education taken as a whole is not adequate to the times and too seldom anticipates the future." A report to be issued by the NEA, proposing cardinal premises for the twenty-first century is the direct and immediate outgrowth of the Bicentennial Committee's belief that "educators around the world are in a unique position to bring about a harmoniously interde-pendent global community based on the principles of peace and justice...." Early in September 1975, a 19-member Preplanning Committee began the task of recasting the seven Cardinal Principles of Education by developing 25 guidelines for the project.

[Ed. Note: Members of the Preplanning Committee read like a "Who's Who of Leading Globalists." It included: former Secretary of Education T.H. Bell, "Mr. Management-by-Objectives," who was responsible for the grant to William Spady of the Far West Laboratory to pilot OBE in Utah, with plans to "put OBE in all schools of the nation"; Professor Luvern Cunningham, Ohio State University, who subsequently served as advisor to the Kentucky Department of Education during its education restructuring in the 1990s; Willis Harman, Stanford Research Institute; Robert Havighurst, University of Chicago; Theodore Hesburgh, University of Notre Dame; Ralph Tyler, Center for Advanced Study in Behavioral Science; Professor Theodore Sizer, Coalition for Essential Schools, which calls for a "less is more" curriculum and removal of graduation standards (the Carnegie Unit); David Rockefeller; Professor Benjamin Bloom, father of Mastery Learning (the international learning method); the late McGeorge Bundy of the Ford Foundation; and others.]

FOUNDATIONS OF LIFELONG EDUCATION WAS PUBLISHED BY UNESCO (UNITED Nations Educational, Scientific, and Cultural Organization) Institute for Education (Pergamon Press: Oxford, N.Y., Toronto, Sydney, Paris, Frank-furt, 1976). In chapter 4, "Theoretical Foundations of Lifelong Education: A Sociological Perspective," Henri Janne described accurately the how, what and why of decentralization (site-based management, charter schools, choice, unelected school councils, etc.) being sold to naïve school boards and citizens as "local control":

> In education a monolithic structure is completely unacceptable as it cre-

ates organizations that, owing to their homogeneity and their ineluctable [inevitable] bureaucratic nature, are averse to change and to individual or local adaptation....

Decentralization of the greatest possible number of decisions is indispensable in a system founded on... education defined as "learning" rather than "teaching."

[Ed. Note: "Learning," as described and defined by the educational change agents, is the process by which students/children are allowed to acquire the knowledge which will be "beneficial" to them personally as they pursue the fulfillment of their particular life roles (jobs). This process is the opposite of the traditional role of education as "teaching" students subject matter which can be used for diversified pursuits later in life.

In the 1977 entry dealing with UNESCO's Development of Educational Technology in Central and Eastern Europe the reader will note that the socialist countries of Eastern Europe had centralized systems of education and had not yet adapted their system to accommodate Henri Janne's proposals for "lifelong learning." Janne explained above how to take a centralized system of pedagogy and ideas and "localize" them in order to change their focus without ever changing the centralized control. This gives an interesting perspective on the oft-seen bumper sticker: "Think Globally—Act Locally."]

1977

[ddd]

"COMPETENCY-BASED EDUCATION: A BANDWAGON IN SEARCH OF A DEFINI-tion," an article by William G. Spady of the National Institute of Education, was published in the January 1977 edition of *Educational Researcher*. Excerpts follow:

In September, 1972, the Oregon State Board of Education passed new minimum graduation requirements for students entering ninth grade in the Fall of 1974 and new minimum standards for local school districts focused on the new requirements in 1974. The thrust of these new requirements and standards involved the introduction of three domains of "survival level" competencies as minimum conditions for high school graduation by 1978: personal development, social responsibility, and career development.... Although largely unintended and unanticipated by those involved, the 1972 Oregon regulations provided the first significant nudge that set in motion across the nation over the next four years a series of actions by state level policy makers and administrators to consider, formulate and implement regulations and procedures that they now associate with the term Competency-Based Education (CBE)....

It is likely, therefore, both that the outcome goals required for graduation in CBE systems will eventually emerge from a tense compromise among the many constituencies in a community regarding the necessary, the desirable, and the possible, and that C-Based diplomas will be viewed with initial if not undying skepticism by colleges and universities.... In short, CBE programs require mechanisms that collect and use student performance data as the basis of diagnosing weaknesses and necessary remediation not only for students but for themselves as well....

According to information compiled by Clark and Thompson (1976), no states outside of Oregon appear to use language consistent with a life-role conception of competency in either their current or pending regulations pertaining to mandated student proficiencies. The possible exceptions refer to the need for occupational and consumer mathematics skills. However, within the next year New York and Pennsylvania may make more decisive moves toward implementing approaches to schooling more fully resembling this conception of CBE. Almost all other states are concerned with capacity-based outcomes in limited basic skill areas (e.g., Arizona, Connecticut, Florida, Georgia, Idaho, Louisiana, Maryland, Nebraska and Tennessee), a slightly broader set of subject area proficiencies (e.g., California, Texas, Virginia and Washington, D.C.) or as-yet-undefined or else locally determined options concerned with some kind of minimum proficiency requirements (e.g., Colorado, Kansas, Michigan and New Jersey). As of October 1976, in only two cases—California and Florida—could students leave school in less than 12 years with a diploma once they passed a state-determined proficiency exam (the Oregon regulations allow local districts to determine whether early graduation will be allowed)....

Aside from Oregon, five states—California, Maryland, Michigan, New York and Pennsylvania—deserve particular attention over the next few years as sites where current thinking about substantial proficiencies or competency-based reforms suggest real promise....

Pennsylvania in a fourth case has been exploring a concept of system reform with a definite Competency-Based orientation. Originally called Community Learning and currently named "Project 81," this program would be centered around facilitating student capacities and competencies in five major areas of activity, with a stress on participation outside the school building where appropriate. The areas include a broad range of basic skills, the world of work and leisure, community governance and involvement, and a broad range of citizen and personal survival skills.

"CONCLAVE OF THE CHANGE AGENTS" BY BARBARA M. MORRIS WAS PUB-lished in the March 1977 issue of *The National Educator*. Excerpts follow from this extremely important article which proves that the federal government has been deeply involved in the funding and implementation of moral/citizenship (values) education:

Early in June 1976, 85 top level members of the educational elite and an assortment of influential change agents met at an invitation only conference in Philadelphia to draft recommendations on how to put "Moral/Citizenship Education" (MCE) programs in every school in the country—public, private and parochial. Conference participants included Humanist values educators Lawrence Kohlberg and Howard Kirschenbaum and representatives of the federal government, foundations, PTA, NEA and the National Council of Churches. The recommendations that resulted from that conference which was sponsored by a Pennsylvania organization called Research for Better Schools (RBS) [a federally funded education laboratory in Philadelphia,

Pennsylvania] have been submitted to the National Institute of Education, with whom RBS has a contract to research, develop and disseminate moral/citizenship education programs....

So shaky is the basis for MCE that much conference time was devoted to trying to decide what to call MCE programs so as to avoid public hostility. Here are some examples of the thinking of conference participants relating to this problem:

- "'Moral/Citizenship Education' as a title can be sold; 'Moral Education' cannot. Avoid such red-flag slogans."
- "We spent three conference days quibbling about the term 'Moral/Citizenship Education.' *That is a major problem.*" [emphasis in original]
- "The concept of self-development (which implies moral development) is more salable and will engender less resistance than moral development."
- "It is important to limit the parameters of what we're engaged in, if not to change the actual title, to avoid religious antagonisms and court action."

THE SCHOOL COUNSELOR, PUBLICATION OF THE AMERICAN PERSONNEL AND Guidance Association, published a special issue on the subject of "Death" in its May 1977 issue (Vol. 24, #5). In this issue a remarkable admission regarding the results of sex education was made which explains clearly the purpose of these controversial humanistic programs: to create the problems sex ed, values ed, drug ed, and death ed were supposed to solve. An excerpt from *The School Counselor* follows:

Helping Students Clarify Values:...

The last goal is to help students clarify their values on social and ethical issues. An underlying, but seldom spoken, assumption of much of the death education movement is that Americans handle death and dying poorly and that we ought to be doing better at it. As in the case of many other problems, many Americans believe that education can initiate change. Change is evident, and death education will play as important a part in changing attitudes toward death as sex education played in changing attitudes toward sex information and wider acceptance of various sexual practices.

[Ed. Note: In light of events in the 1990s, the question arises: What does "doing better at it" mean? The statement "Death education will play as important a part in changing attitudes toward death as sex education played in changing attitudes toward... wider acceptance of various sexual practices" implies that our children benefitted from exposure to "wider acceptance of various sexual practices," when all one has to do is survey the moral landscape to see the devastating effect these programs have had on our children's lives. The same applies to death education and its effect on children's understanding of the value of life, reflected in the increased number of murders carried out by youth.]

JOANNE MCAULEY'S NATIONAL COUNCIL FOR EDUCATIONAL EXCELLENCE, A national organization of concerned parents and educators, was founded in the mid-1970s and, considering the potential it had for holding the line on innovations taking place in American education, its early demise represented a real setback for parents, children, and teachers. Ms. McAuley's May/June 1977 issue of her newsletter, *The School Bell*, is proof that the National School Boards Association was, at one time, a strong proponent of local control, not a "sell out the locals" organization that in the 1990s would support site- and school-based management (taxation without representation) and charter schools. Excerpts follow:

NSBA PRESIDENT TELLS BOARDS: STAND UP TO FEDERAL MEDDLING

On March 27, George W. Smith, immediate past president of the National School Boards Association, warned school board members attending the NSBA convention in Houston that "The Congress and the federal bureaucracy could become the country's master school board unless school board members stand up and be counted." He urged delegates to continue to forge a strong NSBA to convince Congress that local school board members are truly representative, most unselfish, and the best qualified persons to represent the local viewpoint in education.

Smith said local constituencies cannot be forgotten even while the new trust is being built with Congress. "We must not forget our own constituency," he noted. He also advised board members to be aware of—and leery of—proposals for public involvement in public school operations that would shift decision-making authority to "vaguely defined groups of citizens at the school site level." The minister from San Diego cautioned that the power to make a decision must never be divorced from the responsibility for making that decision....

He said school boards must be strong for another reason—to counter the movements of the courts and federal regulatory agencies into the operation of schools. "If we want other governmental units to stop eroding our ability to provide educational governance, we must exercise that ability more often and more effectively." Smith said, "Where we can, we should work together with all segments of the public toward the improvement of the schools. But," he concluded, "our responsibility is to all the people and we must view only the 'big picture.'"

[Ed. Note: Smith's ability to foresee the implementation of site-based management, the down-grading of the importance of elected board members, and the transfer of power to public-private partnerships, etc., is to be lauded! While serving in the U.S. Department of Education this writer attempted to stop federally funded programs to train local school board members in conflict resolution and in how to implement Effective School Research.]

"COMPETENCY TESTS SET IN 26 SCHOOLS: NEW CURRICULUM SHIFTS TEACH-ing Methods in District" was the title of an article which appeared in *The Washington Post* on August 1, 1977. Excerpts follow:

"The materials will be standardized, the lessons will be standardized," Guines said. "We're taking the play out. We're taking the guesswork out. We're putting in a precise predicted treatment that leads to a predicted response." Guines said that the new curriculum is based on the work in behavioral psychology of Harvard University's B.F. Skinner, who developed teaching machines and even trained pigeons during World War II to pilot and detonate bombs and torpedoes. The basic idea, Guines said, is to break down complicated learning into a sequence of clear simple skills that virtually everyone can master, although at different rates of speed. "If you can train a pigeon to fly up there and press a button and set off a bomb," Guines remarked, "why can't you teach human beings to behave in an effective and rational way? We know that we can modify human behavior. We're not scared of that. This is the biggest thing that's happening in education today.".....

According to Thomas B. Sticht, Associate Director for Basic Skills of the National Institute of Education, similar techniques, called competency education or mastery teaching, are now being used in many parts of the country. Since 1973, Sticht said, they have been adopted by the Army and Navy for basic training and to teach entry level job skills. They have been used successfully in college courses, he said, and also to teach mentally retarded children who previously had been classed as "uneducable." "There has to be a well-defined series of objectives," Sticht said, "and a step by step curriculum that gives some way [through Mastery Tests] to know you have met the objectives."...

But the system also has detractors who criticize it as rigid and mechanistic. "We must be very careful," said Lawrence G. Derthick, a former U.S. Commissioner of Education, "about adopting any mechanical system of producing children like objects. There are so many complicating factors in each child—emotional, psychological, the home background, the sensitivity of teachers—there's danger in trying to turn out children like nuts and bolts or steel pins. Human beings are more complex."...

[Ed. Note: William Spady, "father of outcome-based education," served as consultant to the D.C. schools at this exact time, working out of the U.S. Office of Education's National Institute of Education. His position at the time is listed in his curriculum vitae as "Senior Research Sociologist, 1973–1978." With Spady, Thomas Sticht, associate director for basic skills at NIE, also worked on the failed, Skinnerian D.C. school reform. In addition, the reader is urged to refer to the August 8, 1982 *Washington Post* entry which paraphrases Sticht as follows: "Ending discrimination and changing values are probably more important than reading in moving low income families into the middle class." Of further interest, the same Thomas Sticht was president of Applied Behavioral and Cognitive Sciences, Inc., San Diego, California, and has served on the U.S. Labor Department Secretary's Commission on Achieving Necessary Skills (SCANS).]

DEVELOPMENT OF EDUCATIONAL TECHNOLOGY IN CENTRAL AND EASTERN *Europe Studies: Division of Structures, Content, Methods and Techniques of Education* was published and distributed by United Nations Educational, Scientific, and Cultural Organization (UNESCO: Paris: ED–77/WS/133:English Edition) in November of 1977. The author is including excerpts from the "Section on Methods, Materials and Techniques" so that the reader will see how *America 2000/Goals 2000* restructuring is identical to education in the former Eastern European communist countries. The reader must also remember that American education is under the direction of UNESCO due to our membership in the United Nations. Excerpts follow:

> The development of educational technology in the Central and Eastern European countries, as commissioned by the UNESCO Secretariat, is summarised on the basis of the oral and written information supplied by the countries having attended the Budapest International Seminar on Educational Technology in 1976. The countries involved are as follows: People's Republic of Bulgaria, Socialist Republic of Czechoslovakia, Republic of Finland, Republic of Greece, Socialist Federal Republic of Yugoslavia, People's Republic of Poland, People's Republic of Hungary, German Democratic Republic, Union of Soviet Socialist Republics. Data were also supplied by the Socialist Republic of Rumania which could not participate in the Seminar.
>
> The factors exercising a decisive influence on the present standards of the application of educational technology and the strategies and rate of its further spread in the countries listed above are as follows:
>
> a. the overwhelming majority of the countries represented (8 out of 10) are socialist states;
>
> b. except for the Soviet Union and Finland, the nations concerned can be classified into the category of fairly developed countries from the technological point of view.
>
> On the basis of the above factors some of the specific characteristics of the development of educational technology will be underlined. It follows from the essence of the socialist structure of the state in the countries concerned, except Finland and Greece, that their educational system is centralized. This creates an extremely favourable situation for central state measures designed to modernize education. The socialist state possesses the means necessary for education... for the widespread use of methodology based on solid technological foundations and of the media and means of educational technology.... In a situation in which millions of students learn and hundreds of thousands of educationalists teach, on the basis of unified curricula, decisions involving the development of the method to be adopted in education and of the media and aids of educational technology call for very thorough preparatory work....
>
> The socialist countries also have a substantial advantage from the aspect of the development of educational technology because the training and in-service training of teachers rest on a uniform basis. In addition, curricula are uniform in the individual countries and for the different types of schools harmony between the curricular activities and the development of educational technology can be therefore established comparatively easily.

[Ed. Note: A flow chart on page 11 of the study includes under "Factors Influencing the Introduction of Educational Technology" all the components found in American educational restructuring as follows: Adequate Curricula; System of Objectives; Systems of Means of Assessment; Media System; Ensuring Appropriate Facilities (school building, hardware, media); Adequately Trained Teachers (basic training, in-service/further training/information); Research and Development; and International Cooperation.]

1978

PROFESSOR BENJAMIN BLOOM, THE "FATHER" OF MASTERY LEARNING AND developer of the Taxonomy of Educational Objectives, presented a paper entitled "New Views of the Learner: Implications for Instruction and Curriculum" at the 1978 Association for the Supervision and Curriculum Development (ASCD) Annual Conference. The paper was published in ASCD's *Educational Leadership* April 1978 issue (Vol. 35, #7). The following quote explains clearly the reasoning behind UNESCO's requirement that member states, including the United States, incorporate UNESCO's lifelong learning philosophy into their education policies:

> Continuing Learning
>
> Throughout the world, the instruction and curriculum in the schools is being studied to determine its long-term contribution to continuing learning throughout life. The Edgar Faure (UNESCO) report "Learning to Be" has had great influence on this thinking. The Faure report (Faure, 1972) stresses the many changes taking place in all societies and the difficulties individuals have in adjusting to rapid change in the society, in their work, and in their lives. Since, the report continues, it is virtually impossible to anticipate and plan for the changes that will take place, the only adaptive mechanism people have to adjust to and cope with these changes is their ability and interest in continuing learning throughout life....
>
> We, who are responsible for the learning of our students for a ten-to-sixteen-year period, must extend our sights beyond the period that our students are in the schools or colleges. Until we do this and until it becomes a part of our curriculum planning, we will neglect those objectives of education that relate to the entire life of the individual. (pp. 574–575)

[Ed. Note: It is important to recall Bloom's definition of education: "to change the thoughts, actions, and feelings of students." In other words, the above recommendation very simply calls for lifelong brainwashing.]

IN THE AUGUST 1978 ISSUE OF *THE NATIONAL EDUCATOR* BARBARA MORris, editor of *The Barbara Morris Report* and author of many books related to education including her most recent book, *The Great American Con Game*,[12] reported on a speech given at the University of Illinois by Mary F. Berry, assistant secretary in the U.S. Office of Education (1977), regarding Chinese education. The following excerpts from Morris's report are too important to leave out of this book:

> Indeed, what does the U.S.A. stand to learn? Let's take a look.
>
> Red China has eliminated testing and grades. The U.S. is rapidly going the same route. Testing is being downgraded and scoffed at, and grades, where they do exist are just about meaningless.
>
> For the Red Chinese, according to Ms. Berry, truth is a relative concept. In the U.S. schools students are taught the same thing in "values clarification." It's called situation ethics and it means it's okay to lie or cheat or steal or kill when it suits your purpose.
>
> In Red China, according to Ms. Berry, education must serve the masses. Ditto the U.S. Only the semantics are different here. In the U.S. education

is not designed for the benefit of individuals, but for society. "Society" or "masses"—what's the difference?

In Red China, according to Ms. Berry, education must be combined with productive labor and starts at six years of age, with children working at least one hour a day producing voice boxes for dolls. At the middle school level, children make auto parts as part of the school day. We are not at this low level, but Secretary Berry frankly admits, "We will draw on the Chinese model...." We are fast approaching the Chinese model. We have work/study programs and the U.S. Office of Education is working on development of Lifelong Learning programs—another Chinese import. Such programs will enable people to work and study their entire lives for the benefit of the state.

Ms. Berry admitted U.S. Lifelong Learning programs are indeed drawn on the Chinese experience, that such programs are expected to meet "needs for intellectual fulfillment and social growth. It is here that the Chinese have set the pattern for the world to follow, and it is here that American higher education may have its last, best opportunity for growth."

Secretary Berry lamented that the U.S. is only slowly moving into Lifelong Learning, but that "The community college system with its nonconventional enrollment, is one harbinger of change. The traditional extension program is another.... But we have to go beyond them and bring four year institutions and secondary institutions, as well as private instructional facilities into the Lifelong Learning movement."

Ms. Berry is not talking about the future when she recommends radical proposals for U.S. education. A meeting of the National Council for the Social Studies, held in Cincinnati last November, featured several presentations on Communist Chinese education as a model for U.S. education. In one such presentation, teachers learned how the Red Chinese educational system "is related to achievement of national goals and citizenship preparation... how cultural activities and recreational pastimes provide a vehicle for transmitting new social values." Does this help you understand why U.S. schools usually list "worthy use of leisure" or "citizenship education" as a goal of education?

[Ed. Note: Americans, involved in what would seem to be the worthy goal of implementing character, citizenship, or civic education in the government schools or in community groups, or in seeking "common ground" with groups who hold differing views on political, social, and religious issues, should think more than twice before becoming involved in this dangerous dialogue. The reason the dialogue is dangerous is evident when one studies the track record of nations whose citizens have allowed their governments to define morality or good citizenship; i.e., Nazi Germany, the Soviet Union and Red China, to name just a few.]

FIFTH REPORT OF THE NATIONAL COUNCIL ON EDUCATIONAL RESEARCH, funded by the U.S. Office of Education, was published in an issue spanning 1978–1979. The very clear connection drawn between mastery learning and direct instruction, enabling one to understand that they are essentially the same or at least fraternal twins, is the importance of the following excerpt:

> The Learning Research and Development Center (LRDC) at the University of Pittsburgh has developed instructional mastery of learning programs providing individualized instruction in math, science, reading, and early

learning skills. These have been disseminated nationally through Project Follow Through [Direct Instruction/DISTAR] and by Research for Better Schools (RBS). (pp. 28–29)

1979

"Georgia Basic Life Process Skills, ESEA, Title II, Proposed In-structional Time in School Programs," prepared by Lucille G. Jordan, associate state superintendent for Instructional Services of the Georgia Department of Education, was submitted to the U.S. Department of Education for a grant in 1979. The particular curricular programs which received funding under Title II were jointly funded by Exxon Corporation and the U.S. Department of Education. On page 34 of Georgia's grant proposal an extraordinary curriculum graph/chart recommends the following percentages of time be spent at and between 5, 10, 15 and 18 years of age on the following subjects:

> Basic 3 R's: 90% at 5 yrs. Declining to 40% at 10 yrs. Declining to 30% at 15 yrs. Declining to 15% at 18 yrs.
>
> Life Process Skills: (Critical thinking, problem solving, and decision making): 5% at 5 yrs. Increasing to 40% at 10 yrs. Increasing to 70% at 15 yrs. Increasing to 90% at 18 yrs.
>
> Citizenship and Humanities Studies: 30% at 5 yrs. Increasing to 40% at 10 yrs. Increasing to 70% at 15 yrs. Increasing to 90% at 18 yrs.
>
> Science and Technology: 25% at 5 yrs. Increasing to 28% at 10 yrs. Increasing to 30% at 15 yrs. Increasing to 55% at 18 yrs.
>
> Career Education: 20% at 5 yrs. Increasing to 22% at 10 yrs. Increasing to 30% at 15 yrs. Increasing to 55% at 18 yrs.
>
> Health and Physical Education: 10% for ages 5 through 18 yrs.

[Ed. Note: Please note that the "Basic 3 R's" is the only curriculum area targeted for decrease in time spent on instruction. An official of the Georgia School Boards Association cited this graph as being representative of Bloom's *Taxonomy*. Also, why would Exxon, who was in the early 1980s one of the major corporations complaining about illiteracy and workers who are not educated in basic academics, have funded a program guaranteed to water down basic academics? (In a 1976 speech NEA President Catherine Barrett recommended teaching basic skills in only one fourth of the school day.)]

The U.S. Congress fulfilled President Jimmy Carter's promise to the National Education Association by voting for a U.S. Department of Education in 1979. Now the United States which, heretofore, had been represented at international conferences as the unenlightened member of the crowd (no ministerial/socialist status), could join the "big boys" of the international community: the "big boys" being those countries who, since World War II, had been represented at these policy-planning conferences by ministers of education. Interestingly enough, the majority of teacher members of the National Education Association were opposed to the creation of the U.S. Department of Education.

The new Cabinet-level department allowed the former Bureau of Research under the National Institute of Education to become the Office of Educational Research and Improvement (OERI), which would be closely linked to the Paris, France-based Center for Educational Research and Innovation (CERI), part of the United Nations' Office of Economic Cooperation and Development (OECD). OERI's assistant secretary would attend OECD/ CERI meetings at which he would receive his "marching orders" related to international restructuring efforts and programs, all of which were either being implemented or would be implemented in the future in the United States—Effective School Research, site-based management, school-to-work, community education, Concerns-Based Adoption Model (CBAM), etc.

A STUDY OF SCHOOLING IN THE UNITED STATES BY JOHN GOODLAD, PH.D., dean of the Graduate School of Education, University of California, Los Angeles and associated with the Institute for Development of Educational Activities (I.D.E.A., funded by Kettering Foundation), was compiled in 1979 after being researched over a period of several years. Under Dr. Goodlad's direction, trained investigators went into communities in most regions of the country. The sample of schools studied was enormously diverse in regard to size, family income, and racial composition of the student body. The result of the landmark report was *A Place Called School: Prospects for the Future* (McGraw-Hill: New York, 1984) by Goodlad.

In *A Place Called School*, Goodlad proposed pushing high school graduation back to age 16 and having all students take a core curriculum until then. A new "fourth phase of education" would combine work, study, and community service to help ease students' transition into careers, higher education, and adult responsibilities. The following three books were additionally commissioned to be written as a result of this project:

(1) *Schooling for a Global Age*, James Becker, Editor (1979), in the preface for which Dr. Goodlad made the following statement which has contributed to the development of parent-school partnerships:

> Parents and the general public must be reached, also. Otherwise, children and youth enrolled in globally-oriented programs may find themselves in conflict with values assumed in the home. And then the education institution frequently comes under scrutiny and must pull back.

(2) *Communities and Their Schools*, Don Davies, Editor (1981), in which the history of community education at the national and international levels (China, Tanzania, etc.) was covered and the participatory democratic operation of our schools and communities was recommended (government by unelected councils).

(3) *Arts and the Schools*, Jerome J. Hausman, Editor (1980), in which the role of the arts in schools and in society was examined and then the focus shifted to the needs of the individual. *Arts* addressed curricular issues involved in designing and implementing school arts programs and, again, actual programs are discussed and analyzed. The policy implications of implementing the programs described in the book are then discussed along with change strategies for moving from rhetoric to reality.

The four books were published by McGraw Hill. The study itself was funded by the National Institute of Education, U.S. Office of Education and the following foundations: Danforth; Ford; International Paper; The JDR 3rd Fund; Martha Holden Jennings Foundation; Charles Stewart Mott Foundation; Needmor Fund; Pedamorphosis, Inc.; Rockefeller Foundation; and Spencer Foundation. The Advisory Committee for *A Study of Schooling* included the following persons: Ralph W. Tyler, chairman; Gregory Anrig; Stephen K. Bailey; Lawrence A. Cremin; Robert K. Merton; and Arthur Jefferson. The study was conducted under the auspices of the Institute for Development of Educational Activities, Inc. (IDEA) and The Laboratory in School and Community Education, Graduate School of Education, University of California, Los Angeles.

[Ed. Note: In a telephone conversation with a representative of McGraw Hill Publishers in 1982, this writer was informed that all four books were provided to the fifty state education commissioners/superintendents. These four books provide an accurate picture of the role played by the tax-exempt foundations and federal government in the restructuring/social engineering of American society and schools to accommodate the perceived "needs" of the 21st century.]

SENATOR JACOB JAVITS (NY) REQUESTED THAT MR. ARTHUR LIPPER'S address to the World Council on Gifted and Talented Children be printed in the *Congressional Record*, September 5, 1979 (pp. 11904–11905). Senator Javits said in his introduction to the text of the speech:

> Mr. President, the gifted and talented children of our Nation have long been of continuing interest to me for they represent the future leadership of the United States. Last month, in Jerusalem, the World Council on Gifted and Talented Children held its Third Biennial Conference to discuss international cooperative efforts on behalf of the gifted, and to consider research and exchange programs to promote this most precious human resource.... At the Jerusalem conference, Arthur Lipper, III, an investment banker... and great friend of the gifted and talented... forcefully presented the idea that the development of the gifted represents the best hope for future peace and stability in the international political realm.... I urge my colleagues to consider carefully his remarks, and I ask that the text of Mr. Lipper's address to the World Council on Gifted and Talented Children be printed in the Record.

The following excerpts from Lipper's speech reflect a total disregard for the gifted and talented children as individuals who might be capable of deciding for themselves what they wish to do or become. It focuses instead on their "use" by the state to obtain predetermined global goals:

> Some years ago I read the following statement in a school publication:

> > One of America's most tragic wastes of natural resources is the loss of potential for social contribution which is inherent in economically deprived, gifted children.

> > Properly identified at a sufficiently early age, through culture-free, non-verbal testing, the very young child can be provided with the environment,

economic and motivational support necessary for full development as a positive social contributor.

Without such early identification, the socio-economic pressure imposed upon the economically deprived child who possesses superior cognitive ability is likely to result in either a "dropping out" or only a desire to achieve improved personal life style. The chosen or available means of obtaining a better life style may not be socially desirable. Therefore their truly constructive potential, from the standpoint of society [the State, ed.], may be forever lost.

These thoughts seem to me to be applicable to all societies and especially to those less fortunate than America's. Specifically analyzed they are:

1) Identified early enough, poor but gifted children can be given medical, financial and emotional support which probably will lead to the development of positive social attitudes.

2) Not identified and assisted the kids may either not achieve their potential or may use their talents solely for the purpose of bettering their own lives regardless of the means employed or the effects on others.

It is interesting to note the number of proudly proclaimed programs for gifted child identification and development which many of the Socialist and Communist countries have as a stated and de-facto matter of public policy. It is not strange that the capitalist countries, so quick to make use of all other "natural" resources—including the labor of their own and other countries—have been slower to recognize and secure the benefits accruing from the development of their own gifted children.

Perhaps the wealthy nations have not yet sensed the compelling need for broad social progress, based upon the future contribution of the gifted, as have some of the non-capitalist countries.

In closing, Mr. Lipper makes some recommendations, the most alarming of which follows:

Establishment of boarding schools (publicly funded) to house those identified gifted children whose existing home life is non-constructive in terms of their development.

[Ed. Note: Mr. Lipper, in his fervent desire to implement world socialism, seems to have forgotten that individuals, regardless of race, religion, talent, or income, should not be considered property of the State (human resources, human capital, etc.) to be molded and manipulated for the benefit of society as a whole (the State). Also, what and whose criteria will be employed to determine whether "home life is non-constructive"?]

"K–12 Competency-Based Education Comes to Pennsylvania" by John H. Sandberg, director of teacher education for Carnegie-Mellon University in Pittsburgh, was published in the October 1979 issue of *Phi Delta Kappan*. Excerpts from the article follow:

It is too late to stop Project '81, which will run its course and probably will soon be forgotten, but one may hope that other states will think hard before embarking on similar projects.... While it is possible that I misunderstood the meaning or intent of this "major goal" ["gain the skills and knowledge they will need as adults"], it strikes me as being unattainable on its face.... I would argue that we cannot "see that students acquire the competencies they need to be successful in the adult world" because we don't know what they are now much less what they will be ten years from now.... Exchanging courses, credits, and Carnegie Units for "newly defined competencies" will not eliminate this fundamental problem....

Finally, in the case of students who are known to be college bound and are locked into a curriculum that is dictated primarily by college requirements (not life-role expectancies), what is going to give? Will physics give way to lawn mower repair? Chemistry to cooking? Trigonometry to tile setting? Will it really make any difference for these students what the state board requires for graduation as long as Harvard wants math through calculus and two years of a foreign language?... I would be happy to settle for a short list of competencies if I thought we could handle them: Teach children how to read, to write, to do arithmetic, to draw, make music, and to get along with each other.

We are not doing these few things for enough kids now, so perhaps this is what we should be working on instead of making new lists of things we won't know how to do.... I applaud the emphasis that Project '81 gives to making better use of educational resources in the community. But as a Blueprint for structuring public education and for measuring its products, the competency-based approach embodied in Project '81 strikes me as totally ridiculous. A true skeptic might argue that Project '81 may be safely ignored on the ground that the Pennsylvania Department of Education is incompetent to chew, much less swallow, what it has attempted to bite off. Like other grandiose efforts to reform the schools, the project may generate some wind and heat and several billion pieces of paper and then go away, leaving all but the 12 pilot school districts untouched.

Nevertheless, the Pennsylvania Department of Education has already demonstrated, with competency-based teacher education, its competence to effect change—or at least the illusion of change—on a large scale. Project '81 is a much more extensive undertaking whose potential for mischief is incalculably greater. The mischief can occur if Pennsylvanians do not take a long, hard look at where Project '81 is taking them.

INFORMATION REGARDING THE PRELIMINARY PLANNING FOR SCHOOL-BASED clinics was revealed in the October 22, 1979 issue of *Nation's Schools Report* which, under the section "Schools Can Offer Health Services," stated the following:

> Schools with concentrations of Medicaid-eligible students can qualify for federal money if they set up screening and referral programs. A joint effort by the Office of Education and the Health Care Financing Administration could make available to schools some of the $46 million that will probably be spent on screening Medicaid children.
>
> Historically, schools have been excluded from such payments, said Robert Heneson-Walling, in the office of deputy commissioner of the Bureau of Education of the Handicapped. But regulations proposed jointly by the two agencies and published in the *Federal Register* October 4 would allow schools to do the screening and even provide treatment and get paid for it.
>
> "It's never been clear that schools might take this initiative," he told *Nation's Schools Report*. To help interested school officials get started, the two departments will publish a manual in November which will cover rules-

of-thumb for officials to decide whether to undertake the screening, how to do it, and how to get help from state and local agencies.

"It's not an either/or situation for the school district," said Heneson-Walling. There are seven or eight degrees of involvement a school might undertake. Some schools are already involved in extensive health screening services, because of requirements of the *Education for All Handicapped Children Act*, so it would be a natural step for them to become primary health delivery centers. (p. 6)

[Ed. Note: The United States model was given wide publicity at the United Nations/UNICEF-sponsored International Year of the Child Conference. The U.S. Department of Health, Education and Welfare served as co-sponsor of the International Year of the Child's program in the United States. For a glimpse into the future role of the schools in providing health care services turn to the 1999 entry for the "Little Red Riding Hood" version of the government/private sector initiatives outlined in the U.S. Department of Education/U.S. Department of Health and Human Services publication *Together We Can*. The 1999 Congressional proposal to completely fund the *Individuals with Disabilities in Education Act* would go a long way toward universalizing these activities. Increased school violence in the late 1990s is also leading to increases in the number of school psychologists who can be used for "early screening."]

"Big School Changes Proposed" was printed in the Bangor (Maine) *Daily News* on November 30, 1979. The article covered what could easily be described as futuristic plans for Vermont public education. It stated in part:

> Montpelier, VT—A blue ribbon commission has recommended a radical restructuring of education in Vermont with year-round, ungraded schools and a policy of allowing some students to drop out at age 13. In addition, the commission suggested creation of a 4,000-student, residential school for students ages 4 through 19. The state-run school would be a center for educational research and teacher training.... The commission recommends students should be permitted to drop out of formal schooling at age 13, as long as they get a job or enroll in an alternative training program.

[Ed. Note: This extraordinary plan for radical restructuring seemed beyond the pale in 1979. However, it doesn't seem so out of reach in 1999 when most of its recommendations are being introduced nationwide. Year-round school has been proposed in many locales, being adopted in some in 1999. Boarding schools have been openly proposed by former Speaker of the House Newt Gingrich, but have not been widely embraced. However, the concept of allowing students to drop out at age 13 has its parallel in school-to-work efforts which force students to select a career emphasis by the end of eighth grade.]

In the November 1979 issue of *Educational Leadership*, monthly publication of the Association for Supervision and Curriculum Development, "Mastery Learning: The Current State of the Craft" by James Block was published. Excerpts follow:

> Indeed, with the help of dedicated practitioners and administrators, innovative teacher training institutions, progressive national and international educational organizations (ASCD, NEA, NASA, UNESCO, IEA), leading educational publishers (McGraw-Hill, SRA, Westinghouse Learning Corp., Random House), and powerful news media (*The New York Times*, CBS), Mastery Learning has helped reshape the face of contemporary educational practice, research, and theory.... Entire school districts throughout North America (Chicago, Denver, D.C., New Orleans, Vancouver) are actively testing the value of Mastery Learning for their particular educational situation.

[Ed. Note: The above quote by James Block calls to mind the 1921 entry in this book which chronicles the establishment of the Council on Foreign Relations. In that entry a quotation from *Propaganda* by Edward Bernays, Sigmund Freuds's nephew, also remarks on the power of opinion to move an agenda forward:

> It remains a fact in almost every act of our daily lives, whether in the sphere of politics or business, in our social conduct or our ethical thinking, we are dominated by... small number of persons... and technical means have been invented and developed by which opinion may be regimented.]

SUPER-LEARNING BY SHEILA OSTRANDER AND LYNN SCHROEDER, WITH NANCY Ostrander, (Dell Publishing Co., Inc.: New York, 1979) was published. Beneath the title on the cover is an explanation of *Super-Learning* as "New stress-free, fast learning methods you can use to develop supermemory and improve business and sports performance." In reality this "learning technique" is an updated version of ancient practices drawn from many religions and a grab-bag of philosophies, most presented to the chosen rhythms of certain music. The following are excerpts from the book:

> Georgi Lozanov (Lo-san-ov), a Bulgarian doctor and psychiatrist, who didn't set out to be an educator... did set out, following the old adage, to study the nature of man, of the human being in all its potential. Like just about everybody else, he concluded that we're only using a fraction of our capabilities. Lozanov devised ways to open the reserves of the mind and, as a doctor, put them to work to improve the body, to heal mental and physical disease. But in investigating what the whole human being can do, he couldn't help being drawn into creative and intuitive areas. Then still investigating, almost by necessity, he became one of the leading parapsychologists in the communist world. At the same time, Lozanov realized that with his new techniques, the average person could develop supermemory, could learn factual information with unheard-of-ease. (p. 9)
>
> ...Among others, we were going to talk to a Bulgarian scientist, Dr. Georgi Lozanov, who had investigated a number of people with extraordinary mental abilities like Keuni's. Lozanov had come to claim that supermemory was a natural human ability. Not only can anyone develop it, he said, but one can do it with ease. To prove his point there were supposedly thousands of people

in Bulgaria and the Soviet Union who were well on their way to acquiring supermemory of their own. (p.14)

...Dr. Lozanov greeted us in his office. Like the brilliant flowers in the garden outside, the room was awash with bright, vivid colors. As we'd already discovered at the conference in Moscow, Lozanov had a "holistic" sense of humor and a "cosmic" laugh like the Maharishi of TM fame. A lithe, compact man with warm brown eyes and a great cloud of curly, graying hair, he could be as kinetic as a handball one minute and deeply serene the next. "Suggestology can revolutionize teaching," he asserted. "Once people get over preconceived ideas about limitations, they can be much more. No longer is a person limited by believing that learning is unpleasant; that what he learns today he will forget tomorrow; that learning deteriorates with age.".....

He grew philosophical, "Education is the most important thing in the world. The whole of life is learning—not only in school. I believe that developing this high motivation—which comes through the technique—can be of the greatest importance to humanity.".....

"What exactly is the technique of suggestology?" we asked. To create this new "ology," Lozanov and his co-workers had drawn from an almost dizzying array of specialties: mental yoga, music, sleep-learning, physiology, hypnosis, autogenics, parapsychology, drama, to name some. Suggestology's deepest roots lay in the system of Raja Yoga. "There is really nothing new about suggestology," Lozanov explained. "The application is the new thing.".....

Lozanov's suggestology is basically "applied" altered states of consciousness for learning, healing, and intuitive development. (p. 17)

[Ed. Note: Lozanov's methodology has been implemented in school systems across the country—including Henry M. Levin's Accelerated Schools Project participants—and promoted as being physically healthful and psychically helpful. Its roots, as pointed out in the quotes above, are in techniques associated with religion and mind control. In the appendix to *Super-Learning* a "Recap" is written, part of which this writer wishes to leave with the reader so that its connection to what is being presented to teachers and parents in 1999 under the guise of "research-based" theory and practice can be more readily understood:

How does it work? A very specific kind of music has a psychophysicial effect and creates a relaxed, meditative state in the body. Physiological research showed this particular music slows body rhythms to more efficient levels. This music-induced relaxation brings health benefits. It overcomes fatigue and enhances physical and emotional well-being. It's a bit like mantra meditation for it is a mind/body link that helps open up inner awareness. Physiological research also shows this calmed state of the body facilitates mental functioning and learning. The body uses *less* energy, so there's *more* for the mind. [emphasis in original] This particular music induces alert relaxation—alert mind, relaxed body.

How can you, at will, retrieve what you perceive? The answer is rhythm. The connection is made through synchronizing rhythms. Data to be learned is chanted with intonations in rhythm in time to the music. The person learning breathes along rhythmically in a relaxed state. So data, intonations, music, breathing, and body rhythms are all synchronized to a specific rhythmic cycle. The rhythm, intonations, music, and breathing make links with the conscious mind. Harmonized rhythms strengthen the information signal. Conscious awareness of unconscious perceptions is opened up through this link so you become aware of what's in your memory bank.

Finally, superlearning is about learning to learn. There is a snowballing effect once you begin to use the techniques. How do you go about doing superlearning on your own? The process is very simple. In advance, get the music, organize your material and tape it, reading it aloud at slow-paced intervals over the specified music.

Then, just relax and listen to your material as you breathe along to the music.

The roots of the above "learning" process grow deep in the mire of the ancient practices that have come to be called "New Age." The reader is urged to remember the rhythmic chants and sing-song recitations being offered as direct instruction "learning." Again, some of the therapeutic benefits from music and what is called "music therapy" are most often observed among the mentally ill and, for a lack of another designation, the learning disabled. The same areas from which most of the "research-based" data—often called "scientific"—draw their reported "success."]

Steps to Better Writing: A Systematic Approach to Expository Writing by Gene Stanford (Holt, Rinehart and Winston, Inc.: New York, 1979) was published. An exercise from this book is an example of the humanistic influence exerted in a writing textbook format:

> EXERCISE C. In each of the introductory paragraphs below, underline the thesis sentence. Then indicate in the blank which construction (funnel or contrast) was used. Finally, number the factors in the preview of main supporting points....
>
> [Sample paragraph] 2. Too often parents think the way to rear a child is to give him guidance in the proper way to think and act. This "guidance" too often becomes an actual molding of his personality to suit the parent, as is seen in parental lectures beginning with the old clichés, "If I were you I would..." or "When I was your age I...." These parents, while they may have the good of the child at heart, are nevertheless making a grave mistake by trying to compel him to act or think in certain ways. What the teen needs instead is a type of love which gives him the freedom and confidence to develop his own opinions in matters such as religion, morality, and choice of friends. (p. 87)

[Ed. Note: The 1991 article entitled "Seniors' Church Attendance" from *Education Week* (June 12, 1991) shows how successful this type of "academic" curriculum has been in changing our children's values.]

Endnotes:

1   T.I.L.L., 67 East Shore Road, Huntington, N.Y. 11743.

2   See 1998 entry concerning Newt Gingrich's statements about the future of textbooks. Also, see 1974 entry for *A Performance Accountability System for School Administrators* by T.H. Bell.

3   This quote is taken from Danielson's 67-page booklet, *Practitioner's Implementation Hand-book [Series]: The Outcome-Based Curriculum, 2nd Ed.*, by Charlotte Danielson (Outcome Associates, Princeton, NJ, 1992). Charlotte Danielson is presently employed by the Educational Testing Service, Princeton, New Jersey.

4   The Maine Facilitator Center was funded by the U.S. Department of Education and its primary role was to disseminate federally funded National Diffusion Network programs. Since 1994 the NDN has been defunded and its functions have been taken over by the U.S. Department of Education's regional laboratories.

5   This particular "who shall survive" activity is still in use in 1990s NDN programs.

6   The National Diffusion Network catalog, *Programs that Work*, may be purchased for $16.95 by calling Sopris West at 1–303–615–2829.

7   Audiocassette of Lessinger's speech (#612–20129) can be ordered from: ASCD, 1703 North Beauregard St., Alexandria, VA 22311–1714.

8   Sayer, George. *Jack: A Life of C.S. Lewis* (Crossway Books: Wheaton, 1994).

9   Lewis, C.S. "Our English Syllabus" in *Rehabilitations and Other Essays* (Oxford University Press: London, 1939).

10   Ibid.

11   Hooper, Walter, Ed. "Learning in War-Time," in *The Weight of Glory and Other Addresses* (Macmillan Publishing Co., New York, 1980).

12   See Resources page in the Internet version for ordering information for Barbara Morris's *The Great American Con Game*.

THE "EFFECTIVE" EIGHTIES

"Producing a definite or desired *result* [emphasis added]," the first definition for the word "effective" found in *Webster's Dictionary*, is the appropriate definition for the word "effective" as it is used in the title Effective School Research (ESR) or Effective Schools (ES)—which will characterize much of "the effective eighties." This is particularly true as it relates to the Skinnerian "method," often referred to as "What Works" education, more commonly known as outcome/performance/results-based education and mastery learning/direct instruction. The evidence which links OBE to ESR is irrefutable: "Outcome-Based Education incorporates the findings of the Effective Schools Research, linking them together into a comprehensive and powerful model," stated Charlotte Danielson, M.A. in her *Practitioner's Implementation Handbook [Series]: The Outcome-Based Curriculum.*[1]

Whether Effective Schools Research applied to education has been truly "effective" lies in the eye of the beholder and in the beholder's definition of the purpose of education.[2] Disturbing reports continue to surface regarding steep declines in academic test scores in schools which have restructured using the various components of Effective Schools Research. These scores are from schools which, while using ESR, have not yet shifted from norm-referenced (competitive) tests—which compare students' results amongst their peers and which use "A-B-C-D-F" grading—to performance-based (non-competitive) teach-to-the-test assessments. Examples are the "open book test" and "authentic

175

assessment"—which have the students competing against no one but them-selves, giving them as much time as necessary to "master" the competencies.

Once the non-competitive, performance-based assessments are in place, the scores will naturally go up, thus allowing the social change agents to breathe a sigh of relief. The "low test score cat" will have been shoved back into his bag and the media will shout from the rooftops how well our children are do-ing on the new performance-based assessments! As usual, everyone will go back to sleep believing all is well—if they were ever awake to the problem in the first place.

The pre-non-competitive, performance-based academic test score decline should come as no surprise to the change agents in charge of "effective" schools. The "father" of the Effective Schools Research method, or Skinnerian mastery learning, the late Prof. Benjamin Bloom, said in his 1981 book *All Our Children Learning*: "The purpose of education and the schools is to change the thoughts, feelings and actions of students." An even more astonishing statement was made in *The Effective School Report* by one of the leading change agents, Thomas A. Kelly, Ph.D.: "The brain should be used for processing, not storage." With this educational emphasis, academic test scores could have done nothing but decline. If there is anyone reading this book who questions the validity of this writer's claim that America has been "deliberately dumbed down," I urge them to keep these quotes in mind.

Let me pose the following question: How could the writer of this book have written this book had her brain not been used for storage? Could the answer to that question be the reason why the social change agents do not want the brain to be used for storage?

The educationists understand full well what they are doing, since the use of Skinnerian/Pavlovian operant conditioning (mastery learning/direct instruc-tion) does not allow for the transfer of information. All they need is a brain which knows how to immediately process predetermined bits and pieces of information—often nothing more than symbols, simple words or paragraphs, the knowledge of which can be easily measured—as those pieces of information relate to workforce training or a menial job; i.e., pushing a button like a pigeon in Skinner's experiments was trained to push the lever to get its kernel of corn.

That is *not* learning; that is *training* to the point of automaticity, brought about by the above-mentioned animal training. Neither is this training the same as rote learning or memorization. Rote learning or memorization requires storage of information in a brain which has used some reflective thinking to devise a method to recall it. Reflective thinking is essential for learning, allowing the brain to spend time examining the essence of the material with which it is presented.

If Bloom's and Kelly's quotes define what those in charge of educational restructuring are looking for in terms of "results," those same educationists should not be at all surprised or concerned about low test scores. All they have to do is wait for the new performance-based assessments to be put into place nationwide; after which the public—some of whom have been vociferously opposed to outcome-based education—will get off their backs.

Activities related to education in "the effective eighties" were not geared to improving the academic standing of our children. Quite the contrary; every single major government- or foundation-funded activity had as its goal implementation of a global workforce training agenda.

In 1984 Secretary T.H. Bell approved a grant in the amount of $152,530 to the Far West Laboratory for Educational Research and Development (now known as Ed West) at which William Spady was the director. This grant was to carry out a project entitled "Excellence in Instructional Delivery Systems." The cover letter from the Utah superintendent of schools to Secretary T.H. Bell to which the application for grant funding was attached said, "This [the research as a result of the grant] will make it possible to put Outcome-Based Education in place, not only in Utah, but in all schools of the nation." The final report (evaluation) to the U.S. Department of Education regarding the results of this project stated:

> The four models of instructional organization outlined in this casebook are difficult programs to implement. The practices of the ten schools described in the case studies are indeed commendable. Yet we do not offer these ten case studies as "exemplary schools" deserving emulation.[3]

So, what did the change agents do? They put OBE "into every school in the nation."

Such misuse of taxpayer dollars is waste, fraud, and abuse which cries out for a Congressional investigation. Obviously, the intentions of those involved in this grant had nothing to do with the purpose of the project spelled out in the grant applicaton: "To make available to America's educators practical information about what really works well, why it works well, and how it can be made to work well in their local sites." (pp. 6–7) The real purpose of this project was to propose a radical redesign of the nation's education system from one based on inputs to one based on outputs; from one oriented toward the learning of academic content to one based on performance of selected skills, necessary for the implementation of school-to-work, a redesign thoroughly discussed in this book.

Dr. Brian Rowan, a sociologist who served as co-principal investigator with the above Robert Burns on this most fraudulent of federal grants—Utah's "Excellence in Instructional Delivery Systems Project"—explained clearly how deceptive are the claims of those who promote OBE and Effective School Research in a paper entitled "Shamanistic Rituals in Effective Schools." (See the Internet version for Appendix XXVI.) In presenting his paper before the American Educational Research Association prior to his participation in the Utah grant evaluation, Rowan knew full well the project misrepresented itself even before he participated. But, to give credit where credit is due, Rowan at least put in writing the truth about OBE and Effective Schools Research; a truth, which, unfortunately, was made available to only a very small segment of the educational establishment and has remained hidden from the public.

The "effective eighties" saw President Ronald Reagan, who had accused the Soviet Union of being an "evil empire," signing education agreements with the Soviet Union—agreements which are still in effect—and setting up a Task Force on Private Sector Initiatives in the White House which, in effect, started the ball rolling for public-private partnerships (corporate fascism) which are at the heart of the Carnegie Corporation/Marc Tucker/New American School Development Corporation's school-to-work agenda. It is ironic that the U.S. Department of Education, under the stewardship of a Republican administration, effectively transformed the essential character of the nation's public schools from "teaching"—the most traditional and conservative role of schools—to "workforce training"—perceived as liberal and "progressive."

Secretary T.H. Bell fired Edward Curran, a traditional educator who headed up the National Institute of Education and who recommended to President Reagan that NIE—the heart of the "rot" in education—be abolished. Abolishing NIE required only that Secretary Bell give his approval, while abolishing the Department of Education—an election promise President Reagan had made which was incorporated into the Republican Party Platform—required the difficult to obtain approval of Congress. Once Ed Curran was gone, there was no further resistance to the plans of those members of the administration and their corporate cronies (school-business partnerships) who wished to transform the nation's schools from academics to the polytech education being implemented today.

As a conservative Republican, it has not been easy to come to the above conclusion regarding the role of the Republican Party in the "deliberate dumbing down" of America. At the same time, I must add that it is very likely the Democratic Party would have been even more steadfast in implementing the same agenda, had it been in a position to do so. This march to destruction seems to join all forces under its banner.

1980

SCHOOLING FOR A GLOBAL AGE EDITED BY JAMES BECKER (McGRAW HILL: New York, 1980) was published. The preface by Professor John Goodlad is excerpted here:

> Parents and the general public must be reached also [taught a global perspective]. Otherwise, children and youth enrolled in globally-oriented programs may find themselves in conflict with values assumed in the home. And then the educational institution frequently comes under scrutiny and must pull back.

[ddd]

"POLICY ABOUT POLICY: SOME THOUGHTS AND PROJECTIONS" BY LUVERN L. Cunningham was published in the November 1980 issue of *The Executive Review* (Institute for School Executives: The University of Iowa, Vol. 1., No. 2). A footnote on page 1 stated, "The paper was the Walter D. Cocking Lecture presented at the 34th Annual National Convention of Professors of Educational Administration in August, 1980, at Old Dominion University." Some excerpts from Cunningham's "Policy about Policy" follow:

> Local school officials and their constituencies will be facing several critical policy matters in this decade (some new, some enduring). These issues will test severely the structures and processes of policy making within local districts.... Local and state authorities will soon have to develop fresh policies in regard to: the first four years of life; life-long learning; secondary education; equity; classroom control and discipline; global education; languages; human resource development; incentives; testing; and resource acquisition and allocation. I would hope, therefore, that a good many boards would develop policy about policy....
>
> The object of my concern is the improvement of practice within the local units of government (local school districts) where educational policy is developed....
>
> The structure and processes of local district governance and management have changed little over the past century. In many places they appear to be creaking and groaning at the seams and at least warrant inspection if not reform....
>
> Additional steps must be taken to permit better integration of experts into policymaking.... The new professions of civil strategist and systems analyst demonstrate rather well what I have in mind on a broader scale.

The several proposals for changing the governance and management of local school districts which follow are intended to achieve practical objectives.

(1) Pursue policy development processes which are open to, indeed, require the participation of citizens and professionals.

(2) Extend and intensify the citizen role in education policy development and policy making.

[Ed. Note: The writer has selected the two proposals above in order to emphasize Dr. Cunningham's influence on the dilution and diminution of the role of elected school board members. This is the philosophy which Dr. Cunningham took into Kentucky when he served as a consultant during that state's education reform.

Implementation of the above two policies has been responsible for a subtle, gradual, and unhealthy trend towards the council form of government found in undemocratic, socialist countries. Before we know it, if Americans do not vociferously object to this gradual erosion of the elective process, their towns and cities will be run by unelected citizens who are accountable to absolutely no one, since unelected people cannot be removed from (voted out of) office. This writer has always wondered: If members of our communities want so much to serve the community, why don't they run for office? Why do we see so many people signing up to be members of unelected task forces and councils? Is it because they don't want to run the risk of not winning, or is it that an appointed position is one which requires little or no accountability and they won't have to answer for their mistakes?]

[ddd]

Cunningham continues:

...Yehezkel Dror suggests that for purposes of current policy making, the following elements should be standard features of a preferable policy-making method:

(1) There should be some clarification of values, objectives, and criteria for decision making....

(2) Explicit techniques, such as simulation and the Delphi method, should be used as far as they are appropriate, and knowledge from various disciplines should be brought to bear on the issues involved....

The weight of proposal one is not to locate ways to reduce the interference or meddling on the part of school board members in the everyday administration of the school system. The everyday meddling (or involvement if you prefer) of school board members in administrative matters that occurs across the country is understandable. In fact, board members believe deeply that they are serving their constituents when they interfere and meddle. Administrators often have little understanding of or patience for this sense of responsiveness that board members possess. As a consequence considerable institutional energy goes into disputes over the boundaries of board member and superintendent authority and responsibility.

[ddd]

The work of Dr. Cunningham seems to have laid the groundwork for school site-based management which has reduced the role of elected school board members to rubber stampers of decisions made primarily by school personnel and carefully selected politically correct members of the community. Dr. Cunningham served as a consultant to the State of Kentucky's Education Reform Commission in 1989. The following quotes are taken from a memorandum dated November 2, 1989 from Luvern L. Cunningham and Lila N. Carol of Leadership Development Associates regarding *Preliminary Models of Governance for Kentucky*. The recommendations should come as no surprise to those who have read the above excerpts from Cunningham's 1980 paper.

> Each governance model is designed to facilitate the achievement of equal educational opportunity for every learner enrolled in the public schools of the State of Kentucky.
>
> Model One, "Total Educational Governance System for Lifetime Learning, Structural Features and Highlights"—
>
> Policymaking responsibility for a total educational system including higher education is concentrated in a single Board of Regents. A Chancellor would be selected as the administrative head of a newly integrated system encompassing provisions for lifetime learning. Local school districts would be dissolved and site-based control and management instituted.
>
> This model is a complete system of governance for a state system of education.... It is comprehensive and all inclusive, allowing for a thorough approach to accountability.

[ddd]

> This bureau is the central administrative center for lifetime learning. Lifetime learning is a much larger expectation for each citizen than we have acknowledged through policy in the past. Compulsory education statutes usually bracketed the ages of five through sixteen as our expectation for free public schooling in the United States. Lifetime learning on the other hand suggests a reconsideration of the compulsory education requirements pushing taxpayer responsibility both downward and upward through the age ranges. Obviously lifetime learning has tremendous implications for educational finance moving away from traditional concepts of funding toward new ideas such as individual entitlements to be expended throughout the lifetime. Each citizen would have a lifetime learning account to draw on as needed.

[Ed. Note: For a broad view of what this last paragraph could imply, please see "When Is Assessment Really Assessment?" in the Internet version Appendix XI. Many of Luvern Cunningham's proposals were incorporated into Georgia's application to the New American School Development Corporation entitled "The Next Generation School Project." In the 1999 entry dealing with a letter to the editor in Athens, Georgia, some of the details of Georgia's application—which later became a design which was offered by the Georgia 2000 Partnership for school system status leading to grant receiving and education/business partnering under *Goals 2000*—are stated. The reader should compare that letter's contents to Cunningham's proposals.]

COURSE GOALS COLLECTION WAS COMPLETED IN 1980–81 BY THE U.S. Department of Education's Northwest Regional Educational Laboratory in Portland, Oregon, having been initiated in 1971 as the Tri-County Course Goal Project. According to the price list for the collection, 70,000 copies were in use throughout the United States in 1981. Descriptors within the *Collection* state: "The collection consists of fourteen volumes with 15,000 goals covering every major subject taught in the public schools from K–12."

Course Goals Collection, based on "the theoretical work of Bloom, Tyler, Gagne, Piaget, Krathwohl, Walbesser, Mager, and others," blatantly recommends the use of Mastery Learning when it states: "The K–12 Goals Collection provides a resource for developing diagnostic-prescriptive Mastery Learning approaches, both programmed and teacher managed."

This collection also advocates the use of Management by Objectives and Planning, Programming and Budgeting Systems when it asserts

> Perhaps the greatest need addressed by the project is for a sound basis for accountability in education... assistance such as Planning, Program, Budget and Management systems or even general concepts such as Management by Objectives.

The use of values clarification and behavior modification is also encouraged when the *Goals Collection* points out that

> Value goals of two types are included: those related to processes of values clarification; secondly, those representing values, choices that might be fostered in the context of the discipline.

Goals states under "Content" that there is to be *none* because

> [E]stablished facts change, causing many fact-bound curricula to become obsolete during the approximately five-year lag between their inception and their widespread dissemination, and social mobility and cultural pluralism make it increasingly difficult to identify the important facts.

The Course Goals Collection is evidence of illegal federal involvement in curriculum development. The extent of its use nationwide in 1981 is obvious since 70,000 copies were distributed and there were only approximately 16,000 school districts in the nation. Is it any wonder all states now have the same goals?

Charlotte Danielson, M.A., in the appendix to her *Practitioners Implementation Handbook [series]: The Outcome-Based Curriculum, 2nd Ed.* (Outcomes Associates; Princeton, N.J., 1992) entitled, "Classification System for the School Curriculum" acknowledged her use of *the Course Goals Collection* developed by the Tri-County Development Project. In the "Introduction to Outcome-Based Education" to Danielson's *Handbook* she inextricably connects Outcome-Based Education to Effective Schools Research when she says:

> Outcome-Based Education is a system for the organization and delivery of the instructional program in elementary and secondary schools which *assures success for every student* [emphasis in original]. It incorporates the findings of the Effective Schools Research, linking them together into a comprehen-

sive and powerful model. Educators in outcome-based schools know that if they organize their schools properly, and offer high-quality instruction, all students will succeed with no change in standards. (p. 1)

[Ed. Note: Probably the most important quote involving the above Goals Project—at least as it relates to the definition of scientific, research-based instruction—is one found in Indiana Senator Joan Gubbins's excellent report entitled "Goals and Objectives: Towards a National Curriculum?" prepared for the National Council on Educational Research, September 26, 1986 as part of an investigation of the NWREL Goals Project. On page 16 of her report is the following statement:

> I believe the personal valuing goals (included in the Goals Project) would be more properly classified as behavior modification procedures. Therefore, the Project's definition of behavior modification is illuminating:
>
>> [P]rocedures used in programs of behavior modification or behavioral management are based on principles derived from scientific research (e.g., stimulus-response-reinforcement).

Americans supporting the use of mastery learning, outcome-based education, and direct instruction to teach reading, take heed! When advised that such instruction is "scientific, research-based," remember the above U.S. Department of Education definition!]

1981

"A BROAD-GAUGED RESEARCH/REFORM PLAN FOR SECONDARY EDUCATION— in the Tradition of the Eight-Year Study," proposed by The Project on Alternatives in Education (PAE) in 1981, was submitted for consideration and received funding from the U.S. Department of Education and the National Education Association. The project was conducted by leading American change agents, including Mario D. Fantini, John Goodlad, Ralph Tyler, Ronald S. Brandt, Herbert J. Walberg and Mary Ann Raywid. Explanatory cover sheet of the grant proposal was submitted on "The John Dewey Society" letterhead. PAE called for publicly funded choice schools using "effective school [outcome-based education] research" and principles of the Eight-Year Study. These called for "inculcation of social attitudes, development of effective methods of thinking, social sensitivity, better personal-social adjustment, acquisition of important information, consistent philosophy of life," etc.

IN 1981 *OFFICE OF EDUCATIONAL RESEARCH AND IMPROVEMENT: AN OVERview* was prepared by staff members of the U.S. Department of Education for Assistant Secretary Donald Senese's use at Congressional budget hearings. Excerpts from the paper follow:

> Federal funds account for approximately 10 percent of national expenditures on education. The Federal share of educational research and related activities, however, is 90 percent of the total national investment.

The Committee on Coordinating Educational Information and Research

(CCEIR), Council of Chief State School Officers (CCSSO), in its 1980 Mission Statement defined "research" as:

> For purposes of brevity, the term "educational information and research" will be used to include basic and applied research, development, improvement, evaluation, policy study, information systems development, data reporting and analysis, and the dissemination of knowledge and information gained from such inquiry.

[Ed. Note: In other words, just about everything that goes on in the classrooms of American public schools, with the exception of salaries, school buildings, buses and the purchase of equipment, is either a direct or indirect result of funding by the U.S. Department of Education—as research!

Congress has recognized the federal government's supposed limited authority in education. In 1970, *ESEA: General Education Provisions Act* was amended to include a "Prohibition against Federal Control of Education." This section prohibits the federal government from exercising any "direction, supervision, or control over the curriculum, program of instruction, administration or personnel of any education institution, school, or school system, or over the selection of library resources, textbooks, or other printed or published instructional materials by any educational institution or school system." *The Education Amendments of 1976* extended this provision to all programs in the Education Division of the U.S. Department of Health, Education and Welfare.

Although such a prohibition sounds like a restriction against federal control, in effect it leaves out more than it includes; the most important component of federal control being "research" and "development." Who cares whether the federal government is not allowed to extend its long arm down into the choice of curriculum or the selection of resources? The point is that the federal government itself was involved in the development of that curriculum or those resources, teacher training, test development, etc., at one of its research labs or centers, or paid to have it developed by school systems across the nation.]

ASSOCIATION FOR EDUCATIONAL COMPUTING AND TECHNOLOGY (AECT—A spin-off of the National Education Association) received an $855,282 federal contract for "Project BEST" (Better Education Skills through Technology) in 1981. An explanatory brochure states:

> WHAT IS PROJECT BEST? Project BEST is a cooperative effort involving both the federal, state, and local government and the private sector in the planning and use of modern information technologies to improve the effectiveness of basic skills, teaching and learning.

On a sheet circulated within the U.S. Department of Education as an internal document entitled "Project BEST Dissemination Design Considerations," there appeared the following information:

PROJECT DESIGN FEATURES

What We Can Control or Manipulate? = State participation/selection process
Role of advisors
Content of program
Training of state leaders
Resource people utilized
Basic skills content areas emphasized
Perception of need to use technology

BEST's promotional flyer blatantly discussed how the project would serve not just in education, but for other program areas as well, to implement the national/international management system (MBO, PPBS, TQM):

> In addition, the State Team approach and the communications network with professional associations and other groups established by the project will serve as a model for the states in implementing similar efforts in other areas of education, or in such program areas as health, human services, housing, transportation, etc.

William Spady, at that time serving as executive director of the Association of School Administrators, and Dr. Shirley McCune, serving as head of the State Services Division, Denver, Colorado, were listed as members of the advisory board for Project BEST.

[Ed. Note: Project BEST was used as a vehicle to assist in "State Capacity Building"—a process to better enable school oficials, administrators, legislators and others to provide supportive documentation, computer support, and "research" for school reform efforts. State Capacity Building grants have been funded by the U.S. Department of Education and are usually matched with state budget funding.]

***ALL OUR CHILDREN LEARNING* BY PROFESSOR BENJAMIN BLOOM (MCGRAW** Hill Publishing Co.: New York, N.Y., 1981) was published. Excerpts follow:

> In an attempt to maximize curriculum effectiveness... curriculum centers throughout the world have begun to incorporate learning-for-mastery instructional strategies into the redesign of curriculum. (p. 123)

According to Bloom:

> [T]he International Association for the Evaluation of Educational Achievement (IAEEA) is an organization of 22 national research centers which are engaged in the study of education.... This group has been concerned with the use of international tests, questionnaires, and other methods to relate student achievement and attitudes to instruction, social and economic factors in each nation. The evaluation instruments also represent an international consensus on the knowledge and objectives most worth learning. (pp. 33–35)

Another extremely important statement by Bloom in *All Our Children Learning* is found on page 180: "The purpose of education and the schools is to change the thoughts, feelings and actions of students."

HUMAN INTELLIGENCE INTERNATIONAL NEWSLETTER IN ITS MARCH/APRIL
1981 issue reported that critical thinking skills research was taking place
within the United Nations Educational, Scientific and Cultural Organization
(UNESCO), the Office of Economic Cooperation and Development (OECD),
and the World Bank which planned on "increasing the bank's international
education and training budget to about $900 million a year."⁴ The newsletter
related that the U.S. Department of Education's National Institute of Education "has awarded a three-year contract totaling approximately $780,000 to
Bolt, Beranek and Newman, Inc., of Cambridge, Massachusetts to analyze
current programs of instruction on cognitive skills." The July/August issue
of the newsletter contained the following:

> The search for new referential systems and new values modifying existing
> beliefs should be based on modern microbiology. A scientific approach
> should be free from doctrinal bias, and its findings applicable to all man-kind.
> Ideological confrontations between East and West, Marxism and Liberalism,
> Arabs and Jews do have economic, historical, and political bases, but no
> biological basis. These antagonisms have been created by the human brain
> and could be solved by the wiser brains of future man.

[Ed. Note: It should be noted that Marilyn Jager Adams—deeply involved
in "scientific, research-based phonics instruction" through her service on
the Committee on the Prevention of Reading Difficulties in Young Children
for the Commission on Behavioral and Social Sciences and Education of the
National Research Council—has been a long time associate with the above-
mentioned Bolt, Beranek and Newman.]

THE APRIL/MAY 1981 ISSUE OF *TODAY'S EDUCATION*, THE NATIONAL EDU-
cation Association's monthly journal, carried an article entitled "Effective
Schools: What the Research Says" by Michael Cohen, senior associate and
team leader of the Research on Instruction Team of the National Institute
of Education, U.S. Department of Education. Some excerpts from the article
follow:

> According to Ronald Edmonds of the Harvard University Graduate School
> of Education, these [effective school] studies suggest that differences in ef-
> fectiveness among schools can be accounted for by the following five factors:
>
> * Strong administrative leadership by the school principal, especially
>   in regard to instructional matters.
> * School climate conducive to learning [i.e., positive, or "psychologi-
>   cally facilitative," school climate, ed.]; that is, a safe and orderly
>   school relatively free of discipline and vandalism problems.
> * Schoolwide emphasis on basic skills instruction (which entails ac-
>   ceptance among the professional staff that instruction in the basic
>   skills is the primary goal of the school).
> * Teacher expectations that all students, regardless of family back-
>   ground, can reach appropriate levels of achievement.
> * A system for monitoring and assessing pupil performance which is
>   tied to instructional objectives....
>
> ...[T]he five factors identified as contributing to school effectiveness

suggest the classical model of a bureaucratic organization: a goal-oriented organization with a hierarchical authority structure and a central manager who monitors behavior and deliberately adjusts organizational performance on the basis of clear and agreed-upon goals and of feedback regarding goal attainment....

> The principal must be willing to clearly set the direction for the school and to hold the staff accountable for following that direction. The staff, in turn, must be willing to view the principal's direction even if it involves giving up some claims to their own autonomy.

[Ed. Note: The reader should keep in mind that Effective School Research has been used over the past twenty years in inner city schools and schools located in the South; that its track record, if judged by academic test scores, leaves much to be desired. In fact, Washington, D.C. and Secretary Riley's home state of South Carolina—both of which have used Effective School Research—had the lowest academic test scores in the nation, to be followed by many inner city schools, especially those in the southern part of the nation. In this regard, the reader should re-read the 1913 entry containing quotes from Frederick T. Gates, director of charity for the Rockefeller Foundation.]

IN A 1981 ALASKA GOVERNOR'S TASK FORCE REPORT ON EFFECTIVE SCHOOL-ing to The Honorable Jay S. Hammond the following statements were made in regard to mastery learning and direct instruction (highly structured learning activities):

> It has been determined that in the learning of specific skills and factual data that it is possible to enhance achievement by using the approach of mastery learning, wherein instructional objectives are clearly defined—and instructional activities are tied directly to objectives. It has been demonstrated that direct instruction—highly structured learning activity—is effective with certain groups of students. These approaches will assist students with low achievement to move closer to the current mean or average. Yet, a highly structured system of instruction applied to everyone may in fact impede the progress of those students achieving at a level above the current mean or average. The result is that, while variance (or the spread of scores from the mean) is reduced, there is a reduction in both directions. Low achievers may move closer to the mean, but high achievers may well do likewise. The examples presented above regarding achievement may well apply to the operation of schools. If effective schooling practices are too narrow and a rigid system results, variance among districts will be reduced, but the limiting of creativity and the limiting of schools in their ability to adapt to local circumstances will cause reduction in variance from both above and below the mean or average. (pp. 38–39)

[Ed. Note: The introduction to this report which stated: "As part of the Task Force effort several studies were conducted by Northwest Regional Educational Laboratory under contract with the (Alaska) Department of Education," should explain to the reader that the U.S. Department of Education has funded—and continues to fund—mastery learning and direct instruction programs even in the face of evaluative evidence that strongly suggests that average and above average students do not benefit from such educational approaches.]

TWO IMPORTANT CONFERENCES FOR "SCHOOL IMPROVEMENT" WERE SPONSORED by the Northwest Regional Educational Laboratory (U.S. Department of Education) in 1981. They are described below:

> MEETING THE FUTURE: Improving Secondary Schools with Goal-Based Approaches to Instruction. Marriott Hotel, Portland, Oregon. Major addresses: "Alternative Futures for Our Society and Implications for Education" by Dr. Harold Pluimer, Futurist and Educational Consultant, Minneapolis, Minnesota and "School Effectiveness and Implications for Secondary School Improvement" by Dr. Alan Cohen, Professor of Education, University of San Francisco.
>
> Sessions on Innovative Practices: "Improving Goals, Objectives and Competencies; Making the Community a Resource for Learning" ; "Learning through Mastery Techniques; Organizing for Continuous Progress"; "Involving Teachers as Advisors to Students"; "Individualizing Programs for All Students"; "Managing Instruction with Computers"; "Developing Options for Student Assessment"; "Improving Record Keeping and Reporting Procedures"; "Increasing Staff Motivation through Group Planning and Decision-Making"; "Techniques for Managing School Improvement"; "Concerns-Based Adoption Model"; "Force Field Analysis"; "Curriculum Alignment Processes"; "Staff Development Models," and "Wisconsin R&D Center Model for School Improvement."
>
> MICROCOMPUTERS IN TODAY'S SCHOOLS: A Conference for Educational Leaders. Benson Hotel and NWREL Headquarters, Portland, Oregon. Major addresses: "Why We Went for Micros and What Our Community Had to Say about It" by Dr. Billy Reagan, Superintendent, Houston, Texas Public Schools; "Tomorrow's Technology in Today's Schools" by Dr. Dexter Fletcher, World Institute for Computer-Assisted Teaching, and others.

THE NATIONAL EDUCATION ASSOCIATION PUBLISHED *NEA SPECIAL COMMITtee on Instructional Technology Report* which was presented to their 60th Representative Assembly, held July 4–7, 1981. An excerpt from the report related to the problems of programmed learning (computer-assisted instruction) follows:

> In its coming involvement with a technology of instruction, the profession will be faced again with the challenge of leadership—by example and by effective communication—the challenge of convincing the public that education is much more than treating students like so many Pavlovian dogs, to be conditioned and programmed into docile acceptance of a do-it-yourself blueprint of the Good Life.
>
> The problems associated with technology, in its final analysis, are problems of freedom and control. Whose freedom? Whose control? As a result of its study, the committee urges the Association to view the problems and promises of instructional technology not as a single issue but rather as a broad continuum of issues affecting all aspects of education and teaching—from purposes to products, from political pragmatism to professional practice.

Most problems produced by technology have to do with the human use of human beings. In his book, *The Illusion of Technique: A Search for Meaning in a Technological Civilization* (Doubleday: New York, 1978), William Barrette observes that—

> Human creativity exceeds the mechanisms it invents, and is required even for their intelligent direction.... If we try to flee from our human condition into the computer we only meet ourselves there.

"FAMILIES AND SCHOOLS: A SYSTEM OF MUTUAL SUPPORT," A SPEECH delivered in 1981 by Secretary of Education T.H. Bell before a Freeman Institute audience in Utah, included Bell's recommendation that schools should use Professor Lawrence Kohlberg's "Ethical Issues in Decision Making" to teach values. (A synopsis of Kohlberg's Stages of Moral Development is contained in a 1975 entry on the topic.)

[ddd]

EARLY IN 1981 THE PRESIDENT'S TASK FORCE ON PRIVATE SECTOR INITIAtives was installed at 734 Jackson Place, N.W., Washington, D.C. Membership listed on The White House letterhead read like a "Who's Who" of individuals in government agencies, universities, tax-exempt foundations, non-governmental organizations, business, media, labor unions, and religion. The names of some individuals on the task force follow: William Aramony, president, United Way; William J. Baroody, Jr., president, American Enterprise Institute; Helen G. Boosalis, mayor, City of Lincoln, Nebraska; Terence Cardinal Cooke, archbishop of New York; Governor Pierre S. Dupont, Delaware; Senator David Durenberger; Luis A. Ferre, former governor of Puerto Rico; John Gardner, chairman, Independent Sector; Edward Hill, pastor, Mt. Zion Baptist Church; Michael S. Joyce, executive director, John M. Olin Foundation; Edward H. Kiernan, president, International Association of Police; Arthur Levitt, Jr., chairman, American Stock Exchange; Richard W. Lyman, president, Rockefeller Foundation; Elder Thomas S. Monson, The Mormon Church; William C. Norris, chairman and CEO, Control Data Corporation; George Romney, chairman, National Center for Citizen Involvement; C. William Verity, Jr., chairman, Armco Steel, Inc.; Jeri J. Winger, first vice president, General Federation of Women's Clubs; Thomas H. Wyman, president, CBS, Inc.; and William S. White, president, C.S. Mott Foundation.[5]

This totally new and un-American concept of partnerships between public and private sector has been readily accepted by our elected officials who ignore its roots in socialism and its implications for the discontinuation of our representative form of government and accountability to the taxpayers. Under the "partnership" process, determining responsibility when something goes wrong is like pinning jello to the wall.

Such a change in government, if presented in clear language to citizens at the polls, would be rejected. However, when implemented gradually, using the Marxist-Hegelian Dialectic, citizens don't even notice what is happening.

The shift is away from elected representatives. In time, after voters have become even more disenchanted with the candidates and election results, fewer and fewer citizens will vote. At that point a highly-respected member of the public will enter the picture to propose a solution to the problem: some sort of compromise toward parliamentary form of government found in socialist democracies which will be acceptable to Americans unfamiliar with the protections guaranteed by the U.S. Constitution.

One says to oneself, confidently, "This will never happen." Look around you. What do you see? Site-based management in your local schools, trans-ferring decision-making, traditionally exercised by elected school boards, to politically correct appointees and the creation of unelected task forces at all government levels; proposals to "separate school and state" which make no mention of governmental and social structure consequences—efforts to have government money (taxes) pay for services delivered by private religious or homeschools, etc., with no public representation. There can be no account-ability to the taxpayers under a system so alien to the United States' form of representative government.

How clean, neat and tidy. Wholesale destruction of an entire, wonderful system of government without firing a shot.

As a U.S. Department of Education liaison with The White House during the early days of this initiative, this writer inquired of one of President Rea-gan's political appointees whether this initiative was not corporate fascism; a politically incorrect question that resulted in someone else replacing me as Liaison with The White House.

A VERY IMPORTANT NATIONAL ASSESSMENT OF EDUCATIONAL PROGRESS (NAEP) report, in galley stage, entitled *Measuring the Quality of Education: Conclusions and Summary*, was provided to this writer in 1981, shedding light not only on the responsibility of major tax-exempt foundations in the development of a national curriculum, but also on the role of the federal government in setting standards/goals for American education. Excerpts follow from (1) a cover letter signed by Willard Wirtz, former secretary of labor, and Archie Lapointe, executive director of the NAEP, and (2) the report itself:

(1)

In a different sense, this report is designed to meet the responsibilities im-posed at least implicitly by the three foundations which initiated and have supported the project; the Carnegie Corporation, the Ford Foundation, and the Spencer Foundation have become critical and constructive forces in American education.

(2)

Conclusions... Instead of determining "what is being taught" and basing the objectives on this present practice, the controlling question is "what ought to be taught."... It is specifically recommended that caution be exercised against putting the Assessment results in a form that could be misconstrued as constituting national—or "federal"—standards....

Summary... The report reflects most significantly the carefully considered conclusions of the Council of Seven which was established at the beginning of the project. Selected primarily for their recognized responsibility and good sense, they also reflect a variety of experiences and institutional interests: Gregory Anrig, then Massachusetts Commissioner of Education and now President of the Educational Testing Service; Stephen K. Bailey, who is the Francis Keppel Professor of Educational Policy and Administration of Harvard Graduate School of Education; Charles Bowen, Director of Plans and Program Administration for University Relations of the IBM Corporation; Clare Burstall, Deputy Director of the National Foundation for Educational Research in England and Wales; Elton Jolly, Executive Director for Opportunities Industrialization Centers; Lauren Resnick, Co-Director of the Learning Research and Development Center of the University of Pittsburgh; and Dorothy Shields, Director of Education for the AFL-CIO....

...It was the Council's suggestion and eventually its decision to shape the entire report in terms of the Assessment's potential role in developing higher and more effective educational standards. Where we had been timid about this the Council moved boldly. They were right....

...Measuring student achievement is an entirely different business from measuring other aspects of the national condition.... They get to their answers without having to make value judgments. Not so of the measurers of "educational achievement." The key term isn't defined except as they develop its meaning. The rest of this is that once that definition is worked out, the measuring process depends at critical points on what are in significant part value judgments. Whether an educational standard is "better" or "higher" depends on how it consists with ultimate educational purposes...

...Those in charge of the Assessment are in a position to guide their policies entirely by a determination of whatever "quality" means. They face no competition and are subject to no political pressures. Innovation and experimentation are part of the Assessment's authentic tradition. It can provide not only competence but conscience and courage in the implementation of the new national purpose to improve educational standards.

...A statement in the NAEP DESIGN AND DEVELOPMENT DOCUMENT covering the 1979–1980 Reading/Literature Assessment is succinctly descriptive:

> The first step in any assessment cycle is objectives development. The objectives identify the important knowledge, skills, and attitudes within an assessment area which are generally being taught or should be taught in schools. These objectives then become the framework for developing assessment exercises which measure the objectives.

Although there is little public awareness of these steps in the process of setting educational standards, they affect that process vitally and give any standard its determinative character....

...This new emphasis will mean that teaching will be increasingly oriented toward these objectives, which is good or bad depending on their quality [Teach to the test, ed.].

[ddd]...The 1969–1970 Citizenship Assessment included a group task exercise designed to determine, by observing students' group interaction, their ability to "apply democratic procedures on a practical level."... This capacity for innovation and experimentation has been lost, largely as a consequence of budgetary constraints.

...Goals and objectives used for the Connecticut assessments parallel clearly the objectives and subobjectives identified for the National Assessment. Many CAEP items are NAEP items; this was true of all items in the 1979–1980 Connecticut Science Assessment....

...Comparable uses of National Assessment materials have been made in a number of other states. A recent NAEP staff summary lists twelve States as having closely replicated the National Assessment model, and twelve others as having drawn on NAEP offices for technical and consultative advice. There is clear confirmation in this record of not only a substantial service potential, but also of a significant prospect for integrating state and nation-wide assessment programs.

[Ed. Note: As one reads the excerpts in part two of this report, it is important to bear in mind the denials of complicity emanating from the U.S. Department of Education and the respective state departments of education when confronted with charges that the state assessments use test items from the NAEP Test Item Bank. The resistance to such use results from the public's traditional aversion to national tests and national curriculum—with which all of the above entities have denied involvement. Clearly, denial is in vain in light of the evidence contained in this document.]

THE NATIONAL CENTER FOR CITIZEN INVOLVEMENT ISSUED A REPORT ENTITLED *The American Volunteer, 1981: Statistics on Volunteers.* One revealing statement from the report follows:

Volunteer Population: 92 million, 44% of whom work alone in an informal, unstructured environment on projects of their own choice; the rest of whom work in structured activities.

[Ed. Note: Obviously, the major effort related to volunteerism was—and is—to convince the 44% who are, in effect, "doing their own thing," to join in the government-private sector "Points of Light" volunteerism partnership initiated by then-President George Bush, as well as President Bill Clinton's AmeriCorps. That way they will work only on politically correct and government-approved projects.]

MALCOLM DAVIS, THE DIRECTOR OF THE OFFICE OF LIBRARIES AND LEARNing Technology, Office of Educational Research and Improvement at the U.S. Department of Education, in response to this writer's comment in 1981 that computer courseware could allow children to learn at home, responded, "In essence, in the future all education will take place in the home, but the school buildings will be used for socialization purposes." This quote is not exact; however, it represents this writer's recollection of it sixteen years later. I was so stunned by his comment that I recall it often when looking at the issue of "choice" and especially that of homeschooling.

[Ed. Note: This comment was echoed by Alvin Toffler, George Gilder and Lewis Perelman during a Progress and Freedom Foundation conference in

Atlanta, Georgia in August of 1995. This conference preceded and dealt with issues molding the "Contract with America" which Newt Gingrich put forth for Republican candidates to adopt as their platforms in 1996. Lewis Perelman's book, *School's Out* (Avon Books: New York, 1992), deals with this very concept and Perelman attended the conference as an expositor of "conservative" positions on education for the Progress and Freedom Foundation.

A 1992 proposal to the New American Schools Development Corporation (NASDC) from The Center for the New West of Denver, Colorado included a plan from its New West Learning Center Design Team which provided a clear picture of the community of the future. "Home School Families" would be linked to "Public Schools, Communities, Private Schools, Businesses, Alternative Schools, and Higher Education" with the New West Learning Center serving as the "hub" of the wheel, or community. While this proposal was not selected as a recipient of NASDC funding, and, fortunately, has not been funded by any government entity—YET—its description of changes in local governance and relationships of community elements met the criteria established by NASDC. (See the Internet version for Appendix XI and XII.)]

1982

PROFILES IN EXCELLENCE: *1982–1983: SECONDARY SCHOOL RECOGNITION Program: A Resource Guide* (Office of Educational Research and Improvement of the U.S. Department of Education: Washington, D.C., 1982) listed the Kennebunk, Maine High School as one which schools across the nation might wish to emulate. The *Guide* stated that

> The major goal of the school's curriculum is to individualize the learning process for the student. The district is in the process of developing a data bank for students and a testing program for determining expectancy instructional levels for each student. Once this is in place, staff will develop an Individual Education Plan (IEP) for each student to meet individual needs. The major difficulty the school is encountering in implementing this new process is the secondary staff who are trained as subject matter teachers. Teachers need to be retrained to focus on individual needs rather than on content areas.

"FROM SCHOOLING TO LEARNING: RETHINKING PRESCHOOL THROUGH UNIversity Education" by Don Glines was published in the January 1982 issue of the National Association of Secondary School Principals' *Bulletin*.[6] The following are excerpts:

> The implications of these global concerns for schools, educators, and education, are monumental if the views of most future writers are correct. Early recognition of this came in the 1974 book, *Learning for Tomorrow: The Role of the Future in Education* by Alvin Toffler (Random House: New York, 1974), and *The Third Wave* (William Morrow: New York, 1981) [by the same author].
>
> One passage states: "American education is obsolete; it produces people to fit into a reasonably well-functioning industrial society and we no longer have one. The basic assumption driving American education, one both deceptive and dangerous, is that the future will be like the present. Schools are

preparing people for a society that no longer exists. As society shifts away from the industrial model, schools will have to turn out a different kind of person. Schools now need to produce people who can cope with change."...

What do people who will be in their prime in the year 2050, assuming society makes it through the coming transitional decades, need to shape their futures? Is the current curriculum—history, mathematics, science, new versions of Dick and Jane, all taught as separate subjects, really appropriate for the concluding years of the twentieth century? The majority of futures writers have a clear answer: No. They illustrate that instant information retrieval not only ends jobs in the world of work, it ends subjects in the world of learning!...

The potential technology exists to eliminate most current classrooms before the turn of the century, moving from a campus to a community-oriented learning system. A postliterate society is on the verge of arriving; reading will become a luxury, a leisure pastime, or a choice, but not an absolute essential.

Yet, the seventh grade programs in junior high and middle schools continue with the bleakness of 50 years past. Most still require English, history, science, math, and physical education, along with a semester of art and a semester of music. They have period 1, 2, 3 schedules; A, B, C report cards; tardies, notes from home; textbooks. Perhaps even worse is the fact that most colleges still prepare teachers for this antiquity; and administrators, who in spite of the goals professed in graduate courses, continue to perpetuate the system. Is it any wonder that *Learning for Tomorrow* labeled today's education obsolete?

Ron Barnes, in *Tomorrow's Educator: An Alternative to Today's School Person* (Transitions, Inc.: Phoenix, Arizona, 1977), has listed his descriptors of a New Age educator—a person who thinks systematically; accepts and promotes diversity; demonstrates a holistic perspective toward life; strives for self-awareness; promotes interdependence; is comfortable with the unknown; considers human values of highest priority; is experimental; works toward changing schools; has a more open approach to knowledge; and is a true futurist.

OUTCOME-BASED INSTRUCTIONAL MANAGEMENT: A SOCIOLOGICAL PERSPECtive by William Spady was published in 1982, supported by a contract from the National Institute of Education (NIE–P–80–0194). This important paper, which provided a complete overview of the philosophy behind OBE, the organizational dimensions of outcome-based practice, the operational character of outcome-based practice, etc., also carried some interesting comments regarding OBE's relationship to Project Follow Through. Excerpts follow:

> Implications for Follow Through... Despite the limitations of formal validation data sources, however, there is a strong case to be made for implementing fully developed OB [outcome-based] models in Follow Through sites. Philosophically, as well as empirically, this approach is inherently suited to the clientele served by Follow Through programs and possesses an operational character that is well suited for affecting positively both the cognitive and affective outcome agendas sought by a variety of current Follow Through models.
>
> Recognizing that OB practice resembles some of these models, its unique power appears to be that it possesses a fine balance between focus and flexibility, and structure and responsiveness, and that it contains elements

suitable to a variety of student motivational and learning styles without leaning heavily toward any one orientation. That is, it is as inclusionary in its methodology as it is in the conditions for student learning success it tries to establish.

A final point regarding the inherent appeal of OB practice for Follow Through implementation is its basic openness. Public involvement in goal setting, public visibility of objectives and standards, and performance records and reporting systems which describe the actual behavior being sought all help to "demystify" the educational process and facilitate clearer understanding and communication between parents and the school.

The Network for Outcome-Based Schools itself represents a unique and powerful resource for technical assistance and implementation to any sites oriented toward OB practice.

[Ed. Note: The above excerpts should be of interest to those promoting DISTAR/Reading Mastery, the Skinnerian "systematic, intensive, scientific research-based" phonics reading program which was one of the Follow Through models. How ironic that William Spady should say that the outcome-based practice which "conservatives" say they detest is similar to the Follow Through model which they have embraced. It is obvious Spady is not referring to the Open Classroom Follow Through model, since that model did not include "public visibility of objectives and standards, performance records and reporting systems which describe the actual behaviors being sought." In other words, Spady is making it clear that OB practice is a fraternal twin of the Follow Through's Direct Instruction model developed by Siegfried Engelmann, which has also been embraced by "conservatives"!]

"Learning To Read the ECRI Way" by Dennis Bailey was published in *The Maine Times* on January 8, 1982. In the article Bailey points out that

> Patrick Groff, an education professor, wrote in a 1974 issue of *Today's Education*: "So far, mastery learning has not presented the empirical evidence necessary to convince reasonable-minded teachers that all students have the same aptitude for learning every subject."

[Ed. Note: That Professor Groff, professor emeritus, San Diego State University, would make the above comment is interesting in light of recent events; namely, his co-founding with Robert Sweet of the Right to Read Foundation (RRF) which has taken a position in support of the *Reading Excellence Act of 1998*. In supporting this legislation Groff's organization has indicated support for the "scientific, research-based" reading method used in ECRI, the very technique which he says "has not presented the empirical evidence necessary to convince reasonable-minded teachers that all students have the same aptitude for learning every subject." ECRI is the mirror image of Siegfried Engelmann's DISTAR direct instruction, the Skinnerian operant conditioning-based reading program promoted in Right to Read newsletters and on its website.]

William (Bill) Spady, "the Father of OBE," made the following statement during a conference held at the U.S. Department of Education in

1982 (attended by this writer). This writer wrote down verbatim in short-hand Spady's following comment:

> Two of the four functions of Mastery Learning are: Extra: whole agenda of acculturation, social roles, social integration, get the kids to participate in social unit, affective; and Hidden: a system of supervision and control which restrains behavior of kids; the outcome of the hidden agenda should be the fostering of social responsibility or compliance.

"STATE OF PRECOLLEGE EDUCATION IN MATHEMATICS AND SCIENCE" WAS prepared by Paul DeHart Hurd, professor emeritus, Stanford University, for the National Convocation on Pre-College Education in Math and Science, National Academy of Sciences and National Academy of Engineering in Washington, D.C. in 1982. In this paper Prof. Hurd asserts that

> In the Communist countries there are comprehensive examinations at the end of the primary, middle, and secondary schools to assess a student's actual progress. Test results are not interpreted in a competitive sense as to who has done well or poorly compared to other students or a norm, but rather whether a student has mastered the prescribed subject matter. If test results are below expectancy, the student is tutored by the teacher and students. The object is to avoid failures.

[Ed. Note: This definition is striking in its similarity to the definition of OBE/mastery learning/direct instruction, which uses non-competitive, criterion-referenced tests rather than traditional norm-referenced tests which compare students to one another. Another common feature among these techniques is continuous progress whereby students can have all the time and/or tutoring they need in order to "master" the content. Continuous progress is necessary to carry out UNESCO's lifelong learning concept. This "exit exam" process is being legislated into an increasing number of states.]

IN A SPEECH ENTITLED "REGULATED COMPETITION IN THE UNITED STATES" delivered before the top 52 executives in Northern Telecom's Worldwide Corporation meeting, for which the edited proceedings were published in the February 1982 issue of the *Innisbrook Papers*,[7] Harvard Professor Anthony Oettinger of the Council on Foreign Relations made the following extremely elitist statements:

> Our idea of literacy, I am afraid, is obsolete because it rests on a frozen and classical definition. Literacy, as we know it today, is the product of the conditions of the industrial revolution, of organization, of the need for a work force that could, in effect, "write with a fine round hand." It has to do, in other words, with the Bob Cratchits of the world.
>
> But as much as we might think it is, literacy is not an eternal phenomenon. Today's literacy is a phenomenon (and Dickens satirized it) that has its roots in the nineteenth century, and one does not have to reach much farther back to think of civilizations with different concepts of literacy based, for example, on oral, rather than written, traditions.
>
> The present "traditional" concept of literacy has to do with the ability to

read and write. But the real question that confronts us today is: How do we help citizens function well in their society? How can they acquire the skills necessary to solve their problems?

Do we, for example, really want to teach people to do a lot of sums or write in a "fine round hand" when they have a five-dollar, hand-held calculator or a word processor to work with? Or, do we really have to have everybody literate—writing and reading in the traditional sense—when we have the means through our technology to achieve a new flowering of oral communication?[8]

What is speech recognition and speech synthesis all about if it does not lead to ways of reducing the burden on the individual of the imposed notions of literacy that were a product of nineteenth century economics and technology?

Complexity—everybody is moaning about tasks becoming too complex for people to do. A Congressman who visited one of my classes recently said, "We have such low-grade soldiers in the U.S. that we have to train them with comic books." And an army captain in my class shot back: "What's wrong with comic books? My people *function*" [emphasis in original].

It is the traditional idea that says certain forms of communication, such as comic books, are "bad." But in the modern context of functionalism they may not be all that bad.

[Ed. Note: Doesn't the above sound a lot like the Texas Study of Adult Functional Competency, the Adult Performance Level Study, and Secretary of Education T.H. Bell's and William Spady's initiation of dumbed-down competency-based education?

One can't help but wonder if Oettinger—and those social engineers with whom he associates who call the shots in regard to our children's futures—would be happy to have their own children and grandchildren offered such a limited education that they won't even know who Charles Dickens or Bob Cratchit were?]

CHESTER FINN WROTE "PUBLIC SERVICE, PUBLIC SUPPORT, PUBLIC AC-countability" for the March 1982 issue of the National Association of Secondary School Principals' *Bulletin*. Finn became a high profile figure in education circles with his appointment as assistant secretary, Office of Educational Research and Improvement, by Secretary of Education William Bennett. Finn's article was quoted in Barbara Morris's book, *Tuition Tax Credits: A Responsible Appraisal* (*The Barbara Morris Report*: Upland, Cal., 1983):

> Short of scattering money in the streets or handing it out to everyone who wants some, the funding agency must define eligible recipients.... This means, in a word, "regulation," the inevitable concommitant of public financial support.

Finn also believed the government is obligated to recognize that the private schools it helps support are different from public schools—that it is this "differentness" that makes them supportable. The other side of the coin, he says, is the obligation of private schools

> to recognize certain limits to their differentness and certain ways they must

conform to the norms and expectations of a society that values and supports them....

Some, to be sure, like to think they can have it both ways; i.e., can obtain
aid without saddling themselves with unacceptable forms of regulation. But
most acknowledge the general applicability of the old adage that he who
pays the piper calls the tune, and are more or less resigned to amalgamating
or choosing between assistance and autonomy.

On March 29, 1982, at the "closed to the public" annual meeting
of the Council of Chief State School Officers, Secretary of Education T.H.
Bell's top assistant, Elam Herzler, told the assembled fifty state superintendents of education:

> One of the elements of an effective school is to monitor, assess, and feed
> back.... As little as 5 percent of a school budget K–12 would be needed over
> a period of 12 years to enable each student to have his own computer, and
> this is within our cost range.

"Can Computers Teach Values?" by Joseph A. Braun, Jr. and Kurt
A. Slobodzian, assistant professors in the Department of Curriculum and
Instruction of the Northern Illinois University School of Education in Dekalb,
Illinois, was published in the April 1982 issue of *Educational Leadership*.
The following are excerpts:

> In helping children learn how to inquire and examine their own emerging
> value systems, most educators agree that unintentional negative reactions
> by teachers are deleterious to youngsters' self-concept. Couple this with
> potential ridicule from student peers, and one can readily see why values
> education has been a delicate and controversial issue. However, a student
> using CAI [computer-assisted instruction] in the examination, evaluation,
> and acquisition of values would be able to do so with mature guidance in
> an environment free from potential rejection or scorn.
>
> Another pitfall for teachers of values education is the invasion of a child's
> right to privacy. Well-intentioned teachers often expect self-disclosure beyond
> a student's limit of psychological safety (Lockwood, 1977) by demanding
> deeply personal revelations from participants who are not prepared to discuss
> their more private thoughts. The computer, in contrast, has no misguided
> need to get to know "the real you."
>
> The computer, then, is ideally suited to the role of facilitator in values
> education. It inherently possesses the Rogerian [psychologist Carl Rogers]
> qualities of genuineness and congruence. It can even be programmed to
> positively regard anyone who uses it. A student using CAI gains a sense of
> protection as well as a constant source of appropriate feedback while explor-
> ing and integrating feelings, beliefs, and behavior.
>
> Computers have also been programmed to pick out key words from a
> respondent's statements. The computer program then formulates open-ended
> questions from key words, which causes the respondent to focus and further
> clarify feelings. In other words, using a program called "Doctor," Holden
> (1977) describes a conversation between a computer and a troubled young
> woman who began with a common complaint:

Human: "Men are all alike."
Computer: "In what way?"
Human: "They're always bugging us about something or another."
Computer: "Can you think of a specific example?"
Human: "Well, my boy friend made me come here."
Computer: "Your boyfriend made you come here?"
Human: "He says that I'm depressed much of the time."
Computer: "I am sorry to hear that you are depressed."
Human: "It's true, I am unhappy."
Computer: "Do you think coming here will help you not be unhappy?"
Human: "I need some help. That much seems certain."
Computer: "What would it mean if you got some help?"
Human: "Perhaps I could learn to get along with my mother."
Computer: "Tell me more about your family."

THE COMPLETE WORKS OF FRANCIS A. SCHAEFFER: *A Christian Worldview, Volume One, a Christian View of Philosophy and Culture* (Crossway Books: Westchester, Ill., 1982) was published. In a treatise entitled "A Christian View of Philosophy and Culture: Back to Freedom and Dignity," noted Christian scholar and theologian Dr. Francis Schaeffer warned of B.F. Skinner and his methods:

Skinner says that up until the present time all of humanity has considered man to be in some sense autonomous—that is, that there is in each individual an "ego" or mind or center of consciousness which can freely choose one or another course of action. But, Skinner says, autonomous man does not exist, and it is the task of behavioral psychology to abolish the conception.... Skinner declares that everything man is, everything man makes, everything man thinks is completely, 100 percent, determined by his environment.

After the publication of *Beyond Freedom and Dignity* [1972], when he [Skinner] was at the Center for the Study of Democratic Institutions, he spoke at Westmont College in Santa Barbara, California. There he said, "The individual does not initiate anything." In fact, he said that any time man is freed from one kind of control, he merely comes under another kind of control. Christians consider that man is autonomous in that he is significant, he affects the environment. In behavioristic psychology, the situation is reversed. All behavior is determined not from within but from without. "You" don't exist. Man is not there. All that is there is a bundle of conditioning, a collection of what you have been in the past: your genetic makeup and your environment. But Skinner goes a step further, subordinates the genetic factor, and suggests that man's behavior can be almost totally controlled by controlling the environment.... Some behaviorists would differ with him on this last point. How is it that the environment controls behavior?

Here Skinner brings up the concept of "operant conditioning." This notion is based on his work with pigeons and rats. The basic idea is that "when a bit of behavior is followed by a certain consequence, it is more likely to occur again, and a consequence having this effect is called a reinforcer." (p. 27) That is, for example, "anything the organism does that is followed by the receipt of food is more likely to be done again whenever the organism is hungry."

There are two kinds of reinforcers: negative reinforcers which have adverse effects, and positive reinforcers whose effect is positive. Skinner contends that only the positive reinforcers should be used. In other words, in order to reinforce a certain kind of behavior, one should not punish; he should reward. If a person is surrounded by an atmosphere in which he gets a sufficient reward for doing what society would like him to do, he will automatically do this without ever knowing why he is doing it.... Within the Skinnerian system there are no ethical controls. There is no boundary limit to what can be done by the elite in whose hands control resides.

The reduction of man's value to zero is one of the important factors which triggered the student rebellion at Berkeley and elsewhere in the 1960s. Those students sensed that they were being turned into zeros and they revolted. Christians should have sensed it long before and said and exhibited that we have an alternative.... We are on the verge of the largest revolution the world has ever seen—the control and shaping of men through the abuse of genetic knowledge, and chemical and psychological conditioning.

Will people accept it? I don't think they would accept it if (1) they had not already been taught to accept the presuppositions that lead to it, and (2) they were not in such hopelessness. Many of our secular schools have consistently taught these presuppositions, and unhappily many of our Christian lower schools and colleges have taught the crucial subjects no differently than the secular schools.

Schaeffer's "Conclusion" follows:

What do we and our children face? The biological bomb, the abuse of genetic knowledge, chemical engineering, the behavioristic manipulation of man. All these have come to popular attention only a few years ago. But they are not twenty years away. They are not five years away. They are here now in technological breakthroughs. This is where we live, and as true Christians we must be ready. This is no time for weakness in the Church of Christ. What has happened to man? We must see him as one who has torn himself away both from the infinite-personal God who created him as finite but in his image and from God's revelation to him. Made in God's image, he was made to be great, he was made to be beautiful, and he was made to be creative in life and art. But his rebellion has led him into making himself into nothing but a machine. (pp. 374–384)

AN ARTICLE ENTITLED "GRADUATES LACK TECHNICAL TRAINING, STUDY Warns—By 1990, 2 Million May Not Have Essential Skills Needed for Employment in 'Information Society'" was published in the May 12, 1982 issue of *Education Week*. This article clearly placed the responsibility for the transformation from traditional academic education to workforce training at the feet of the Carnegie Corporation-spawned Education Commission of the States (ECS) and the National Assessment of Educational Progress (NAEP). This article fired one of the first shots across the bow of traditional academic education. It clearly defined the new "education" landscape when it described the need for Benjamin Bloom's Taxonomy (high level skills of critical thinking; i.e., evaluation, analysis, synthesis, application, etc.) versus "low level basic skills," emphasizing the use of the brain for processing, not storage (explained by Thomas Kelly in the January 1994 issue of *The Effective School Report*). The terminology in this article would, eleven years later, be reflected in the major *Goals 2000* restructuring legislation, the *Elementary and Secondary Reauthorization Act of 1994* (H.R. 6) which referred to the learning of basic academic skills and the emphasis on repetitive drill and practice in elementary school as a "disproven theory." Some excerpts from this enlightening article follow:

> "Unless the decline of high-order skills among high-school students is reversed," warns a new report from the Education Commission of the states, "as many as two million students may graduate [in 1990] without the essential skills required for employment in tomorrow's technically-oriented labor force."
>
> "Information Society: Will Our High School Graduates Be Ready?" was prepared by Roy Forbes, director of the National Assessment of Educational Progress (NAEP) and Lynn Grover Gisi, a research assistant and writer with NAEP. Its intention, the authors say, is to "stimulate research and communication among the groups concerned with technology's impact on education."
>
> The Forbes-Gisi report reviews labor-force projections, summarizes recent National Assessment findings, and outlines "recent corporate, educational, and legislative actions" designed to address the problem.
>
> Arguing that the computer chip will replace oil in the U.S. economy, and will form the basis for a new information society, the authors say that the "basics" mastered by the high-school gaduates of the future will have to include more complex skills than minimal reading, writing, and computing. Among the higher-level skills the information age will require, they argue, will be "evaluation and analysis, critical thinking; problem-solving strategies, including mathematical problem-solving, organization and reference skills; synthesis; application; creativity; decision-making given complete information; and communication skills through a variety of modes." ...The data from the National Assessment provide convincing evidence that by the time students reach the age of 17, many do not possess [the above listed]... higher-order skills. The "elements of the problem," says the report, are:
>
> - Foreign competition. The age of high technology is rapidly changing the roles of production and other countries are responding—faster than the U.S.—by upgrading their educational programs on a national level. The U.S. educational system, says the report, "poses unique problems by its inherent commitment to diversity and emphasis on local and state control."...
>
> - Students. Technology used for educational purposes has the potential to reshape instructional delivery systems, the report says, and that may result in a decentralization of learning from traditional schools into homes, communities and industries....
>
> - Responsibilities and relevance. Education must become more relevant to the world of work, the report contends, and this requires "informational feedback systems on the successes of students who have completed the required curriculum. Quality control has focused on the inputs into a system—teachers and textbooks, for example—and not the outcomes. Thus there has been no attempt to incorporate long-term information into the management system's program planning." The report's authors agree with a report of the Southern Regional Education Board that American schooling no longer lacks

the basics rather the "complexities that make for mature learning, mature citizenship, or adult success.".…

Unless the U.S. can keep pace, the report contends, its "position as a leader of technology and competitor for world markets will be severely threatened."

Cooperative Efforts

Only cooperative efforts involving all segments of society will solve the problem, the report states. In particular, it calls on American industry and labor to play a greater role.…

…"Industries cannot afford to pass up these opportunities and others because their future existence will depend upon it.… Clearly we are not cultivating the raw materials, our future workers, who are vital not only for economic progress, but ultimately for economic survival."

[Ed. Note: There are many responses this writer could make to the above article, but the first of which is that the statement "Clearly we are not cultivating the raw materials, our future workers"—our children!—is the most offensive of all. The use of those words alone when referring to human beings should tell the reader that something is very, very wrong in the United States of America. One has more respect for their pet animals than to refer to them as "raw materials."

Secondly, the report's agreement with the Southern Regional Education Board "that American schooling no longer lacks the basics" defies logic! From a region which consistently scores at the bottom of the heap, this is particularly repugnant. The idea that "higher order skills" should be the focus of our educational efforts can only be the product of the thinking of persons who are not concerned with whether or not students can read, write, or compute unless it is to perform a workforce function. Without a basic ability to read, write and compute on a broad base, it is impossible for anyone to have substance about which to "think critically"! Thinking critically—making choices and comparisons—requires a base knowledge that is either acquired through study (as in the case with most children who are students) or through life experience (which adults, but not children, can claim).

Lastly, the use of technology to decentralize "learning" from traditional schools into homes, communities and industries should raise a tall, red flag for successful homeschoolers. These folks are talking about government control of this process.]

THE INTERNATIONAL CONFERENCE FOR PARENT/CITIZEN INVOLVEMENT IN Schools was held July 22–25, 1982 at the Hilton Hotel, Salt Lake City, Utah. A letter to Secretary Bell dated February 25, 1982 requesting conference funding contained an impressive list of supporters on its letterhead, including: Scott Matheson, governor of Utah; Mrs. Barbara Bush, honorary chairperson, National School Volunteer Program; T.H. Bell, U.S. secretary of education; Dr. Don Davies, Institute for Responsive Education; Dr. Carl Marer, National Committee for Citizens in Education; Dr. M. Donald Thomas, superintendent of schools, Salt Lake City, Utah, and education representatives from Canada and Australia.

Dr. Donald Thomas, originally on the board of directors of *The Effective School Report*, and executive director of the Network for Effective Schools, is a well-known change agent. Thomas has traveled to Russia under the auspices of U.S. Secretary of Education Lamar Alexander and Dale Mann of Columbia University, to work with Russia on implementing international education restructuring.

The above-mentioned letter to Bell also stated:

> The "think tank" session will be by invitation only to leaders in the movement. Its purpose will be to assess the current status of parent/citizen involvement in the schools; to identify trends and directions of the movement for the 80s; and finally to plan further positive action to support the continuation of the movement.

One of the attachments to this conference correspondence included many pages related to Effective School Research and a listing of the components necessary for education restructuring. The list included:

- mastery learning/direct instruction
- expectations
- climate
- motivation
- measurement diagnosis
- assessment
- class management
- discipline
- classroom organization
- pupil conditions/rewards
- praise
- parent involvement, etc.

Those connected with such research are listed as follows: Michael Rutter, England, Effective School Study; the late Harvard Professor Ron Edmonds; professors Benjamin Bloom and John Goodlad; Larry Lezotte; Donald Thomas; and others.

A second attachment on National Coalition for Parent Involvement in Education (NCPIE—Alexandria, Virginia) letterhead stated that NCPIE was facilitated by the National School Volunteer Program and funded by Union Carbide Corporation.

A MEMO WAS SENT TO SECRETARY OF EDUCATION T.H. BELL FROM THE ASsistant secretary, Office of Educational Research and Improvement, regarding "upcoming events for July 31–August 31" which listed:

> AUGUST 5—President Reagan is scheduled to hold a press conference in which he will announce an initiative involving the National Diffusion Net-

work and the National Health Screening Council for Volunteer Organizations, Inc. This collaboration, called PARTNERSHIP, links schools with the media, local businesses, government and hospitals in a school improvement effort.

[Ed. Note: This activity was cancelled due to prompt grassroots opposition in the D.C. area consisting of a memorandum to the White House informing the President of concern nationwide related to the process known as "community education" and public-private partnerships.]

A **U.S. Department of Education memorandum to Secretary Bell** dated October 5, 1982 stated:

> President Reagan is scheduled to visit P.S. 48, an elementary school in the Bronx, New York City. During his visit the President will meet Dr. Ethna Reid, Director of the Exemplary Center for Reading Instruction, a program in the National Diffusion Network. Dr. Reid will be at P.S. 48 to train staff members in the use of ECRI.[9]

[Ed. Note: Whether the President, a very busy man, met with Dr. Reid or not, is insignificant. What IS highly significant, however, is WHY this extraordinary effort was made to introduce the President of the United States to Dr. Ethna Reid of Utah. In retrospect, scheduling President Reagan to meet with the developer of the "chosen" teaching method which incorporates Skinnerian mastery learning and direct instruction makes sense.]

U.S. Secretary of Education T.H. Bell's Commission on Excellence published *A Nation at Risk: The Imperative for Educational Reform* in 1982. This report laid the groundwork for the controversial restructuring Americans face today. Initially, the commission engaged in a slick, expensive propagandistic roadshow, intended to mobilize American opinion in favor of the umpteenth reform since the federal government seized control of education in 1965, causing steep declines in academic test scores. The recommendations were couched in terms Americans would accept; i.e., mastering basic skills, more homework, etc. Its hype was best illustrated by the following excerpt:

> If an unfriendly foreign power had attempted to impose on America the mediocre educational performance that exists today, we might well have viewed it as an act of war.... We have, in effect, been committing an act of unthinking, unilateral educational disarmament.

[Ed. Note: The rhetoric worked. Spending increased. Ideas, which would never have been accepted had a crisis not been deliberately created, were embraced without question. These included doing away with the only valid criterion for measuring student academic achievement—the Carnegie Unit—with its required four years of math, four years of English, four years of history, etc., in order to graduate from high school. Of interest was an informal comment made by Secretary Bell at the initial (closed to the public) commission meeting in July of 1981. Secretary Bell commented that one had to "create conflict in order to obtain one's objectives."

The conflict was indeed created between the conservatives (falsely represented by big business interests) and the liberals (the left-wing tax-exempt foundations and leadership of the teacher unions, etc.), in order to be able to come to a compromise (arrive at the consensus or common ground) which represented what the United Nations and its educational agencies had been promoting since 1945. The U.N. agenda included socialist lifelong learning and training for the global workforce. This consensus required—and succeeded in obtaining—partnerships/mergers between individuals and groups that had formerly had nothing in common—especially the partnership between government schools and business. Such a partnership is required by socialist/fascist forms of government.]

THE CENTER FOR EDUCATIONAL RESEARCH AND INNOVATION (CERI),[10] WHICH is attached to the Organization for Economic Cooperation and Development (OECD) in Paris, France, held an International School Improvement Project (ISIP) conference in Palm Beach, Florida in 1982. Many of the key components of the United States' education reform movement (effective schools movement) were discussed by delegates from member countries. The main topic appeared to be a subject entitled "CBAM" about which absolutely nothing was said in the invitational papers sent to delegates planning to attend.

The writer was bewildered by the term "CBAM" until it appeared in the U.S. Department of Education-funded project "Changing Teacher Practice, Final Report of an Experimental Study—Gary A. Griffin, Principal Investigator, Susan Barnes, Sharon O'Neal, Sara E. Edwards, Maria E. Defino, Hobart Hukill—Report No. 9052, Research and Development Center for Teacher Education, The University of Texas, Austin, Texas 78712." Within the project report there is discussion of the application of "behavioral science for systems improvement." The "Changing Teacher Practice" project contained the "Concerns-Based Adoption Model" (CBAM), which illustrated the extent of psychological manipulation undergone by teachers who resist change. The following excerpt explains the purpose of "Concerns-Based Adoption Model" as a support tool to assist teachers through the painful process of "change":

> The Concerns-Based Adoption Model (CBAM) provides a structure for staff development planning which focuses on the process of change as a personal experience (Hall & Loucks, 1978, Note 19). The perceptions, feelings, motivations, frustrations, and satisfactions of teachers about an innovation are identified and classified according to a developmental scheme of stages. The process of change by which a person moves through these stages is attended to so that an innovation can be implemented. Concerns-based staff development recognizes and accepts as legitimate the concerns of the person involved in the change process. Change is regarded as long term and developmental, and individuals are perceived to need support as they experience change. In this model any process or product that the teacher has not previously encountered is regarded as an innovation for that teacher. (p. 37)

[Ed. Note: The information regarding the ISIP conference in Palm Beach is taken from a July 9, 1982 letter from J.R. Gass of the Organization for Economic Cooperation and Development of the Center for Educational Research and Innovation to Donald J. Senese, assistant secretary for the Office of Educational Research and Improvement, U.S. Department of Education. Such international meetings at which international education/workforce training agenda items are discussed take place regularly. OERI and CERI are closely connected in the work they carry out for OECD, UNESCO and the United Nations.]

"BETWEEN CLASSES—WHAT COST, ACCOUNTABILITY?" BY TERRY L. FOR- thum, teacher and editor of the state newspaper of the Arizona Federation of Teachers, was published in the October 1982 issue of the *The Arizona Forum*. Excerpts follow from this thought-provoking article:

> If accountability becomes the ultimate goal of education and all areas of education are reduced to "components" measurable by standardized testing, education will no longer be a learning process but a cloning process for both the teacher and the student. The priority questions for education in the future may well be: Why can't Johnny think? Why can't Johnny enjoy? Why can't Johnny feel? Why can't Carbon Unit J smile?... [See the "Consolidation" cartoon on this book's flyleaves, ed.]
>
> The panic caused by educational studies of the Why Can't Johnny Read variety has created a new educational priority—ACCOUNTABILITY. In its purest form, accountability aids the profession and the professional in main- taining standards of excellence. The results of any attempt to "monitor" the profession and therefore make it accountable can only be as valid, however, as the instrument or process which produces the results....
>
> Accountability is the central election issue in the race for Superintendent of Public Instruction [Mr. Forthum is referring to reform opponent Ann Her- zer's bid to unseat Carolyn Warner as superintendent of public instruction, ed.]. The present administration has established pilot programs throughout Arizona which can measure student progress as defined by the testing instrument, therefore making the school and instructor accountable. The evaluative program, developed nationally and piloted in other states before reaching Arizona, can in fact establish a criteria for testing accountability. That it works is not the issue. The issue is how it works. The issue is not "should education be accountable" but should education make B.F. Skinner methodology the model for establishing educational accountability?

EDWARD CURRAN, DIRECTOR OF THE NATIONAL INSTITUTE OF EDUCATION, was dismissed by Secretary T.H. Bell in 1982 due to Curran's recommen- dation to President Reagan that the National Institute of Education—the research and development arm of the U.S. Department of Education—be abolished. President Reagan was out of the country at the time of Curran's dismissal. When President Reagan was elected Dr. Curran left his position as headmaster of the Cathedral School for Girls in Washington, D.C., first to work on the education department transition team and later to assume the directorship of the National Institute of Education.

Curran's courageous recommendation would not have required Con- gressional approval, as did the proposal to abolish the U.S. Department of Education; an executive order by Secretary Bell was all that was required. Abolishing NIE could have removed much of the controversial federal government influence in our local schools. In an article entitled "Success Eludes Old Research Agency," *Education Week* (December 9, 1982) quoted Dr. Curran as follows:

> NIE is based on the premise that education is a science whose progress depends on systematic *"research and development."* As a professional educator, I know that this premise is false.

1983

"A RELIGION FOR A NEW AGE" BY JOHN DUNPHY, WRITTEN FOR THE JANUary/February 1983 issue of *The Humanist*, the journal of the American Humanist Association, lifts the veil of respectability from humanism and humanistic ethics. Excerpts follow:

> I am convinced that the battle for humankind's future must be waged and won in the public school classroom by teachers who correctly perceive their role as the proselytizers of a new faith: a religion of humanity that recognizes and respects the spark of what theologians call divinity in every human being.
> These teachers must embody the same selfless dedication as the most rabid fundamentalist preachers, for they will be ministers of another sort, utilizing a classroom instead of a pulpit to convey humanist values in whatever subjects they teach, regardless of the education level—preschool day care or a large university.
> The classroom must and will become an arena of conflict between the old and the new—the rotting corpse of Christianity, together with all its adjacent evils and misery, and the new faith of Humanism, resplendent in its premise of a world in which the never-realized Christian idea of "love thy neighbor" will finally be achieved.

EDUCATION FOR RESULTS: IN RESPONSE TO A NATION AT RISK, VOL. 1: Guaranteeing Effective Performance by Our Schools (SAFE Learning Systems, Inc.: Anaheim, Cal., 1983) by Robert Corrigan was published. In its 500-page how-to manual, Corrigan's S.A.F.E. [Systematic Approach for Effectiveness] model was described. Corrigan explains:

> The following successive phases were performed to test out the theoretical concepts of increased mastery learning effectiveness: Phase 1. To design and to extensively field-test a group instructional learning-centered program applying those programmed instructional principles postulated by Skinner and Crowder to be combined with the techniques of System Analysis for installing required system-wide managing-for-results processes including the accountable performance by teachers, principals and support personnel. This program would be "packaged" for use by teachers to deliver predictable achievement of defined mastery-learning objectives. (p. 155)

[Ed. Note: This program was endorsed by—among others—Bill Spady (Mr. OBE), the director of the controversial Far West Laboratory Outcome-Based Education Project (the Utah Grant) and Professor Homer Coker of the University of Georgia, who developed—with National Institute of Education funds—a controversial standardized teacher evaluation instrument with 420 teacher characteristics (competencies/behaviors). This book's Internet version has Appendix VI which contains extensive quotes from this important trail-blazing project.]

FROM THE FIRST NEWSLETTER, *OUTCOMES*, PUBLISHED BY BILL SPADY'S Network for Outcome-Based Schools in 1983, came the article "Four Phases in Creating and Managing an Outcome-Based Program" by John Champlin of the Department of Educational Administration of Texas Tech University in Lubbock, Texas. The fact that mastery learning is outcome-based education is made clear in the following excerpts:

> "Outcome-Based" was conceived during discussions in 1979 when our attention centered around how Mastery Learning could be better managed and made more likely to survive, despite many ill-conceived design and implementation attempts. Those participating proposed that an advocacy network be established. This founding group of a dozen or so concluded that more support for Mastery Learning would be likely if this new network focused equally on outcomes as well as process. They argued that instructional delivery systems needed to be sufficiently flexible and responsive to produce a wide variety of outcomes, not just the existing limitations of basic skills programs. This decision was considered critical in view of limited success in efforts to operationalize competency-based concepts during the 1970s.... Out of these dialogues emerged the Network for Outcome-Based Schools, a loose configuration of researchers, teachers, principals, school superintendents and college professors whose goal was to advocate and implement Mastery Learning as a vehicle for producing the capabilities and responses necessary for students to attain varied outcomes. The Network has been a vigorous proponent of all of the identified components of Outcome-Based (OB) programming since its inception....
>
> INITIATE COMMUNITY REEDUCATION AND RENORMING ACTIVITIES— Any new program development absolutely requires provisions to foster community understanding. Many well-intended change efforts have fallen upon the rocks because the community didn't understand it, challenged it, and built up so much pressure that it was easiest for staff to revert to the safe harbor of the status quo. This community effort should be designed both to reeducate and to renorm parents and the general public. It is important that your community know what you intend to do, why it is happening, and exactly what they can expect as it progresses. I believe a district will win some degree of tolerance and patience if it involves the community in this way. To expect residents to passively accept any modification after the fact or by edict is a serious error. Think of renorming the community the same way you conduct similar efforts in the school environment. Don't challenge the community, co-opt them. (pp. 36–7)

THE U.S. DEPARTMENT OF EDUCATION FUNDED TWO IMPORTANT PROJECTS in 1983: 1) "Framing a Future for Education" for Kansas; and 2) "Strategic Planning and Furthering Excellence in Millard Public Schools" for Nebraska, both of which were assigned to Dr. Shirley McCune of the MidContinent

Regional Educational Laboratory (McREL) as project director. These two projects, based on the work of the New Age Naisbitt Group founded by John Naisbitt who authored *Megatrends,* served as national pilots for OBE restructuring of America from a "representative democracy" to a "participatory democracy—moving from a left versus right politics to a politics of the radical center," in Dr. McCune's words. McCune became famous (or infamous) during the National Governors' Association conference in Wichita, Kansas in 1989 when she said,

> What we're into is the total restructuring of society. What is happening in America today and what is happening in Kansas and the Great Plains is not simply a chance situation in the usual winds of change. What it amounts to is a total transformation of society.... Our total society is in a crisis of restructuring and you can't get away from it. You can't go into rural areas, you can't go into the churches, you can't go into government or into business and hide from the fact that what we are facing is the total restructuring of our society.

[Ed. Note: In the 1996 entry regarding McCune's book, *The Light Shall Set You Free* (Athena Publishing, Alpha Connections: Santa Fe, New Mexico, 1996), McCune expressed her belief that "each individual is a co-creator with the Divine."]

[ddd]

COMPUTERS IN EDUCATION: REALIZING THE POTENTIAL WAS PUBLISHED BY the U.S. Department of Education in June, 1983. Under the subtitle "Expert and Novice Thinking" the authors speculate:

> Recent studies in science education have revealed that students approach learning with many prior conceptions based on their life experiences, which can be obstacles to learning. These conceptions are very resistant to change. We need to understand why students' conceptions persevere so strongly and how best they can be modified.

"THERE HAS BEEN A CONSPIRACY OF SILENCE ABOUT TEACHING: B.F. SKINner Argues that Pedagogy Is Key to School Reforms" by Susan Walton was published by *Education Week* in its August 31, 1983 issue. Excerpts from this extremely enlightening article follow:

> Improving methods of teaching would do more to help public education than would lengthening the school day or any of the other reforms proposed by the National Commission on Excellence in Education and other groups that have recently issued reports on education. So argues B.F. Skinner, the Harvard University psychologist whose pioneering theories about and studies on the "conditioning" of behavior have had a substantial impact on education. Still a source of controversy 40-odd years after Mr. Skinner began his research, those theories have been instrumental in the development of mastery learning and the "teaching machines" of the 1960s. The behavioral scientist's work has also been an integral part of the debate over individual-

ized instruction.... Central to Mr. Skinner's thinking on education are the notions that children should be allowed to learn at their own pace and that teachers should rely on "reinforcers" or rewards, to strengthen patterns of behavior that they want to encourage. Mr. Skinner argues that computers, as they are most commonly used, are essentially sophisticated versions of the "teaching machines" of the 1960s.... Pointing to recent articles and reports on how to improve education, Mr. Skinner argues that one central fallacy is that it is more important for teachers to know their subject matter than to know how to teach it. Mr. Skinner also advises that educators stop making all students advance at essentially the same rate.... No teacher can teach a class of 30 or 40 students and allow each to progress at an optimal speed. Tracking is too feeble a remedy. We must turn to INSTRUMENTS [emphasis in original] for a large part of the school curriculum. The psychologist also urges educators to "program" subject matter. "The heart of the teaching machine, call it what you will, is the programming of instruction—an advance not mentioned in any of the reports I have cited," he writes. He argues "the reinforcing consequences of being right" will eventually prompt students to do what they are supposed to do, but to elicit the behavior the first time, their behavior must be "primed" and "prompted." "Programmed instruction," Mr. Skinner contends, makes "very few demands on teachers."

[Ed. Note: Had the above interview occurred a year later, Skinner would have known that *A Nation at Risk*'s ultimate recommendations would be to implement Skinnerian mastery learning (OBE) "in all the schools of the nation."]

MAINE ASSOCIATION FOR SUPERVISION AND CURRICULUM DEVELOPMENT in-service training was attended by this author in 1983. Dr. S. Alan Cohen led the training. Cohen taught research and curriculum design in the Department of Curriculum and Instruction at the University of San Francisco, California, and was president of SAC Associates, a private consulting firm in systems analysis, evaluation and curriculum design. The following information was contained in a flyer handed out at the in-service training:

His [Cohen's] curriculum research generated the concept of High Intensity Learning, an application of systems theory to classroom management. Today, thousands of schools around the world operate his High Intensity Learning Centers in reading and math. He co-authored the Random House series, the first commercially published basal program developed on the Mastery Learning model. A second Mastery Learning program, published in 1978, teaches pupils how to score high on standardized tests. In 1979 Dr. Cohen authored, designed and published a series of graduate textbooks under a SAC subsidiary, Mastery Learning Systems (MLS). Cohen was one of the architects of the Job Corps Curriculum System. Has been consultant to the Right to Read Office, U.S. Office of Education Office of Economic Opportunity.... His work as consultant and author to Random House and to 20th Century's B.F. Skinner's Reading Program reflects an unusual synthesis of radical behaviorism and humanistic approach to curriculum design....

...[W]ith Harry Passow and Abe Tannebaum of Teachers College, Columbia University, Dr. Cohen formed the education task force in the first War on Poverty, Mobilization for Youth. Since that time, his training in learning psychology has been applied to research, materials and systems development, writing and teaching in three major areas: systems applications to curriculum, teaching the disadvantaged and learning disabilities.

During the in-service training, this writer recorded verbatim Cohen's following points:

> In 1976 Block and Burns published in the American Educational Research Association research, around the world on mastery learning. United Nations Educational, Scientific and Cultural Organization (UNESCO) is committed to Mastery Learning all over the world. We have evaluated data worldwide.... Loyola University is the information center for Mastery Learning. Amazing amount of data from all over the world that tells the obvious.... You can account for 97 out of 100 things you give in a test.... Teaching kids to discriminate between long and short "a" is bad... mundane.... Design assessments to fit what teachers are doing.... Avoid misalignment of conditions of instruction and conditions of assessment....
>
> [Referring to the Iowa and California tests] Start teaching to them or stop using them. Find out what they truly measure.... Same issue as defining what you are teaching.... How do you get teachers to measure precisely what they teach? You must have an A and that better be different than B, C. and F because not everyone can get to Harvard. They can't buy the fact that every kid can get an A.... Way we guarantee no discrimination is to teach and test.... Between 1969 and 1971 Omaha, Nebraska implemented mastery learning curriculum citywide. Has best curriculum management I've seen anywhere.... New kind of report card... listed competencies describing what kids can do and described standardized test scores vs. norm-referenced.... Key components of mastery learning are: a) careful control of cues (stimuli), what you bring to student; b) careful control of reinforcers; c) kids on task; and d) recycling (correctives).

THE COMING REVOLUTION IN EDUCATION: BASIC EDUCATION AND THE NEW *Theory of Schooling* (University Press of America, Inc.: Baton Rouge, 1983) by the late Eugene Maxwell Boyce, former professor of educational administration, Bureau of Educational Studies and Field Services, College of Education at the University of Georgia, was published. An excerpt follows:

> In the communist ideology the function of universal education is clear, and easily understood. Universal education fits neatly into the authoritarian state. Education is tied directly to jobs—control of the job being the critical control point in an authoritarian state. Level of education, and consequently the level of employment, is determined first by level of achievement in school. They do not educate people for jobs that do not exist.... No such controlled relationship between education and jobs exists in democratic countries. (p. 4)

[ddd]

NORTHWEST REGIONAL EDUCATIONAL LABORATORY (NWREL) PUBLISHED *Effective Schooling Practices: A Research Synthesis—Goal-Based Education*

Program in the mid-1980s. [Goal-based education = outcomes-based education] NWREL is a federally funded laboratory whose role has always been to develop goals for American education. An excerpt from *Effective Schooling Practices* follows:

> Incentives and Rewards for Students Are Used to Promote Excellence:
>
> 1. Systems are set up in the classroom for frequent and consistent rewards to students for academic achievement and excellent behavior; they are appropriate to the developmental level of students; excellence is defined by objective standards, not by peer comparison.
> 2. All students know about the rewards and what they need to do to get them. Rewards are chosen because they appeal to students.
> 3. Rewards are related to specific achievements; some may be presented publicly; some should be immediately presented, while others delayed to teach persistence.
> 4. Parents are told about student successes and requested to help students keep working toward excellence. Brophy (1980); Brophy (1981); Emmer (1981); Evertson (1981); Hunter (1977); Rosswork (1977); Rutter (1979); Walker (1976).

[Ed. Note: An example of the pervasiveness of Skinnerian operant conditioning, with its rewards/reinforcement system, is found in the Effective School Research on "school climate." The definition of "positive/effective school climate" has varied; one definition being "psychologically facilitative environment"—Skinner to the core. The Charles F. Kettering Foundation Ltd. (Dayton, Ohio) *School Climate Profile*, based on Eugene Howard's Colorado Model, contains a mark-off sheet with blocks in which data are arranged by "Almost Never, Occasionally, Frequently, and Almost Always" to score behavior. Under "Program Determinants" from "Definitions of Climate Terms" in Howard's Colorado Model, we find this wording:

> 2. INDIVIDUALIZED PERFORMANCE EXPECTATION AND VARIED REWARD SYSTEMS:
>
> Practices are identified whereby staff members recognize individual differences among pupils. Everyone is not expected to learn the same things in the same way or in the same length of time. Rewards are sufficiently available so that all pupils, with effort, may expect to be positively and frequently recognized by the school.]

RESEARCHER AND WRITER K.M. HEATON, IN HER REVISED EDITION OF AN article entitled "Preconditioning for Acceptance of Change" explained very clearly in 1983 how radical change in our republican form of government has been brought about at the local level through the use of psychopolitics.[11] The following are excerpts from Mrs. Heaton's article:

> Variants of these control strategies have been, and are being, used on every front in this war. A case in point: In the early seventies, a textbook was developed by a think tank in Berkeley, with the authority of the Governor's [Ronald Reagan] office, and coordinated by the Council on Intergovernmental

Relations, which provided an elementary course in the use of psychopolitics "to provide the operant mechanism to change events in local government" (a direct quote). Named as the essential elements for planned change were:

- development of a climate for change;
- a crisis of major importance;
- a catastrophe having a physical effect on community;
- mounting cost of government, and/or major services;
- and/or collapse of government's ability to deal with these.

The Politics of Change (TPOC) then proceeded to suggest how to create these elements. TPOC offers prima facie evidence of a deliberate, calculated scheme to disinform, mislead, manage and control the destiny of local government in California and its citizens, without regard for legal, moral or ethical considerations.

1984

DURING JANUARY AND FEBRUARY OF 1984, THIS WRITER—WITH THE HELP of grassroots activists and several officials in the U.S. Department of Education—organized witnesses and testimony to be presented at the U.S. Department of Education "Hatch Amendment" hearings held in seven cities: Seattle, Washington; Pittsburgh, Pennsylvania; Kansas City, Missouri; Phoenix, Arizona; Concord, New Hampshire; Orlando, Florida; and Washington, D.C. These hearings were held "pursuant to the notice of proposed rulemaking to implement Sec. 439 of the *General Education Provisions Act (The Protection of Pupil Rights Amendment)*."

This *Amendment* is usually referred to as the "Hatch [Sen. Orrin] Amendment," although the senator who originated it and was most involved in the initial important wording was the late Senator Edward Zorinsky (D.-Neb). As the *Amendment* went through the Congressional committee process, Zorinsky's most important wording was weakened or deleted.

The weakened wording which attempted to address long-standing problems experienced by parents and good educators follows:

Protection of Pupil Rights, 20 U.S. Code Sec. 1232h, Inspection by parents or guardians of instructional material....

(a) All instructional material, including teachers' manuals, films, tapes, or other supplementary instructional materials which will be used in connection with any research or experimentation program or project shall be available for inspection by the parents or guardians of the children engaged in such program or project. For the purpose of this section "research or experimentation program or project" means any program or project in any applicable program designed to explore or... develop new or unproven teaching methods or techniques....

Psychiatric or psychological examination, testing or treatment:...

(b) No student shall be required, as part of any applicable program, to submit to psychiatric examination, testing or treatment, or psychological examination, testing or treatment, in which the primary purpose is to reveal information concerning political affiliations; mental and psychological

problems potentially embarrassing to the student or his family; sexual behavior and attitudes; illegal, anti-social, self-incriminating and demeaning
behavior; critical appraisals of other individuals with whom respondents
have close family relationships; legally recognized privileged and analogous
relationships, such as those of lawyers, physicians, and ministers; or income
(other than that required by law to determine eligibility for participation in a
program or for receiving financial assistance under such program); without
the prior consent of the student (if the student is an adult or emancipated
minor), or in the case of an unemancipated minor, without the prior written
consent of the parent.

At the annual meeting of the American Educational Research Association held in New Orleans, Louisiana in April of 1984, Brian Rowan,
Ph.D. in sociology, presented a paper entitled "Shamanistic Rituals in Effective Schools." The work on this "curious" paper was supported by the
National Institute of Education, U.S. Department of Education (Contract
#400–83–003). Rowan should be noted as one of the principal investigators
involved in the infamous 1984 grant to Utah (See later 1984 entry for Utah
grant) to implement William Spady's Outcome-Based Education program,
the purpose of which was to "put OBE into all the schools of the nation."

The "curious" nature of this paper is derived from Dr. Rowan's implied
criticism of the very Effective Schools Research with which he is so closely
associated. The importance of Rowan's paper lies in Rowan's professional
credentials and willingness to bring to the debate table a discussion of the
legitimacy of claims of "effectiveness" made by those associated with the
Effective Schools movement (William Spady, et al.), including promoting
outcome-based education, mastery learning and direct instruction—all of
which are required by Effective Schools Research. This presentation helps
one to better understand the dismal academic results to be found in schools
using Effective Schools Research; i.e., most often urban schools attended
by underprivileged and minority children.

The following quotes are taken from "Shamanistic Rituals in Effective
Schools" which can be found in its entirety in the Internet version of this
book in Appendix XXVI:

> We begin with one of the most common shamanistic rituals in the effec-
> tive schools movement, the glowing literature review....
>
> ...Lacking a systematic understanding of the scientific pros and cons of
> effective schools research, naïve individuals are left only with the powerful
> and appealing rhetoric of the reviewers.... The experienced shaman knows
> to avoid the scrutiny of scholars, for this can raise objections to the "sci-
> entific" basis of ritual claims and divert attention away from the appealing
> rhetoric. Instead, the shaman cultivates the practitioner who needs a simple
> and appealing formula.
>
> Thus, any experienced shaman can find "effective" schools....
>
> The ritual is particularly suited to application in urban or low performing
> school systems where successful instructional outcomes among disadvan-
> taged students are highly uncertain but where mobilized publics demand
> immediate demonstrations of success. The uncertainties faced by practitioners

in this situation can easily be alleviated by what scholars have begun to call curriculum alignment [teach to the test]....

Thus, the art of measurement can be used as an aid to shamanism, especially in urban schools plagued by the uncertainties of student performance. Student variability in performance can be reduced, and relative performance increased, not by changing instructional objectives or practices, but simply by changing tests and testing procedures.

THE OFFICE OF EDUCATIONAL RESEARCH AND IMPROVEMENT OF THE U.S. Department of Education in 1984 approved a grant from the Secretary's Discretionary Fund in the amount of $134,459 (Grant No. 122BH40196) to Vanderbilt University to implement Vanderbilt's proposal entitled "National Network for Educational Excellence." This project covered a period from October 1984–October 1985 to use a computer-based network of fifty superintendents to collect and exchange information about "effective" practices and to encourage national dialogue about increasing school "effectiveness," so as to promote educational excellence. (Quotation marks have been added around the words "effective" and "effectiveness" to alert the reader to the fact that this grant was another effort to implement "Effective Schools Research" based on Skinnerian psychology. Rowan's remarks in the entry prior to this one cast an interesting light on this information.) At the time this grant was made, Chester Finn was professor of education and public policy at Vanderbilt University. Finn would shortly thereafter be named assistant secretary to the Office of Educational Research and Improvement under Secretary of Education William Bennett who, in 1985, provided over $4 million to implement Effective School Research nationwide.

A LETTER TO PRESIDENT RONALD REAGAN WAS WRITTEN BY WILLARD W. Garvey, executive director of the National Center for Privatization, dated April 6, 1984.[12] An excerpt follows:

Privatization is now an idea whose time has come.... The knowledge, communication and computer industry can make political representatives obsolete. Privatization might well be the theme for the 200th anniversary of the Constitution. Privatization is essential for national salvation.

The following notation was printed on the letterhead of the above-mentioned letter:

The National Center for Privatization is supported by the following groups and individuals: Heritage and Reason Foundations; Pacific and Manhattan Institutes; VOLUNTEER; National Center for Citizen Involvement; International Executive Service Corps; United Way with its Services Identification System; National Legal Center for the Public; churches; labor unions, Peter Drucker* and Milton Friedman.

---

* See the Update to the Revised and Abridged version of this book for more information about Peter Drucker and his effect on education policy.

THE SPRING 1984 ISSUE (VOL. 7, NO.4) OF *EDUCATION UPDATE* FROM THE Association for Supervision and Curriculum Development carried the following statements:

> One comprehensive study concludes that counseling can have marked deleterious effects on problem students. Joan McCord, a Drexel University sociologist, undertook a 30-year follow up study of a classic, highly respected study on juvenile delinquency—"The Cambridge Somerville Youth Study." In the original study (first report in 1948) an experimental group of 253 high-risk problem boys were given extensive counseling. A control group matched as to behavior, history, and family background received no counseling. In 1975 Professor McCord contacted the original participants and compared the circumstances of the experimental and control subjects. The experimental subjects were, among other things, found more likely to commit criminal acts, be alcoholics, suffer from mental illness, die younger, and have less prestigious jobs than the control group.

[Ed. Note: The results of this study match the negative results discussed in the May 1977 issue of *The School Counselor*, American Personnel and Guidance Association's Special Issue on Death, which said,"Death education will play as important a part in changing attitudes toward death as sex education played in changing attitudes toward sex information and wider acceptance of various sexual practices." In other words, counseling, sex ed and death ed have negative effects, if, as one would hope and expect, the purpose of such programs is to help young people live happy and stable lives. This is particularly disturbing in light of increased student violence which has taken place in the nation recently.]

STEPHEN BROADY OF TARKIO, MISSOURI PRESENTED TESTIMONY IN 1984 AT the U.S. Department of Education's Region VII hearing on "Notice of Proposed Rulemaking to further implement Section 439 of the *General Education Provisions Act*, 34 CFR, Parts 75, 76, and 98, 20 U.S.C.A. Section 2132(h) 20 U.S.C. 1231e–3(a)(1), 1232h (*Hatch Amendment*)." Broady's statement exposes the controversial nature of the two leading mastery learning programs—Exemplary Center for Reading Instruction (ECRI) and Project INSTRUCT—both of which use Skinnerian operant conditioning and both of which submitted claims of effectiveness which have been questioned by persons involved in implementing and evaluating the programs. The third program, DISTAR (Direct Instruction for Systematic Teaching and Remediation), which is similar to ECRI, is the highly recommended "scientific, research-based" phonics program so popular with conservatives in the late 1990s. The following are some excerpts from Stephen Broady's testimony:

> I am a farmer currently engaged in the operation of over one thousand acres of prime farm ground. I became interested in education after my wife and I observed emotional change in our daughter while she was attending a rural public school using an "approved" federal educational project... "Project INSTRUCT"... approved for funding in the amount of $710,000 and for nationwide use by the Joint Dissemination Review Panel on May 14, 1975 (JDRP #75–37).

Although Project INSTRUCT is only one of over 300 "approved" educational projects, Project INSTRUCT and the educational project upon which it is based, the Exemplary Center for Reading Instruction (ECRI), are the most widely used mastery learning educational projects in the United States.

...These mastery learning systems use a type of psychological manipulation based on the Skinnerian ideology of rewards and punishments, and individual feelings are irrelevant.... More commonly referred to as "behavior modification," the Skinnerian ideology which is used in the teaching techniques of these mastery learning systems, breaks down the process of learning into small bits of information and actually codes a type of behavior that is desired into the learning process itself.

The real objective of these mastery learning systems with their behavior modification, is a deliberate attempt to make children conform to an artificial environment which is more suited to the thinking of the school than to the needs of the children.

These federally funded mastery learning systems require the use on young children of a highly structured curriculum, test and re-test with the use of criterion tests, stopwatches, direct eye contact, physical contact, and psychological manipulation until the so-called "mastery" of the subject is achieved. These ideas and practices form a complex philosophy in which the "authoritarian" concept predominates.

In the early part of 1983, I obtained the evaluation report of Project INSTRUCT from the superintendent's office of the Lincoln Public Schools. At that time I was unaware the so-called behavior modification based on Skinner's rewards and punishments was used on my daughter.

The evaluation results clearly referred to behavioral objectives which were... established for: (a) students; (b) parents; (c) administrators; (d) media specialists; (e) project staff; (f) teachers; (g) paraprofessionals and volunteers, and (h) prospective teachers.

The wholesale use of behavior modification is part of Skinnerian psychology. As it was outlined in the evaluation, Project INSTRUCT includes rewards and punishments, not only for school children, but for anyone who comes in contact with the school system itself.

The *Evaluation of Project INSTRUCT, Executive Summary*, written by Carl Spencer, project director for Lincoln Public Schools, also explains that

> Project INSTRUCT grew from beliefs that to reduce reading failure reading programs must (1) be diagnostic and prescriptive so that failure does not begin to occur, (2) be implemented by regular teachers in regular classrooms, (3) provide direct rather than indirect teaching, (4) correlate instruction in all language skills, particularly reading, spelling and handwriting....

The intent and emphasis in 1970 was on behavioral indices and concrete ways of showing accountability; and the data would suggest that the reading of the students themselves may not have increased, but the impact of Project INSTRUCT in the Lincoln, Nebraska Publish Schools seems to be very extensive and influential.

[Ed. Note: Project INSTRUCT accomplished its major objective—it developed and installed a less than successful reading program in Lincoln, Nebraska using a model which could be transported to other districts. It also had considerable impact upon the district as a whole, on schools outside of

Lincoln and even on the Nebraska State Department of Education. In assessing this impact as a whole, Dr. Ronald Brandt, assistant superintendent for instruction, has said of this project, "Project INSTRUCT made a lasting contribution to instruction in the Lincoln Schools by helping us improve our planning capabilities and by furthering the concepts of focused instruction and mastery learning."

It should be noted that Dr. Ronald Brandt went on to become the executive editor of the Association for Supervision and Curriculum Development's (ASCD) publication *Educational Leadership*. ASCD could be considered the most influential education organization in the world, outside of UNESCO.]

DAVID W. HORNBECK, CHAIRMAN OF THE BOARD OF TRUSTEES OF THE CARNegie Foundation for the Advancement of Teaching and Maryland's state school superintendent, oversaw the implementation of Project BASIC in 1984. Project BASIC was based on the very controversial Management by Objectives (MBO/PPBS) that is thoroughly discussed in this book.

One of the more controversial graduation requirements in Project BASIC was "the worthy use of leisure time," which was later given the more acceptable and politically correct label of "arts and recreation"—another semantic deception at work. However, Hornbeck's penultimate controversial recommendation—one which would reverberate from coast to coast, resulting in heated debate at local school board meetings—was his recommendation to the Maryland State Board of Education that community service become a mandatory graduation requirement. Many objections were raised on the grounds that that recommendation constituted involuntary servitude, thus making it unconstitutional.

[Ed. Note: In this writer's opinion, David Hornbeck is a soft-hearted, highly paid "should-have-been" Presbyterian minister do-gooder who approaches his job with missionary fervor rooted in theologian Reinhold Niebuhr's idea that a good Christian must strive to correct any unjust status quo. However, his mission seems to be to help implement a socialist world government, increasingly referred to as "The New World Disorder," as was the goal of the do-gooder Federal Council of Churches in 1942, working toward all being equally poor, miserable and illiterate.

Should the elitist power brokers, for whatever reason, feel they need the expertise of the Hornbecks of this world, please spare those least able to protect themselves—the minorities and disadvantaged—from the change agents' experimentation.]

AN ARTICLE ENTITLED "INDUSTRIAL POLICY URGED FOR GOP" WAS PUBLISHED in *The Washington Post* on May 14, 1984. Excerpts follow:

> SAN FRANCISCO (UPI)—A conservative study group founded by supporters of President Reagan is about to issue a report that advocates Republicans shed some of their deep-rooted antipathy to a planned economy.
>
> An industrial policy accepted by both political parties and by business and labor is essential to revitalize America's dwindling clout in the world

economy, according to the study's editor, Professor Chalmers Johnson of the University of California.

"The Industrial Policy Debate" is to be issued today by the Institute for Contemporary Studies, a think-tank founded by presidential counselor Edwin Meese, Secretary of Defense Caspar Weinberger and other Reagan supporters.

"What we are really trying to pose is a serious debate that has become stupidly politicized by both parties," Johnson said. "We are trying to get the question of an industrial policy for the United States to be taken seriously by people who don't really believe in it—above all Republicans.

"Americans must come to grips with economic policy or go the way of England. We have probably got a decade before it becomes irreversible."

In the United States, he said, "The whole topic we are trying to address is so caught up with politics and the particular positions of industries that it is very hard to disentangle what we mean by economic policy."

While the Democrats are "planning to throw money at the northern Midwest 'rust' belt" to get votes, Johnson said many Republicans "are painting themselves into a corner by attacking the very concept of industrial policy—arguing that it violates the sacred principles of private enterprise and free trade."

He cited as a valid and successful national economic policy "the kind of government-business relationship" that has made Japan a leading economic force in the world. "A government-business relationship is needed in a competitive capitalist economy," he said.

"Reaganomics without an accompanying industrial policy to guide it, has been costly," Johnson said.

[ddd]

IN 1984 JACQUELINE LAWRENCE GAVE TESTIMONY BEFORE THE SUBCOMMITtee on Education, Arts and Humanities of the Senate Committee on Labor and Human Resources which held hearings on *Senate Joint Resolution 138*, a bill establishing a commission on teacher education. Excerpts from Mrs. Lawrence's testimony follow:

> My name is Jacqueline Lawrence. I am a parent from Montgomery County, Maryland....
>
> Prior to the 1960s, American public schools placed major emphasis on the intellectual development of our children, on their mastery of basic skills such as reading, writing and mathematics. Competency in physics, biology, chemistry, and chronological factual history was required. Cognitive learning and scholarly objectivity were stressed as the basic approach to education at all levels. As a result, our nation produced a large, well-educated middle class—our greatest strength.

[Ed. Note: Mrs. Lawrence's comments regarding the "major emphasis on intellectual development prior to the 1960s" remind the writer of a scholarly ancient history textbook used in a high school history course at the Rockland, Maine District High School as late as the early 1970s. (It took a while for the change agents to penetrate a fishing community on the coast of

Maine!) The textbook written by Professor James Breasted, an Egyptologist and Semitic scholar, is a fascinating and extremely well written history of Ancient Greece, Egypt, etc., with few black and white photographs, quizzes at the end of each chapter, and text written for college level students. That was only 25 years ago! It would be virtually impossible to find a textbook of that scholarly level in public high schools or in most colleges today. This writer has nothing but a feeling of tremendous sadness pondering the vapid education landscape Americans seem so willing to accept for their offspring. It is my constant hope that American apathy in this regard is due to their not knowing what has happened, and that once they know, they will—all of them—collectively and individually attempt to reverse this situation.]

Mrs. Lawrence continued:

> It is public knowledge that since the 1960s academic standards have declined. Why? Quite simply, over the past 20 years our schools have not placed emphasis on academic achievement. There has instead been a shift toward psychological development and social adjustment of students in the affective domain, that is, their feelings, attitudes, and opinions.
>
> The shift began in 1965 with the passage of the *Elementary and Secondary Education Act* (ESEA).... Since 1965, billions of federal dollars have been allocated to educational theorists and curriculum developers to alter the course of public education. The blueprint for the process of educational reform may be found in a series of guides known as *Pacesetters in Innovation*.... From this has come a nationwide information network of ERIC clearinghouses (Educational Resource Information Centers) and the National Diffusion Network of laboratories for the dissemination of federally funded classroom materials and curriculum.
>
> With the new programs came a retraining of the teachers. A prime example: in 1969 the Office of Education began financing model teacher education programs known as the Behavioral Science Teacher Education Program (BSTEP–OE 5803) to introduce to the classroom methods employed by the behavioral scientists, the sociometrist, and the psychiatrist.
>
> Such methods are the most coercive and manipulative known to man today. They were originally developed and used for treating mentally disturbed in mental institutions and the criminally insane in prisons. The techniques are role-playing, psychodrama, sociodrama, simulation games, guided fantasy, diary-keeping, situation attitude scale tests, encounter groups, magic circle, and behavior modification such as isolation, time-out boxes and coffins, as well as operant conditioning. These are techniques to influence by clinical, hospital procedures the thinking processes of children in a compulsory classroom setting.
>
> In addition to training teachers, a special cadre of sensitive manipulators, known as change agents, were trained to facilitate the process of change and to identify forces which resisted change.
>
> The change agent serves as a catalyst for teacher and citizen awareness and attempts to gain support for educational change.
>
> Dr. John Goodlad's *Report to the President's Commission on School Finance, Issue #9*, "Strategies for Change," dated October 1971, explains that the change agent is the decision-maker. He decides which changes a school will make. The report states that five to fifteen percent of the people in a

given community are open to change. They are the Early Majority and can be counted on to be supportive. A second group, 60 to 90 percent, are the Resisters; they need special attention and careful strategies. Also there are Leaders, formal and informal, and their support is critical for effecting change.

In a diagram from the report... you will note that the change agent creates the Early Majority and influences the Leaders, and then gets both of these groups to act in concert with him to level a triple attack on the Resisters.

Goodlad's report to the President expressed concern about the willingness of the people to change: "People cannot be forced to change until they are psychologically ready."...

...Even if we assume for the sake of argument that change agents are gifted with infinite knowledge and wisdom, their methods are in conflict with the political principles of democracy. Their changes in curriculum and methods and goals of education have not come as a result of democratic discussion and decision.

In this vein, it is interesting to note that the Maryland State Teachers Association has lobbied against proposed state legislation for parental access to classroom materials because teachers "would be ineffective as change agents."...

...Moreover, education is now termed psycho-social, psycho-medical, humanistic, affective and/or diagnostic and prescriptive. Educators diagnose the child's emotional, intellectual, perceptual and conceptual development levels. Dr. Benjamin Bloom explains that what educators are classifying is the intended behavior of students, or as he puts it, "the ways in which individuals are to act, think, or feel as a result of participating in some unit of instruction."

In order to bring about desired attitudinal changes in students, teachers must first know where a child is in his or her attitudes and opinions. Various tactics and techniques are used in classrooms to make a child reveal himself to his teacher and peers. The examples I use below are nationally used and have received federal funding:

- Magic circle, talk-in, contact or group discussions: The teacher gathers the children into a circle where they are encouraged to discuss personal feelings about one another, their parents, and home life. Family size, advantages, disadvantages, comparison of toys, vacations, and clothing may be discussed. Family conflicts, worries and fears are often revealed.
- Inside-Out: A nationally-used elementary social studies program encourages students to discuss their feelings before, during and after their parents' divorce; their personal reactions to the death of a friend, pet or relative; what your friends think of you; what adults think of you and what you think of yourself.
- Logbooks: These are workbooks used in conjunction with many language arts textbooks. They are vehicles for children to reveal their reactions to short stories, often dealing with emotions and moral dilemmas. There are no right answers, only personal responses. Sometimes the logbooks guide the child into a response. For instance:

> Even if your family is a happy one, you're bound to feel sad... or even lonely. When might a person be lonely even if he is part of a family? Loneliness is listening to your parents

arguing. Loneliness is when you come home and there's no one there. Loneliness is....

Perhaps the most frequently used strategies for self-revelation are the diary and role-playing. These techniques were introduced into American public schools by an Estonian teacher, Hilda Taba, and a Romanian psychiatrist, Jacob Moreno.

[Ed. Note: In 1957 a California State Senate Investigative Committee exposed the work of Hilda Taba, Jacob Moreno and others. In spite of this exposure, these people continued to receive tax dollars and access to schools nation-wide. Hilda Taba's program has remained in use by key change agents from 1960 to 1999. Bruce Joyce and Marsha Weil's *Models of Teaching* mentions her work as well as that of many other sociologists, behavioral psychologists, etc. As a school board director in 1976, the writer found materials related to the above-described programs and many others described by Mrs. Lawrence in a box given to her by a home economics teacher. Needless to say, the writer was shocked to find that behavior modification was being introduced into the curriculum under the innocent-sounding "home economics" label.]

The U.S. Office of Education gave grants to Taba to develop an elementary social studies program to improve the social adjustment and personality development of children. She had worked in reform schools and mental institutions with Moreno and found that role-playing and diaries were successful tools to learn where a child stood in his beliefs, attitudes, and social interactions.

The diary has been used for years in Russia and China for self-revelation, self-evaluation, and self-criticism. More recently the personal diary was found in Guyana throughout the Jim Jones compound.

Montgomery County, Maryland, requires its students to keep a diary from kindergarten through grade nine. Diaries are an important psychological instrument. They provide a precise record and personality profile of the child, his family members, neighbors and peers—information needed by the teacher or therapist to alter a student's behavior or attitude. It is important that the writing be free-style and spontaneous, coming directly from the emotional feeling area of the child. Diaries are not corrected for form, grammar or spelling....

A teacher manual for values education suggests 15 kinds of diaries for use in the classroom; some examples are a budget diary, religion diary, hostility and anger diary, low points diary, affectionate and tender feelings diary, and a time diary....

In the psycho-social approach to education, the child is taught concepts through the use of psychotherapy. For example, to better understand the social problem of prejudice and to teach children through experiential learning, blond children in a fifth grade (age 10) were asked to sit in the back of the room for one week, totally isolated, not permitted to participate in the classwork. For a one-and-a-half hour period each day, brown-haired students were instructed to pick on, insult, make fun of or taunt the blonds. Needless to say, taunting spilled over onto the playground with some of the blonds being told, "You can't play with us." At the end of the week, blonds were given candy bars as a reward for their suffering, but the browns, who in bullying were obeying the teacher's instructions, were given nothing. How does a child react to being punished or deprived for carrying out his assignment?

How much learning went on in that classroom for five days? Some children enjoyed taunting and bullying. Was the week spent on such "experiential learning" quality time? What about the seven and one-half hours spent in taunting? Would this time have been better spent on academic learning?...

Educators use the even more volatile psycho-drama for attitudinal change. One example is the concept that we must prune away defective persons in order to improve the quality of life for the remainder of the group. This drama involves murder. Many variations are found. I first came across this psychodrama theme in a federally funded home economics curriculum guide... containing the exercise "Whom Will You Choose?" It goes as follows: 11 people are in a bomb shelter with provisions sufficient to last 11 persons two weeks or six persons a month. The group is told that five persons must be killed. They are instructed to accept the situation as fact, that is, to concern themselves with life/death choices, not with attacking the logic or probability of the situation. A profile is given of each person in the shelter. Problem people, such as the athlete who eats too much, the religious type with "hang-ups," the pregnant or ill are generally killed. Survivors tend to be those trained in medicine, engineers, and pacifiers.

[Ed. Note: Jacqueline and Malcolm Lawrence had just returned from their Foreign Service assignment in Europe and were appalled to encounter what had happened to American education in their absence. The Lawrences organized "Parents Who Care" and began to confront the school district with what they had discovered. Due to the broad publicity generated by the group's assertions and activities, Edward Hunter, former intelligence service operative and author of two books on his coined word "brainwashing" as practiced pre- and post-World War II[13]—*Brainwashing* and *Brainwashing in Red China: The Men Who Defied It*—approached the Lawrences with a request to examine the curriculum materials about which they had become concerned. Hunter took the materials for a period of time and upon returning them, informed Jackie and Malcolm that they were indeed examples of methods and techniques used in Russian and Chinese brainwashing. (The Maryland State School Board also made a statement regarding the fact that Maryland's teachers were not trained to use "psychoanalytical techniques in the classroom.") The psycho-social technique for confronting prejudice (isolation of the blonds) should be especially disturbing in light of increased concern over schoolyard taunting and increased school violence at the close of this century.]

"E.C.S. at 20: The Compact's Potential Is Still to Be Realized" by Thomas Toch was an article from *Education Week* (October 24, 1984) which covered the early history of the Education Commission of the States. The excerpts warrant repeating:

"Some degree of order needs to be brought out of this chaos," wrote James B. Conant, the President of Harvard University, in 1964 in reference to education policymaking in this nation. "We cannot have a national educational policy," he added in his book *Shaping Educational Policy*, "but we might be able to evolve a nationwide policy." The solution, Mr. Conant concluded, was a "new venture in cooperative federalism," a compact among the states to create an organization to focus national attention on the pressing education issues of the day. The following spring, the Carnegie Corporation and the Ford Foundation awarded a grant to Terry Sanford, who had recently left the governorship of North Carolina, to transform the Conant idea into reality. John W. Gardner was Carnegie's president at the time. A preliminary draft of the compact was completed by July and endorsed by representatives from all 50 states and the territories in September. Within five months, 10 states had ratified the agreement, giving it legal status. Out of the compact was born the Education Commission of the States (ECS)....

"We invented a little device to get the compact approved quickly," Mr. Sanford, now the president of Duke University, said recently. "We didn't need money from the legislatures, we had plenty of foundation funding, so we agreed that the governors could ratify it by executive order.".…

But since the establishment under Governor James B. Hunt [also of North Carolina] of the Commission's Task Force on Education for Economic Growth two years ago, ECS's role has begun to change. The task force's report *Action for Excellence* joined *A Nation at Risk* and the Carnegie Foundation for the Advancement of Teaching's *High School* as principal voices in the chorus of reform. It gained Gov. Hunt and several other "education governors" who were linked to ECS wide national publicity, and, in making a series of specific reform recommendations, thrust ECS into the policy-making arena.

[Ed. Note: The multi-million dollar contract to operate the National Assessment of Educational Progress, awarded to the ECS in 1969, was transferred to Educational Testing Service (ETS) in 1983. This move was significant due to Carnegie's deep involvement in establishing, funding, and directing ECS's and ETS's activities. Essentially, this move gave Carnegie Corporation and Carnegie Foundation for the Advancement of Teaching extensive control over the direction and content of American education as a whole and individual state policy making in paticular with regard to education. Dennis Cuddy, Ph.D.—rightly, it seems—refers to the U.S. Department of Education as the "Carnegie Department of Education."]

THE PRESIDENTIALLY APPOINTED NATIONAL COUNCIL FOR EDUCATIONAL Research (NCER) issued two "Policies on Missions for Educational Research and Development Centers," dated June 14 and October 25, 1984, shortly after regional hearings had been held regarding the need for regulations to implement the *Protection of Pupil Rights Amendment* (PPRA). The following are excerpts from NCER's two policy statements:

JUNE 14, 1984. In the past two decades, federally funded research and curriculum projects have frequently provoked considerable controversy. This is primarily a result of deeply divergent philosophical views on the nature and purpose of public education in this country. During this period, the views of the general public were, for the most part, excluded from serious consideration as educational research came to be viewed as the observation and measurement of the education process using the largely quantitative techniques of modern social science [Skinnerian behaviorism].

OCTOBER 25, 1984. Insofar as it represents a broad spectrum of interests, including parents who have a serious stake in the outcomes of federally funded educational research, the Council affirms that the fundamental philosophical foundation for such research should be the unambiguous recognition and respect for the dignity and value of each human person.

For the past fifteen years the U.S. Department of Education has ignored the testimony taken at the regional hearings, the views spelled out in the above-mentioned policies, as well as the requirements of the PPRA. The two policy statements represent a strong position taken by the National Council, which oversaw the research activities of the former National Institute of Education prior to its being incorporated into the Office of Educational Research and Improvement (OERI). The Council had quite obviously read the important testimony regarding Skinnerian mastery learning/direct instruction which was given at the regional hearings on the PPRA. The Council took a stand on the most important question facing us today in education: Are we, as free Americans, going to continue to accept the succinctly expressed definition of educational research included in the last sentence of the June 14 policy, a definition which is undeniably behaviorist and part of the behavioral psychologists' vocabulary—"observation and measurement of the educational process using the largely quantitative techniques of modern social science"? Or do we agree with the Council that the fundamental philosophical foundation for such research should be the "unambiguous recognition and respect for the dignity and value of each human person"?

As a complete counterpoint to the strong policy position taken by the council, the following information should be carefully considered. Professor Robert Glaser, professor of psychology and education and co-director of the Learning Research and Development Center of the University of Pittsburgh, was for all intents and purposes put in charge of the Commission on Reading in 1983. It was Glaser who appointed members to the Commission on Reading, thereby wielding considerable influence on the recommendations resulting from that Commission's report, *Becoming a Nation of Readers*, for which Glaser wrote the foreward and which was published under the auspices of the National Academy of Education's Commission on Education and Public Policy with sponsorship from the National Institute of Education. That report was probably the most important study which set the stage for the *Reading Excellence Act of 1998* (REA), setting in motion numerous activities which resulted in a determination that only proposals which were based on "scientific research" would be accepted for funding under the REA. In the foreward to *Becoming a Nation of Readers*, Glaser said:

> In teaching, as in other professions, well-researched methods and tools are essential. This report makes clear the key role of teachers' professional knowledge. Research on instructional pacing and grouping and on adaptation to children's accomplishments has contributed to new ideas that can help all children master the basics and then attain levels of literacy far beyond the basic competencies. **[ddd]**

Professor Glaser's credentials are uniquely important, placing him in a position of prominence regarding what method of instruction will be used in American classrooms—one based on the worldview that man is a human being, created in the image of God, with conscience, soul, intellect, creativity, free will, or one based on the new psychology of learning ("scientific," evolutionist, "research-based")—the worldview that man is an animal whose behavior can be manipulated by creating the necessary environment to bring about predictable, predetermined, neurologically conditioned responses. (The reader should refer to the Internet version for Appendix III, "Excerpts from *Programmed Learning: Evolving Principles and Industrial Applications*," which is a report of a 1960 seminar of businessmen and social scientists to discuss programmed learning and its application to business, at which professors B.F. Skinner, Arthur A. Lumsdaine and Robert Glaser were the speakers and discussion leaders. Robert Glaser was also a research advisor to the American Institute for Research at that time. Several pages of this report of the seminar are devoted to Glaser's "Principles of Programming.")

According to the following quote from an official Mission, Texas, school memorandum to concerned parents, Exemplary Center for Reading Instruction (ECRI), the fraternal twin of DISTAR (Direct Instruction for Systematic Teaching and Remediation), led the pack as far as Robert Glaser's National Commission on Reading was concerned:

> In 1986 ECRI was evaluated as playing a primary role in the United States becoming a nation of readers. The Regional Laboratory for Educational Improvement (sponsored by the U.S. Office of Educational and Improvement) published *Implementing the Recommendations of Becoming a Nation of Readers*. This document makes a line-by-line comparison of 31 reading programs, including ECRI. ECRI received the highest score of all 31 programs in meeting the specific recommendations of the National Commission on Reading.

Siegfried Engelmann's DISTAR (Reading Mastery) and ECRI are both based on the very sick philosophical world view that considers man nothing but an animal—an "organism" (in Skinner's words)—responsive to the manipulation of stimulus-response-stimulus immediate reinforcement or rewards to bring about predetermined, predictable behaviors. Skinner's quote about making a "pigeon a high achiever by reinforcing it on a proper schedule" is repeated often in this book to impress on the reader the horrifying aspect of animal training masquerading as education in these programs.

The National Research Council's *Preventing Reading Difficulties in Young Children*, compiled by Catherine E. Snow, M. Susan Burns, and Peg Griffin, Eds. (National Academy Press: Washington, D.C., 1998) acknowledged G. Reid Lyon, Ph.D., chief of the Learning Disabilities, Cognitive, and Social Development Branch of the National Institute of Child Health and Human Development of the National Institutes of Health (U.S. Department of Health and Human Services) who supports behaviorist reading programs like ECRI and DISTAR (Reading Mastery) as well as instruction based on so-called "medical and scientific research." Other individuals mentioned in *Preventing Reading Difficulties* who were involved in the promotion of DISTAR include Edward Kame'enui, Department of Special Education of the University of Oregon and Marilyn Jager Adams. These two individuals also served on the Committee on the Prevention of Reading Difficulties in Young Children, and

Adams is mentioned in *Becoming a Nation of Readers*. (See 1998 Herzer critique of *Preventing Reading Difficulties in Young Chil*dren.)

What does all of this tell the reader? Perhaps the same thing that is suggested to this writer: that the *Reading Excellence Act* will provide the funding and technical assistance to implement across the nation not just reading programs, but all curricula—including workforce training—in the mode of DISTAR and ECRI, which are based on "scientific, medical research." It is difficult to come to any other conclusion.

In light of this information, the *Reading Excellence Act of 1998* should be repealed. It is an unconstitutional curriculum mandate in violation of the *General Education Provisions Act of the Elementary and Secondary Education Act of 1965*. Call your congressmen and senators and ask that they support legislation to repeal this *Act*.

IN 1984 *SCHOOLING AND TECHNOLOGY, VOL. 3, PLANNING FOR THE FUTURE: A Collaborative Model, An Interpretive Report on Creative Partnerships in Technology—An Open Forum* by Dustin H. Heuston, World Institute for Computer-Assisted Teaching (WICAT) was published (Southeastern Regional Council for Educational Improvement: Research Triangle Park, North Carolina, 1984) under a grant from the U.S. Office of Education, HEW, National Institute of Education. An excerpt from "Discussion: Developing the Potential of an Amazing Tool" in *Schooling and Technology* follows:

> We've been absolutely staggered by realizing that the computer has the capability to act as if it were ten of the top psychologists working with one student.... You've seen the tip of the iceberg. Won't it be wonderful when the child in the smallest county in the most distant area or in the most confused urban setting can have the equivalent of the finest school in the world on that terminal and no one can get between that child and the curriculum? We have great moments coming in the history of education.

[Ed. Note: The comment regarding the computer's role as a "top psychologist" is as disturbing as is the idea of "no one getting between the child and the curriculum." These ideas lay to rest the publicly stated purpose of the words "parent-school partnerships" which represent a superb example of semantic deception.]

HOW TO MEASURE ATTITUDES BY MARLENE E. HENDERSON, LYNN LYONS Morris and Carol Taylor Fitz-Gibbon, Center for the Study of Evaluation of the University of California, Los Angeles (Sage Publications: Thousand Oaks, Cal., 1984) was published. Funded by the National Institute of Education, the table of contents follows:

- An Introduction to the Measurement of Attitudes and Attitude Change
- Selecting from among Alternative Approaches to Collecting Attitude Information
- Self Report and Reports of Others
- Interviews, Surveys and Polls
- Logs, Journals, Diaries and Reports

- Observation Procedures, Sociometric Procedures, Various Names for the Attitude You Want to Measure
- Reference Books that List, Describe, or Evaluate Existing Measures
- Validity and Reliability of Attitude Instruments
- Validity: Is the Instrument an Appropriate One to Measure? What You Want to Know
- Names and Addresses of Publishers of Attitude Measures

[ddd]

GRANT APPLICATION FROM FAR WEST LABORATORY FOR EDUCATIONAL RE-search and Development to the U.S. Department of Education for "Excellence in Instructional Delivery Systems: Research and Dissemination of Exemplary Outcome-Based Programs" was approved by T.H. Bell in 1984. William Spady, director of the Far West Laboratory, carried out this project—which came to be known as the infamous "Utah Grant." The following cover letter from Utah Superintendent of Public Instruction Leland Burningham to Secretary of Education T.H. Bell, dated July 27, 1984, is reproduced in its entirety:

Dear Secretary Bell:

I am forwarding this letter to accompany the proposal which you rec-ommended Bill Spady and I prepare in connection with Outcome-Based Education.

This proposal centers around the detailed process by which we will work together to implement Outcome-Based Education using research veri-fied programs. This will make it possible to put outcome-based education in place, not only in Utah but in all schools of the nation. For those who desire, we will stand ready for regional and national dissemination of the Outcome-Based Education program.

We are beginning to see positive, preliminary results from some of the isolated schools in Utah which have implemented Outcome-Based Education. These positive indicators are really exciting!

We sincerely urge your support for funding the proposal as presented.

Warmest regards,

G. Leland Burningham
State Superintendent of
Public Instruction

Attached to the grant application was Spady's "Summary of Professional Experience" which included "Senior Research Consultant to the Washington, D.C. schools" during 1977–1978—the same time the D.C. schools imple-mented mastery learning.

In a *Washington Post* article dated August 1, 1977, entitled "Competency Tests Set in 26 Schools," Thomas Sticht—who was later named to U.S. Secretary of Labor Elizabeth Dole's Secretary's Commission on Achieving Necessary Skills (SCANS)—was also mentioned as an associate director at the National Institute of Education (NIE) at the time mastery learning was implemented in the D.C. schools. The *Post* article quoted Sticht extensively, verifying that he and Spady were both deeply involved in the implementation of the new mastery learning curriculum. Later, in 1987, *The Washington Post* again paraphrased Sticht as follows:

> Many companies have moved operations to places with cheap, relatively poorly educated labor. What may be crucial, they say, is the dependability of a labor force and how well it can be managed and trained, not its general educational level, although a small cadre of highly educated creative people is essential to innovation and growth. Ending discrimination and changing values are probably more important than reading in moving low income families into the middle class.

[Ed. Note: What an extraordinary comment from someone supposedly involved in helping inner city students learn the basic skills! Nine years later, in an article in the March 5, 1996 issue of the *Washington Times*, the extent of academic damage caused by the Mastery Learning programs initiated by Spady and Sticht in 1977 was revealed:

> In the verbal portion of the 1995 Scholastic Achievement Test (SAT) D.C. public school students scored 342 out of a possible 800—86 points below the national average. On the math portion of the SAT, District public school students scored 375 out of a possible 800—107 points below the national average.

In 1999 the Washington, D.C. schools are using the same mastery learning/direct instruction method which caused the problem to solve the problem! In addition, the same *Washington Times* article stated that present Secretary of Education Richard Riley's home state of South Carolina, which probably has been more deeply involved in Effective Schools Research than any other state with the notable exception of Mississippi, had the next lowest scores.]

Important: The "Excellence in Instructional Delivery Systems" grant (the "Utah Grant") evaluation report, entitled *Models of Instructional Organization: A Casebook on Mastery Learning and Outcomes-Based Education* and compiled by project director Robert Burns (Far West Laboratory for Educational Research and Development: San Francisco, April 1987), stated in its "Conclusion" that:

> The four models of instructional organization outlined in this casebook are difficult programs to implement. The practices of the ten schools described in the case studies are indeed commendable. Yet we do not offer these ten case studies as "exemplary schools" deserving of emulation. Rather, they describe educators who have attempted to go beyond current curricular, instructional or organizational arrangements found in the majority of schools today. They have accepted the challenge of translating a difficult set of ideas into actual practice. And while they may not have always been completely successful, their experiences have provided us with ideas about how to begin moving closer to the ideal of successful learning for all students.

[Ed. Note: The above wording is similar to wording in the evaluation of

Project INSTRUCT, another model mastery learning program (1975). Neither mastery learning project had positive "academic" results. One can only conclude that academic achievement was not the intent. The documented results were changes in "curricular, instructional and organizational arrangements" in the schools involved so that they could become performance-based, necessary for school-to-work training.

Lack of positive results indicated in the evaluation of the mastery learning/outcome-based education experiments in schools—including the much-touted Johnson City, New York's Outcomes-Driven Developmental Model—did not deter the educators/sociologists from implementing outcome-based education/mastery learning in "all schools of the nation."

In assembling this research on mastery learning/outcome-based education/direct instruction programs and their evaluations, it appears that academic achievement has not been the desired object or the result of the use of these "What Works" methods and curricular thrusts. There are no longitudinal studies or long-term results indicating that the newly trumpeted "scientific, research-based" criteria for program development is valid criteria. The lack of evidence should serve as a clear warning to parents and good educators to steer clear of any programs or program development based on any of the above-mentioned models, or on the Skinnerian method called for by Effective Schools Research. (See the Internet version for Appendix XXVI.)]

DAVID HORNBECK, SUPERINTENDENT OF MARYLAND'S PUBLIC SCHOOLS, IN testimony before the Maryland State Board of Education in 1984 attempted to "mandate community service at state-approved places." During Hornbeck's testimony he quoted the late Ernest Boyer, then-president of the Carnegie Foundation for the Advancement of Teaching, as saying, "In the end the goal of service in the schools is to teach values—to help all students understand that to be fully human one must serve."

THE JULY 1984 EDITION OF THE EFFECTIVE SCHOOL REPORT CARRIED AN article entitled "Effective Schools for Results" by Dr. Robert E. Corrigan and Dr. George W. Bailey. Excerpts follow:

> Over the past thirty years there have been three primary programs related to the design and implementation of effective schools and successful learning results. Each of these research efforts focused on different aspects or variables in the following areas: behavioral change and the application of learning theory to produce successful learning results; the identification of sociological factors operating in effective schools; teaching strategies to effect learning, and the combination of these variables and practices in a systematic approach to achieve learning and management results.... The following professionals and groups have initiated successful educational programs which can work together as a common system to deliver predictable success for every learner—the ultimate criterion of an effective school program: Wilbur Brookover and Ron Edmonds of the Effective Schools Research Movement; B.F. Skinner, Norman Crowder, Robert and Betty O. Corrigan, 1950–1984, Mastery Learning Practices; Madeline Hunter, 1962–1984, Mastery Teach-

ing Practices; R.E. Corringan, B.O. Corrigan, Ward Corrigan and Roger A. Kaufman, 1960–1984, A Systematic Approach for Effectiveness (SAFE) for district-wide installation of Effective Schools....

Skinner proposed that it is feasible to deliver predictable learning mastery results when teachers performed the following programmed actions to design and implement lesson plans or curricula. These design and teaching steps describe the general process steps of learner-centered mastery learning instruction.

[Ed. Note: Included in step 3 of the above-mentioned learner-centered mastery learning instruction is: "Provide immediate feedback as to the correctness of learner responses, provide for immediate correction of errors, and control the progress of learning as students proceed in small steps along the tested learning path to master the learning objectives and criteria with predictable success."]

The article continues:

The ultimate benefits to be derived through the installation of this mastery of skills delivery system will be the predictable success of all future graduates to master relevant skills to enter and succeed in society. Graduation skill standards would be continually evaluated and, where necessary, will be revised based on new skill requirements established by industrial, civic, and academic leaders either (a) to get and hold jobs, (b) to advance to higher education, and/or (c) to be self-sufficient following graduation.

[Ed. Note: How much clearer could the Corrigans be in describing the need for Skinnerian mastery learning/direct instruction in order to implement school-to-work? (See the Internet version for Appendix VI.)]

DR**. T**HEODORE **S**IZER**'**S **C**OALITION OF **E**SSENTIAL **S**CHOOLS **(CES)** WAS founded in 1984. Major Coalition principles are:

- Focus on helping adolescents to learn to use their minds well....
- Less is more: Each student should master a limited number of essential skills areas of knowledge....
- School goals should apply to all students....
- Teaching and learning should be personalized; each teacher should have no more than 80 students....
- Scrap the time-honored feature of the American education system: graduation requirements based on the so-called Carnegie Units, or the "seat time" students spend in various subject areas....
- Students should be active workers [student-as-worker philosophy]....
- Students should be able to demonstrate mastery of skills and knowledge.

The Coalition of Essential Schools (CES) was established at Brown University. From twelve "charter" schools in four states, CES by 1993 grew to include more than 130 member schools in nearly thirty states. Along with the Education Commission of the States, the CES sponsors Re:Learning, a partnership with participating states to build support for essential school change at the state and district levels.

Ten years later evaluation studies have found that gains weren't measurable. Even so, philanthropist Walter H. Annenberg pledged to donate $50 million to the Annenberg Institute for School Reform, run by Sizer and based at Brown University.

It is important to mention that the majority, if not all, of the major education reform projects have failed to improve students' academic test scores. Notable examples are: Johnson City, New York—the Outcomes-Driven Development Model (ODDM) by John Champlin; William Spady's Far West Laboratory Utah Grant, "Excellence in Instructional Delivery Systems: Research and Dissemination of Exemplary Outcomes-Based Programs"; and Marc Tucker's National Center on Education and the Economy (NCEE), which moved from Washington, D.C. to Rochester, New York in 1988 to "help" that city's much-heralded reform movement. *The Rochester Democrat and Chronicle* of March 14, 1993 in an article entitled "A City's Dream Unfulfilled"—after five years of Tucker's "help"—reported the following:

> Since Rochester's schools started reform, fewer graduates have received the more stringent Regents diploma. In 1986–87, 23.1% of graduates had Regents diplomas, and 17.5% graduated with them last year [1993].

JOHN I. GOODLAD CLEARLY STATED THAT HOW A STUDENT FEELS ABOUT school is more important than test scores in an article entitled "A Cooperative Effort Is Needed: Can Our Schools Get Better?" (originally published in *Phi Delta Kappan*, January, 1979 when Dr. Goodlad was dean of the Graduate School of Education at the University of California, Los Angeles, and re-published in *Education Digest* on November 1, 1984.) Excerpts follow:

> It seems to my associates and me that how a student spends time in school and how he feels about what goes on there is of much greater significance than how he scores on a standardized achievement test. But I am not sure the American people are ready to put a criterion such as this ahead of marks and scores. And so it will be difficult for schools to get better and more difficult for them to appear so....
>
> Adherence to norm-referenced [competitive] standardized test scores as the standard for judging student, teacher, and school performance has led to a stultifying approach to accountability.

IN A PERSONAL LETTER TO CHARLOTTE ISERBYT FROM STEVEN M. HERSEY, executive director of the Maine Association of Christian Schools dated November 17, 1984,[14] Hersey enclosed portions of a testimony by Kevin Ryan, professor at Boston University, regarding Boston University, the country of Portugal and the World Bank. Professor Ryan was called to testify for the Maine State Department of Education in a legal hearing against the Maine Association of Christian Schools. The following excerpts from Ryan's testimony are important due to the disclosure by Ryan of his role in the development of a teacher-training faculty system—modeled after that of the United States—for Portugal immediately after the communist takeover of that country. One might ask why a communist country like Portugal should choose the American teacher education curriculum to accomplish its political and philosophical goals. Portions of Ryan's testimony follow:

A. I [Ryan] am a professor of Education [at Boston University] and I teach graduate courses and supervise dissertations. But I'm there primarily now to work on a project to help a Portuguese Minister of Education develop a teacher-training faculty system....

Q. ...Could you describe what it is you're doing?

A. Well, the Portuguese nation had a social revolution [communist take-over] in 1974, and at that time they decided that their educational system was very inadequate, that it was not democratic, that the mandatory compulsory age of education was only to the fourth grade, and they mandated a system of education not unlike the United States in terms of compulsory education up to grade 12 and an elementary through high school division. The country was very interested in this. They also wanted to be part of the European Economic Community. But, unfortunately, Portugal was a poor country, and the World Bank said to them, you will not be admitted into the European Economic Community until you get in place a modern school system. And they [the World Bank] have come through with a good deal of financial support for that.

   An important part of that is the development of a teacher training infrastructure. Now, what that means is that Portugal, which has, as of right now, a very small and very sort of casual teacher education method, is establishing 12 regional teacher education institutions at the university level positions; and they looked to the rest of the world for help on this, and they put out a request for proposals.... Boston University... was chosen... to train the faculties of these 12 new institutions....

Q. Now when the proposal was first made... was it contemplated that Boston University might do all the training of Portuguese teachers themselves?

A. Yes, I did. My feeling is that in this particular project the stakes are enormously high. The 120 people who are currently right now being selected for these roles in these 12 institutions are going to be there for 20 or 30 years; so that the course they have on teaching or supervision is going to set an intellectual and training agenda for them for a number of years. They are going to go on and train all these teachers with what they learned.

Q. And do you have any responsibility with respect to the curriculum that will be used in the program to develop a teacher training instruction?

A. Well, the Portuguese did a lot of study on their own, and they looked at various curricula for teacher education.... I think one of the reasons they selected Boston University was because the curriculum that they wanted taught seems to be one like an American teacher education curriculum. And we have their indication of what courses they want, and the sequence. And we—and this happened before I was there—we went with our course outlines and, in a sense, negotiated with them to a mutual satisfaction about what the content of what the various courses would be.

Q. Do you belong to any professional associations?

A. I am a member of the American Educational Research Association;
I am a member of Phi Delta Kappa; I am a member of the Network
of Educational Excellence; I was a member of the Master of Arts in
Teaching Association—in fact, I was president, before it—before—I
think it's defunct now.

[Ed. Note: Of interest is the fact that Paulo Freire, the well-known radical
Brazilian educator who wrote *Pedagogy of the Oppressed*, was also a consultant to the government of Portugal at the time of its revolution. (See August
19, 1986 entry for *New York Times* article.) As of 1992 Professor Kevin Ryan
is reported to be involved in and the director of the Center for the Advancement of Ethics and Character at Boston University.]

AN ARTICLE ENTITLED "OBSERVING THE BIRTH OF THE HATCH AMENDMENT
Regulations" by Bert I. Greene and Marvin Pasch was published in the
December 1984 issue of *Educational Leadership*, monthly journal of the
Association for Supervision and Curriculum Development. Excerpts from
the article follow:

> However, from the day the Hatch Amendment was passed, the written con-
> sent requirement lay dormant, that is, until 1984. As Charlotte Iserbyt, an
> education activist and former Department of Education employee, [stated]
> in a memorandum to her conservative allies dated 10 January 1984:
>
>> The only tool available to us to protect our children in the government
>> schools is a federal law, the Hatch Protection of Pupil Rights Amendment,
>> passed unanimously by the U.S. Senate in 1978, for which the Office of
>> Education promised regulations in early 1979.... I know that many of
>> you, for good reason, feel that the Hatch Amendment has been useless.
>> Of course it has been useless. Any statute which has no mechanism for
>> enforcement is nothing more than a scrap of paper....
>
> Iserbyt then turned her attention to the reason why regulations have not
> been promulgated:
>
>> Although excellent regulations were drafted in 1982 by conservatives in
>> the Office of the General Counsel (who have been subsequently fired
>> by Secretary Bell), they have not seen the light of day since Bell doesn't
>> like them and he also does not want to offend his educationist friends by
>> signing off on regulations that will disturb their modus operandi—their
>> persistent efforts to change the values, attitudes and beliefs of students
>> to conform with those necessary to bring about a socialist/humanist one
>> world government.
>
> As Iserbyt clearly saw, it is through regulations that responsibilities be-
> come clarified, procedures for grievance and redress established, and penalties
> for non-compliance stated. Therefore, the importance of regulations cannot
> be overstated.... Interestingly, Iserbyt had notification of the proposed regu-
> lations prior to 10 January as evidenced by an Urgent Alert she sent to her
> "Education Group Leader Activists." Her guidance... included suggestions
> related to the scope of the soon-to-be published regulations. She argued:
>
>> It was the intent of Congress to cover all the mindbending techniques
>> and materials used in our children's classrooms, in special education and

guidance, not just the narrow and difficult to define areas of psychological and psychiatric testing or treatment.

She provided a set of quotable commentaries for her contacts as they prepared oral or written testimony....

Some people who testified argued that the techniques being used in our schools can be likened to those used in Russia, Red China, and Nazi Germany....

A potentially major educational change has occurred, and the education profession failed to block it.

[Ed. Note: Anyone following or involved with the Anita Hoge/ Pennsylvania case will tell you that the U.S. Department of Education—under secretaries of education William Bennett and Lamar Alexander—pulled out all the stops, at every level, to thwart Hoge's efforts and those of other parents who tried to use this law. Such an assault on those who paid the bills—and provided the children ("resources") upon whom they experiment even today—was, and is, criminal.]

1985

ON MARCH 6, 1985 *EDUCATION WEEK* PUBLISHED AN ARTICLE ENTITLED "Half of Chicago Students Drop Out, Study Finds: Problem Called Enormous Human Tragedy." (Return to 1968 *Learning and Instruction* entry for details of the Chicago Mastery Learning debacle.)

EFFECTIVE SCHOOLS DEVELOPMENT IN EDUCATION ACT WAS INTRODUCED into Congress on March 8, 1985. An excerpt from the Extension of Remarks in the House of Representatives by Hon. Augustus F. Hawkins of California follows:

Mr. Hawkins: Mr. Speaker, there are public schools in this Nation which evidence continuous improvement and growth in the academic achievement levels of their students, for each day that these students are in the school.... Where are these public schools? They are in Jackson, MS; Spencerport, NY; Los Angeles, CA; New York City; Glendale, AZ; Richmond, VA; Pittsburgh, PA; Hartford, CT; Portland,OR; and many other cities throughout the Nation.

What they have in common is a determination to improve pupil performance, pupil behavior, and the effectiveness of teaching and learning in their schools. They are adherents and advocates of the late Professor Ron Edmonds's—of Michigan State University and Harvard University—effective school principles, which emphasize the belief that while public schools realistically can't control what happens in their surrounding communities, public schools can control what happens within their "four walls."

[Ed. Note: This particular legislation, which originally called for a whopping $230 million over a three-year period, did not pass. However, similar effective schools legislation, H.R. 747, passed and provided $4.5 million over a three-year period during William Bennett's tenure as U.S. Secretary of Education.

The above schools—especially Jackson, Mississippi, the home of *The Effective School Report* and one of the first inner city schools used as an effective schools (ML/DI) research experiment—which have been using mastery learning for a long period of time would provide an excellent list for Congress to use in an investigation of inner cities' norm-referenced test scores!]

THE DALLAS MORNING NEWS OF MARCH 23, 1985 RAN AN ARTICLE EN-titled "Teachers' Group to Develop New Curriculum" by Karel Holloway of Boston. An excerpt follows:

> The National Education Association is beginning an 18-month program to develop a new school curriculum designed to assure that students master basic skills, NEA President Mary Futrell announced Friday. "The association first will survey scholars to determine what they believe constitutes 'mastery' in reading, writing, mathematics and social studies. Using criteria from the scholars and the findings of current education research studies, the associa-tion will develop experimental strategies to teach the mastery skills at five schools that will be selected from throughout the nation. The results of the programs tried at the five schools will determine the shape of the new cur-riculum," Mrs. Futrell said in a speech to the Education Writers Association. That curriculum then will be tested for three years at 24 schools nationwide.... The Mastery In Learning Project will be funded by $600,000 from the NEA and donations from other foundations. Nine education research institutes will participate in the project.

Summit Christian Academy of Dallas, Texas included the above article in a promotional flyer on which it typed the following additional information regarding the use of mastery learning:

> The purpose in sending you this article is to evidence that truly we did cre-ate "TOMORROW'S EDUCATION TODAY" five years ago at a cost of over four million dollars. We employed over 250 dedicated Christian writers and editors to create the LIFEPAC curriculum. Each had an average of five years classroom teaching experience, and over 75% held Masters degrees or higher, and 40 held Doctorate degrees. Truly, there is no finer curriculum in the market place today. For comparison between our curriculum, A.C.E., A-Beka, Bob Jones and others, please write to: Summit Christian Academy, 13789 Noel Road, Suite 100, Dallas, Texas 75240.

[Ed. Note: This article proves the extensive use by Christian educators of the same Skinnerian mastery learning used and recommended by the National Education Association. How can Christian educators, opposed to the teaching of evolution, support a teaching method based on Darwin's theory of evolu-tion? Dr. Francis Schaeffer was right on target when he said: "Many of our secular schools have consistently taught these presuppositions (evolutionary theory) and unhappily many of our Christian lower schools and colleges have taught the crucial subjects no differently than the secular schools."]

EDUCATION DAILY OF APRIL 5, 1985 PUBLISHED AN ITEM ENTITLED "TEACH-ers Influence Students' Values through Writing Assignments" which stated in part:

Researchers attending the annual meeting of the American Educational Research Association here said writing can be used to clarify students' values and even alter their views on controversial subjects.

But teachers can also use writing to manipulate a student's viewpoint and attitude on controversial issues, said a researcher who has studied how writing changes attitudes. "You can generate attitude change by writing," said John Daly of the University of Texas. Daly said his research showed that writing an essay about an issue helps students clarify their own views. But when asked to write an essay arguing a position opposing their values, the students are lead to change their minds....

...And the greater the effort a student puts into a writing assignment, the greater the change in attitude, Daly concluded.

Daly's finding disturbed some educators, who said they were concerned that teachers have the power to alter students' values. "It can be dangerous when we know that educators have the power to influence kids' minds," said Barbara Mitchell of the University of Pennsylvania.

THE MAY 1985 *EDUCATION UPDATE* FROM THE ASSOCIATION FOR SUPERVISION and Curriculum Development contained a revealing article "Promising Theories Die Young" about the late Madeline Hunter, University of California at Los Angeles education professor and the nation's best known Mastery Teaching teacher trainer. Dr. Hunter was a psychologist who served more than twenty years as principal of the Experimental Laboratory Elementary School at UCLA. (John Goodlad also served at UCLA's lab school.) Hunter's views on Instructional Theory Into Practice (ITIP) and on dialectical thinking follow:

> Madeline Hunter, UCLA education professor and research interpreter, told a huge, doting audience that educational theorists and practitioners "badly need each other" and that it is high time to tap each other's strengths rather than zap each other's perceived flaws. Hunter said that she is particularly conscious of this schism because "I'm part of both but not really one or the other." Hunter has been a school psychologist, principal, researcher, and, in ASCD immediate Past President Phil Robinson's words, "one of the most able... teachers of teachers." Hunter delivered three mandates for the next decade: 1. Unite educational theory and practice; 2. Recognize, integrate, and use all three kinds of knowledge; and 3. Move toward dialectical thinking.

Under the article's subtitle, "Three Kinds of Knowledge," Hunter's presentation to the audience was covered as follows:

> When she was a school psychologist, Hunter said, she had an exchange with a teacher who had rebuked a student for making a silly remark:
>
> Hunter: What did the smart-aleck want?
> Teacher: Attention.
> Hunter: Have you ever heard of Pavlov?
> Teacher (amazed): What do slobbering dogs have to do with it?

In the same *Education Update* article, under subtitle "Toward Dialectical Thinking," Hunter's presentation reported:

Hunter advised educators to move toward dialectical thinking, which means, she said, that with empathy, you "embrace the most convincing argument... against your own conclusion. Dialectical thinking will move us from right and wrong to better in this set of circumstances." Moving into this "thoughtful uncertainty," Hunter said, does not mean obligatory abandonment of one's own position, but she said, the advantage is that "where we take an opposing point of view and hold it in tension with our own point of view, each builds correction into the other." Hunter nudged educators to come out of "armed camps... where we're not collaborating" so that "I understand why you think it's right for your students to line up while I think it's better for them to come in casually." And she concluded, "To respectfully address another person's point of view is a master, master step. Until we accomplish it in our own profession... I see very little hope for it in our community, in our cities, in our nation, and in the world."

The validity of Hunter's claims of success for her ITIP mastery teaching program was questioned by Robert Slavin of Johns Hopkins University in his paper entitled "The Napa Evaluation of Madeline Hunter's ITIP: Lessons Learned," published in *Elementary School Journal* (Vol. 87, No. 2: University of Chicago, 1986). Slavin says in part, "Although teachers in the program changed their behavior and students' engaged rates improved, program effects on student achievement were minimal."

Robert Slavin followed up on his critique of Hunter's claims of success for her mastery teaching program with his report funded by the U.S. Department of Education entitled *Mastery Learning Reconsidered*, published by the Center for Research on Elementary and Middle Schools, Johns Hopkins University (Report No. 7, January 1987). An excerpt from the abstract of the report follows:

> Several recent reviews and meta-analyses have claimed extraordinarily positive effects of mastery learning on student achievement, and Bloom (1984a, b) has hypothesized that mastery-based treatments will soon be able to produce "two-sigma" (i.e., two standard deviation) increases in achievement. This article examines the literature on achievement effects of practical applications of group-based mastery learning in elementary and secondary schools over periods of at least four weeks, using a review technique, "best evidence synthesis," which combines features of meta-analytic and traditional narrative reviews. The review found essentially no evidence to support the effectiveness of group-based mastery learning on standardized achievement measures. On experimenter-made measures, effects were generally positive but moderate in magnitude, with little evidence that effects maintained over time. These results are discussed in light of the coverage vs. Mastery dilemma posed by group-based mastery learning.

[Ed. Note: Slavin's critiques echo the negative results of mastery learning discussed elsewhere in this book. Unfortunately, ten years later Slavin received his mastery learning/direct instruction crown in 1999 when Slavin's program "Success for All," which also uses mastery learning/direct instruction, was accepted as one of the nationally recognized programs for use in restructuring.]

THE EFFECTIVE SCHOOL REPORT'S MAY 1985 ISSUE CONTAINED AN ARTICLE entitled "Principal's Expectations as a Motivating Factor in Effective Schools." An excerpt follows:

> The principal expects specific behavior from particular teachers which should then translate into achievement by the students of these teachers; because of these varied expectations, the principal behaves differently toward different teachers; i.e., body language, verbal interactions and resource allocations. This treatment also influences the attitudes of the teacher toward the principal and their perception of the future utility of any increased effort toward student achievement. If this treatment is consistent over time, and if the teachers do not resist change, it will shape their behavior and through it the achievement of their students.... With time teachers' behavior, self-concepts of ability, perceptions of future utility, attitude toward the principal and students' achievement will conform more and more closely to the behavior originally expected of them.

EDUCATION DAILY OF JUNE 12, 1985 PUBLISHED "SWEEPING OVERHAUL OF Minnesota Education System Proposed." Excerpts follow:

> The Minnesota Business Partnership, an organization of 60 corporations, commissioned an education consulting firm to study the state education system and plan improvements. The result is the Minnesota Plan, the business community's proposals to radically restructure the state's education system. The plan was outlined Monday at a National Institute of Education seminar in Washington, D.C. by Paul Berman, President of BW Associates, which conducted the study. The proposal would make kindergarten through sixth grade the elementary level, set up grades seven through 10 as the common high schools, and create specialized programs for grades 11 and 12. Students would have to master a core program of communication, social studies, science and math until the 11th grade, and pass state competency exams at the end of the sixth and 10th grades. Moreover, the plan would eliminate state-mandated courses and allow districts and schools to determine course requirements. Under the plan, 11th and 12th grade students could take courses at post secondary institutions, technical or vocational schools or even private corporations....
>
> Despite the worries of business leaders in the partnership... most legislators don't feel a major restructuring is necessary. "Most of us feel the system is changing and responding to needs. But it is not in need of drastic change." But Berman counters that since "the best teachers are leaving at age 30 now," teacher improvement plans would help overburdened staff and increase student-teacher contact. Teaching teams composed of a lead teacher, teaching assistants and adjunct teachers would work with 120 students. This would allow for individual student learning programs and removal of student counselors.... "It's not a fantasy no matter how radical it is," Berman contends, adding that the public does not realize that "reforms we start today are not going to be in effect for 20 years. It takes time to modernize." (p. 6)

[Ed. Note: In retrospect it seems, to this writer at least, that Minnesota was clearly out front in its early adoption of performance-based school-to-work agendas. (See the Internet version for Appendix X.)]

NORTH CAROLINA'S COMPENTENCY-BASED CURRICULUM, "BASIC EDUCATION Program," was introduced in 1985. A few of its more unusual "basic" competencies, involved students entertaining allegiance to a world constitution and a world government rather than to the *U.S. Constitution*. Excerpts follow:

> FIFTH GRADE: Develop a flag, seal, symbol, pledge and/or national anthem for a new country.... Design a postage stamp to be used worldwide. The stamp should denote what the world would need to make it a better place....
> SIXTH GRADE: Draw national symbols for an imaginary nation....
> SEVENTH GRADE: Understand the need for interdependence....
> NINTH GRADE: Write a constitution for a perfect society.

A NATIONAL EDUCATION ASSOCIATION (NEA) PRESS RELEASE FOR JUNE 28–July 3, 1985 described in considerable detail the purpose of its Mastery In Learning project.[15] It was explained that Mastery Learning is

> a concept first proposed a generation ago by Harvard psychologist Jerome Bruner.... A growing body of research and educational reform proposals came from such respected educational analysts as Mortimer Adler [developer of the Paideia Proposal and long-time advocate of a one-world government, ed.], John Goodlad, Theodore Sizer, and Ernest Boyer who have all sought to translate Bruner's work into classroom reality.

Also revealed in an NEA booklet on mastery learning is the fact that

> Mastery Learning is one of many instructional models. Others include Active Teaching, Direct Instruction, Student Team Learning, Socratic questioning, coaching, creative problem solving, Bruner's Concept Attainment Strategy, and Madeline Hunter's Target Teaching Approach. These models incorporate research on effective teaching, and all may be explored by the schools associated with the project.

[Ed. Note: Jerome Bruner and B.F. Skinner were the developers of the highly controversial, federally funded curriculum *M:ACOS (Man: A Course of Study)*.]

EDUCATION WEEK OF AUGUST 28, 1985 CARRIED THE ARTICLE "PROPONENTS of Mastery Learning Defend Method after Its Rejection by Chicago" which quoted Benjamin Bloom, often cited as "the father of Mastery Learning," as saying that some 50 million children around the globe are taught with a mastery learning approach. In addition, University of California Professor James H. Block is quoted as saying he "doesn't know of any major urban school system in the United States that has not adopted some kind of mastery learning program."

[Ed. Note: James Block's statement underscores the need for a Congressional investigation requiring the U.S. Department of Education to provide longitudinal/norm-referenced test scores for all "major urban school systems" that have used mastery learning/direct instruction over the past thirty years. (See the Internet version for Appendix XXVI.)]

[ddd]

MAINE'S STATE DEPARTMENT OF EDUCATION 1985 ASSESSMENT OF EDUCAtional Progress [MAEP] test item bank, based in part on National Assessment of Educational Progress (NAEP) test items, included the following correct answer as to why the Soviets occupied Eastern Europe after World War II:

> [Correct answer]
> Soviet occupation was primarily a result of the Soviet Union's desire for security along its borders.

[Ed. Note: One cannot help but wonder how the international community would have responded to the United States' occupation of Canada, Mexico, Cuba, the West Indies, Greenland, and Iceland in order to "secure its borders."]

[ddd]

IN 1985 THE U.S. DEPARTMENT OF EDUCATION, THROUGH THE SECRETARY'S Discretionary Fund under Secretary William Bennett, approved the promotion of and funding for development of a character education program by the Thomas Jefferson Research Center (TJRC) of Pasadena, California. The grant was for a "teacher training project demonstrating the viability of a district-wide educational program involving... the TJRC." Through the grant, the TJRC, founded in 1963, would apply its character education curriculum "across all segments of the [Pasadena] district's grade levels... expanding the effort to parents and community, and... to other school districts, and to share... methods and approaches with other educators and institutions nationally." Community service projects for elementary, middle, and high school students "are seen as extensions of classroom activity and essential elements in... the range of values being stressed." The TJRC's federally funded demonstration "character education" program included "Personal Responsibility Skills and Ethical Decision-Making."

National dissemination was expected to be effected through regional and national workshops, education conferences, computer conferences, and through TELE, "an electronic learning exchange... a computerized network of educators... involved with exemplary programs and computer assisted instruction programs within California and... across the nation." The promotional literature for the TJRC's middle and high school Achievement Skills programs and the text of the teacher's manual for its middle school Achievement Skills program (1984) explicitly stated that "the basis for the programs lies in the motivational theories of [Abraham] Maslow."

In *Religion, Values, and Peak Experiences* (Ohio State University Press: Columbus, Ohio, 1964) Maslow stated that "each person has his own private religion... which may be of the profoundest meaning to him personally and yet... of no meaning to anyone else... each person discovers, develops, and retains his own religion." An examination of the TJRC's middle school Achievement Skills reveals not only the program's base in Maslow's psychological theories, but also the program's ties to consciousness-altering methods. Early in the semester-long program, students are told that "we are going to study some psychology. We are going to study our selves or our *minds* [emphasis in original]. Each of you is going to get a chance to look at yourself as if you were a psychologist." Repeatedly throughout the program, students are exposed to self-hypnosis, guided imagery, visualization techniques, and relaxation therapy—tools used in psychosynthesis (defined by Roberto Assagioli as the formation or reconstruction of a new personality). In his book *Psychosynthesis*[16] as mentioned earlier in this book Assagioli notes

> the possible dangers of the exploration of the unconscious. The first and foremost is the release of drives and emotions which were locked in the unconscious and which can flood the conscious ego before it is ready and prepared and competent to contain, control and utilize them. It is the situation of the "apprentice sorcerer."
>
> ...We think that cases of suicide or of the development of psychotic states can be due to the premature and uncontrolled release of explosive drives and emotions from the unconscious.

The middle school Achievement Skills program also utilizes what are psychotherapeutic values clarification techniques: role playing, open-ended questions, and moral dilemmas. These same values clarification methodologies form the basis of the K–6 "character education" component funded by the grant. Psychologists have warned educators about the dangers of unbridled use of role-playing techniques by untrained people, for the very reasons Assagioli cites as well as others.

The K–6 materials were developed by the American Institute for Character Education (AICE) of San Antonio, Texas, and are marketed nationally. *The Teacher's Handbook* (1983) from AICE indicates that the program is another "how to learn instead of what to learn" program and admits to the use of values clarification, the promotion of self-disclosure and the creation of a classroom climate where "there are no right answers to any one problem."

U.S. PRESIDENT REAGAN AND SOVIET PRESIDENT GORBACHEV SIGNED AN agreement in 1985 calling for

> cooperation in the field of science and technology and additional agreements in other specific fields, including the humanities and social sciences; the facilitation of the exchange by appropriate organizations of educational and teaching materials, including textbooks, syllabi and curricula, materials on methodology, samples of teaching instruments and audiovisual aids, and the exchange of primary and secondary school textbooks and other teaching materials.... The conducting of joint studies on textbooks between appropriate organizations in the United States and the Ministry of Education of the U.S.S.R.

At the same time, the Carnegie Corporation signed agreements with the

Soviet Academy of Sciences which resulted in "joint research on the application of computers in early elementary education, focusing especially on the teaching of higher level skills and complex subjects to younger children."

The U.S.-Soviet education agreements were discussed in an article entitled "U.S. and Soviets to Share Insights on Computers" by Fred M. Hechinger, education editor, in the December 10, 1985 issue of the *New York Times*. The article states in part:

> A meeting of American and Soviet educational computer experts has produced an agreement to exchange specialists involved in the improvement of elementary and secondary education.
>
> The initial American-Soviet exchange is intended as a first step toward cooperation among education reformers from a number of countries, including Britain and Japan. One goal is to reduce the present emphasis on training computer programmers, and stress instead the computer's potential to restructure the education of young children, beginning in third grade or earlier.
>
> Several issues are listed for joint investigation. They include computer-based methods to develop creative abilities of primary school pupils, creation and testing of software for use in primary school, and proposals for the restructuring of the curriculum and of teaching methods through the use of computers in the early grades.
>
> Additional issues include evaluation of the training of teachers in the use of computers and elimination of teachers' fear of computers, and creation of Soviet-American pilot projects for joint experiments.

[Ed. Note: On December 20, 1985, during a "Contact America" radio interview with U.S. Secretary of Education William Bennett, co-host Malcolm Lawrence asked Bennett if he was involved in the United States-Soviet education exchanges. Bennett responded, "No. I'm not in that loop." Pray tell, what "loop" was he in during his tenure as the top official dealing with American education? The writer was informed by the U.S. Department of State that both agreements were still in effect after the so-called break-up of the Soviet Union. (See the Internet version for Appendix XXIII.)]

1986

THE FACT FINDER OF PHOENIX, ARIZONA ON JANUARY 1, 1986 (VOL. 46, No. 4) carried an article entitled "Shocking U.S. Agreements to Let Soviet and Red Chinese Educators Indoctrinate America's Children." (See the Internet version for Appendix XXIII.) Excerpts follow:

> We now have proof that agreements have been made with the Soviets for nearly 30 years to have their educators work with ours in planning curricula for America's school children. This is a shocking addition to what we have already learned about the many ways that the Soviets are carrying out their secret war for world domination.
>
> Early in October, we learned that two Communist educators are already here in Phoenix, teaching and conferring with educators at Central High School. Boris Bayev is a 41-year old principal of a Soviet secondary school at Ulyanovsk, USSR. A teacher from Red China is also at Central High.

EDWIN FEULNER, PRESIDENT OF THE HERITAGE FOUNDATION (CONSIDERED by some to be the foremost "conservative" think tank in the nation), chaired the United States Information Agency's (USIA) Commission on Public Diplomacy in 1986. The annual report carried a cover letter from Feulner as chairman encouraging the acceptance of its recommendations. Under "Educational and Cultural Programs, Exchanges and International Visitors" the report states in part:

> The Commission urges USIA, the Department of State, and the relevant private sector organizations to move quickly to develop specific programs for U.S.-Soviet exchanges pursuant to the General Exchanges accord, other exchange initiatives undertaken at the Geneva Summit, and the agreement by President Reagan and General Secretary Gorbachev to review these programs at their next meeting.

[Ed. Note: The Heritage Foundation later established an office in Moscow, ostensibly to oversee Russia's "hoped-for" evolution from Communism to free market economics.]

NATIONAL ACADEMY OF EDUCATION AT THE HARVARD GRADUATE SCHOOL of Education (Cambridge, Massachussetts), sent out an informational letter in 1986 entitled "ACLS [American Council of Learned Societies]-USSR Ministry of Education Commission on Education" describing joint U.S.-Soviet education activities. An excerpt which details an extraordinary agenda for cooperation with "The Evil Empire" follows:

> Scholars from the American Council of Learned Societies and the Ministry of Education of the Soviet Union met in the United States in 1986 and agreed to establish a Commission on Education that will be responsible for joint scholarly relations in pedagogy and related fields between the United States and the Soviet Union. Some major joint U.S.-Soviet project themes are: Methods of Teaching and Learning School Science and Math Subjects Using Computers; Theory of Teaching and Learning; Psychological and Pedagogical Problems of Teaching in the Development of Pre-School and School-Age Children; and Problems of Teaching Children with Special Needs.

THE FEBRUARY 1986 ISSUE OF THE EFFECTIVE SCHOOL REPORT CARRIED the first of a twelve-part series entitled "Implementing Effective Schools: Commitment—The First Step." An accurate description of the Pavlovian/ Skinnerian methods required by Effective Schools Research is found in this article. Excerpts follow:

> Effective schools research is conclusive beyond any doubt that all children can learn. Practice now reveals that any school can be led, through a systematic process of training for behavioral change, to effectiveness. Neither research nor practice suggests that the process of becoming effective is easy....
>
> The task of leading a school from ineffectiveness to effectiveness is monumental; however, it can be done. And the research proves that it can be done without wholesale changes of personnel. Ron Edmonds said that

we must assume that the teacher and staff are at least as educable as the children they teach....

Change in an effective school must be dramatic if the school is to become effective. The mind-set of many if not most employees within the building must change. Effective school behaviors must be demonstrated by all. These behaviors are observable, measurable, and transferable; therefore, they can be learned. In-depth and highly structured training will precede improved outcomes.

The trauma experienced by a school that sets a course of effectiveness will be substantial, and will require the implementation of a rigid, highly structured, and sequenced program with all research-based elements in place.

[ddd]

CAROL BARBER, OUTCOME-BASED EDUCATION/MASTERY LEARNING CONSULTANT from Houston, Texas wrote "Outcome-Based Education/Mastery Learning: What Is It? Why Do It? How Do You Do It?" which appeared in the Spring (Vol. 5, No. 3) 1986 issue of *Outcomes*, the quarterly journal of the Network for Outcome-Based Schools. The following are excerpts:

OBE/ML: WHAT IS IT?

As discussed by others in this issue, there is considerable overlap in many of the school reform movements sweeping the country today. Frequently, outcome-based education and mastery learning are used interchangeably or as synonymous phrases. While there are certainly many commonalities in the two movements, they also are very different.

One way to differentiate OBE from ML from other effective school practices is to visualize an umbrella and its various parts. The umbrella includes: 1) a canopy; 2) a center pole to support the canopy; and 3) a set of hinged ribs radiating from the center pole. The umbrella gives us a perfect analogy for comparing many of the school reform movements. Outcome-based education is represented by the canopy of the umbrella. The OBE ideas represent possible reform of the total school system.... When a district moves into OBE, it is ready to examine belief systems of staff, students, parents; placement of students; grading and reporting policies; curriculum issues; certification processes; instructional methods; etc., etc., etc. In other words, OBE means an approach to reform within the *total* [emphasis in the original] school system; i.e., the umbrella under which all practices of school operation will occur.

The center pole supporting the umbrella represents the mastery learning ideas. Mastery learning supports the OBE movement in that it is the main vehicle upon which to begin the change process in the belief system, curriculum organization and instructional strategies. Mastery learning provides us with the support and processes needed to begin the total OBE reform in our schools.

The set of hinged ribs radiating from the center pole can be viewed as any of the many *effective school movements* [emphasis in original] and/or strategies available to us. Strategies such as Dr. Hunter's Mastery Teaching, Hopkins' Student Team Learning, Johnson and Johnson's Cooperative Learning, Joyce's Teaching Models, Good's TESA, and many others, represent effective practices which are totally compatible and will certainly enhance an OBE/ML program.

...Realistically, one could implement any one of the above-mentioned strategies without having ML in operation; indeed one can implement ML without having OBE. However, when OBE is implemented, ML must be applied.

"REPORT TO THE SECRETARY OF EDUCATION WILLIAM BENNETT, APRIL, 1986. Transforming American Education: Reducing the Risk to the Nation" was issued by the National Task Force on Educational Technology. The memo was distributed at an Ohio State School Board caucus. An excerpt follows:

> For 1990–2000: The improvement and transformation of education to Mastery Learning will demand continuing support. The nation needs to recognize that the education of its citizens provides the basis for the economic, social and cultural health of American society. Enlightened national self-interest should justify the support of the well-planned educational transformation that the Task Force proposes.

ON MAY 5, 1986 *THE ST. LOUIS GLOBE-DEMOCRAT* RAN AN ARTICLE EN-titled "School Officials Upset by New State Plan" which reported that local educators objected vociferously to a new state plan that required them to give standardized tests in seven core subjects to students in the third, sixth, eighth, and tenth grades. Excerpts from this article follow:

> Local educators are stepping up their criticism of what they claim is state interference in the way local schools teach children.... The tests are required by the *Excellence in Education Act of 1985*, a reform bill that educators have largely supported. But school officials claim the testing component will force them to change their curriculum so students learn material in the same order the tests are given [teach to the test]. They claim 70 to 80 percent of the curriculum in local schools could be determined by the new tests....
>
> "We are not opposed to the concept of teaching children the fundamental facts that they ought to know. The issue is who controls the curriculum," said Kirkwood School District Superintendent Thomas Keating. Keating and other superintendents aired their complaints at a joint meeting last week of the Cooperating School Districts of the St. Louis Suburban Area and the Missouri School Boards Association....
>
> ...One of the harshest critics of the test plan is Ferguson-Florissant Superintendent Daniel B. Keck, who said the districts may just as well replace their school names with "Department of Elementary and Secondary Education, State of Missouri, Local Annex."...
>
> Keck, however, said the state has bypassed elected school board members and established a direct "pipeline" to local schools. He said administrators are accountable to whoever sets the curriculum.... "To whom am I as the chief executive officer of a school district responsible: to you, or DESE?" Keck said. "In this particular system, there are no checks and balances. That is bad governance." He said the media will create public pressure to excel on the new tests.
>
> Keck said the legislature has "inadvertently" transferred accountability for

educational quality to itself. He predicted that if the test scores aren't satisfactory, the state will lower the standards "until the legislature looks good.".…

…"And the same number of kids will walk out the door functionally illiterate," he said.

One of the test items (objectives) found in Missouri's Educational Objectives, Grade 12, resulting from passage of Missouri's *Excellence in Education Act of 1985*, follows:

> Given a description of an individual with a debased character, such as a child murderer or a person who has set fire to an inhabited building, students should reject suggestions for punishment which would detract from the dignity of the prisoner.

In the May 15, 1986 issue of *Education Daily* an article related to student assessment reported that "Secretary Bennett names study group to evaluate student assessment" and lists "Chairman Lamar Alexander, Governor of Tennessee and Chairman, National Governors Association, and Hillary Rodham Clinton, First Lady of Arkansas and partner in the Rose law firm" amongst members of the study group.

An article entitled "Carnegie Teaching Panel Charts 'New Framework'—Grants Totaling $900,000 Made to Press Reforms" written by Lynn Olson appeared in the May 21, 1986 issue of *Education Week*. The announced "New Framework"—amongst other things—carved in stone the methodology which teachers would be required to use in order to obtain board certification. Excerpts follow from this extremely important article:

> The Carnegie Corporation of New York announced here last week that it has awarded two major grants, totaling nearly $900,000, to forward the recommendations of the Carnegie Task Force on Teaching as a Profession.
>
> Last year, the corporation created the Carnegie Forum on Education and the Economy, a multi-million dollar initiative designed to help chart U.S. education policy during the next 10 years. The forum assembled the 14-member task force on teaching as one of its first initiatives. The foundation awarded $817,000 to Stanford University for a 15-month research project to develop prototypes of the kinds of assessments the task force's proposed National Board for Professional Teaching Standards might use to certify teachers.…
>
> …According to David A. Hamburg, president of the corporation [psychiatrist and negotiator of the Carnegie-Soviet Education Agreements], the grants illustrate Carnegie's commitment to the task force's work.…
>
> The 15-month Stanford study is the "opening gambit in a long and complex campaign to develop assessments for use by the national board," said Lee S. Shulman [deeply involved with the Chicago Mastery Learning debacle, ed.], principal investigator for the study and a professor of education at Stanford.…
>
> "Two major 'products' will come out of the Stanford study," said Mr. Shulman. First, it will create, field test, and critique several "prototype" assessments—most likely in the areas of elementary-school mathematics and secondary-school history.

Second, it will develop a protocol for how to develop such assessments in the future.... As part of its work, the Stanford project will do the following:

- Commission about 20 experts to write papers summarizing the knowledge and skills that the prototype assessments should measure.
- Conduct "wisdom of practice" studies of outstanding teachers to determine through interviews and observations what it is that they know and can do....
- Bring together people from around the country who are doing state-of-the-art assessments in other fields, such as those for airplane pilots and foreign-service jobs, to determine what assessment techniques are applicable to teaching.
- Bring together experts in the fields to be tested—such as elementary-school math teachers, teacher educators, and mathematicians—to get their advice on what the assessments should measure and how.

In addition, the project will have a steering committee representing key stakeholders in the creation of such assessments as well as experts in testing and in the subject areas to be tested.

Members of the Task Force included: Lewis M. Branscomb, Chairman, Vice President and Chief Scientist of the International Business Machines Corporation; Alan K. Campbell, Executive Vice President and Vice Chairman of A.R.A. Services, Inc. of Philadelphia; Mary Hatwood Futrell, President of the National Education Association; John W. Gardner, former Secretary of Health, Education and Welfare and founder of Independent Sector; Fred M. Hechinger, President of the New York Times Company Foundation, Inc.; Bill Honig, California State Superintendent of Public Instruction; James B. Hunt, former Governor of North Carolina, former Chairman of the Education Commission of the States and a lawyer with the firm of Poyner and Spruill; Vera Katz, Speaker of the Oregon House of Representatives; Governor Thomas H. Kean of New Jersey; Judith Lanier, Dean of the College of Education at Michigan State University; Arturo Madrid, President of the Tomas Rivera Center of Claremont (California) Graduate School; Shirley M. Malcolm, program head, Office of Opportunities in Science, American Association for the Advancement of Science; Ruth Randall, Commissioner of Education in Minnesota; Albert Shanker, President of the American Federation of Teachers.

AN ARTICLE IN THE MAY 21, 1986 ISSUE OF *EDUCATION WEEK* ENTITLED "Researchers Leery of Federal Plans for Collaboration—Fear 'Cooperative' Link a Path to 'Intervention'" by James Hertling discussed possible federal control of education research. Some excerpts follow:

The Education Department's decision to form a collaborative relationship with its new research and development center on reading has revived the debate over what control the government should have over the work of educational researchers receiving federal money....

...But the cooperative agreement outlined in the April 22 Federal Register announcing the competition for the new center on reading research and education mandates government involvement in all stages of the center's work: "developing the agenda, specifying anticipated outcomes, setting research priorities, altering research objectives on the basis of preliminary finding, and receiving final results."

"There's nothing we have heard that makes a cooperative agreement acceptable," said Laurie Garduque, director of governmental and professional liaison at the American Educational Research Association.

[Ed. Note: The above excerpts are important due to their identification of Secretary William Bennett's U.S. Department of Education as the source of the Skinnerian "scientific research-based" reading instruction ultimately used as the criteria necessary for funding of proposals under the *Reading Excellence Act of 1998*.]

"CARNEGIE REPORT ON EDUCATION: 'RADICAL BLUEPRINT FOR CHANGE'" by Nancy Garland was published in the *Bangor* [Maine] *Daily News*, June 28–29, 1986. The article stated in part:

> The leader of the 600,000-member American Federation of Teachers, [Al] Shanker said many Asian and European countries are changing the way they educate their children to meet the rapidly changing needs of industry. American industries will lose ground if schools cannot produce employees with skills useful in those industries.

PAULO FREIRE'S INFLUENCE ON WORLD EDUCATION, INCLUDING EDUCATION in the United States, is revealed in an interesting article entitled "Radical Theorist Takes His Message to the World" published in *The New York Times* August 19, 1986. Some excerpts follow:

> Within days of the triumph of the Sandinista Revolution in July 1979, Nicaragua's new leaders had tracked down the Brazilian educator Paulo Freire at the university where he was lecturing in the United States and had issued him an invitation to come to Managua to help reorganize the country's education system and design its new literacy program.
> When Portugal underwent its revolution in 1974 its new Government made a similar offer to Mr. Freire, as did Chile's Institute for Agrarian Reform during the period just before the election of Salvador Allende Gossens there.[17]
> Newly independent nations in Africa, ranging from Angola to Tanzania, have also sought the advice of the man regarded as perhaps the foremost literacy expert and radical educator in the world.
> "It's something that pleases me," Mr. Freire said recently as he passed through New York City, on his way to a series of workshops and seminars at American universities. "At times, I have been criticized by some philosophers of education, who place me in postures that they classify pejoratively as revolutionary...."
> Mr. Friere (pronounced FRAYree) first became widely known in this country with the publication *Pedagogy of the Oppressed* more than 15 years ago. He has argued that it is not education which shapes a society, but rather society which molds education to fit the ends and interests of those in control. In his view, education, particularly the process of learning to read and write, "can become an instrument of social transformation by making those at the bottom of society aware of their plight and the reasons for it."
> In practice, refined through literacy campaigns among peasants in the Brazilian Northeast beginning in the late 1950s and later on four continents, Mr. Freire and his many disciples have relied on words like "hunger" or "land,"

chosen for their relevance to the pupil's own political and social situation, to teach peasants and workers to read and write. The objective is to develop among them what Mr. Friere calls "a critical comprehension of reality."

...But Mr. Freire also argues that his distinct education has considerable relevance in the industrialized nations of the capitalist world. Mr. Freire's methods have been adapted in the United States by feminist, Hispanic and black groups that operate adult literacy programs or train teachers. Even some corporations, such as Consolidated Edison in New York, have at various times used his techniques in education programs for new workers with low levels of formal education.

"I am not a technician of literacy, as many people apparently saw me in the beginning," he said. "I am an educator who thinks globally.".…

To some of his critics, including the Reagan Administration, Mr. Freire's emphasis on the practical has been taken to an absurd extreme in Nicaragua, where second graders count not apples or oranges but hand grenades and rifles to learn arithmetic.

[ddd]

THE NEW YORK TIMES OF AUGUST 31, 1986 CARRIED AN ARTICLE ENTITLED "Study Says 33% of Young Adults Are Illiterate." Excerpt follows:

> Results from College Graduates: The most recent Federal study was conducted by two private groups, the Educational Testing Service and the National Assessment of Educational Progress, at a cost of $1.8 million. In testing basic skills at various levels, the study found that one in three young adults with a college degree from a two- or four-year school failed to answer this question correctly: If one purchased a sandwich for $1.90, a bowl of soup for 60 cents, and gave the cashier $3, how much change should he receive? The answer is 50 cents. (p. 28)

GEORGE ROCHE, PRESIDENT OF HILLSDALE COLLEGE, HILLSDALE, MICHIGAN, and chairman of the National Council on Educational Research, a presidentially appointed council overseeing the activities of the National Institute of Education, requested an investigation into the controversial Northwest Regional Educational Laboratory's (NWREL) Tri-County K–12 Course Goals Project which was initiated in 1971. Joan Gubbins, a former Indiana state senator and chairman of the council's Improvement and Practice Committee, researched the Goals Project, prepared, and submitted her report entitled "Goals and Objectives: Towards a National Curriculum?" to the Council on September 26, 1986.

Although Senator Gubbins's important report could have been used as a brief documenting the illegality of NWREL's role in development of the *Course Goals*, it evidently fell on deaf ears. Had the premise of this report—that the goals were based on humanistic no right/no wrong philosophy and the method was based on Skinnerian operant conditioning—been accepted by Secretary of Education William Bennett and his Assistant Secretary Chester

Finn, American parents and teachers might have seen a most welcome change in the course of American education, as well as an end to outcome-based education, its dumb-down values-changing curriculum, and global workforce training.

However, William Bennett and Chester Finn were promoting outcome-based education and had no desire to pull the plug on their own agenda. In fact, four days after Senator Gubbins presented her report to the council, Secretary William Bennett announced a $4.5 million grant to provide behaviorist effective school training for school districts across the nation. The October 1986 issue of *The Effective School Report* announced that

> Bennett awarded the money from his Secretary's Discretionary Fund for the commitment phase of the School Effectiveness Training Network (SET/Net), the largest Effective School training program ever undertaken. "I see this project as an indication of what school districts, large and small, can do together in improving schools," Bennett said in a Sept. 30 news conference. "This effort shows a real commitment to helping all children learn through the Effective School process, a process that is based on research and What Works."

Secretary Bennett's reluctance to acknowledge the problems associated with NWREL's Goals Project as pointed out by Senator Gubbins is better understood when one reads the Project's definition of behavior modification:

> [P]rocedures used in programs of behavior modification or behavioral management are based on principles derived from scientific research (e.g., stimulus-response-reinforcement).

"Scientific, research-based" teaching with roots in Skinnerian behavioral psychology is the common thread running through the fabric of all Effective School Research; including that promoted by the U.S. Department of Education under Secretary William Bennett's direction. Senator Gubbins's fine paper could not be allowed to cast a shadow on "a process that is based on research and What Works."

TIME FOR RESULTS: GOVERNORS' REPORT ON EDUCATION WAS PRESENTED to the 1986 National Governors' Association annual meeting in Wichita, Kansas. Then-Governor of Tennessee Lamar Alexander chaired the meeting and outlined a plan to restructure schools in America. There was a heavy emphasis on retraining of teachers in Skinnerian practices, merit pay/incentives/rewards, etc.

"THE COOPERATIVE UMBRELLA" IS THE TITLE OF A SHEET FROM A PACKET of materials distributed at a Cooperative Education conference for teachers in Northwest Indiana in 1986. The sheet was copied from *Circles of Learning: Cooperation in the Classroom, Rev. Ed.* by D.W. Johnson, R.T. Johnson and Edith Johnson Holubec (Prentice-Hall: Englewood Cliffs, N.J., 1986). An excerpt follows:

BASIC ELEMENTS OF COOPERATIVE LEARNING

Positive Interdependence
Students must feel that they need each other in order to complete the group's task, that they "sink or swim" together. Some ways to create this feeling are through establishing mutual goals (students must learn the material and make certain group members learn the material), joint rewards (if all group members achieve above a certain percentage on the test, each will receive bonus points), shared materials and information (one paper for each group or each member receives only part of the information needed to do the assignment), and assigned roles (summarizer, encourager or participator, elaborator).

1987

[ddd]

NORTH CENTRAL ASSOCIATION OF COLLEGES AND SCHOOLS (NCA): *MICHIgan Committee's Outcomes Accreditation* was published in 1987. The brochure demonstrates clearly the shift from academic education to performance/outcome-based affective education focusing on changes in the behavior of the individual student over time. Excerpts from this important publication follow:

The NCA's Outcomes Accreditation model has generated considerable interest among Michigan educators. It is a process that follows many of the principles of the "Effective Schools Research" and results in schools focusing their activities on improving student success....

Outcomes Accreditation [OA] is a school-based accreditation and evaluation model that helps schools document the effectiveness of their programs. Schools are required to target their evaluation efforts by measuring changes in student behavior; i.e., outcomes. OA serves as an alternative to the NCA's traditional evaluation formats. OA was adopted for use by NCA member schools in April 1987. Rather than focusing on "inputs" or what the school contributes to the educational process, OA examines "student outcomes" or the influence the school has on the students it serves....

Schools identify no more than five areas in which they want to focus their improvement activities. Target goals are written for each area. Three of these target goals focus on cognitive or basic skill areas, and two goals address affective concerns or how students behave or feel about themselves. The goals are written in such a way that changes can be measured over time. Student outcomes are measured by comparing desired levels of student performance with present performance....

Examples of specific data sources include: criterion- and norm-referenced test results, anecdotal records, attitude inventories, teacher-made tests, student participation rates, writing samples, and attendance and enrollment figures.... Next, faculty committees establish the desired levels of student performance. Although external sources such as state-mandated goals, national averages or goals developed by textbook publishers might be helpful in formulating performance expectations, educators need to base desired performance levels on their knowledge of each child. The discrepancy that exists between current and desired student performance then serves as the focus of the school improvement plan.

AT THE SECOND ANNUAL NATIONAL OUTCOME-BASED EDUCATION CONFER-
ence, held February 12–14, 1987 in Tempe, Arizona, a notebook was distributed which contained a flow chart describing how mastery learning works.
The notebook contained materials generated by the following presenters: Part
I, William Spady; Part II, Lawrence A. Rowe; Part III, Kathleen A. Fitzpatrick;
and Part IV, Janet N. Barry. This writer has converted the flow chart which
was in the notebook to written text in order to provide a graphic (rat maze)
description of the behavior modification method behind mastery learning
and direct instruction. The chart's description follows:

MASTERY LEARNING BREAKS THE FAILURE CYCLE

At the top of a circle is the word "TASK," which has an arrow pointing towards LACK OF UNDERSTANDING, which has two parts: 1) change presentation and 2) use alternative material. 2) has two arrows: one towards TASK
COMPLETION SUCCESS and the other towards DIFFICULTY. DIFFICULTY
has two parts: 1) peer tutoring and 2) shorten assignments. 2) has two arrows: one towards TASK COMPLETION SUCCESS and the other towards
FAILURE. FAILURE has two parts: 1)change environment and 2) change
curriculum. 2) has two arrows: one towards TASK COMPLETION/POSI-
TIVE FEEDBACK, and the other towards NEGATIVE FEEDBACK. NEGATIVE
FEEDBACK has two arrows: 1) use self-pacing, self-checking, and 2) group
discussion of goals. 2) has two arrows: one towards ATTAINABLE GOAL/
POSITIVE FEEDBACK, the other towards POOR SELF CONCEPT. POOR SELF
CONCEPT has two arrows: 1) provide successes and 2) positive feedback.
2) has two arrows: one toward RAISED SELF ESTEEM and the other LOW
MOTIVATION. LOW MOTIVATION has three arrows: 1) provide choices, 2)
choose relevant materials, and 3) utilize interests. 3) has two arrows: one
towards HIGHER MOTIVATION/WILLINGNESS TO TRY and the other toward
BEHAVIOR PROBLEMS (Task Avoidance). BEHAVIOR PROBLEMS has three
arrows: 1) provide choices, 2) contracting, and 3) group goal setting. 3) has
two arrows: one toward RECHANNELLED BEHAVIOR DIRECTED TOWARD
SKILL ATTAINMENT and INADEQUATE SKILLS. INADEQUATE SKILLS has
two arrows: 1) prescriptive curriculum and 2) modified environment. 2) has
two arrows: one towards SKILLS ATTAINED/NEW TASK ATTEMPTED, and
the other back to start, "TASK."

EDUCATION DAILY OF MAY 21, 1987 COVERED THE CARNEGIE FOUNDATION
for the Advancement of Teaching's award of $817,000 to Lee Shulman of
Stanford University, formerly involved in Chicago's Mastery Learning failure,
for his forthcoming work on assessments for new teachers.

KATHY L. COLLINS, LEGAL COUNSEL FOR THE IOWA DEPARTMENT OF EDUCA-
tion, wrote an article entitled "Children Are Not Chattel" for the American
Humanist Association's journal *Free Inquiry* in the Fall of 1987 (Vol. 7, No.
4, p. 11) and stated that

Christian parents who want the freedom to indoctrinate their children with
religious education do not understand that the law that prevents them from
legally teaching their kids prevents someone else from abusing them....

Certified teachers are state-mandated child-abuse reporters. When children are allowed to be kept at home, there may be no outside contact, no help for the abused child.

[Ed. Note: This portentous article was published just as the homeschooling movement in America began mushrooming. Parents responded to the failures of the latest fads in the classrooms by pulling their children out of public schools to instruct them at home. Many educators viewed the rise of home education with alarm. Parental rights and constitutional religious freedoms posed a direct threat to the "it takes a village to raise a child" philosophy which was to become embedded in every state's education reform plan during the 1990s.]

[ddd]

DAVID W. HORNBECK OF THE CARNEGIE FOUNDATION FOR THE ADVANCEMENT of Teaching and Maryland's state superintendent of instruction, whose credentials lie in theology rather than in education, presented his proposal for a new public education system for the nation in the November 17, 1987 issue of *The Montgomery County* [Maryland] *Journal*. The *Journal* carried an article entitled "State Education Chief Pushes Revolutionary Plan for the Nation" that, amongst other things, "would let students enroll in schools of their choice and even sue the state over low-quality education." Excerpts follow:

"The model state law would create a situation in which it's the school's fault and not the kid's if the school is unsuccessful. If it's not a successful school, you can leave it." The system would let a student cross district lines in search of better public education....

Hornbeck's presentation Saturday at an Asheville, North Carolina meeting aroused just a few criticisms, which were mainly concerned with the proposal's wording, said Jay P. Goldman, spokesman for the school chief's council. "This follows years of massaging and reworking it," he said....

...The new rights proposals are directed toward all children, but special measures target those considered "at risk of educational failure." In the early years, low-income children would be identified as at risk; in later years, achievement would provide the definition.... "We're trying to take a step away from kid-bashing," Hornbeck said. "Society and the schools fail the kids."...

...Hornbeck, who said he is waiting for the council vote before discussing the issue with Gov. William Donald Schaefer and Maryland legislative officials, said he expects local school officials across the country to resist the proposals.

"If the council adopts this, you will have the superintendents of the United States saying we want to create new rights and routes that may well lead to the courts," Hornbeck said....

...One of the plan's goals is to eliminate spending differentials from district to district, ranging about $2,000 per pupil from highest to lowest in Maryland. "That means $50,000 more behind one classroom of 25 kids than another," Hornbeck said.

[Ed. Note: Did we understand Mr. Goldman correctly? "This follows years of massaging and reworking"? Why does one need "years of massaging and reworking a proposal" which supposedly is in the best interests of the traditional American teacher and the children he or she teaches? Obviously, this proposal by Hornbeck was a radical one which would focus not on traditional education, but on producing or molding a "product," your child—who is now being referred to as "human capital" by Hornbeck—your child, whose workforce skills and politically correct attitudes, values and beliefs would entitle him to a Certificate in Mastery in order to be hired by and able to increase the profits of a corporation.

References to "special measures target those considered 'at risk of educational failure'" are unsettling. If our children reject the "education" to which they are subjected, they will immediately be labeled "at risk," thus subjecting them to the behavior modification programs and operant conditioning techniques normally used for special education.

When Hornbeck says, "Society and the schools fail the kids," are we to believe "It's the environment, stupid"? Everything that goes wrong in our great nation is now blamed on the "environment"; from people's choices to smoke or not to smoke, drink or not to drink, murder or not to murder, study or not to study. According to Skinnerian behaviorist thinking, since humans are to be thought of as animals, not having free will and, therefore, not being responsible for their actions, they would be incapable of making complex decisions, of deciding "yes" or "no." We are on a slippery slope when we accept this "the environment is responsible" line of thinking.

Hornbeck's proposal parallels the 1999 passage of "choice" legislation in Florida, under Governor Jeb Bush's direction. Delivery of failing grades to schools will be the trigger for funding for moving students to schools of their "choice"—including private or religious schools.]

1988

ON FEBRUARY 22, 1988 CLARENCE THOMAS, CHAIRMAN OF THE EQUAL Employment Opportunity Commission (EEOC), who would shortly thereafter be appointed by President George Bush to the U.S. Supreme Court, signed off on an EEOC Policy Notice regarding protection from mandatory New Age training in the workplace. The Policy Notice explained:

1. SUBJECT: Policy statement on "new age" training programs which conflict with employees' religious beliefs.
2. PURPOSE: This policy statement is intended to provide guidance in the handling of cases where an employee objects to participating in the training program because it utilizes techniques or exercises which conflict with the employee's religious beliefs.
3. EFFECTIVE DATE: Upon Receipt.
4. EXPIRATION DATE:
5. ORIGINATOR: Title VII/EPA Division, Office of Legal Counsel.
6. INSTRUCTIONS: This notice supplements the instructions in #628 of Vol. II of the Compliance Manual, Religious Accommodation, and should be inserted after p. 628–630.

[Ed. Note: This Policy Notice extends to all government employees who resist manipulative New Age training which is based on the behavioral techniques and behavior modification described in this book. Held captive in the classroom due to attendance laws, why haven't our children been provided the same protection from the mind-bending curricula and methods used on government employees in the workplace? Why are not American teachers provided this protection from the mind-bending, brain-numbing, in-service sessions which violate their constitutional rights? The *Protection of Pupil Rights Amendment* which passed the U.S. Senate unanimously in 1978, for which regulations were drafted and approved in 1984, has proven to be useless since the educational bureaucracy refuses to enforce it and has consistently stonewalled when parents have attempted to assert their rights under the law.]

THE *EFFECTIVE SCHOOL REPORT*'S MARCH, 1988 ISSUE PUBLISHED "INTER-national Congress for Effective Schools Draws Participants from 13 Nations to London" which heralded Effective School Research as representing "the" chosen organizational and pedagogical vehicle for the operation of the world's schools. Excerpts follow:

> Representatives from thirteen countries came to London in January for the inaugural meeting of the International Congress for Effective Schools. In the United States, the Effective Schools Movement was begun to improve public schools for children from low income families. Thirty American states have used effective schools precepts as part of their reform efforts.
>
> Effective schools activities were reported from Australia, Canada, England, and Wales, Germany, Hungary, Ireland, Israel, the Netherlands, Norway, Scotland, Sweden, South Africa, and the United States. Dale Mann, a professor at Teachers College, Columbia University, and the founding chairman of the International Congress, said that the 130 registrants were using effective schools ideas in school improvement work that ran the gamut from early childhood education to high school reform.
>
> The Congress will meet next in January, 1989 in Rotterdam. A special section of the program will offer legislators an opportunity to share their perspectives on school improvement. The Rotterdam meetings will be organized by a team led by D.A.A. Peters (Projectleider, Project Onderwijs en Social Milieu, Burg, Van Walmsumeg 892, 3011 MZ Rotterdam, the Netherlands 010–4113266).[18]

[Ed. Note: By this time the reader is all too familiar with *The Effective School Report* and Effective School Research, as well as its role in the dumbing down of public school children, particularly those from low income families. The international change agents "used" these children (experimented on them—starting with children in Jackson, Mississippi where *The Effective School Report* was originally located) prior to recommending that all children be subjected to the Skinnerian dumb down methods (OBE/ML/DI).

From this time on the reader will encounter entries in this book dealing with Effective Schools Research exchanges with Russia and China, thereby closing the circle on the implementation of Effective Schools Research on a global basis. Also of importance is the reference to the inclusion of England and Wales, not only in the original National Assessment of Educational Progress (NAEP) 1981 paper by Archie Lapointe and Willard Wirtz, but in the 1994 *National Issues in Education: Goals 2000 and School-to-Work* entry which reveals that

> In 1991 Lamar Alexander, working with Chester Finn and others who were familiar with the work of British Prime Minister Margaret Thatcher in enacting a national curriculum in England and Wales, convinced Bush to endorse the idea of national standards for education.

Of interest here is that the National Assessment of Educational Progress (NAEP) had been working on assessment for many years, dating back to 1980, with Clare Burstall of Wales, U.K. Also, one might ask why the United States would want to copy the English education system in light of the poor performance of its students on basic skills tests. The December 9, 1988 issue of *The Wall Street Journal* carried an editorial entitled "And You Thought American Schools Were Bad!" in which Theodore Dalrymple, the pen name of British physician Anthony Daniels, said that

> In eight years in medical practice in an English slum (in which lives, incidentally, a fifth of the population of the industrial English city where I work) I have met only one teenager of hundreds I have asked who knew when World War II was fought. The others thought it took place in the early 1900s or the 1970s, and lasted up to 30 years.

Another recurrent theme, which will become evident throughout the rest of this book, will be the growing emphasis on what Utah's Superintendent Burningham referred to as "research-verified programs." This term will change subtly as Effective Schools programs are referred to as "scientific, research-based," implying that they are "acceptable and desirable"—or as Secretary of Education William Bennett explained, "What Works."]

DR. SUE E. BERRYMAN, DIRECTOR OF THE INSTITUTE ON EDUCATION AND the Economy at Teachers College, Columbia University, New York, presented a paper entitled "Education and the Economy: A Diagnostic Review and Implications for the Federal Role" at a seminar on the federal role in education held at the Aspen Institute, Aspen, Colorado on July 31–August 10, 1988. Under acknowledgments one reads:

> This Seminar was sponsored by The Carnegie Corporation, The Ford Foundation, The Hewlitt Foundation, The Primerica Foundation, and the Rockefeller Brothers Foundation. This paper is based heavily on, and could not have been written without, research conducted under the auspices of The National Center on Education and Employment, funded by the Office of Research, Office of Educational Research and Improvement of the U.S. Department of Education. The paper also relies on research funded by the National Assessment of Vocational Education.

An excerpt from Dr. Berryman's resumé, which was attached to her paper, follows:

1973–1985 Behavioral Scientist, Behavioral Sciences Department, The RAND
Corporation, Santa Monica, California, and Washington, D.C.

> Analyzed individuals' educational and employment choices and the
> nature and consequences of military, corporate, and federal human
> resource policies.

The table of contents of Dr. Berryman's report is reproduced here:

Excerpts from the body of the paper follow:

[ddd]

WHO SHOULD LEARN?

The skills just described are generic in that, in general, they cut across
industries and occupations. Thus, everyone needs to learn them, not just
some people. This does not mean that everyone needs to learn them in the

same way. It does mean that for these skills, our educational objectives for everyone need to be roughly the same.

The idea has been most problematic for higher order cognitive thinking. Like other industrialized nations, the United States has harbored two quite distinct educational traditions—one concerned with elite education, the other with mass education. As Resnick [Lauren] (1987a) points out, these traditions conceived of schooling differently, had different clienteles, and held different goals for their students. Thus, although "...it is not new to include thinking, problem solving, and reasoning in someone's curriculum, it is new to include it in everyone's curriculum."...

WHEN SHOULD THEY LEARN?

Early. We usually think about preparing students for the labor market during high school. However, we are talking generic work-related skills here, not occupationally specific ones; for these high school is too late. It is implausible to think that high school sophomores educated in a passive learning regime for the first nine years of their schooling can learn to self-regulate their learning in the tenth year. We can make analogous arguments about learning how to learn, about learning how to function effectively in teams, or about learning how to resolve conflicts.

For example, as Resnick (1987a) notes, the most important single message of modern research on the nature of thinking is that the kinds of activities traditionally associated with thinking are not limited to advanced levels of development.

> These activities are an intimate part of even elementary learning....
> In fact, the term "higher order" skills is probably itself fundamentally misleading, for it suggests that another set of skills, presumably called "lower order," needs to come first. This assumption... implicitly... justifies long years of drill on the "basics" before thinking and problem solving are demanded.... Research suggests that failure to cultivate aspects of (higher order cognitive) thinking may be the source of major learning difficulties even in elementary school.

This section relies heavily on pioneering work in cognitive psychology, cognitive science, and cognitive anthropology on non-school learning and its implications for how we structure formal learning. At the heart of this research is the presumption that intelligence and expertise are built out of interaction with the environment, not in isolation from it. This work implicitly challenges our traditional distinctions between "head" and "hand," between "academic" and "vocational" education, between "education" and "training," and between school-based and work-based learning.

Coming out of this stream of research is a much clearer sense of how school-based learning and non-school-based learning differ from each other. In a bravura synthesis of the work in this field, Lauren Resnick (1987b) delineates four broad contrasts between in-school and out-of-school mental activity that raise profound questions about the utility and effectiveness of schooling for all non-school activity, including work of all types and for all learners, whether at-risk, or not-at-risk. They stimulate us to rethink—radically rethink—how we teach in school.

The first contrast is between individual cognition in school versus shared cognition outside. Although group activities occur in school, students are ultimately judged on what they can do by themselves. Much of the core activity of the school—homework or in class exercises—is designed as individual work. For the most part, students fail or succeed at a task independently of what other students do (aside from grading on a curve). By contrast, a great deal of activity outside of school is socially shared: work, personal life, and recreation take place in social systems in which what one person is able to do depends fundamentally on what others do and in which "successful" functioning depends upon the mesh of several individuals' mental and physical performance. This contrast argues for much more team and co-operative learning, the student being accountable for both individual and team performance. (p. 21)

[Ed. Note: The above emphasis on group learning, group cooperation, etc., reminds me of a comment made by a lady in the audience when I was giving a speech on education restructuring with its emphasis on the need for cooperative learning and how cooperative learning is used in communist countries. She recounted an incident which occurred while visiting relatives in the Ukraine (part of the former Soviet Union). A fire broke out in the house one evening and, instead of her relatives using their individual brains and ingenuity to put it out, (assuming individual responsibility), everyone sat on the couch and frantically stared at one another, not knowing how to deal with the situation.]

THE EAST GIBSON COUNTY (INDIANA) GROUP, KNOWN AS "JEANNIE'S Group," opposed the use of *Tactics for Thinking*, developed by Robert Marzano in 1988.[19] After long and heated discussions with the school system, the superintendent suddenly notified the group that he had arranged for a debate to be held in two days! Short notice, considering the fact that he carefully neglected to inform them until the day of the debate that they would be debating outside experts. And, experts they were—no less than Ronald Brandt of the Association for Supervision and Curriculum Development (ASCD) and Professor Ed Jenkins of Indiana University. A firsthand account of a portion of the debate follows:

[Pat Burkhart, one of the East Gibson County Group debaters] "We would like to do some demonstrations for you.... The first one is yoga (demonstrated).... The second exercise is self hypnosis.... These instructions... came from an article in *The Readers' Digest* (demonstrated).... The third exercise is a semi-trance. This is the semi-trance in the Norman-Lindsay book *Human Information Processing* referenced by Marzano in *Tactics for Thinking*, 'Unit 1: Attention Control' (demonstrated).... The fourth exercise is the Involuntary Attention-Orienting Reflex. These steps come from the book *The Working Brain* by Alexandr Luria [of Russia] which is also referenced in the *Tactics for Thinking* manual by Marzano (demonstrated). The last exercise is Marzano's Attention Control in the *Tactics* manual. As a volunteer, we have an 8-year-old child who understands the difference between acting and reality. We thought this appropriate—to use a child—since Marzano does. The difference is, our child knows what we are doing, but Marzano's victims don't.

"Please tell us what is the difference? The thing that is really silly is that we are supposed to believe that this is higher order learning—that it is learning to learn.... This is learning to have your conscious mind sedated and using only your unconscious mind which processes everything indiscriminately.... There isn't much going on here besides a form of self-hypnosis."

In conclusion, the opponents of *Tactics for Thinking* asked Joan Gubbins, former Indiana state senator and presidentially appointed member of the National Council for Educational Research, to read the following:

> If we turn to Marzano's conclusions at the end of his evaluation, he states, and I quote: "These findings can not be considered stable." Do you understand what all of this says? Marzano himself says his evaluation of this experimental program is unreliable.... Nothing is said about improvement of performance on standardized achievement tests by the students used in this field testing. However, in a program Marzano reported on in 1984 [he admitted that] "a decrease in math and reading achievement was indicated on standardized tests."

THE AUGUST 1988 ISSUE OF *EDUCATION UPDATE,* PUBLISHED BY THE Association for Supervision and Curriculum Development (ASCD), carried an article entitled "Tactics for Thinking Attacked in Washington, Indiana" which said, in part:

> *Tactics for Thinking,* a framework for teaching thinking developed at the Mid-continent Regional Educational Laboratory (McREL) and published by ASCD in 1986, has recently been the target of critics who argue that it "brainwashes" children and advances a "New Age" agenda of one-world government. The problems first occurred in Battle Ground, Washington, and have surfaced in at least one other Washington community and in two Indiana towns.
>
> *Tactics,* according to ASCD Executive Editor Ron Brandt, "gives teachers a practical way to teach their students to think well." The program teaches 22 skills divided into three categories: Learning-to-Learn Skills, Content Skills, and Reasoning Skills.... For example, a unit of the program on "attention control" describes how adult learners are able to disregard distractions and concentrate on a particular subject, which helps their performance. The *Tactics Trainer's Manual* suggests an exercise in which participants can be voluntarily controlled. Although the strategy may seem ordinary, critics of *Tactics* in East Gibson, Indiana, said it "is the same technique used by hypnotists, used in mind control, and in New Age meditation."
>
> ...Marzano denied that *Tactics* is controversial or contains sensitive material, asking, "How can teaching kids to control their attention in class so they can learn more be controversial?"
>
> Paul Drotz, an assistant superintendent in the South Kitsap, Washington school district where *Tactics* was challenged, said that "the vocabulary used in the program left us pretty open to attacks. I could change 12 words and local critics would have a difficult time attacking it." Judy Olson, a consultant hired by the Washington ASCD to train teachers in *Tactics,* said she advised trainees to call one unit "pay attention" rather than "attention control." Because of the controversy, however, the Washington ASCD will no longer provide *Tactics* training, although it will still build awareness of it, members of the group's governing board said.
>
> ...Marzano said that development and field testing of *Tactics* was "typical," and that the screening process, which included review by eight nationally recognized experts in critical thinking, was more thorough than normal.... ASCD has sold more than 17,000 teacher's manuals, 3,600 trainer's guides

and 550 videotapes since it began publishing the program. Marzano estimates that 20,000 teachers have been trained in the program.

Brandt suggested that school districts involve board members, teachers, and the community early on in deciding whether and how *Tactics* might be used in the system. ASCD will continue to closely monitor any instance in which the program is challenged. Anyone knowing of such incidents should write Brandt at ASCD headquarters, 1703 Beauregard St., Alexandria, VA 22311–1714.

[Ed. Note: The *Tactics* program, or a similar critical thinking program using another title, could well be part of the curriculum in each of the 16,000 school districts in the nation, since it takes only one of those 20,000 teachers in each district to train other teachers. It was, however, not adopted in East Gibson County, Indiana.]

THE AUGUST 11, 1988 EDITION OF *EDUCATION DAILY* COVERED THE National Citizens Alliance Press Conference held at the National Press Club in Washington, D.C. Excerpts follow:

GROUP ASKS EDUCATION DEPARTMENT TO STOP FUNDING "MIND-CONTROL" CURRICULA, END SOVIET EXCHANGES

A citizens group headed by a former Education Department official asked ED to stop promoting curriculum the group says controls students' minds.

The National Citizens Alliance (NCA), a group of parents and teachers, alleged at a Washington, D.C. news conference yesterday that ED is promoting "mind-control" curricula that use hypnosis-like techniques to foster concentration.

NCA wants to "get the federal government to stop pouring millions of dollars" into the "development of mind-control programs currently sweeping through American schools," said Charlotte Iserbyt, who served as senior policy advisor in ED's Office of Educational Research and Improvement from 1981 to 1982 and is NCA's East Coast coordinator. Iserbyt called on Education Secretary William Bennett and other federal officials to:

End federal funding and promotion of programs such as *Tactics for Thinking*, which is used in Indiana schools.[20] NCA says the curriculum "employs hypnotic-like processes and altered states of consciousness techniques on children";

Cancel the education portion of the 1985 exchange agreement between the United States and the Soviet Union, which NCA says allows dissemination of "communist propaganda" through global teaching methods and the joint development of textbooks and computer software; and

Force Pennsylvania to ask parental consent before using its Educational Quality Assessment test, which NCA says uses "psychological and psychiatric testing" in violation of the federal *Protection of Pupil Rights Amendment* [Anita Hoge case against the Pennsylvania Department of Education].

NCA also criticized ED's National Assessment of Educational Progress for tracking student attitudes and behavior, saying that obtaining such information violates privacy rights and could lead to behavior modification nationwide.

Secretary Bennett's spokesman Loye Miller said he is not aware of the complaints to which NCA refers. An OERI spokesman declined to comment.—Christopher Grasso

A MAJOR REPORT ENTITLED *THE FORGOTTEN HALF: PATHWAYS TO SUCCESS for America's Youth and Young Families* was published by the W.T. Grant Foundation's Commission on Work, Family and Citizenship.[21] The November 23, 1988 issue of *Education Week* carried an item on the report which stated that service projects and community service were recommended as a requirement for graduation. An excerpt from the article follows:

> The report recommends that schools and communities "establish attractive service opportunities" for young people and either include service projects as part of the curriculum or require a specified amount of community service as a requirement toward graduation. The report also encourages "partnerships between business and state and local governments that provide opportunities for job training."

A RECAP OF A **1988** INVITATIONAL CONFERENCE IN THE **U.S.S.R.** ENTITLED "Children, Computers and Education," written by David Porteous, contract coordinator for the School of Social Work, University of Connecticut, West Hartford, Connecticut, was published in the 1988/1989 issue of *T.H.E. Journal* (technology journal).[22] Excerpts follow:

> Recently, educators from the United States, Canada, West Germany and the Netherlands met with counterparts from the Soviet Union and Bulgaria in an historic first—an invitational conference in the U.S.S.R. titled "Children, Computers, and Education."
>
> The word "informatics" is used in Russian to denote the principles underlying the operations of computer hardware and software. Informatics seems to encompass the electronic and algorithmic systems of computers. Dr. Alexey Semenov of the Soviet Academy of Sciences said algorithmic thinking is embedded in the Soviet's educational system and fundamental to their understanding of cognition. This fits with the Soviet schools' high regard for mathematics and physics....
>
> Semenov's presentation on the history and present status of algorithmics in Soviet schools started with the fact that their schools have used programmed instruction since the 1960s.... As might be expected, LOGO is held in high esteem in the Soviet Union and Seymour Papert works with some Soviet schools....
>
> There was hope among the leaders with whom we talked that computers will become seen and used in more diverse ways throughout the curriculum. Certainly the goals of Gorbachev's Perestroika include the restructuring of schools, along with other institutions and the economy, and a subsequent technological boost to the country. With the broad curriculum reforms and structural changes occurring in schools today and in the near future, the computer could expedite this process....

MODEL SCHOOL

Most schools have one or more sponsors, such as factories, institutes, universities, which provide materials, professional assistance and a place for students in the upper forms to do practical work for three to four hours a week, including computer programming. School #344 has close ties with a university and a technical institute, for instance [same as USA School-to-Work proposals, ed.]....

...The informatics curriculum, with objectives broader than computer use, is taught even when students do not have access to a computer....

We were told that this conference, from Leningrad to Moscow to Zvenigorod, had begun to open many minds as to what is possible with computers and children beyond the formal informatics curriculum. Professional respect and relationships have developed among participants. We could not have heard better news for our efforts to achieve a major step towards a productive global discussion of how all children can benefit from an informed use of CAI [computer-assisted instruction/programmed learning] in the world's classrooms.

1989

IN AN ARTICLE IN THE JANUARY 25, 1989 ISSUE OF *EDUCATION WEEK* Chester E. Finn, Jr., former head of the U.S. Department of Education's research branch, told business leaders in Washington that he favored the development of a "national curriculum."

RUSHWORTH KIDDER, PRESIDENT OF THE INSTITUTE FOR GLOBAL ETHICS with offices in Camden, Maine, and London, England, wrote *Reinventing the Future: Global Goals for the 21st Century*, published by The Christian Science Publishing Society (MIT Press, Cambridge, Mass, 1989) which covered the dialogue between 35 notables from 12 nations gathered at "Wingspread" in Racine, Wisconsin in April of 1989. *The Christian Science Monitor*, the Johnson Foundation and the University of Maryland-Baltimore County sponsored the event. In his book Kidder stated that the conference included "everything that sounded like a reasonable goal for the year 2000," among which were the following: "Educate children in the context of one world; Develop educational curricula that reflect the realitites of global interdependence; Promote community service; Inculcate a healthy skepticism for authority; Reduce the share of GNP (Gross National Product) devoted to military spending; and Strengthen the role of the United Nations and other multilateral forums."

In a July 5, 1994 letter from Mr. Kidder to Mr. David Zanotti, president of the Northeast Ohio Roundtable, Kidder described the work of his Institute for Global Ethics as follows:

> The Institute for Global Ethics is an independent, non-profit educational organization specifically dedicated to promoting the discussion of ethics in a global context. Taking a journalistic rather than an academic approach, we see our task as responding to the ever-growing need for identifying and describing standards of ethical values throughout the world. We don't dictate what those values should be. Instead, we try to help discover what they actually are—and to promote their discussion and application in ways that are non-threatening, inclusive, and conflict-resolving.

The Institute has a national board of directors, an international advisory council, a network of nationwide and global connections, and a membership base of some 2,500 individuals in the United States and around the world. Some of our activities [from which the writer has selected only a few, ed.] include:

- **Global Values Survey**. We are currently carrying out a multi-country survey of values and ethics to help us understand the core values that unite various cultures as well as the different ways each culture defines an ethical decision. The pilot survey, carried out among samples of business leaders in Japan, India, and the United States, was completed in June. We're now laying plans to launch a full-scale survey of individuals in business, politics, medicine, journalism, and other sectors of society in 12 nations. [The Institute was awarded a $450,000 grant from the W.K. Kellogg Foundation of Battle Creek, Michigan to accomplish this survey, ed.]

- **Education**. The Institute works actively with several school districts and educational organizations in the United States on character education, seeking ways to help schools and communities find the core, shared values among their constituencies that can form a basis for discussions of ethical issues in the schools. We've produced an award-winning half-hour video, *Personal Ethics and the Future of the World*, designed for use in schools and with audiences of all ages. And we've also published a booklet, *Character Education: Lessons from the Past, Models for the Future*, by Professor James Leming of Southern Illinois University.

- **Seminars**. We are currently working with several clients (including the J.M. Smucker Company, Lancaster Laboratories, Inc., and the Council on Foundations in Washington, D.C.) to provide ethics training programs. We have trained more than 1,000 executives and managers in day-long, intensive seminars, and developed a train-the-trainers program as well. Our goal is to encourage what we call "ethical fitness"—which, like physical fitness, needs to be practiced, developed and applied.

- **Radio**. Our newest venture is a one-hour Public Radio program titled "Let's Be Honest—Ethical Issues of the '90s." Featuring a three-person panel and a moderator, the program focuses on the moral and ethical aspects of a specific topic drawn from the week's news and encourages on-air telephone calls from listeners. Pilot versions of the program, aired on Maine Public Radio, have been very well received, and plans are afoot to develop a version of the program for a national audience.

[Ed. Note: Kidder's Global Ethics program is another example of the problem with character education as a whole: basing character, values and ethics on consensus decisions by a group instead of absolute, enduring principles.]

KENT TEMPUS WROTE "EDUCATION IN THE FUTURE: 21ST CENTURY SCHOOLS Will Offer Learning for All Citizens" for *The Muscatine* [Iowa] *Journal*'s April 22, 1989 issue. Excerpts follow:

Schools in 21st Century Iowa will be hubs of their communit[ies], providing broad learning opportunities for all citizens, according to the director of the Iowa Department of Education. William Lepley says future schools will be centers for family and social services as well. "Society in the year 2010 has realized that the school is the single societal institution that can truly be an advocate, a resource, and a catalyst for children and families, as well as learners of all ages," Lepley said.... Students' evaluation will improve. Instead of grades, students will be assessed not on the work they complete, but on the skills they master, he explained.

Community service will be a graduation requirement. Also, educational opportunities are available for all citizens from preschool to adults. The school year won't be restricted to 180 days of 5–1/2 hours each, because flexible schedules and teacher contracts will permit year-round learning, he said. "Teachers in ideal schools are managers of the learning environment," Lepley said. "The teacher has been given the tools to be able to diagnose learning needs and to prescribe appropriate activities." Schools themselves will change too, Lepley noted. The ideal school houses social agencies such as health, job, and human service agencies, child care and serves as the community's senior citizen volunteer center, he said. And adults come to ideal schools—open round the clock—for educational opportunities ranging from childbirth and parenting classes to pre-retirement planning, he added. In the ideal community, Lepley said, the superintendent coordinates children and family services, in addition to education.

[Ed. Note: Lepley used the term "hub" in this article and in a pamphlet distributed widely across Iowa to describe the school of the future which will encompass numerous social service agencies, health care, job training, child care, etc. This concept mirrored the Community Education plans promoted by the Mott Foundation of Michigan and incorporated into federal grantmaking under the *Elementary and Secondary Education Act of 1965*.

A multitude of state reform plans in the early 1990s include diagrams of this same plan, exhibiting the school as the center (or "hub") of the community; significantly, some diagrams show churches, recreation and other private aspects of life encompassed within the "hub" concept. With the advent of school-to-work programs, the concept has been expanded to include "one-stop training centers" for workforce development and placement. Children who don't pass the proficiency assessments will be sent through these "centers" for services and remediation which will rely on operant conditioning methods to ensure "success".

Substitute "government" for schools like this "hub" plan and what political/economic system do we have? Who exactly asked for—voted for?—this alien "education" system which places our citizens and communities under the control of the unelected school superintendent?]

BARRY BEAR, A MILDLY RETARDED 11-YEAR-OLD INDIAN BOY LIVING ON A reservation and being taught at home by his mother, was declared a "child in need of assistance" (CINA) by a landmark Iowa Supreme Court decision on May 17, 1989. Barry Bear was removed from his home when the court cited "his parents' failure to exercise a reasonable degree of care in supervising him" because he was not in school. His parents had been previously jailed for violating the state's compulsory attendance (truancy) law. This precipitated the filing of a CINA petition, leading ultimately to the legal challenge which resulted in the Iowa Supreme Court decision. According to "The Tama Story: Educational Tyranny in Iowa," an article by Samuel Blumenfeld,[23] the following occurred:

> [The State of Iowa] wanted to establish a legal precedent whereby home-schooled children could be removed from parents found guilty of violating the compulsory attendance law.
>
> The juvenile law states that a child in need of assistance is a child (1) whose parents physically abused or neglected the child, (2) a child who "has suffered or is imminently likely to suffer harmful effects as a result of the failure of the parent... to exercise a reasonable degree of care in supervising the child," or (3) a child who is in need of treatment for serious mental illness or disorder.
>
> Definition two is the one the State decided could be effectively used to prosecute Barry Bear's parents. It is also vague enough, wide enough to include fundamentalist Christian home schoolers. After all, the State can always get humanistic psychiatrists, psychologists, guidance counselors, and other "experts" to testify that keeping a child out of public school can cause "harmful effects" by depriving the child of needed socialization....
>
> ...Barry was taken from his family and placed in foster care.

[Ed. Note: This ominous decision was supposed to have created court case precedent in Iowa and around the country. A handful of heroic homeschoolers stopped these efforts; at the same time foiling a truancy bill in the Iowa legislature that would have allowed—even mandated—a homeschooled child to be removed from his parents and placed into foster care. The Barry Bear case provides a snapshot of the future, of the "penalties" that will be imposed on parents who fail to comply with various aspects of compulsory attendance and testing laws. The full weight of this "hammer" will be felt when school-to-work certification requirements and newly proposed "performance-based" national standards and assessments for "accountability" and "quality" are imposed on *all* children, including the homeschooled. It should be noted that no national organization assisted in the grassroots homeschoolers' resistance, on behalf of the Bear family, to these aggressive state actions.]

THE NATIONAL GOVERNORS' ASSOCIATION (NGA) EDUCATION SUMMIT WAS convened in 1989 by President George Bush at the University of Virginia in Charlottesville, Virginia. The NGA unveiled *America 2000*—now known as *Goals 2000*—and its six national education goals (which have now been increased to eight). These goals have served to carve into stone controversial "education" practices thoroughly exposed in this book, and to lay the foundation for activating school-to-work initiatives. The goals are as follows:

> GOAL 1. By the year 2000, all children will start school ready to learn.
> GOAL 2. By the year 2000, the high school graduation rate will increase to at least 90 percent.

GOAL 3. By the year 2000, all students will leave grades 4, 8, and 12 having demonstrated competency over challenging subject matter including English, mathematics, science, foreign languages, civics and government, economics, arts, history, and geography, and every school in America will ensure that all students learn to use their minds well, so they may be prepared for responsible citizenship, further learning, and productive employment in our Nation's modern economy.

GOAL 4. By the year 2000, the Nation's teaching force will have access to programs for the continued improvement of their professional skills and the opportunity to acquire the knowledge and skills needed to instruct and prepare all American students for the next century.

GOAL 5. By the year 2000, United States students will be first in the world in mathematics and science achievement.

GOAL 6. By the year 2000, every adult American will be literate and will possess the knowledge and skills necessary to compete in a global economy and exercise the rights and responsibilities of citizenship.

—Later Additions—

GOAL 7. By the year 2000, every school in the United States will be free of drugs, violence and the unauthorized presence of firearms and alcohol and will offer a disciplined environment conducive to learning.

GOAL 8. By the year 2000, every school will promote partnerships that will increase parental involvement and participation in promoting the social, emotional, and academic growth of children.

[Ed. Note: In 1999, ten years later, the National Education Goals Panel recommended changing the name *Goals 2000* to *America's Goals* since the goals would not be reached by the year 2000—thanks to intense opposition to *Goals 2000* from teachers and parents, who considered it a corporate/federal takeover of the nation's schools.]

THE JULY 5, 1989 ISSUE OF *THE NEW YORK TIMES* CARRIED AN ARTICLE by Edward B. Fiske entitled "Lessons—in the quiet world of schools, a time bomb is set for 1993 on certifying teachers." An excerpt follows:

The new national system will not replace those now in use. Rather, it will offer a new voluntary credential to experienced teachers willing to undergo classroom observations and a battery of sophisticated new tests of their pedagogical expertise. The system is modeled on professional specialty boards in, say, medicine, through which doctors who are already licensed to practice obtain an additional prestigious credential.... For each of these credentials the task is to figure out "what teachers should know and be able to do." Then designers must devise ways of measuring teachers using new techniques like video simulations of classroom situations. All in all, it's a five-year, $50 million project for which the National Board [National/Carnegie Board for Professional Teaching Standards] is seeking Federal, corporation and foundation support.... The National Board has thus signaled that four years from now it intends to start issuing credentials based on the image of a teacher who would have a hard time functioning in most public schools today. The choice would seem to be either to back away from this image or put pressure on schools to change.... David Kearns, Chairman of the Xerox

Corporation and a member of the board, believes schools should change. "Schools must find ways of driving decision-making down to the people who actually do the teaching," he said.

[ddd]

AN ARTICLE ENTITLED "THE DECADE OF THE NINETIES" BY DONALD THOMAS, executive director, Network for Effective Schools, was published in *The Effective School Report* for August 1989. Under the subtitle "Educational Implications" Thomas says

Operate schools on a year-round basis; train citizens and students in skills and processes of effective participation in government; develop public policy toward private education....

Desirable future conditions: The economy will be more of an equilibrium economy with less dependence upon money, and more dependence upon the production and exchange of goods and services. There will be an increased movement toward cooperation and responsibility for the well-being of others. The civil rights of all individuals will be respected and taught in homes and schools; a value system will emerge that will give basic human values—i.e., liberal arts, caring for others, etc.—their proper place. There will be fewer single family dwellings. Industry will take more responsibility for education, particularly for job training....

...[D]evelop curricula to involve students in anticipating and planning how to welcome newcomers; use community education to help citizens anticipate and prepare for newcomers; design and implement statewide parent education and education for responsible parenthood; institute widespread, effective public education programs on family life; ensure that human caring will become the focus of curriculum at all levels; develop courses in futuring with future centers in high schools; involve schools with water commissions, air quality commissions, city councils, county commissions, legislatures and governmental agencies, focusing on economics, ecology, environment and culture as an integral part of the learning; teach and practice a win-win philosophy in schools [Deming's TQM] in the place of the present win-lose philosophy....

CITIZENSHIP
Necessary Quality: Protecting each other from distractive forces.... These are qualities that can best be learned through practice and experience. Our schools must, therefore, give young people the opportunities for service to others, practice in public service, and adherence to personal responsibilities. The basic values of a good and free nation can be learned by young people when appropriate conditions exist as schools form partnerships with community agencies for public service projects to be a part of schooling; rewards are provided for encouraging young people to perform community service; community service is recognized as a necessary learning option....

The year 2000 is very near. The sooner we begin the task of improving student achievement and citizenship, the sooner we will achieve the national objective for adequately preparing our young people to live in the 21st century; to be broadly literate in a world community; to be highly skilled in an ever-changing work environment; to be human in a society of individuals striving for personal satisfaction and security. To achieve this goal we will need to think differently about schools, about children and about education. We, as a nation, must see education as a lifelong process, as occurring in the total community, and as being the responsibility of everyone.... Our national survival depends on it; the world expects it, and the children of the world require it.

[Ed. Note: Leaving aside the focus on political correctness, one should be concerned over the total lack of emphasis on—or even mention of—academics. It would be a grave mistake to dismiss this article as the totalitarian ravings of a lesser-known change agent spoken to his closest change-agent associates. Dr. Thomas, a close friend of the late former Secretary of Education T.H. Bell and present Secretary Richard Riley, is one of the most important change agents in the world. He has been responsible for controversial restructuring in several states and has been involved in exchanges with the former Soviet Union and Eastern European nations which are implementing Effective School Research. Again, it was he who recommended a $50.00 fine for parents who refused to volunteer in schools—both in South Carolina and in Utah.]

"APPROPRIATE EDUCATION IN THE PRIMARY GRADES: A POSITION STATEMENT of the National Association for the Education of Young Children" (NAEYC) was published and distributed in 1989.[24] Excerpts follow:

INTEGRATED COMPONENTS OF APPROPRIATE AND INAPPROPRIATE PRACTICE IN THE PRIMARY GRADES

Appropriate Practice. The curriculum is integrated so that children's learning in all traditional subject areas occurs primarily through projects and learning centers that teachers plan and that reflect children's interests and suggestions. Teachers guide children's involvement in projects and enrich the learning experience by extending children's ideas, responding to their questions, engaging them in conversation and challenging their thinking.
Inappropriate Practice. Curriculum is divided into separate subjects and time is carefully allotted for each with primary emphasis given each day to reading and secondarily to math. Other subjects such as social studies, science, and health are covered if time permits. Art, music, and physical education are taught only once a week and only by teachers who are specialists in those areas.

Appropriate Practice. The goal of the math program is to enable children to use math through exploration, discovery, and solving meaningful problems. Math activities are integrated with other relevant projects, such as science and social studies....
Inappropriate Practice. Math is taught as a separate subject at a scheduled time each day. A math textbook with accompanying workbooks, practice sheets, and board work is the focus of the math program. Teachers move sequentially through lessons as outlined in the teacher's edition of the text.... Timed tests on number facts are given and graded daily. Competition between children or groups of children.... is used to motivate children to learn math facts.

RENEWAL OF U. S.-SOVIET EDUCATION/CULTURAL AGREEMENTS IN 1989 called for placing statues of Soviet cultural figures on United States territory.

IN 1989 THE ASSOCIATION FOR SUPERVISION AND CURRICULUM DEVELOP-ment's (ASCD) Elementary Global Education Framework entitled "Elementary Education for the 21st Century: A Planning Framework Based on Outcomes" announced on its title page the following:

> The realities of the globally interconnected and culturally diverse world of the 21st century require an education for all students that will enable them to see themselves as—

HUMAN BEINGS
whose home is
PLANET EARTH
who are citizens of a
MULTICULTURAL DEMOCRATIC SOCIETY
in an increasingly
INTERCONNECTED WORLD
and who
LEARN, CARE, THINK, CHOOSE, and ACT
to celebrate life on this Planet
and
to meet the global challenges confronting Humankind

> Key global challenges at the outset of the 21st century are in the areas of improving and maintaining the quality of the ENVIRONMENT, improving and maintaining HEALTH AND WELL-BEING, assuring HUMAN RIGHTS, and reducing VIOLENCE AND CONFLICT.

This ASCD framework was used by the Eugene, Oregon School District 4J as a guide for development of their Education 2000 Elementary Integrated Curriculum K–5.[25] Excerpts from the "Guide" to be used by teachers involved in curriculum implementation follow:

District 4J Mission

Investing in Students
Creating the Future
Eugene's Elementary Program's Mission
To Instill in Each child

- a sense of self worth
- a respect for the earth and all peoples
- and a commitment to the pursuit of life-long learning....

One of the five priorities established in the District's future planning report in 1988–1989 addressed the need to design an appropriate education for an information age.... Some of the skills and knowledge that students will need to acquire include:

1. managing information and learning to learn (i.e., problem solving, critical thinking, applying knowledge, making decisions and judgments);
2. understanding and participating in the arts;

3. interpersonal and intrapersonal skills;
4. global perspectives; and
5. using appropriate technology....

After careful consideration of the educational needs of students preparing for the 21st century, the writing committee defined its task as developing a more conceptual-based curriculum with essential skills at its core. A conceptual-based curriculum is structured around broad-based themes that allow for the integration of skills and subject matter rather than emphasizing disjointed, small, unrelated chunks of information.

Curriculum Strands
How is the content of the curriculum organized?
In place of the eight traditional disciplines around which the former curriculum was organized, the Education 2000 Curriculum is organized around three curriculum strands.... 1) The Human Family, 2) Our Planetary Home and Its Place in the Universe, and 3) Understanding and Fulfillment of the Individual.

Core Skills
What skills are included in the curriculum? Core essential skills include physical, social, and thinking skills incorporating language arts and mathematics.

Major Themes and Concepts
What major themes and concepts are included? The Education 2000 Curriculum includes six major themes: Communities, Change, Power, Interactions, Form and Systems.

Characteristics of the Curriculum
What are some of the characteristics of the new curriculum? First, it expands the traditional understanding of "basic skills" to include dimensions of thinking as well as language arts, mathematics, physical and social skill development.

It shifts what is required from many individual bits of content to major themes and related concepts.... With the former curriculum, elementary students were expected to master 2,175 separate bits of information that included skills, concepts and content organized within eight discrete disciplines. The new K–5 Education 2000 Curriculum requires mastery of only six major themes, 60 concepts and 132 core skills organized within three curriculum strands. This revision greatly reduces the fragmented nature of the former curriculum and significantly decreases the number of specific requirements to approximately one-tenth of the original number.

[Ed. Note: ASCD's involvement in this local school district's curriculum was a logical follow up to its involvement from the beginning in Robert Muller's *World Core Curriculum*, upon which District 4J's curriculum was based. According to an article entitled "Educator Proposes a Global Core Curriculum" by Susan Hooper which appeared in the November 27, 1985 issue of *Education Week*, Gordon Cawelti, executive director of ASCD, in an address to educators from twelve Western nations and Japan, urged them to press for the development of a world core curriculum based on knowledge that will ensure "peaceful and cooperative existence among the human species on this planet." *Education Week* explained, "Cawelti's world core curriculum would be based on... proposals put forth by Robert Muller,

Assistant Secretary General of the United Nations, in his recent book *New Genesis: Shaping a Global Spirituality."*

Of additional significance is the fact that Willard Daggett's International Center for Leadership in Education discussed the Eugene District 4J in an article entitled "Cyber High School" in its March 1998 issue of *Model Schools News*. Regarding the Center's selection of Cyber High School, Eugene 4J School District, Eugene, Oregon as one of its model schools, the article states:

> For the first time in human history, teacher, learner, and learning material do not have to be in the same place at the same time. This concept has the potential of revolutionizing education, considering the fact that where students live has always been the single greatest factor influencing the quality of their education, albeit one often overlooked. The truth of the matter is that what street they lived on, what town they lived in, what state and country determined what classes they could take, the quality of teachers they could expect, and who their classmates would be. But all that is about to change.... Courses offered also include several inventive multidisciplinary subjects such as "Baseball: Its Impact on American Society and World History through Film," not to mention the fact that all of the courses offer a global classroom and a multi-cultural perspective.]

THE AUTUMN 1989 ISSUE OF *THE 2020 NEWSLETTER* PUBLISHED BY IM-TEC, a Norwegian education association,[26] revealed the fact that as they push forward with their own International Learning Cooperative, Europeans were embracing the American *Tactics for Thinking* program developed by the U.S. Department of Education's MidContinent Regional Laboratory (McREL). Of interest is the fact that Shirley McCune (referenced several times in this book) was senior director of McREL at the time the activities described in *The 2020 Newsletter* were taking place. This newsletter illustrated clearly the extent of internationalization of not only curriculum, but instruction, assessment and administration. IMTEC reported:

> The IMTEC training program for school-based development consultants is going on at present in two countries: Germany... the Netherlands. We are also planning a renewed program in Norway. We are also in the planning stage of this program in the U.K.

A section of IMTEC's newsletter entitled "Cooperation with McREL" made the following statements:

> The Second "School-Year 2020" International Conference held in Colorado, October 1988, was a joint undertaking by McREL (the MidContinent Regional Educational Laboratory) and IMTEC....
>
> Our cooperation with McREL will continue. A Development Group represented by people from McREL and IMTEC is presently working on new programs building on McREL's Achieving Excellence Program (A+) and IMTEC's IDP, the Institutional Development Program....
>
> McREL's A+ is a site- or school-based management system. It organizes and uses research-based knowledge to increase educational efficiency, effectiveness and excellence.... The A+ management system also provides unique assessment tools for maintaining progress and redirecting energy.

Pilot programs of A+ will take place in the Netherlands, in the UK, and most likely Norway during 1989/90....

THINKING SKILLS

IMTEC is presently developing a new "Thinking skills" program, building upon development work in several countries. Central to our interest has been the "Tactics" program developed by McREL.

[Ed. Note: The above relates to Effective School Research, OBE, ML, PPBS, etc.; what is being sold to Americans as "local control" or "localism" is in fact "global." In addition, the "Tactics" program is the same *Tactics for Thinking* discussed in the 1988 "Jeannie's Group" entry in this book.]

SOVIETS IN THE CLASSROOM: AMERICA'S LATEST EDUCATION FAD WRITTEN by this writer in 1989 (published four years after the fact by America's Future, Inc.), details the U.S.-Soviet and Carnegie-Soviet education agreements. (For full text of this pamphlet, see the Internet version for Appendix XXIII.) Two excerpts dealing with the specific agreements follow:

The agreements call for "Cooperation in the field of science and technology and additional agreements in other specific fields, including the humanities and social sciences; the facilitation of the exchange by appropriate organizations of educational and teaching materials, including textbooks, syllabi and curricula, materials on methodology, samples of teaching instruments and audiovisual aids... exchange of primary and secondary school textbooks and other teaching materials... the conducting of joint studies on textbooks between appropriate organizations in the United States and the Ministry of Education of the U.S.S.R.".…

2. The Carnegie Corporation's exchange agreement with the Soviet Academy of Sciences has resulted in "joint research on the application of computers in early elementary education, focusing especially on the teaching of higher level skills and complex subjects to younger children." ("Higher level skills" is often a euphemism for "critical thinking skills.") Carnegie's 1988 one-year $250,000 grant is funding implementation of this program, coordinated on the American side by Michael Cole, director of the Laboratory of Comparative Human Cognition at the University of California, San Diego.

AN ARTICLE IN THE SEPTEMBER 9, 1989 ISSUE OF *THE WASHINGTON TIMES* entitled "China Says Educators Sowed Seeds of Unrest" placed blame on teachers for the student democracy protests which resulted in the Tiananmen Square massacre. Excerpts follow:

BEIJING (AGENCE FRANCE-PRESSE)—In a front-page editorial, the intellectual *Guangming Daily* said teachers had used their classrooms to spread "bourgeois liberalization," the standard code word for undesirable Western influences....

   …"We must clearly understand that the teaching rostrum is provided by the people and the Communist Party and that it is sacred," the newspaper said. "The people's teachers have the right to spread Marxist theory, communist morality and knowledge of the Four Modernizations," it added. "Teachers have no right to spread bourgeois liberal tendencies."

Yesterday's editorial came as efforts by the authorities to put fresh emphasis on political education have been moving into high gear and just days before the 40th anniversary of Communist China on October 1.

On Tuesday, 40 teachers at Beijing University, which had been a hotbed of student unrest, were forced to take up shovels and clear scrub from a campus playing field as part of the push for political re-education through manual labor....

...The premier also defended a new government plan to send graduating students to farms and factories for a year, saying it was meant to "improve feelings toward laboring people."

"We hold that young students should, first of all, work in 'grassroots' units to obtain practical experience," Mr. Li said.

Many students have privately said they dread and scorn the scheme.

ON SEPTEMBER 10, 1989 *THE WASHINGTON POST* RAN AN ARTICLE ENTITLED "China Orders Manual Labor for Students: Beijing Moves Again to Control Citizenry" which mirrored and elaborated on the above-excerpted article of September 9. The *Post* reported:

The mandatory labor requirement is the latest in a series of measures taken by the government to punish, restrict and reeducate Chinese students, particularly those in the capital, since the democracy movement was crushed by the army in early June.

...The newly announced measure is reminiscent of the approach taken by the Chinese government in the 1950s, when students worked for several hours a week either in factories or in workshops established on school premises.... In another development, students at two leading Beijing universities this week revealed that students will be required to take a test of their political reliability before being allowed to formally enroll.

[ddd]

IN 1989 SHIRLEY MCCUNE, SENIOR DIRECTOR OF THE U.S. DEPARTMENT of Education-funded MidContinent Regional Educational Laboratory (McREL), told the teachers in South Kitsap, Washington: "The school of the future must be far different than that of today to meet the changing needs of society." The following excerpts are taken from an article entitled "Schools of the Future" which was published in the *Bremerton* [Washington] *Sun* on October 14th:

When you walk in the building, there's a row of offices. In one are drug counselors. One is for social security. Another, family and child psychologists. Yet another has a doctor and nurse who do well-child exams.

In the cafeteria, senior citizens mingle with students having lunch. Oldsters and youngsters are sometimes paired for school projects, like oral history.

There's a child-care center, and tied into it are classes for teenagers where they learn the importance of child-nurturing skills.

In the gym, homemakers are taking exercise classes. After work, more men and women will show up for their fitness workout.

These are "community learning centers, not just schools." "Schools are no longer in the schooling business" but rather in "human resource development," she said.

Dr. McCune was in South Kitsap to talk about something everyone's hearing a lot about these days—"restructuring" schools. Her speech kicked off a full day of teacher training. Across the state, most teachers were taking part in local or state-sponsored training.

In South Kitsap, workshop choices reflected the wave of the future Dr. McCune described. They dealt with topics such as celebrating differences in learning styles, using whole language approach, using cooperative learning, and integrating technology with curriculum.

Endnotes:

1   *Practitioner's Implementation Handbook [series]: The Outcome-Based Curriculum, Second Ed.*, by Charlotte Danielson (Outcomes Associates: Princeton, NJ, 1992).

2   See Appendix XXV in the Internet version entitled "Shamanistic Rituals in Effective Schools" by Brian Rowan who says, among other eye-opening comments, "Thus, any experienced shaman can find 'effective' schools."

3   *Models of Instructional Organization: A Casebook of Mastery Learning and Outcome-Based Education*, Robert Burns, Ed. (Far West Regional Laboratory for Educational Research and Development: San Francisco, April 1987).

4   *Human Intelligence International Newsletter* mailing address is: P.O. Box 1163, Birmingham, MI 48012.

5   The Mott Foundation was one of the early initiators and heavy financial supporters of un-American community education and the unelected advisory council concept. Mott still retains its role as leader of this movement, which is now international and borrows much of its organizational structure from communist China.

6   At the time he wrote the article, Glines was assistant to the director of the Office of Instructional Support and Bilingual Education of the State of California Department of Education, Sacramento, California. This article was adapted with permission from an article published in *The California Journal on Teacher Education* (Spring, 1980).

7   Copies of the February issue of the *Innisbrook Papers* can be ordered from: Corporate Relations Department, Northern Telecom Limited, 33 City Centre Drive, Mississauga, Ontario L5A2A2.

8   The reader should not dismiss this last comment by Oettinger as a flippant remark. For more information on "the new flowering of oral communication" read *ComSpeak 2050, How Talking Computers Will Recreate an Oral Culture by Mid-21st Century* by William Crossman, e-mail: WillCross@aol.com.

9   Information taken from Charlotte T. Iserbyt's *Back to Basics Reform Or... OBE Skinnerian International Curriculum* (Charlotte Thomson Iserbyt: Bath, Maine, 1985).

10 Center for Educational Research and Innovation: Rue Andre-Pascal, 75775, Paris, France.

11 K.M. Heaton's article can be accessed at ameriandeception.com.

12 Private collection of the writer.

13 *Brainwashing* (Capp Clark Publishing Co., Ltd.: Toronto, 1971) and *Brainwashing in Red China: The Men Who Defied It* (Vanguard Press, Inc.: New York, NY, 1973).

14 Private collection of the writer.

15 For more information on this project, write: Mastery in Learning Project, National Education Association, 1201 16th Street, NW, Washington, DC 20036.

16 Roberto Assagioli, *Psychosynthesis: A Manual of Principles and Techniques* (Viking Press: New York, 1965).

17 Like Paolo Friere, Kevin Ryan of Boston University was invited by and received a contract from the newly-established Portuguese government, after its communist revolution in 1974,

to train teachers so that Portugal could meet the European Community admission requirements. Professor Ryan is prominent in the character and moral education movement in the U.S. in the 1990s.

18 For more information on the Rotterdam meetings and/or the International Congress for Effective Schools, write: A.A. Peters or Professor Dale Mann, or Professor Terry Astuto at Teachers College, Columbia University, New York, NY 10027, or call 212-678-3726.

19 Regarding the next few entries dealing with the Tactics for Thinking curriculum and Higher Order Thinking Skills (HOTS), this information was provided by Jeannie Georges who gave testimony at The National Citizens Alliance press conference and who has written extensively on the subject.

20 Ibid.

21 Single copies of the report, *The Forgotten Half: Pathways to Success for America's Youth and Young Families*, may be obtained free from: William T. Grant Foundation Commission on Work, Family and Citizenship, 100 Connecticut Avenue, NW, Suite 301, Washington, DC 20036-5541.

22 This conference is another example of an activity associated with the U.S.-Soviet education agreements signed in 1985. This particular conference very likely took place as a consequence of the Carnegie Corporation's exchange agreement with the Soviet Academy of Sciences, resulting in "joint research on the application of computers in early elementary education, focusing especially on the teaching of higher level skills and complex subjects to younger children."

23 *The Blumenfeld Education Letter*, April 1990 (Vol. V., No. 4).

24 A copy of this NAEYC publication (#578) is available by sending $.50 to: NAEYC, 1509 16th St., NW, Washington, DC 20036, or by calling 202-232-8777.

25 Oregon School District 4J, 200 N. Monroe, Eugene, OR 97402. Margaret Nichols was superintendent of schools for District 4J.

26 IMTEC is located at: Dynekilgata 10, 0569, Oslo 5 Norway.

8

THE NOXIOUS NINETIES

Many quotes in this book point toward implementation of radical restructuring of the nation's schools in "the noxious nineties." The one entry this writer believes best illustrates this plan and how it would be implemented throughout the remainder of the 20th century and into the 21st century is taken from *Conclusions and Recommendations for the Social Studies* (Charles Scribner's Sons: N.Y., 1934). This study was funded to the tune of $340,000 by the Carnegie Corporation of New York, quite a sum of money in 1934 dollars! Professor Harold Laski, the philosopher of British socialism, said of this report: "At bottom, and stripped of its carefully neutral phrases, the Report is an educational program for a Socialist America." An important and revealing excerpt from *Conclusions and Recommendations* follows:

> The Commission was also driven to this broader conception of its task by the obvious fact that American civilization, in common with Western civilization, is passing through one of the great critical ages of history, is modifying its traditional faith in economic individualism [free enterprise], and is embarking upon vast experiments in social planning and control which call for large-scale cooperation on the part of the people.... (pp.1–2)
>
> ...Cumulative evidence supports the conclusion that in the United States and in other countries the age of "laissez faire" in economy and government is closing and that a new age of collectivism is emerging. (p. 16)

That a "new age of collectivism" has emerged and is being implemented right now under our very noses in "the noxious nineties," with little or no outrage from the public or our elected officials, can only be attributed to the "deliberate dumbing down" of Americans, who haven't been taught the difference between free enterprise and planned economies (socialism); between "group thinking" and individual freedom and responsibility.

The late Norman Dodd in 1986 made an extremely pertinent and important observation regarding Americans' growing preference to "think and act collectively" and the resulting dangers. Mr. Dodd's comments were made upon his receipt of the National Citizens' Alliance Americanism Award presented by Senator Jesse Helms. This award recognized Dodd's courageous work as research director for the 1953 Congressional investigation of the tax-exempt foundations. In Dodd's words:

> What is happening I can best explain by describing to you where you would end up if you could sponsor a resumption of the inquiry into the effect of foundation-type organizations in this country. If that were to be done, you would come into possession of proof... exposing a fundamental truth which has never been put into words.

> I shall try to recite that truth to you and you can take it home and act on it as a premise. This truth is that whenever a people show by their actions that they prefer to think and act collectively, their dynasty becomes a reenactment of the story of the Fall, as told to us by God through Moses.... We are now in a position where we can see that it is that dynastic effect which you are experiencing today.

> We have a task and that task is to sponsor an inquiry which would pull out into the open the proofs which show that it is that dynasty that is being worked out by us as a people, unwittingly, in complete ignorance....

> I wish I could help you... think about that truth because it has never been put into circulation. It now deserves to be, and it is persons like yourselves [dear readers] who can contribute to the circulation of that particular finding which the foundations, in their zeal, have actually made understandable. They [the foundations] have made a mistake.... The mistake they have made is now represented by their determination to cooperate with the Soviet Union educationally.

1990

Secretary's Commission on Achieving Necessary Skills (SCANS—U.S. Department of Labor) was established in 1990 and concluded its work in May of 1992. SCANS was conceived by Roberts T. Jones, assistant secretary of the Employment and Training Administration (ETA), through his parentage of the seminal study *Workforce 2000*. He and then-Secretary of Labor Elizabeth Dole created the commission and Arnold Packer served as executive director. SCANS was established by Secretary Dole to determine the skills that young people need to succeed in the world of work.[1] The Secretary's Commission on Achieving Necessary Skills published four reports "intended to define the know-how American students and workers need for workplace success... in communities across the United States." The reports are:

1. *Learning a Living: A Blueprint for High Performance*—"why change is needed"
2. *What Work Requires of Schools*—"defines the five competencies and three-part foundation that constitute the SCANS know-how"
3. *Skills and Tasks for Jobs*—"a tracing of the relationship between the SCANS competencies and skills and 50 common occupations"
4. *Teaching the SCANS Competencies*—"unites six articles that give education and training practitioners practical suggestions for applying SCANS in classroom and workplace"

Learning a Living: A Blueprint for High Performance, the first report from SCANS, asserts that "The Commission's fundamental purpose is to encourage a high performance economy characterized by high-skill, high-wage employment." The following controversial component of SCANS, which angered parents and ignited fires of protest across the nation, is found on page 65 of *Learning a Living*:

HYPOTHETICAL RESUMÉ

Jane Smith	Date of Report: 5/1/92
19 Main Street	Soc. Sec.: 599–46–1234
Anytown	Date of Birth: 3/7/73
Home Phone: 817–777–3333	Age; 19

SCANS Personal Qualities	Average Rating	No. of Ratings
Responsibility	Excellent	10
Self-Esteem	Excellent	10
Sociability	Excellent	8
Self-Management	Excellent	7
Integrity/Honesty	Good	6

Since when did the federal government assign itself the responsibility of grading citizens on "personal qualities"? Since our government began to consider citizens "human capital" or "resources"? Are citizens useful for anything besides potential workers? The above resumé also included the number of points Jane earned toward her "Certificate of Initial Mastery" as well as a record of volunteer and work experience. The bureaucrat at the U.S. Labor Department who wrote this part of the report explained:

> Because this information would be extremely useful to employers in making hiring decisions and to colleges in evaluating applications, students would have a strong motivation to learn the SCANS foundation skills and workplace competencies, and employers and colleges would have a strong incentive to require them.

Nine years later the hypothetical SCANS resumé would become reality as exemplified by Ohio's Career Passport which is a collection of student records that showcase past performance. The Passport includes a resumé, transcript, narrative identifying career goals and activities, as well as any diplomas, awards, certifications, licenses and community involvement.

The aforementioned information regarding this Career Passport is taken from a May 25, 1999 letter from the Akron Regional Development Board to area employers which states that Ohio's companies can sign on as employers who "ask for the Career Passport." This letter continues as follows:

> By joining the more than 3000 businesses nationally that are requesting records, you help drive home the message that accountability, initiative, and motivation are traits that companies seek in job candidates.
>
> The Akron Regional Development Board, and The Greater Cleveland Growth Association, Cleveland Tomorrow, the Ohio Department of Education Career Educators, and Regions 8 and 9 School-to-Work have teamed up with the National Alliance of Business (NAB) to encourage employers to use school records as part of their hiring process. The national campaign called "Making Academics Count," will help students, parents and educators become more aware of the importance of requisite workplace skills.
>
> Help send the message to area students by completing the enclosed reply form and returning it via fax to 330–379–3164. We will count you as an organization that wants young people to realize the importance of education and work skills....
>
> You can learn more about this initiative online at www.makeacademics count.org or www.c-e-a.org/ohiocdm.htm. On behalf of the Akron Regional Development Board and employers across our region, we encourage you to promote higher achievement by endorsing the "Ask for the Career Passport" program.

At this point it is important to recall the fact that one of the members appointed to the SCANS which originated this type of career passport was Thomas Sticht, Ph.D., infamous for the following quote which parents should ponder, especially if they feel that "techademics" are the answer to their children's upward mobility. Sticht's statement paraphrased in the August 1, 1987 issue of *The Washington Post* bears repeating here:

> Ending discrimination and changing values are probably more important than reading in moving low income families into the middle class.... What may be crucial [companies say] is the dependability of the labor force and how well it can be managed and trained—not its general education level, although a small cadre of highly educated, creative people is essential to innovation and growth.

[ddd]

THE WASHINGTON POST PUBLISHED "TYING PROFESSIONAL PAY TO PRODUCtivity" by Elizabeth Spayd in its January 28, 1990 issue in which Ms. Spayd covered the use of behavior modification in the workplace in order to increase productivity. Some excerpts follow:

> "One CEO I know says to employees, 'If you tell me I can't measure what you're doing, I'm not sure I need you here,'" recalls Michael Emig, a compensation consultant with Wyatt Co. in Washington. "The fact is, any work that people are paid to do can be measured. The trick is to go in with an open mind."... To help ensure that productivity goals are met, the paychecks of top managers now reflect their ability to meet department goals,

a compensation plan that eventually will spread throughout the hospital. According to Arthur Andersen & Co., which consulted Pekin Memorial on its plan, the keystone to implementing productivity bonuses is putting everything in measurable terms, considering such factors as accuracy, speed, cost, quality—even creativity.... Once the job has been quantified, the next step is to examine the processes by which work is done, dividing them into those that add value and those that don't. Those that don't should be eliminated.

Studies show white-collar workers on average spend 75 percent of their time doing non-value-added tasks, Skwarek said. But defining the waste and eliminating it are two different things. And for productivity to increase, proper employment of the compensation lever is critical.

A bank teller might be rewarded for the number of customers processed in a week, but penalized for every customer who complains about service. In jobs where it's difficult to measure the output of a *single worker* [emphasis in original], compensation might be linked to a group's ability to meet certain goals, an increasingly common approach.

Whatever the approach, Wyatt's Emig encourages companies to think big—meaning bonuses as high as 25 percent of salary.

"The basic idea is borrowed from B.F. Skinner, who taught us that behavior which is positively reinforced will be repeated," says Emig. "But it doesn't work if people don't consider the money worth striving for."

[Ed. Note: Is it politically incorrect to ask how the United States became the most productive nation in the world without using the above-outlined ridiculous Total Quality Management system based on Skinner's operant conditioning?]

THE NATIONAL CENTER ON EDUCATION AND THE ECONOMY (NCEE) ISSUED in 1990 a proposal to the New American Schools Development Corporation (NASDC) entitled "The National Alliance for Restructuring Education: Schools and Systems for the 21st Century." The report was stamped "CONFIDENTIAL." On the cover page NCEE's partners in this venture are listed as follows: States of Arkansas, Kentucky, New York, Vermont, and Washington; Cities of Pittsburgh, PA; Rochester, NY; San Diego, CA; and White Plains, NY; Apple Computer, Inc.; Center for the Study of Social Policy; Commission on the Skills of the American Workforce; Harvard Project on Effective Services; Learning Research and Development Center at the University of Pittsburgh; National Alliance of Business; National Board for Professional Teaching Standards; New Standards Project; Public Agenda Foundation; and Xerox Corporation.

[Ed. Note: NCEE's proposal is heavily excerpted in Appendix XII of the Internet version of this book. The last few pages of excerpted materials which relate to "staff development" could have been written by the late Madeline Hunter, master teacher trainer who has translated "theory into practice" in her "Instructional Theory Into Practice: ITIP."[2] These excerpted materials prove that NCEE's National Alliance for Restructuring Education, in conjunction with the University of Pittsburgh's Learning Research and Development Center and the National Board for Professional Teaching Standards, has selected "the method"—Skinnerian operant conditioning—to train teachers so that, as robots, they will all teach exactly the same way.]

WORLD CONFERENCE ON EDUCATION FOR ALL, SPONSORED BY THE WORLD Bank, United Nations Educational, Scientific, and Cultural Organization (UNESCO), and others, was held March 5–9, 1990 in Jomtien, Thailand. "Outcomes" were approved at this conference, and the Education for All Forum Secretariat advertised the "World Declaration on Education for All" and "Framework for Action to Meet Basic Learning Needs" as the agenda for discussion at the World Conference.[3] Important and significant institutional membership in the Education for All Coalition included: American Association of School Administrators (AASA); Association for Supervision and Curriculum Development; International Reading Association [which was the prime mover behind the dumb-down Whole Language reading instruction, ed.]; and the National Education Association.

[ddd]

THE MARCH 28, 1990 ISSUE OF *EDUCATION WEEK* RE-PUBLISHED "A ROAD Map for Restructuring Schools," a one-page list of principles of restructuring and steps for policy makers to use. Developed by the Education Commission of the States (ECS) and the National Governors' Association (NGA) and signed by Jane Armstrong, director of policy studies for ECS, this "Road Map" was a result of two regional workshops to discuss strategies for redesigning state education systems to meet national performance goals. Excerpts follow:

> PRINCIPLES OF RESTRUCTURING... Restructuring requires risk-taking and experimentation in order to transform schools into dynamic, self-renewing organizations....
>
> STEPS FOR POLICY MAKERS TO TAKE... Develop a specific and demanding statement of what basic skills, thinking skills, knowledge, attitudes and behaviors you want all students to have when they complete school....

- Student outcomes should meet employability criteria suggested by business and industry.
- Build a coalition of business, community, education and political leaders... to bring external pressure on the education system for productive change.
- Sell the agenda to policy makers and the public.
- Identify and train spokespersons to advocate system restructuring.
- Get business and political leaders to carry the restructuring banner.
- Provide flexibility, encourage experimentation and decentralize decision making.
- Use incentives to encourage risk taking and experimentation.
- Decentralize authority by encouraging site-based management.
- Redesign teacher and administrator education.
- Redesign teacher education to model instruction for an active learning classroom.

- Develop programs that focus on content knowledge and new forms of pedagogy.
- Link schools with universities and other sources of information to help teachers expand their knowledge of teaching and learning.
- Strengthen the clinical experience by placing teacher candidates in schools that are restructuring.
- Provide time for teacher renewal, collaboration and the acquisition of new skills, understandings and attitudes.
- Provide incentives for teachers to receive national board certification.
- Develop multiple ways to measure progress to avoid "high stakes" testing and teaching to a single test.
- Develop "outcomes-based" accreditation procedures.
- Provide rewards for high-achieving schools and sanctions for low-achieving schools.
- Create programs that engage students in community service.
- Collaborate with other social service agencies to fully serve the needs of all children.
- Encourage parental involvement.
- Create public school choice plans.
- Provide incentives to reward accomplishments.
- Align and revise state policies to support restructuring.
- Develop business/education partnerships. Use technology to explore new ways to deliver instruction… not as an "add-on" to the traditional lecture, recite, test method of instruction.
- Be prepared to handle policy decisions on jurisdiction over distance learning; i.e., teacher certification, textbook and curriculum approval.

The ECS/NGA Restructuring Workshops were supported by grants from the American Express Foundation, ARCO Foundation, BellSouth Foundation, Carnegie Corporation of New York, Control Data Corporation and The John D. and Catherine T. MacArthur Foundation.

IN 1990 MARC TUCKER'S NATIONAL CENTER ON EDUCATION AND THE Economy (NCEE) of Rochester, New York published *America's Choice: High Skills or Low Wages!* which asserted that

> Once youth centers are established, we propose that the child labor laws be amended to make the granting of work permits to young people up to age 18 contingent on either their possession of a certificate of initial mastery [CIM] or their enrollment in a program leading to the certificate. At first glance, this may seem draconian. But in the long run this requirement will benefit our youth and ultimately the nation.

[Ed. Note: The "Certificate of Initial Mastery" (CIM) is a device which is copyrighted to the private sector National Center on Education and the Economy to be used by the public schools—and a moneymaker for NCEE.]

THE STATE OF MAINE TOOK A LEADERSHIP POSITION IN THE IMPLEMENTATION of a school-to-work system in 1990. The following excerpts from *The School to Work Revolution* by Lynn Olson (Perseus Books: New York, 1997) relate to the first steps taken to implement this new corporate fascist system of governance. Olson recalled Maine's activity as follows:

John Fitzsimmons, the President of the Maine Technical College System and former state labor commissioner in Maine during the 1980s, traveled to Germany and Denmark in the early 1990s, along with the then-Governor John R. McKernan, Jr. [husband of U.S. Senator from Maine Olympia Snowe], to get a first-hand view of European apprenticeships. The governor and Fitzsimmons were so impressed by what they saw that they plotted the outlines for a Maine initiative on paper napkins on the transatlantic flight home. In February 1993 the Maine Youth Apprenticeship Program—now called Maine Career Advantage—accepted its first 12 students. By 1996 the initiative had spread to 276 students, 108 high schools, and 197 businesses. An additional 850 students were involved in career-preparation activities such as job shadows, developing portfolios, and summer internships.

"I really believe, in my state, the future lies in the quality of the skilled workforce," Fitzsimmons told me in 1994, a strong Rhode Island accent still lingering in his voice. "We will not compete with a North Carolina Research Triangle or with Massachusetts's Harvard and M.I.T. and their ability to be international research areas. We will be the producers of goods. And I take great pride in that because if we're able to produce high-quality products, it will mean high-wage jobs for our people."

POLYTECHNICAL EDUCATION: A STEP BY ROBERT H. BECK, UNIVERSITY OF Minnesota, was published in 1990. Beck was under contract to the National Center for Research in Vocational Education, University of California, Berkeley and was supported by the Office of Vocational and Adult Education through a U.S. Department of Education grant for $4 million [*Carl D. Perkins Vocational Education Act*, Grant #V051A80004–88A, September.[4]] Had this report not cost $4 million in taxpayers' money, one could dismiss it as just another effort by the federal government to keep its education researchers occupied. Why would the government spend such an enormous amount of money on a government project describing the Soviet polytech system unless the government was considering putting the same polytech system in place in the United States?

Recent workforce training legislation in Congress does indeed call for the implementation of the Soviet/German/Danish polytech system.

[ddd]

DAVID W. HORNBECK, MEMBER OF THE BOARD OF TRUSTEES OF THE CARNegie Corporation and a partner in the Washington, D.C. law firm of Hogan and Hartson, delivered a paper entitled "Technology and Students at Risk of School Failure" at the Council of Chief State School Officers' (CCSSO) 1990 Technology Conference in Minneapolis, Minnesota April 29–May 2. The paper was commissioned by the CCSSO and was distributed by the federally funded North Central Regional Educational Laboratory (NCREL) in Elmhurst, Illinois. Excerpts from this paper follow:

> In March, the Kentucky legislature enacted the most aggressive and far-reaching education legislation in memory. They identified six goals for their

schools (President Bush's Six Ambitious Goals adopted by the Governors February 25). The goals include not only math, science, social studies and English but, more significantly, they emphasize such things as thinking, problem solving, main ideas and integration of knowledge. Kentucky, however, went further. They are building a new set of assessment strategies that are performance based; they have adopted a system of rewards and sanctions that will impact on the schools' staffs in proportion to the schools' success in increasing the proportion of successful students in a school or the failure to do so. The President, the Governors and now a state legislature have made decisions that reflect the future.

The fact is that corporate America is becoming increasingly involved in the policy and politics of elementary and secondary education. The Committee for Economic Development was the first major corporate player. They were joined by the National Alliance of Business. Most recently, The Business Roundtable, which is composed of the nation's 201 largest corporations, has recognized their vital interest in American public education. Each corporation has "adopted" a state where each corporation will concentrate strong effort. Moreover, they have declared that the effort will be of at least ten years' duration....

...There are numerous ways technology, and I initially refer to the computer, can assist.... The computer motivates. It is non-judgmental. It will inform a student of success or failure without saying by word or deed that the student is good or bad. The computer individualizes learning, permitting mastery at one's own pace.... The computer gives prompt feedback....

Let's turn then to more specific contributions computers can make. First, it is clear that the basic skills of students can be enhanced. In a presentation to the U.S. Senate Committee on Labor and Human Resources in 1987, Robert Tagaart, relying on work done by himself, Gordon Berlin, and Andrew Green, identified ten elements that research prescribes to teach basic skills effectively. They include:

- individualized, self-paced instruction
- competency-based, open entry/open exit approaches
- use of multiple media and methods, including computers
- frequent feedback and positive reinforcement
- accountability of teachers and learners
- efficient management to maximize time on task
- individual attention and one-on-one instruction
- supportive services and learning environments
- linkages to work, training, and other activities

[Ed. Note: Kentucky's experience with its new set of performance-based assessment strategies was a disaster. An article in the June 26, 1997 *Louisville Courier-Journal* datelined Frankfort, Kentucky stated that

Nearly all elementary and middle schools in Kentucky received incorrectly low test scores last fall, and fixing the error will mean that teachers will get an estimated $2 million in additional reward money.... While the error by Advanced Systems in Measurement and Evaluation, Inc., amounts to a small change in the schools' actual scores—an average of about 1 point on a 140–point scale—there could be serious consequences for the state's test, which has already been at the center of controversy. Critics seized upon the mistake as evidence that significant changes are needed in the testing system created by Kentucky's 1990 school reform law.

The March/April, 1997 issue of *Kentucky Citizens Digest* carried an article entitled "Are Basic Skills a Casualty of KERA?—Are state tests causing teachers to underemphasize basic skills?" which revealed that

> If two recent reports are any indication, basic skills among students may very well be a casualty of education reform in Kentucky. A report from RAND, a prominent national research organization, found that tests now being used under KERA (called KIRIS tests) are causing public school teachers to de-emphasize basic skills instruction in Kentucky schools. "The subject areas for which the most teachers indicated a decrease since KIRIS began," said the report, "were art, social studies, science, and reading. Eighty-nine percent of the teachers indicated that these changes were due largely to KIRIS."]

LAMAR ALEXANDER, FORMER GOVERNOR OF TENNESSEE, SECRETARY OF EDU-cation in President George Bush's administration, and Republican presidential candidate in 1999, was quoted in *Southern Living* (Vol. 25, No. 6, June 1990) in an interview when he was serving as president of the University of Tennessee as saying:

> I suggest we create a brand-new American school, as different from today's schoolhouse as the telegraph was from The Pony Express. Such a school would probably start with babies and go through the eighth grade. It would be all year long. It would be open 6 a.m. to 6 p.m. Every child would have his or her own computer and workstation. Every child would have a team of teachers that would stay with that child until graduation....
>
> We already spend more money than any country per pupil on education. I just don't think we spend it well.

[ddd]

DR. M. DONALD THOMAS, IN AN ARTICLE IN *THE EFFECTIVE SCHOOL RE-port*'s September, 1990 issue entitled "Education 90: A Framework for the Future," said in part:

> From Washington to modern times, literacy has meant the ability to read and write, the ability to understand numbers, and the capacity to appreciate factual material. The world, however, has changed dramatically in the last 30 years. The introduction of technology in information processing, the compression of the world into a single economic system, and the revolution in political organizations are influences never imagined to be possible in our lifetime.... Literacy, therefore, will be different in the year 2000. It will mean that students will need the following [the writer has selected some key requirements from a much longer list, ed.]:
>
> • Appreciation of different cultures, differences in belief systems and differences in political structures....

- An understanding of communications and the ability of people to live in one world as one community of nations....
- In a compressed world with one economic system... it is especially important that all our people be more highly educated and that the differences between low and high socio-economic students be significantly narrowed....
- Education begins at birth and ends at death....
- Education is a responsibility to be assumed by the whole community....
- Learning how to learn is more important than memorizing facts....
- Schools form partnerships with community agencies for public service projects to be a part of schooling....
- Rewards are provided for encouraging young people to perform community service.

"WORLD CLASS SCHOOLS AND THE SOCIAL STUDIES" BY CORDELL SVENGALIS from *Social Studies Horizons* (Iowa Department of Education: Des Moines, Iowa, Vol. 3, No. 1, Fall 1990) was published. The following excerpts reveal a significant definition of "World Class education," one of the popular "buzz words" used to describe and promote education reform during the early 1990s:

As part of a nationwide trend, the Iowa Department of Education has become involved in the movement to develop a world-class educational system for the schools of our state....

Few would argue with the need to greatly improve the educational system we now have, and to help students acquire the skills they will need to become better integrated into the global community. We have not only become globally interdependent, we have come to recognize our global interconnectedness. Therefore, a World Class education program would have as one of its major objectives the development of skills and understandings grounded in an ethical/moral context. This ethical/moral context would be based on the idea of assuming a sense of responsibility toward our interrelated planetary future....

Perhaps the most compelling vision of our time is that of a *sustainable society* [emphasis in original]. Our global society, in terms of the environmental degradation, explosive population growth in the Third World, energy shortages, pollution, conflict, crime, drugs, poverty, and just sheer complexity, is not sustainable into the 21st century.... Students need to understand these things as part of their World Class education.

This particular issue of *Social Studies Horizons* also reported on the 1990 Chicago Conference on Holistic Education, which issued a document called "The Chicago Statement" calling for a radical change in education. An excerpt asserts that

The time has come to transform education so as to address the human and environmental changes which confront us. We believe that education for this new era must be holistic. The holistic perspective is the recognition that all life on this planet is interconnected.... Holism emphasizes the challenge of creating a sustainable, just and peaceful society in harmony with the Earth and its life.

Dr. Svengalis of the Iowa Department of Education was involved in the production of a *Catalogue of Global Education Classroom Activities, Lesson Plans, and Resources*. The curriculum came under fire from the Iowa Farm Bureau because of its open advocacy of vegetarianism and environmentalism, according to the Iowa Farm Bureau's *Spokesman* (September 19, 1992) article entitled "State Role in Global Education Resource Guide under Review." Also included in the global education curriculum were themes of pacifism, population controls, international global government, and Gaia worship. Fourth and sixth graders could be assigned to "[t]alk about the ideas of a 'living' Earth using Lovelock's Gaia hypothesis." Dr. James Lovelock made the radical "scientific" proposal that the Earth was both an entity and a deity.

According to education reform researchers Marla Quenzer and Sarah Leslie, environmental "outcomes" were supplanting traditional academics. In an article published in the May 1993 issue of *Free World Research Report* entitled "The Myth of a Competitive World-Class Education," Quenzer and Leslie refuted the idea that "world-class" education is competitive and academically challenging. Under the new reforms they found an emphasis on cooperation and sustainability based upon extreme environmentalism and "a kind of 'New Age' soup of pantheism, Hinduism, Taoism and Buddhism." They cited an article entitled "Global Framework for Local Education" from *Holistic Education Review* (Spring 1991):

> This author, Joel Beversluis, states "that educational objectives [should] transcend the accumulation of facts, the learning of skills, and even the preparation for work and life in the world as it is. Rather, at its best, education will assist, like a midwife, in the transformation of the mindsets—the consciousness—of students...." Beversluis asks, "Is it not time for the community of educators and educational publishers to recognize that the respectful study of diverse cosmologies, value systems, and religions has a legitimate and even necessary place in the curriculum?" He then proceeds to list these new "global" values....
>
> Just what values are being talked about? This turns out to be the pivotal question. Beversluis spells it out for us. He lists as negative values: "individualism, nationalism, free enterprise, unlimited growth and progress, and competitive achievement." The values he lists as positive are "interdependence, diversity, cooperation, equilibrium, and limits." The values that he lists as negative are foundational to western civilization and are based upon a rich Judeo-Christian heritage. The values he lists as positive can be found in Iowa's proposal for "World-Class Education under 'Examples of Core Concepts'" and are an integral part of Iowa's Global Education goals. Not surprisingly, these same values crop up in all the new state "outcomes" lists as well.

[Ed. Note: For more information on the connection between extreme environmentalism, sustainability, and the deliberate dumbing down of America, see the Internet version for Appendix XXVII.]

THE 1990–91 (WINTER) ISSUE *OF OUTCOMES,* AN EDUCATIONAL JOURNAL devoted to discussion of Outcome-Based Education and the problems associated with its implementation (teachers', administrators' and community resistance) published a remarkable article entitled "Paradigm Change: More Magic than Logic" by John C. Hillary. The reader should remember that the manipulation of classroom teachers and administrators discussed in this article is standard operating procedure in most schools undergoing "restructuring." Excerpts from Hillary's article in *Outcomes* follow:

> The deeper changes that frustrate leaders and threaten followers are planned second-order changes.... These changes intentionally challenge widely shared assumptions, disintegrate the context of "organization" and, in general, reframe the social system. This, in turn, generates widespread ambiguity, discontinuity, anxiety, frustration, confusion, paranoia, cynicism and anger as well as temporary dysfunction. Such trauma often builds to the point that leaders abandon their efforts.

> The most disruptive changes—second order changes—on the other hand, call into question the entire context of organization. Such multidimensional changes not only challenge the content of each domain but also disrupt the alignment among them. Paradigm change is therefore not only traumatic in and of itself, but also challenges other attributes and disintegrates the relationship among all domains. The eventual outcome of such change is "transformed" or "renewed" organization.

> The new vision for schooling suggested by contemporary educators represents a significant "second order" challenge to school organization.

> The leader of planned second order change will be regarded as out of context by the organization. If he thinks and behaves in accord with a vision that requires second order changes, he has no choice but to violate or challenge the established culture, mission/purpose, and paradigm of the organization. From the existing frame of reference, such behavior will be seen as illogical. Powerful and pervasive psycho-social forces will bear down on the renegade in a relentless organizational effort to bring him back into alignment. Unless the leader succeeds in progressively bending the pervasive frame, persistence is increasingly risky.

> During second order change, the organization must face and hopefully pass through a period of widespread psychological ambiguity, social disconnectedness and general confusion.... The requisite disintegration of the existing culture, mission/purpose, and paradigm disrupts the organization's frame of reference. During this time, there is little or no clear and consistent context to guide the thinking and behavior of members. In social systems, this condition produces dysfunction, anxiety, frustration, disequilibrium, and systemic chaos.

> The instigator of second order change must consistently behave in ways that will not make sense when framed by the existing context. With time and leadership, the organization environment must move from initially and naturally selecting against the innovation to selecting for the innovation. The extinction of the old way of doing business is the desired outcome. Hence and with time, the risk should gradually shift away from the innovator and toward those who persist in holding on to "the way it's always been."

[Ed. Note: The writer, over a fairly long period of years, has come to the conclusion that many of America's best administrators and teachers have been waging a "silent" war against the above change agent activities, and that had they not been so engaged, the public education system would have been destroyed long ago.]

1991

"AMERICA 2000 PLAN," WRITTEN IN 1991 AND DESIGNED TO IMPLEMENT the Carnegie Corporation's restructuring agenda, was presented to the American people by President Bush's Secretary of Education Lamar Alexander. The plan proposed to radically restructure American society and was prepared by, amongst others, Chester Finn—former assistant secretary, Office of Educational Research and Improvement, and associated with Education Excellence Network (Hudson Institute). Secretary Alexander claimed, "The brand new American school would be year-round, open from 6 to 6, for children 3 months to 18 years." The slim booklet containing *America 2000: An Education Strategy (Rev.)—Making This Land All That It Should Be* was published by the U.S. Department of Education and portions of this publication follow:

> Message from President George Bush
> April 18, 1991
>
> To those who want to see real improvement in American education, I say: There will be no renaissance without revolution.
> We've made a good beginning by setting the nation's sights on six ambitious National Education Goals—and setting for our target the year 2000.... For today's students, we must make existing schools better and more accountable. For tomorrow's students, the next generation, we must create a New Generation of American Schools. For all of us, for the adults who think our school days are over, we've got to become a Nation of Students—recognize learning is a lifelong process. Finally, outside our schools we must cultivate communities where learning can happen....
>
> EXECUTIVE SUMMARY
> The strategy anticipates major change in our 110,000 public and private schools, change in every American community, change in every American home, change in our attitude about learning. The strategy will spur far-reaching changes in weary practices, outmoded assumptions and long-assumed constraints on education. It will require us to make some lifestyle changes, too....
> *America 2000* is a national strategy, not a federal program. It honors local control, relies on local initiative, affirms states and localities as the senior partners in paying for education, and recognizes the private sector as a vital partner, too.
> The federal government's role in this strategy is limited—wisely—as its part in education always has been. But that role will be played vigorously. Washington can help by setting standards, highlighting examples, contributing some funds, providing flexibility in exchange for accountability and pushing and prodding—then pushing and prodding some more.
> The *America 2000* strategy has four parts that will be pursued simulta-

neously. For tomorrow's students, we must invent new schools to meet the demands of a new century with a New Generation of American Schools, bringing at least 535 of them into existence by 1996 and thousands by decade's end....[19]

THE CHALLENGE: America's Skills and Knowledge Gap

Introduction:

As a nation, we now invest more in education than in defense. Nor is the rest of the world sitting idly by, waiting for America to catch up. Serious efforts at education improvement are under way by most of our international competition and trading partners.

While more than 4 million adults are taking basic education courses outside the schools, there is no systematic means of matching training to needs; no uniform standards measure the skills needed and the skills learned.

[Ed. Note: Carnegie's Marc Tucker took care of matching training to needs when his *Human Resources Development Plan for the United States*, developed by the National Center for Education and the Economy, was unveiled in 1992. (See the Internet version for Appendix XVIII.) As far as keeping track of the progress of our "international competition and trading partners" is concerned, the *North American Free Trade Agreement* (NAFTA), the *General Agreements for Tariffs and Trade* (GATT), and international co-ordination of ISO 9000 and 1400 through the United Nations will ensure that we maintain "computability."]

[ddd]

AN ARTICLE ENTITLED "SENIORS' CHURCH ATTENDANCE" WAS PUBLISHED IN the June 12, 1991 issue of *Education Week*. The central premise of the article was summed up in the following quote:

High school seniors in 1990 were much less interested in, and involved with, organized religion than were their counterparts in the 1970's, according to data compiled by the Institute for Social Research (ISR) at the University of Michigan.

[Ed. Note: The Institute for Social Research (ISR) is, interestingly enough, the same institute that was involved in Ronald Havelock's *The Change Agents' Guide to Innovation in Education* which instructed educators how to "identify resisters" and how to sneak controversial sex, drug and death education into curriculum despite parental objections. The article reveals that the schools were highly successful in their efforts to indoctrinate students in non-absolutist, humanistic values. It should come as no surprise that the average American in 1991, subjected to values clarification in the schools of the 1960s, 1970s, and 1980s, is non-judgmental regarding immoral behavior. For example: in 1999 President Clinton, according to the polls, retained the confidence of 60–75% of the American people during his investigation and even after his impeachment trial revealed flagrant immoral activity.]

A SAMPLE "21ST CENTURY REPORT CARD" WAS A HANDOUT AT THE AUGUST, 1991 Association for Supervision and Curriculum Development (ASCD) Network conference in Traverse City, Michigan entitled "Creating the Twenty-First Century." Descriptive excerpts—which originally led this writer to believe this sample report card was a joke until able to verify its actual existence—follow:

> DaVinci Elementary School
> Principal: R.B. Fuller
>
> [After each of the following categories there is a mark A through F as a grade, ed.]
>
> Spatial Relationships; Intuition; Insight; Generates Ideas Freely; Daydreaming/ Reverie; Gestalt Perception; Esthetic Sensibility: color, form, music, poetry
>
> Teacher's Comments: school psychologist suggests remedial imagination
>
> Work Habits: Able to transcend space/time limitations; Is flexible; Listens attentively—with third ear; Follows directions unless better idea occurs; Completes assignments—when useful; Makes good use of time: fantasizing, creating, meditating.
>
> Citizenship: Accepts responsibility; Respects authority—if there is justification for respect; Respects rights and property of others; Shows empathy/telepathy;
>
> Teacher's signature:
> Parent's signature:

Bonnie Newhouse, a Traverse City, Michigan wife and mother of four children who had served on the junior and senior parent advisory committees as well as the district advisory council, wrote an article for the *Traverse City Record-Eagle*'s March 18, 1992 issue which included the following information related to change agent tactics to implement restructuring promoted at the ASCD meetings:

> In a study done by the U.S. Senate Republican Policy Committee on Illiteracy, September 1989, they conclude: "For the past 50 years, America's classrooms have been used by psychologists, sociologists, educationists and politicians as a giant laboratory for unproven, untried theories of learning, resulting in a near collapse of public education."
>
>   This "collapse" was also referred to by William Spady in his address to the ASCD High School Futures Planning Consortium III August 1991 meeting in Traverse City. He spoke of prominent educators talking of WHEN the public education system collapses, not IF [emphasis in original]. He also shared with the audience that he was one of three given a grant by the Danforth Foundation with the assignment to transform America's high schools.
>
>   What does all this really mean for our students? From the information gathered and rhetoric offered, perhaps the most significant was found in yet another ASCD Network conference held the previous week, "Creating the 21st Century"; an example of a 21st Century Report Card [was presented]....

We are seeing a major shift away from academics toward attitudes and values. The question is, who will determine which outcomes your child must have to graduate? If all this seems farfetched, one has only to read some of the information presented at the ASCD workshops: "Learners' behavior must show... Learners' attitudes must demonstrate... Learners will advocate for collaborative change."

Most enlightening was a session titled, "How to develop the 'desired state' for your high school." A more accurate title may have been "How to manipulate teachers, parents and the school board to accomplish your agenda." Among the suggestions: use teachers in these pilots that are the kids' favorites; introduction of special education in the classrooms will help in overcoming the barrier of the closed door; how do you deal with people who sabotage your plan? Do little things to include them, give them power, let them be co-chairs.

THE GEORGIA PUBLIC POLICY FOUNDATION, A STATE AFFILIATE OF THE Heritage Foundation, published *Reach for the Stars: A Proposal for Education Reform in Georgia* by Matthew J. Glavin in October of 1991.[5] Excerpts follow:

[Preface] The Georgia Public Policy Foundation wishes to thank the Hudson Institute for sharing much of their original research that constitutes the basis for this plan....

[Foreword] *Reach for the Stars* proposes step-by-step how we can take the education bull by the horns and steer it toward success. For parents, it means an end to excessive school taxes and the beginning of accountability on the part of the school system.... I urge you to read this report with an open mind and an eye toward change. If Georgia hopes to continue another decade of growth, it must begin preparing now. *Reach for the Stars* outlines the necessary steps to ensure Georgia's future. As citizens, we can not afford to miss this opportunity.

> William Bennett
> Former Secretary of Education
> October, 1991

[Ed. Note: The introduction to *Reach for the Stars* quotes the late Al Shanker, long-time president of the nation's second largest teacher union—American Federation of Teachers—as if Shanker would be recommending any changes or restructuring other than that proposed by the Carnegie Corporation. The reader should refer to the 1986 entry which quoted from an article entitled "Carnegie Report on Education: Radical Blueprint for Change" which appeared in the June 28–29, 1986 issue of *The Bangor* [Maine] *Daily News*. This article identified Shanker as a willing accomplice of Carnegie's plan (the Marc Tucker/National Center for Education and the Economy plan) to restructure education.]

In the following excerpts from *Reach for the Stars* the writer has related the statements to outcome-based education, education restructuring, school-to-work, site-based management, etc., all of which concerned parents and teachers have been led to believe are anathema to conservatives:

And we need a system of measuring achievement that will tell parents how well their sons and daughters are doing compared with what they need to know to get ahead—not compared to what a kid in another county or another state knows [outcome-based education which replaces norm-referenced testing with criterion-based testing, ed.].

It's time to shift the power back to the teachers and principals [site-based management which abolishes the power of elected school boards, ed.].

Under the Georgia Public Policy Plan, "ready for life" means having the knowledge and skills to be successful in life as a citizen, employee and person. Earning a basic high school diploma should mean one is ready for life [UNESCO's lifelong learning and elements of competency-based/outcomes-based education, ed.].

Second, create a new statewide assessment system which: (a) measures the extent to which individual students are meeting the standards; (b) provides information on school performance for parent selection of schools; and (c) gives employers an objective and meaningful way to assess the capabilities of job applicants by requiring a uniform exit assessment to earn a high school diploma [the controversial National Assessment of Educational Progress which measures students' attitudes and beliefs, and school-to-work, SCANS, ed.].

Academic standards should include knowledge, concepts, and skills that all students, college-bound and job-bound, need to master [school-to-work, mastery learning, ed.].

These standards are currently being developed at the national level by the National Education Goals Panel (NEGP) [no local representation, ed.].

The academic standards will: (a) identify the core competencies that all students should master at key transition points in their education careers, and (b) identify the skills and knowledge that students must master to earn a high school diploma.... These academic standards will also include knowledge and skills needed for responsible citizenship; personal skills required to get, keep, and progress on a job; and social skills needed to work with others on a job [Certificate of Initial Mastery, lifelong learning, SCANS, OBE, mastery learning, and school-to-work, ed.].

In conjunction with the National Education Goals Panel, a new voluntary nationwide examination system is being developed based on the five core subjects that are tied to the new national academic standards. Georgia should adopt this new examination system as soon as it is available for implementation. [This "voluntary nationwide examination system," which circumvents local control, has metamorphosed into a mandated nationwide examination for which legislation has been before Congress since 1997, ed.]

The State of Georgia should take this opportunity to request that the NAEP reauthorization... include a provision allowing any state that wishes to use the NAEP tests on a school-by-school basis to do so [NAEP was not designed to be a school-by-school comparison, ed.].

There are three integral and inseparable concepts that will "free the teachers" and "free the parents"—Deregulation, School Autonomy and Parental Choice.

[Ed. Note: How can there be "freedom" for parents and teachers when schools are run by unelected (unaccountable) councils which must conform their curriculum to *Goals 2000*—national standards, national tests, resulting in a nationalized (socialist) education system?]

One of the guiding philosophies of this plan is that government funding for K–12 education should be targeted to the child—not the school district. Each and every school-aged child will be entitled to public support for his or her education. Parents can use the child's publicly funded "scholarship" at any school where the child meets admission requirements. Exceptions would be schools that fail to meet state performance standards, or private schools that choose not to participate.

[Ed. Note: Targeting funding to the child according to the child's Individual Education Plan (IEP) and meeting the state requirements fits in nicely with school-to-work. Won't a child whose career path is that of a fireman receive less funding than a child whose career path is that of an engineer?]

Under the Georgia Public Policy Foundation recommendations the local districts must divest themselves of operating control of the schools [site-based management and charter schools, ed.].

Each autonomous public school organizes as a non-profit corporation with a board selected by the teachers and other certified staff of the school.

[Ed. Note: This proposes a complete change of government, resulting in loss of representation by publicly elected representatives.[6] This is the Carnegie Corporation's plan spelled out in *A Nation Prepared: Teachers for the 21st Century*[7] which proposed the total restructuring of the teaching profession and Luvern Cunningham's disastrous Kentucky model.]

"Company Schools," schools that are sponsored at the work site for students who come to work with a parent but which are also open to local students [school-to-work, ed.].

The curriculum in most American schools is geared toward the lower rote skills and is far less challenging than curricula in many other countries. [The reference to "lower rote skills" is a reference to basic skills—reading, writing, and arithmetic—and the rote learning of those skills. In 1994 H.R. 6, the controversial legislation that had parents up in arms, referred to "lower rote skills" in this same derogatory manner. The funding in H.R. 6 was definitely geared toward OBE/mastery learning/direct instruction and multi-cultural programs, ed.]

[Ed. Note: This report could have been written by UNESCO and the U.S. Department of Education with assistance from the Carnegie Corporation and the teachers' unions—American Federation of Teachers (AFT) and National Education Association (NEA). It incorporates most of the essential elements of OBE, *America 2000*, *Goals 2000*, the New American School Development Corporation's charter schools, and SCANS.]

Human Capital and America's Future: An Economic Strategy for the Nineties (Hopkins Press: Baltimore, Md., 1991) edited by David W. Hornbeck and Lester M. Salamon, was published. The following quotes confirm the worst fears of parents related to education reform and dumbed down outcomes which are referenced by the change agents as "world class." *Human Capital* explains that

[E]mployer beliefs about the superior capabilities of educated people turned

out NOT to be confirmed in practice [emphasis in original]; educated employees have higher turn-over rates, lower job satisfaction, and poorer promotion
records than less educated employees. (p. 7)

Education researcher Judith McLemore of Alabama excerpted and commented upon David Hornbeck's statements in "New Paradigms for Action,"
chapter 13 of *Human Capital* :

> Programs proposed to "cope with *human capital* problems" include "Initia-
> tives to alleviate poverty" (p. 360) which include "income transfers.".... The
> gap between "the haves and the have-nots is growing." Economic prosperity
> of the nation is "heavily dependent" upon stability. (p. 362)
>
> Fastest growing "segment of the work force" is "women, blacks and
> hispanics, whom we have historically served poorly," and not "white males"
> whom we have historically served relatively well.... At present, "schools
> and other *human capital* related institutions contribute to the growing gap
> between the *rich and the poor*." (p. 363)
>
> The alteration of our *human capital development* institutions must be as
> fundamental as the changes in our economic institutions and other parts of
> our social fabric.... It is imperative to "improve the school success of young
> people with whom we have failed historically." (p. 364)
>
> "What are the basic tools we have available to initiate and sustain real
> change?"... 1. Demonstration projects... 2. Charismatic leaders... 3. Money
> (p. 365)... 4. Lawsuits (p. 366)... 5. Labor contracts... 6. Legislation. (p. 367)
>
> "It is not possible to achieve the kind of outcomes we envision without
> being specific as to what those outcomes are. Moreover, it is necessary to
> define the quality and scope of the desired outcomes. Using the *Job Training
> Partnership Act* as an example... one of the frequent criticisms of its outcome
> definition is that it encourages 'creaming.' If, however, the outcome sought
> and rewarded was not just job placement, but job placement for the most
> difficult to serve and job placements of a certain quality in terms of pay and
> future prospects, one would quickly eliminate that charge.... Crafting out-
> comes can be a very tricky process ... to achieve the high graduation rates
> reflecting higher achievement levels will require success with the same young
> people with whom we have failed even with lower standards." (pp. 369–370)
>
> "What we teach should basically be the same for ALL students." (p. 375)
> [all emphases in original]
>
> "New Paradigms for Action" makes it clear that in the future the "sys-
> tem" (not the student) will be responsible for student success... and the
> students will be followed (data collection system from birth until death?).
> The "system" will be rewarded or penalized for the success/failure of those
> "difficult to serve" including whether or not they get high paying jobs after
> schooling ends.

In order to drive home her point that our children, as human capital,
are nothing but pawns in the hands of the state/business community,
McLemore refers to the foreword to Alexander Frazier's book *Adventuring,
Mastering, Associating: New Strategies for Teaching Children* (Association for
Supervision and Curriculum Development: Washington, D.C., 1976), written
by Delmo Della-Dora, president of ASCD (1975–1976), which said, "This
work represents Alexander Frazier's attempt to describe what he calls an
equal rights curriculum for all children." On page 83 Frazier said, "Our goal

is the removal of inequality among children who have been undertaught, overtaught, mistaught, or not taught some things at all." On page 15 he said, "Jefferson saw the public school as an agency for finding talent to serve the state. In the same way, the school could recruit for the business and industrial establishment."

VIRGINIA BIRT BAKER'S PAPER, WRITTEN IN 1991,"EDUCATIONAL CHOICE— The Education Voucher, Tax Credits, and the Nonpublic Schools" explains very clearly that educational "choice" is a Trojan Horse carrying government control of all schools and schooling. Excerpts follow:

> "Education is an emotional issue," he said. "We're staying away from the word 'voucher' because 'educational choice' sounds a little more palatable to parents. Educational choice is giving students and their parents a voucher... and we want to mobilize a significant number of people... to get the camel's nose under the tent.... We've got to prepare for the long term... so we can strengthen our position and that of our friends."
>
> So reported a leader of a covert "new right" Dallas think tank at a recent White House Conference on Education. The pro-choice activists are vociferous proponents of tuition tax credits and the education voucher, and we wonder why they want to "improve the schools' and parents' attitudes" by confounding our intellectual inquiries with an emotional and illusory word change.
>
> The Associated Press has reported that... President George Bush said, "Choice will be a critical element in education reform for years to come." This recent upsurge in support of "choice" and the voucher program is nothing new and deserves closer scrutiny by parents and especially by private and home school patrons....
>
> The Private School Trap—
> To parents who have been paying taxes to support government schools, it sounds wonderful to be able to choose the better school not necessarily in their neighborhood. To parents who have been paying taxes to government schools and paying the tuition costs to send their children to private schools, a tax break or a government-paid incentive would be a welcome relief from financial strain, seemingly encouraging a sort of free-market approach to education. But stop and think: The state has its fangs into private and home schools now; what will it be like when schools are recipients of "choice" money?
>
> The truth of the matter is, once private education accepts tuition tax credits/vouchers it can no longer remain "private," because through government regulations, it will be forced to become one and the same with its public counterpart.

THE UNITED STATES COALITION FOR EDUCATION FOR ALL (USCEFA)—AN outgrowth of World Conference on Education for All, Jomtien, Thailand—met October 30–November 1,1991 in Alexandria, Virginia. President Bush's wife, Barbara, was named honorary chairperson. One of the keynote speakers at the event was Deputy Minister of Education Elena Lenskaya, Republic of Russia.[8] The purpose of this conference was to "involve the United States in reform of education/community renewal worldwide." The same United

Nations outcomes as those recommended at the Jomtien conference were adopted. According to "The Mission Statement":

> USCEFA is comprised of a diverse group of international, domestic, governmental and non-governmental groups, associations, and individual education, business, media and health leaders. The Coalition was created as an outgrowth of the World Conference on Education for All, where official delegations from 156 countries achieved a worldwide consensus to launch a renewed worldwide initiative to meet the basic learning needs of all children, youth and adults.[9]
>
> The Coalition is taking this worldwide consensus and bridging between the initiatives for reform in other countries and the goals for education reform in the United States. [This statement flies in the face of change agent assurances at the local and state level that goals are locally developed, ed.]
>
> It strongly believes that the improvement of education is essential for improving the quality of life for the world's people and for sustainable economic development; and for these reasons, this organization is committed to improving the state of basic education in the United States and developing countries by creating new partnerships for educational reform....
>
> Through seminars, publications, media events, conferences, networking and the dissemination of information, the U.S. Coalition for Education for All is working to meet the goals set by the World Conference on Education for All. Members of the Board of Directors include:
>
> President: Janet Whitla, Education Development Center, Inc.[10]
> Vice President: Stephen F. Moseley, Academy for Educational Development, Inc.
> Secretary: Richard Long, International Reading Association
> Treasurer: John Comings, World Education, Inc.
> Clifford Block, Far West Regional Laboratory for Educational Research and Improvement
> David Dorn, American Federation of Teachers
> Alan Hill, Apple Computer, Inc.
> Gary Marx, American Association of School Administrators
> Thomas Shannon, National School Boards Association
> Daniel Wagner, National Center on Adult Literacy, University of Pennsylvania

NEW AMERICAN SCHOOLS DEVELOPMENT CORPORATION (NASDC) WAS established in 1991. President George Bush requested that the business community raise funds to support development of "radical, break-the-mold" schools (one in each Congressional district) which would in the future be known as "charter schools" (public school "choice" schools).[11] The Request for Proposals from NASDC required that

> Design teams should define the scope and focus of their own work. Student age-grouping may be unconventional, and designs may serve students younger than five years of age and older than eighteen; students need not all be assembled in a single building or at a particular time of day; the school day and school year may be redefined. The duties of administrators, teachers, volunteers, parents, and all other adults may be changed.... The design may entail major changes in community governance, community structures

and the functions of other institutions such as public health agencies and welfare departments. Alternatively, designs may adopt conventional arrangements for any of above.

THE EFFECTIVE SCHOOL REPORT'S NOVEMBER 1991 ISSUE CARRIED AN ARticle entitled "A Letter from Russia." The following excerpts illustrate the extent of damage resulting from the 1985 U.S.-Soviet and Carnegie education agreements and other exchange agreements:

Editor's note: Don Thomas, executive director of the Network for Effective Schools, journeyed to Russia in September as part of a contingent of American educators traveling under the auspices of the U.S. Department of Education (Secretary Lamar Alexander). Dale Mann of Columbia University was a part of the delegation. After initial meetings in Moscow, Thomas traveled to the City of Sochi to meet with Russian educators. One of his contacts was Professor Victor Nouja, a school administrator from Rostov-on-Don. The following letter is a follow-up communication from Nouja, who is eager to establish contacts with American educators for the exchange of information and teaching on school management practices:

Dear Mr. Thomas:

How are you and your family? Now that we have returned from the first East-West International Workshop in Sochi (Russia) to our native city, Rostov-on-Don, my friends and I want to thank you for the opportunity you gave us to learn about the experiences of school reform and educational management in the state of South Carolina and the evaluation of schools in South Carolina. I am sure your experience will be very helpful for us.... There are many teachers and school principals who are very interested in taking part in different projects. But, we would like to have our own project—"Rostov-South Carolina-Utah." Me and my boss had a very long and promising talk with our city authorities about our possible contacts. And they promise to undertake sponsorship of the international teacher training and school management program.

Now some words about goals of the project. The first is—to exchange our experience in school management and especially in evaluation of school activity. The second is—to transfer your experience of using computer systems in both teaching and school management. The third goal—exchange of teaching experience. Now we begin to work with groups of teachers who are ready for actions in this project.

Mr. Thomas, I'll be very happy if you send a letter and tell me your vision on points I have described. If there is no objection and difficulties to start this project then we need to find time and place we could meet and discuss details. It might be either your town in South Carolina or our native city Rostov-on-Don. At that meeting we'll be able to work out a program or project and sign something like an agreement on form and the matter of the project. Our city's authorities are ready to take part in this business. I hope we could organize this meeting this winter or early in spring time. Mr. Thomas, I have a big favor to ask of you... papers and some tests for accreditation of schools.

Signed Victor Nouja, 344103 Stz Sodzujestva NeF, ap 170, Rostov-on-Don, USSR, Russia

BRITISH COLUMBIA TEACHERS' FEDERATION[12] IN 1991 PUBLISHED "WHAT is the Market Model?" Excerpts from this interesting flyer made available to Canadian teachers follows:

> AIMS: The Market Model aims to reduce learning to an instrument serving social power. More specifically public education is enlisted in the Market Model to serve the needs of corporate capital in an information age of global production.
>
> FEATURES:
> 1. In Canada the market model started in higher education, and is now moving to secondary schooling.
> 2. Cuts in government funding, with corporate funding targeted to particular projects.
> 3. Purpose of education—to compete economically in the international marketplace.
> 4. Demands that public education be redesigned to serve as a knowledge producer for private corporations in the national economic competition.
> 5. Textbook production and distribution under control of private corporations.
> 6. Academic teachers are conceived as "business persons" who provide goods and services under Free Trade Agreement and NAFTA.
>
> RHETORIC:
> "New Reality"
> Competition, Market Discipline
> "The Campus as Corporation" (Strangeway, 1984)
> Curriculum Products
> Resource Units or Resource Packages
> Uniform Standards Skills
>
> MAIN SOURCE: McMurtry, John, Journal of Philosophy of Education, Vol. 25, No. 2, 1991. PD95–0016

[Ed. Note: Many of McMurtry's ideas are to be found in so-called "conservative" think tanks' papers on education restructuring. Number 6 under "Features" is particularly offensive in that the idea of teachers becoming "private contractors" instead of school system employees is being discussed and proposed around many a policy maker's table in this country. What a peculiar thing. If teachers are being trained not to concentrate on subject matter or "lower level skill development," what would they have to market? The ability to "train" students to perform certain tasks in a certain way in a certain period of time? Market Model Maniacs?]

1992

THE EFFECTIVE SCHOOL REPORT'S FEBRUARY 1992 ISSUE CARRIED AN ARTICLE entitled "Free Education in a Free Society" by Nick Zienau of England's Educational Consultancy. It reads in part:

> This article describes a project which began at a conference organized in September 1991 to discuss possibilities for projects between East and West

which might assist the process of educational reform in Russia and the other republics formerly of the USSR.... An important part of becoming convinced that this was worthwhile was to discover that there was a common set of values and ideas about the changes facing education systems whether in Russia, the U.S. or Europe.... A key theme for us was, therefore, that those ideas which hitherto have been seen as progressive alternatives and often dangerously radical in educational theory and practice will increasingly become part of mainstream education practice and thinking.

A second key principle was the idea that increasingly education will cease to be a state monopoly and must have a relationship with the free market. This seems related to the idea of individual enterprise and choice. Our belief is that it is helpful to educational reform and therefore to this project to form collaborative relationships between the state and organizations acting in the free market. This will help to allow individual autonomy, enterprise, etc., to flourish and allow relationships between those involved in reform not to be based on fixed budgets and supply side economics. It will require us to have clear contracts between participants. If we have ideas about how to go about training teachers, we will learn these best from each other by doing it together and that only in this way can the project be effective as an educational intervention between nations, between innovators or between individuals.

...We believe in an exchange of learning and in the idea that there is likely to be as much that the West can learn from eastern partners as the other way around. We believe that a key to what this learning might be about is that the West's knowledge of how to do things in education, how to make changes for instance in the technology, is matched by pedagogic systems and theories which have been highly developed in Russia. We believe that these theories and practices can form the basis of radical curriculum innovation and organizational reform.

Finally, we believe in a project that has an organic structure. It will have two nodes, one in the east and one in the west, and it will span three continents. It will have a core structure which must have a small financial base and it will have participating organizations and individuals. However, the form of the organization must be one in which projects can be developed from the center core and not controlled by it. Participants should be free to create these without relying on central funding or permission as long as they can fit into this set of agreed values which the project will develop.

First among these is the theme of teacher education (both pre- and in-service). We see this as the key way of changing and influencing education....

Thirdly, we hope to gain the active involvement of industry and commerce. It will be the concern of the project to encourage such collaboration on both sides, both in the Eastern consortium and in the Western consortium. We understand it as an important way of ensuring that education is relevant to society, understood and cared about, and seen as connected to sources of wealth creation in society. Certainly in the East and also, we would venture, increasingly in the West, active involvement of industry and commerce is essential in order to obtain the funds and commitment necessary for educational reform to succeed. This means that in practice we will take every available opportunity to involve actively avant-garde leaders of industry and commerce both in funding, supporting and implementing the project. The important criteria for collaboration must be that there is sufficient congruence of ethics and values about the goals and methods of the project.

Fourthly, in order to "practice what we preach," we believe that our meetings and projects events do actively demonstrate and work with the pedagogic systems, that the learning should be managed in a conscious way. We therefore will make it a feature of the project that we focus on the skills and strategies of managing learning in an international context whether it be in the seminars, conferences, exchange trips or consultations. Fifth, it will be important to formulate structures and models of organization that encourage independence and autonomy through small groups.... The education reform process will be built on the work of many small groups making their own decisions. We will need to build into our project structure of contract making, interdependence with autonomy and hold it within a regulated and boundaried field of action. These kinds of structures and models are new forms of organization for both East and West and represent a move away from hierarchy and role-dominated cultures.

The Consortium activity has the official support of the Minister of Education for the Russian Republic, Dr. Edouard Dneprov, and a close liaison has been established with the Ministry. On the Western side, the consortium at present includes consultants, trainers, and researchers from the UK, Netherlands and the USA who aim in the first place to act as a bridge into the various educational networks in the West. These will include higher education initiatives, networks of alternative schools, organizations involved in innovative teacher training, consulting organizations, industrial and commercial organizations concerned with pedagogical innovation. They are also currently working to obtain funding and support among possible private and public sector sponsors.

Signed Nick Zienau

[Ed. Note: Considerable space has been devoted to quotes from *The Effective School Report* due to their obvious close relationship to activities in American education restructuring; i.e., choice, charter schools, school-business partnerships, school-to-work legislation, The New American Schools Development Corporation, site-based management, merger of public and private sectors, and the Skinnerian workforce training methodology. This important article justifies the validity of concerns expressed by Americans opposed to the U.S.-Soviet and Carnegie-Soviet education agreements signed in 1985 by President Reagan, Mikhail Gorbachev, Carnegie Corporation and the then-Soviet Academy of Sciences, respectively.]

"BEIJING JOURNAL: PERSONAL FILE AND WORKER YOKED FOR LIFE" BY Nicholas D. Kristof was published in *The New York Times* on March 16, 1992. This article described the Chinese dangan as part of a web of social controls that ensures order in China. Excerpts follow:

BEIJING—As part of China's complex system of social control and surveillance, the authorities keep a dangan, or file, on virtually everyone except peasants. Indeed, most Chinese have two dangans: one at their workplace and another in their local police station.... "School records and grade transcripts," she began, offering a foreigner a rare look into the dangan system, "Entry into the Communist Youth League and the Communist Party. Family members and photo. Promotions and level of work. Performance evaluations. That kind of thing. About 10 times."

A file is opened on each urban citizen when he or she enters elementary school, and it shadows the person throughout life, moving on to high school, college and employer. Particularly for officials, professors and Communist Party members, the dangan contains political evaluations that affect career prospects and permission to leave the country.... The dangan affects promotions and job opportunities, and it is difficult to escape from because any prospective employer is supposed to examine an applicant's dangan before making a hiring decision.

[Ed. Note: Sounds like the U.S. Secretary of Labor's Commission on Achieving Necessary Skills resumé for "Jane Smith" which grades Jane on a 1–10 basis on honesty, etc., and which includes her community service activities. Oregon's legislation stating that employers could not hire potential employees unless they had a Certificate of Initial Mastery did not pass. However, the very idea that it was proposed means that that is exactly what is intended. The above article is important because of U.S. educators' official visits to China and the fact that the U.S. Department of Education's contract for the SPEEDE Express (an electronic data exchange system to be used for transfer of student records, etc.) is the beginning of the transfer of personal data on students to various agencies, prospective employers, etc.]

FILLING THE GAPS: AN OVERVIEW OF DATA ON EDUCATION IN GRADES K *through 12* was published by the National Center for Educational Statistics (U.S. Department of Education, Office of Educational Research and Improvement: Washington, D.C. [NCES 92–132], 1992). On page 5 one finds a most extraordinary and revolutionary definition of teacher "quality" which transfers the responsibility for learning from the student to the teacher. Excerpts from *Filling the Gaps* follow:

TEACHERS
Beginning in the 1980s, NCES collected detailed information on the characteristics and qualifications of teachers....

But the term "qualifications" is not synonymous with "quality." The characteristics that contribute to good teaching are many, and no single configuration of traits, qualifications, or behaviors unvaryingly produces optimal student outcomes in all situations. NCES teacher surveys have concentrated on collecting data on "qualifications," rather than trying to define "quality." In order to define and measure "quality," characteristics and qualifications of teachers must be related to growth in student achievement.

[Ed. Note: If the bottom line regarding "quality teaching" is "growth in student achievement" one must assume that extraordinary measures will be necessary to bring about such "growth in student achievement" and the only measures that exist are those associated with the Skinnerian operant conditioning method used in mastery learning/direct instruction/outcome-/results-/performance-based education, all of which are synonymous with the new definition of "achievement." The Skinnerian method identifies each and every minute component of the subject to be learned and measures each and every response by the student and teacher, leaving much real learning out of the picture. It is evident that the teacher will also be "trained" in the same way the student is "trained" in order to become a "quality teacher" who never deviates from the script and whose every action, including facial expressions and body gestures, can be precisely measured, accounted for, and evaluated.

As a teacher, you WILL perform, or you will lose your job.

As a student, you WILL achieve, unless you are unwilling to be trained like an animal, in which case you may be sent to some form of "boot camp" for "re-education."

In order to accomplish the above, you, as a teacher, WILL teach to the test.]

> Perhaps the most important data gap in understanding how teachers affect the educational process is the lack of a good definition of "teacher quality.".... The National Education Statistics Agenda Committee... has recommended that OERI fund special studies to improve the measurement of, among other things, "important school processes including... methods of training teachers and assessing their competence."
>
> Another gap relates to the assessment of teacher quality....
>
> The qualifications measures that NCES does not collect cannot currently be related to measures of student achievement.... Development of a measure of "teacher quality" would be hastened by obtaining student outcome measures that could be linked to the rich nationally representative data on teacher qualifications.... These data are collected from information available in school records.... This student records form, if found feasible, could provide the data necessary to improve our understanding and measurement of "teacher quality."

[Ed. Note: In addition to data-gathering based on teach-to-the-test produced student performance measures of "teacher quality," *Filling the Gaps* also outlines other data gathering that is related to the "quality" measure—quality of life. According to *Filling the Gaps*:

> Socio-economic status (SES) of students is important for understanding, among other things, student outcomes including achievement test scores and graduation rates.... [C]ompletion in 1993 of the project to map decennial census information to school district boundaries will enable most elementary/secondary data to be linked to school district SES measures for analysis.

The original 1981 Census Mapping Project, a joint venture between the National Center for Education Statistics and the U.S. Census Bureau, was kept a highly guarded secret for a long time. One can only speculate as to the reason—perhaps it is related to the fact that exchanging information of this type between government agencies has been, technically, illegal. (The reader may remember the cries of protest that surfaced in the mid-1980s over the idea of the IRS tracking unpaid student college loans by sharing data from the U.S. Department of Education. The justification for continuing to illegally share interagency data was lost in the shuffle as the dust settled over that debate. Perhaps the 1981 Census Mapping Project was used as justification for "on-going practice constitutes acceptable practice.") However, it is important to note the fact that the SES measures projected for the 1993

NCES-U.S. Census project are to be arrived at by analyzing data collected on the "community"—or school district—level.

NCES maintains a series of *Educational Records Series* handbooks containing the computer coding numbers, categories, and specific pieces of information gathered and recorded about anything connected with schools—including *Handbook VIII: The Community*. This handbook, while having its contents merged into later versions of others in the series, originally contained the coding for all community "quality of life" information, including factors producing socio-economic status data and a chapter entitled "Attitudes, Values and Beliefs." This handbook provided the vehicle for profiling a "community"—defined as a "school district" by the Census Mapping Project—for planning of programs by Community Education practitioners. (*Community Education's Effect on Quality of Life* by W. James Giddis, Diana Page, and George L. Mailberger [Center for Community Education at the University of West Florida: Pensacola, Fla., 1981], p. 8.)

Profiling a community for "Attitudes, Values and Beliefs" is useful for those education change agents steeped in the methods taught in Ronald J. Havelock's *The Change Agents' Guide to Innovation in Education*, regularly taught at the National Training Laboratory's programs and other leadership training seminars for teachers, administrators, board members, elected or appointed officials, and other "first-level adopters" of new education reform/ restructuring proposals. The data gathered through the Census Mapping Project, among other things, assists in identifying those in a local community defined as "resisters" to controversial programs.

Efforts to require "accountability" based on "measurements of teacher quality" have much broader consequences than most policy makers have imagined. Defining terms can lead to understanding that some recent reform efforts are based on faulty premises, to say the least.]

COMMUNITY LEARNING INFORMATION NETWORK, INC. (CLIN) WAS INCORporated in 1992. CLIN's 22-page publicity packet stated in part:

> CLIN was incorporated in April of 1992, with a bi-partisan "Blue Ribbon" board of directors to implement a community-linked learning technology and information delivery system. CLIN has attracted a following in a substantial number of communities and involves a broad range of industries and interests (including educators, small and large businesses, hospitals, National Guard and Reserves, various government agencies, public housing, and inner city organizations and telecommunication providers) in implementing the CLIN concept. CLIN has been recognized by the White House and senior members of Congress and currently has legislation marked for testbed projects. CLIN has also developed international projects to include an approved project with the People's Republic of China sponsored by the highest levels of the Chinese government.[13]

[Ed. Note: United States government assistance to the Chinese Communist government will ensure an even tighter control of that government over every aspect of its citizens' lives. The transfer of medical records, personal information, etc. over CLIN networks should be of great concern to Americans who value their right to privacy. U.S. Senator Phil Gramm of Texas (R.) has been the chairman of the board of directors for CLIN—a public-private venture.]

TEXAS RESEARCHER BILLY LYON WROTE *CONNECTIONS AND CONFLICTS OF Interest (Or, There Ought To Be an Investigation!)* in 1992.[14] This extraordinary piece of research, which discusses in detail the private, for-profit design team projects selected by the New American School Development Corporation (NASDC) and the connections of those involved, also presented new information on vouchers (educational "choice"). The preface is presented below in its entirety:

PREFACE

This paper began as a revision and update of the original article, "$$$ 'Choice' For Profit? $$$," about the Edison Project. Since writing that article, however, the eleven "Design Teams" have been selected by the New American School Development Corporation and the released embargoes received, giving more fodder for grist. To be perfectly honest, some of the connections were just too irresistible to ignore. Each one led to another and this paper has grown like over-leavened dough. The "Design Teams," new information from *America 2000*, proposed legislation, and a little digging in some old files, provided further insight into the voucher proposals. This paper is about vouchers (educational "choice") as much as anything, but from a different perspective. The Design Teams give you an idea of what kind of "private schools" the vouchers may eventually be used for.

For those who received the earlier "Choice for Profit?" article, Appendix A contains additional information on Time-Warner, Benno C. Schmidt and Chester Finn, Jr. The material on James S. Coleman in Appendix B is especially significant.

By no means, does this paper cover all connections, or even all the "Design Teams." We're sure that those who are left out will not be offended. A chart is enclosed which, hopefully, will help you see some of these connections.

As you read this paper, keep in mind that in the beginning of talks on education reform/restructuring, all that citizens were demanding was a return to traditional basics. They wanted their children to be able to read!

This writer has, with much difficulty, selected only a few important quotes from Billy Lyon's report. "With much difficulty" due to the report's containing nothing *but* vital information and documentation on a subject which has everything to do with our children's futures and that of our nation—"choice." Excerpts from this fine report follow:

THE EDISON PROJECT, TIME-WARNER & WHITTLE COMMUNICATIONS:

Chris Whittle's Edison Project is an initiative to build a national, private, for-profit school system. Time-Warner has been not only a full partner in the Edison Project, but owned 50% of Whittle's principal company, Whittle Communications LP. Other initial Edison Project partners and financiers were Phillips Electronics and Associated Newspapers Holdings, which agreed to spend up to $60 million for the three-year study. Team members of The Edison Project include: Yale University President Benno C. Schmidt, Jr.; Lee Eisenberg, former editor-in-chief of *Esquire* (Whittle was once co-owner); Dominique Browning, former assistant managing editor of *Newsweek Magazine*; Vanderbilt University professor and former assistant secretary of education in the Reagan Administration Chester E. Finn, Jr.; and John Chubb of the liberal Brookings Institution and Center for Education Innovation....

NASDC DESIGN TEAMS:

NASDC is the private, non-profit corporation set up by American business leaders at the request of President Bush to develop a new generation of American schools by contracting with and supporting the most promising "break the mold," "start from scratch," curricula design teams. Even though NASDC is non-profit, the eleven winning design teams are "for profit." NASDC is part of *America 2000*, President Bush's education restructuring strategy....

Clinton Administration Secretary of Education Richard W. Riley calls NASDC and *Goals 2000 (Educate America Act)*, a powerful combination for "change and improvement." NASDC Executive Management Council Chairman Kearns says the two working in partnership "will provide systemic change in education." ("NASDC FACTS," New American Schools Development Corp., no date, received 9/13/93)....

In a *Wall Street Journal* (6/5/92) article Benno Schmidt, president of the Edison Project, discussing what is wrong with present schools and how projects such as the Edison Project might improve things, claims that "schools have wavered from liberal educational purposes... leav[ing] little room for the free play of young people's curiosity... and the cultivation of the imagination...." He asked, "What might result if children came to school as toddlers or even earlier, rather than as five- or six-year-olds? What if parents were systematically involved and actually worked regularly in schools? What if students taught other students much more? What if schools were open 12 hours a day, 12 months a year? What if... a school system across the nation was completely tied together technologically, and could take advantage of systemwide experimentation?..." [What if we just taught students how to read and write well and compute 2 plus 2 without a calculator? B. Lyon]

CHESTER FINN:

Dr. Dennis Cuddy, in *Now is the Dawning of the New Age New World Order*,... said: "In the book *We Must Take Charge*, not only does Finn advocate a national curriculum, but he also writes:

> The school is the vital delivery system, the state is the policy setter (and chief paymaster), and nothing in between is very important. This formulation turns on its head the traditional American assumption that every city, town, and county bears the chief responsibility for organizing and operating its own schools as a municipal function. That is what we once meant by local control, but it has become an anachronism no longer justified by research, consistent with sound fiscal policy or organizational theory, suited to our mobility patterns, or important to the public.
>
> Every student must meet a core learning standard or be penalized, according to Finn, who says perhaps the best way to enforce this standard is to confer valuable benefits and privileges on people who meet it, and to withhold them from those who do not. Work permits, good jobs, and college admission are the most obvious, but there is ample scope here for imagination in devising carrots and sticks. Drivers' licenses could be deferred. So could eligibility for professional athletic teams. The minimum wage paid to those who earn their certificates might be a dollar an hour higher.

Cuddy refers to a U.S. Department of Education "White Paper" (probably prepared largely by Finn)... with a cover letter saying "Assessment can be used as both a carrot and stick".... Under the White Paper's section "Intervening in Academic Bankruptcy" it indicates that some school districts may be unwilling to meet their educational responsibilities, and in those cases, state intervention may mean "replacing district superintendents and local school boards with state-appointed officials." This is the same "state takeover" of local schools not meeting certain state standards that Carnegie persuaded the National Governors' Association to recommend when Lamar Alexander was its chairman in 1986.

Dr. Cuddy then reminds us that "Leading conservatives around the country were warned about the Alexander/Finn educational philosophy, but most refused to oppose the nomination of Lamar Alexander as Secretary of Education."

JOHN CHUBB:

Team member John E. Chubb, senior fellow with the Brookings Institution, was a participant at the 1989 White House Workshop on Choice in Education at which he also introduced speaker Governor Rudy Perpich of Minnesota. Chubb is on the Executive Committee of the Center for Educational Innovation, "an independent project of the Manhattan Institute for Policy Research... [whose goal]... is to improve the educational system in America by challenging conventional methods and encouraging new approaches... seeks to accomplish this through... research, discussion and dissemination directed at a broad public audience. The Center's work is made possible by grants and gifts from the following: Karen and Tucker Anderson, The Chase Manhattan Bank, Exxon Education Foundation, The Lauder Foundation, The Rockefeller Foundation and others." (From "Education Policy Paper, Number 1, Model for Choice: A Report on Manhattan's District 4, Manhattan Institute for Policy Research" included in the notebook entitled *Choosing Better Schools: Regional Strategy Meetings on Choice in Education* which came from the U.S. Department of Education, Office of Intergovernmental and Interagency Affairs, Jack Klenk, special advisor.)

John Chubb is one of a 14-member task force who issued a study that "proposed a set of bold, innovative solutions designed to bring about... improvements in Texas public schools," entitled *Choice in Education: Opportunities for Texas* (March, 1990). In addition to Chubb, "Members of the Task Force producing this study included... Dr. John Goodman, president of the National Center for Policy Analysis, Dallas; Allan Parker, associate professor of law, St. Mary's University, San Antonio; Dr. Linus Wright, former under secretary of education; Dr. Kathy Hayes, associate professor of economics; and Fritz Steiger, president, Texas Public Policy Foundation [Heritage Foundation state affiliate, ed.]." (Texas Public Policy Foundation REPORT, Summer, 1990, Vol. 11, Issue 11, pages 3–4.) Dallas Eagle Forum also reportedly co-sponsored the John Chubb-Terry Moe conferences in March, 1990....

VOUCHERS ("CHOICE"), EDISON PROJECT AND NASDC DESIGN TEAMS:

Since vouchers (educational "choice") are important to the success of this scheme to "privatize" and "decentralize" education through "Design Teams," the Edison Project and other private programs, with the assistance of waivers and "flexibility," vouchers need to be examined in the new context.... Mainstream news sources have pointed out that vouchers will benefit

Chris Whittle's Edison Project, as well as any "privatized" school projects. Examples are:

> *Newsweek* (6/8/92)—"There's no question that Whittle schools could be extremely rewarding... if Congress approves a voucher system...."

> *Time* (6/8/92)—[owned by Time-Warner]—"...the Bush Administration strongly supports the concepts that underlie the Edison Project.... Many observers believe Whittle's long-term plan anticipates the use of these (voucher) funds. If adopted, the reform (vouchers) could funnel billions of public dollars into private schools...."

CHUBB & CONSERVATIVES:

Most conservatives have been conspicuously silent on John Chubb's partnership in The Edison Project, and the benefits to be accrued from government voucher assistance. Many call this "privatization" of education, leaving the impression that it is "free market enterprise," which is absolutely ridiculous since the venture is taxpayer funded and, consequently, government controlled! Chubb's role may now be an embarrassment to those, who with great fanfare and publicity, sponsored his tour around the country extolling the virtues, but not the consequences, of education "choice." Nor were people informed of Chubb's liberal connections. And, only later did people learn of the other "designs" on "choice" money which came to light with the introduction of *America 2000*, The Edison Project, and the other for-profit programs. The Design Teams projects were probably part of a veiled plan that drove the promotion of vouchers to begin with—from top down. Before letting the cat out of the bag, however, it was necessary to garner support for the strategy, especially from Christian conservatives. "Choice" had to be sold to them as beneficial. And, so it was. Many fell for it, following certain leaders. John Chubb was at the top of the sales team.... [John Chubb is also a supporter of the Skinnerian DISTAR/Reading Mastery program developed by Siegfried Engelmann and thoroughly discussed in this book, ed.]

LAYING THE GROUNDWORK:

Regional strategy meetings on choice in education were held in the fall of 1989, following the White House Workshop on Choice in January, where John Chubb, Dennis P. Doyle, Joe Nathan, Governor Rudy Perpich of Minnesota, Governor Tommy Thompson of Wisconsin, and then-Governor of Tennessee Lamar Alexander were speakers. At the strategy meetings, research papers, position statements, and policy analyses were presented and the information compiled in a large notebook entitled, *Choosing Better Schools: Regional Strategy Meetings on Choice in Education*. The notebook contained two "Education Policy Papers," from the Center for Educational Innovation (CEI), a project of the Manhattan Institute for Policy Research. The list of CEI Executive Committee members included John Chubb, Senior Fellow, Brookings Institution, and Joe Nathan, Senior Fellow, Humphrey Institute of Public Affairs. Among the CEI supporters were... The Chase Manhattan Bank, Exxon Education Foundation... The Rockefeller Foundation.... (THIS ISN'T GRASSROOTS CONSERVATISM, FOLKS!) CEI's Education Policy Paper #2, "The Right to Choose," contained presentations by John Chubb, Joe Nathan, Chester Finn, Jr., and James S. Coleman.

James S. Coleman has been busy, too. His work penetrates the entire educational environment, including restructuring. He's been quoted in educational materials for at least 25 years. Recently, a paper by Coleman, entitled "Parental Involvement in Education," was included with the *America 2000* issues paper, "What Other Communities Are Doing, National Educational Goal #1," distributed after the third *America 2000* satellite town hall meeting (7/28/92).... Coleman gives yet another reason for approving "choice," one less publicized. He said that the "choice system" would give the school more authority, making it possible to require more of parents and children by having them accept and obey a set of rules as a condition of entering and continuing in the school....

PRIVATE VOUCHERS:

Does the information just presented tell us something about the evolution of arguments for vouchers; from one of assisting those in private schools to that of aiding the poor who can't afford a private school? Does it explain why all voucher legislation/amendments are directly or indirectly connected to Title I, Chapter I of ESEA, which addresses the "Disadvantaged"? Does it suggest that the purpose of the whole scheme is "homogenization" through more integration, economically and socially... for total equality through redistribution of wealth and children, via vouchers?...

G.I. BILL FOR CHILDREN, OR INTEGRATION BY VOUCHER?
Recall these statements:

> Albert Shanker, American Federation of Teachers—"It may be that we can't get the big changes we need without choice."
> President George Bush—"Choice is the one reform that drives all others."
> Former U.S. Secretary of Education Lauro Cavazos—"President Bush and I are determined to use the power of choice to help restructure American education."

A MESSAGE FROM PRESIDENT GEORGE BUSH WAS DELIVERED REGARDING *THE National Youth Apprenticeship Act* (House Doc. #102–320, *The Congressional Record*) on May 3, 1992. Excerpts follow:

I am pleased to transmit herewith for your immediate consideration *The National Youth Apprenticeship Act of 1992*.... This legislation would establish a national framework for implementing comprehensive youth apprenticeship programs.... These programs would be a high-quality learning alternative for preparing young people to be valuable and productive members of the 21st century work force.... There is widespread agreement that the time has come to strengthen the connection between the academic subjects taught in our schools and the demands of the modern, high technology workplace.... Under my proposal, a student could enter a youth apprenticeship program in the 11th or 12th grade. Before reaching these grades, students would receive career and academic guidance to prepare them for entry into youth apprenticeship programs.... A youth apprentice would receive academic instruction, job training and work experience.... Standards of academic achievement, consistent with voluntary national standards, will apply to all academic instruction, including the required instruction in the core subjects of English, mathematics, science, history, and geography. Students would be expected to demonstrate mastery of job skills....

My proposal provides for involvement at the Federal, State and local levels to ensure the success of the program. Enactment of my proposal will result in national standards applicable to all youth apprenticeship programs. Thus, upon the completion of the program, the youth will have a portable credential that will be recognized wherever the individual may go to seek employment or pursue further education and training....

I believe that the time has come for a national, comprehensive approach to work-based learning. The bill I am proposing would establish a formal process in which business, labor, and education would form partnerships to motivate the Nation's young people to stay in school and become productive citizens.... I urge the Congress to give swift and favorable consideration to the *National Youth Apprenticeship Act of 1992.*

AN ARTICLE BY LAURA ROGERS ENTITLED "IN LOCO PARENTIS, PART II—THE 'Parents as Teachers' Program Lives On" was published in the September 1992 issue of *Chronicles*.[15] Ms. Rogers rendered all Americans a great service by providing a seminal work on this totalitarian program. Excerpts from her excellent article follow:

For the uninitiated, the PAT [Parents as Teachers] program was begun in Missouri in 1981, ostensibly for the purpose of curbing the high dropout rate and winning back parental support for the public school system. In 1985 the state legislature mandated that the PAT program be offered to all schools and children in Missouri and since then the PAT program has been proposed in at least forty other states. Simply put, the program pivots on assigning to all parents and children a "certified parent educator." This state employee evaluates the child (under the guise of educational screening), assigns the child a computer code classification, and initiates a computer file that the state will use to track the child for the rest of his or her life. All of the computer code designations label the child to some degree "at risk," and there is no classification for "normal." The state agent conducts periodic home and school visits to check on the child and the family, dispensing gratis such things as nutritional counseling, mental health services, and even food. Schools under the PAT program provide free day and overnight care. The "certified parent" might forbid the biological parents to spank their child, and might prescribe, if the child is deemed "unhappy," psychological counseling or a drug such as Ritalin. If the parents refuse the recommended services or drugs, the state may remove the child from the home, place him in a residential treatment center, and force the parents to enroll in family counseling for an indefinite period.

ON NOVEMBER 11, 1992, SEVERAL DAYS AFTER THE 1992 PRESIDENTIAL election, Marc Tucker, director of the National Center on Education and the Economy in Rochester, New York, wrote a letter to Hillary Clinton on NCEE letterhead in which he outlined a lifelong, (socialist) workforce agenda, most of which—interestingly enough—had no problem being approved by a Republican-controlled Congress within three years.[16] (See the Internet version for Appendix XV and XVIII.) The letter's introductory paragraph stated:

I still cannot believe you won! But utter delight that you did pervades all the circles in which I move. I met last Wednesday in David Rockefeller's [Jr.] office with him, John Sculley [Apple Computer executive] et al. It was a great celebration. Both John and David R. were more expansive than I have ever seen them—literally radiating happiness. My own view and their's is that this country has seized its last chance....

...We propose, first, that the President appoint a national council on human resource development.... It would be established in such a way to assure continuity of membership across administrations, so that the consensus it forges will outlast any one administration.... Second, we propose that a new agency be created, the National Institute for Learning, Work and Service.

AMERICAN FEDERATION OF TEACHERS AFFILIATE, THE PHILADELPHIA FEDeration of Teachers, stated its opposition to Outcome-Based Education (OBE) in a November 20, 1992 letter to Pennsylvania state senators as follows:

OBE should be a pilot project at best, and tested in several schools as a welcome addition to the existing Carnegie Units. It should not be implemented statewide because it could be a costly disaster. OBE has no grade designations. OBE has minimal "benchmark" designations. There are no time designations. For example, a student completes all English requirements in one and one-half years. This student is not required to further develop English skills in the remaining two and one-half years of his/her high school career. There are NO safety nets for students. OBE is really non-graded schools and non-graded classrooms. It is a very dishonest approach to slipping this whole structure into place. Parents, teachers, and students have a right to honestly discuss these very important educational plans. We would appreciate your support in the closing days of this legislative session to block any implementation of Outcomes-Based Education here in the Commonwealth of Pennsylvania.

SCHOOL'S OUT: A RADICAL NEW FORMULA FOR THE REVITALIZATION OF America's Educational System by Lewis J. Perelman was published (Avon Books: New York, 1992). The book's cover stated that

Dr. Perelman earned his doctorate in social policy at the Harvard Graduate School of Education. A Senior Fellow of the Discovery Institute, he was formerly Director of Project Learning 2000—a study of restructuring education and training sponsored by nine U.S. corporations and foundations.

George Gilder, author of Wealth and Poverty, also recommended the book by Perelman as follows: "A compulsively readable rush to a vital new paradigm for technology and learning. You will never think of schools in the same way again." In the preface of School's Out, Perelman reveals that

Unlike others who channeled their disaffection into calls for "reform," by 1970 I was convinced that the education system could not be amended but needed to be entirely replaced by a new mechanism more attuned to the technology and social fabric of the modern world. This conclusion was nurtured by many sources, but especially influential were the works of B.F. Skinner, George Leonard and Jay Forrester. The work of Skinner and his disciples showed that the processes of learning could be analyzed, understood, and organized to serve the individual learner's needs.... Inspired by such ideas, I returned to Harvard in 1970 and spent the next three years in an intense and largely independent study of most of the key questions that underlie this book: What is learning and how does it work? What technologies can facilitate learning, and how do they work? How does learning fit in with the overall processes of human economy and ecology? And most important, how do you transform or replace established human institutions?...

Of the several Harvard and MIT faculty who contributed to my exploration of these questions, I particularly benefited from the aid and encouragement of Wassilly Leontief, Harvey Liebenstein, Jay Forrester, Ithiel deSola Pool, B.F. Skinner, and Paul Yivisaker.... After leaving Harvard, I continued my research for another year with support from a grant from the Rockefeller Brothers Fund and presented the results of the whole five years of study in my first book, *The Global Mind*, published in 1976. (p. 8)

[Ed. Note: In 1994 Dr. Perelman served as education specialist for the Progress and Freedom Foundation's First Annual Meeting in Atlanta, Georgia, "Cyberspace and the American Dream."[17] The Progress and Freedom Foundation published Alvin and Heidi Toffler's book, *Creating a New Civilization: The Politics of the Third Wave*, which carried a foreword by U.S. Representative and soon-to-be Speaker of the House Newt Gingrich (R., GA). On page 96 of the Toffler's book, the Progress and Freedom Foundation issued this invitation:

If you have read and been influenced by this or by any of their works, they—and we—would like to know about it. Especially if you have ideas for how to speed the transition to a Third Wave America, please send them to us.]

1993

THE 1993 ANNUAL REPORT OF THE HERITAGE FOUNDATION OF WASHINGTON, D.C., dedicated to their twentieth year celebration, revealed the following:

The idea of the *North American Free Trade Agreement* (NAFTA) originated with Heritage Fellow Richard Allen and has long been advocated by Heritage policy analysts.... The idea of creating a North American free trade zone from the Yukon to the Yucatan was first proposed by Heritage Distinguished Fellow Richard Allen in the late 1970s, refined by then Presidential candidate Ronald Reagan, and further developed in a major 1986 Heritage Foundation study. (p. 4)

[Ed. Note: The *North American Free Trade Agreement* got the ball rolling for the development of skills standards by the newly formed National Skills Standards Board, endorsed by the U.S. Labor Department Secretary's Commission on Achieving Necessary Skills (SCANS) study originated under Labor Secretary Elizabeth Dole, and eventually led to the *School-to-Work Opportunities Act* and the dumbing down of American education curriculum for workforce training. With all of this emphasis on "standards" it should be pointed out that NAFTA allows exchanges of all categories of professionals, with those coming from Mexico and Canada having met their own countries' standards, not necessarily equal to those required in the United States. If this process evolves the way most of these exchange processes have in the past, that disparity will be addressed in one of two ways—by changing U.S. standards to match foreign standards, or by altering both NAFTA nations' standards to align with international standards like ISO 9000 or ISO 1400 monitored by UNESCO. This should be of concern to professional organizations in the United States.]

"Schoolroom Shuffle: Trailing in Education for Years, Kentucky Tries Radical Reforms—Grades 1 through 3 Become One Class with No Texts, Desks or Report Cards—Some Parents, Principals Balk" by Suzanne Alexander was published in *The Wall Street Journal* (A–6) on January 5, 1993. Some excerpts follow:

> Lexington, Kentucky—Teachers work in teams, using children's literature to teach spelling, reading and writing. For math and science, students are taught to analyze instead of memorize.
>
> "We've turned education topsy-turvy," says teacher Beverly Dean, gazing around her classroom at children studying on pillows, a couch and a rocking chair.
>
> Indeed, Kentucky has become a giant laboratory for school reform.
>
> "We have redefined the basics and challenged every assumption you have about learning," says Faye King, principal of Stanton Elementary School in eastern Kentucky. "It's radical and its comprehensive. But we can't do any worse, so why not go for the best."...
>
> In some cases, public schools themselves are resisting change. Longfellow Elementary Center in rural Mayfield, Ky., has postponed combining its kindergarten through third grades while it pleads with state officials not to force it to do so next year. "It's almost humanly impossible to teach when you put so many age (and ability) levels in one classroom," says principal Elsie Jones. She adds that without grades, parents won't know at what level their children are performing, and should the students move away, their new schools may have difficulty placing them in the appropriate grade....
>
> Although its fourth and fifth grades remain traditional, changes in what were the lower grades (in Picadome Elementary) have transformed the atmosphere in those classrooms. "This is my 19th year of teaching, and this is my best year," says Barbara Evans, trying to keep order within groups of noisy six and seven-year-olds racing to complete math, cursive writing and art assignments with a dinosaur theme.

Total Quality for Schools: A Suggestion for American Education by Joseph C. Fields was published (ASQ Quality Press: Milwaukee, Wis., 1993). This book was given to selected local school boards in districts implementing reform/restructuring. Excerpts follow:

> Educators must confront this age-old question of whom to serve and resolve this question in favor of the customer and the American culture, political system, and economic system.... (p. 19)
>
> Schools must think in terms of futures, always 10 to 20 years ahead of today. Schools that are constant in their purposes must change to meet customer requirements. Schools must deal with the problems of today as well as the problems of tomorrow to assure Americans that they will be in the education business of the future. As the number of private schools increases, as school vouchers and schools of choice develop, and as schools

take on more and more social responsibilities, it is questionable whether or not certain schools will be in business in the future....

Businesses will not buy from uncertified vendors. This idea might contain some merit for educators. The state of Tennessee, in its original Career Ladder Program for educators, required a portfolio of specifications, quality assurances, work standards, and process control in addition to several site visits from evaluators who were unfamiliar with the evaluated teacher. Consider too the "parent as vendor" of a precious resource, the child. In the internal customer concept, the parent is serving the teacher. Teachers could identify reasonable specifications for parents relative to the home learning environment and certify parents who will cooperate. (p. 48)

[Ed. Note: The above statement is absolutely appalling! In the words of Cynthia Weatherly in her article "Privatization or Socialization?":

We are misled when we believe that education is a commodity or service to be "purchased" by "consumers." This tends to make the public believe that education is market-driven. Compulsory attendance laws make education anything but market-driven! More importantly, the concept of consumer/purchaser does not correlate to our relationship to our elected officials who are legal overseers of the process. Have we lost sight of what our relationship to government is? Education is a trust, not a commodity. These are our children, and their futures; parents are not "shopping" for education, but are fervently searching for someone to whom they are willing to entrust the task of providing an academic education for their children.

As charter schools develop, the temptation will be for private industry to take a more direct role in funding and developing programs for these schools which will produce workers who can fill the corporations' needs. These schools, then, have the potential of becoming "corporate academies" with a narrow focus and limited curriculum base. This is accomplished through the school-business partnerships growing into corporate funding to accomplish its task. As this potential reality develops, the specter of true socialism—the combining of the private and public sectors to produce goods and services—takes on discernible size and shape....

B.F. Skinner once mused that the functions of government in the future would be educational. In the above scenario we see that the reverse of that prediction can be true as well—in the future the functions of education will be governmental. Let us remember that the true purpose of education is the intrinsic enhancement of the individual. Let us not reduce education to limited learning for lifelong labor and our great country's heritage of freedom to a footnote in history.

In addition, at the Sixth Annual Model Schools Conference—sponsored by Willard Daggett, director of the International Center for Leadership in Education—in Atlanta, Georgia in July of 1998, a participant who is an assistant principal at a middle school in Southern California made this comment to a reporter regarding mechanisms to encourage parental involvement and support in the education of children:

One way to make sure that parents attend conferences at school and support the educational process for their children would be to dock a certain part of their tax deduction for their children. There could be a scale of activities

in which the parents would be required to have documentation—perhaps
a sign-off at the school—of participation before they would be allowed to
claim their tax deductions for their children. I agree with Daggett that we
may have to employ some measures that seem extreme.[18]

Returning to a final quote from *Total Quality for Schools: A Suggestion
for American Education*:

> In all this interpretation, schools are not free. They require responsible com-
> mitment from everyone. Citizens would no more be allowed to put obstacles
> in the way of public educators than to interfere with public medical, police,
> or fire protection personnel who are doing their duty. (p. 53)]

IN 1993 THE U.S. DEPARTMENT OF EDUCATION'S NATIONAL CENTER FOR
Educational Statistics (NCES) described in a handout a joint project between
NCES and the Council of Chief State School Officers (CCSSO) to develop
an electronic data link between education and the "world of work" called
"SPEEDE Express." This linking process would facilitate local "industry
partnerships" and would prepare for the use of an "international standard"
for exchanging student records.[19] An excerpt from the handout follows:

> In 1989, building on projects completed in Florida and Texas,[20] work began
> on the development of a national (eventually, an international) standard
> for exchanging student records more efficiently. This system would tap into
> the sophisticated automation of many education agencies and institutions.
> The Standardization of Postsecondary Education Electronic Data Exchange
> (SPEEDE) is intended to assist school districts (grades pre-kindergarten
> through 12 and postsecondary educational institutions in the United States
> and Canada) in the process of transmitting student academic records (tran-
> scripts) from one educational institution, agency, corporation, or other
> recipient.

M. DONALD THOMAS'S "PLAN FOR ACTION" ENTITLED *THE EMPOWERED
Educational System for the 21st Century—Establishing Competitiveness,
Productivity, Accountability and Equity in South Carolina Education* was
presented to the South Carolina legislature in 1993. Included among other
radical recommendations in Thomas's plan was: "Board authority to require
parents (guardians) to provide services to schools which their children attend."

In a videotape of Thomas making these assertions at a school board
meeting, a parent asked the question, "What would the penalty be if parents
didn't wish to perform such services?" Thomas responded, "Fifty dollars!"
He then went on to claim that he had instituted such a requirement in a
school system in Utah without resistance.[21]

PETER SHAW WROTE "THE COMPETITIVENESS ILLUSION: DOES OUR COUNTRY
Need to Be Literate in Order to Be Competitive? If not, Why Read?" for the
January 18, 1993 issue of *The National Review*. The following quotes are
from page 41:

The technological society does not particularly depend on education. A glance at the record shows us that the rapid growth of the United States into the world's greatest industrial power coincided with a steady drop in reading levels running from 1930 to the present. Regna Lee Wood a teacher, pointed out in an article in *NR* (Sept. 14th) that this falling off was followed by a related, long decline in SAT scores beginning in 1941. Technological society turns out to work in the opposite way from that usually supposed: namely, by actually requiring less rather than more education of its workers. This is because modern industry depends on reducing human error, which means reducing dependence on the individual worker's expertise and judgment. In building or maintaining electronic devices, workers who once installed or rewired electrical circuits now plug in modular components consisting of machine-printed circuit boards.... The future role of literacy in the workplace has been succinctly stated by Pierre Dogan, the president of Granite Communications, a company that is now "developing software for hotel housekeeping." It seems that "so long as maids can read room numbers, they will be able to check off tasks completed or order supplies by simply touching pictures on the screen." Dogan points out that "you can create a work program with prompting including iconic [picture] messages." In fact, he logically concludes, "you can use an illiterate workforce."

[Ed. Note: This article provides an excellent explanation of why large multinational corporations such as BMW's owner, Mercedes-Benz, etc., are settling in those states which have for many years been used as national pilot/experimental laboratory states for Skinnerian mastery learning/training in leisure and life/work skills. Among those states are Southern states which were part of the early General Education Board's "benevolent effort" to reform the South after the Civil War, including Alabama, Mississippi and South Carolina (present Secretary of Education Richard Riley's home state which has produced the second lowest standardized test scores in the nation).

These states are also a part of the Southern Regional Education Board (SREB) consortium, which has produced and dispersed an educational approach called "techademics" outlined in a program and book entitled *High Schools That Work*, written by Dr. Gene Bottoms of the SREB. (Bottoms was once employed by the Georgia Department of Education when Georgia was implementing competency-based education, the forerunner of outcome-based education, and later ran for state superintendent, unsuccessfully.)

In 1994 Dr. Bottoms addressed the Second Model Schools Conference in Atlanta—sponsored by the International Center for Leadership in Education, Inc. and directed by Dr. Willard Daggett—explaining how the *High Schools That Work* model operated through integrating academic and vocational studies. As Dr. Bottoms explained, a survey by the Committee for Economic Development had revealed that students preparing to go to work right out of high school had an inflated opinion of their abilities. "Techademics" seeks to integrate academic subjects with vocational subjects by eliminating the theoretical aspects of these courses (such as English, math and science) which would be taught in college preparatory classes, and uses instead Daggett's "Application Model" to learn how to apply this information directly to work-related tasks. In Dr. Bottoms's words: "To significantly improve the achievement of vocational completers, SREB and its partners believe that any model for integrating academic and vocational studies must change the high school's focus from ability as the key to academic success to effort as the key" (direct quote from page 110 of the *Second Model Schools Conference Proceedings*).

Some additional quotes from Dr. Bottoms's address to the participants at the Model Schools Conference bear repeating here for the light they may shed on the integration of educational reform as such reform relates to charter schools/choice and "techademics":

> Take language arts, math, science, and vocational teachers off for a three-day weekend together. Take their books and make them find common materials they teach. Break down barriers of ignorance and form a team....
>
> ...Teams went into industries to see what business needs....
>
> ...Decentralization and site-based management are the keys. These schools stretch time on task—standards firm but time flexible. Need a longer day, week, and year for extra help....
>
> ...Basic principle: an ungraded academic core with a career emphasis. The NAEP is used in measuring achievement....
>
> ...Each student has the same English teacher for four years....
>
> Can't carry out Deming's principles in present structure—must change to accommodate TQM.... Break out of state cultures—cross state lines!]

[ddd]

IN THE UNITED STATES COALITION FOR EDUCATION FOR ALL'S (USCEFA) publication *EFA Today* January-March, 1993 issue, Russell Bong of the National Training Laboratory's Institute for Applied Behavioral Science (NTL) wrote an article entitled "Overcoming Resistance and Facilitating Change: The NTL Institute's Approach."[22] An extraordinarily blatant, and some might consider frightening, explanation of the purpose of the National Training Laboratory can be found in the following excerpted material:

> Founded in 1947, the NTL Institute was affiliated with the National Education Association during its first 20 years of operation. The Institute became independent in 1967 and today serves as a nonprofit professional membership organization of applied behavioral science experts.... Dedicated to developing and applying scientific methods to behavior modification, the Institute facilitates productive change at the individual, social, organizational, and macro-system levels....
>
> To elaborate, attitudes are primarily shaped by values and beliefs, which, in turn, are shaped by both perceptions and misperceptions. NTL's approach seeks to fundamentally change personal attitudes, which it does by reshaping underlying beliefs and by eliminating dysfunctional misperceptions....
>
> It all comes down to a basic tenet: In order to facilitate change on a larger level, individuals must first work for change on a personal level. To become a true and effective agent of change, one must facilitate change within oneself.

In 1993 Dr. Beau Fly Jones, a senior director of the North Central Regional Educational Laboratory (NCREL) in Oak Brook, Illinois and a strong advocate and practitioner of Skinnerian mastery learning, wrote "The Unfolding of an International Partnership: A Story of Russia and the U.S." published in *EFA Today* (No. 2, January–March, 1993). Excerpts follow which illustrate the extent of controversial exchange activities due to the 1985 U.S.-Soviet and Carnegie-Soviet agreements in education:

> Well-designed exchanges often involve strong emotions, including caring, empathy, and the excitement of discovery, and individuals may return from such exchanges not only with cognitive paradigm shifts, but also with life-changing values and interests.
>
> This has been the case with the NCREL involvement in Russia.
>
> In January 1992, the Russian Ministry of Education assumed control of the former Soviet Ministry's responsibilities. Dr. Edward Dneprov, the new minister, initiated massive reforms focusing on decentralization, democratization, and the demilitarization of the Russian school system.
>
> NCREL's relationship with the new Russian Ministry began with an invitation to join the Metropolis Project, a collaboration among schools in Chicago, Moscow, and Amsterdam. The objective of the Project is to identify and develop successful models of systemic change in an urban context. To this end, the Project involves research, training, and exchanges of school staff in the three cities. Themes that guide these efforts are authentic learning, global education and strategic teaching....
>
> ...Metropolis schools were being selected, and one of the highlights of the delegation's February tour was the signing of a Letter of Cooperation between the Russian Ministry and the Chicago Public Schools....
>
> Existing exchanges between the U.S. and Russia tend to focus on university students or the teaching of foreign languages. For that reason, one of the major problems in obtaining funding for the Metropolis Project was that it involved a new level of exchange, this time between Russia and U.S. teachers and administrators, as well as a change in the nature of the exchange, which would focus on school reform and school-based training.

James Collins and Martin Haberman echoed Eugene Boyce in the February 1993 issue of *The Journal of Associating Teacher Educators* in an article entitled "The Future of the Teaching Profession" when they said

> Schooling is now seen as primarily job training and, for this reason, quite comparable to schooling in non-democratic societies. Once education is redefined as a personal good and as emphasizing preparation for this world of work as its first purpose, our schools can appropriately be compared with those in the U.S.S.R.[23]

[ddd]

The March 3, 1993 issue of *Education Week* ran the article "Center Lists Skills Both Disabled, Non-Disabled Should Have." An excerpt follows:

A federally funded research center has unveiled a list of academic and life skills it says all students—disabled as well as non-disabled—should have upon leaving school. The wide-ranging list compiled by the National Center for Educational Outcomes at the University of Minnesota includes 25 outcomes for what young people should gain from school and 77 indicators of whether those outcomes are being achieved. "We ought to be trying to achieve the best possible outcomes for all kids," said James E. Ysseldyke, the director of the Center. "We shouldn't have a separate system of outcomes and educators for disabled kids.".... The life skills identified by the Center include the ability to get along with others, to be responsible for one's self, and to successfully manage daily life. Upon leaving school, the indicators say students should be able to make "healthy lifestyle choices," to cope with stresses, and to volunteer in their communities, among other outcomes.

[Ed. Note: The above makes sense in light of the fact that "scientific research-based" (behaviorist/operant conditioning) direct, systematic phonics (DISTAR or Reading Mastery) is the phonics reading program developed for special education students, which will be used for all students under the *Reading Excellence Act of 1998* passed by Congress. This also foreshadows the emphasis on full funding for the *Individuals with Disabilities in Education Act* (IDEA) in the 1999 debates over the reauthorization of the *Elementary and Secondary Education Act* (ESEA).]

[ddd]

THE EFFECTIVE SCHOOL REPORT'S MAY 1993 ISSUE CARRIED "DIALOGUES in International Education" by Nick Zienau which discussed a conference in Sochi, Russia organized by the Ministry of Russia and a Norwegian network known as IMTEC which works with the U.S. Department of Education's Midcontinent Regional Educational Laboratory (McREL), the developer of *Tactics for Thinking*. Nick Zienau is a senior partner in Zienau Consulting which together with Cascade International of San Francisco is organizing the upcoming conference. The Russian partner in this enterprise is Eureka Free University, Moscow.

[ddd]

AN INTERVIEW WITH KEN HAZLIP AND JAMES BLOCK WAS INCLUDED IN THE Fall 1993 issue of *Outcomes*, the Outcome-Based Education movement's journal mentioned in previous entries in this book. Excerpts from that interview follow:

> *Jim*: To stay on this point about labels, this movement, this idea set, has made several choices of labels. At one time it was called Mastery Learning, another Outcomes-Based Education, and now Partners for Quality Learning. Yet much of what has driven this movement under the OBE label has not changed from Mastery Learning and what has changed still comes from the research done under the Mastery Learn-

ing rubric. Will this new Quality Learning label stimulate a better idea base than the old label OBE?

Ken: I doubt it. The power of our movement still derives from the original Mastery Learning idea....

Jim: When we were a Mastery Learning movement, we were concerned with schools and school districts. As we move to quality, we start to see linkages between school and the workplace....

Ken: Our school environment certainly does not look like this. The irony of the linkages you describe is that we will have to look to industry to "fix" problems that we have imported from old industrial practices because we were trying so hard to look like factories years ago.

Jim: I am a little surprised by your response. It seems to me that one of the characteristics of the workplace is that it is organized to produce a product.... Surely you are not arguing that the workplace and the workworld is the same kind of place that we should generate for kids in our schools?

Ken: Again, it depends on the level of health that the workplace presents us.

Jim: So what we are in the business of doing is just generating little workers? Where do the kids come into the equation of this process?

Ken: Kids should drive the terms forming the equation. We should be looking at them and their needs to determine how best to work with them, not forcing them into the mould our traditional classrooms and traditional methods require.... Most workplaces are still 180 degrees away from this, however—they are negative, coercive, demanding. But many in the American workplace are reinventing or reengineering that workplace. Many are beginning to look at the "old" research that John Champlin mentioned in our summer interview—Getzels and Guba and their organizational development work, Herzberg's motivation-hygiene work, and Deming's ideas [TQM]. In reinventing the workplace, they believe it can be caused to be both productive and satisfying for the worker. We can create that in the classroom and have kids who are challenged, motivated, and excited to be there....

Jim: ...Our movement has based its efforts on the research, but apparently the research in this case is perceived as either out of date or out of fashion. Why do we need to look outside to industry for models that we have described inside the ML/OBE field?

Ken: So many of the concepts presented by business gurus about workplace change are summed up very well in Mastery Learning's basic beliefs.

Jim: Is it that people within the Mastery or the Outcomes movement can only go so far, or do we need a swift kick from the outside?

Ken: As far as our mental models go, experience and environment have put burdensome blinders on us, and many will not see the implications of ideas until they are approached from a different perspective. I would rather we did not need so many detours, but if Deming gets us closer to better schools, then we "do" Deming. I incorporated his ideas and many business models when I was directing a district's restructuring efforts. We all want the research to drive our efforts, but our movement's Mastery Learning research exists in a broader context, and education research just does not have a lot of credibility among too many educators. The reasons are mostly poor ones, but they exist nonetheless and form a real barrier to change. If Deming presents an idea without the research prejudice baggage attached, I will start with Deming and end up teaching the group about the research.

A LETTER FROM LAWRENCE W. LEZOTTE, PUBLISHER OF *EFFECTIVE SCHOOLS Research Abstracts*, was written to his colleagues in September, 1993. An excerpt follows:

> First, whether or not you have been engaged in this debate as yet, you need to become familiar with the concerns and issues of the Christian Coalition. You must be prepared to respond to its challenges, which are often based on half truths and misinformation. These issues must be carefully and clearly explained to those citizens who wish to hear the educators' point of view. This will require all of us to be familiar with the research on such important topics as Mastery Learning, Continuous Progress, and De-Tracking—to mention just a few. Second, to develop mainstream community involvement, I strongly recommend that school and district leaders create a task force to study the issues related to school reform and be prepared to present their views along with the views that will be presented by the Christian Coalition. I truly believe that if educators have to debate the coalition alone, more often than not, educators will lose the debate on school reform. We need to make sure that a broad cross-section of our citizens are involved in the important debate on the future of public education and, in turn, the future of our nation.

[Ed. Note: While this author thinks it is remarkable that Dr. Lezotte would admit to being at a disadvantage in combatting "resisters," it is somewhat unfortunate that he should give credit to only one organization as being responsible for the opposition which restructuring has encountered. A broad cross-section of the country—including teachers and administrators in public schools—has been in the camp of the "resisters" when it comes to restructuring. The writer finds it hard to believe that the educational establishment—with the extraordinary resources at its disposal—was unable to obtain the support of the community, and found it necessary to use Ronald Havelock's change agentry on the citizenry.

In writing this letter Lezotte evidently fired the first shot of warning to the education community, for not six months after Lezotte's letter was written, a researcher downloaded from the internet the National Education Goals Panel's *Community Action Toolkit*, which contained instructions for combatting community resistance to restructuring. It provided recommendations for action by specific community entities—the press, civic organizations, religious entities, and business—and samples of letters to the editor, advertisements, supportive flyers, and public service announcements, for use in building support for local educational restructuring. One of the most distasteful results of this effort was the recommended manipulation of the religious community. (See the Internet version for Appendix XIV.)]

THE IMPACT ON EDUCATION OF THE UNITED STATES SIGNING THE *NORTH American Free Trade Agreement* was discussed in an article entitled "USIA's

Grants Go to Schools in NAFTA Nations" published in the September 12, 1993 edition of *The Washington Times*. Some excerpts follow:

> United States Information Agency Director Joseph Duffey attending a four-day "implementation" conference at Vancouver, British Columbia, yesterday announced the first North American three-way university affiliation grants to involve exchanges of faculty and staff among Canadian, Mexican and U.S. universities for teaching, lecturing, research and curriculum development.
>
> "We often have university affiliation grants," Mr. Duffey said in an interview before he left for Vancouver. "This is the first time we've decided to start awarding three or four a year that involved three countries in North America."... Each USIA award will carry about $100,000, plus travel and per diem expenses, for exchanges of faculty, administrators and educational materials.
>
> The agreement, part of the broadened dialogue that has come out of the North American Free Trade Agreement, will support an array of projects focused on history, economic development, international trade and the environment.
>
> "What we seek to do is, among other things, nothing less than dismantling barriers to academic mobility," Mr. Duffey said in a speech at the conference.
>
> Mr. Duffey said he expects the North American countries to succeed in achieving a sense of regional community where the quest for a common community of nations in Western Europe has foundered.
>
> "We're trying to reverse the tradition of nationalism and people, who in looking to their identity, look backwards to the past," he said. "Instead, we want them to look to the future." (p. A–5)

THE FOLLOWING LETTER FROM UTAH GOVERNOR MICHAEL O. LEAVITT AND his State Superintendent of Public Instruction Scott W. Bean, dated September 30, 1993, gave a clear picture of the role of the governors of the individual states in implementing United Nations Educational, Scientific and Cultural Organization's (UNESCO) lifelong learning "cradle-to-grave" agenda in the United States. Utah's state report, "A Utah Perspective on the National Education Goals," was written and edited by Dr. David E. Nelson of the Utah State Office of Education who was also involved in the 1984 Utah OBE grant. Some excerpts follow:

> At the education summit in Charlottesville, Virginia, in September 1989, the nation's governors agreed to establish national education goals and a system to assess and monitor progress toward achieving them. Today, September 30, 1993, the anniversary of the historic summit, the National Education Goals Panel will issue its third annual education report. The report will focus on national and state progress toward achieving the education goals set in 1990 by the President and the governors. This progress report will inform the nation on how well we are doing on each of the goals. The governors also agreed to report individually on efforts of their respective states related to their state's performance toward achieving the national goals.
>
> Our own report, "A Utah Perspective on the National Education Goals," is issued to citizens of the state of Utah to inform them on the progress being made in our state toward the national goals. Because the goals are "cradle to grave" and cover the preschool years and the after school years,

the information has been compiled from many state agencies. Meeting all of these six goals will require the coordination and work of all state agencies.

IN LONNIE HARP'S ARTICLE "WIDELY MIXED TEST RESULTS LEAVE SOME in Kentucky Puzzled," which appeared in *Education Week*'s October 13, 1993 issue, the problems with the national reform leader's implementation of its widely-acclaimed restructuring—*Kentucky Education Restructuring Act* (KERA)—were outlined. An excerpt follows:

> As Kentucky moves toward implementation of its path-breaking system of rewards and sanctions for schools, state students have handed officials a hard-to-read snapshot of the progress of reform.
>
> Results of the second year of a new open-ended assessment system, released last month, produced widely mixed results and, in the case of older students, some troubling declines.

THE NOVEMBER 15, 1993 ISSUE OF *THE ATLANTA CONSTITUTION* CARRIED an article entitled "Ware Students Are Drawn to Swampy Experiment: Magnet School Makes Okefenokee Its Lab." Outlining what could be interpreted as the use of magnet/charter schools in a school-to-work scenario, excerpts follow:

> The Ware County School of Agriculture, Environmental and Forestry Sciences is an experiment in educational excellence that was years in the dreaming and application-pending stages.
>
> The concept was to create a magnet school unlike any other in the Southeast, a school where the study of sciences most important to the surrounding land would be incorporated into almost all the curricula. That would produce graduates oriented toward the disciplines most needed by employers in the region's forestry and agriculture industries.

IN 1993 THE SCHOOL TO WORK OPPORTUNITIES ACT PASSED THE HOUSE of Representatives without a roll call vote. [It passed the Senate in 1994, ed.] This legislation called for Soviet/German full employment/quota-type system, incorporating the Danish model for polytech education. Anyone familiar with this legislation will recognize the similarity between its wording and the late Professor Eugene Boyce's definition of communist polytech education (found in this book's 1983 entry for *The Coming Revolution in Education*) which states that the communists "do not educate people for jobs that do not exist. No such direct, controlled relationship between education and jobs exists in democratic countries."

IN A CRITIQUE OF H.R. 6—*THE ELEMENTARY AND SECONDARY EDUCATION Reauthorization Act of 1993*—Cynthia Weatherly wrote in a memo to this writer:

> HR 6 is an omnibus bill originally presented to Congress in January 1993 as a reauthorization bill for *The Elementary and Secondary Education Act of 1965*. The first and last paragraphs of this 901–page tome are the only parts of the

original bill which remain. 886 pages are printed in italics, which means that there are 886 pages of new language, otherwise known as "new law." *Goals 2000* and the National Education Goals Panel form the framework for HR 6. All of the education proposals in HR 6 are constructed in such a way as to cause "the nation to meet the national education goals." Therefore, instead of a reauthorization bill for *ESEA 1965*, HR 6 becomes the implementation bill for *Goals 2000* and the School-to-Work bills. One of the most controversial components included in HR 6 deals with basic pedagogy in which the framers deny the need for basic skills acquisition before engaging in more complex tasks. References to more controversial components follow:

> [T]he "disproven theory that children must learn basic skills before engaging in more complex tasks continues to dominate strategies for classroom instruction, resulting in emphasis on repetitive drill and practice at the expense of content-rich instruction, accelerated curricula, and effective teaching to high standards. Use of low-level tests that are not aligned with curricula fails to provide adequate information about what children know and can do and encourages curricula and instruction that focus on the low-level skills measured by such tests.

> [H.R. 6] Provides for restructuring of our nation's education and social services delivery systems.... Local schools may use federal funds to serve as centers for delivery of education and human services for members of the community; unaccountable consolidation of programs; waivers of laws, outcome-based education language and practices; parents as partners skill training; i.e. "All parents can contribute to their children's success by helping at home and becoming partners with teachers so that children can achieve high standards." Requires school-parent compacts that outline how parents, staff and students will share responsibility for student achievement and means by which school and parents will build and develop a partnership, etc.; facilitates school-to-work transition; encouragement to pursue public school choice, and development of charter schools.

WELCOME NEWS ON THE OUTCOME-BASED EDUCATION FRONT WAS REPORTED in an article entitled "In Littleton, Colorado, Voters Expel Education Faddists," which appeared in the November 18, 1993 issue of *The Wall Street Journal*. Excerpts from this article which illustrate how David overcame Goliath in the late twentieth century and reveal the extent of controversy raging in Littleton over its school system's adoption of "outcomes-based education" (OBE) follow:

> There [Littleton, CO.], a slate of three "back-to-basics" candidates crushed another coalition, including two incumbents, that supported a host of trendy educational reforms and was backed by the educational establishment. All 15 principals, for example, released an open letter to voters denouncing the insurgent slate. Yet the margin of victory was nearly 2 to 1. What had so galvanized voters? The fact that their district is a national leader in implementing "outcome-based education" (OBE) and that officials there had, as the journal *Education Week* explained in a pre-election article acknowledging the contests' significance, "pioneered new performance assessments and standards for high school graduation."

> ...Having acknowledged that American schools are in need of improve-

ment, a growing number of educators are gravitating toward the view that
the fault lies in too much emphasis on "content knowledge" and not enough
concern, to quote the Littleton principal again, with "decision-making skills,
thinking skills, and the ability to find and use information." Or, to quote the
Littleton elementary principals' letter, students "must do more than spell
and compute. They must be able to reason, persuade and solve problems."

Nevertheless, OBE proponents, with their emphasis on "thinking skills,"
repeatedly contrast their theory with an approach that hasn't been in vogue
for decades, one of perpetual rote learning in which all creativity is stifled.
Education Week is typical in presenting this caricature. It described the
Littleton reforms as nothing more than encouraging students "to focus on
problem-solving rather than memorization"—as if a nation in which only
32% of 17-year-olds in a 1986 survey could place the Civil War in the correct
half-century was in danger of stuffing too many facts into students' heads.

Across America, school districts are considering, or putting in place,
reforms similar to those in Littleton. Educators, often with the best of intentions, are rewriting report cards to include fuzzy criteria such as self-esteem
and interpersonal relationships. They are denigrating standardized measurements of knowledge and the memorization of facts. To be sure, not all of the
rethinking is misguided, but some of it amounts to dubious experimentation
on children. Littleton proves that with the proper candidates, the movement
toward a vague, "skill-oriented" curriculum can be stopped in its tracks.

[Ed. Note: Very regrettably the above refreshing and impressive victory over
the bureaucracy was short-lived. Slick change agent tactics managed to
bring at least one new supposedly anti-reform, back-to-basics board member
"on board" what one hoped to be a sinking ship, thus assuring a return to
implementation of the "nationally-detested" OBE. Littleton, Colorado became
one of Willard Daggett's Model School systems and a national model for
implementation of outcome-based education.

Six years later Littleton tragically made front-page news nationally and
internationally when on April 20, 1999, two teenagers at Columbine High
School killed twelve students and one teacher, wounding many others with
shotgun blasts, automatic pistol fire, and homemade pipe bombs, after which
they took their own lives. This was the worst of what has become a rash of
school violence against fellow students and teachers by young people. The
sites of this lengthening list of tragedies are also sites of schools and school
systems which have been restructured and embraced the outcome-based/
performance-based/mastery learning concepts of schooling, with all the
programs and methods with which they are associated. This writer, in a
letter to the editor published by several national journals, discussed what
she perceives to be a possible cause of such violence. The text of this letter
is reprinted here in its entirety:

> An important question should be examined in regard to the tragedy in
> Littleton, Colorado. "What was going on inside the brains of the two boys
> who committed this terrible crime?"
>
> Not only should Americans point the finger at violent television as a
> reason for copycat violence. They should examine the effects of computers
> and computer games on the human brain. I am no expert, but the computer is

an operant conditioning machine and no less than the late Harvard Professor B.F. Skinner, the father of operant conditioning, referred to it as "his box." Operant conditioning bypasses the brain with all the important functions which distinguish man from an animal: memory, conscience, imagination, insight, and intuition, functions by which human beings know absolutes and truths and are able to know God.

Use of computer programming (simulation/virtual reality) to train individuals to fly an airplane, perform surgery, etc. serve a very useful purpose. On the other hand, the same simulation/virtual reality computer war game videos which allow the individual to engage in killing in a bloody and violent atmosphere, played over and over again, desensitize the individual to the evil act of killing, whereby the individual, as a programmed robot, finds it increasingly easy to carry this distorted vision of reality outside into other areas of his life, such as a school building or playground. If that individual happens to be full of hatred, it doesn't take much imagination to figure out what "programmed" action he or she may take in order to vent that hatred and frustration.

The use of computer-assisted instruction in school, which unfortunately has been accepted as the alternative to traditional education, should also be of some concern to those seeking an answer to school violence. The same operant conditioning, upon which school programs for all disciplines is based, can be used for training an individual to perform. Skinner said "I could make a pigeon a high achiever by reinforcing (rewarding) it on a proper schedule" and "What is reinforced (rewarded) will be repeated." Such "training" is not "education" in the traditional sense since it does not transfer. With traditional academic "education" a student is capable of transferring what he learns to other areas of his life, at some future time. He can store the information for future use; it is in his brain where it is able to be reflected upon, where his soul, memory and conscience are able to influence the information and decisions he makes.

Not so with operant conditioning where no such transfer occurs. Children who spend their school years "learning" (being "trained") in this manner can be expected to experience a certain frustration and dehumanization in their behavior since the creative functions of the brain are being constantly cut off. Operant conditioning experiments on animals have caused similar frustration and violent behavior.

If Littleton, Colorado schools are anything like other schools around the nation, they are using the highly controversial "scientific research-based" Outcome-Based Education/Mastery Learning/Direct Instruction based on Skinnerian behavioral psychology, which is necessary for School-to-Work programs and workforce training. OBE and computer-assisted instruction go together as a hand fits in a glove. The combination amounts to a most lethal concoction for our children.

I fear that unless we examine the use and effect of video games and the use for twelve years of computers in the classroom we may experience more Littletons. Is it too far-fetched to assume that he who is trained like an animal may just end up behaving like an animal?]

EDDIE PRICE, A 39-YEAR-OLD SOCIAL STUDIES TEACHER WITH SEVENTEEN years of teaching experience, wrote "A Reign of Terror—Impressions of KERA" which appeared in the December, 1993 issue of *The Hancock Clarion* of Hawesville, Kentucky. Excerpts from his important and, one might point out, extremely courageous article follow:

> I would never do anything to jeopardize my teaching career or, even more importantly, the security of my family, but I MUST speak out against what I perceive as a massive wrong in education—the Kentucky Education Reform Act (KERA).
>
> The perpetrators of KERA began inundating our schools with mountains of regulations, restrictions, and KERA mandates.... When we expressed our concerns we were told "Be patient.... Give KERA a chance.... Teachers, we need your help. This is a partnership."
>
> KERA's Outcomes appeared to throw the hard, objective, factual subject matter out the window in favor of affective goals (more concerned with emotions and feelings). Our curriculum would have to be pared down and structured around values and attitudes.
>
> When teachers voiced concerns about not meeting the Valued Outcomes, they were "soothed" with the explanation that schools would be given the chance to improve. "A 'Kentucky Distinguished Educator' will be sent to your building to help you grow." Then I learned that this official had the absolute power to declare the school "A School in Crisis"! The principal, and individual teachers could be eliminated with the single stroke of a pen. Past performances, evaluations, educational degrees, experience, awards, student achievement outside of KERA would mean nothing....
>
> When I sat down and read the entire history of KERA's evolution, I realized that our lawmakers and, even worse, our public had been skillfully and strategically duped. KERA had been slickly packaged in deceptive language of "glittering generalities" that the public seemed eager to swallow in the name of reform. Who could argue with such glossy words as "excellence," "revamping," "progress," "outcome-based," "self-esteem," etc., unless they are "traditional," "hidebound," "inflexible," and "resistant to change"? I realized that our distinguished and infallible commissioner basked in the full limelight of a press he had masterfully managed. Kentucky newspaper editors had been appointed to state committees in the name of "progress" and their editorials provided—free of charge—an excellent soapbox from which to indoctrinate the public. Pro-KERA articles and comments have no problem making headlines while others with opposing views must pay exorbitant sums for "political advertisements." School principals and test scores can be subjectively manipulated from above to bring down the Kentucky Distinguished Educators upon schools "not politically correct." For a "dissident," teaching in the public schools today is similar to living under a Stalinist "Reign of Terror."
>
> This is all so incredibly un-American that someone, maybe the FBI again, must investigate our legislature to discover how and why such a massive piece of legislation passed without more discussion. How many millions have already been squandered? How many millions more? No one truly had a chance to examine it fully. The public education hearings held across the state were structured around a preconceived plan devised by a national organization—the Pritchard Committee. The whole thing was rammed down the public's throat before anyone could mobilize. Most concerned were placated by the false notion that parents and teachers would have more control with the "depoliticalization" of education. The end result? Our local, elected school boards (those most responsive to a community's needs) were virtually

stripped of their power while state control drastically tightened. The state now mandates the outcomes, approves the curriculum, trains the teachers, and judges the performance of students—all of which must conform to KERA.

[Ed. Note: Had the media, over the past ten years, been willing to publish the many articles and letters to the editor which mirrored Eddie Price's concerns, the national restructuring effort would be dead in its tracks. Even with censorship of opponents' views, restructuring has run up against intense opposition and is "in deep trouble." An article which appeared in the October 10, 1998 issue of the Louisville, Kentucky *Courier Journal* entitled "Kentucky Schools Test Scores Vary Little from Last Year" shows that KERA has been a total flop, as have all the other multi-million dollar, corporation-backed state reform acts implemented across the country. Wherever Carnegie's David Hornbeck goes one can expect a first-class academic flop! Of course, flops are essential in order to convince the public that "workforce training" is the solution—the deliberate dumbing down at work.]

1994

U.S. COALITION FOR EDUCATION FOR ALL: A HISTORY WAS PUBLISHED IN 1994 by the U.S. Coalition for Education for All based in Washington, D.C. Excerpts from that publication follow:

> U.S. delegates from government agencies and non-governmental organizations participated in the 1990 World Conference and helped to prepare the Education for All (EFA) goals and action plan. In February 1991 the U. S. Coalition for Education for All (USCEFA) was created to promote EFA awareness and activities in the United States and to serve as a link to the global EFA movement.... In 1991, USCEFA held its first major conference, "Learning for All: Bridging Domestic and International Education."...
>
> ...From this conference the USCEFA's agenda unfolded. USCEFA organized a symposium entitled "Integrating Social Services and Education: A Look at Collaboration and Delivery." At the first meeting of the International Consultative Forum on EFA, U.N. sponsors singled out USCEFA as a model for national initiatives supporting basic education worldwide. This forum selected USCEFA to lead an international task force to explore the involvement of media in education....
>
> USCEFA's 1994 main events included: a symposium entitled "The Educational Implications of NAFTA" [*North American Free Trade Agreement*] that addressed educational issues emerging in the wake of the signing of the NAFTA agreement; co-sponsorship of a global teleconference entitled "Global Interdependence: the United States and the Third World." USCEFA's most prominent 1994 event is its December conference; "The Revolution in World Education: Toward Systemic Change." This conference explores systemic change in education and the achievement of educational goals and outcomes around the world.... USCEFA will continue to cooperate internationally to keep the spirit of the Jomtien Conference alive and to make Education for All a reality at home and abroad.

"To OBE or Not to OBE?" was the question posed by Marjorie Le-
dell, associate of William Spady's in his High Success Network, in her article
for *Educational Leadership*'s January 1994 issue. From page 18 we read:

> Finally, raise the real issue and depend on democracy. Don't let "to OBE
> or Not to OBE" or "to implement or not implement efforts to improve student
> learning" cloud the overdue national debate about whether public education
> should exist or be replaced with publicly funded private education.

The January 1994 issue of *The Effective School Report* carried an
article entitled "Alternative Assessment of Student Achievement: The Open
Book Test" by Thomas A. Kelly, Ph.D. An excerpt follows:

> All classroom tests should be open book tests.... We are moving toward
> higher level thinking and away from memorization of facts. Give them the
> facts. Once we leave school, we can use references any time we want. We
> are no longer required to memorize endless lists of facts, formulas, etc. Open
> book tests will move school activities much closer to real life activities. The
> human brain should be used for processing, not storage.

[Ed. Note: Initially the writer's reaction to this quote was disbelief, and then
plain revulsion over what can only be referred to as a pervasive mindset
found in those educators who have been "transformed" into managers of
the learning process, total quality technicians, etc. A true understanding of
the significance of Dr. Kelly's statement came to me only after GenYvette
Sutton, a fine researcher from Pennsylvania, made the following percep-
tive comments as part of her contribution to a video entitled "The Truth
behind Outcome-Based Education" in which this writer also participated.[24]
In the segment of the video dealing with the dangers of Skinnerian operant
conditioning used in computer programming, the new emphasis on critical thinking, and Dr. Kelly's comments regarding the brain being used for
processing and not for storage, Sutton said

> True education should expand all the faculties of the mind: memory,
> conscience, imagination, insight, intuition and brain. When you just process
> information, you deny or cut off those other functions of the mind and re-
> duce it to the brain alone, which is just simply [responding to stimuli]. The
> danger is unbelievable....
> Columbia Teachers College held a symposium on "Knowing: How We
> Come to Know Things" and how important this is. Some speakers said that
> much that is being done in education denies these other functions of the
> mind and reduces them to the [responsive] brain alone. They reminded us
> that those other functions—memory, conscience, imagination, insight, and
> intuition—are the functions by which we know absolutes and truths, [discern
> right from wrong], and are able to know God.

Outcome-based education, because it concentrates on the "end product"
of its process, can be said to restrict the student's mental functioning to the
level Kelly described as "processing." The predetermined goals and outcomes
prevent the student from using brain functions which make him unique as
a human being. Success in an outcome-based environment is restricted to

performing prescribed tasks to the point of automaticity. The functions of memory and creativity are not used, nor are they considered necessary to succeed in an OBE program or any program that uses Skinnerian mastery learning or direct instruction. Predictability is the bottom line for OBE, limiting the student to only those responses which are prescribed. When trained by OBE methodology, the student cannot fail unless he employs creativity and produces an unpredicted response. In an OBE environment, he can believe only that which is acceptable. The most predictable outcome, over time, is frustration—and ultimately, low achievement and behavior problems. We should be reminded that robots, although generally reliable, have no feelings and are not governed by conscience.

What a chilling thought.]

EDUCATION WEEK CARRIED AN ARTICLE IN ITS MARCH 16, 1994 ISSUE entitled "Back to the Future—with Funding from NASDC and Direction from the Hudson Institute, the Modern Red Schoolhouse Updates an American Icon for the 90's" by Lynn Olson. Excerpts follow:

> Of all the design teams funded by the New American Schools Development Corporation in 1992, the Modern Red Schoolhouse was the one with the closest ties to the Republican Administration then in power and its ideological heart....
>
> ...Its chief sponsor is the Hudson Institute, a public policy center based in Indianapolis that made its reputation analyzing national security issues. Hudson's board of trustees includes former Gov. Pierre S. du Pont, IV, of Delaware and former Vice President Dan Quayle.
>
> William J. Bennett, a U.S. Secretary of Education under President Ronald Reagan, served as chairman of the design team. Bennett, an outspoken proponent of private school choice, left the project last year when he formed Empower America, a conservative think tank based in Washington. Bennett once described the Modern Red Schoolhouse to *The Washington Times* as a "conservative plan with the three C's at its core: content, character, and choice."
>
> Yet, in many ways, the Modern Red Schoolhouse defies political or ideological labels. Some of its instructional approaches, such as multi-age homerooms and self-paced learning, would be considered "radical" by observers on both sides of the political aisle.

PRESIDENT CLINTON SIGNED *GOALS 2000 ACT* ON MARCH 24, 1994. THIS legislation laid a large portion of the groundwork for radical restructuring of the nation's schools from the teaching of academics to workforce training.

MICHIGAN'S STATE BOARD OF EDUCATION ADOPTED THE FINAL VERSION OF the *Communication Arts Framework for the High School Proficiency Test* in April of 1994. Extensive excerpts from the *Framework*, representative of standards adopted throughout the country intended to assist students in entering the workforce or in pursuing higher education, follow:

Assessment Framework for the Michigan High School
Proficiency Test in Reading

INTRODUCTION

One of the more widely used methods of control is legislatively mandated graduation standards that require students to pass state mandated tests (Berk, 1986).... The lesson seems to be that if tests remain inadequate, so will the curriculum they influence.

The challenge for Michigan is to create a reading/communication arts framework for curriculum and assessment that does not narrow the curriculum. To prevent this from happening, the Model Core Curriculum Outcomes in Reading, the foundation upon which the proficiency test is based, must be incorporated into a framework that is consistent with the emerging trends in the field. The Model Core Curriculum Outcomes in Reading are derived from the Michigan Reading Association's definition of reading (Wixson & Peters, 1984). The definition provided a theoretical foundation for changing reading instruction and assessment in the state. It is based on a constructivist view of reading that posits, "Reading is the process of constructing meaning through the dynamic interaction among the reader, the text, and the context of the reading situation." (Wixson & Peters, p. 4)...

While the constructivist perspective is a useful way to view the reading process, it must be expanded to include the social dimension of learning. This perspective is best illustrated by the work of Vygotsky (1978). He contended that higher cognitive learning is rooted in social connections; and as a result, knowledge is socially constructed as learners engage in holistic and authentic activities (Englert & Palincsar, 1991; Palincsar & Klenk, 1992)....

A common feature of the constructivist and socioconstructivist views of reading is the importance placed on metacognition—purposeful, effortful, self-regulated, active, intentional learning.... What is called for is a vision of curriculum that incorporates a socioconstructivist view of reading into a curriculum framework that defines the context for constructing meaning in a way that is consistent with the Model Core Curriculum.

A New Vision

For too long a period of time the reading/communication arts area has avoided the question: *Is there a content to reading/communication arts?* [emphasis in original]... At the elementary level the predominate focus is process—reading, writing, viewing, listening and speaking. While literature has recently assumed a more prominent role, the ideas and issues that persist and recur over time are relegated to a secondary level of importance. As a result, literature instruction at the elementary level is haphazard at best (Walmsley & Walp, 1992).

At the middle and high school levels the emphasis is primarily on content, content which is often narrowly defined by literary studies of the canon. Instruction resembles more of a transfusionist's perspective in which students receive information much in the same way patients receive blood (Applebee, 1989; Crews, 1992). Taught in this manner, content is memorized, regurgitated, and trivialized. When this occurs, the high school literature curriculum becomes decontextualized and fragmented (Purves, 1992). In this context the primary goal is to understand a novel, short story, poem, or play; the result is that the literary work becomes the end rather than a means to the end. What is absent from both the process and content perspectives is the application of knowledge in authentic ways. What is needed is a vision of reading/communication arts curriculum that more explicitly defines the context for constructing meaning in a more meaningful way, one that fosters active learning in authentic contexts such as the home, community, and the workplace.

An Expanding View of Text

[T]here is more to developing a curriculum than content. The ideas, themes, issues, and problems that make up the content of text must be placed in a framework that is linked to other considerations such as: what is to be learned, how it is to be learned, in what context it is to be applied, and how is it to be assessed? The framework becomes the common thread that ties together all the components of the instructional system.

...The context in which this type of learning occurs is prescribed by a reading/communication arts curriculum that provides students with learning opportunities. These learning opportunities... apply their existing knowledge to issues and problems that result in new understandings, to synthesize and communicate what they have learned, to generate new knowledge or creative applications, and to think critically about the content and make decisions or take actions that relate to it. This type of innovative curriculum points the way toward higher, richer levels of knowing that are assessed in authentic ways.

Overview of the Framework

The primary goal of the Reading/Communication Arts Framework described in this document is to develop independent, self-sufficient, lifelong learners whose understandings and capabilities allow them to become personally, socially, and civically involved in the world around them... requires the integration of disciplinary knowledge with learner characteristics that promote positive attitudes and dispositions. These elements... guide the systematic delivery of the curriculum. Student achievement of the goals is determined by an assessment system that uses authentic performances to evaluate student proficiency. (See Figure 1)

Figure 1
Communication Arts/Reading Framework for Curriculum and Assessment
GOALS
RESOURCES
DISCIPLINARY KNOWLEGE LEARNER CHARACTERISTICS *Literary Knowledge *Dispositions of Thoughtfulness *Discourse Knowledge *Metacognitive Knowledge *Process Knowledge *Attitudes and Perceptions
AUTHENTIC APPLICATION OF KNOWLEDGE *Engaging *Meaningful *Functional *Integrated
READING OUTCOMES
CURRICULUM CONSIDERATIONS
ASSESSMENT SYSTEM *Model Tasks *Portfolio *On-Demand Tasks

[Ed. Note: The material that was emphasized in the *Assessment Framework for the Michigan High School Proficiency Test in Reading* above is an excellent explanation of the Whole Language philosophy. When education materials refer to "authentic" applications of learning, that means reading or any other learning which is "applied" in a real world setting; for instance, manuals of instruction for operation of household appliances, or letters to the editor concerning a topic which has been discussed in the classroom and about which the student has formulated an "acceptable" position. Anywhere the *Michigan Framework* mentions "social dimensions of learning" or "socio-constructive views of learning" it is saying that learning has to be applied in a social setting or have a social end. In this context, learning for the sake of learning and without prejudice regarding a social point of view is unacceptable. There must be a "social construction" taking place for the learning to be meaningful. This is a good illustration of how children obtain a social/political point of view which is often contrary to that of their parents.

The reference to and building upon the work of Vygotsky indicates the waywardness of the *Michigan Framework*. L.S. Vygotsky was a Soviet psychologist and mentor to the infamous psychologist of the same origin, A.R. Luria. Vygotsky and Luria conducted research in the teaching of higher level skills—known in this country as Higher Order Thinking Skills (HOTS)—which deals with the changing of attitudes, values and beliefs. "Constructivist" learning is a term which Vygotsky used when training teachers to "build on the knowledge that children have already obtained" and which is often mistaken to mean building one concept upon another. This could not be further from the truth. With Vygotsky in mind, the building of knowledge is always in a particular direction—that which has been determined by the social/political outcomes desired by the one who is teaching or directing the student's efforts. The *Michigan Framework*—and most other states' frameworks—are based on the idea that the "method of control" is a state-mandated test which reflects the curriculum—teach to the test.]

EDUCATION WEEK PUBLISHED THE ARTICLE "SUCCESS WITH COALITION RE-forms Seen Limited in Some Schools" by Debra Viadero of New Orleans on April 13, 1994. An excerpt follows:

> Some of the first studies to look at the acclaimed Coalition of Essential Schools reform network suggest that some participating schools are having limited success in implementing its ideas.
>
> Five studies on coalition schools were presented here last week during the annual meeting of the American Education Research Association. Collectively, they draw on the experiences of 24 schools nationwide. The coalition currently has nearly 160 member schools.
>
> Four of the five studies suggest that, while some teachers have made profound changes in their teaching styles as a result of involvement in the coalition, few, if any, of the schools studied have implemented its philosophy wholesale. Some schools, facing teacher dissension or financial or district pressures, have abandoned it.

THE NATIONAL SCHOOL BOARDS ASSOCIATION (NSBA) RECOMMENDED RADI-cal changes for local school boards at its annual meeting in New Orleans in April of 1994. An article entitled "N.S.B.A. Endorses All Alternatives to Traditional School Governance" in *Education Week* for April 13, 1994 relates the following:

"A New Framework for School Governance" endorses school-based decision-making, charter schools, and other alternatives to traditional governance structures, provided they meet local needs.... Much of the report focuses on improving the alignment of government services at all levels so that children can meet high academic standards.

In addition to the national education goals, the new report advocates the creation of national goals for child and youth development.... Establishing explicit, substantive goals based on children's needs will allow providers to coordinate services more effectively and insure that help is available to those in need.

[Ed. Note: What a difference seventeen years can make! On March 27, 1977 the immediate past president of the National School Boards Association warned school board members "to be aware of and leery of... proposals for public involvement in public school operations that would shift decision-making authority to 'vaguely-defined groups of citizens' at the school site level," which is exactly what NSBA meant when it called for "alternatives to traditional governance structures" in 1994.]

SCHOOL-TO-WORK TRANSITION IN THE UNITED STATES: THE CASE OF THE *Missing Social Partners—A Report of the Governance and Finance Team of the Comparative Learning Teams Project* (Center for Learning and Competitiveness, School of Public Affairs of the University of Maryland: College Park, Md., 1994) was prepared by Robert W. Glover, team leader for the Center for the Study of Human Resources, and Alan Weisberg, Foothill Associates, with assistance from team members: Andrew M. Churchill, Jobs for the Future; Sharon Knotts Green, Motorola, Inc.; Robert McPherson, Center for the Study of Human Resources; Janet Lewis, Hewlett Packard Corporation; Quint Rahberger, Oregon Bureau of Labor and Industries; Mark Scott, Center for Learning and Competitiveness; and F. Eugene Scott, Sutter Health Systems. This document was published as a joint project of the Center for Learning and Competitiveness (CLC) and The Greater Austin [Texas] Chamber of Commerce.

The CLC Advisory Board includes the following persons: The Hon. William E. Brock,[25] chair, senior partner of The Brock Group; Dr. Anthony P. Carnavale, director of Human Resource Studies, Committee for Economic Development; Nancy S. Grasmick, state superintendent of schools for the State of Maryland; Dr. Herbert J. Grover, professor of education, University of Wisconsin at Green Bay; Mayor Vera Katz, Portand, Oregon; Eugenia Kemble, assistant to the president for educational issues, American Federation of Teachers/AFL-CIO; The Hon. John R. McKernan, Jr., governor of Maine; Hilary C. Pennington, president, Jobs for the Future; William B. Rouse, chief executive officer, Search Technology, Inc.; and, Marc Tucker, president, National Center on Education and the Economy. Anne Heald is the executive director of the CLC.

Excerpts from *School-to-Work Transition in the United States* follow:

In February 1993, CLC brought together 25 leading experts from state and federal organizations as well as international leaders, to identify the most pressing questions and problems that confront policymakers and practitioners working to build school-to-work transition systems in the United States. The outcome of that meeting was a consensus that there were five areas in need of immediate in-depth attention:

- Building a System: Governance and Finance
- Developing Standards, Assessment and Credentialing
- Building Partnerships: The Role of Economic Actors
- Designing Quality Programs
- Providing Career Guidance

To address these issues, and with the generous financial support of the German Marshall Fund of the United States, CLC initiated its Comparative Learning Teams Project. CLC issued a request for proposals nationwide, and respondents were asked to select one of these areas as the focus for an international learning investigation, developing levels of inquiry in substantial detail and with specific outcomes for their trip. The capacity of teams to effectively disseminate their findings in a way that would positively impact on the development of school-to-work systems in the United States was a key selection criteria.

CLC awarded grants to five organizations in the school-to-work transition field who led, planned and supported a Comparative Learning Team. The grants enabled each team of at least nine people to visit two European sites where sophisticated school-to-work transition teams operate. Each comparative learning team participated in carefully planned 12– to 14–day working sessions in Germany, Denmark, the United Kingdom, Switzerland and Sweden, where they gained direct access to their foreign counterparts and first-hand exposure to European systems....

Already, the work of the comparative learning teams has had an impact on system-building in the United States. Team members were able to build on their European experience when designing state systems under the guidelines of the new Federal School-to-Work Opportunities Act. Officials in the Departments of Labor and Education, working on school-to-work policies, were briefed.... Participants have spoken at numerous conferences, and published comments in newspapers and newsletters. Key findings of the teams are guiding further policy work around key issues such as the engagement of industry in school-to-work programs and in the design of skill standards....

For over a decade American policy leaders have looked to Europe for insight into how to move young people effectively from school to the workforce, while providing them with relevant and valuable skills. The impressive achievements of European systems triggered much enthusiasm in this country about the potential positive impact of reform here.

Now with the passage of the school-to-work legislation, and with states actively attempting to build school-to-work transition systems... the international experience remains highly significant. Issues that challenge American policymakers in building systems, such as developing appropriate funding mechanisms, engaging industry partnership and ensuring relevant standards, have long been at the core of investigation in Europe....

...As states and sites move to implement comprehensive reform in the United States under the auspices of the School-to-Work Opportunities Act, all five reports will provide valuable information and insight into the best international lessons.... We want to express our thanks to the lead organizations for the project: The Austin [Texas] Chamber of Commerce, the New

Standards Project [Marc Tucker's National Center for Education and the Economy program], The Council of Chief State School Officers, the National Alliance of Business, and the Northwest Regional Educational Laboratory.

The following quote from an article in the May 14, 1984 issue of *The Washington Post* entitled "Industrial Policy Urged for GOP" sheds some light on behind-the-scenes activities which have led to acceptance of corporate-fascist workforce training necessary for a planned economy:

> A conservative study group founded by supporters of President Reagan is about to issue a report that advocates Republicans shed some of their deep-rooted antipathy to a planned economy. The "Industrial Policy Debate" is to be issued today by the Institute for Contemporary Studies, a think tank founded by Presidential Counselor Edwin Meese, Secretary of Defense Caspar Weinberger, and other Reagan supporters.

It should also be pointed out that Secretary of Defense Caspar Weinberger served as Secretary of the U.S. Department of Health, Education, and Welfare in the Nixon Administration in 1973, and that he oversaw the development and publication of the Planning, Programming, Budgeting and Evaluation Systems (PPB[E]S) *State Educational Records and Reports Series* handbooks which document the establishment of the central planning system for the USA. One of the handbooks included in this series entitled *Financial Accounting: Classifications and Standard Terminology for Local and State School Systems* stated in its preface:

> Another project funded by the Office of Education from 1968 to 1971 was the development of a program, planning, budgeting, and evaluation conceptual design under the sponsorship of the Association of School Business Officials' Research Corporation.... The emphasis in this project is on the development of a goal-oriented system for evaluating programs.[26]

[Ed. Note: One can't resist asking the politically incorrect questions: When were the American people asked if they wanted to exchange our free enterprise system for the socialist school-to-work system identified with European countries? When was the decision made, and by whom, that the United States would benefit from a planned economy, when this nation has served as the lighthouse for the world, beckoning millions to its shores to benefit from the upward mobility provided by the free enterprise system? By this time the reader should seriously question the legitimacy of the "lead organizations" for the Comparative Learning Teams Project—organizations that this book has documented to be involved in "the deliberate dumbing down" of America.]

A PAPER ENTITLED "ISSUE FOR DESIGNING A SYSTEM OF SKILL STANDARDS and Certification for the American Workforce: On What Basis Should Occupation/Skill/Industry Clusters Be Organized?" by Robert W. Glover of the Center for the Study of Human Resources, University of Texas at Austin, was prepared for the U.S. Department of Labor in May of 1994. Mr. Glover has contributed to several national and international studies, including

America's Choice: High Skills or Low Wages![27] and was the author of the Texas Department of Commerce's publication entitled *Developing a System of Skill Standards for the State of Texas* (January 1993). Excerpts from Glover's paper follow:

The Appeal of Setting National Standards as a Device To Reform and Upgrade American Learning Systems

In its report published in June 1990, the Commission on Skills of the American Workforce placed the development of skill standards and certification on the table as a major policy instrument for improving the education and training preparation of the American Workforce.... Specifically, the Commission's first recommendation called for "A new educational performance standard... for all students, to be met by age 16... established nationally" (p. 69)... [and] described the new assessment system as focusing on thinking-based achievement rather than routine skills. This new certification, which has come to be called the Certificate of Initial Mastery was envisioned as a cumulative assessment and certification process involving a variety of assessments, including a portfolio of performances and projects. It was to be administered by an independent examining organization and focus on "thinking-based achievement, not routine skills."

Recommendation number 3... called for the development of "a comprehensive system of Technical and Professional Certificates and associate's degrees for the majority of our students and workers who do not pursue a baccalaureate degree" (*Commission on Skills of the American Workforce*, 1990, p. 77).

The Certificate of Initial Mastery aims to cover general workplace skills whereas the envisioned system of Technical and Professional Certificates and associate's degrees was aimed at assessment and certification of specific occupational skills. The two types of certification are parallel and complementary.... The two sets of skills are related but separable. Obtaining a Certificate of Initial Mastery was considered by the Commission as a gateway or threshold conveying eligibility to compete for Technical and Professional Certificates.

The Commission on Skills of the American Workforce recommended that the Certificate of Initial Mastery be "benchmarked to the highest standards in the world" [undefined, ed.] (p. 69). Likewise the standards of Professional and Technical Certificates should be "at least equal to those set by other advanced industrialized nations" (p. 77).

Since the publication of *America's Choice: High Skills or Low Wages!* in June 1990, considerable progress has been made toward moving the concept of a cumulative portfolio of tests, projects, and achievements into reality. Within a short year, public opinion about national testing made a remarkable transformation from high negative to positive (Marshall and Tucker, 1992). The Secretary's Commission on Achieving Necessary Skills (SCANS), chaired by William Brock (who also served as co-chair of the Commission on Skills of the American Workforce [U.S. Secretary of Labor]), developed an innovative taxonomy of transferable generic skills applicable to all workforce entrants in a high performance economy. The New Standards Project, under the direction of Marc Tucker of the National Center on Education and the Economy and Lauren Resnick of the Learning and Development Center at the University of Pittsburgh, working with a consortium of 19 states and 6 local school districts, is developing new approaches to assessment toward the creation of a certificate of initial mastery (National Center on Education and the Economy, 1994a, 1994b, and 1994c). Now the recommendations of the Commission are embodied in the *Goals 2000* legislation recently passed by Congress and signed into law.

As an amplification of the above report, the writer would like to quote from the presentation by Paul F. Cole, secretary-treasurer of the New York State AFL-CIO Chapter, at the Second Annual Model Schools Conference in Atlanta, Georgia in 1994. Mr. Cole's statements included:

> I worked on the critical thinking skills portion of the Secretary's Commission on Achieving Necessary Skills (SCANS) report. The fundamental revolution in the workplace called for restructuring of education to meet the challenge....
>
> Value-added students produce a high performance environment....[28]
>
> We must go from norm-referenced to criterion-referenced testing. Educational equality is the goal. We must benchmark nationally. Office of Educational Research and Improvement (OERI) study on standards reflected these changes to be made:
>
> 1. Setting standards
> 2. New assessments—portfolios, authentic assessment
> 3. System of credentialing
> 4. Curriculum frameworks
>
> Some industries are devising standards for school achievement. Queens Aviation High School, [Queens] New York, meets FAA standards. National Skill Standards Board is working on integrating comprehensive skill standards....
>
> Manipulation of symbols is a skill used with computers rather than direct observation of information. This will affect how we teach reading.

[Ed. Note: This last statement regarding reading should be considered very seriously. What changes in the teaching of reading have been promoted of late? Primarily, the "scientific, research-based, direct, systematic" Skinnerian behavioral approach characterized by direct instruction—and funded under the *Reading Excellence Act* in 1998. Is this emphasis an outgrowth of SCANS-related policies adopted by "partnerships" between government and business interests at the expense of real educational opportunities for children? In 1981 Professor Anthony Oettinger said in a speech that "in the modern context of functionalism, they [comic books], may not be all that bad" for instruction. Comic books and Paul Cole's "manipulation of symbols" have much in common. (See the Internet version for Appendix XI and XXV.)]

PRESIDENT BILL CLINTON SIGNED THE *SCHOOL-TO-WORK OPPORTUNITIES Act of 1994* on May 4, 1994. This law provided seed money to states for development of local partnerships of business, labor, government, education and community organizations to develop school-to-work systems.

THE *WASHINGTON POST* CARRIED AN ARTICLE ENTITLED "TRYING TO CATCH Up on Their Reading: Tutors Find What Students Miss" in its May 25, 1994 edition. Excerpts from this article follow:

Students are selected for the program by English teachers, counselors, and principals.... Sykes said the D.C. school system will establish "gates," or assessments at grades 3, 5, 6, 8 and 9. There will be no student who will move beyond that gate unless they have shown mastery skills to move to the next level. Sykes said the school system also is developing a statewide reading curriculum that would alleviate the problem of students missing lessons when they change schools in the District.

The students who are enrolled in the Sylvan Center [a private contractor which uses mastery learning, ed.] at Anacostia High School said they are proud to go there. There is no stigma attached to the program. In fact, they said, their friends want to know how to join them in a learning environment where the teachers pay close attention... and give them treats... don't seem irritated when they don't understand and congratulate them for every step of progress they make. "This program gives you confidence. It's fun to learn like this. If you do good, they give you awards."

Tarenia Rogers, 15, a tenth-grader, said the program gives her some-thing to look forward to when she goes to school. "It's like a job," she said. "When you come in here and work, *you get paid*" [emphasis in original]. When students score well or complete assignments, teachers reward them with tokens that can be used to buy products such as beads, basketballs and T-shirts at the Sylvan "store"—a display counter that stands in one corner of the classroom.

[Ed. Note: This is the school system in which William Spady and Thomas Sticht served as consultants in the implementation of the now infamous Mastery Learning program in 1978, and which in 1996 had the lowest test scores in the nation. Interesting that Washington, D.C. schools—like Chicago which experienced the "human tragedy" due to mastery learning—are again implementing the same Skinnerian rat training method for "tutoring" its inner city children. (See the Internet version for Appendix XXV.)]

THE CONFERENCE BOARD PUBLISHED *BUSINESS AND EDUCATION REFORM: The Fourth Wave—A Research Report* (CB Report No. 1091–94–RR) in 1994. Founded in 1916, The Conference Board was established with a two-fold purpose: 1) to improve the business enterprise system and 2) to enhance the contribution of business to society. To accomplish this, The Conference Board strives to be the leading global business membership organization that enables senior executives from all industries to explore and exchange ideas of importance concerning business policy and practices. The Board has offices in New York City, Brussels, Belgium, and Ottawa, Ontario, Canada. Some excerpts from this extremely important, 41-page document from The Conference Board follow:

A study of business involvement in systemic education reform shows that such reform:
- is a long-term, complex and politically charged process requiring on-going commitment
- demands that business collaborate with other important stakeholders to effect real reform
- requires clearly stated and explicit goals that place children first

- emphasizes structural changes within schools, communities and the public policy process.

[ddd]

...The business community now stands at a critical juncture in its involvement in school reform, with two significantly different pathways developing. The first, evidenced by the emergence of charter schools, privatization initiatives, and emphasis on school choice involves stepping outside the current system and attempting to improve education by starting anew. Businesses that choose this path accept the premise that the current system is irretrievably broken and cannot possibly be repaired by those working within it.

[ddd]

...Collaboration involves formal working relationships among business and school officials, social and human service agencies, parents and other relevant stakeholders to reform schools by changing the systems in which they are embedded, the reward structures that perpetuate them, and the defining features (e.g., curriculum, school days, performance measurement) of the schools themselves. The critical assumption is that the schools can be transformed from within....

In effect, blame for the problems of national competitiveness and for the problems of children in a complex and changing society is moving away from schools toward a more honest assessment of what is producing the so-called crisis in our schools. The answers often lie outside the schools themselves.

Since schools reflect society, it may be necessary to rebuild the community infrastructure in new ways, by using the school itself as a community resource....

...School days remain, for the most part, shorter than those of other industrialized nations, and the school year remains on an agrarian calendar. The structure of schools tends to isolate teachers not only from each other, but also from other important stakeholders, such as parents, businesses, social service and civic agencies, and community organizations that might take up some of the social and family burdens that have been placed on schools. Subjects are still predominantly taught in rote memorization fashion in short bursts of activity of 45–50 minutes. Often little time is devoted to staff or curriculum development.

In part, this situation exists because, as Chester Finn has stated, "people aren't changing their behavior at the 'retail' level of education." The explanation for this inability to change is due, in part, to public attitudes about education and schooling. These attitudes, which research shows are pervasive, mean that, rhetoric aside, fostering serious organizational change in schools has been difficult to accomplish....

MODELS OF COLLABORATION FOR SYSTEMIC REFORM

Case 1: Re:Learning—Monsanto, Southwestern Bell, Emerson Electric and Hallmark's Support for Systemic Education Reform

The group determined that the goal would be active student learning with demonstrations of student accomplishment, which is a fundamental aspect of the Common Principles of the Coalition of Essential Schools. The principles provided a foundation upon which all of the group's efforts could build, with particular attention devoted to the aspect it deemed most critical to actually achieving their goals: development of the teachers who work in the restructured schools.

The organizational framework the coalition chose to achieve its goal was Re:Learning, a national effort to address education reform by redesigning the total education system. Re:Learning, begun in 1988, includes the Coalition of Essential Schools, the Education Commission of the States, and all member schools, districts, and states....

Case 5: Partnership for Kentucky School Reform

The state of Kentucky is identified as being on the leading edge of the school restructuring and reform movement. Faced with the *Kentucky Education Reform Act* (KERA), which was intended to radically restructure schools because the system had been declared unconstitutional, business leaders in the state rallied together with educators and government leaders.

This type of collaboration was not new: Leaders in these three sectors had been interacting for a number of years, particularly concerning issues of education in the Louisville area and surrounding Jefferson County. Indeed, Louisville had been one of the 12 National Alliance of Business Compact Cities, funded to develop ways for these sectors to work together to improve education.

KERA represents a long-term and systemic approach to school reform. Among other things, the act guarantees a certain level of funding on a per-student basis, establishes mechanisms to equalize school financing, and introduces school-based management at each school along with major curriculum revisions and an entirely new primary school program.

One of the more innovative approaches embedded within KERA is the establishment of family resource centers and youth services centers within schools in poor areas. This "one-stop shopping" approach is meant to ensure that children are able to learn when they are in school because their families are receiving needed services. Additionally, all four-year-olds are required to attend preschool. A strict accountability system accompanies and supports the implementation efforts. One characteristic of KERA is its emphasis on high expectations for children.

KERA, coupled with the Business Roundtable's efforts to involve the business community in state-level advocacy, galvanized the business community into action. In the fall of 1990, the CEO's of three companies, John Hall of Ashland Oil, David Jones of Humana, and Kent C. "Oz" Nelson of United Parcel Service, established the Partnership of Kentucky School Reform. With the inaugural meeting held in March 1991, more than 50 leaders joined together to solidify their support for successful implementation of the innovative KERA. The group represented a non-partisan cross-section of business, government, civic, and education leaders, all making a commitment to improve the quality of education in the state through a statewide information campaign combined with local activities to support the reform movement.

[Ed. Note: KERA has become a case study in how educational reform went *astray* in a state that "was on the leading edge of the school restructuring and reform movement," and how it brought *grief* to parents, students, teachers and legislators. It was also a case study that involved a key, if not *the* key education change agent—who is not even an educator—David W.

Hornbeck, who took his marching orders from Marc Tucker's National Center on Education and the Economy (NCEE).

To add insult to injury, Hornbeck left Kentucky's sinking KERA ship to become superintendent of the Philadelphia, Pennsylvania school system where his tenure in Pennsylvania was equally controversial and destructive, resulting in the school system's being declared unable to function, wanting the state to take it over pending its "re-establishing" itself. Is it the role of the Hornbecks of this world to destructure schools, enabling them to be restructured according to the needs of the global economy?

Are the Hornbecks of the world brought in specifically for that purpose?

Additionally, one could ask why The Conference Board, and business interests in general, find the work of particular change agents and their tactics so appealing and positive? Is it because the change agent puppets are performing perfectly for their puppeteers who consider our children "human capital resources" to be trained, allowing the multinational corporations to spin off profits as a result? Take the case of a school system in New Mexico; the local school board rejected the Re:Learning Project only to be heavily pressured by the governor and a CEO of a multinational corporation—and others—who absolutely insisted on the implementation of Re:Learning. These folks had just returned from the "Charlottesville Summit" where they had received their marching orders under *America 2000*.[29]]

IN *THE READING* (PENNSYLVANIA) *EAGLE/TIMES* ON JUNE 25, 1994 AN article by Stephanie Ebbert entitled "School Exams Likely to Have Russian Origin" stated the following:

> Teachers in the former Soviet Union, who played host to visiting U.S. educators, express interest in exchanging tests and course material to compare students' aptitudes and curriculum.... Wyommissing School District students may soon be taking tests drawn up by teachers in the former Soviet Union.
>
> Dr. Charles R. Walker, superintendent, has established ties with educators in St. Petersburg, the former Leningrad, as a result of an April excursion there. Walker, one of 32 educators who, along with their spouses, took a 10-day educational trip to visit schools in St. Petersburg and Moscow, returned with contacts, fax numbers from Russian schools, and plans to establish ties to ensure students are competitive on a global scale.
>
> Teachers there expressed interest in exchanging tests and course material to compare students' aptitude and curriculum in the two countries, Walker said. In one public school that Walker visited the board had recently decided to mandate that students wear uniforms to try to contain the forces of commercialism, at least during the school day, he said.

[Ed. Note: Although dress codes are proper—and many private schools require an identifiable uniform to distinguish their schools' students from others—many government schools in urban areas in the U.S. are beginning to require uniforms. With the advent of: reduced time for recess; encouraging military personnel to function as teachers or instructors; the use of police to monitor school corridors and to teach the unsuccessful DARE (Drug Abuse Resistance Education) program; and the concept of our children being labeled "human capital resources" for the government-promoted school-to-work scheme, the idea of uniforms for public school students is more than a little disturbing.]

THE SECOND ANNUAL MODEL SCHOOLS CONFERENCE, SPONSORED BY THE International Center for Leadership in Education, Inc. (ICLE—whose director is Dr. Willard R. Daggett, previously employed as a co-trainer with William Spady at Outcome-Based Education training sessions sponsored by Spady's High Success Network) was held June 26–29, 1994 in Atlanta, Georgia. Representatives of the educational systems of China, Denmark, England, France, Germany, Japan, and Russia were included as presenters at the conference.

Of special interest was the presentation given by Su Lin, founder and chairwoman of China International Intellectual Resources Development Center for Children (CICC).[30] This school has branches in the United States, Germany, and other countries to facilitate the immersion of its Chinese students into the culture as well as the language of other countries. Excerpts from her presentation follow:

> It is CICC's task to be engaged in educational reforms, to establish organizations of intercultural communications, and to integrate educational institutions with enterprises. Therefore, CICC's systems engineering of education is an enormous constitution [composition] of education and technology, theory and practice, experimentation, organization, and management.
>
> CICC has been incorporated into an international group.
>
> We stress the following aspects:
>
> 1. The kind of citizens required by the 21st century will constitute our essential consideration of educational receivers, aims, and contents.
> 2. We must do experiments in the search for a new education model.
> 3. The greatest characteristics of the 21st century will be the internationalization of education. With that in mind, we aim to develop our education in an international environment, as education is supposed to be an open system.
> 4. China is carrying on its social reforms, encouraging individuals and the non-governmental sector to run education. [Privitization, vouchers, charters, etc., ed.]
> 5. The secure job policy makes education a closed and extremely stable system, closed to competition. Our curriculum is out of date. Education reforms are imperative in China....
>
> Sincere love of children is the principle upon which CICC is constructed....
>
> I am strongly against parents or teachers who impose their own views and demands on the children. Education is a noble job that calls for devotion and dedication with no reservation. Chances and conditions for education should be equal for every child....
>
> The cultural, economic, and educational levels for the minorities in Hainan are relatively low. With these factors in mind, CICC intentionally enrolls students from these minorities for educational experimentation and research....
>
> The aim of CICC is to develop children into persons with sound personality for the 21st century. To this end we incorporate the following features:

1. Standardization—a series of educational activities designed, organized, and managed according to educational principles and social needs to achieve a desired end.
2. Complying with natural law—all educational activities must obey the natural physiological and psychological development of children. Tampering with these laws leads to failure, as in the medieval missionary schools and family education.
3. Exploitation—exploiting the tremendous potential capacities of children.
4. Succession and systemization—treat the developmental process as a systemic whole.

...Personality is the synthesis of a person's mental and physical qualities. Our proposal is that elementary education should be globally oriented.... This is the inexorable result of international economic development.

Education reforms conducted by CICC include the shortening of the whole educational period to fifteen years of schooling. Weekday boarding is one of the educational facilities of CICC. They [the students] are required to board at school on weekdays and go back home by school bus on weekends. We provide boarding for the following reasons:

1. Most people are too busy working to pay enough attention to the education of their own children.
2. Many of the children come from broken families. The boarding school is a place they can turn to for comfort. Some even prefer to stay at school on weekends.
3. Many parents are not well-educated themselves and know nothing about how to bring up their own children.
4. China has a "one-child" policy as a way of controlling the birthrate. It is statistically shown that problems such as self-centeredness, stubbornness, and dependence are some common characteristics of only children nowadays. CICC provides boarding to strengthen the children's sense of equality, solidarity, and independence.

We have established a school for the parents, where people can learn how to educate their own children. The overall plan for CICC has Moon Lake as the hub of the community with the educational center around it. CICC has organized itself into a self-supported international group corporation of educational institutions and enterprises by opening businesses and services in children's education, science and technology, medicine and health, legal, insurance, trade and tourism.

[Ed. Note: Do the above outlines remind the reader of the New American Schools Development Corporation's criteria for schooling in the United States through charter schools that bear many of the above characteristics? Can the reader recognize the Chinese equivalent of "at-risk" categories that our country is targeting for educational funding? Does reference to boarding schools remind the reader of the November 1979 article in *The Bangor* (Maine) *Daily News* about radical changes proposed by a Vermont task force which included boarding schools, a center for educational research and teacher training, and elements of the school-to-work agenda for the 1990s?

The above Chinese model, describing the school as the "hub" of the community, bears much resemblance to the community education programs of the past twenty-five years or so. While the Chinese still use the word "children" instead of this country's substitute "human capital resources," one must not lose sight of the environment—political, economic, and religious—in which the above extreme, communist and coercive "educational solutions" are suggested and established. The reader should also bear in mind that this program was presented at Willard Daggett's ICLE "Model Schools" conference.]

"SCHOOLS: INTO THE FUTURE" IS THE TITLE OF AN ARTICLE WHICH RAN IN *The Oregonian* [Portland, Oregon] on September 8, 1994 and carried a subtitle as lead-in which read "Oregon's school-reform plan is one of the country's most ambitious—and this year it really kicks into gear." Since Oregon was the first state to implement the *Goals 2000 Act* (signed by President Clinton on March 31, 1994) and the *School-to-Work Opportunities Act* (signed by Clinton May 4, 1994), before quoting from the article in *The Oregonian*, the writer wants to quote from the first paragraph of the radical *Goals 2000 Act*:

PUBLIC LAW 103–227
March 31, 1994
103rd Congress

To improve learning and teaching by providing a national framework for education reform; to promote the research, consensus building, and systemic changes needed to ensure equitable educational opportunities and high levels of educational achievement for all students; to provide a framework for reauthorization of all Federal education programs; to promote the development and adoption of a voluntary national system of skill standards and certification; and for other purposes.[31]

Excerpts from the "Schools: Into the Future" article which enable the reader to comprehend the controversial nature of *Goals 2000*:

Efforts to make learning more relevant by breaking down walls between schools and the adult world are bringing the most visible changes. At Portland's Roosevelt High, for example, students will choose career paths early in their high school years and actually will follow them into the workplace with real-world experiences such as internships and job-shadowing programs. At Grant High, students will learn directly from Cellular One workers. And at Marshall High, business leaders will serve as mentors to individual students, guiding the choices that will affect their futures in the world of work.

Oregon's law, like President Clinton's Goals 2000 reform legislation, aims to dramatically raise the education levels of students schools failed to reach in the past. This year, Portland Public Schools will embark on a plan to push all students into an academic regimen equal to that traditionally reserved for the college-bound, says Jack Bierwirth, Portland Public Schools Superintendent.

It will do so by aggressively following Oregon's school-reform blueprint. The state plan attempts to reach the forgotten half in two ways:[32] by requiring all students to meet high academic standards and by blending academics with new vocational paths that lead to further studies and good jobs.

Because of the state plan's scope and high standards, the American Legislative Exchange Council last month chose Oregon as one of eight states to receive its A+ award in education.

Replacing the Diploma

Oregon's reform plan will require students to earn two certificates of mastery to graduate—one at about the end of their sophomore year and the second about two years later. This year's eighth-graders will be the first class to earn certificates instead of diplomas.

Reformers say the distinction is central to the changes education faces: diplomas are based on course credits or the time students put in. But certificates, they say, are based on standards or what students know and can do.

Another article in the same September 8, 1994 issue of *The Oregonian* was entitled "Model Program Links Classroom to Workplace." This article by Courtenay Thompson deals with a pilot project to implement school-to-work requirements of the *Oregon Educational Act for the 21st Century*. The following are excerpts from that article:

> In the blood splatters of murder victims, David Douglas High School senior Chrissy Ballantine is learning about both forensics and her future.
>
> A student in the school's innovative Law Network course, the 17-year-old is exploring careers by learning to interpret blood splatters with the help of a Multnomah County forensic specialist. Last year, she also analyzed the book *Lust Killer*, a true-crime novel by Ann Rule about Jerome Brudos, an Oregon serial killer.
>
> Not standard classroom fare, but Ballantine raves about the two-year course, a pilot program to implement school-to-work requirements of the Oregon Educational Act for the 21st Century.... "We were doing an excellent job of providing a well-rounded college prep education," said Anthony Palermini, David Douglas superintendent. "But it wasn't relevant to 25 to 30 percent of our students."
>
> As a result, the district began developing what it calls Project Stars—"Students Taking Authentic Routes to Success"—in which students select one of six general career areas, or "constellations," to concentrate their electives. Students will work toward certificates of advanced mastery, a key measure of academic success under state-mandated school reform.... The career focus would start in the seventh grade, when students would take a career-orientation class. Students would select their constellation by the time they hit high school.

[Ed. Note: The fact that Oregon's school-to-work reform plan received the American Legislative Exchange Council's (ALEC) highest educational award *should* come as a surprise since ALEC is an association created by "conservatives" (Paul Weyrich) in 1981 as a counterpart to the liberal, Rockefeller-spawned ACIR (Advisory Commission on Intergovernmental Relations); both organizations draft "model" legislation for use by state and federal legislators.]

ON NOVEMBER 2, 1994 *EDUCATION WEEK* PUBLISHED AN EDITORIAL LETTER by this writer entitled "Viewing Reform Partnerships as Big Brother's Intrusion." A portion of the letter follows:

> Don Davies ("Partnerships for Reform," *Commentary*, October 12, 1994) just doesn't get the message: Smart Americans don't like partnerships with the government; and if public schools aren't "government," what are they?

Evidently there are still enough politically savvy (educated) Americans who reject such partnerships, having studied government intrusion in the home and family in countries such as Cuba, the former Soviet Union and Eastern bloc countries, and especially in Communist China, from which some of Don Davies's community-education research apparently has emanated.

The Community Learning and Information Network, Inc., or CLIN, incorporated in 1992 and supported by major corporations and education associations, will make Professor Davies's dream come true. He "won't have to worry about citizens who 'resist'" *Goals 2000* reform (don't want to dance with the government). According to the CLIN fact sheet, "The CLIN concept is to implement a community-linked learning-technology and information-delivery system that uses... two-way interactive video, networked computer-assisted learning, video programming, multimedia, interactive cable, and electronic mail (including electronic video mail) based on an 'open systems' architectural approach. CLIN, Inc.'s goal is [to] link every public and private school in the United States, as well as every institution of higher education and corporate and industrial training sites."

An information packet from the Community Learning and Information Network states: "CLIN has also developed international projects, to include an approved project with the People's Republic of China sponsored by the highest levels of the Chinese government."

Professor Davies's concerns about lack of parental and taxpayer support for reform will also be dealt with when the National Goals Panel's 235-page *Community Action Tool Kit*, the intent of which is to psychologically manipulate taxpayers into supporting *Goals 2000*, hits our communities. The *Tool Kit* recommends, among other techniques, these: "Describe allies and opponents; identify change agents; get the president of Hewlett Packard to write the chairman of the school board a letter supporting the proposal." It also provides a case study of how Christian ministers were manipulated into supporting *Goals 2000* in Edmonds, Washington.

Alexander Solzhenitsyn, the famous Soviet dissident, issued an important warning when he said, "Coexistence on this tightly knit earth should be viewed as an existence not only without wars... but also without [government] telling us how to live, what to say, what to think, what to know, and what not to know."

So-called "peace" is breaking out all over the world. How long this type of peace will last will depend on the patience freedom-loving citizens have with Global Big Brother's intrusion into the privacy of their homes and families.

CHALLENGERS FOR INSIGHT IN ITS NOVEMBER 1994 NEWSLETTER PUBLISHED an article entitled "Susan Kovalik's Integrated Thematic Instruction" which enables the average parent or teacher to understand a new teaching model based on "brain compatible learning" for outcome-/performance-based education.[33] This critique of Kovalik's model was written by education researchers Marilyn Boyer and Barbara Volkman of Indiana.[34] Since this article describes a new and most controversial method which may well be used extensively throughout the nation, this writer has included it in its entirety so that the reader can use it for educational purposes:

SUSAN KOVALIK'S INTEGRATED THEMATIC INSTRUCTION
By Barbara Volkman and Marilyn Boyer

Controversy continues to rage throughout Indiana over a state-supported teaching model for Outcome-/Performance-Based Education. Many traditional teaching methods are being eliminated as public school classrooms experiment with new teaching techniques based on *brain-compatible learning*, such as those promoted in the 1992 Integrated Thematic Instruction: The Model (ITI) developed by Susan Kovalik and Associates of Arizona.

A memorandum was sent to all Indiana superintendents, inviting them to attend a lunch/conversation with Susan Kovalik in Indianapolis on November 10, 1994 during the 7th National Conference of the American Association of School Librarians. [It stated in part that] ITI is of great interest to parents in Indiana and elsewhere, since *"Susan is well known as a writer, facilitator, and president of one of the largest inservice training organizations in the United States,"* according to the invitation.

Kovalik's material shows a strong connection to the New Age philosophies of Eastern mysticism and Western occultism. Indiana has for several years been putting in place the new age curriculum that contains all of the psychological/educational processes necessary to achieve in the student the desired *state, national and international outcomes*.

Master teacher Barbara Pedersen, an associate of Susan Kovalik's from Central Elementary School in Lebanon, Indiana, has brought the ITI model to Indiana classrooms through the Indiana Department of Education-supported C.L.A.S.S. (Connecting Learning Assures Successful Students) project. Pedersen not only trains and coaches teachers in many schools in Indiana, but now has expanded to include Kentucky teachers.

The ITI model's approach to teaching uses a single theme (yearly, monthly, weekly) to tie together various areas of instruction such as science, math, history, and reading. Thematic teaching is not new. What is new, says Kovalik in her 1992 ITI manual, is that, "The entire ITI Model—curriculum development and instructional strategies—has been selected and organized with great care to fit how the brain learns" (p. 3).

This type of thematic model, based on human brain research, is called *brain-compatible learning.* However, a close look behind the model at the books that Kovalik cites as brain research reveals that ITI is not based on valid scientific studies, but rather on educational theories tied to psychic phenomena research.

The mind, claims Kovalik, is designed to learn from the experience and complexities of the natural world, and thus she rejects the logical, sequential (traditional) teaching approach to learning. According to Kovalik, the goal of school districts and school boards should be to provide students with a brain-compatible learning environment by eliminating policies that support brain-antagonistic elements (i.e., a textbook for every student, traditional evaluation/grading, and sequential curricula presented in a logical manner).

Opponents of the ITI model list the following major criticisms: 1) New Age ideas and practices including yoga relaxation, visualization, and guided imagery leading to altered states of consciousness; 2) Tribes, a cooperative learning model predominantly centered on social (peer group) development rather than individual academic achievement; 3) academic deficiencies traced to emphasis on *exploration of the complex, random, chaotic "real world"* instead of concentrated on sequential, logical teaching of subject matter through textbooks; 4) controversial nature of certain themes (political, religious, paranormal, etc.) and overemphasis on themes; and 5) teaching methods and curriculum linked to questionable brain research (i.e., *Brain-Compatible Classroom*).

The ITI model encompasses six main brain research theories:

(1) Triune Brain—Paul McLean's evolutionary theory of mankind's *three separate brains* of varying ages. This is a key component and rationale for providing a stress-free brain-compatible learning environment.

(2) Accelerated Learning—the speed up memory learning by teaching directly to the subconscious mind derived from George Lozanov's Suggestology, which is based upon research from yogis and psychics. The ITI model has all of the parts of this type of Accelerated Learning—yoga relaxation, visualization, guided imagery and special effects of music. Lozanov's method is also called SALT (Suggestive Accelerative Learning and Teaching [which supports Stanford's Henry Levin's Accelerated Schools efforts]) and Integrative Learning.

(3) Left Brain/Right Brain Thinking—a theory to develop the intuitive side of the right brain by accessing the subconscious mind. There is no consensus in the research to support this theory. Although some scientists have claimed to validate the roles of the left/right brain hemispheres, others would disagree. "We don't have one shred of evidence that something as high-level as creativity could be allocated to one side of the brain or the other," says Levy (professor of biopsychology at the University of Chicago). "Attempts to apply what is known about hemispheric differences to the enhancement of learning are premature.... That was the conclusion of the fourteen-member panel of researchers from the National Academy of Sciences that recently completed a broad view of 'brain asymmetry'" (*The Omni Wholemind Newsletter*, Vol. 1, No. 4, March 1988).

(4) The Seven Intelligences—redefines intelligence to include music, dance, sports, etc. Howard Gardner, departing from traditional education, theorizes that humans have seven intelligences that are associated with brain locations. They are *logical-mathematical*, *linguisitic*, *spatial*, *bodily-kinesthetic*, *musical*, *intrapersonal*, and *interpersonal*. Gardner labels what has been traditionally called a human talent as an intelligence. Parents should have grave concerns about labeling a student's personal beliefs and his/her interaction with others as intelligences, because the state can then do the developing and assessing of them. This is one of the dangers of Outcome-Based Education since the learner outcomes often include the student's attitudes and beliefs.

(5) Personality Types/Learning Styles—Pedersen refers to the importance of learning styles. One of the methods of identifying/teaching to learning styles used in Indiana as well as many other states is the 4MAT system of instruction developed by Bernice McCarthy. 4MAT is based on theories from education, psychology, neurology and management. The system includes four types of learners: Imaginative, Analytic, Common Sense and Dynamic. McCarthy teaches to the learning style of the student with left/right mode techniques.

(6) Brain-Compatible Learning, a phrase coined by Leslie Hart, author of *Human Brain and Human Learning*. Hart believes humans learn best from the rich, random, chaotic "real world" instead of concentrated, sequential, logical teaching of subject matter through textbooks.

Replacing traditional teaching methods with occult techniques that teach directly to the subconscious mind opens the door to possible mind control (brainwashing). It appears that some education reformers think children can learn better in this hypnotic state which allows all material into the mind. Children can then absorb any agenda the school (state) wishes to teach without the brain discriminating the validity of the material.

Authors' Update (recent developments since this article was written):

Howard Gardner has now expanded to eight and a half intelligences by adding naturalist and half of spiritual.

The following recent publications show that educators continue to misapply the brain theory and research that even the scientific community still disputes:

A Celebration of Neurons: An Educator's Guide to the Human Brain by Robert Sylwester is published by the Association for Supervision and Curriculum Development (ASCD) in 1995 as a major guide for educators. Sylwester notes that educators must not make the mistake of left/right brain books, workshops and curriculum that often went far beyond the research findings. He sees misinformed or uninformed people making major policy decisions for educators. However, he maintains that application of this research is an important step for educators even though the applications are not clear, the issues are complex, and educators generally lack the scientific background to understand or build a curriculum utilizing the research.

The Education Commission of the States has held 16 workshops in the last year on the implications that neuroscience may have for state policymakers who may be getting carried away on brain research. ("Education Policymakers Embrace Brain Findings—Scientists Question Rush to Apply Brain-Research Findings," by Linda Jacobson, *Education Week*, April 8, 1998) [all emphases in original]

JOHN OMICINSKI, GANNETT NEWS SERVICE, WROTE "MULTICULTURALISM IS a Worthy Goal, but America Still Needs Americans" which appeared in the Sunday, November 20, 1994 issue of the *Detroit News*. Omicinski's article covered a speech by Librarian of Congress James Billington at the 75th anniversary of Georgetown University's School of Foreign Service.[35] A few interesting excerpts from the article follow:

> Will America lead the world into the 21st century? Not the way things are going, says Librarian of Congress James Billington. [Not] in a country afflicted with a lazy, ill-defined multiculturalism filling up with African Americans, Korean Americans, Japanese Americans, he suggests. And his bottom line is simple: America doesn't work without Americans.
>
> As a custodian of the library and its 105 million items, Billington is caretaker of the world's largest depository of human culture. He also is one of Washington's sharpest minds, an expert on Russian history as well as America's heritage, and an even rarer breed—a straight talker.
>
> The arsenal of information we command ought to qualify the United States as an unchallenged cultural superpower, Billington says. But this imposing mother lode of words isn't of much use if U.S. residents are too indolent, too self-satisfied, too culturally balkanized to use it, he says....
>
> Is America an idea or a nation?

The sharpening split between left and right makes that a cutting-edge question in the current cultural wars. And Billington comes down on the side of nationhood largely because America's good ideas don't much matter if there's no nation to push them.

Gathering the world's civilization to itself, the United States should be primed to set a model for the world. But it isn't working that way, said Billington. A gaggle of voices—all given equal weight in a society that may have forgotten its traditional values—has turned America into a dizzy spin. "Unfortunately, we seem to have lost our national compass somewhere on the road to the next millenium," Billington said. "We are getting ever more lazy.... Many of our great institutions of higher learning seem to have become indifferent to—even contemptuous of—their historic function of transmitting a basic understanding of their own culture from one generation to the next.

"In place of the expanding, inclusive America, which adds without subtracting, the ideological multiculturist would create a balkanized America and a continuous process of subtraction from any sense of common tradition or shared values.... This kind of multiculturalism is the denial rather than the fulfillment of true pluralism, which in the great American tradition assumes a variety of authentic and deep convictions rather than a... uniformity of relativistic indifference."

Billington sees a single language as the ultimate national glue. Though English is on its way to dominating the world, America's left-wing elitist intellectuals say it shouldn't be America's *lingua franca*. "In any country that endures, there must be a unum as well as a *pluribus*," said Billington.

That's not all.

Billington says a national idea also requires a "clearer understanding than our educational system has often done in recent years of our durable constitutional system and public institutions and of our distinctively Judeo-Christian roots.... The bridges to other cultures will not be solid unless they begin with casements that are sunk deep into one's own native ground."

Leaders of our governments, schools and universities have much to answer for, perhaps even the death of the American nation. Billington's speech is another reason to demand better from them, or show them the door.

EDUCATION WEEK OF NOVEMBER 23, 1994 RAN THE ARTICLE "EDUCATION, Religious Groups, Seek Common Ground." Excerpts follow:

The leaders of several national education associations and conservative religious and citizens' groups have been meeting behind the scenes in an effort to find common ground on school reform and end their increasingly hostile debate.... An encouraging sign—and surprising turnabout—in the debate between school-reform leaders and their conservative opponents has been the recent partnership of William G. Spady, a leading advocate of outcomes-based education, and Robert L. Simonds, the president of the Costa Mesa, California-based Citizens for Excellence in Education, which says it has about 250,000 members nationwide. In many ways, the two men represent polar opposites in the debate over the direction of schools. Yet in recent months, they have made plans to sponsor jointly a non-profit National Center for Reconciliation and Educational Reform at the University of Northern Colorado in Gruel....

In many areas, CEE-affiliated activists support a back-to-basics agenda, opposing whole language instruction, open-ended assessments and teaching strategies that stray from the drill-and-practice routine. But after building a constituency that has seen its job as fighting against the tide, Mr. Simonds said, it is time to work with educators on better choices.... "We are not opposed to Bill Spady's theory of outcomes-based education. There are a lot of good ideas in it," Mr. Simonds said.

IN A LETTER DATED DECEMBER 12, 1994 FROM WILLIAM SPADY OF THE High Success Network to Dr. Nancy Grasmick, Maryland state superintendent of schools, a copy of which was very likely sent to the 49 other state school chiefs, Spady made the following statements:

> With both the federal government and state bodies pushing harder than ever to improve the focus and effectiveness of what happens at the local level, major educational reform seems inevitable—except for one new factor: the open resistance by citizens' groups to a host of "progressive" reform ideas and initiatives....
>
> When we met in March, Dr. Simonds was a staunch opponent of virtually everything I advocated in terms of outcomes-based educational change and restructuring. Today, to the amazement of many educators and policy makers, he is in agreement with the basic components and principles articulated in the enclosed document developed by Dr. Kit Marshall and myself. More importantly, he and I have joined forces to form a National Center on Educational Reconciliation and Reform—an endeavor that colleagues across the country tell us is badly needed....
>
> We would be delighted to discuss the feasibility of working with you and your constituents to bring this program to your state and to generate a broad base of support for reconciliation and reform. This could be done either under the auspices of the *Goals 2000* initiative or through other sponsorship.

COTTAGE GROVE, OREGON'S SOUTH LANE SCHOOL DISTRICT PLOUGHS AHEAD as the nation's certificate in mastery pack leader. According to an article entitled "Cottage Grove Endures Trials, Triumphs as It Tests New School Plan" in the December 13, 1994 issue of *The Oregonian*:

> Parents are still fighting the changes. Students will mutter about being guinea pigs. Teachers—even those who back the reforms—groan about the workload.
>
> Last spring, Cottage Grove High School handed out the state's first certificates of initial mastery to 81 sophomores. The certificate, keystone in the 1991 reform act, is designed to measure students on what they've learned and what they can do, as opposed to what courses they have taken.
>
> Much of the criticism arises from the way ninth-graders were thrust cold into the new program two years ago. They worked on team projects that would be graded jointly, took more responsibility for their own learning and developed portfolios of their classwork. And, more significantly, they had to meet higher academic standards.
>
> Timm Wagner, 16, failed to get his certificate last year because, he says, his teammates on a group project didn't get their work done. "I don't like it," he says. "If I'm doing a job, I should get fired if I do something wrong, not if somebody else does something wrong."

SCHOOL-TO-WORK PROGRAMS PROMOTED BY BUSINESS IS THE SUBJECT OF AN
article entitled "Leading Business Executives Create Council to Promote S-
T-W Programs" in the December 14, 1994 issue of *Education Week*. Some
excerpts follow:

> Some of the nation's leading corporate executives last week announced that
> they have formed a group to promote business involvement in school-to-
> work programs.
> Members of the National Employment Leadership Council will work
> with the U.S. Education and Labor departments to implement school-to-
> work programs in their own companies and encourage other firms to do the
> same. Whether many businesses take them up on the offer could determine
> the prospects for work-based learning in the United States. The new council
> provides the strongest signal to date that the private sector may be ready to
> support such programs....
> But the council stopped short of releasing numeric goals for how many
> firms it hopes to recruit or how many training slots they would provide....
> Jerome Grossman, the chairman and C.E.O. of the New England Medical
> Center, said the council hopes to set numeric objectives within the next two
> months.
> The council's staff is housed at the Institute for Educational Leadership,
> a non-profit group based in Washington.
> The following companies and C.E.O.'s are charter members of the council:
> Ford Motor Co., Alan Trotman; American Express Travel Related Services
> Co, Inc., Roger Ballou; Atlanta Life Insurance Co., Jesse Hill, Jr.; BellSouth
> Corp., John Clendenin; Charles Schwab Corp., Lawrence J. Stupski; Cybernet
> Systems Co., Heidi Jacobs; Eastman Kodak Co., George Fisher; H.J. Russell
> & Co., Herman J. Russell; ImmunoGen, Inc., Mitchell Sayare; Manpower
> Corporation, Mitchell Fromstein; McDonald's USA, Ed Rensi; New England
> Medical Center, Jerome H.Grossman; Pacer Systems, Inc., John C. Rennie;
> Peavey Electronics Corp., Melia Peavey; Phillips Display Components, Dr. Iva
> Wilson, president; Siemens Corporation, Albert Hoser, president and C.E.O.;
> the Taubman Company, Al Taubman, chairman; Thom McAn Shoe Company,
> Larry McVey, president; UNUM Corporation, James F. Orr, III, chairman and
> C.E.O.; and Will-Burt Company, Harry Featherstone, chairman and C.E.O.

WEDNESDAY, DECEMBER 28, 1994 ISSUE OF *THE WALL STREET JOURNAL*
carried an article under its column Critical Thought entitled "Acclaimed
Reforms of U.S. Education Are Popular but Unproven—Ted Sizer's Methods
Stress Reasoning over Rote: Gains Aren't Measurable—Ambiguity and Faculty
Battles." Sizer's Coalition of Essential Schools, considered by many to be
the centerpiece of national education reform, proves to be more workable
in theory than in practice. Some excerpts follow:

> In the crusade to revitalize high schools, no one has attracted more atten-
> tion—or money—than Theodore R. Sizer, professor of education at Brown
> University and creator of Essential Schools. But as Dr. Sizer's adherents
> and donations pile up, so too does research challenging the effectiveness of
> coalition schools. Five recent, little-publicized studies, including a five-year
> research project sponsored by the coalition itself, suggest that Dr. Sizer's
> ideas may be a lot more workable in theory than in practice....

Not since John Dewey, whose writings shaped the 20th century U.S. curriculum, has one person's philosophy taken hold in so many classrooms, educators say. More than $100 million has poured in from education foundations and donors such as AT&T, Exxon and Citicorp. Anecdotal evidence from some coalition schools points to improved attendance rates, lower dropout rates, better test scores or more students going to college.

But even coalition officials concede such evidence is spotty. They also haven't tried to determine comprehensively whether coalition students are learning more, despite pressure to do so from some benefactors. Grant Wiggins, the coalition's former research director, says he remains unconvinced that coalition schools are better. "It has always been my sense that it's not better. It's not worse; it's just different," explains Dr. Wiggins, who says he quit the coalition in 1988 because of "a combination of burnout and frustration."

1995

[ddd]

IN AN ARTICLE ENTITLED "RUSSIAN TEACHER REVIEWS WORK IN SAD 53" which was published in the January 12, 1995 issue of *The Bangor* (Maine) *Daily News*, Brenda Seekins explains all too clearly the extent of cooperation between Russia and the U.S. in school-to-work (planned economy) activities. According to Seekins's research these activities were not confined to ivory tower musings, but had penetrated education at the local level. Some excerpts follow:

PITTSFIELD—Russian exchange teacher Tanya Koslova addressed the SAD 53 board of directors Monday night to express her appreciation for the opportunity to work with the district and Maine Central Institute [MCI—deeply involved with workforce training, ed.].

She offered an overview of the work she had done in the district over the past four months, spending two months with children in kindergarten through grade eight and the balance of her time at MCI.

She particularly enjoyed students who participated in her Russian humanities class who were "highly-motivated and eager students."[MCI Headmaster] Cummings told the board that MCI will be the recipient of the School-to-Work funding in conjunction with the Maine Youth Apprenticeship Program.

The school could receive up to $8,000 to provide staff training to better integrate academics with the program provided by apprentices' worksites.

MACHIAVEL PEDAGOGUE OU LE MINISTERE DE LA REFORME PSYCHOLOGIQUE *[Machiavellian Pedagogy or the Ministry of Psychological Reform]* by Pascal Bernardin (Editions Notre-Dame des Graces: Paris, 1995) was published. This book deals with United Nations Educational, Scientific, and Cultural Organization's (UNESCO) role in the transformation of education worldwide from a system based on academic instruction to one in which the purpose is nothing but conditioning for acceptance of world government (New World Order). Monsieur Bernardin discusses brainwashing techniques such as cognitive dissonance and the group process, and is highly critical of the role played by American and European behavioral psychologists in the transformation of the world's schools from places of learning to mental health clinics for brainwashing. The following are excerpts from this writer's translation from the French version:

> The general philosophy of the pedagogical revolution is exposed, without detour, in the publications of the international organizations (UNESCO, OECD, Council of Europe, Commission of Bruxelles...)....
>
> This pedagogical revolution attempts to impose an ethic for the creation of a new society and to establish an intercultural society. The new ethic is nothing more than a remarkable presentation of a communist utopia. A study of the documents leaves no doubt, under cover of ethics and behind a rhetoric and remarkable dialectic, of a communist ideology for which only the presentation and the means of action have been modified.... Also it is no surprise that the level of scholarship will continue to go down since the role of the school has been redefined so that its principal mission is no longer intellectual but social formation....One no longer gives students intellectual tools for liberation but imposes on them values, attitudes, and behavior using psychological manipulation techniques.

SALEM, OREGON'S *THE STATESMAN JOURNAL* OF FEBRUARY 4, 1995 carried an article entitled "Service Learning Projects Match Students with Needs in the Salem-Keizer Community." Excerpts follow:

> Service learning is a method through which students learn values, citizenship, and skills by performing a variety of community services. On any given school day, hundreds of Salem-Keizer teens leave their classrooms to visit local businesses, nonprofit agencies and other community organizations or activities.
>
> The students aren't on field trips—they're visiting their service sites, where they perform a variety of community service work, also referred to as "service learning." It is here that students are learning the meaning of citizenship and service. They're also becoming more aware of their role in the community.
>
> "Service learning demonstrates the partnership between the school district and the community. Students learn firsthand about the needs and issues of our community—the homeless, the hungry, the elderly, and environment—while they work toward meeting those needs," explains Pat Abeene, Volunteer Services coordinator for the district.
>
> Abeene said service learning takes various forms. These range from the district's Youth Community Service Program—in which high school students get [selective or elective] credit for community service—to individual school projects integrated into the regular curriculum.
>
> Other service sites offered through the program include the Boys and Girls Clubs, nursing homes, the Humane Society, and Oregon state parks.... Another example of service learning was the McNary Area Service Learning Project. The successful project teamed eight Keizer schools in the collection of 6,000 recyclable milk jugs from area homes—a service currently unavailable

through Salem-Keizer disposal companies. [See June 7, 1998 *The Statesman Journal* entry for the effect of this experiment, ed.]

THE FOLLOWING STATEMENTS WERE PUBLISHED IN **1995** IN THE **MARYLAND** State Department of Education's *MSDE Bulletin* (Vol. 6, No. 3) entitled "Keeping You Current on Education Reform in Maryland":

SEEKING COMMON GROUND ON SCHOOL REFORM

William Spady, a leading proponent of outcomes-based education, and Robert Simonds, head of a Christian group that has led the fight against OBE, made a joint presentation before the State Board in February to discuss their 10-months' dialogue of reconciliation....

Early in their discussions, which began at a meeting last March of the Association of Supervision and Curriculum Development (ASCD) the two men agreed that the public schools are essential to democracy and must be strengthened....

The two men have come to agreement on a set of components and principles for school reform, which Spady calls the "High Success" model. They agree that specific reform alternatives should include the following components:

* Quality performance standards
* Future-focused planning
* Extensive community involvement
* Continuous improvement strategies
* Challenging learning experiences
* Advanced instructional processes
* Real-life learning assessments

Both men had praise for Maryland's reforms. Simonds said, "The Maryland Learning Outcomes are what parents want."...

Several education associations (including the Association for Supervision and Curriculum Development, the American Association of School Administrators, the National School Boards Association, the National PTA) have joined with the Citizens for Excellence in Education and other conservative groups to continue the search for common ground on education.

[Ed. Note: Robert Simonds's co-option by the very groups responsible for at least thirty years of failed, so-called "reform," is beyond this writer's comprehension.[36]]

"CONTENT OF OUR KIDS' TESTS SHOULDN'T BE SECRET" BY MARGARET Sitte, columnist, ran in the March 3, 1995 issue of *The Bismarck* (North Dakota) *Tribune*. Excerpts follow:

In 1990 North Dakota eighth-graders scored highest in math on the National Assessment of Educational Progress. Questions of psycho-analysis have surfaced, however, leaving many parents to ask, "What exactly is the NAEP?" Senator Bob Stenehjem, R., Bismarck, thinks it's time to find out, and he has introduced SB 2308 allowing parents the right to see it.

Anita Hoge, a Pennsylvania mother of three, listened intently one day in

1986 as her ninth-grade son came home complaining, "I've just taken the weirdest test in the world. It was so hard. You couldn't answer the questions."

"The prospect of working most of my adult life depresses me. Check 'yes,' 'no,' or 'sometimes.'"

Being a concerned parent, Anita marched to school and demanded to see the test, the Pennsylvania Educational Quality Assessment. She was refused. A feeling in the pit of her stomach told her something was terribly wrong.

Anita called other parents, and together six women embarked on an extensive investigation that lasted several years.

Berit Kjos's *Brave New Schools* (Harvest House Publishers: Eugene, Ore., 1995), in discussing Anita Hoge's case, states:

> Anita Hoge, a native of Pennsylvania, is no stranger to concerned parents or to the educational establishment. While her story has encouraged thousands of parents across the country, it has also brought anxiety to the change agents who hoped to conceal their strategies until they accomplish their purpose. Anita's courageous search for answers to mystifying school practices has given us a glimpse of an educational process designed to conform all children to the new, politically correct version of "appropriate mental health."
>
> Anita's journey will take you through a maze of white papers and technical documents and expose the true nature of contemporary education: social engineering. It will give you an inside look at the deceptive testing mechanism designed to measure the attitudes and values of our children and make sure every student will demonstrate the pre-planned nonacademic "outcomes." Unwilling to give up in the face of overwhelming opposition, Anita has become a living demonstration of the hope that "one person can make a difference." (p. 206)

[Ed. Note: Anita Hoge filed a lawsuit against the U.S. Department of Education, the Pennsylvania State Department of Education and others, using the federal *Protection of Pupil Rights Amendment*. The outcome of her suit was delayed by the U.S. Department of Education's tactics until the statute of limitations expired, thus its acknowledgment that her suit was legitimate served only as a moral victory. The Pennsylvania Department of Education continued to stonewall Mrs. Hoge's efforts to uncover the privacy-invading components of its statewide assessment test, discontinuing its use for a time and later changing the name of the test—as good change agents are wont to do!

For further information, see the 1964 discussion of the origins of the NAEP; 1988 National Citizens Alliance press conference at the National Press Club; 1998 Ohio Supreme Court favorable decision in Steve Rea's challenge to the Ohio Department of Education; and the Internet version for Appendix IV.]

THE BISMARCK (NORTH DAKOTA) SUNDAY TRIBUNE CARRIED AN ARTICLE entitled "Test Board Tackles Secrecy Stigma" by Jeff Olson in the March 5, 1995 issue. Excerpts follow:

> A Bismarck legislator's bill to let parents inspect a national student achieve-

ment test sent the exam's governing board scrambling for a new public access policy.

New policy directives give parents a look at old test questions and demographic background questions, but maintain high security for National Assessment of Educational Progress [NAEP] exam questions still in use. They were approved Friday in Washington.

Should Sen. Robert Stenehjem's bill become law, director of the NAEP, Archie LaPointe, said it would mean the end of the exam in North Dakota. National test results wouldn't waver because North Dakota students are a sliver of the nation-wide test sample. But LaPointe feared copycat legislation could seriously disrupt NAEP operations in other Great Plains states.

National Assessment personnel came from the Educational Testing Service at Princeton, N.J., a private company under contract to the federal government which sponsors the NAEP.[37]

ETS staff and governing board members from across the country said they were surprised by Stenehjem's bill. North Dakota children have dominated state-by-state comparisons in the NAEP.

But the 25-year-old program has been peppered with accusations that it amounts to psychological testing, and is not the anonymous comparison of academic achievement as prescribed by law. Parents are also upset that they can't have easy access to active test questions.

"The NAEP just isn't worth it," said Stenehjem, a Republican who sponsored SB 2308. "There is too much secrecy and there are too many intrusive background questions."

Parents from Pennsylvania, Nebraska, Iowa and other states have complained bitterly about the NAEP for several years. But no one has scared the governing board with legislation. Until now.

"**EDUCATORS, RELIGIOUS GROUPS CALL SCHOOL TRUCE—THEY AGREE TO** Disagree on Hot Issues of '90s" by Sally Streff Buzbee was published in the March 22, 1995 issue of *The Atlanta Constitution*. What the article actually said is that the left and the right will meet at the middle (common ground, or what Shirley McCune refers to as "the radical center"). This is an excellent example of the Hegelian Dialectic at work. Some pertinent excerpts follow:

> ARLINGTON, VIRGINIA—Educators and religious parents fighting a bitter "culture war" over the future of America's public schools signed a pledge Tuesday to tone down their rhetoric and cooperate for children's good....
>
> ...[T]he 17 groups, ranging from the conservative Christian Coalition to the liberal People for the American Way, pledged to work to solve disputes before they become lawsuits and to improve communication and respect each other's positions.
>
> The agreement could influence debates likely in Congress this year over school vouchers and school prayer. But the agreement will be aimed at solving disputes that have divided communities in recent years.
>
> "The statement is eagerly awaited," said Charles Haynes, a visiting scholar at The Freedom Forum First Amendment Center. He brought the groups together with help from the non-partisan Association for Supervision and Curriculum Development (ASCD).
>
> "People in Vista, California, and in many other communities have been

saying 'We want it now,'" Haynes said. The Vista school district near San Diego has been fighting over the teaching of evolution and creationism.

"This is going to give all these local districts something to look at, something to help guide them." Haynes said.

"Several prominent groups, including the conservative Focus on the Family and the liberal American Civil Liberties Union, did not sign the statement of principles," Haynes noted.

"I don't think any of them are against it in theory, but thought it was vague," he said.

In part, the agreement will clarify for local teachers, principals and parents what the Supreme Court has ruled is allowable in public schools, such as the fact that religious groups have equal access to school rooms for after-school meetings.

"Far too often, constitutionally protected religious liberties are being denied," said Robert Simonds of Citizens for Excellence in Education.

The agreement basically says, "Public schools should not be hostile to religion," said Education Secretary Richard Riley, who also signed it.

[Ed. Note: This writer questions the use of the word "non-partisan" when referring to ASCD, since ASCD—a spin-off of the National Education Association—is not a political party. Also, anyone who uses the ASCD to bring groups together on the issue of religion is behaving like whomever put the wolf in charge of the henhouse. As far as the people in Vista, California saying, "We want it now," what is it they want now? Why have they hung out the white flag in the war courageous parents across the nation have been fighting since 1945 to hold the line on the issue of "coming to common ground" on values?

Allowing religious groups to have equal access to school rooms for after-school meetings is actually the "camel's nose under the tent" for state regulation of religious activities and the introduction of all sorts of religions into the school's curriculum. Remember that Secretary Riley said that "Public schools should not be hostile to religion" and even witchcraft is a state-recognized religion.]

"WHY THE EDUCATION DEPARTMENT MUST GO" BY GORDON S. JONES, former under secretary of education in Secretary T.H. Bell's department of education, was published in *The Washington Times* on April 7, 1995. Jones said in part:

> To put the matter in its starkest terms, state school superintendents like the Department of Education because they are getting, on average nationwide, almost half of their funding and staff courtesy of the federal taxpayer. The state of Michigan, for example, receives 77 percent of its operating budget from the Department of Education; its counterpart in Iowa has 81 percent of its staff paid for by Uncle Sugar.

[Ed. Note: One of the primary reasons for abolishing the U.S. Department of Education is to cut down to size the bloated and dictatorial state departments of education which receive their marching orders from Washington.]

THE SUNDAY NEW YORK TIMES MAGAZINE OF APRIL 30, 1995 PUBLISHED "Who'll Teach Kids Right from Wrong?—The Character Education Movement Thinks the Answer Is the Schools" by Roger Rosenblatt. This article describes very clearly the pros and cons of a very controversial subject—the character education movement of the late 1980s and 1990s.

Rosenblatt devotes a good bit of space to Thomas Lickona, a developmental psychologist and a professor of education at the State University of New York, who is an acknowledged leader of the burgeoning character education movement. Lickona has recently established the Center for the 4th and 5th R's (Respect and Responsibility) at State University of New York-Cortland, which is becoming something of a national center for the study and development of character education curricula.

In the *New York Times* article Rosenblatt said that

> Character Education represents an effort to teach moral behavior to primary and secondary school students in a time perceived to be morally rudderless and to be without such teaching in local communities or in the home. Across the country, teachers are confronting children with moral dilemmas and asking them to think and talk. The felt need for this kind of education is so deep and widespread that it spurred a movement that has attracted as many former activists of the 1960s—Lickona is one—as it has conservative thinkers and politicians of the 1980s. (Supporters include Barbara Jordan, Barbara Bush, Marian Wright Edelman, Jesse Jackson, Tom Selleck and Nathan Glazer)....
>
> ...Richard Baer, Jr., of Cornell University has found fault with the content of some courses (bland pablum) and complained to Rosenblatt that there is no empirical evidence that character education actually improves character. Baer's main concern is that the public schools will become centers of a culture war between those on the the the right who believe that character education must incorporate religion and those on the left who do not want religious teaching at all....
>
> ...Besides Lickona's center at Cortland, there is the Josephson Institute of Ethics in Los Angeles which supports a Character Counts Coalition. Amitai Etzioni, a leader of the Communitarian movement, has devoted the energy of his Communitarian Network to advance the cause. Boston University has established the Center for the Advancement of Ethics and Character specifically to develop character education. All this is in addition to the work of individual schoolteachers and educators at the university level who are turning the idea that values can be formally taught into a field of study—Kevin Ryan, Director of the Center for the Advancement of Ethics and Character Education at Boston University; Kevin Walsh at the University of Alabama; William Damon at Brown University, and others. Kevin Ryan says: "We've had 10 years of talking about school reform. This issue is at the *heart* [emphasis in original] of school reform." For Kevin Walsh, the ultimate purpose of character education is nothing less than "to prepare the next generation to inherit society."

Rosenblatt identifies the following states as being involved in implementing character education: Mississippi, New Hampshire, New Jersey (the N.J. Dept. of Education has endorsed a set of "core values" and set up a council to define commonly accepted values). He lists St. Louis, Seattle, Chicago,

San Antonio, and Frankfort, Kentucky as cities and towns involved in character education and concludes by saying, "Classes in character education are held in rural and suburban schools, like those around Lansing, N.Y., and in inner-city schools, like Theodore Roosevelt High School in the Bronx."

In discussing the problems associated with character education, Rosenblatt asks what happens when two moral rights collide? A teacher might well begin complicating things, talking of exceptions and degrees, but a teacher also wants to avoid sliding into the moral relativism that created the mess that character educators are trying to fix. Rosenblatt then reveals the contradiction in Lickona's argument regarding moral relativism when he says, "Deciding to do his [Lickona's] dissertation on children's moral thinking, he was drawn... to Lawrence Kohlberg of Harvard, a major figure in the late 1960s on the subject of moral reasoning." The reader is urged to review this book's 1975 entry which describes Kohlberg's "Ethical Issues in Decision Making" for an understanding of the "moral relativism which created the mess that character educators," including especially Lickona, are supposedly correcting.

[Ed. Note: Curriculum is not the answer. The hiring of competent teachers whose lifestyles are exemplary and who exhibit civilized behavior (respectful, courteous, caring, loyal, etc.) is the best and safest way for schools to encourage morality in our children. Such an atmosphere, in combination with literature which helps students understand that moral behavior is something to emulate, not disdain, would do more than all the "character," "civics," "citizenship" and "values education" being discussed by the carefully selected task forces representing all degrees of political persuasion being set up to create the dialectic necessary to reach "common ground" on consensus values.

A careful reading of Rosenblatt's article is recommended as the first step towards an understanding of the pitfalls Americans face as they enthusiastically join forces to solve problems which clearly, short of violating the First Amendment, cannot be dealt with successfully in the classroom.]

LOOKING BACK, THINKING AHEAD: AMERICAN SCHOOL REFORM 1993–1995 was published by the Hudson Institute's (Indianapolis, Ind.) Educational Excellence Network (Chester Finn, William Bennett, Lamar Alexander, Diane Ravitch) in 1995. An excerpt follows:

> The report decries the backlash against outcomes-based education.... Many state outcomes are inappropriate... but... unfortunately, an awfully important baby [mastery learning] could go down the drain with the OBE bath water, and the country could find itself returning to an era when inputs, services, and intentions are the main gauge of educational quality and performance.

[Ed. Note: This quote exposes the hypocrisy of those policymakers "opposing OBE"; they oppose the outcomes, but not the *Skinnerian method*. As explained elsewhere, the outcomes can be changed overnight, whereas once all teachers have been trained or retrained in Skinnerian mastery learning, there can be *no* return to academic freedom for teachers or students.]

COMMITTEE FOR ECONOMIC DEVELOPMENT (CED) 1995 YEARBOOK ENTITLED *Putting Learning First: Governing and Managing the Schools for High Achievement* was published. This 60-page report called for school choice, charter schools, and social services delivered through schools or in collaboration with schools.

THE NATIONAL EDUCATION GOALS PANEL *COMMUNITY ACTION TOOLKIT* WAS developed and distributed by the U.S. Department of Education in 1995. The *Toolkit* was to be used for brainwashing, coercing and coalescing communities into accepting *Goals 2000*, H.R. 6, school-to-work, UNESCO's lifelong learning, etc. *Toolkit* instructions discussed how to deal with resisters. Elected officials, governors, and others were involved in production and dissemination of this 300 + page "How To" *Toolkit*, which used Professor Ronald Havelock's *The Change Agent's Guide to Innovations in Education* techniques to brainwash themselves and their constituents, especially targeting the religious community. (See the Internet version for Appendix XIV.)

"THE SHOCKING BELIEFS BEHIND EDUCATIONAL STRATEGIC PLANNING" BY Michael Jacques was published in the August 1995 issue of *The Interpreter*. Jacques, a concerned parent from West Allis, Wisconsin, has provided some very "hard-to-come-by" information regarding The Cambridge Group, an international strategic planning center for education reform. Excerpts from this informative article follow:

> Strategic planning seems to be the driving force at the local level for Outcomes-Based Education (OBE)/*Goals 2000*. Most school districts... have a facilitator trained by The Cambridge Group, which is an international strategic planning center for education out of Montgomery, Alabama. *The Facilitator's Training Manual* states under "The Urgency of Change" on p. 4:
>
> > Education must declare its magnanimous intent and omnipotent ability to serve as the surrogate family.

"Strategic Planning" is defined:

> Either no one can see or will acknowledge the fact that the real task of reformation is the radical transformation—a re-creation—of every facet of the American education system—its purpose and scope, its governance, its teaching and learning dynamics, its curricula, its time and place—all with a new dedication to developing the original genius in the mind of every student. This means a complete change of all education paradigms, of definitions, of disciplines, of vocabularies—perhaps values. This is the meaning of reform. And that is the meaning of strategic planning.... (p. 20)
>
> The advent of this new age, and the discovery that human beings now have both the capacity and the inclinations to re-create themselves in their own image according to their own imaginations... specifically it has demanded a redefinition of the human being.... (p. 28)

Urgency of Change
Spiritual: once confined only to that thought to be religious and other
worldly; forbidden in the world of practicality and reality; a relationship between someone and God or something. Now, a realization of the
pneumapsychosomatic nature of every person; the practical reality of
the human spirit when manifested in self-esteem, motivation, aesthetic
appreciation, manners and respect, as well as reverence; and *a priori* an
ultimate relationship between people....

   The fact is that all American institutions—the Constitution, the Bill
of Rights, the legislative and judicial branches of government, the education system, and other aspects of the current established order—were
predicated on a mono-cultural society. It will be interesting to see how
long the present systems can exist in a polyglot society. (p. 29)

Mr. Jacques ends his article by quoting from the Wisconsin Independent
School Board Association: "Only the village idiot would consider letting the
entire village in on the task of raising his children."

"THE LANGUAGE OF OBE REVEALS ITS LIMITATIONS" BY GRETCHEN SCHWARZ
was published in the September 1995 issue of *Educational Leadership*, Association for Supervision and Curriculum Development's (ASCD) journal. Ms.
Schwarz is assistant professor of curriculum and instruction at Oklahoma
State University, Stillwater, Oklahoma. Excerpts from Schwarz's refreshingly
objective critique of OBE follow:

In contrast, the language of Outcome-Based Education (OBE) seems limiting
and dehumanizing. Many educators not associated with the Religious Right
are highly critical of OBE, as am I, but for different reasons.... In response
to the March 1994 issue of *Educational Leadership*, which portrayed OBE in
a positive light, I would like to consider the language of OBE as revealed in
*Choosing Outcomes of Sig*nificance by William Spady. Individual words and
phrases jump out at me as a reader. Following are terms that Spady used
frequently and that particularly troubled me... "outcomes, generalizable,
Discrete Content Skills, microforms of learning, Structured Task Performances,
components in a larger block of curriculum, competence, mental processing,
performance enablers, execution, Higher-Order Competencies, technical and
strategic Life Performance Roles."...

   Such mechanistic, instrumentalist language has a constraining effect on
me as a reader, just as OBE has a constraining effect on school reform. This
list reads like the terminology of the CEO or the social engineer—very much
in the management-oriented, positivist-behaviorist tradition....

   ...With OBE, outside experts prescribe what is best for students and teachers, who remain essentially voiceless. Uniform outcomes are designed and
implemented in a curriculum that reduces thinking to mental processing....

   All the bottom-line language reminds the reader of the boardroom. Of
course, Spady's High Success Network is a business. But children are neither
customers nor products, and a school is not a business....

   OBE language is the scientistic, industrial language of Tyler and Skinner
as documented by Callahan (1962) in *Education and the Cult of Efficiency*.
Ultimately, the language of OBE is controlling, narrow, mechanistic, and
finally, impoverished. Our students and teachers deserve more than OBE
has to offer.

[Ed. Note: Professor Schwarz's comment that OBE "reduces thinking to mental processing" calls to mind the Thomas Kelly quote: "The brain should be used for processing, not storage."]

A REAFFIRMATION OF FAITH IN MAINE'S PUBLIC SCHOOLS, EDITED BY MARgaret L. Stubbs, Ph.D., of the Maine Department of Education in Augusta, Maine, was published in 1995. This document revealed the extraordinary thrust towards a partnership between religious institutions and the public schools. *Reaffirmation of Faith* also describes the socialist (planned economy) nature of workforce training in Maine. Excerpts follow:

> Religious and spiritual institutions have the responsibility to cultivate within their organizations the values they hope will guide their constituents' lives in a changing world that offers not only opportunity and beauty but also great danger, and in so doing have a complementary role to play as community participants in systemic school change....
>
> Before hiring a student, even for part-time work, review each student's work portfolio; the portfolio should contain vital information as to the student's school attendance record, achievement and assessment, sample writings, letter of recommendation, etc....
>
> ...Two-year degree programs in regional Vocational/Technical Centers for public high school graduates.... Courses would be based on an assessment of the work needs of the region. The particular courses would "sunset" once the needs of the area were fulfilled and new courses for the associate degree would be offered to fulfill new assessed needs for the area.

[Ed. Note: The last two sentences regarding "assessment of the work needs of the region" and courses "sunsetting" once the needs of the area were fulfilled show that Maine has adopted the same system described by Professor Eugene Boyce when he said in communist countries education is "directly tied to jobs.... They do not educate people for jobs that do not exist. No such direct controlled relationships between education and jobs exists in democratic countries" (see 1983 Eugene Boyce entry). Suppose your child wants to take a course that has "sunsetted"? Will he/she have to leave the state in search of such a course, or be deprived of the opportunity?]

H.R. 1617 OR THE *CAREERS ACT (CONSOLIDATED AND REFORMED EDUcation, Employment, and Rehabilitation Systems Act)* passed the U.S. House of Representatives in September of 1995. The law calls for four consolidated job training programs to replace formerly existing programs: youth development and career preparation; adult training; adult education and literacy; and vocational rehabilitation. This legislation was based on school-to-work legislation passed in 1994. Four block grants for job training were tied together at state and local levels to form one cohesive system organized around a single plan submitted to the federal government.

Under this plan states would develop one-stop delivery systems, business-led unelected local workforce boards, and voucher programs to allow them to maintain "top-notch state-of-the-art job training programs." State legislatures would be bypassed and money would be driven to states and communities (in most cases 80% funding is spent locally). H.R. 1617 gave enormous power to state governors and removed the power of local school boards to determine what is best for their students. Labor market information systems, funded by the federal government to increase availability of information provided to those who need additional job training, would be strengthened.

To promote accountability, the *CAREERS Act* set up a system of goals and performance indicators to ensure that states, communities, service providers, and "clients" are all focused on results. The *Act* consolidated or eliminated more than 150 program authorities. This legislation fulfilled requirements outlined in Marc Tucker's letter to Hillary Clinton following the November 1992 election. H.R. 1617 represented a radical change in America's free economic system. (See the Internet version for Appendix XV.)

IN 1995 REPORTS OF OUTCOME-BASED EDUCATION FAILURES CONTINUED TO surface: Chicago, Illinois; Johnson City, New York; Utah OBE Project; Kentucky; Pasco, Washington; California; Rochester, New York (Carnegie National Alliance for Education and Economy—Marc Tucker/David Hornbeck pilots); Cottage Grove, Oregon (first high school in nation to issue the Certificate of Initial Mastery, which originated and is copyrighted by Marc Tucker's Center for Education and the Economy); Ted Sizer's Coalition of Essential Schools (funded by Carnegie's Education Commission of the States and multi-millionaire Walter Annenberg); inner cities—most of which used Mastery Learning—especially Washington, D.C.; and Secretary of Education Riley's home state of South Carolina (lowest test scores in the nation). These failures and troubling consequences were reported in major newspapers, magazines and education-related journals.

[Ed. Note: The writer predicts that once schools have been manipulated into substituting non-competitive criterion-referenced testing for competitive norm-referenced testing, the dismal test score scenario will be a thing of the past, as a result of the proposed "quality" teach-to-the test measures of educational achievement being put in place. Then, all parents can plaster their cars with "My Child Is an Honor Student" bumper stickers.]

TRI-CITIES FOUNDATION FOR ACADEMIC EXCELLENCE (TFAE) OF PASCO, Washington issued a press release in 1995 entitled "Survey of Former Pasco, Washington Teachers Gives Outcomes-Based Education Insights" which read as follows:

> In 1988 the Pasco School District piloted OBE and has since been used as an OBE role model for education reform across Washington State and the nation. During the 1992–93 and 1993–94 school years, the Pasco School District lost more than one hundred teachers. Tri-Cities Foundation for Academic Excellence (TFAE) surveyed these former teachers to obtain their insights on the OBE program and establish whether or not the OBE philosophy and the manner in which it was implemented were influential factors in their leaving the District. Are teachers currently being coerced or forced to leave the Pasco

School District if they are not using the Outcomes-Based Instructional Model? The following results represent responses from teachers in a district used as a model for Washington state's now-mandated Outcomes-Based Education and OBE across the nation:

- 68% responded children did not benefit from Outcomes-Based Education;
- 86% responded Outcomes-Based Education divided teachers and created polarized camps;
- 27% stated that they were asked to leave if they didn't agree with Outcomes-Based Education.

The survey was designed for complete confidentiality and anonymity.[38]

[Ed. Note: Barbara McFarlin-Kosiec, Ph.D. in Educational Leadership, a veteran teacher in the Pasco School District, has filed suit against the district due to its non-renewal of her contract. The non-renewal was based on the vice-principal's opinion that she failed to use the instructional process of OBE in the classroom. Ms. Kosiec's suit is based upon her belief that her constitutional rights have been violated; i.e., in order to continue teaching in the district she was required to go along with an alien philosophy and to hold certain politically correct attitudes and beliefs.[39]]

NATIONAL ISSUES IN EDUCATION: GOALS 2000 AND SCHOOL-TO-WORK EDITED by John F. Jennings, general counsel for education for the Committee on Education and Labor of the U.S. House of Representatives (Phi Delta Kappa: Bloomington, Ind., and Institute for Educational Leadership: Washington, D.C., 1995) was published.[40] The following are comments by Mr. Jennings which reveal some heretofore closely guarded secrets related to the roots of *Goals 2000* and the *School-to-Work Opportunities Act*:

Now there is a measure of national agreement that there should be voluntary national standards.... All the major education organizations, all the major business groups, the nation's governors, the current Democratic president, and the former Republican president have all advocated this concept. The purpose of this book is to explain why and how this agreement came about by focusing on two major legislative initiatives of the Clinton Administration: the *Goals 2000 Act* and the *School-to-Work Opportunities Act*. The Clinton initiatives are rooted in the Bush legislation and in the summit conference held by President Bush with the nation's governors in Charlottesville, Virginia, in 1989, in which then-Governor Clinton took part. At that event the governors and the President agreed on the concept of national goals for education, the first ever to be devised.

While previously there had been some acceptance of the idea that the federal government had a role in dealing with special needs children and with certain problems in education, there had not been agreement in this century that the national government had a legitimate concern about the general state of education. And, it is important to point out, the governors did not universally endorse the idea of expanding the influence of the federal government in education. Some—probably most—hoped that some new way could be found to raise the issue of education to a level of national awareness without relying on such past practices as federal grants. The tension created by trying to find this new way permeated the debate that took place during the next five years.

President Bush complemented his meeting with the governors by sending to Congress legislation that he believed would reform education. That bill contained a number of small-scale programs seeking to change a few schools and practices. The Democratic House and Senate reluctantly passed a version of Bush's bill. However, very conservative Republican senators subsequently filibustered the final bill; and the initial Bush school reform initiative died in 1990.

In 1991 Lamar Alexander was appointed secretary of education by President Bush, and he substantially revised the bill that the Senate had killed the year before. Alexander, working with Chester Finn and others who were familiar with the work of British Prime Minister Margaret Thatcher in enacting a national curriculum in England and Wales, convinced Bush to endorse the idea of national standards for education.

[Ed. Note: Of interest here is that the National Assessment of Educational Progress (NAEP) had been working on assessment for many years, dating back at least to 1980, with Clare Burstall of Wales, U.K.]

The internationalization of education, with its exchanges of data systems, curricula, methods, technology, teachers, etc., is essential for the implementation of the international socialist management and control system being put in place right now. A fascinating book entitled *Union Now: The Proposal for Inter-Democracy—Federal Union* (shorter version) by Clarence Streit (Harper Brothers Publishers: New York and London, 1941) described plans for the reunification of the United States and England, the first stage of which is presently being expanded to include the European Community and former (?) communist countries in Eastern Europe.

Our nation's replication of the English education system, as proposed by Lamar Alexander and Chester Finn, coincides with the proclaimed desire of Andrew Carnegie in 1886 to "create two nations out of one people" (return the United States to the "mother" country—England). Carnegie's corporation of the same name and all of its subsidiaries have been the principal organizations in charge of American education. Through funding of the most important entities controlling American education—the Educational Testing Service, the National Assessment of Educational Progress, the Education Commission of the States—and through its most important exchanges with the "former" Soviet Union, Carnegie's power, influence, and point of view have been strongly felt throughout this century. Lenin would be pleased indeed with the accomplishments of the Carnegie Corporation in promoting what Lenin referred to as international socialism through the creation of individual regions and later through the amalgamation of those regions into an international socialist system; i.e., one world government.

The following quote from Andrew Carnegie's *Triumphant Democracy or Fifty Years' March of the Republic* (Charles Scribners Sons: New York, 1886) is thought provoking:

Time may dispel many pleasing illusions and destroy many noble dreams, but it shall never shake my belief that the wound caused by the wholly un-looked for and undesired separation of the mother from her child is not to bleed forever. Let men say what they will, therefore, I say, that as surely as the sun in the heavens once shone upon Britain and America united, so surely is it one morning to rise, shine upon, and greet again the reunited state, the British-American union.

Jennings's revelations from *National Issues in Education* continue below:

> The governors and the President had agreed on national goals for education in 1989, but they had not proposed national standards for education. Therefore, Bush's second reform plan moved national involvement in education to a more advanced stage....
>
> A Republican president proposing such national standards in education was the education policymaking equivalent to the reshaping of foreign policy when President Nixon went to China. Richard Nixon had made a career out of attacking Communism and calling liberals sympathizers of that ideology; and then he—not a liberal—opened the doors to "Red" China, the same doors that he had spent 25 years locking.

[Ed. Note: It was also under Nixon's watch that the National Institute of Education was created and it was he who carved the nation into ten regions, facilitating the change in our constitutional governance from a constitutional republic to a participatory democracy—through the regional government process necessary for world government. The late Senator Edmund Muskie (D.-Maine), referred to as "Mr. Metro" by those opposed to regional government, said Nixon had accomplished what several democratic administrations had been unable to accomplish!]

Jennings continued his fascinating account as follows:

> Democratic Presidents Kennedy and Johnson had proposed a major expansion of federal aid to education in the 1960s and had achieved the enactment of historic legislation that created the current array of federal programs. But they were dogged along the way by criticism from conservatives who asserted that the liberals were really trying to nationalize education. Now, 25 years later, it was a self-proclaimed conservative Republican, not a liberal Democrat, who was advocating a monumental movement away from local control of education.
>
> Despite the importance of the second Bush legislation, it ran into the same problem as the first. A Democratic Congress reluctantly passed the bill in the House and the Senate, but the conference report again was filibustered by very conservative Republican senators who were not as impressed as were Bush, Alexander, and Finn with the accomplishments of Margaret Thatcher in establishing a national curriculum.

[Ed. Note: The writer would like to repeat the quote from Theodore Dalrymple (pen name for Dr. Anthony Daniels), the British physician who wrote for *The Wall Street Journal* in 1988 the following observations concerning the deplorable condition of the English education system which Bush, Alexander and Finn wished to emulate:

> In eight years in medical practice in an English slum (in which lives incidentally a fifth of a population of the industrial English city where I work)

I have met only one teen-ager of hundreds I have asked who knew when World War II was fought. The others thought it took place in the 1900s or the 1970s, and lasted up to 30 years.]

National Issues in Education also includes a chapter by U.S. Secretary of Education Richard W. Riley. Riley provides two delicious morsels regarding the "bipartisan" atmosphere surrounding the birthing of *Goals 2000* and the *School-to-Work Opportunities Act*:

> The National Goals Panel was actively opposed by Congress which felt no ownership and resented the non-voting status of Congressional members.... (p. 5)
> ...Truth was the reform movement at the national level had no statutory basis. Even ten years after the report *A Nation at Risk*, there had been little federal response. The National Education Goals, three years after their announcement, had no legal standing of any kind. No federal initiative, no funding or flexibility had been enacted to provide states, communities, or schools with the assistance they needed to reach these important goals. Most troubling of all, as attractive as the goals were, as important as they were, as essential as they were, in the final analysis they represented nothing more than a political agreement between a former President and the nation's governors. We decided to take the seeds of interest we had inherited and transform them into a national movement—a movement in which states and local districts with a clear vision of where they wanted to go could count on the American people and the federal government as partners in the journey. Thus the *Goals 2000—Educate America Act* was conceived. (p. 6)

[Ed. Note: The reader by this time recognizes the fact that the American people did not buy into *Goals 2000*/School-to-Work, that the government was compelled to use its change agent manual—the bag of tricks in the *Community Action Toolkit*—to implement the restructuring and get key legislation passed. (See the Internet version for Appendix XIV.)]

IN DECEMBER OF 1995 THE FOLLOWING INFORMATION WAS EXCERPTED FROM United States Information Agency Internet sources and put into summary form by education researcher and writer Joan Masters of Bowie, Maryland:

> DECEMBER 3, 1995: MADRID, SPAIN—U.S. President Bill Clinton, president of the European Commission Jacques Santer, and Prime Minister of Spain Felipe Gonzalez, who is also president of the European Union's Council of Ministers, formally endorse a New Transatlantic Agenda (NTA). The NTA would enable the two sides, the US and the EU, to join forces to deal with a wide range of international, political and economic issues. The New Agenda's "joint action" has some one hundred "initiatives" aimed at achieving four broad objectives:
> 1. Promoting peace, development and democracy around the world;
> 2. Responding to global challenges;
> 3. Contributing to the expansion of world trade; and
> 4. Building bridges across the Atlantic.
> With little or no national debate the United States is committed to become the European Union's "partner" in solving most of the world's problems. Only the enlargement of NATO receives wide coverage. (On September 9, 1997, 133 of the United States' "leading foreign policy experts and states-

men" signed the New Atlantic Initiative Statement on NATO enlargement.
These signers cover a broad range of America's well-known nationalists and
internationalists. John O'Sullivan, editor of William F. Buckley's "conservative" journal *National Review*, resigned his position to become founder and
co-chairman of the New Atlantic Initiative.)

DECEMBER 21, 1995: WASHINGTON, D.C.—Dr. Joseph Duffey, Director of the
United States Information Agency (USIA) and Mr. Jeronimo Saavedra
Acevedo, minister of science and education of Spain, signed an agreement
between the United States of America (U.S.) and the European Community
(EC) establishing a cooperation programme in higher education and vocational education and training. This agreement is in keeping with the fourth
NTA objective—"Building bridges across the Atlantic"—and establishes a
"formal basis for the conduct of cooperative activities in higher education and
vocational education and training." The annex of this seven page Agreement
reveals that the US/EC will form a consortia to support education institutions and vocational training establishments undertaking joint projects. Each
consortium will be supported by seed funding and will mutually agree upon
eligible subject areas. Activities eligible for support may include: frameworks
for student mobility, including work placement; structured exchanges of students, teachers, trainers, and administrators; joint development of innovative
curricula; and transatlantic cooperation. Among other things too numerous to
mention here, the joint consortia projects will be made available for the use
of "a wider audience." *No longer called citizens*, the Agreement acknowledges
"the crucial contributions of education and training for the development of
human resources capable of participating in the global knowledge-based
economy." [emphasis in original]

By 1996 grants were already being given to US colleges and universities
for such projects as: "Global Dimensions in Health Care;" "Atlas"—a project
for environmental management; and "US/EU Export Development Program,"
a feature of which is the use of student mobility, "not just for academic purposes, but also as part of an export development program designed to facilitate
more transatlantic trade for local business and industry." Another very interestingly named project, given out to seven different American institutions,
is called "Work World 2000: An International Strategy for School-to-Work
Transitions." Using simulations of both American and European workplaces
and company models, students will learn the structures of international business and follow up with transatlantic exchanges and internships.

DECEMBER 1995: BRUSSELS, BELGIUM—Representatives from the nations of the
European Union release their study group report called *Accomplishing Europe
through Education and Training*. For Americans to understand the inherent
dangers of throwing in our lot with the socialistic states of Europe, especially
in the field of education, this report needs to be studied in depth. It's no
secret that some conservatives in the U.S. believe that a European education
is far superior to what has been offered in our public education system in the
last thirty years. And this may be right, at least academically. On the other
hand, there are those who believe many of the "innovations" we are plagued
with, such as sex education, originated in Europe, especially in England.
One European group doing studies on "multi-media" materials complains
that most of the educational software in the EU comes from the US. So, it is
difficult to know for certain which continent created the propaganda horrors

inflicted on our children today in the classrooms of our respective countries. But whatever the truth, much as the Soviet Union once tried to create the "Soviet Man," the European Union study group report is laying out a plan to develop the "European Union Citizen."

The report reminds its readers of the history of pagan times and the great philosophers of Greece, then recalls Europe's Christian roots, implying that the Union of Europe's ancient nations has now begun a new age; education of the Union's children must change to accommodate this modern era of globalisation and dissemination of information technologies. For Americans, who cut their milk teeth on the ideals of independence and freedom, and the belief that anyone who works hard can overcome anything, even class, one sentence is particularly chilling. The report says, "Trends in work/ employment practices and the emergence of a learning society will be even more instrumental in defining everyone's place, as a function of skills and knowledge built up throughout life." But with all the talk of the information society and "life-long learning," these European educators predict that "ever-increasing ecological pressures will prompt a radical re-think of our model of economic growth with increasing emphasis on 'sustainability.'" This contradictory vision of economic growth and environmental sustainability may yet be the un-doing of the New World Order on both sides of the Atlantic.

1996

THE *CHICAGO* *TRIBUNE* OF FEBRUARY 14, 1996 CARRIED THE ARTICLE "School Plan Skips over the Basics." Some excerpts follow:

> Yet for all their specifics, school leaders said Tuesday that they will not spell out many details on how they will implement their version of direct instruction, a back-to-basics instructional approach that has won national acclaim for improving student achievement at other inner city schools....
>
> Chicago school officials were so impressed with the approach, which uses scripted lessons delivered in a rapid-fire manner, that a contingent of them flew last year to Houston to see how direct instruction helped one of the schools post some of the highest test scores in Texas.... But for now, Chicago school leaders said they need more time to "customize" direct instruction to fit the local needs....
>
> "The educational plan is a big plan, and it's comprehensive," said Paul Villas, chief executive officer of the schools. "We've looked at a lot of solutions and direct instruction is just one of them.".... DeChico maintained that they remained enthusiastic about the direct instruction approach....
>
> One other top school official indicated that the early draft of the education plan included only a few lines about it. The reason, according to the source, was because of complaints, particularly from local teachers, that the approach is too time-consuming and stunts teacher creativity.... The administrator suggested that school leaders may have been swayed by teacher complaints that direct instruction requires too much of teachers, who would have to study the scripted lessons nightly for the next day....
>
> Villas said that by June, school leaders will be ready to trot out details on how they will use direct instruction.

[Ed. Note: Where are the norm-referenced test scores that prove student achievement in inner city schools? Or, has enough time passed (16 years) that the change agents can count on parents and teachers having such short memories that they have forgotten that 18,000 inner city students dropped out of high school due to the same "rat lab" Chicago Mastery Learning experiment to which they were subjected between 1968 and 1981?]

THE CHICAGO TRIBUNE RAN THE ARTICLE "CITY SCHOOLS DROPPING IOWA Skills Tests" on March 7, 1996. An excerpt follows:

> The new test would assess whether students have mastered what they have been taught.... One potentially contentious issue remains: direct instruction, a strategy aimed at forcing low-achieving schools to accept a curriculum based on scripted lessons and recitation.... "I can't imagine that the majority of the teachers in our school would at all be willing to implement direct instruction," said Julie Wopestehoff, Executive Director of Parents United for Responsible Education.

AN UNTITLED ARTICLE APPEARED IN *THE CHICAGO SUN TIMES* ON MARCH 8, 1996. An excerpt follows:

> Determined to show that all Chicago public school students can succeed, DePaul University is waiting for the stroke of Governor Edgar's pen to kick off plans for its own charter school.... "These children can learn at the same rate as the children of Ph.D.'s.... We have a list of things we can choose from. There's direct instruction, whole language, team learning, cooperative learning," said Barbara Sizemore, Dean of DePaul University's College of Education, Chicago.

[Ed. Note: Well, well. This quote stripped the Empress and her change agent associates of whatever clothing they had left—which wasn't much due to this type of "bait and switch" technique having been used on parents over and over again. Create the problem; parents scream; impose a solution they would never have accepted in the first place; parents gratefully accept it, not knowing the only difference between the solution and what they had before is a new label.

Some parents understood the manipulative mastery learning method. This writer has boxes full of letters from teachers, doctors, and parents in Texas, Ohio, Arizona, Indiana, etc., deploring the serious negative effects of mastery learning—sickness and stress. But when the change agents substituted the "direct instruction" label for the failed "mastery learning" label, how could parents be expected to recognize the deceit?

Actually, it does take some kind of nerve to propose a solution which only fourteen years earlier had been *discredited as a failure* in Chicago, and which has put Chicago, Washington, D.C., and South Carolina at the bottom of the heap as far as test scores go. If one checked all the other inner city schools that have used this Skinnerian method, one would find only minor differences between their low test scores and those of the three mentioned above.

Dean Sizemore was telling parents and teachers something—something very important. She was obviously very proud of the menu being offered to the naïve charter school parents and children in Chicago—the menu to be offered to all schools in the nation. The implementation of site-based management (unelected, hand-picked councils) would assure approval of Sizemore's controversial outcome-based education which consisted of cooperative learning and Engelmann's direct instruction/DISTAR/SRA/mastery learning in conjunction with literature-based whole language instruction, etc.—a delicious concoction to be sure, guaranteed to further dumb down our children.

Parents, Direct Instruction is *not* back-to-basics (teacher-directed instruction of content, with the teacher teaching in the front of the classroom). It is fast-forward into the world of global workforce training, where the teacher will be in front of the classroom chanting, *not* instructing; your children will be expected to "perform" like rats or pigeons, *not* learn academic content.

Parents want teachers to teach content which their child can relate to other parts of his/her life for complete understanding; they want their child to be able to make connections between what he/she learns and past knowledge, to be used in the future. Chanting back what a teacher chants is *not* learning—it is training. There can be no transfer of knowledge when bits and pieces of information which relate to nothing are all the "robots" can repeat. Parents don't want teachers to be controllers or directors, and they surely don't want their children to be passive learners chanting back answers like parrots, mimicking what a teacher says. Such *training* considers your child as nothing but a raw resource to be prepared and molded as a product. Traditional education, which allows for give and take between teacher and student (creativity) is the last thing in which the corporate/education elite is interested.

This new type of education (training), in conjunction with mandatory community service, workforce preparation starting in elementary school, mandatory uniforms for America's school children, new school board policies regarding fighting in school which will allow the police to come to the school and drag your children into holding tanks for further prosecution, etc., sends chills down the back of this writer. It brings to mind the ugliness of a recent era in history which many seem to have forgotten.]

IN-SERVICE TEACHER TRAINING WAS HELD IN CHICAGO, INDIANAPOLIS, AND Minneapolis during the first part of May in 1996. The flyer advertising these events stated the following:

NATIONAL EDUCATION INSTITUTE PRESENTS

Using Research-Based Teaching Techniques to Increase Student Learning:
Or How to Teach Anyone Anything

PROGRAM AGENDA:
The three key parts of direct instruction; discover the major and minor differences between direct instruction and traditional teaching methods.
National consultant, teacher and trainer Adrienne Allen to conduct the training sessions.

[Ed. Note: This flyer was received from a homeschool mom who said the "research-based" training was for homeschoolers. The above quote presents a very different picture from that being circulated throughout the nation which describes direct instruction as a "traditional" teaching method.]

"DUMBED-DOWN SATS DISGUISE DEFICIENCIES—THE FAULT, DEAR EDUCA- tor, Is Not in Our Tests," by George C. Roche, president of Hillsdale College in Hillsdale, Michigan, was published in the July 5, 1996 issue of *Human Events*. Dr. Roche's article underscores the success of the internationalist change agents' relentless efforts to dumb down our children and, in turn, our nation. The following excerpts are most enlightening:

> "SAT Scores Rise Strongly after Test Is Overhauled" read a *Wall Street Journal* headline. The continuation of the article carried the title "SAT Scores Post Strong Increase." Good news?
>
> Hardly. The "higher" scores came from a "dumbed-down" test. Students now have an extra half hour to complete the "new" Scholastic Aptitude Test. They now use electronic calculators and answer fewer questions in general and fewer multiple-choice math questions in particular. Reading passages now ask definitions from context. And the difficult antonym section (involving knowledge of words that are opposite in meaning), calling for linguistic and intellectual subtleties long lost, has been dropped entirely.
>
> ...Here's the College Board's rationale for the changes: "Students taking the SAT in the 1990s are substantially different from those who took the test in the 1940s when the scale was created. Continuing to force-fit their scores to a scale established for a very different group of students reduces the interpretive value of the score within the population for the sake of slavish consistency to the original scale and comparisons over time."
>
> They'd like you to be persuaded by exaggerations like "force-fit" and "slavish" and breeze past their statement that today's students are "substantially different" from those who took the test in 1940. I'd like you to be persuaded that the College Board just admitted that the educational system's "substantially different" students are really "substantially deficient."
>
> ...The history standards of the government's new *Goals 2000* program, drenched in political correctness, highlight America's admitted faults and leave out much that is positive. OBE students going through the *Goals 2000* program wouldn't have much of a chance with the older, tougher SAT test, but the easier version, plus the "recentering" changes now in place will help disguise actual deficiencies.
>
> Putting an artificially higher number on actually lower academic performance only highlights the problems facing American education. You can fiddle with the figures forever, but as long as education "professionals" refuse to be honest with our citizens, matters can only get worse.

[Ed. Note: Not only did Dr. Roche vent his frustration with the new SAT, *The New York Times*, in an article entitled "Defining Literacy Downward" in its August 28, 1996 issue, stated: "The S.A.T. turns poor performance into a new norm."]

[ddd]

"PARENTS TURN TO TUTORS: REBELLION AGAINST WHOLE LANGUAGE" BY
Rosalind Rossi and Sharon Cotliar was published in *The Chicago Sun-Times*
on August 12, 1996. Excerpts follow:

> Jean Iovino, owner of eight Sylvan Learning Centers in the suburbs, said
> the number of beginning readers in her centers has skyrocketed in the last
> five years.... Many parents suggest that the shift from phonics to the "whole
> language" philosophy of reading instruction is behind the drop in scores....
> "Our business has increased 20 percent a year every year for the past four
> years," said Vickie Glazar, spokeswoman for Maryland-based Sylvan Learn-
> ing Systems.

[Ed. Note: Sylvan Learning Centers use mastery learning/direct instruction. The *Reading Excellence Act of 1998* (H.R. 2614) contains the legally
questionable call for the use of Sylvan Learning Centers: "Tutorial service
providers might include public agencies, non-profit private organizations,
and profit-seeking private business firms (e.g., Sylvan Learning Centers)."]

"A GUIDE TO COMPETING TEACHING METHODS" BY ROSALIND ROSSI WAS
published in *The Chicago Sun-Times* on August 12, 1996. A portion of "A
Guide" follows:

> Direct Instruction: A method of instruction in which the teacher directs
> lessons in carefully sequenced steps. In one of its most conservative forms,
> developed by Siegfried Engelmann of the University of Oregon, teachers use
> textbooks with child-tested scripts to teach phonics in small steps, and chil-
> dren repeat back words, or give answers as a group in fast-paced, rhythmic,
> "choral chants." Often includes heavy use of workbooks. Complaints about
> direct instruction: The Engelmann method, used alone, has been accused
> of turning teachers into robots, of robbing children of the joy of reading real
> books at an early age and of emphasizing sound over meaning.

DR. SHIRLEY MCCUNE, PROJECT DIRECTOR FOR THE MID-CONTINENT RE-
gional Educational Laboratory (McREL) wrote *The Light Shall Set You Free*
(Athena Publishing, Alpha Connections: Santa Fe, New Mexico, 1996), in
which she revealed her theological connections with New Age guru Alice
Bailey. Excerpts from McCune's book underscore the fact that the U.S. taxpayer is paying the salaries of social engineers with bizarre beliefs who are
wreaking havoc in curriculum development and organizational restructuring
of the nation's schools. Excerpts follow:

> Those who journey into the Light will move with us in the ethers to live
> in the Fifth Dimension and above. Those who choose to stay in the lower
> vibrations will be provided for accordingly also. The Earth will be cleansed
> in the next decade for the purification must be complete.... The way to the
> Light is to increase your vibratory frequency.... This point of Light stimulates
> each breath we take.... The Light is within.... This tremendous source of
> power can be accessed only by going within the mind's eye and by listen-
> ing to the silence.... This path requires a whole new curriculum and set of
> guidelines to describe our existence.... The Light is within us always, silently

waiting to be discovered, to show us the way back to our divinity.... Each individual is actually a co-creator with the Divine.... The date for entry into the Fifth Dimension is scheduled for the year 2012, says Kuthum [An alleged "ascended master" who supposedly transmitted his ideas to Madame Blavatsky, founder of the Theosophical Society and author of *The Secret Doctrine* and *Isis Unveiled*, ed.]....

...We are entering the Age of Aquarius.... The goal for all of humanity who will enter the new millenium is to become androgynous.... Educational systems, businesses, political structures, and governments all built on self-serving principles, for example, are crumbling, only to be re-born through tremendous pain into higher forms. Thus, we are witnessing "the end of the world" and we do not even recognize what we see. Standing on the threshold of the Aquarian Age... we can align our bodies and our behaviors to create harmony and consistency with the God within us.

"UNDERSTANDING OUTCOME-BASED EDUCATION," AN ARTICLE WRITTEN BY Jerry L. Haddock, Ed.D., regional director for Southern California/Southern Nevada and director of curriculum for the Association of Christian Schools International (ACSI), and Sharon R. Berry, Ph.D., a director of curriculum of ACSI, was published in 1996 and circulated throughout the ACSI network of Christian schools.[41] Excerpts follow:

MASTERY LEARNING

Developed from Skinnerian psychology, Mastery Learning proposes that students should be taught until they have learned a subject no matter how long it takes. Believing that all learning could be broken into minute, successive steps of behavior, thousands of objectives for each subject area were published in voluminous books. The difference in Outcome-Based Education is a specification of a smaller number of more general outcomes. For example, there are 36 outcomes specified for graduation in the Littleton, Colorado project....

On the last page of the article—as a part of a larger category entitled "Where Do We Stand?"—under the title "Mastery Learning" the authors assert:

This [mastery] is also an important part of the Christian school. No, not in the sense that secular OBE proponents advocate, but with a Christ-honoring emphasis. One that says every student is important enough to have an appropriate instructional program and a teacher who is sensitive enough to do what is necessary to ensure that the student masters curriculum at his/her ability level. The distinction here is that we should not require all students to learn at the same rate. God has given each of us different talents and abilities. To the best of our ability we ensure that students achieve basic standards, with all students being challenged to reach their potential. As Dr. Bruce Wilkinson, author of "The 7 Laws of the Learner," has emphasized, "If a student hasn't learned, the teacher hasn't taught."

[Ed. Note: It is difficult to understand ACSI's support for a method of teaching which is clearly based on Darwin's theory of evolution (that man is an animal), which uses Skinnerian stimulus-response-stimulus operant conditioning. How can Christian educators and parents oppose the teaching of evolution at school board meetings across the country and then return to their homes/schools the next day and use a method of teaching/learning which is based on the evolutionist theory which they oppose? Personally, this writer does not agree with Dr. Wilkinson's statement concerning the student and teacher. Sometimes, no matter how well a teacher may teach, the student may not be interested in learning.[42]]

ANITA HOGE DEVISED AND DISTRIBUTED WIDELY "FIVE MAGIC QUESTIONS Enable Parents to Debate the Issues" in 1996 as a tool for parents' groups to use in testimony before state legislatures and local school boards. The text of the pamphlet follows in its entirety.

FIVE MAGIC QUESTIONS ENABLE PARENTS TO DEBATE THE ISSUES

Education regulations or laws state which standards or outcomes your child needs to meet to graduate. Many of the outcomes are vague and subjective. Look at the verbs. This shows why these outcomes are impossible to measure objectively. An example under a category like "Citizenship" states, "All students will negotiate and cooperate with others." The Five Magic Questions parents can use to win the debate when outcomes reflect subjective or vague areas are:

1. *How do you measure that outcome?* If an outcome states that "all children must have ethical judgment, honesty, or integrity," what exactly is going to be measured? How do you measure a bias in a child in order for him to graduate? Must children be diagnosed? Will they be graded by observation or pencil or paper tests? How will performance or behavior be addressed?

2. *How is that outcome scored or what is the standard?* What behavior is "Appropriate" and to what degree? For example, how much self-esteem is too much or not enough to graduate? Can government score the attitudes and values of its citizens?

3. *Who decides what that standard will be?* The state has extended their mandated graduation requirements or exit outcomes down to the individual child. This bypasses all local autonomy. What about locally elected school directors? Will they become obsolete? Are we talking about a state or government diploma?

4. *How will my child be remediated?* What are you going to do to my children to change them from here to there in their attitudes and values in order to graduate? How do you remediate ethical judgment, decision-making, interpersonal skills, environmental attitudes? What techniques will be used? What risks are involved? What justification does the state have to change my children's attitudes?

5. *What if parent and state disagree on the standard or how it is measured in the classroom?* Who has the ultimate authority over the child? What about privacy? Can parents opt out of a graduation requirement of the state?

All children must meet the same fixed standard of "future citizen" or not graduate, go to college, or get a job. Your child is human capital. This is why the state wants control of the graduation requirement—and that is why local school boards must create policy to stop the state from exerting power over elected officials. Ask this question: Do you want equity in opportunity, or do you want equity in standards?

[ddd]

IN THE SEPTEMBER 1996 ISSUE OF *VITALITY* AN ARTICLE ENTITLED "EDUCA-tion: Why the 'Dumbing Down' in the Schools?" by Rep. Henry Hyde, chairman of the Republican Platform Committee, was published. Congressman Hyde, in an excellent critique of *Goals 2000, School-to-Work* and *CAREERS* legislation, asserted:

> This concept has been around since at least the 1960s and perhaps as far back as the 1930s. It has been tried in many schools over the last 20–30 years, to the detriment of our children. In the 70s, it was called "Mastery Learning" under the supervision of Professor Benjamin Bloom, and now it is known as "Outcomes-Based Education" (OBE). State school superintendents have learned to call OBE by other names because of its bad reputation which precedes it, but the concepts are all the same.

[Ed. Note: Representative Henry Hyde seems to be one of the few congressmen who understands the "method." This writer wonders if he is aware of the fact that the Chicago schools are using the method under the label "direct instruction"—and that Chicago schools have signed an education agreement with Russia?]

IN THE SCHOOL WATCH COLUMN OF *THE ATLANTA CONSTITUTION* THE TOPIC of the day for October 14, 1996 was "Teaching Politics." Excerpts follow:

> Teachers are finding innovative ways to interest students in becoming well-informed voters. Many teachers form a seating chart based on alphabetic order, but Linda Morrison uses another method. In her current issues class at North Cobb High School, liberals sit on the left side of the room and conservatives sit—where else?—on the right. Morrison's technique is one of many methods teachers are using to educate students on electoral and political processes.
>
> "When you combine what we do in here with their American government class, it makes everything a lot more interesting for the students," said Morrison, a former Cobb County Teacher of the Year.
>
> At the beginning of the year, Morrison gives her class a political orientation test, which charts how conservative or liberal a student is on several issues. The more liberal your views, the farther to the left of the room you sit. Those with moderate views sit closer to the middle, and conservatives sit on the right.
>
> "Our main textbook is *Newsweek*," Morrison said. "Whatever the current issues are, we discuss them. All I usually do is referee."

OCTOBER 21, 1996 *THE NEW YORK TIMES* PUBLISHED AN ARTICLE ENTITLED "Carnegie Foundation Selects a New Leader," Lee Shulman, Ph.D. For further information about the "new leader" the reader should re-read the 1968 entry on "Learning and Instruction... Chicago Mastery Learning" in which the behavioral psychologist Lee Shulman was deeply involved.

1997

ON JANUARY 25, 1997 THE FIRST PLENARY SESSION OF THE NATIONAL COM- mission on Civic Renewal was held. Funded by the Pew Charitable Trusts, the Commission operates out of the Institute for Philosophy and Public Policy, a research center at the University of Maryland at College Park. One common theme running through the numerous reports produced in 1998 as a result of the Commission's study of the "deplorable" lack of citizen involvement, crying out for partnerships, etc., was that elected officials are no longer able to meaningfully contribute to the decision-making process when seeking answers to societal problems.

Those chosen to promote political and social "action" in our "needy" communities came from all political persuasions—a clever technique which made the Commission seem all-embracing and allows for public ownership of the projects selected for implementation and encouragement. When one had Ernesto Cortes, Jr. of the Industrial Areas Foundation representing the political left and former Secretary of Education William Bennett representing the political right—which is increasingly controlled by "neoconservatives"— it was not unreasonable to expect that discussions would result in reaching "common ground" politics of the "radical center," which is an abandonment of principle by both the right and the left. A list of high profile Americans involved in the National Commission on Civic Renewal will be included at the end of this entry.

NOTE: The reader should be warned that this is a very lengthy entry. The writer is of the opinion that it is about a pivotal gathering that has given assistance to the move toward socialism in this country. Please read all.

Why is the National Commission on Civic Renewal being created at this time? The Commission says that

> In spite of recent improvement in the economy, both experts and ordinary citizens have become increasingly troubled about what they see as a decline in the strength of our social fabric and in the quality of our civil and civic life. Basic institutions at the family and neighborhood level have come under intense pressure; voting and other forms of community and political participation have declined; Americans' trust in large institutions and in one another has plunged. The Commission will seek to address these ills: by gathering and assessing information and advice from a wide range of voices; by inventorying, studying, and highlighting promising civic organizations and initiatives around the country; and by offering specific recommendations for improving our civic and civil life.

Statistics published in a 1982 National Center for Citizen Involvement report quoting from a 1981 issue of *The National Volunteer* stated that 44% of Americans work as volunteers outside of an organization—"doing their own thing," so to speak—not the volunteerism the elite involved in commissions similar to the National Commission on Civic Renewal are interested in promoting.

The writer will wager that the above-referenced "ordinary" citizens were not consulted on this elitist project. "Ordinary" citizens are too involved in trying to make a living, "meeting the payroll," and being part of that "44%" to find time to be herded around by change agent planners, participating in projects which more often than not do not significantly affect the lives of those most in need. If the reader feels that the writer of this book is going overboard with her use of the word "elite," hold onto your seat while we make an ascent into the rooftop conference room of a Washington, D.C. club where one of the meetings held by the Commission took place. Hear ye! Hear ye! Theda Skocpol, professor of government and sociology at Harvard University, is about to give testimony before the Commission:

> My research on the past and present of U.S. civic engagement suggests that *this Commission should look upward, not downward.* [all emphases in original] Too much money in politics, too great a reliance on staff-led groups, *too much top-down manipulation—and far too few incentives for leaders to organize or engage in dialogue with actual groups of fellow citizens across the nation*—these are Americans' sense of disconnection from shared civic life. You won't find the answers you seek in purely local groups, or among the less privileged. You must look to America's powerful and best-educated elites—to folks like all of us sitting in this room. What is [it] that we [businesspeople], professors, foundation heads, think tank impresarios, and religious and political leaders are doing that we should not be doing? Equally pertinent, what new things should we elites do? America's best educated, wealthiest, and most powerful leaders are the ones who are failing our fellow citizens—because we have withdrawn from the group settings in which we would have daily chances to work with, and discuss the nation's concerns, with most of our fellow citizens.

The writer has an answer for Ms. Skocpol: stop trying to social engineer "the locals" into accepting solutions which "the locals" never asked for and probably would not want if they were informed of the real purpose of the so-called "solutions." Skocpol refers to the activities of "tax-exempt foundation heads and think tank impresarios." She would be wise to remain silent on that score, considering the severe damage done by those very entities to the preservation of freedom in our nation. The Commission seems to have made a big mistake publishing Skocpol's paper. Its condescending, elitist tone surely will not help to get their project off the ground—perhaps that is best for all of us.

Excerpts from *The Final Report of the National Commission on Civic Renewal: A Nation of Spectators—How Civic Disengagement Weakens America and What We Can Do about It* (1998) follow:

> Defining the Challenge of Civic Renewal.
> In America we do not depend on kings, clerics, or aristocrats, or (for that matter) on technocratic elites or self-appointed leaders to serve as the "vanguard" for the rest of us. [This is a strange comment in light of the makeup and conclusions of the Commission and its expert consultants, ed.]...

> We believe that the capacity for democratic citizenship must be nurtured in institutions such as families, neighborhoods, schools, faith communities, local governments, and political movements—and therefore, that our democracy must attend carefully to the health of these institutions....
>
> We believe that building democracy means individuals, voluntary associations, private markets, and the public sector working together—not locked in battle.

[Ed. Note: First, the writer thought that the United States was a constitutional republic, not a democracy. Secondly, again we find the reference to the public sector and the private having to join together; i.e., partnerships, which the reader should recognize as corporate fascism/socialism. This is the first time the writer has been informed that the above-mentioned groups have been "locked in battle." The next thing we will hear is that in order for "democracy" to flower, *a la* Red China, we must all participate in sensitivity training/conflict resolution/encounter group sessions.]

> We believe that democracy means not only discussing our differences, but also undertaking concrete projects with our fellow citizens to achieve common goals.... (p. 7–8)

A New Movement.
New organizations are refocusing the attention of families, schools, and communities on the formation of civic character....

> ...But we believe that the current level of mistrust [of government and large institutions, ed.] is inconsistent with civic health. Americans cannot love their country if they have contempt for its government.... (p. 10–11)

Meeting the Challenge of Civic Renewal.
The goals of civic renewal are straightforward: to strengthen the institutions that help form the knowledge, skills, and virtues citizens need for active engagement in civic life; to remove the impediments to civic engagement wherever they exist; and to multiply the arenas for meaningful and effective civic action.... (p. 12)

Individuals.
We therefore challenge every citizen to become an active member of at least one association dealing with matters of local neighborhood, church, or community concern. [Is this a challenge to the "44%" who cannot presently be tracked and controlled in their "civic and volunteer" service? ed.]...

Families.
It means sweeping away impediments to adoption. It means dramatically reforming foster care and establishing a national norm that no child should spend more than one birthday without a permanent home in a stable, loving family. It means a massive new partnership among the public, private, and voluntary sectors to provide adult mentors for one million young people now languishing on waiting lists across our land.

[Ed. Note: "A national norm"? Who keeps track and evaluates? Who decides what is a "stable, loving family"? "Massive new partnership"? "Adult mentors for one million young people... on waiting lists"? What waiting lists? To be adopted, to have a mentor? These partnerships mean that government will coordinate the activities of the private and voluntary sectors to accomplish enforceable standards in the area of family life. The Commission also acknowledged that a healthy mistrust of government is essential for a "democracy." This writer believes it to be essential for the preservation of freedom as well. Perhaps what our nation needs is an even higher level of citizen mistrust which would result in more people going to the polls to vote out rascals.]

Neighborhoods.

Every neighborhood should assume responsibility for matters of significant local concern, emphasizing areas where neighbors can do meaningful civic work together. For example: neighborhood crime watches; cleaning, repairing, and patrolling public parks; escort services for students walking from home to school in the morning and back in the afternoon.... (p. 13)

...We applaud the efforts of organizations such as the National Civic League, the Center for Democracy and Citizenship, the Civic Practices Network, the Center for Living Democracy, the Pew Partnership for Civic Change, and [Heritage Foundation's, ed.] *Policy Review: The Journal of American Citizenship* to identify promising community-based empowerment efforts, to make this information available to communities searching for usable models, and to weave together local activities into a wider community-based movement for civic renewal.

Schools.

First, we add our voices to others—such as the Communitarian Network, the Character Counts! Coalition, the Character Education Partnership, and the Center for Civic Education—in support of a far greater emphasis on civic and character education. We believe that our schools should foster the knowledge, skills, and virtues our young people need to become good democratic citizens....

While the National Commission has not reached agreement on mandatory community service for high school students, we are impressed with the ways in which well-designed community work carefully linked to classroom reflection can enhance the civic education of students.... Every state should require all students to demonstrate mastery of basic civic information and concepts as a condition of high school graduation. [Citizenship, OBE-style, ed.]

In addition to their role in forming civic competence and character, we believe that the overall performance of our schools has important effects on our civic condition. To cite but one example: students consigned to failing schools are far less likely to achieve full participation in civic life. Free citizens must be educated. For this reason, we offer some proposals to improve teaching and learning....

...Despite the political and substantive difficulties, the federal government should spur the development of a voluntary national testing system with high standards and make it available for adoption (or adaptation) by states and localities. (p. 15)

The federal government, states, and localities should cooperate to increase parental choice through such measures as open enrollment and public school choice within districts (and even beyond). Within five years, every state should enact meaningful charter school legislation, and the federal government should dramatically increase its support for charter schools. (pp. 14–16)

Note: While the National Commission has focused its report and rec-ommendations on areas of substantial agreement, we note an important area of ongoing disagreement among us.

Some members of the National Commission advocate public support for parental choice broadened to include private and religious schools, especially for low-income students now trapped in failing systems. These members believe that wider choice will enhance educational opportunity and accountability, improve quality, help get parents more involved in their children's schooling and catalyze civic engagement. They consider school choice to be a crucial and necessary step toward civic renewal and self-government.

Other Commission members believe that public schools have been, and continue to be, vital meeting grounds in which future citizens learn to respect and work with one another across their differences. These members fear that choice widened beyond the bounds of public schools could diminish support for public education, further fragment our society, and weaken our democracy.

We were not able to resolve these differences. (Not surprisingly, our nation's representatives have not yet reached common ground, either.) But we do agree on the civic standards and principles that should be employed in public deliberation on school choice, and we call for con-tinued civil dialogue on this question.

Faith-based Institutions.

Faith-based institutions should take full advantage of new opportunities under federal law to receive public support for activities such as job search programs, "second chance" homes for unmarried teen parents, child care, and drug treatment, while maintaining their religious character. The federal government should broaden this new partnership with faith-based institutions to cover the maximum feasible range of social services....

The federal government should revise the tax code to increase incen-tives for charitable contributions and to recognize the charitable efforts of all Americans, including poor and low-income families....

Individual faith-based institutions should band together into community-wide coalitions to achieve important civic objectives....

...We call for the mobilization of public, foundation, and corporate sup-port for new ventures, such as John Dilulio's Jeremiah Project, which will help gather credible data about the effectiveness of faith-based activities, mobilize resources, and direct them to promising faith-based programs.

[Ed. Note: This is the most frightening "partnership" proposal of all. When the government "partners" with another entity, it is always the government who sets the standard—and enforces it. While there may be worthwhile efforts that many churches in a community can agree upon and work to-gether to accomplish, again, this should be decided on the local level by the churches involved without any coordination by any other entity to satisfy its goals and aims. Gathering "credible data" about "faith-based activities" so that resources can be directed to "promising faith-based programs" is exactly what the writer was referring to earlier when she cautioned the reader about partnering churches or "faith-based institutions" with the government.]

The following high profile individuals are involved in the National Commission on Civic Renewal project:

- **Co-Chairman William Bennett**, former U.S. Secretary of Education, and co-director of Empower America, an organization dedicated to promoting "conservative" principles and ideas. Secretary of Education Bennett funded the American Institute for Character Education/ Thomas Jefferson Research Center's very controversial, no right/ no wrong answers character education program based on Abraham Maslow's Hierarchy of Needs and Self-Actualization. When confronted with information concerning the U.S.-Soviet education agreements signed during his tenure, Bennett said, "I'm not in that loop."

- **Co-Chairman Sam Nunn**, former U.S. Senator from Georgia, was deeply involved in the passage of National Service legislation to lay the groundwork for a nationwide "civilian service corps" by offering generous higher education benefits in exchange for one or two years of public volunteer service. Though Nunn served as chairman of the Senate Armed Services Committee, the "volunteer service" legislation he sponsored was in no way involved with military service to this country.

- **Executive Director William A. Galston**, professor of government in the School of Public Affairs, University of Maryland at College Park and director of the University's Institute for Philosophy and Public Policy. From January 1993 through May 1995, Galston served as deputy assistant for domestic policy to President Clinton. Galston was also deeply involved in the drafting of *Goals 2000*. Prior political experience includes: chief speech writer for former Independent Party presidential candidate John Anderson's National Unity Campaign in 1980; issues director for Democratic presidential candidate Walter Mondale's campaign; senior advisor for then-Senator Al Gore's campaign for the Democratic Party's presidential nomination; and since 1989 served as senior advisor for the Democratic Leadership Council and the Progressive Policy Institute.

- **Lamar Alexander**, former governor of Tennessee, former U.S. Secretary of Education, former and present candidate for the Republican Party nomination for President of the United States.

- **Elaine Chao**, Distinguished Fellow, The Heritage Foundation. Until recently, Elaine Chao was president and chief executive officer of United Way of America.

- **Ernesto Cortes, Jr.**, Industrial Areas Foundation (IAI), Southwest regional director. Founded more than fifty years ago in Chicago by the late Saul Alinsky, the IAF is a non-profit organization, originally operating throughout the Catholic Church in the U.S., designed to provide leadership training to poor and moderate income people in more than forty broadly based, multi-ethnic organizations in the United States and the United Kingdom. (Go to www.lospequenos.org

or to www.catholicmediacoalition.org for Stephanie Block's articles and research dealing with the highly controversial activities of the Industrial Areas Foundation.)

- **Amitai Etzioni**, professor at Georgetown University, founder and chairman of The Communitarian Network, is involved with the Education For All (EFA) activities both nationally and internationally, the Character Education Partnership, and the activities of the Freedom Forum First Amendment Foundation (Vanderbilt University). According to *Webster's New World Dictionary* (1976) a "communitarian" is "a member or advocate of a communistic community." Communitarianism is the social philosophy of the Skinnerian Walden II experimental commune at Los Horcones, Mexico.[43]

- **John Gardner**, professor of education at Stanford University in California, has served as former president of the Carnegie Corporation of New York, which—as the reader knows—has had virtual control over American education since the early 1900s.

- **Peter C. Goldmark, Jr.**, was elected the eleventh president of the Rockefeller Foundation in June 1988. Goldmark is a member of the Council on Foreign Relations.

- **Oz Guiness**, Senior Fellow with The Trinity Forum. Guiness headed up the controversial Williamsburg Charter Character Education Project whose work was continued by Charles Haynes of the Freedom Forum First Amendment Foundation at Vanderbilt University.

- **Michael S. Joyce**, president and chief executive officer of The Lynde and Harry Bradley Foundation in Milwaukee, was former leader of the John M. Olin Foundation in New York and the Goldseker Foundation in Baltimore. A strong supporter of parental choice in education, Joyce spent six years with the Educational Research Council of America and was a contributing editor to a textbook series on the social studies. Joyce served on the Presidential Transition Team in the Reagan Administration and in 1993 joined with William Kristol to found the Project for the Republican Future.

- **Richard D. Land**, president-treasurer of the Ethics and Religious Liberty Commission of the Southern Baptist Convention, the agency for "applied Christianity" (social and moral concerns) for the Convention.

- **His Eminence Bernard Cardinal Law**, Archbishop of Boston since 1984. He was created Cardinal by Pope John Paul II in May 1985.

- **Edwin Lupberger**, chairman of the U.S. Chamber of Commerce and member of the U.S. Chamber's Center for Workforce Preparation, also serves on the board of the Committee for Economic Development (CED) and is Louisiana's Honorary Consul of the Federal Republic of Germany.

- **Bruno V. Manno**, executive director of the National Commission on Philanthropy and Civic Renewal, is closely associated with Vanderbilt University and the Hudson Institute. Manno has served as assistant secretary of education for policy and planning and as director of planning for the Office of Educational Research and Improvement under Secretary of Education Lamar Alexander in 1986.

- **Sanford McDonnell**, chairman of the Character Education Partnership and McDonnell Douglas Corporation.

- **Michael Novak**, currently holds the George Frederick Jewett Chair in Religion and Public Policy at the American Enterprise Institute. Mr. Novak has received numerous awards, including the Templeton Prize for Progress in Religion (1994).

- **Lester Salamon**, director of the Institute for Policy Studies at The Johns Hopkins University, and was the co-editor of *Human Capital and America's Future* with David Hornbeck.

- **Robert Woodson, Sr.**, founder and president of the National Center for Neighborhood Enterprise which has been in the forefront of the movement to "empower" low-income Americans. In 1990 Woodson received the high-profile John and Catherine T. MacArthur Fellowship. He is a board member of the American Association of Enterprise Zones and the Commission on National and Community Service.

[Ed. Note: The writer cannot help but compare this commission and its *raison d'etre* with former President Dwight Eisenhower's American Assembly, which developed the pre-determined, socialistic "Goals for Americans" in 1960. As to the meeting of minds on "common ground," Shirley McCune (referred to previously in this book as a major education change agent with the Mid-Continent Regional Educational Laboratory) quoted from The [John] Naisbitt Group's training materials regarding political philosophy at an educational restructuring presentation to the Millard, Nebraska School District[44] when she explained that basic shifts related to restructuring move across a continuum: Naisbitt listed "From" and "To" as being "left vs. right politics" resulting in "a politics of the radical center." This is an excellent illustration of the Hegelian Dialectic at work and is the basis of the activities of the National Commission on Civic Renewal.]

[ddd]

THE MAY 1997 ISSUE OF *THE EFFECTIVE SCHOOL REPORT* CARRIED AN article entitled "The Future of Hong Kong Is Linked to Education." Excerpts follow:

> The information to be presented will come from a major report recently issued by the Education Commission established by the Central Government of Hong Kong in 1983. The major reference will be *Education Commission Report No. 7, Quality School Education*, issued in November, 1996.
>
> As one reads each [article] in the series of articles, the obvious and continuous reference to the effective schools movement becomes more than apparent. It serves us well to understand that just as the effective schools correlates were developed within our realm of the world, so it is these same

correlates have been adopted throughout the world to improve the quality and design of education.

A blue ribbon commission was formed in April, 1996 to make recommendations on the development and establishment of quality school education. Three broad principles served as the bases for the work of the committee. They included the following:

- Ways to relate school funding to performance[45]
- Roles of key players in the school system and
- Their relationship with one another.

Beyond the primary principles established by the committee are six objectives which may appear to many educators as fundamental objectives for any school system in any nation. These primary objectives include:

- to enhance the community's appreciation of the need for quality school education;
- to inculcate a *quality* culture in the school system [emphasis in original];
- to provide a practical framework for key players in the school system to achieve the aims of education in an effective, efficient and accountable manner;
- to recommend an integrated strategy for quality assurance;
- to reward or give recognition to performing schools; and
- to assist or take appropriate remedial action regarding under-performing schools to encourage initiatives and continuous improvement.

In its deliberations, the committee reviewed large volumes of overseas and local literature on the effective schools movement, quality assurance measures and school management approaches. Members of the committee participated in visits to study the operation of education throughout the world.... The [Education Commission] report was primarily a product which offered a plan to develop performance indicators for the school system.... Society has accepted the responsibility to provide an education for each and every child and to structure such an education according to their individual abilities and aptitudes.... As a leader in international commerce, the community of Hong Kong, especially the business community, recognizes massive changes in world trade and production. As businesses throughout the world, including nations in North America and Europe, have restructured their businesses and production systems, Hong Kong has emerged as one of the world's foremost financial centers, a hub of regional telecommunications, transport and trading, a leading tourist and convention destination and a major exporter of professional services to the world, especially mainland China. Along with its transformation, Hong Kong commerce now demands a labor force which is "informed and knowledgeable, highly qualified and specialised, with advanced skills and the ability to think independently and to communicate well." (p. 5)

[Ed. Note: Surprise! Surprise! The reader should go to the Internet version for Appendix VI for the SAFE effective school international pilot project carried out in Korea in 1970 to see that many of the "effective school correlates" referred to above were *exported* from the U.S. to other parts of the world.]

"THE GOAL OF HONG KONG SCHOOLS—ESTABLISHING QUALITY IN ITS Schools" was the feature article in the June/July, 1997 issue of *The Effective School Report*. This article continues the explanation of the transformation of Hong Kong's educational system which began in last month's issue. Excerpts follow:

> ...Excellence is found in the innovations and outstanding performance which distinguish one school from others.

> School Choice Should Be Made Available

> Hong Kong's education system provides parents with a choice of different types of schools. The perception of parents and students of the educational process, and the satisfaction of members of the community with outcomes are also useful indicators of the quality of education.

> Excellence is not confined to achieving outstanding academic results or promoting the self-esteem of students. For instance, some schools might achieve excellence by developing the potential of low achievers and producing value-added results.

> In order to build a quality culture in schools, a number of measures must be taken. They include:

> - translating the goals into achievable, observable and measurable quality indicators;
> - having a school funding system which is efficient and equitable, which meets basic needs and which is related to performance;
> - providing incentives to recognize and encourage initiatives and the pursuit of excellence.

> Aims

> To prepare students to become responsible citizens and maintain high moral standards....

> Output Indicators

> Output indicators may start with value-added performance in three areas; academic achievement; students' self-esteem; and perception of the school teachers, parents and students. As a start, these three types of output indicators may be developed first, followed by the development of indicators in other domains such as the students' ability for self-learning, social and communicative skills, moral attitudes and civic-mindedness. In order to encourage continuous improvement, the sooner the various indicators are developed, the better....

> Value-Added Concept of Output Indicators

> We suggest that in assessing the performance of a school, it would be more appropriate and fairer to bring in the concept of value-added achievement rather than simply looking at absolute performance. Value-added performance can be assessed in a number of areas. For example, it would not be appropriate to compare the academic performance of different schools if they admit students coming from different backgrounds. The value-added concept allows comparison of students as they enter a school and as they leave. The same concept can be applied across the output indicators. The focus will be on a student's progress over the years.

> (Information used in this series has been derived from the publication, *Education Commission Report No. 7—Quality School Education*, prepared

by the Hong Kong Task Group on School Quality and School Funding and the Hong Kong Education Commission, chaired by Professor Rosie Young, November, 1996.)

[Ed. Note: Anyone the slightest bit familiar with educational restructuring, *Goals 2000*, or school-to-work programs will understand from the above excerpts, the extent of the internationalization of education and the duplicity of those—including the media—who deny that restructuring is international. Rudyard Kipling's "East is East and West is West" has been successfully repudiated by those involved in training the global workforce. A more appropriate Kipling quote might be one from *London Truth*, reprinted in the Middlebury, Vermont *Register* of March 1899, which follows: "Pile on your brown {white, black, red, pink, yellow} man's burden to satisfy your greed."]

ATLANTIC MONTHLY'S JULY 1997 ISSUE CARRIED THE ARTICLE "THE COMputer Delusion" by Todd Oppenheimer. Excerpts follow:

> There is no good evidence that most uses of computers significantly improve teaching and learning, yet school districts are cutting programs—music, art, physical education—that enrich children's lives to make room for this dubious nostrum, and the Clinton Administration has embraced the goal of "computers in every classroom" with credulous and costly enthusiasm....
>
> The noted psychologist B.F. Skinner, referring to the first days of his "teaching machines," in the late 1950s and early 1960s wrote, "I was soon saying that, with the help of teaching machines and programmed instruction, students could learn twice as much in the same time and with the same effort as in a standard classroom." Ten years after Skinner's recollections were published, President Bill Clinton campaigned for a "bridge to the twenty-first century... where computers are as much a part of the classroom as blackboards." Clinton was not alone in his enthusiasm for a program estimated to cost somewhere between $40 billion and $100 billion over the next five years. Speaker of the House Newt Gingrich, talking about computers to the Republican National Committee early this year, said, "We could do so much to make education available twenty-four hours a day, seven days a week, that people could literally have a whole different attitude toward learning."... In a poll taken early last year U.S. teachers ranked computer skills and media technology as more "essential" than the study of European history, biology, chemistry, and physics; than dealing with social problems such as drugs and family breakdown; than learning practical job skills; and than reading modern American writers such as Steinbeck and Hemingway or classic ones such as Plato and Shakespeare....
>
> Interestingly, shop classes and field trips are two programs that the National information Infrastructure Advisory Council, the Clinton Administration's technology task force, suggests reducing in order to shift resources into computers. But are these results what technology promoters really intend? "You need to apply common sense," Esther Dyson, the president of EDventure Holdings and one of the task force's leading school advocates, told me recently, "Shop with a good teacher probably is worth more than computers with a lousy teacher. But if it's a poor program, this may provide a good excuse for cutting it. There will be a lot of trials and errors with this.

And I don't know how to prevent those errors."[46] The issue, perhaps is the magnitude of the errors.

Alan Lesgold, a professor of psychology and the associate director of the Learning Research and Development Center at the University of Pittsburgh, calls the computer an "amplifier," because it encourages both enlightened study practices and thoughtless ones. There's a real risk, though, that the thoughtless practices will dominate, slowly dumbing down huge numbers of tomorrow's adults. As Sherry Turkle, a professor of the sociology of science at the Massachusetts Institute of Technology and a longtime observer of children's use of computers, told me, "The possibilities of using this thing poorly so outweigh the chance of using it well, it makes people like us, who are fundamentally optimistic about computers, very reticent."...

Clifford Stoll, the author of *Silicon Snake Oil: Second Thoughts on the Information Highway* (1995), told *The New York Times* last year, recalling his own school days in the 1960s, "We loved them because we didn't have to teach, and parents loved them because it showed their schools were high-tech. But no learning happened."...

Reading programs get particularly bad reviews. One small but carefully controlled study went so far as to claim that Reader Rabbit, a reading program now used in more than 100,000 schools, caused students to suffer a 50 percent drop in creativity. (Apparently, after forty-nine students used the program for seven months, they were no longer able to answer open-ended questions and showed a markedly diminished ability to brainstorm with fluency and originality.)

What about hard sciences, which seem so well suited to computer study? Logo, the high-profile programming language refined by Seymour Papert and widely used in middle and high schools, fostered huge hope of expanding children's cognitive skills. As students directed the computer to build things, such as geometric shapes, Papert believed, they would learn "procedural thinking," similar to the way a computer processes information. According to a number of studies, however, Logo has generally failed to deliver on its promises....

Judah Schwartz [a physicist], a professor of education at Harvard and a co-director of the school's Educational Technology Center, told me that a few newer applications, when used properly, can dramatically expand children's math and science thinking by giving them new tools to "make and explore conjectures." Still, Schwartz acknowledges that perhaps "ninety-nine percent of the educational programs are terrible, really terrible."...

Opinions diverge in part because research on the brain is still so sketchy, and computers are so new, that the effect of computers on the brain remains a great mystery. "I don't think we know anything about it," Harry Chugani, a pediatric neurobiologist at Wayne State University, told me. This very ignorance makes skeptics wary. "Nobody knows how kids' internal wiring works," Clifford Stoll wrote in *Silicon Snake Oil*, "but anyone who's directed away from social interactions has a head start on turning out weird.... No computer can teach what a walk through a pine forest feels like. Sensation has no substitute."...

In *Silicon Snake Oil* Michael Fellows, a computer scientist at the University of Victoria, in British Columbia, was even blunter. "Most schools would probably be better off if they threw their computers into the Dumpster."...
The problem is that technology leaders rarely include these or other warnings in their recommendations. When I asked Dyson why the Clinton task force

proceeded with such fervor, despite the classroom computer's shortcomings, she said, "It's so clear the world is changing."

[Ed. Note: "The world is changing" is the response change agents are trained to use when confronted by common sense taxpayers who ask why dumb projects are being funded. The writer can't possibly recall the number of times her change agent superintendent responded with those exact words! The reader can rightfully accuse the writer of this book of an anti-computer bias and of selectivity in choosing quotes to prove her point. I stand "guilty" on all counts. Those interested in computer-assisted instruction should get a copy of the above article so they will not be overly influenced by this writer's selection of quotes.]

AN ARTICLE ENTITLED "'REAL-LIFE' SCHOOL ELIMINATES BOOKS" APPEARED in the September 1, 1997 issue of *The Washington Times*. The article reveals the extent to which American public schools are doing away with books.

> WALKERSVILLE, MD—Third-grader Billy Horn had a math problem his mother couldn't help solve, so she asked for the source.
>
> "I said, 'Where's your book?' and he said, 'They don't have books,'" Joan Horn said.
>
> Like most people schooled in the 1960s and 1970s, Mrs. Horn assumed her children would learn their lessons as she did, from heavy books with problems at the end of each chapter.
>
> But textbooks play a smaller role, even a minor one, in modern education.
>
> "We're trying to make school look more like real-life experiences and have assignments that are intriguing and captivating and problem-solving," said Jerome Strum, Billy's principal at Glade Elementary.

ON SEPTEMBER 24, 1997 TEXAS CHRISTIAN ALERT NETWORK (TCAN) issued a memo entitled "Communism Comes to Texas Public Education." TCAN had received the following excerpted analytical summary by Chris Patterson, reseacher, of the Texas version of the national school-to-work legislation. The first paragraph of the alert warned that:

> This nationally mandated program will differ very little from one state to another so persons in all states should read the following very carefully and decide whether you want the federal government to have absolute control of your child and his/her career, from the cradle to the grave.

> TEXAS SCHOOL-TO-WORK SYSTEM
> by Chris Patterson

> Introduction
> In November 1996, Texas received a $61 million dollar federal grant to implement a School-to-Work (STW) system. With this grant, Texas joined the group of 36 states which participate in a national workforce development program. The national program is designed, regulated and initially funded by the federal government. The objective of this program is to coordinate workforce development with economic, educational and welfare plans within

and between states of our nation. STW introduces "major changes or a radical transformation of the purpose, content and structure of public schools."

Key Components of STW
Employer needs and skill standards drive STW as curriculum and instructional practices are modified to prepare students to enter the local workforce....

Academic education and vocational instruction are fully integrated. Curriculum is founded upon performance-based standards. Academic subjects incorporate instruction related to personal and career goals. Both work and school-based instruction are designed according to local workforce needs. "All students will engage in STW."...

Students will be prepared for, certified and placed in post-secondary education or jobs which reduce mismatches between students/education and education/workplace, incorporating:

- Career awareness kindergarten through 6th grade.
- Choice of career pathway by no later than 8th grade.
- Work-based learning which includes mentorship, job-shadowing, volunteer service, school-based enterprise, apprenticeship, internship and paid work experience.
- Students will be required to acquire the following as conditions for graduation: certificates of initial and/or advanced mastery.
- Workplace competencies and paid work experience in career field.
- Statutory requirements will be established for schools to adopt block scheduling.
- Health and human services will be integrated with school and work-based learning.
- An electronic data tracking system will be developed for all students.

The only elected official responsible for STW governance is the Governor of Texas. The Texas Skills Standards Board recommends standards and certification to the Texas Council on Workforce & Economic Competitiveness....

The Council exercises statutory authority to develop, maintain and enforce STW....

The Council delegates authority to the Texas Workforce Commission to direct activities of participating organizations, including: the Texas Education Agency, Higher Education Board, Human Services, Rehabilitation Commission, Commerce Department, Commission for the Blind, National & Community Services, and Veterans Education. The Texas Workforce Commission governs twenty-eight Local Workforce Development Boards which direct local implementation of STW....

Proponents of STW Claim:
The objectives of STW are to provide students with:

- Rigorous academics;
- Opportunity for highly skilled, highly-paid jobs;
- Participation in STW is optional for both students and businesses.

Opponents of STW Claim:
Academics are diluted and academic achievement will decrease because:

- Curriculum standards are performance- or outcomes-based;
- Academic learning is displaced by personal, social and workplace competency instruction;
- Block scheduling results in less course content and lower test scores;

- Ability Grouping (including Honors Courses) which increases student achievement is prohibited;
- Traditional liberal arts education is replaced by vocational training;
- Students will be identified and trained for low skill, low pay jobs. Less than 15% of workforce requires a Bachelor's Degree;
- Leading 5 targeted occupations identify cashiers, janitors/cleaners, sales clerks and registered nurses;
- Participation is not fully voluntary—the state is pursuing legislation to make STW a condition of graduation.

Vocational and academic instruction are integrated; students are not provided an opportunity to select academic course work which is not integrated. Private sector funding is required to support STW (matching funds of $20 million will be required in 1997 and will increase to a projected $45 million in 2001). According to the STW grant proposal, Texas has no immediate plans to tax businesses to force participation as is done in Europe, but areas will be required to raise private funds.

STW Poses Troubling Questions:

- Should the government direct the development of curriculum, implementation of instructional practices and establishment of a data collection system for schools?
- Should the government through schools identify, train, certify and place workers?
- Should educational policies be established without the authority of state school boards, local district boards and legislators?
- Should the purpose, structure and means of public education be "transformed" without public debate and consent?
- Should the government establish a national plan for economic management?

[Ed Note: The reader should be aware that the "only elected official responsible for STW governance is the governor of Texas." The sitting governor of Texas at that time—who received the $61 million grant for Texas to implement its School-to-Work system—was none other than George W. Bush. Bush became President of the United States and pushed through the infamous *No Child Left Behind Act*.]

ON OCTOBER 14, 1997 THE CENTER OF THE AMERICAN EXPERIMENT BREAKfast and Luncheon Forum Series of Minneapolis, Minnesota held its meeting at the Radisson Plaza Hotel. The flyer announced the appearance of Chester E. Finn, Jr., who would speak on "Reforming Education—Why Do Bad Things Happen to Good Ideas?" Excerpts from the flyer read:

Join us for an American Experiment Breakfast Forum at which Chester E. Finn, Jr., discusses why conservatively inspired school reforms frequently get morphed into anti-intellectual and statist mush. Why are basically good ideas such as outcomes-based education and national standards often turned upside down by educational establishmentarians? What does this track record portend for school choice? How can future hijackings be averted? Dr. Finn is president of the Thomas B. Fordham Foundation and also serves as John M. Olin Fellow at the Hudson Institute. Quite likely the nation's most prolific education critic, he is the author of a shelf of books and writes regularly for *The Wall Street Journal, Commentary* and other publications.

[Ed. Note: The flyer conveniently omitted the fact that Chester Finn was one of the architects of President George H. W. Bush's *America 2000*, which is the foundation document for President Clinton's *Goals 2000* "real" conservatives so thoroughly detest. The author includes this information regarding Finn as proof that the dialectic (right vs. left meeting at the radical center) has been accomplished. The "neo-conservatives" have seized the high ground, and are developing and supporting socialist programs initially proposed by the liberals. An example being the flyer statement "basically good ideas such as 'outcomes-based education,'" which is shocking coming from a supposedly "conservative" organization and speaker. The exceptions are choice, vouchers, magnet/charter schools, which give the *appearance* of originating with conservatives—which will also track your child into a preplanned future. This alien (socialist) concept is, however, supported by the multinational corporations, foundations, education union leadership, and institutionalized educational research and development change agents for global workforce training purposes.

As an example of the above collaboration toward global workforce training taking the place of education, please refer back to the 1976 entry for NEA's "Cardinal Principles Revisited, 1976," which included on its panel: David Rockefeller, Chase Manhattan Bank; McGeorge Bundy, Ford Foundation; Francois Blanchard, Syndicat National des Enseignements de Second Degre (France); Lester Brown, Worldwatch Institute; Willis Harman, Stanford Research Institute; Fred Jarvis, National Union of Teachers (England); Sally Swing Shelley, United Nations; Sir Walter Perry, The Open University (England); and Joe H. Foy, Houston Natural Gas Co. The author has selected the above, primarily non-educator individuals, from a lengthy list to help the reader understand how the education establishment at the very top is "in bed with," or more likely controlled by, leading international think tanks and multinational corporations.

The author would also like to point out that the American Experiment organization in Minnesota is another state affiliate of the neo-conservative Heritage Foundation.]

"Clinton Charm Gets Rio Workout" was the title of an article for *The News & Observer* of Raleigh, North Carolina on October 16, 1997. Excerpt follows:

> By stressing the importance of education, Clinton identified a passion shared by his Brazilian host, President Fernando Henrique Cardoso, a university professor who has earmarked a portion of the unexpected earnings from Brazil's massive privatization project to improve public schools. The two governments agreed to a "partnership for education" in which the United States will help Brazil develop standardized testing of its public schools' performance, U.S. and Brazilian classrooms will be linked by computer, and

a commission will be set up to oversee a new student exchange program and promote private sector investments in schools.

H.R. 2614, THE *READING EXCELLENCE ACT,* PASSED THE **U.S.** HOUSE OF Representatives in November of 1997.[47] For the first time in U.S. history legislation has been passed which mandates a particular method of teaching. Excerpts from the abstract of the legislation follow:

SELECTION OF READING AND LITERACY GRANT APPLICATIONS
Applications from Reading and Literacy Partnerships will go to the Secretary of Education, who would forward them to a Peer Review Panel for initial approval. The Peer Review Panel will consist of experts in the field of reading who are appropriate to evaluate such grant applications. Members would be selected by the National Institute for Literacy (NIFL) in consultation with the National Research Council (NRC, a division of the National Academy of Sciences); the Child Development and Behavior Branch (CDBB) of the National Institutes of Health; and the Secretary of Education. NIFL, NRC, CDBB and the Secretary would also be members of the Peer Review Panel. A priority would be given to applications from states that have modified or plan to modify state teacher certification in the area of reading to reflect reliable, replicable research on reading.... In selecting an applicant, the Reading and Literacy Partnership must give priority to subgrantees that form a partnership with a local Head Start program or a community-based organization (CBO) working with children to improve their reading skills, or state or federally funded preschool programs or family literacy programs.

INFORMATION DISSEMINATION
The National Institute for Literacy would head up the effort to disseminate information on reliable, replicable research on reading to all recipients of Federal financial assistance under ESEA, Head Start, IDEA, and the *Adult Education Act.* In doing so, NIFL would build upon applicable information networks currently in existence including OERI (Office of Educational Research and Improvement, U.S. Department of Education) and those established by states and private sector entities. The panel may assist any reading and literacy partnerships to determine whether applications for subgrants meet the requirements of this *Act* relating to reliable, replicable research on reading.

AUTHORIZATION
There would be a total of $260 million available for this *Act.* For more detailed information, visit the worldwide web at http://www.house.gov/eeo/.

[Ed. Note: Legislating a particular method to teach reading would never have been possible had the Hegelian Dialectic not been used. Workforce training requires that Skinnerian operant conditioning (programmed learning) be implemented in the schools. The only way to get that method accepted was:

(1) Create the problem: introduce Whole Language which is guaranteed to hinder children's ability to learn to read and causes parents to scream for a solution—any solution!

(2) Right on schedule, the social change agents responded with a predetermined solution which necessitated the use of Skinnerian direct instruction (programmed learning) to teach reading.

Little have parents realized that Skinnerian direct instruction and Skinnerian mastery learning are identical twins with very bad track records which caused William Spady et al. to rename them "Outcome-Based Education" in the early 1980s.

In order to assure passage of the *Reading Excellence Act*, Douglas Carnine, Ph.D., director of the Follow Through Direct Instruction Model in the University of Oregon's Department of *Special* Education which is associated with the National Center to Improve the Tools of Educators (NCITE) funded by the U.S. Department of Education's Office of *Special* Education, sent a letter to "Concerned Friends" requesting they lobby for passage of H.R. 2614. The author has deliberately emphasized the word "special" in special education because the fact that direct instruction programs are designed for special education students should not be lost on the reader, since *all* students—not just those needing special education—will be exposed to the direct instruction process and the Skinnerian operant conditioning method. (For more information regarding direct instruction, please refer to the Internet version for Appendix II, III, VI, XVII, XX, XXI, XXV, and XXVI.)

The following critique of DISTAR, Engelmann's Direct Instruction special education program, by a special education teacher in Florida should serve as a warning for those who do not understand the implications of using special education programs on all children.[48] The teacher points out that DISTAR was:

1. Developed for teaching the severely impaired (retardation and neurologically impaired).
2. NOT suitable EVER for regular education.
3. Is political "goosestepping"—group training.
4. Purely "mechanical" system—"authoritarian."
5. For NORMAL intelligence to SUPERIOR intelligence—a DISASTER. Teacher pounds away (scripted); children become bored; "frigidity" sets in and children tune out. Become the next behavior problems [emphasis in original].
6. We would be deliberately creating behavioral (mental) dropouts.

You can teach (the teachers) DISTAR in two days ("mechanistic"). Teachers don't have to know anything about language development. "El cheapo" response to whole language debacle.]

[ddd]

FORMER VICE PRESIDENT DAN QUAYLE JUMPED ON THE PUBLIC-PRIVATE partnership bandwagon, extending it to include the government and churches "dancing together" to help the less fortunate in our society, as reported in the November 13, 1997 issue of *The* (Louisville, Kentucky) *Courier Journal.* The following are some excerpts from "Quayle Backs Church-Government Partnerships":

Sounding like a preacher and a politician, former Vice President Dan

Quayle told about 5,000 people in Louisville last night that the government should use churches and other "faith-based institutions" to administer help to the poor, the homeless, the abused and the neglected....

He said everyone supports the concept of church-state separation, but "The Constitution protects religion from government. It's not the other way around."...

He told them that inner-city churches must become partners with the government to fight crime, deliver nutrition and restore family values, said Jefferson County Republican Party Chairman Bill Stone, who arranged the meeting and attended it with Quayle.

[Ed. Note: Mr. Quayle, have you been living under a rock ever since 1965 when the *Elementary and Secondary Education Act* passed and all the government's values-destroying education programs and methods became a part of our local schools' curriculum? Mr. Quayle, did you understand the intrusive, far-reaching effects of *America 2000* developed by the administration for which you served as vice president?]

1998

THE AMERICAN INSTITUTE FOR CHARACTER EDUCATION (AICE), A LEADING developer of character education materials, funded by grants from the Lilly Endowment as well as other foundations and best known for its development of materials for the Thomas Jefferson Research Center's controversial character education program, transferred its assets to Learning for Life in 1998. Information downloaded from Learning for Life's website reveals that Learning for Life is extending AICE's curriculum development efforts into the area of "school-to-careers" (school-to-work). One of its brochures states that

Learning for Life can provide the basis for operating and meeting the goals of the *School-to-Work Opportunities Act of 1994*. The *Act* has three basic components that are used to accomplish its goals: school-based learning, connecting activities, and work-based learning.

Before a School-to-Careers program is developed, an assessment is conducted to determine precisely how the Learning for Life program can help the school or school system help the students address the transition from school to careers. Only after this is done can a program be designed to help meet the school's needs.

Learning for Life will become a catalyst for establishing relationships between community-based organizations, including both for-profit and not-for-profit organizations, and the local school district, selected schools, and students....

Some of Learning for Life's connecting activities are listed as:

- Camps, retreats, conferences and workshops
- COPE courses, with team building, leadership, self-reliance, respect for self and others, and self-esteem
- Community-wide service projects, such as food drives, crime prevention programs, and service learning
- Program resources, such as leadership development workshops and scholarship opportunities

- Ethics in Action in Exploring: Five components that assist with the development of ethical decision-making.

[Ed. Note: The last "connecting activity" listed in Learning for Life's materials should be of particular concern for parents upset over the Thomas Jefferson Research Center Curriculum.]

IN 1998 THE EUROPEAN COMMISSION DIRECTORATE GENERAL OF EDUCATION, Training and Youth in Brussels, Belgium announced the availability of their Leonardo da Vinci Programme Cooperation in Higher Education and Vocational Education Document entitled "Cooperation in Higher Education and Vocational Education and Training between the European Community and the United States of America—Third Call for Proposals. Launching Date: 17 February 1998." Excerpts from the announcement taken from the Internet follow:

On 23 October 1995, the Council adopted a decision concerning the conclusion of an agreement for cooperation in higher education and vocational training between the European Community and the United States of America. The Cooperation Programme aims to add a new European Community/United States dimension to student-centered cooperation and bring balanced benefits to both the European Community and the United States.
Transatlantic cooperative activities eligible for support are:
- Development of organisational frameworks for transatlantic student mobility, including work placements, which will provide adequate language preparation and full academic recognition;
- Joint development of innovative curricula, teaching materials, methods and modules including those exploiting the new education technologies;
- Other innovative projects, including the use of new technologies and distance learning, which aim to improve the quality and cost-effectiveness of transatlantic cooperation in higher education and vocational education and training.

ECUMENICAL NEWS INTERNATIONAL's NEWS HIGHLIGHTS (LONDON-ENI) OF February 19, 1998 reported that the World Bank and the world's faiths promise to work together: "The World Bank and the world's major religions [agreed] to establish joint working groups on development issues, it was announced at the end of a high-level, two-day dialogue at Lambeth Palace." (Refer back to the *Time* article entry of 1942.)

[ddd]

THE BOSTON GLOBE CARRIED AN ARTICLE ENTITLED "SUSPICIONS ABOUT THE Statewide Tests" by Jeff Jacoby in the May 7, 1998 issue. The article contained such good information that much of it is included here:

I was going to write a column expressing my reservations about the MCAS, a 15-hour-long series of tests now being administered to fourth-, eighth-, and tenth-graders in every Massachusetts public school. I was going to point out that for all the ink and air time being devoted to the Massachusetts Comprehensive Assessment System, as it's formally called, little is actually known about it. I was even going to suggest that with all the uneasy questions the MCAS raises, parents ought to exercise their legal right to keep their children from taking it.

For one thing, I was going to call attention to the spotty record of Advanced Systems, the Dover, N.H., company hired to devise and grade the 210,000 tests being administered this month. Advanced Systems lost its $32 million contract with the State of Kentucky after botching the scores of more than 1,000 elementary and middle schools. The state launched what the magazine *Education Week* called "a sweeping audit" of the company's performance, scrutinizing "how the mistake could have gone undetected for many months."

Kentucky wasn't the only state where Advanced Systems failed. Scores in Maine were miscalculated, too. In New Hampshire, skepticism runs so high that the state Senate wants an elaborate regimen of supervision over every aspect of Advanced Systems' operations. Has the company cleaned up its act, I was going to ask, or is Massachusetts also going to wind up with shoddy and unreliable data?

But incompetent scoring was the least of my concerns.

I was going to highlight the copycat nature of these "assessments." Other states have been administering similar tests, always linking them to the federal *Goals 2000* and School-to-Work laws, both of which are considerably more creepy and New-World-Orderish than their innocuous names suggest. The very word "assessment" conveys something beyond mere measurement of academic achievement. Parents in state after state have discovered that their kids are being evaluated not just on their knowledge of language, math, and science, but on what they think, how they behave, and the way they were raised.

Would the MCAS, I was going to wonder, be as full of fuzzy PC questions on "feelings" and "attitudes" as tests elsewhere have been? If not, why have officials balked at a simple amendment to the *1993 Education Reform Act* providing that the MCAS "shall be designed to avoid the gathering or measuring of individual student attitudes, beliefs, or behaviors"? No one, I was going to say, could object to a clarification so straightforward—unless the purpose of the assessments is in fact to probe students on matters that are none of the state's concern.

Such as? Well, the Pennsylvania Educational Quality Assessment instructed students to react to statements like "I often wish I were somebody else" and "I don't receive much attention at home." To measure their "tolerance," students were presented with 35 situations—"Your sister wants to marry a person whose religion is much different from yours from your family" [sic], "You are asked to sit at a table with retarded students in the lunchroom"—and asked how comfortable or uncomfortable each would make them.

The California Learning Assessment System included loaded questions like this: "European Americans discriminated against Chinese immigrants because of ethnic and cultural differences. By yourself, think about an instance of discrimination that you know of. It could be a situation in which a person or a group of people is treated unfairly because of age, color, customs, or some other quality or belief. What could be done to help solve this problem?"

Kentucky told fourth-graders to imagine themselves Indians at the time the first pioneers arrived and to write "how you would have felt when you saw the pioneers cutting down trees and clearing land." Rhode Island grilled students on how often they like being in school ("Never? Sometimes? Always?"), whether they are happy with themselves "as a person," and how socially active their parents are.

I was going to quote the sweeping phrase in the Massachusetts ed-reform law that empowers the Department of Education to assemble a dossier on each student comprising "basic demographic information, program and course information, and such other information as the department shall determine necessary." I was going to describe the extraordinary secrecy that surrounds these tests in many states. Parents and school committee members are forbidden to see them, or are allowed to do so only if they sign nondisclosure agreements. The College Board isn't so mysterious about its SATs (each year it releases the previous year's tests). So why are many states so furtive about their "assessments"?

I distrust the MCAS. I am more than somewhat skeptical of the motives behind it and was going to write a column saying so.

But I have been persuaded not to jump to conclusions. I have been urged to wait for this first MCAS to play itself out, to see whether students report being asked anything dubious or improper. I have been reminded that this year's tests will only set a bench-mark—that not until 2003 will the tests actually have an impact on students' ability to graduate.

So, I'll hold my doubts in abeyance. For now. I can always write that column another time.

"SOUTH CAROLINA TAKES TO HEART COACH'S SHOT AT 'HORRIBLE' SCHOOLS" was an article with a Clemson, South Carolina dateline which appeared in *The Atlanta Journal-Constitution* on May 15, 1998. Some excerpts follow:

> Educators and politicians screeched when they heard former Clemson University basketball coach Rick Barnes say he was packing up his family and moving to Austin, Texas in part because South Carolina schools are "horrible."...
>
> Ever since the late 1970s, when current U.S. Education Secretary Richard Riley became governor, education reform has been a top issue in South Carolina. Yet, over nearly two decades, the state has remained—along with several other Southern states—at the bottom of national rankings....
>
> Moreover, South Carolina schools regularly win the U.S. Department of Education's Blue Ribbon, showing excellence in student achievement and teacher performance. Three elementary schools in fast-growing Greenville County won the award last year.

[Ed. Note: South Carolina can claim the dubious distinction of having been the home state of Effective Schools Research change agent Donald Thomas, promoter of U.S.-Soviet pedagogy exchanges, and U.S. Secretary of Education Richard Riley, former state school superintendent and governor of South Carolina during the adoption phase of the state's OBE/school-to-work experiments. The above article is most telling in that it proves that the southern states which adopted the late Professor Ron Edmonds's Effective Schools Research and its components (mastery learning/direct instruction/outcome-based education/cooperative learning, etc., etc.) in the mid-1970s have the lowest test scores in the nation. The philosophy behind Effective School Research, that "all children can learn if provided with the necessary 'environment' and enough time" is no more, no less than the outcome-based education philosophy which has by 1998 been implemented "in all schools of the nation." How can South Carolina have the lowest test scores and win Blue Ribbons?

The Effective School Report, the journal from which this writer has frequently quoted— and the one and only journal which consistently deals with OBE, TQM, Effective Schools, etc.—was born in Jackson, Mississippi in the early 1980s. Former Secretary of Education T.H. Bell served on the board of directors of its parent company, Kelwynn, Inc., the Effective Schools training company which published *The Effective School Report*. It should come as no surprise that Jackson, Mississippi schools served as the first guinea pig schools for implementation of Effective School Research.

The fact that South Carolina and Mississippi, two of the southern states most deeply involved in mastery learning over a long period of time, have such low academic test scores should be adequate justification for Congress to call for an investigation of the consequences of adopting effective school research and outcome-based education, *if*, and the writer repeats *if*, academic performance is what is being sought by the education bureaucracy and the Congress which funds public education. Surely, if the departments of education in those southern states which implemented Effective School Research had performed longitudinal studies tracking the children who went through those schools, education policy planners would have evidence that Effective School Research falls far short of the claims made by its proponents, most of whom benefit financially from such promotion. (See the Internet version for Appendix XXVI.)

This writer has a question for Coach Barnes: Couldn't his family's move to Austin, Texas, which is implementing the same Skinnerian method under another label (direct instruction), be a wonderful example of jumping from the frying pan into the fire—especially since Austin, Texas is also deeply involved (a leader) in non-academic school-to-work?]

A VERY INTERESTING ARTICLE ENTITLED "TAKING TECHNICAL ASSISTANCE on the Road" was published in the Spring 1998 issue of *Early Developments* (Vol. 2, No. l), a publication of the Frank Porter Graham Child Development Center at the University of North Carolina at Chapel Hill.[49] This center is funded in part by UNC and partly by PR/Award No. R307A60004 administered by the Office of Educational Research and Improvement, U.S. Department of Education. Excerpts from the article follow:

> By the early 1990s, Frank Porter Graham's researchers were at work in the People's Republic of China, Eastern Europe, and the former Soviet Union. For example, in 1995 Shelley deFosset and Pat Trohanis began working with the privately financed Step by Step program which was aimed at creating early childhood education demonstration projects initially in 17 emerging democracies of Central and Eastern Europe and the former Soviet Union.
>
> Step by Step founder and sponsor, George Soros, through his Open Soci-

ety Foundation, wanted to create a childhood education project that would ultimately lead to a new participatory citizenry beginning with the youngest members of society, its children.[50] Educators and parents in the countries involved have been enthusiastic—and, by the end of the second year Step by Step was in 1,500 classrooms serving over 37,500 children and families. Most countries have been successful in getting local funding for the programs.

Through a subcontract with Children's Resources International of Washington, D.C. which is the Open Society's technical assistance arm for the Step by Step project, de Fosset and Trohanis have hosted two groups of Russian teachers and administrators in the United States, and deFosset estimated that she's visited Russia "16 or 17" times. While in the U.S. Russians received training and visited numerous preschool programs. "When we're in Russia, we do training in the cities in Russia—and then we visit programs and provide feedback on existing programs," said de Fosset.

MARILYN PEASE OF NEW BEDFORD, MASSACHUSETTS WROTE AN ARTICLE FOR the May 22, 1998 issue of *The Standard-Times* of New Bedford entitled "MCAS Tests Undermine Rights of Parents" which deals with the same subject covered by Mr. Jacoby's May 7 column, but from a parent's perspective. Excerpts follow:

Once upon a time, Americans lived in a republic, where the voice of the minority carried as much weight as the voice of the majority because of a representative government. Laws and rights applied to individuals whether one, one hundred, or more people exercised their rights as opposed to marching lockstep or allowing themselves to be herded.

Along comes the Massachusetts Comprehensive Assessment System. The Department of Education wants us to believe that it's mandated for all 4th, 8th, and 10th graders and that the law has not provided for students or parents to "opt out." However, the law also does not specifically prohibit parents from exempting their children from the assessment; doing so would be a usurpation of parental authority and responsibility.

The state Supreme Court recognizes that children are not mere creatures of the state. Those who nurture and direct their destiny have the right to prepare them for additional obligations. Furthermore, Public Law 96–88, Title I, Section 101, number 3 states: "Parents have the primary responsibility for the education of their children and states, localities, and private interests have the primary responsibility for supporting that parental role."...

I submitted my intent in writing to exempt my son from MCAS. Despite my lack of permission, the test was administered to him, regardless. Whatever happened to parent/school partnerships? What if parents expect the public schools to provide factual information for their children to assimilate instead of the assessment of opinions their children are expected to synthesize, opinions that are being scored toward state standards, and opinions that will consequently be remedied until that standard is achieved?

We the People are allowing a major paradigm shift to occur, in which the state will be directing student destiny based on his or her performance on the MCAS. This correlates with MGL Chapter 69, Section 1D (I), which parents may review but not contest. Did parents knowingly relinquish their rights and authority upon enrolling their children in public schools?

Mr. Rick Atkins from the DOE's Accountability and Evaluation Services agreed that the law does not prohibit a parent from exempting their child from the MCAS. However, he said the child would receive a score of zero, which would be averaged with and thus would affect the entire school district. (Is that in the law, or another arbitrary and capricious rule the DOE spontaneously made up? Did our local educrats bother to ask?)

By refusing to exempt any child from the MCAS upon parental request, one might presume that their child is being exploited by the public schools so as not to bring down the average scores of the entire district. It appears that fundamental civil liberties are also being violated, but who cares? It's only one person, maybe a few. I guess it's easier to perpetuate the deception than to acknowledge it. Then We the People would have to do something about it.

[ddd]

THE SPRING 1998 ISSUE OF ASSOCIATION FOR SUPERVISION AND CURRICULUM Development's *Curriculum Update* was devoted to arts education and the main article was entitled "Arts Education: A Cornerstone of Basic Education." This writer, always a supporter of music and art in the public school curriculum, was educated regarding the real purpose of arts education when reading *Arts and the Schools* by Jerome Hausmann, one of the four books commissioned for John Goodlad's federally and foundation-funded *The Study of Schooling*. (See 1979 Schooling in the United States.) The *Curriculum Update* article exposes these same "reformed" purposes for arts education as devised by those contributing to America's dumbing down. Excerpts follow from this enlightening article:

CLAIMING ITS PLACE IN THE CORE CURRICULUM
"Today's school gatekeepers think of arts education as they experienced it, as holiday art or as recreation, not as a cognitive process," says Leilani Lattin Duke, director of the Getty Education Institute for the Arts. By studying the arts, students can develop capacities for critical thinking and problem solving, she explains.

"The arts represent forms that humans have created to convey their feelings, their visions, their aspirations, and their values," says Elliot Eisner, professor of education and art at Stanford University. "The presence of arts in the schools makes it possible for children and adolescents to learn how to read the images that arts provide.... Children need to be able to look at art and images and to recognize their historical and cultural significance in order to understand the message being conveyed."

Once children can interpret these sometimes confusing messages, they will need to learn how to manage them. "A lot of what is taught in school suggests that there are correct and incorrect answers to questions, as evidenced by the use of multiple-choice and true/false tests," explains Lehman. "In the real world, questions aren't posed that way." For example, questions about how to achieve world peace or end world hunger don't have any easy answers. The arts naturally require people to seek multiple solutions.

[Ed. Note: The writer understands and appreciates the artist's legitimate role of creating a painting or writing music as an expression of his own feelings about life. That is what makes art so special. However, social engineers should not use art to promote their own agendas in the classroom. The reader is urged to turn to the 1970 entry which quotes from Leonard S. Kenworthy's paper, "The International Dimension of Education: Background Paper II Prepared for the World Conference on Education," which says in part:

> For example, the writer has found tremendously effective a 10-minute film on the United Nations, entitled "Overture." There is no narrative in this film; the pictures are shown against a background of music, with the Vienna Symphony Orchestra playing the *Egmont Overture.* It is a powerful learning device and moves its viewers in a way few other approaches touch them.

Anyone familiar with Chairman Mao's brainwashing in Red China understands the use of theatre, art, and music to indoctrinate citizens.]

THE BUSINESS SECTION OF THE MAY 27, 1998 ISSUE OF *USA TODAY* CARried an article entitled "Schools Learn Lessons in Efficiency from Business." Excerpts follow:

> The biggest experiment, however, involves the public school system itself. In one of the most ambitious attempts yet to take something that works in business and apply it to public education, the 19 schools here expect in six months to become the first school district in the world to be ISO 9000 certified.
>
> ISO 9000, a sort of Good Housekeeping Seal of Approval for businesses, is a way of enforcing excellence that has been embraced by businesses worldwide.... But because the Lancaster [Pennsylvania] schools have identified their customers to be students and parents, ISO 9000 by definition must also force improvements in curriculum, teaching methods and anything else that leads to the ultimate goal of higher academic achievement.
>
> There is growing optimism in education circles that this could be the landmark experiment that finally marries education to a nuts-and-bolts business tool. ISO 9000 proponents say it will enforce discipline, not upon the students, but upon an unwieldy system. It will enforce consistency so that average teachers closely resemble the best.
>
> Will it work? Mixed signals abound. Interviews find Lancaster teachers and principals sold on ISO 9000—but unable to articulate how it will affect the classroom. That's a red flag to the business world.
>
> The U.S. Department of Education is so hopeful that it is funding the Lancaster experiment with $800,000 in federal grants. [With a per pupil expenditure of $18,000 a year, the Lancaster School District is having a hard time making ends meet and was at the beginning of 1999 saddled with $95 million in debt, ed.] It will be the first school district to get certified, although the Brandywine district in Delaware is not far behind.
>
> The New Jersey State Legislature wants the state's entire public school system to be ISO 9000 certified and has enacted a waiver from state monitoring to those that implement it. However, only four of 600 school districts are so far considering it.
>
> Success is far from certain. ISO 9000 is laden with flowcharts and statistics and comes steeped in manufacturing terminology guaranteed to make teachers cringe. Curriculum is a "process control." "Scrap" is a lost learning opportunity.
>
> The biggest roadblock has been the inability of educators to fully under-

stand it. There have been workshops for two years, but many still are unable to cite examples about how it has changed the classroom.

That's a warning sign to Kurt Landgraf, chairman of DuPont Europe, who has a master's degree in education. At this stage in ISO 9000 training, every employee "should be able to tell you exactly what they're doing differently," he says.

But Robert Bowen, the business consultant the school district hired to implement ISO 9000, says he's not worried. He knows first-hand that ISO 9000 is difficult to grasp because he's spent a decade unsuccessfully trying to explain to his parents what he does for a living....

Business leaders hesitate to get their hopes up. Throughout the 1990s schools have dabbled in continuous improvement and other pieces of total quality management (TQM). But despite those methods, U.S. 12th graders finish ahead of only Cyprus and South Africa in the international Math and Science Survey, says IBM CEO Louis Gerstner.

Trade magazine *Quality Progress* said the number of public schools surveyed that had TQM projects in 1997 dropped 32% from 1996.

"We lost our way," says Mary Schutz, a principal in Wagon Mound, N.M. where teachers were once as excited about TQM as Lancaster's are about ISO 9000.

He (William Kiefer, the Lancaster schools' ISO coordinator) also promises solid evidence by this fall that academic achievement is on the rise in Lancaster.

So far, such evidence does not exist.

[Ed. Note: When the writer attended the 1992 National Governors Association "Quality in Education" Conference held in Minneapolis, Minnesota, the session designed for school and other public officials was facilitated by a representative of IBM. During the question and answer period, a superintendent inquired about what to do when the expense of processing older teachers through staff development was not yielding changes in their behavior or level of acceptance of "reform." The facilitator, without a second thought, pointed to the TQM flowchart on the wall behind her and indicated a box marked "Waste Management." She then answered, "You watch them; you document their mistakes; then you get rid of them." That is the TQM/ISO 9000 process at work.]

ASSOCIATION FOR SUPERVISION AND CURRICULUM DEVELOPMENT'S JUNE 1998 issue of *Education Update* carried a "Message from the Executive Director" subtitled "South Africa Tackles Ambitious Curriculum Reform Effort." Revealing excerpts follow:

In March 1998, I traveled to Cape Town, South Africa, as a participant in the Comparative Human Relations Initiative Consultation, funded by the Ford Foundation through a grant awarded to the Southern Education Foundation in Atlanta, Georgia.... South Africa's education system is crippled by the legacy of apartheid as it struggles to deal with issues of inequity and quality.... Consequently, the brew of raised expectations among the ever-growing numbers of the poor and the government's inability to respond portends trying times ahead.

The new government is trying to respond to this situation through an enterprise called the National Qualifications Framework (NQF), an innovative education and training paradigm that uses outcome-based education to prepare students to be lifelong learners. Subsequently, a massive curriculum reform effort entitled Curriculum 2005 was initiated in January of the 1998 academic year in all primary schools. But the solid vision behind Curriculum 2005 has been marred by inadequate implementation of strategies and resources.

Various public and private groups have either supported or criticized the government's decision to implement Curriculum 2005, which is based largely on the tenets of outcome-based education. Sangaliso Mikhatshwa, Deputy Minister of Education, asserts that "this system offers much in South Africa's move away from the rote learning and content-driven curricula of the past." He further contends that it represents a "head, hands, and heart approach," as learners are required to indicate what they have learned in terms of knowledge, skills, and attitudes.

It is still too early to predict whether these difficulties represent mortal wounds to the government's education reform plans or merely predictable roadblocks along the way to successful innovation. The one thing that is certain about South Africa is the predictability of the unpredictable. Still, there are insurmountable courage, hope, and optimism among South Africa's peoples.

[Ed. Note: The language in this article—particularly the wording "offers much in South Africa's move away from the rote learning and content-driven curricula of the past"—parallels and echoes that of the opening pages of H.R. 6, the reauthorization of funding for the *Elementary and Secondary Education Act*, which called for funding programs and curricula which would not address so-called "lower order skills." This language is interpreted to mean memorization of facts and basic academic skills as we have always known them. In addition, the reader should understand that outcome-based education is based on Effective Schools Research, the basis for international education reform, and that it has generated intense opposition abroad as well as in the United States of America.[51] The writer also assumes that language contained in International Loan Agreement guidelines issued by the World Bank to facilitate "development" in South Africa may have contributed to the adoption of this internationally accepted (mandated) Skinnerian method. (See November 17, 1984 Maine Association of Christian Schools' letter regarding Kevin Ryan, Portugal, and the World Bank, and the Internet version for Appendix VI which relates to Korea and the World Bank.)]

THE JUNE 7, 1998 ISSUE OF OREGON'S *STATESMAN JOURNAL* PUBLISHED AN article entitled "Salem-Keizer Test Scores Fall." Excerpts follow:

Salem-Keizer student scores dipped for the second consecutive year in a prominent achievement test, dragging district scores further below the national average.... "We can't and shouldn't try to make any excuses for it," said Dan Johnson, the district administrator spearheading education reform efforts. "It's fairly consistent across each of the categories in terms of the decline."

"Some averages fell to the 40th percentile or lower."... District administrators were hard-pressed to pinpoint reasons for the falling scores.

Johnson attributed it partly to school reforms and a phenomenon he called the "change curve." Schools that shift their teaching approaches often witness dips in scores while they're trying to make changes in the classroom.... Candalaria has worked hard to improve students' creative thinking when approaching math problems.... But by focusing on new skills, teachers might have given less attention to basic math computation, where scores are dropping, she said.

[Ed. Note: Please refer to the February 1995 entry.]

THE ATLANTA CONSTITUTION RAN AN ARTICLE ENTITLED "GINGRICH: TAPS for Textbooks—He Says Computers Will Replace Them" in its June 9, 1998 edition. Excerpts follow:

[Newt] Gingrich, speaking Monday at the Supercom trade show at the Georgia World Congress Center, said the onrush of technology will make textbooks obsolete.

"One of the goals should be to replace all textbooks with a PC," the Georgia Republican said. "I would hope within five years they would have no more textbooks."

Personal computers are the new focus for learning and students should be given one when they enter first grade, he said.

That suggestion drew immediate fire from Washington, D.C.-based author Harriet Tyson, who wrote *A Conspiracy of Good Intentions: America's Textbook Fiasco*.

Gingrich has distorted technology's value, she said. "He is like a 16-year-old who just fell in love with computers. He is not a techie. He's just in love with techies."

Gingrich, a former college professor who peppers his talks with references to writers such as Peter Drucker, W. Edwards Deming and Alexis de Tocqueville, also called for an overhaul of the nation's schools. Gingrich urged that schools be judged in a business context.

Gingrich argued that Internet connections should often be available to replace the traditional lecture by a professor. In contrast to the old-style teaching model, the Net would be accessible 24 hours a day, he said. "We have to become a learning society."

[Ed. Note: The following quote from the 1971 *The Individualized Learning Letter* entry echoes the views of Newt Gingrich:

Down with textbooks! Textbooks not only encourage learning at the wrong level (imparting facts rather than telling how to gather facts, etc.), they also violate an important new concern in American education—Individualized Instruction.

This is also another instance which reminds us of the gravity of the consequences of H.R. 6 (reauthorization of the *Elementary and Secondary Education Act of 1965*) and its assertions that "lower order skills" (memorization and basic academics) should not be funded or promoted.]

THE TRI-CITY HERALD OF KENNEWICK, WASHINGTON CARRIED "GROUP Supporting Paula Jones Case Sues Pasco Schools" by Wendy Culverwell in its June 11, 1998 issue. The article tells us that

> The organization that is paying Paula Jones's legal bills in her sexual harassment case against President Clinton filed suit Monday against the Pasco School District.
>
> The suit contends the district violated the constitutional rights of a former teacher who objected to outcome-based education.
>
> In the action filed in U.S. District Court in Spokane, the Rutherford Institute alleges the district wrongfully terminated Barbara McFarlin-Kosiec and violated her constitutional rights to free speech and free exercise of religion. The complaint seeks economic damages.
>
> Ken Rice, the Kennewick attorney who represents the district, said the district hasn't been served with the complaint, but he doesn't believe the suit has merit. He said the district would defend itself vigorously.
>
> According to the press release issued by the Rutherford Institute, McFarlin-Kosiec was forced to resign as a teacher in 1995 because of her opposition to outcome-based education. She was a veteran teacher when she was hired in 1993 to teach at Mark Twain Elementary.
>
> The lawsuit was filed by Greg Casey and Bruce Gore, Spokane attorneys affiliated with the Rutherford Institute.... The Institute describes itself as an international, non-profit civil liberties organization specializing in the defense of human rights.
>
> Neither McFarlin-Kosiec nor her attorneys could be reached for comment Wednesday.

[Ed. Note: The reader will recognize the name of Barbara McFarlin-Kosiec as one of the teachers who reviewed and endorsed *the deliberate dumbing down of america*. Who better could understand the consequences of opposition to the restructuring paradigm shift?]

THE WASHINGTON TIMES OF JUNE 11, 1998 PRINTED AN ASSOCIATED PRESS article entitled "Congress to Expand Education Savings." Important excerpts follow:

> House and Senate negotiators agreed yesterday on a bill to expand tax-favored savings accounts for educational expenses, including tuition at private and religious schools, and to erase a ban on President Clinton's proposed national standardized tests. The deal removes an obstacle to President Clinton's plan for voluntary national tests in fourth-grade reading and eighth-grade math. Negotiators deleted an amendment passed by the Senate in April that would have banned the standards-based tests unless specifically authorized by Congress and would have converted some Education Department programs into block grants.
>
> The negotiators also tacked on a reading bill, supported by Mr. Clinton, that must be signed in order for $210 million to be spent starting July 1 for research, teacher training and grants to help improve reading instruction.

[Ed. Note: Although the above legislation did not become law, the importance of this entry relates to (1) the removal of the ban on national testing and (2) the approval of legislation which will mandate a particular method of reading instruction, Skinnerian Direct Instruction in the *Reading Excellence Act*, which did pass a few months later in November of 1998 as part of the omnibus budget.]

[ddd]

CONTINUING HER EXCELLENT WORK AS "WATCHDOG" ON BEHALF OF OHIO taxpayers, State Board of Education member Diana Fessler—an articulate opponent of the school-to-work philosophy—wrote a letter dated June 22, 1998 to U.S. Secretary of Education Richard Riley and U.S. Secretary of Labor Alexis Herman in regard to her being barred from a meeting sponsored by the National School-to-Work Office of the U.S. Department of Education on June 14–18, 1998 in Cleveland, Ohio. Ms. Fessler's letter is reproduced in its entirety in order to relay the complete details of her experience.

Dear Secretaries Riley and Herman:

I am a duly elected member of the Ohio State Board of Education (SBE) with approximately one million people residing in my district. Section 3301.07(C) of the Ohio Revised Code directs the SBE to administer and supervise the allocation and distribution of all state and federal funds for public education in Ohio. Accordingly, I have an obligation to be fully informed regarding education matters affecting my constituents.

Seeking to stay abreast of School-to-Work (STW), I made arrangements to attend a meeting sponsored by the National School-to-Work Office (NSTWO) on June 14–18, 1998 in Cleveland, Ohio. Forty-three states and Puerto Rico were represented. I was formally introduced and welcomed from the podium by Ohio's STW director, and I attended the Sunday through Tuesday morning sessions without incident.

On Tuesday afternoon, Ivan Charner of the Academy of Educational Development (operator of the NSTWO's Learning Center) told me I could not attend his closed "strategy" meeting for the eight states that received first-round STW money. I find it incredible that those who claim that STW is good for kids, good for the economy, good for our nation, and worthy of replication find it necessary to conduct the public's business behind closed doors, and I told him so. A woman nearby said, "Well, the FBI meets behind closed doors," and I thought to myself, "Good grief, this is worse than I thought; these people think a STW meeting is on par with an FBI operation."

Mr. Charner referred me to Ms. Irene Lynn, Interim Director of the NSTWO. She confirmed that I was not welcome, saying: "It is just not an open meeting; it is a non-public meeting." I asked, "Who is paying for this meeting?" and she acknowledged that taxpayers were. I asked who decided to keep me out and she said that she had. I asked what the NSTWO was trying to hide, and she said it was just a "working meeting," and that government workers often get together for such meetings, and nothing was hidden.

These were not routine staff meetings. Participants had flown in from all across the country to meet in a swanky hotel, at taxpayers' expense, to identify and discuss "obstacles" that they face in moving the STW agenda forward and to develop "strategies" to overcome those "obstacles."

Ms. Lynn attributed the "problem" to my "not understanding STW" and used the common, and offensive tactic of characterizing those who do not blindly embrace STW as being "misinformed" or "lacking in understanding." When I pointed that out, Ms. Lynn corrected herself and acknowledged that the "problem" is philosophical in nature, not informational.

It is no secret that I have serious reservations regarding the STW system. I have researched it extensively, and I have made that research available to my constituents via my web site—to the chagrin of STW devotees who seek to hide the full scope of STW from the American people for as long as possible using whatever means necessary. Thus, they attempt to conduct the people's business behind closed doors, or only in the presence of the Enlightened. This bureaucratic tyranny undermines rational, open disagreement—the hallmark of civil liberty in the arena of government.

To reaffirm that there was a concerted effort to bar me from the meeting, on Wednesday morning I entered the Communications Task Force meeting room and stood at the back of the room. Stephanie Powers, Director of Communication & Public Affairs, Office of the Assistant Secretary, U.S. Department of Labor, Employment & Training Administration; and Peter Woolfolk, Special Assistant for Communications, Vocational and Adult Education, Office of the Assistant Secretary, U.S. Department of Education, insisted that I leave.

One can only wonder what NSTWO was trying to accomplish by barring me from the meeting. One might reasonably conclude that the decision to oust me was considered to be the lesser of two evils; i.e., the repercussions of doing so being less problematic than risking full disclosure of what took place during the meetings. I also found it troubling when Ms. Powers said that I need to understand that "Congress has provided for these business meetings"—implying that Congress would approve closed-door STW meetings.

Ms. Powers said that she knew that we did not agree on STW. As I told Ms. Powers, STW is not the issue—it is whether the general public, through their elected representatives, have access to critical public information regarding the work being done to re-shape our schools, our economy, and our system of government. She had no reply. Knowing that the meeting would have been "shortened" had I stayed, I left the hotel, but there are still questions that need to be answered:

- By what authority did Mr. Charner, Ms. Lynn, Ms. Powers, and Mr. Woolfolk bar me from the meetings?
- Why was it imperative that the public's business be conducted behind closed doors?
- And, if STW is indeed good for kids and essential for the good of the economy, why must the details be kept hidden from public scrutiny?

NSTWO has yet to provide me with copies of Ohio's Urban/Rural Opportunities Grants, claiming that they cannot do so unless the grantees give the NSTWO permission to do so. Any attempt to make the release of public records contingent on the one seeking the information first getting permission from the recipient of federal funds is absurd, but it does illustrate the extent to which your employees will go to restrict the flow of information. Therefore, pursuant to the FOI Act, please see that I get a copy of each Ohio UROG grant including the budget narratives and appendices, as well as the following documents relevant to the June 14–18 STW meeting in Cleveland: the communication from legal counsel regarding closed-door meetings; all RFP's, SGA's, and contracts (including facilitation and technical assistance) with appendices and the budgets; a list of all disbursements including date, amount, vendor, and purpose; all notes taken by staff and "recorders"; all overheads, handouts, background materials, audio tapes, and videos, and candidate applications, including resumes and appendices, of those applying for the position of Director of the NSTWO.

This is not a letter of complaint; it is a declaration: your people are out of control. This letter also serves as formal notification that concealment of public information, unless required for national security, will not be tolerated. Furthermore, I am seeking legal counsel to determine if any state or federal laws have been broken regarding this matter.

The purpose of government is to serve the interests of the people—not to develop legislative agendas, refine implementation strategies, and create marketing plans behind closed doors. Apologies from bureaucratic bullies who willfully prevented me from gathering the background information to enable me to carry out the duties of my office would be meaningless. Ms. Lynn, Ms. Powers, Mr. Woolfolk, and Mr. Charner should be fired and their positions filled by people who have a firm understanding of, and respect for, how representative government is supposed to work.

Please give this letter your prompt attention. I look forward to receiving your personal letter of reply.

On behalf of my constituents,

Diana M. Fessler
Ohio State Board of Education—Third District[52]

CC: Senators Lott, Ashcroft, DeWine, Glenn; Representatives Gingrich, Armey, DeLay, Boehner, Hyde, Hoekstra and Graham

THE JUNE 1998 ISSUE OF *THE CHRISTIAN CONSCIENCE* CARRIED AN ARTICLE by education researcher Bettye Lewis of Michigan entitled "Violence in the Schools: Part 2—Achieving National Education Goal Six." In this article Lewis asserted that "Goal 6 may be the most diabolical goal in the *Goals 2000: Educate America Act*, since it is this goal which will strip away individual freedoms in favor of the collective world community (New World Order). Will Americans wake up and refuse to relinquish their unalienable (God-given) constitutional rights? Or will they continue in apathy as they increasingly become drones in the coming New World Order?" Excerpts of Lewis's article follow:

The Michigan Strategy Proposal for Drug and Violence Free Schools and Communities states:

Michigan now has one of the Nation's most aggressive and comprehensive long-term strategies to reach Goal 6: "By the year 2000, every school in America will be free of drugs and violence and will offer a disciplined environment conducive to learning."

Governor John Engler and the Michigan State Board of Education have worked jointly to provide leadership and establish a clear plan of action to enable our schools and communities to create safe, disciplined and drug free learning environments for our children by the year 2000. It will demand local community action, greater coordination, and careful targeting of $17 million in federal Drug Free Schools and Communities Act (DFSCA).[53]

Throughout this document the Communitarian agenda is apparent. This philosophy assigns responsibility to the community, not the parents, for the development of the child.... The section on "Action Items" refers to State and Local Goals and shows us how dictatorial the state and federal Government have become toward recipients of *Drug Free Schools and Communities Act* funds. Notice there is no choice—"the school district *will....*"

Every school district will develop a local school-community coalition and advisory team. The data banks established for continual assessment and analysis will be the controlling factor, not only regarding the individual, but the school and the community, establishing community norms as well.... As one reads this proposal for accomplishing Goal 6, it becomes clear this document became the foundation for the Bias Crime Response Task Force Report. Surveys, marketing and a media blitz will be used to convince the public that violence is out of control and every community must be used to address the problem and fully implement Goal 6. Five years ago—1993—this document (Michigan's Strategy Proposal) cited the State Goal to be:

> Every school-community drug education advisory team will review current needs assessment and problem statements, undertake and complete a comprehensive needs assessment with data sufficient to identify, alter or select prevention programming and utilize data to plan evaluations of program impact by June 1994. The state will compile a county by county risk and protective factor profile as a local resource and for comparative data.

The State Goal reveals just how extensive the databanks will be and how the data will be used as a means to dictate how every school/community will address the problem and develop prescribed national norms. The target date, June 1994, aligned perfectly with the *1994 Student Data Handbook: Elementary, Secondary and Early Childhood* and the *1994 Staff Data Handbook: Elementary, Secondary and Early Childhood.*[54] These data handbooks were first developed in 1974.... One of the original ten data handbooks was on community and number-coded community values—the values every U.S. community was eventually to embrace as their norms.[55]...

...The systems change and the implementation of the School-to-Work system will force the continual assessment of children to analyze the progress being made toward the elimination of all bias, individualism and privacy. Common unity cannot prevail unless all children develop the predetermined behavior, attitudes, and values for existence in the interdependent global society of the future.

The federal government is up to its old trick of creating a problem—which they certainly have done by limiting discipline in schools, subjecting children to certain learning experiences, requiring inclusive education which requires juvenile offenders in tethers to be in the regular classroom, requiring group consensus decision making and problem solving. The violence problem has been advertised for quite some time, and the rigged survey results will be used to continue the media blitz to gain public acknowledgment of the problem. The solution to the problem was planned long before *Goals 2000*, but the objective was state enforcement and control.

Most of the plan has already been implemented. Remember, everything is to be in place by the year 2000. We already have alternative schools, after-hours programs, full-service schools, day care, peer mediation, community service, character education, health education, uniforms in some schools, etc.

Goal 6 data banks on violence and bias crimes open the public square to drowning in the flood waters of the collective. Laws will be of no importance as norms become dictated by the federal government via their data collection system. These norms are becoming very evident: a new type of family (the community), gun control… efforts to modify the values of Christians or any faith that disagrees with the norms of anti-individualism, population control, promotion of the world community over nationalism, with survival only through cooperation, collaboration and consensus. (pp. 14–23)[56]

[Ed. Note: Lewis's exposé of what is taking place in Michigan is a most valuable warning for all Americans. In order to fully understand the significance of her exposé, substitute the names of *your* children, *your* town, *your* county and *your* state and you will feel chills race down your spine.]

DR. LAWRENCE W. LEZOTTE, SENIOR VICE PRESIDENT OF EFFECTIVE SCHOOLS, Okemos, Michigan, presented a paper entitled "Learning for All—What Will It Take?" at the Sixth Annual Model Schools Conference sponsored by Willard Daggett's International Center for Leadership in Education, Inc., at the Renaissance Waverly Hotel and Cobb Convention Centre in Atlanta, Georgia, June 28–July 1, 1998. An excerpt from Dr. Lezotte's paper follows:

A single school, as a system, can control enough of the variables to assure that virtually all students do learn. The distinguished educational researcher Robert Gagne said that the essential task of the teacher is to arrange the conditions of the learner's environment so that the process of learning will be activated, supported, enhanced, and maintained.

[Ed. Note: Quoting from the 1969 entry in this book entitled *Improving Educational Assessment and an Inventory of Measures of Affective Behavior*, the writer wishes to draw the reader's attention to a most revealing statement from "The Purposes of Assessment" by Ralph Tyler:

Now, as the people from conditioning have moved into an interest in learning in the schools, the notions of behavioral objectives have become much more specific. As far as I know, one cannot very well teach a pigeon a general principle that he can apply to a variety of situations. The objectives for persons coming out of the Skinnerian background tend to be highly specific ones. When I listened to Gagne, who is an intelligent and effective conditioner, talk about human learning objectives, I wince a good deal because he sets very specific ones. I know that we can attain levels of generalization of objectives that are higher than that.

Making the connection between Lezotte, Gagne, and Tyler should help the reader understand that the restructuring going on in this nation's schools reflects the use of Skinnerian operant conditioning (OBE/ML/DI). Lezotte, one of the leaders of today's restructuring movement, has made this clear by his reference to Gagne, conditions and environment. The high profile that Lezotte maintains with his Effective Schools organization and his consistent appearance at Willard Daggett's meetings and seminars—and Daggett's close former association with William Spady of OBE fame—should demonstrate to the reader that all of these participants and promoters of the restructuring movement are "singing the same tune," as it were, and they sound exactly like Skinner's operant-conditioned pigeons. Lawrence Lezotte has also served on the board of directors for *The Effective School Report*—this very important and relatively unknown (to the public) journal.]

THE *ATLANTA CONSTITUTION*'S JULY 1, 1998 EDITION CARRIED AN ARTICLE by Doug Cumming entitled "Georgia Schools OK Tracking Systems" which confirmed the worst fears of education researchers tracking Planning, Programming, Budgeting Systems (PPBS) and Management by Objectives (MBO) for over twenty-five years. Excerpts from this revealing article follow:

> Taking its biggest step yet to create a powerful new computer information system that can track every state education dollar down to the attendance rates and test scores of every Georgia classroom, the State Board of Education approved two major computer contracts Tuesday.
>
> The two contracts, for as much as $31 million over the next 12 months, along with a related contract tabled until July 9, will give school systems quicker access to information.
>
> "For example, the new systems will let school systems instantly report students who are absent for two consecutive weeks or suspended for drugs, alcohol, or guns. This will allow the state to immediately revoke their driver's licenses under a law that took effect this year.
>
> "That's just a taste of what is possible. In the future, by linking student records, staff records and funding formulas, the new system will also allow local schools and state policymakers to see how well teachers and students are performing within specific programs.
>
> "We know that in education for too long, programs have been implemented, and there was never any comprehensive measurement," said Miriam V. Holland, director of administrative technology for the state Department of Education.
>
> "The state goal over the next few years is to be able to pinpoint the cause of academic weaknesses such as the recent failure rate on the science portion of the state's graduation exam," she said.
>
> Bonnie Knight, head of business and technology for the Rockdale schools, said she is excited about what will be possible when a new student-information system is introduced and linked to the accounting system. Then, teachers can punch up on their own computer, within security limits, family and student records, and administrators can access the kind of information that private businesses normally use to determine the cost-effectiveness of any program. Knight says she knows of no other state that is linking student records with state and local school accounting systems.
>
> James Mullins, a lobbyist for DeKalb County schools, which uses its own information systems, said the new system will put increasing pressure on systems like his to adopt the state's system. He said many local systems quietly worry that the proposed new system could eventually give the state the power of a "Big Brother" to control local schools directly.

[Ed. Note: The legitimate concern expressed by James Mullins of DeKalb County regarding "Big Brother" comes as a timely warning for naïve Americans who see nothing wrong with providing any and all information—social security numbers, fingerprints, personal data—to anyone who requests it, even, and especially, your local school officials. The reader is urged to re-read the 1972 entry in this book which quoted from "Schools to Try New Program" published in the Tallahassee, Florida *The Ledger* for the Cecil Golden comment which likened PPBS/MBO—of which the above article is the fulfillment—to an atom bomb: "[L]ike those assembling the atom bomb, very few of them understand exactly what they are building, and won't until we put all the parts together."]

[ddd]

THE JULY 9, 1998 ISSUE OF THE SOUTH BRISTOL, MAINE *LINCOLN COUNTY Weekly* published an article entitled "Darling Center Hosts UNESCO Conference" which illustrates the extent to which even the smallest towns in our nation are being affected by international education policies. The article states in part:

> While the majority of residents and visitors in the area celebrate Damar-iscotta's past 150 years, a fledgling group of international visitors gather at the Ira C. Darling Marine Center to plan for the future.
> Participants in the third International Working Conference on Information Technology in Education Management (ITEM) have come from 18 countries, including Australia, Japan, New Zealand, China and the Netherlands, to share their research on integrating information for education management....
> ..."One very important aspect of this work is how integrated information influences or informs the decisions of school administrators and policy makers," said Ray Taylor, the conference coordinator and a former superintendent of the Augusta school district....
> While the Darling Center hosted the meeting, School Union 74, UNESCO (United Nations Educational, Scientific and Cultural Organization), and a North Carolina company, OR/ED Laboratories, also supported the week's events.
> "Most of the participants work with national information systems for education, with Great Britain, Israel, Hong Kong, and New Zealand, having among the most advanced systems," Taylor said.
> Speakers debated the benefits of standardizing student and school infor-mation across regions. Such information systems benefit students by tracking their academic achievement, as well as administrators who have individual children continually entering and leaving their schools.
> "This goes beyond counting cheese and buses," one participant remarked. "We want to create consistent data on local, regional and national levels."
> [And international? ed.]

THE JULY 11, 1998 ISSUE OF *THE WASHINGTON TIMES* CARRIED AN ARTICLE entitled "Classroom Brain-Watchers?" by Kathleen Parker which discussed the federal government's plan to prevent school violence by "adding psy-choanalysis to our teachers' laundry list of responsibilities." Excerpts follow:

> I have a healthy paranoia toward government, born most likely of having been reared by a misanthropic WWII pilot with a bomb shelter. Let's just

say, when government bureaucrats knock on my door and say, "We want to help you," I get the same feeling I got as a little girl when the old man down the street reached over his cyclone fence to offer me a piece of candy. Not "No, thanks," but "Run!"

When they come knocking to say they want to help my children, I reflect wistfully on moats.

Such that when I recently heard about the federal government's plan to prevent school violence by adding psychoanalysis to our teachers' laundry list of responsibilities, I began pricing drawbridges.

Judging from the absence of news stories on the subject, you may have missed your future. President Clinton first mentioned the plan in his June 13 radio address to the nation. Education Secretary Richard Riley mentioned it again a couple of weeks ago during the Safe and Drug Free Schools Conference in Washington, D.C.

Mr. Clinton has directed Mr. Riley and Attorney General Janet Reno to work with the National Association of School Psychologists to develop a framework—"early warning guide"—to help teachers and principals identify which kids are most likely to bring Grandpa's deer rifle to school one of these days.

The plan also calls for expanding links between schools and local psychological communities so children identified as "troubled" have access to counseling.

Because the guide is in the early planning stages, details are skimpy. No one knows yet how danger signs will be defined or recognized, according to a Department of Education spokesperson. Right off, I'd have to say it's pretty easy to tell which kids are dangerous without creating a psychological bureaucracy. In nearly all recent school shootings, as Mr. Clinton pointed out, the shooters announced their plans in advance.

In other words, if a kid says, "I'm going to blow everybody away tomorrow because they've been picking on me since nursery school," you might assume trouble. If, on the other hand, a third-grade boy draws a picture of a ship exploding with bodies flying in all directions, punctuated by red ink blots, you might assume you've got a normal third-grader on your hands.

But you can bet that won't be the thinking once the warning guide is in the hands of extremely well-meaning educators and counselors, some of whom have the judgment and perception of parakeets. That third-grader will wind up in some counselor's office for analysis and reprogramming before you can say "Freud."

Paranoid? You bet.

My own child—a kind, sensitive 13-year-old whose disinterest in guns rivals his interest in hanging up wet towels—drew incredibly violent pictures during his grade-school years. The exploding ship with exploding bodies comes to mind. How might a newly trained teacher—especially a female teacher without sons—interpret such a drawing?

Clearly a sociopath. Get that boy downtown!

Will any child who talks about guns be sent to the "thought police"? What about playing cowboys and Indians, or "Star Wars" during recess? Does this qualify a child for re-education? What sort of records will be kept?

Even Mr. Riley expressed concerns about the plan. "We need to be very cautious about the idea of sorting out our children and labeling them," he said in the speech. "Too many children are already being sorted out in our schools and too often this approach to education has been harmful to minority youth."

Not to mention harmful to freedom. Can mandatory psychological profiling be far behind? The potential for abuse of power and thought control is the stuff of science fiction. But that's just the thinking of a paranoid. I probably just need a little psychotherapy.

And a big moat.

IN THE JULY 14, 1998 *CONGRESSIONAL RECORD* CONGRESSMAN HENRY HYDE (R., IL) included a very important article written by D.L. Cuddy, Ph.D., former senior associate with the U.S. Department of Education and consultant to the North Carolina House Select Committee for Federal Education Grants. Cuddy wrote "Education: The New Transatlantic Agenda" which appeared in the July 2, 1998 issue of Dunn, North Carolina's *The Daily Record*. Excerpts follow:

> The White House released a statement May 18 at the conclusion of the U.S.-European Summit in London, indicating that "through the New Transatlantic Agenda (NTA), created in 1995, the United States and the European Union have focused on addressing the challenges and opportunities of global integration."
>
> One part of this "global integration" in 1995 was the agreement between the U.S. and the European Community establishing a cooperation program in higher education and vocational education and training.
>
> The agreement, signed December 21, 1995, called for "improving the quality of human resource development... transatlantic student mobility... and thus portability of academic credits." In this regard, a joint committee would reach decisions by consensus.
>
> As part of the NTA, the United States and European Union then convened a major conference, "Bridging the Atlantic People-to-People Links," May 5–6. 1997, calling for "thematic networks for curriculum development," and further stating that in an information-based global economy, "governments too are obliged to adapt their economic, training and social welfare programs."
>
> The conference final report noted that in the United States, ACHIEVE has been one of the organizations at the forefront of defining key issues in this regard and developing strategies to address them.
>
> ACHIEVE has been measuring and reporting each state's annual progress in establishing internationally competitive standards and business leaders involved have indicated their commitment to consider the quality of each state's standards when making business location or expansion decisions.
>
> The "Partners in a Global Economy Working Group" of the conference discussed "what redesigning of curricula is required... (i.e., what career skills are needed)... portability of skill certificates... institutionalizing cross-national learning/training activities."
>
> Most people debating STW in America are familiar with the role of Marc Tucker, president of the National Center on Education and the Economy. He's also on the National Skill Standards Board (NSSB).
>
> On the National Skill Standards Board website under international links, one finds "Smartcards Project Forum," under which one reads: "The Tavistock Institute and the European Commission are working on a feasibility study

to research the effect of using Smartcards in competence accreditation. The study will be carried out in the USA and parts of Europe."

The project involves assessing and validating students' skills, with information placed on personal skills Smartcards, which "become real passports to employment."

If without a passport one cannot enter a country, does this mean that without a skills passport, one may not be able to get a job in the future?

In October 1997, the Tavistock Institute (and Manchester University) completed the final report for the European Commission and described in a report summary were the relevancy of *Goals 2000*, SCANS... typology with its "profound implications for the curriculum and training changes that this will require," valid skills standards and portable credentials "benchmarked to international standards such as those promulgated by the International Standards Organization (ISO)."

The report summary went on to say that "there is increasing attention being focused on developing global skill standards and accreditation agreements" and there will be "partnerships between government, industry and representatives of worker organizations ... [and] a high degree of integration... embedding skills within the broader context of economic and social activity and specifically within the areas of secondary education work-based learning and local and regional economic development.... The NSSB, *Goals 2000*, STW Program are all combining to act as a catalyst to promote the formation of partnerships to develop skills standards. In this regard, a system like O*Net can be seen as the glue that holds everything together."

O*Net is a new occupational database system sponsored by the U.S. Department of Labor's Employment and Training Administration and is being piloted in Texas, South Carolina, California, New York and Minnesota. It includes information such as "Worker Characteristics" (abilities, interests and work styles) and "Worker Requirements" (e.g., basic skills, knowledge and education).

CHRISTINE BURNS, A VETERAN TEACHER OF OUTSTANDING CHARACTER, REPUtation and credentials, labeled the St. Louis Career Academy a "diabolical gauntlet of pandemonium" in an article entitled "School-to-Work Academy: A 'Model' for Chaos" which appeared in the July 1998 issue of *The Education Reporter*. Excerpts follow:

The Career Academy... was touted by education reformers as the wave of the future—the "New Urban High School"—with the intent that it will eventually be open 24 hours a day. The Career Academy was designed to be one of five "break-the-mold" School-to-Work model high schools in the U.S. that are to be replicated throughout the country.

In May of this year, the Career Academy's facade of "success" and "achievement" began to crumble when one of its teachers came forward to paint a sordid picture of chaos, confusion and ineptitude at the school, calling it "a diabolical gauntlet of pandemonium" for its students.

Mrs. Burns, after eight months' teaching at the academy, desired only to "get out of it" and be "rid of the problem." But then the school district told her to read, critique and sign off on a document entitled "Building the Foundation for Life-Long, Self-Directed Learning" which according to Burns was "full of lies, suppositions and half truths." Realizing that she could not sign the document, she says that neither could she "walk away without someone, somewhere, knowing what I believe to be the truth about what is happening, or rather, not happening at the St. Louis Career Academy."

Mrs. Burns drafted a rebuttal to "Building a Foundation" which she sent to the school's principal, the CED Superintendent, the court-appointed vocational education monitor, and the school district's seven board members. The rebuttal charges the school with "lying about students gaining in academic achievement." It contends that "the school relies too heavily on computers, that computer labs are typically chaotic and poorly controlled due to lack of manpower," and that "destruction and theft of equipment are commonplace." "Students cheat on computerized tests to advance to their next 'tier' (grade)," she wrote, adding that "the school lacks practical in-classroom teaching, order and discipline." She charged that "children at the academy have been part of a giant School-to-Work experiment for the past two years, subjected to unproven and unorthodox practices and procedures, like rats in a maze."

Though the Career Academy has attempted to refute Mrs. Burns's charges, "Building the Foundation"'s 37 paragraphs provide some clues as to their validity. Paragraph 9 refers to the school's staff and students as remaining "intensely involved in an on-going process of self-creation." Paragraph 26 whines that: "In spite of an explicit court mandate to 'break the mold,' the academy continues to come under attack from proponents of the old system." Yet paragraph 30 admits that "students have learned they can fool the computer by 'smart guessing' or by memorizing answers for retests. Some students wonder how much of their learning they will retain. Others have 'maxed out' on the English and math programs, and do not feel challenged by their supplemental work."

BILL CARLSON, AN EDUCATION RESEARCHER FROM TEXAS, COVERED THE School-to-Career Academy Conference held July 23–24, 1998 at the Airport Hyatt Hotel in Burlingame, California. Carlson's article should be in the hands of parents and small businessmen who have been subjected to the skilled manipulation of the change agent promoters of STW. Excerpts from Mr. Carlson's article, "Impressions and Concerns: A Preliminary Report" follow:

The School-to-Career (STC) "academy" featured two keynote speakers, J.D. Hoye and Willard Daggett. Hoye bills herself as J.D. Hoye, President, Keep the Change, Inc. Her web site (http://inet.ed.gov./offices/OVAE/hoye.html) identifies her as the Director of the National School-to-Work (STW) Office in Washington, D.C. (Note: STC and STW as used in this report convey the same meaning.) Hoye's former involvement was with the Oregon Department of Education and Office of Community College Services, Oregon, arguably and tragically the most OBE-impacted state in the nation.... Both speakers are extremely smooth and clever STW marketers. Both have a passion for ALL children to learn and seem convinced that STW will "level the playing field." (It must, however, be mandatory that ALL children experience STW. Why?)

Hoye gives the message that our current education system does great for 25–30% of the students. She wants a level playing field for ALL students. She points to a book called *The New Basics* as a guide. She plays down memorization, abstract and theoretical teaching because they don't stick as well as cooperative project completions. Now is the time to promote STC throughout our communities because it "sunsets in 2001." Be creative in finding ways to "convince" skeptics, especially parents. Involve them in the process and they will believe the ideas generated were their own. Administrators should make sure, as far as possible, that hiring, promotion and retention policies coincide with promotion of school-to-work goals.

Students are the best communicators of the need for change and STW. Periodically, a student was brought out to give a "first-hand example" of our need to change, change, change to STW. She describes what we are doing (promoting school-to-career) as "the most important thing happening on our planet!"

Willard Daggett was clearly the featured event. (web site—http://www.daggett.com) He was introduced as one who is "taking on the task of promoting school-to-career in California." If Dr. Daggett is the King of STW, Hoye is certainly the Queen. Daggett touts himself as being the President of the International Center for Leadership in Education, Inc.

He offered thanks to educators for "hanging in there" in spite of all of the criticism. His advice to the audience was, "Don't put the spin on STC as STC, but put the spin on 'The Basics' in relation to school-to-career." (Fool 'em?) In order to effect change (the key word, again!), you must have a passion to change. Basic conditions to create change: 1. Have passion, 2. Have data, 3. Have leadership, and 4. Have staff development. Using these four ingredients, you will have successful models to help market STC. Some of the 255 subject areas in our schools should be taken out. "In America, when something goes into the curriculum, it never comes out." Examples given (I believe) to take out: some of the requirements in math, science, social studies, etc. He wants schools to make room for information that now "doubles every nine months!"

Daggett says reading for entertainment should be mostly replaced with reading and writing technical manuals and emphasis should be placed on procedure and process.... Daggett said that the time has come to create controversy.... He has discussed with neurosurgeons (He has one in the family.) whether death is inevitable, or, with the advance of biotech, an option. Heavy stuff!... In one of the "breakout" sessions that I attended, the focus was on how to sell STW to an unaware community. For the past four years, educators, school board members, teacher unions, and some employers have been the targets of repeated STW indoctrination. Now, parents, students and others must somehow be hauled in. One lady said she thought the name (STW) should be changed because a conservative group called "the Eagle Forum" is openly and effectively critical of STW.... Following skeptical comments, the same lady concluded that, "Now, for sure, we'll have to change the name" and call STC something other than STC. (Fool 'em!)...

I haven't heard speakers like this since the radical 1960's era when those demanding "change" wore long hair, headbands and sandals, not a suit and tie. Daggett and Hoye continued to "evangelize" the vast cult-like following of those who now support radical changes to our schools. Citizens are paying BIG-TIME for this experiment in social control, but too few know much about STC. And probably would want no part of it if/when it's ever fully explained to them.

I don't.

DR. KEN WILLIAMS, AN ELECTED TRUSTEE TO THE ORANGE COUNTY DEPART-
ment of Education and board-certified family physician in Santa Ana, California, wrote the following August 27, 1998 letter to the *American School Board
Journal* regarding the School-to-Work Career Inventory and Assessments.
Dr. Williams's incredible experience exposes the dangerous implications of
the use of psychological assessments, etc., to predict an individual's career
potential. The full text of Dr. Williams's letter follows:

> Dear Sir:
> I am writing you as an elected Trustee to the Orange County Department of
> Education in California regarding the STW Career Inventory and Assessments.
> I was asked to share this information with you because of my concerns with
> the STW program.
>
> Last year, I took a computer-assisted career inventory program at the
> local high school here in Orange County to determine what career pathway
> I would have been encouraged to take if I were a freshman.
>
> To my surprise, the career inventory programs encouraged me to follow a
> career pathway that would lead to one of the following occupations: 1) Auto
> Muffler Installer, 2) Plasterer and Drywall Installer, 3) Glazier, 4) Cement
> Mason, 5) Auto Body and Fender Repairer, 6) Railroad Brake Operator, 7)
> Bus Driver, and 8) Modeling.
>
> Now, let me state that I am not degrading any of these occupations. The
> good people of this nation who are engaged in these fields are hard working
> Americans who deserve our respect. My concern is that when I took this
> career assessment and inventory, I answered all twenty or so questions with
> the idea that I wanted to be a family physician practicing in the city of Santa
> Ana, California, where I took the career program at the local high school
> (where a STW program is in place).
>
> In conclusion, I wonder how many smart and talented kids from tradi-
> tionally disadvantaged minority groups in this inner city are being directed
> into low wage and low skill jobs, instead of into professional and graduate
> schools. Is this the ultimate, "in-your-face" federal program that will take
> away liberties and freedoms from our people?
>   Sincerely,
>   Dr. Ken Williams

WILLIAM J. BRAUN, SR., ISSUED A PRESS RELEASE DATED AUGUST 29, 1998
from Cleveland, Ohio concerning a landmark education case, *State ex rel.
Stephen Rea v. Ohio Department of Education*. The press release discussed
the successfully argued Stephen Rea court case regarding the status of certain
tests and assessments being declared public records:

> Stephen Rea, relying on the *U.S. Freedom of Information Act* and the *State of
> Ohio Availability of Public Records Law*, requested copies of sensitive testing
> materials used on his daughter at West Branch High School, Beloit, Ohio.
>
> His continued requests fell upon deaf·ears, all the way up to the State
> Superintendent of Schools. Rea argued that all classroom materials generated
> with government-funded dollars constituted public records *per se*.
>
> He would be allowed to view the requested materials, but only if he
> agreed to sign a secrecy agreement that carried a fine and imprisonment

clause if violated. On 28 August 1996, Rea filed a complaint with the Ohio Supreme Court, which was accepted for trial.

Rea sought judicial judgment against the Ohio Board of Education on four issues. The case was tried *in mandamus*. In a powerfully worded majority opinion, the Court ruled in favor of Rea and his daughter. (*State of Ohio, ex rel: Stephen Rea, et al v. Ohio Department of Education. Case No. 96–1997, in Mandamus.*)

Tomorrow's battles will shift abruptly from school superintendents' offices and Department of Education conference rooms to State and Federal Court Chambers, where they are more likely winnable, including the recovery of reasonable fees and court costs.

[Ed. Note: Despite winning this case, by 1999 the Department of Education and The Ohio State University have failed to comply with the Ohio Supreme Court ruling requiring the providing of all of the documentation requested by Steve Rea. In a letter dated December 4, 2004 from the U.S. Department of Education to Mr. Rea, the DOE stated that "only if James actually took the test without Mr. and Mrs. Rea's consent would there be a basis for a complaint under the PPRA." In other words, the DOE was now contending that a child would actually have to take the test before the PPRA could be applied—and they did not uphold informed written consent. In 2004 another decision adversely affected Rea's case. In that case the "intellectual properties" argument was revived. In 2009 a teacher initiated a lawsuit in order to view the test and was denied access.]

"WORKFORCE INVESTMENT ACT PUTS AMERICA ON ROAD TO FASCISM— Hillary's Global Village and the New World Order Are Officially Instituted by Congress" by Jim Day appeared in the August, 1998 *St. Louis Metro Voice* monthly. Excerpts follow:

> "Few bills which we consider will have a greater impact on more Americans than the Workforce Investment Act (H.R. 1385) we pass today."—Sen. Edward Kennedy (*Congressional Record*, July 30, 1998, p. S 9490).
>
> [PUBLISHER'S NOTE: Truer words were never spoken in relation to gaining total control of the citizens of the United States and turning our nation into a fascist state. If you think this is an outlandish statement, read this article. What you are about to read is the absolute truth which is backed by more documentation than you could ever hope to read.]
>
> On July 30 Senators Edward Kennedy (D) MA, Jim Jeffords (R) VT, Mike DeWine (R) OH, Paul Wellstone (D) MN, Christopher Dodd (D) CT, and Jack Reed (D) RI, unanimously passed by a voice vote the Conference Report on H.R. 1385—the *Workforce Investment Act of 1998*—the latest version of "The CAREERS Act." A voice vote only requires a majority of those present to pass or reject a bill. The report was then sent back to the House of Representatives for review.
>
> According to the *Congressional Record*, only six senators spoke on the floor. Due to the fact that no roll call vote was taken, it is not known if any other senators were present in the chamber at the time.
>
> Late in the afternoon the next day, July 31, without any notice, when most congressmen were on planes headed home, five congressmen, again by a voice vote, unanimously approved H.R. 1385, paving the way for President

Clinton's signature on August 7. The five congressmen were William Clay, Sr. (D) MO, Howard P. "Buck" McKeon (R) CA, William "Bill" Goodling (R) PA, Dale Kildee (D) MI, and Matthew Martinez (D) CA.

Again, due to the fact that no roll call vote was taken, no one knows how many other, if any, congressmen were present at the time of the vote. These 11 men and President Clinton have just created and signed into law legislation which converts America's free market economic system to a controlled or managed market system—the same type of economic system which was established by Nazi Germany.

[Ed. Note: President Clinton, on August 7, 1998, signed this controversial school-to-work/job training bill, the final version of the infamous *CAREERS Act* which grassroots activists had worked hard to kill for over four years and had thought they had put to rest in the summer of 1996 when Senator Trent Lott refused to bring it up for a vote. These same activists were taken by surprise when Rep. Howard P. (Buck) McKeon, proclaimed conservative from California, appeared out of nowhere like a stealth bomber, reintroduced and assisted to pass similar legislation in April 1997—this time titled *The Employment Training and Literacy Enhancement Act of 1997*. Activists had little time to mount an effort to down this nasty stealth missile, allowing it to go on to the Senate which, in turn, passed it in August of 1998.]

THE NATIONAL ACADEMY OF SCIENCES AND THE U.S. DEPARTMENT OF Education-funded *Preventing Reading Difficulties in Young Children*, Grant No. 0235501 (National Academy Press: Washington, D.C., 1998), was critiqued by Ann Herzer of Arizona, M.A., reading specialist. Herzer literally lobbed a well-justified grenade at those so-called "experts" involved in the research and writing of the book, whose credentials indicate their long-term involvement in programs for special education and in the promotion or development of Skinnerian operant conditioning programs to teach reading and other subjects. Mrs. Herzer's critique follows in its entirety:

> The National Academy of Sciences is a private, non-profit organization which was granted a Charter by Congress in 1963. The Academy advises the government on scientific and technical matters. (p. iv)
>
> The following three groups are named on the title page for the above book:
>> (1) Committee on the Prevention of Reading Difficulties in Young Children;
>> (2) Commission on Behavioral and Social Sciences and Education and
>> (3) National Research Council.
>
> Apparently the first committee mentioned was responsible for the report (the book) and members were "Chosen for their special competencies and with regard for appropriate balance." (p. ii)
>
> The Acknowledgments read like a *Who's Who of Government Change Agents and Behavioral Scientists*. Reid Lyon (National Institute of Health—NIH) with whom I spoke regarding the *Reading Excellence Act*, is listed, as are members connected with NIH's labs, several members from the U.S. Department of Education, the Carnegie Corp., etc, etc., etc.
>
> During the information-gathering phase, a number of people are mentioned who made presentations to the committee on programs that focused

on prevention of reading difficulties. They did not say who selected the presenters. I am familiar with two names: Ethna Reid (*Keyboarding, Reading and Spelling*) and John Nunnary (*Success for All*). I will never forget Reid's government-sponsored (NDN) program, the *Exemplary Center for Reading Instruction* (ECRI). The 1978 week-long ECRI workshop I attended started my investigation into the Skinnerian Mastery Learning/Direct Instruction programs. *Success for All* is one of the New American Schools Development Corporation programs, selected and approved by Presidents Bush and Clinton for restructuring education, which also uses Skinnerian Direct Instruction.

Several professional associations were mentioned along with groups, including Save the Children International.

Some members of the Committee are worth mentioning: Marilyn Jager Adams who wrote *Beginning to Read: Thinking and Learning about Print* (a real Pavlovian bell-ringer disguised under phonics) and Edward J. Kame'enui, special education, University of Oregon and associate director of the federally funded National Center to Improve the Tools of Educators (NCITE)—the same center with which Douglas Carnine (who was involved with the failed Follow Through federal program and the government-sponsored Skinnerian S-R-S program DISTAR—(Direct Instruction System for Teaching and Remediation) is connected. DISTAR is now being touted by the government change agents and the radical right Heritage Foundation as a Direct Instruction "scientific" program for teaching phonics (of all things) to pre-K–3rd grade students.

Members and their qualifications are mentioned as follows: Catherine Snow, M.A. and Ph.D in psychology from McGill University (Canada); Marilyn Jager Adams, visiting professor at Harvard University School of Education and a previous research scientist at Bolt, Beranek and Newman, Inc.; Barbara T. Bowman, co-founder and president, the Erickson Institute in Chicago, Illinois, recent appointee to the Great Books Foundation and the National Board for Professional Teaching Standards; M. Susan Burns, formerly on the faculty at the University of Pittsburgh; Barbara Foorman, University of Texas, Houston Health Science Center and also principal investigator of the Early Intervention Program of the National Institute of Child Health and Human Development, consulting editor for the *Journal of Learning Disabilities* and a member of the New Standards Project; Claude N. Goldenberg, a research psychologist in the Department of Psychiatry, Biobehavioral Sciences at the University of California, Los Angeles; William Labor of the University of Pennsylvania, currently engaged in several research programs funded by the National Science Foundation and the National Endowment for the Humanities; Richard K. Olson, associate director of the Center for the Study of Learning Disabilities funded by the National Institutes of Health; Charles A. Perfetti, a senior scientist at the Learning Research and Development Center at the University of Pittsburgh; etc., etc., etc., who are supposed to give this hand-picked committee an "appropriate balance."

The "treatment" suggested in both of the above-mentioned books [Jager's *Beginning to Read* and *Preventing Reading Difficulties*] for teaching young children to read appears to have been designed for the mentally retarded to severely handicapped children—not average children.

This group is proposing language training from birth. Apparently parents are to be trained as though *none* have any normal/natural instincts in child rearing or language. HIPPY, PAT (Parents as Teachers) and other home-bound programs are now proposed for the "at risk"—the poor and minority children, but how long will it be before the radical behavioral scientists demand home visits and training for all children and their families as was mandated in the former Soviet Union?

In my opinion, the individuals involved in producing the two above-mentioned books and especially the U.S. government, who supplies the grant money, are not interested in children learning to read but only in training and programming them for the planned global workforce. Otherwise programs like DISTAR, ECRI and Madeline Hunter's *Essential Elements of Instruction* would have been exposed and stopped long ago.

When I evaluated the Texas Alternative Document (TAD), I was not aware of the significance of TAD until Reid Lyon and others responded on the internet education loop. These individuals apparently are supporting the Skinnerian DISTAR, or similar programs, as a method to teach reading through the distribution of TAD. TAD is now being pushed in Nebraska as curricula for language arts. I predicted it would be the national model for restructuring and teacher training. DISTAR is now training teachers in California, according to *Education Week*. The big emphasis nationally is on "teacher training," especially in Reading—"re-training," *not* "education"—is the emphasis [emphasis in original].

[ddd]

THE SEPTEMBER 16, 1998 ISSUE OF *THE WASHINGTON TIMES* CARRIED AN article entitled "New Tack Taken on Religion in Schools: Group Seeks End to Secular Bias" which chronicles the publication of a new guidebook, *Taking Religion Seriously across the Curriculum* co-authored by Charles Haynes of the First Amendment Center at Vanderbilt University and Warren Nord of the University of North Carolina (Association for Supervision and Curriculum Development and the First Amendment Center: Washington, D.C., 1998). The opening paragraph of the article is very telling:

> A group of educators and policy advocates yesterday united around a "new consensus" on teaching about religion in public schools, calling it a long-shot agenda but the most likely to satisfy all Americans....
>
> ..."If this book is the next step, it's a big step," said Diane Berreth of the Association for Supervision and Curriculum Development (ASCD), which advises public schools on teaching.
>
> The "new approach" seeks a middle ground between totally secular schools and those where the local majority religion is promoted by school officials. "Religion is still not taken seriously in the public school curriculum," said Charles Haynes, a co-author of the new guidebook.
>
> Warren Nord, a University of North Carolina humanities professor and co-author, said, "A full education must acknowledge different ways of knowing reality, from the scientific and economic to the religious and moral."... Miss Berreth of ASCD said a few pilot schools must test the new agenda to prove its effectiveness. "This may be a role of [charter schools]," she said.

[Ed. Note: The above two authors made their remarks at a symposium with five other panelists. The event was sponsored by the Freedom Forum and the ASCD, which published the 220-page book with the First Amendment Center at Vanderbilt University.

If anyone out there believes a book published by the Association for Supervision and Curriculum Development (a spin-off of the National Education Association which consistently issues tirades about Christians who believe in sound moral values) could come up with anything the purpose of which is not to make further inroads into the *destruction* of whatever absolutist values our children still have, then I suggest they have been living under a rock ever since the 1940's when the drive to eliminate absolutist moral values from our schools started. The ASCD was heavily involved in the mind-altering curriculum *Tactics for Thinking*.

Researchers and activists involved in following the circuitous path taken by those who want to remove religious-based absolute values from this planet, starting in the schools, have thrown roadblocks in their way every time they surfaced with a new sugar-coated version of their sugar-coated values-destroying curriculum. How many more times must citizen researchers leap forward to expose this fraudulent crowd which has used semantic deception (given its programs the following misleading labels) and operated as the following entities:

- "Character Education" in the early 1970's (which advised those involved not to use the "red flag" word "values");

- The Public Education Religion Study Center at Wright State University's "comparative religion" curriculum (which was funded by Religious Heritage of America, Inc. and the Lilly Endowment of the Eli Lilly Corporation);

- the appointed Maryland Values Commission, another project shared with Religious Heritage of America;

- the American Institute for Character Education (AICE), funded by the Lilly Endowment;

- the Williamsburg Charter proposal which led to the First Amendment Center's curriculum "Teaching about Religion," and now, *Taking Religion Seriously across the Curriculum*, which a high school teacher from San Diego, California said should be "mandatory reading" for all public school instructors.]

AN ARTICLE ENTITLED "U.S. ANNOUNCED EXCHANGE PROGRAMS" APPEARED in the September 18, 1998 edition of the *Odessa* (Russia) *Post* which heralded the results of the U.S.-Soviet Education Agreements signed in 1985 and numerous planning activities since 1985. Excerpts follow:

> The program is administered by the U.S. Information Service. The American Council for Collaboration in Education and Language Study (ACCELS), the International Renaissance Foundation, and the International Research and Exchanges Board for Scholars (IREX) will be responsible for processing applications, selecting candidates and administering the exchange and scholarship programs....

...ACCELS will administer the U.S.-Ukraine Awards for Excellence in Teaching, which will bring 15 Ukrainian teachers of English and American Studies to the United States... in the summer of 1999. Finalists selected from participating regions can also win computer equipment, copiers or internet access for their schools....

...[N]ot only can Ukrainians find out more about the American way of life, our values, beliefs, hope and ambitions, Americans will also learn more about Ukraine and Ukrainians.

"A QUESTION OF EFFECTIVENESS" BY ANDREW TROTTER WAS PUBLISHED IN the October 1, 1998 issue of *Education Week*'s special report entitled *Technology Counts '98—Putting School Technology to the Test*. This important special issue should be read in its entirety for an understanding of the plusses and minuses of using technology in the classroom. One interesting chart on page 9 indicated that when the public and teachers were asked "How much do you think computers have helped improve student learning?" members of the public, in contrast to educators, were nearly twice as likely to say "A great amount"(MCI Nationwide Poll on Internet in Education, 1998).

THE OCTOBER 7, 1998 ISSUE OF *EDUCATION WEEK* CARRIED A FULL-PAGE advertisement for the Sixteenth Annual Effective Schools Conference to be held in March of 1999. This writer has copied the advertisement in order to illustrate that any concern for academic instruction for American school children is a thing of the past. (The semantic deception will be obvious.)

SIXTEENTH ANNUAL
EFFECTIVE SCHOOLS CONFERENCE

LEARNING FOR ALL—WHATEVER IT TAKES
March 4–7, 1999
Willard Daggett, Larry Lezotte, Ray Gollarz, Michael Fullan, John Jay Bonstingl, Ernest Stachowski, Douglas Reeves, Alan November, Spence Rogers, Sandi Redenbach, Robert Slavin

NSCI
NATIONAL SCHOOL CONFERENCE INSTITUTE[57]
Phoenix, Arizona
Pre-Conferences:

Leading Learning for All
Making the Right Changes at the District Level to Assure Successful, Sustainable School Reform—with Larry Lezotte

Educational Accountability in Complex School Systems
The Challenges of High Standards, Accurate Assessments, and Meaningful Accountability with Douglas Reeves

CONTENTS
• Correlates of Effective Schools
• Developing the Leadership Team
• Meaningful Educational Accountability
• Creating Positive School Climate

- Managing Change to Implement Standards
- Instructional Strategies to Enhance Achievement
- Infusing Technology
- Ensuring the Success of All Children
- Effective School Improvement Planning
- Quality Teaching in the Classroom
- Communication Literacy
- Classroom Success—Applying Brain Research
- Motivating Students
- Assessments as a Performance Tool
- Quality and Equity in the School
- Site-Based Decision Making
- Learning Organizations

AN ARTICLE ENTITLED "CHARACTER EDUCATION CATCHING ON AT SCHOOLS— Respect, Responsibility Emphasized" by Anu Manchikanti was published in the October 9, 1998 issue of *The Washington Times*. Excerpts follow:

Character education is a national movement to bring universal virtues into the classroom.

At Wasatch, a character education program has been in place for two years.

Thomas Lickona, director of the National Center for the 4th and 5th Rs (respect and responsibility), says a moral decline in youth reflects a character crisis in the United States.

In his 1997 State of the Union Address, President Clinton called for schools to teach character and mold children into good citizens. Most recently, Vice President Al Gore announced $2.7 million in grants for 10 states under the Partnerships in Character Education Pilot Projects Program. The grants should allow states to work with school districts in developing curriculum and providing teacher training for character education programs. Iowa, New Mexico and Utah have received such grants.

"It isn't a separate curriculum or an add-on or an extra thing," said Kristin Fink, character education specialist at the Utah State Office of Education. "It's really something that should be woven into everything we do."

According to Kevin Ryan, director of the Center for the Advancement of Ethics and Character at Boston University, the potential for character education exists in all curriculum to engage children in moral thought.

For instance, physical education teachers might emphasize the importance of playing fair in athletics, or science teachers may stimulate discussion about the ethical issues involved in genetic cloning.

"They're going to either learn good character or bad character," Mr. Ryan said. "It's all an inevitable part of life that schools will have an impact."

But Murray Philip, a school board member in Nashville, Tennessee questions the idea that character can be taught. "Who are we to decide what is good character, and what is bad character?" he said. Mr. Philip doubts that character can be taught because he feels it is learned through adversity and experience. Many argue that the job of teaching character lies in the hands of families rather than schools. "There's an awful lot of kids who are not being taught anything at home," Mr. Ryan said. "There's no such thing as a morally neutral school."

[Ed. Note: In response to the statements by Thomas Lickona, it is hard for this writer to accept Mr. Lickona as a leader in the area of moral education considering his promotion of the late Lawrence Kohlberg's humanistic "Stages of Moral Development" and morally relativistic character education program "Ethical Issues in Decision Making."

As for Clinton's 1997 State of the Union speech, with the recently concluded impeachment trial and the events which precipitated it, there are no words to adequately express the irony of Clinton's calling for the schools to teach "character." Also, can one really imagine a government-developed character education program or one that would be allowed to be used in government-supported schools which would be effective, when government-supported "scientific research" is based in an evolutionary perspective of our children being trainable animals? Children observing teachers and others in authority exhibiting good character is the best "character education." Also, allowing school boards to hire teachers whose lives incorporate high moral character would do much to contribute to the solution of this problem.

After having read and said all of the above, the writer would like to issue degrees in rocket science for all the parents who understand the problem!]

[ddd]

THE FOLLOWING NEWS ITEM WAS CARRIED BY *USA TODAY* IN ITS OCTOBER 12, 1998 issue:

> SALT LAKE CITY, UTAH—The Utah School Boards Association has asked a judge to declare the '98 *Charter Schools Act* unconstitutional. Charter schools are funded with public education money, but are exempt from many of the restrictions on public schools. The lawsuit alleges local school boards have control over schools in their boundaries, and that by reaching within those boundaries, the state is creating a new school district without a public vote.

[Ed. Note: Hats off to the Utah School Boards Association. When education activists/researchers in their many speeches across the nation referred to charter schools as "taxation without representation" the silence in conservative audiences was "deafening."]

IN 1998 THE NORTHWEST REGIONAL EDUCATIONAL LABORATORY, ONE OF the ten laboratories across the nation supported by contracts with the U.S. Department of Education's Office of Educational Research and Improvement (OERI), provided the following information on its "Education & Community Services: Emerging Issues" website (http//www.nwrel.org/pscc/emerging.html). For the reader who may, understandably, want to have an up-to-date report on the status of the restructuring of the nation's schools, through school-to-work and the merging of education and workforce training with social services (systemic change), there is probably no better source than the Northwest Regional Educational Laboratory. "Emerging Issues" as of October 16, 1998 follow:

Twelve major emerging issues have been identified from an analysis of recent policy reports and validated by a focus group of state leaders as having a significant impact on education in the Northwest:

1. Acknowledging fundamental shifts in teaching and learning. A view of students as active learners... emphasis on cooperative and applied learning.

2. Dealing with the rising threat of violence. High incidence of violence, substance abuse, and gang-related crime are causing schools to review discipline policies, implement special curricula, and work increasingly with law enforcement and other community agencies.

3. Assuring a sound infrastructure for education. A growing student population is on a collision course with an aging and inadequate physical and fiscal infrastructure.

4. Strengthening the connection between education and work. Relationships between education and work are being re-examined and restructured.... [M]arketplace requires workers with higher levels of complex skills.

5. Garnering support for education reform. Education reform, like all change, is generating anxiety and opposition. Educators are increasingly attempting to involve parents and community members in open, honest discussion.

6. Changing expectations for education decisionmaking and governance.... [I]ncreased community collaboration, school site councils, and service integration efforts are altering and redefining many traditional governance and decisionmaking processes. [No approval of voters, ed.]

7. Using standards as a means to systemic change. Consensus that piecemeal changes in schooling are not adequate to meet the challenges of the future is giving rise to a growing emphasis on standards and assessment at all levels of the education system.

8. Strengthening support and respect for teachers.... [T]eachers are the critical element in providing quality education, and that their task is becoming more complex and difficult as they face increased expectations in teaching a more diverse student body.

9. Supporting young children and their families. Educators are defining their role in working with families to ensure the healthy early development of children.... [Does their role include interference in family life? ed.]

10. Increasing community collaboration and service integration.... [C]hange occurs only with the full commitment of the community, schools are getting involved in collaborative efforts with many other types of organizations. [This collaboration, integration, etc., represents a change in governance without approval of the voters, ed.]

11. Harnessing new technologies.... [C]omputers in schools are putting technology in the forefront of efforts to fundamentally change the role of students from passive to active learners and the role of teachers from information givers to facilitators and coaches. [Clearly a shift from academic education to performance-based workforce training, ed.]

12. Shifting the focus from risk toward resiliency. Realizing that the vast majority of children develop into successful adults, educators

and other service providers are shifting their attention from deficit program models that address specific risk factors toward program approaches that focus more on enhancing positive factors. [If the reader understands #12, please contact the writer, ed.]

"CHARTER SCHOOLS BILL NOW LAW" REPORTED *THE ARIZONA REPUBLIC* IN an AP report appearing in its October 23, 1998 issue. Excerpts from this news item, which identifies the Democratic Party with a Republican initiative, follow:

> President Clinton on Thursday signed the *Charter School Expansion Act of 1998* to speed the development of high-quality charter schools, a key element of his education agenda. The law authorizes up to $100 million a year over the next five years for the planning and expansion of charter schools. Clinton cited the charter schools legislation as an example of bipartisan cooperation....
>
> Clinton has set a goal of 3,000 charter schools nationwide by the time he leaves office. There now are about 1,000.
>
> Charter schools tend to be smaller and custom-designed. Under charter schools laws, depending on the state, parents, community activists, teachers or even private companies may set up schools under a special agreement or charter. The schools might emphasize a particular curriculum such as arts or technology, or more traditional teaching methods using repetition and drills, or experimental methods that let children learn at their own pace.

[Ed. Note: Charter schools are obliged to adhere to federal guidelines; i.e., *Goals 2000*, etc. Individuals familiar with charter school legislation consider them unaccountable to the taxpayers due to their being run by unelected councils; taxation without representation.]

A NATIONAL INSTITUTE ON CAREER MAJORS WAS ANNOUNCED NOVEMBER 4, 1998 by the National School-to-Work Office. The accuracy of predictions made by anti-school-to-work citizens—that their children's academic education would be watered down, if not eliminated, once the Marc Tucker Plan moved out of its planning stage and into the following action mode—is demonstrated by the following:

> Just one month after it announced that all 50 states were "on board" to receive federal School-to-Work Implementation Grants, the National School-to-Work (STW) Office has now announced (Nov. 4) a National Institute on Career Majors to be held in Chicago, Illinois on February 4–6, 1999.
>
> "The purpose of the Institute is to bring together State Teams to strategically design a plan to implement career majors at the State and local levels." To participate, states are asked to assemble "an interagency team of 6–10 members representing State level policy-makers around education and labor; business and industry; educators at the secondary and postsecondary level; and include representatives from a local-level partnership that is currently building a STW system around career majors."
>
> Activities will "focus on strengthening the capacity of education and business leaders to develop a standards-based curriculum leading to high skills, high wage, high demand occupations. Through individual team facilitation,

each State Team will develop or revise a plan to organize school learning around career majors."

Attendance at this institute is limited to 15 teams, but more are sure to follow. Funds are being provided for team travel. Funds are also going to be made available to states at a later date to host similar career majors institutes for their local STW partnerships.

The event will take place at the Fairmont Hotel... Chicago, Illinois.

"NEW MODEL FOR TEACHER EDUCATION—WITH FOCUS ON CONTEXT AND Workplace: Project Could Better Prepare Students" by Michael Childs was published in the November 9, 1998 issue of *Columns* (p. 2), a University of Georgia faculty newsletter. Excerpts from the article follow:

> University of Georgia's College of Education is beginning a three-year project that will attempt to bring together classroom and real-life work experiences in a way that could change how teachers are taught and what they're taught to teach. The project could better prepare students for the challenges they are likely to face in the changing workplace of the 21st century.
>
> The college will develop and pilot-test a new teacher-education model that will place prospective teachers not only in the context in which they will work—the classroom—but also in the context of where their students will work—community and workplace settings in business, industry and the professions.
>
> "Teachers need to understand much more of the pedagogy. Teachers need to understand how it applies in life settings," says Dean Russell Yeany. "We don't just want to perpetuate academic learning—at some point it has to be applied to the workplace...."
>
> ...A long-term goal is to have a much more effective school-to-work transition for students.
>
> "Schooling should transition right into work and I think schooling has become so academic that it isn't transitioning well into work," says Yeany.
>
> Funded for 18 months by an initial $864,000 grant from the U.S. Department of Education, the Teacher Development Pre-Service Model of Excellence Initiative is one of the college's largest and most ambitious projects ever.
>
> "This is a big investment by the federal government to develop a model they hope will become available to other colleges," says Yeany.
>
> A student orientation to area business and industry will include both on-site and virtual observation of manufacturing and business processes.

THE NOVEMBER 16, 1998 EDITION OF *THE ATLANTA CONSTITUTION* CARRIED an article entitled "Education in a Relaxed Atmosphere: Brain-Based Method—Teaching Trend Emphasizing Creativity, Flexibility and Informality Growing in Area Schools" by Delbert Ellerton. The activities described in the article are typical of the exercises promoted by Sheila Ostrander, Lynn Schroeder with Nancy Ostrander in their book *Superlearning 2000* (Dell Publishing: New York 1994), an updated version of their earlier book *Superlearning*. The following are excerpts from the article:

> At the front of Amanda Neff's softly lit, first-grade classroom in Henry

County, a plant sits next to the glass case that is home to Riley, a small black rat snake.

As Riley slithers around inside the glass box at Wesley Lakes Elementary School, a group of students eagerly crowds around.

Riley is just one of the several ways Neff is bringing life to her classroom by teaching students in ways that emerging research says they naturally learn. Instead of just reading books about snakes, the students have the real thing right before them.

Teachers such as Neff are part of a national group embracing an approach formally called brain-based learning. The trend, which surfaced in California in the 1980s, is based on teachers being flexible and creative. It also is based on the belief that eliminating the sterile, institutional environment encourages children to relax and learn.

In addition to using Riley, the snake, as an educational tool, Neff softens the mood in her Wesley Lakes classroom by dimming the bright overhead fluorescent lights and turning on lamps in corners of the room. She plays soft music on a computer CD player throughout the day....

"It's making children feel more comfortable and taking away the threat. They're more open. They don't shut down on me when I ask them something," Harris said.

Harris's students sit in groups of three in an arrangement educators call "tribes." The setup is said to encourage teamwork. Teachers in Henry and Clayton counties have received brain-based learning training through staff development workshops. One such workshop in Clayton County is called "Symphony on Styles" and focuses on effective teaching methods for students' diverse learning styles, said Bobbi Ford of Clayton's staff development department....

In October, Ford attended a brain-based learning conference in California which drew educators from Sweden, Canada, Australia, South Africa and Mexico....

...Teachers in Coweta, Fulton and Carroll counties also use brain-based techniques. One Coweta school plays classical music over the intercom.

A newly formed statewide brain-based learning advisory council met in Athens last month, attracting 23 interested educators. The council is building a network to provide information about brain-based learning, said Judith Reiff, an early childhood education professor at the University of Georgia who is on the council.

[Ed. Note: Even though the reader can read the roots of *Superlearning* in this book's earlier, 1979 entry, the writer would like to repeat a section of *Superlearning 2000* that gives an explanation of what it is:

What is Superlearning?

These are the Superlearning core techniques that vastly accelerate learning and brighten performance. Techniques that can help you take charge of change.

- Get into a stress-free, "best" mindbody state for what you are doing.
- Absorb information in a paced, rhythmic way.
- Use music to expand memory, energize the mind, and link to the subconscious.

- Engage your whole brain, your senses, emotions, and imagination for peak performance.
- Become aware of blocks to learning and change, then flood them away.

Not even a multiple personality would want to use all the exercises and ploys offered in this book. The idea is to give you a choice. You don't need to pick up very many to flesh out the basic Superlearning protocols. First and foremost, Superlearning involves a new sense of your self and your possibilities, a new perspective—a twenty-first century point of view.

In the first chapter of *Superlearning 2000* on pages 8–9 we find the following quotes:

> Five pages, that's all we devoted to Lozanov learning when we wrote about our Communist odyssey. (See *Psychic Discoveries Behind the Iron Curtain*, 1970; updated and to be republished, 1995.) Inquiries roared in from everywhere, even the Pentagon's Institute of Defense Analysis. Western mind-groupies rushed to Sofia [Bulgaria], while a handful of pioneering educators began the hard work of adapting the Communist learning system to North America.
>
> A genuinely powerful new way to learn, to expand memory, to excel began to emerge in Des Moines, Toronto, Atlanta. By the late 1970s an innovative psychologist, Dr. Donald Schuster of University of Iowa at Ames, founded the Society for Accelerative Learning and Teaching (SALT). Now there are professional societies in a dozen countries, including the very international Society for Effective Affective Learning (SEAL) in England. At the time only a few professionals had moved outside of establishment lines. What about all the other people who always wanted to color outside the lines? We took what was proven and devised something that wasn't: a do-it-yourself system. Superlearning, open to everyone. The generic name is accelerative or accelerated learning.
>
> Basic Superlearning draws from Lozanov and his sources, ancient ones like Raja Yoga, contemporary ones like Soviet science.... And we got lucky. We came across another "ology": Sophrology, "the science of harmonious consciousness," a cornucopia of routes to excellence still almost unknown in America, developed by Alfonso Caycedo, a Spanish M.D. every bit as innovative as Lozanov.

[Ed. Note: These last sentences remind this writer of the early work of Roberto Assagioli, author of *Psychosynthesis*. The reader should also be made aware that Henry Levin of Stanford's Institute for Accelerated Learning does indeed advocate the Superlearning (SALT, SEAL) method for its member schools.]

"COMING SOON TO A SCHOOL NEAR YOU: FORCED LABOR" BY PAUL Mulshine, columnist, was published in the November 29, 1998 issue of the Newark, New Jersey *Star-Ledger*. Excerpts from Mulshine's article follow:

> Imagine a state that uses its school system not to produce independent-minded, broadly educated citizens, but compliant workers trained to behave. A state where, in their early teens, children are forced to make a lifelong decision from 14 government-sanctioned career possibilities with such depressing

titles as "waste management," "administrative services" and "manufacturing, installation and repair." A state where students in the government schools are forced to spend one day a week toiling in menial labor.

The old Soviet Union? China?

Nope. New Jersey.

I wish I were making this up. But I'm not. This is a fair summation—minus the jargon—of the School-to-Work program that the state is planning to impose on us next year. You can veiw it on the Internet at http://www.state. nj.us/njded/proposed/standards/stass2.htm. See for yourself.

NINA SHIKRAII REES OF THE HERITAGE FOUNDATION, WASHINGTON, D.C., wrote an article entitled "Time to Overhaul the *Elementary and Secondary Education Act of 1965*" which recommended a major shift in the traditional philosophy of education from an emphasis on inputs to an emphasis on outputs. An abstract of her article which was published in a Heritage Foundation Press Release dated December 2, 1998, follows:

> During the reauthorization process of the 1965 *Elementary and Secondary Education Act*, the 106th Congress has a historic opportunity to change the course of K–12 education. Congress needs to shift the goals of the ESEA from one confined to inputs to one focused on achievement. Congress can make this happen by sending more federal dollars to the classroom instead of to education bureaucracies; empower parents, teachers and principals; boosting the quality of teachers; and allowing flexibility and demanding accountability. Sending money to the same old federal education programs will waste precious education tax dollars and allow American students to fall even further behind their counterparts in the developed world.

[Ed. Note: If what Ms. Rees recommends is authorized by the 106th Congress, the course of K–12 education will be more than changed. It will be eliminated, to be replaced by K–12 school-to-work training, required by NAFTA and GATT, both of which are supported by Ms. Rees's employer, the Heritage Foundation. As sensible as the above recommendations may appear at first sight, as one moves carefully through the text one can identify key words which should raise red flags for those opposed to the philosophy behind *Goals 2000* and the *School-to-Work Opportunities Act*.

When Ms. Rees says "Congress needs to shift the goals of the ESEA from one confined to inputs to one focused on achievement" she really means she supports outcome-based education, since the word "achievement" as she has used it means "outcome." She then goes on to recommend all the "nasties" associated with Marc Tucker's National Center on Education and the Economy which are also associated with all recent restructuring legislation, as well as with outcome-based education: "empowering of parents, teachers, and principals"; "sending more federal dollars to the classroom"; "boosting the quality of teachers"; "allowing flexibility"; and "demanding accountability."

Of special interest here is her recommendation to boost the "quality of teachers." The reader is urged to turn to the 1992 entry regarding *Filling the Gaps* for the new millenium definition of "quality of teachers."

Note also how this report uses the word "achievement." This is the alternative to focusing on "inputs"—the legal requirement of most state constitutions with regard to their responsibility to the public to "offer," "make available" or "furnish" educational *opportunity* to all citizens. Most of our state constitutions—unless they have changed in the last few years—do not require the state to be responsible for each student's success, because the state cannot ensure what is a personal responsibility. States are responsible for the provision of everything necessary for a child or student to have the *opportunity* to achieve academic success—"inputs." (This has traditionally been known as the Carnegie Unit requirement.) It is when the state becomes the guarantor of success—Ms. Rees's "achievement"—that parents have felt the stifling hand of the state in the area of privacy and personal freedom.

Sending more "dollars to the classroom" may sound like returning to local control, but is in fact the reverse since it bypasses not only state legislators—who presumably represent their constituents at the state level—but also local school boards who traditionally have made decisions at the central office building level—not at the school building level—on how their constituents' tax money could best be spent.

Much damage has been done over the years under the guise of "accountability." Exactly to whom does the Heritage Foundation want the schools to be accountable? Parents and taxpayers who have had no say whatsoever in restructuring plans, or the international business community which initiated and supports the recommendations spelled out in most of Heritage Foundation's reports, including its call for the use of Skinnerian Direct Instruction (DISTAR) as presently implemented in Houston, Texas at Thaddeus Lott's Model Wesley Elementary School, and which is on a roll across the nation since the passage of the *Reading Excellence Act?*]

CENTER ON EDUCATION AND WORK OF THE UNIVERSITY OF WISCONSIN published a paper in 1998 entitled "Changing Admission Procedures in Four-Year Colleges to Support K–14 Reform."[58] The paper lists as the principal investigators: L. Allen Phelps, University of Wisconsin-Madison and David Stern, University of California at Berkeley. Christine Maidl Pribbenow, University of Wisconsin-Madison is listed as project director. The following project areas are listed as: Postsecondary; competency-based admissions; secondary; integrated curriculum; and performance-based assessment. Excerpts from the project abstract follow:

> This one-year (1998) National Center for Research in Vocational Education (NCRVE) project consists of a number of specific research questions which will be addressed through the work of investigators at both U.C.-Berkeley and U.W.-Madison. The purpose of this project is to review existing research on performance-based assessment in education and discuss the use of these assessments in college admissions. This review will provide a broader understanding of the ways in which school-to-work and other K–14 reforms are being accommodated in the higher education admission policies and processes being adopted by institutions, particularly those with selective admissions criteria.

At U.C.-Berkeley, investigators will identify 4–5 states that are beginning to develop new processes for admission and placement using performance-based assessment. Through a series of surveys, on-site and telephone interviews, the following will be examined: [Two of five areas of interest have been selected to illustrate the intent, ed.]... (3) Various approaches taken by select high schools in response to the initiative... and (5)The alignment of state K–12, K–14, or K–16 educational standards and industry and occupational standards with these assessments.

At U.W.-Madison, investigators will complete quantitative and qualitative analyses of the early efforts to develop performance-based admissions and their initial effects on student experiences and outcomes in postsecondary education.... Essentially, the goal is to generate evidence that illustrates the innovative developments, benefits and limitations of using performance-based assessments for college admissions that support models of continuous, seamless learning focused simultaneously on careers and college. Researchers intend to conduct the following studies:

- Examine the efficacy, validity and reliability of the CBA for admitting high school graduates with intensive, career-focused high school experiences.
- Explore the link between college experiences with earlier career-related learning as provided and documented in the CBA process.

Both the U.C.-Berkeley and U.W.-Madison researchers will use their research to write a proposal for consideration by the governing boards and administrative leaders of four-year colleges and universities, both public and private. A meeting will then be convened with high-level representatives of four-year colleges and universities to discuss this proposal. The investigators' findings will also be used to complete a report which reviews research and current practice, analyzes performance-based admission efforts, and discusses the proposal regarding the use of performance-based assessment. Finally, one or two briefs will be published which summarize the findings and/or proposal in a reader-friendly format for policymakers, university governing boards, university faculty and administrators.

[Ed. Note: The reader should be aware that the above project is just one of many efforts to change the focus of higher learning from liberal arts, theoretical and applied arts to a continuation of the school-to-work focus. The National Center for Educational Statistics published a new handbook in its *Educational Reports Series* in 1993 which outlined the new "crosswalks" of course descriptions at the postsecondary or college/university level. These crosswalks reflect the transition to performance-based coursework from academic/theoretical coursework. The result is a complete refocusing of postsecondary education toward behavioral performance rather than encouraging the traditional emphasis on academic knowledge acquisition.]

"A GOVERNOR WITH PRINCIPLE WOULD REJECT SCHOOL-TO-WORK" BY PAUL Mulshine was published in the December 6, 1998 issue of the Newark, New Jersey *Star-Ledger*. Excerpts from Mulshine's article follow:

Christine Whitman once wrote that Republicans believe that "government should only do what individuals can't do for themselves and that government decisions should be made as close to the people they affect as possible."

A wonderful philosophy. There's a problem, though: By that standard, our governor is not a Republican....

...Her administration's latest travesty, the School-to-Work proposal, is just the latest in a long line of thoroughly un-Republican concepts backed by Whitman. Since I wrote about the proposal last week, a couple of things have happened. Assemblyman Scott Garrett, a Republican from Sussex County, announced the introduction of a bill that will prohibit forced labor in schools. Also, the Homdel Board of Education held a meeting Wednesday night at which people came from all over the state to raise objections to the idea. It was a pivotal event. Never in my 22 years of journalism have I seen a proposal get knocked around by so many different people for so many different reasons.

A freshman at Holmdel High School said that her friends were in a panic. The requirement that all juniors and seniors spend a day a week working would mean they'd have to miss classes. This would harm their chances of getting into college, the girl said. She asked that most Republican of questions, "How come we have no say in this?"

A guy in a sweat suit from a nearby town raised another objection: "The school is not the state's. The school is mine, and they tell me it's not mine. I didn't see them at the bake sale."

A school superintendent said that he'd fled Ohio because of a similar program there that was destroying the high-achieving schools by turning them into vocational centers. Several people objected to a requirement that students choose a career in the sophomore year of high school.

One cited a study that showed that the typical college student changes majors three times before settling on a field....

...This is an amazing thing Whitman's people have invented: A concept that offends practically everyone. Usually a political idea has a core constituency—bleeding heart liberals, tightwad conservatives, public employee unions, whatever. But this one riles people up across the board. It does make the bureaucrats happy, though....

...It would be wonderful, just once, to see Christie Whitman denounce a bad idea not because of poll results but because of principle. Close your eyes. Try to imagine Christie Whitman uttering the words, "This is wrong. Trenton should not impose ideas like this on the people of New Jersey."

You can't imagine it? Me neither.

ON DECEMBER 23, 1998 MAINE'S COMMISSIONER OF EDUCATION J. DUKE Albanese sent a memorandum to all superintendents of schools related to the *Maine Aspirations Benchmarking Initiative*. Excerpts from this memorandum, which reveal the extent of Maine's transformation of its schools from academics to workforce training and of its educational bureaucracy's disregard for student privacy follow:

> Sponsored by Webber Energy Fuels, the $300,000 initiative is directed by the University of Maine/Maine Principals' Association Research Partnership, in collaboration with the National Center for Student Aspirations and the Maine Department of Education.
>
> The Initiative has the potential of surveying the entire population of students in grades 6 through 12 in Maine public schools, providing an un-

paralleled database portraying the status of student aspirations in Maine and the conditions that nurture, delay or prevent their development.

The Initiative expands and elaborates on the highly successful Student Aspirations Survey. The approximately 30-minute survey will provide schools with information and insight, from their students' perspectives, in areas of the total learning environment, including:

- aspirations
- conditions in schools
- challenging behaviors
- school climate
- parent-school interaction
- parental support and guidance

The Initiative is highly relevant to the Maine Learning Results. While the Learning Results allow the measurement of achievement, the Benchmarking Initiative will allow the measurement of motivation to achieve. The Initiative will enable schools to begin to assess themselves as related to the Guiding Principles which have not yet been addressed in content standards. Survey questions strongly relate to Guiding Principles II and IV—a Self-Directed and Life-Long Learner, and a Responsible and Involved Citizen, respectively. The Initiative will provide baseline data on career development and help schools and the standard of career preparation....

...Schools participating in the Initiative will receive several important benefits—all at no cost: 1) schools will receive detailed informative reports of their students' responses, providing an assessment of the school dynamics and their effect on aspirations, motivation, and learning; 2) broader reports based on the data will provide the opportunity for schools to compare their profiles against state and regional profiles; 3) schools can take advantage of responsive programs and technical assistance to create or strengthen aspiration conditions in areas of need identified by schools; and 4) schools will receive assistance in monitoring the impact of reform efforts, including a follow-up survey toward the end of the project to check against the baseline data, an important, but often neglected step in the action research process.

1999

THE FEDERALLY FUNDED NORTH CENTRAL REGIONAL EDUCATIONAL LABORA-tory (NCREL), which serves seven states in the Midwest, published "New Times Demands New Ways of Learning" in its Winter-Spring issue of *Ed-Talk*. This article "is intended to offer a way to evaluate the effectiveness of various technologies and technology programs against the backdrop of new research on learning." Some excerpts follow:

"Learning" here does not mean how well students perform on standardized tests. That's not learning, as researchers and educational reformers are coming to understand it. There's a dynamic shift occurring in this country as we move from traditional definitions of learning and course design to models of engaged learning that involve more student interaction, more connections among schools, more collaboration among teachers and students, more involvement of teachers as facilitators, and more emphasis on technology as a tool for learning. It is in this context that our framework operates; it is this type of engaged learning that technology must support to be effective....

In place of these old assumptions, researchers are positing new ways of looking at learning that promote:

- engaged, meaningful learning and collaboration involving challenging and real-life tasks; and
- technology as a toll [requirement] for learning, communication, and collaboration.

The traditional learning model is not relevant to real student needs.

These attributes contrast sharply with the discrete, low-level skill, content, and assessment methods that traditional ways of learning favor. The new workplace requirements for learning are incompatible with instruction that assumes the teacher is the information giver and the student a passive recipient.

The new requirements are at odds with testing programs that assess skills that are useful only in school.

Technology in support of outmoded educational systems is counterproductive.

The reliance on standarized tests is ludicrous. Technology works in school not because tests scores increase, but because technology empowers new solutions.

There are no definitive answers about the effectiveness of technology in boosting student learning, student readiness for workforce skills, teacher productivity, and cost effectiveness. True, some examples of technology have shown strong and consistent positive results. But even powerful programs might show no effects due to myriad methodological flaws. It would be most unfortunate to reject these because standardized tests showed no significant differences. Instead, measures should evaluate individual technologies against specific learning, collaboration, and communication goals.

What is effective learning and how can it be measured?... [Barbara Means of SRI International] identified seven variables that, when present in the classroom, indicate that effective teaching and learning are occurring. These classrom variables are:

- children are engaged in authentic and multidisciplinary tasks;
- assessments are based on students' performance of real tasks;
- students participate in interactive modes of instruction;
- students work collaboratively;
- students are grouped heterogeneously;
- the teacher is a factilitator in learning; and
- students learn through exploration.

We took these variables and reorganized them into a set of eight categories of learning: tasks, assessment, instruction, learning, context, grouping, teacher roles, and student roles.

Centralized systems are likely to inhibit learning to the extent that they use the transfer mode of learning and instruction. This model assumes that the central source holds most of the important information and that it is the student's job to transfer the information from this central source to his or her location and "learn" it.

[Ed. Note: The above text provides an excellent, if not depressing, overview of the transformation from education to workforce training. The timing of this article is interesting in light of other reports, some of which are referred to in this book, exposing the limits of computer technology in the teaching of the important basic academic skills. The above article also admits the lack of supportive research on the "effectiveness of technology in boosting student learning," but still insists that the methodology should not be rejected just "because standardized tests showed no significant differences." Instead, the answer is to use this unconfirmed technology to accomplish limited learning tasks in an attempt to convince the reader that this "new" type of "education" should be embraced by all. In addition, does the reader notice how the educational system "transformation" explanations become more and more convoluted and difficult to understand as this process continues?]

ROSIE AVILA, A SCHOOL BOARD MEMBER IN THE SANTA ANA UNIFIED SCHOOL District, Santa Ana, California, wrote an interesting but frightening article entitled "Parent Report Cards" regarding the implications of parent education programs that was included on an education website on the Internet January 10, 1999. Some excerpts follow:

> As a school board member I have discovered just how they will implement *the U.N. Convention on the Rights of the Child*, the new global parenting code....
>
> I noticed every time they talked about parent involvement (a goal of *Goals 2000*) it was in the context of parent education, what parents need to do at home to help their children succeed in school. Parents are called partners with the schools....
>
> Federal funding mandates parent education. Every one of our schools has a parent education program; 300–400 parents at a time are going through these.... All parents are required to sign a Parent Compact, agreeing to do certain things at home, "provide a study space, put the kids to bed on time, read with them," etc. So, parents are trained, then have to sign an agreement.
>
> Then I saw a bill pass in Sacramento at the State level. It was first described as a "parent report card," but I understand there was objection and so it was redefined, but passed anyway.... I read an article in the *Better Homes and Gardens Magazine* describing the new "parent report card." It said students would give information to their teachers, and parents [would be] graded on students' grooming, sleep habits, and attendance at school meetings, etc. The article said, "Students would be empowered by signing off on their parents' report card," and that "Children knew when their parents were flunking."
>
> Our school district received a $1.1 million dollar grant under "safe schools," another goal of *Goals 2000*. It said we would not have any violence or drugs in schools in the new century and that prevention was the key. Quoting Janet Reno, "Students acted up when they had neglectful parents" and that we could spot them in the early grades. So, if a parent was deemed to be neglectful (failed on their report card, was what I figured), they would have to go through the SARB (Student Attendance Review Board) and have a meeting at the police department with someone from the District Attorney, Child Protection Service, Social Services, School Counselors, etc. Here they would be given their court-ordered program to improve their parenting.
>
> So, there it was. A global parenting code: the *Convention on the Rights of the Child*, federally funded parenting courses with a required Parent Compact

through Chapter One, a State Parent Report Card, and a local punishment or coercion policy redefining the role of the SARB to include neglectful parents.

They have most of the system in place here in California. They just need that ratification of the *U.N. Convention on the Rights of the Child.*

[Ed. Note: The above information regarding report cards for parents should come as no surprise given the following recommendation made by neo-conservative Chester E. Finn, Jr., in an article condensed from the Heritage Foundation's *Policy Review*; Summer 1986, No. 37, pp. 58–61 (reprinted in *Education Digest* on January 1987, p. 4).]

> 6. *Parents must be enlisted in the work of the school and in the education of their children.* Along with endorsing over to the school their child's tuition grant, parents must be asked to assume certain elemental responsibilities, both for such mundane matters as discipline and attendance and for such specific ones as providing the child with a place to do his homework and checking each night to make sure it is done. Just as parents should have the right to evaluate—and choose among—schools, so too should teachers and principals have the right to appraise parents' performance with respect to the education of their children. What about a section in the child's report card where the school team can "grade" the parents' performance?

Really, Mr. Finn? This seems to be a bizarre approach to "school choice"— "endorsing over to the school their child's tuition grant, parents must be asked to assume elemental responsibilities." Ms. Avila's concern about the liberal international influence in public schools seems to have found its way into the "conservative solution."]

An Educator's Guide to Schoolwide Reform (Educational Research Service: Arlington, Virginia, 1999) was prepared for publication by American Institutes for Research under the direction of Rebecca Herman as project director. The *Guide* was produced under contract to the American Association of School Administrators, the American Federation of Teachers, the National Association of Elementary School Principals, and the National Education Association. The "overview" of the *Guide* states in part:

> This guide was prepared for educators and others to use when investigating different approaches to school reform. It reviews the research on 24 "whole-school," "comprehensive," "schoolwide" approaches.
> THIS GUIDE IS NOT MEANT TO ENDORSE, FAVOR, OR DISCREDIT ANY OF THE APPROACHES. Rather, it is designed to assist those who want to critically examine the most widely available schoolwide reform approaches. Schools can improve their performance in a variety of ways, not just by using a schoolwide approach. However, educators interested in these approaches should find the guide useful.

This book has repeatedly dealt with the Skinnerian, scientific, research-based method of teaching and learning, therefore, the writer lists below only the four out of 24 programs recommended by the *Guide* which clearly use this method. They are:

1. Coalition of Essential Schools

2. Direct Instruction

3. Modern Red Schoolhouse

4. Success for All

Since much already has been written about Siegfried Engelmann's Direct Instruction in this book, the writer will focus on Robert Slavin's "Success for All." The following excerpts from "Ready, READ!" by Nicholas Lemann, which appeared in the November 1998 issue of *The Atlantic Monthly*, give the reader a clear picture of how a direct instruction/mastery learning classroom marketed as "Success for All" functions:

> Success for All, Accelerated Schools, and the School Development Program, all designed by university professors—the first two have each been adopted by more than a thousand schools across the country, and the third by 700....
>
> ...By the end of this school year the Success for All organization will have a budget of $30 million and will operate in more than 1,100 schools all over the country. Among its customers are the Edison Project which is private [publicly funded charter school]; the state of New Jersey; and the cities of Houston, Memphis, and Miami....
>
> ...The prevailing criticism of Success for All is that it is designed to produce higher scores on a couple of tests chosen by Slavin, for which the control-group schools don't train their students; the gains it produces, according to critics, are substantially limited to the first year of the program.
>
> Success for All tells schools precisely what to teach and how to teach it—to the point of scripting, nearly minute by minute, every teacher's activity in every classroom every day of the year.
>
> ...Teachers must use a series of catch phrases and hand signals developed by Success for All.... At every level Slavin's programs greatly reduce teacher autonomy, through control of the curriculum.... People usually describe Success for All with terms like "prescriptive," "highly structured," and "teacher-proof"; Slavin likes to use the word "relentless." One education researcher I spoke with called it "Taylorism in the classroom," after Frederick Winslow Taylor, the early twentieth-century efficiency expert who routinized every detail of factory work....
>
> A few minutes in a Success for All classroom conveys the Parris Island feeling of the program better than any general description could. It is first grade—the pivotal year. The students read the first page of the story loudly, in unison. The teacher says, "Okay, next page. Finger in place, ready, read!" After a few minutes of this students have finished the story. Not missing a beat, the teacher says, "Close your books, please. Let's get ready for vocabulary." She moves to a posted handwritten sheet of words and points to herself. "My turn. Maze, haze, hazy, lazy. Your turn." She points to the class. The students shout out the words in unison: "Maze! Haze! Hazy! Lazy!"
>
> Then the teacher announces that the students are going to do "red words"—Success for All lingo for words that students can't decode from their phonemic components. "Okay, do your first word," she says. The students call out together, "Only! O (clap) N(clap) L(clap) Y(clap). Only!" After they've done the red words, the teacher says, "Now let's go to our meaningful sentences." The students read from a sheet loudly and in unison the definitions of three words and then three sentences, each into their cooperative learning

groups to write three sentences of their own, using each of the words. "If you work right, you'll earn work points for your work team! You clear?" Twenty voices call out, "Yes!"

Last year, when I was there, the school was phasing in uniforms.

[Ed. Note: Brown shirts?]

In a Letter to the Editor printed in the *Athens* (Georgia) *Daily News/Banner Herald* of January 18, 1999, Priscilla Carroll, former elementary school teacher, responded to a letter to the editor from Professor Carl Glickman of the University of Georgia, author of books on school reform, which dealt with changes in local school board responsibilities as a result of the adoption of block scheduling, one of the reform components resulting from Clarke County (Athens) School District being designated as a "Next Generation School" district. Mrs. Carroll responded that

> Some of the Next Generation School Project power structure changes state:
> a) Local boards will not manage, operate nor make decisions for running schools.
> b) Local boards will be advised by created community teams or collaboratives.
> c) Local boards must let go... presiding over student or employee grievance hearing.
> d) Grievance hearings will be delegated to "duly appointed mediation and arbitration panels."
> e) Local boards won't decide field trip requests, student transfers, challenges to library books, school calendar decisions, bus routing problems and athletic program concerns.
> f) Local boards must "move away from... hiring, firing and promoting employees."
> g) Local boards "will be freed of constraints and obligations that impede their ability to address the global issues which are more worthy of their time."
> h) Local boards must "give up the role of keeper of the purse" (won't control education money).
> i) The local "appointed" school superintendents (LSS), are to be trained and controlled by the state.

[Ed. Note: When Georgia's radical "break the mold" Next Generation School Project proposal was not accepted as one of the original New American School Development Corporation (NASDC) design teams, corporate and non-profit "partnership" funding was generated to accomplish the Project within the state. Mrs. Carroll's comments were paraphrased from the "Next Generation School Project" manual. Professor Luvern Cunningham would be pleased to see how his recommendations to get rid of school boards are being carried out across the country.]

"School to Work Gets Poor Grade in Study" by Mark Shrug and Richard Western of the University of Wisconsin at Milwaukee, professors who conducted a study for the Wisconsin Policy Research Institute, ap-

peared in the January 19, 1999 issue of *The Milwaukee Journal Sentinel.*
Excerpts follow:

> More than $195 million, almost all federal money, was spent from 1991 to
> 1998 in Wisconsin on programs under the label School-to-Work, but it has
> had almost no demonstrable impact on the state's schools or economy.... It
> has had no identifiable impact on the academic learning of K–12 students
> in Wisconsin and it has involved too few students in its core, work-based
> learning activities to register a significant aggregate impact on Wisconsin's
> workforce.
>
> Many school districts, including MPS (Milwaukee), generally have
> dropped the term. And attention, some suggest, has shifted to different
> policies, particularly proficiency testing and a looming statewide test that
> all students will have to pass to graduate.
>
> The study says one of the few tangible accomplishments of School to
> Work was that 347 students had graduated from apprenticeship programs
> statewide. But, the study says, that was equal to 1/10,000th of the state
> workforce in 1996.... The study says there was no "reliable evidence" that
> School-to-Work had accomplished any of its major goals.
>
> Grants were used ($30 million) for teacher training, apprenticeships,
> job shadowing and connections between schools and individual businesses.
>
> James H. Miller, president of the policy research institute, said, "As with
> most bureaucratic educational reforms, School-to-Work sounds terrific, but
> in reality it is all style with absolutely no substance."

[Ed. Note: Let's hope that the old adage "You can lead a horse to water,
but can't make him drink" will play itself out in regard to school-to-work.

However, leadership in the homeschool community seems to have embraced at least a portion of the school-to-work proposition. While apprenticeship has been promoted to homeschoolers as an alternative to "electives"
by some homeschool organizations and leaders (Bill Gothard, Doug Phillips
et al.), now the apprenticeship concept is being embraced at the post-high
school level by none other than Michael Farris of Home School Legal Defense
Association. In his announcement about the forthcoming establishment of the
Patrick Henry College in Purcellville, Virginia, Farris stated in an interview
with Andrea Billups of *The Washington Times* (May 17, 1999):

> "I wanted to break out of the educational box like I've helped to do with
> K-through-12 education."...
>
> ...Initially, the school will offer a lone undergraduate major in govern-
> ment, featuring an apprenticeship program designed to give students practical
> experience in public policy and service....
>
> As a part of their curriculum, Patrick Henry students will work on
> faculty-supervised research and writing projects for congressional offices,
> state legislators, federal agencies, think tanks and advocacy groups.
>
> "We are combining a traditional liberal arts model with a white-collar
> version of vocational training," said the school's provost and academic dean,
> Brad Jacob, a lawyer and professor who served as the CEO of the Christian
> Legal Society. "It all comes from the ivory tower concerns, where students
> learn theory but don't know beans about how to work in the workplace....
> We believe in mentoring and disciplining."

This should come as no surprise in light of Mr. Farris's previous public enthusiasm for apprenticeships expressed at his organization's National Home Educator's Leadership Conference in Orlando, Florida in 1995. During a "debate" with William Spady, Farris lauded the Swiss educational system as a "very successful national model."[59] The Swiss system is committed to apprenticeships, with 75% of its students never going to high school or college but into apprenticeships after the eighth grade. Their K–8 system prepares students to enter apprenticeships, certainly limiting career employment choices and movement.

The bottom line is this: "apprenticeship" *is* "workforce training." Skipping over traditional academic high school and college subjects, or watering down a liberal arts college education to accommodate its "application" to a workplace setting, constitutes the "deliberate dumbing down" of homeschoolers. Could school-to-work at the college level be the "camel's nose under the tent" for STW at K–12 level for homeschoolers?]

THE JANUARY 1999 ISSUE OF *COMMUNITY UPDATE* PUBLISHED BY THE U.S. Department of Education provided an update on activities being held by the Religion and Education Partnership (first established in 1995). The following excerpts describe the involvement of "the church in the state" and "the state in the church"— something heretofore not spelled out in government publications. The U.S. Department of Education announced that

> Religious leaders, educators, members of the higher education community, and students came together at Spalding University in Louisville, Kentucky on December 11, for the fourth Religion and Education Summit supported by the Partnership for Family Involvement in Education....
>
> More than 500 participants gathered in Louisville from Kentucky, Ohio, Indiana, and Tennessee to hear U.S. Secretary of Education Richard W. Riley participate in a town hall discussion on three important topics: family involvement in education, school safety, and preparing young people for college and careers. Programs that support these initiatives were presented in small group gatherings where participants could speak to practitioners from Tampa, Florida; Birmingham, Alabama; and Louisville, Kentucky. A materials fair featuring model programs, community services, information about the public schools in the area, and materials produced by the Partnership for Family Involvement in Education was open throughout the summit.
>
> The goal of the Religion and Education Summit was to bring together leadership representing faith communities and elementary, secondary, and higher education to discuss issues of concern to the community and to build partnerships to bring about changes needed for the benefit of all children. Previous summits were held in Lawrence, Massachusetts; Wilmington, Delaware; and St. Petersburg, Florida. Partnerships formed at these summits have continued to work together to improve education and strengthen family and community involvement in local schools. To obtain information on how to plan and hold a Religion and Education Summit, email partner@ed.gov.

[Ed. Note: The writer suggests that parents involved in such partnerships re-read "Little Red Riding Hood" and retrace Little Red Riding Hood's steps to Grandma's house in the woods. Particular attention should be given to

Red Riding Hood's finding The Big Bad Wolf in Grandma's bed wearing Grandma's night cap!]

SPEAKING OF "LITTLE RED RIDING HOOD," THE JANUARY 24, 1999 ISSUE of *The Gwinnett Daily Post* of Lawrenceville, Georgia contained an article by staff writer Laura Ingram entitled "Clusters Promote Community Growth." This article describes a second-step phase of a "systems change" effort outlined in a joint publication from the U.S. Department of Education and the U.S. Department of Health and Human Services, *Together We Can*. The article, which illustrates the shift from representative (elected) governance to regional (unelected) governance with its "Big Bad Wolf" use of partnerships to accomplish its goals, is included in its entirety below:

> Unique groups called Community Cluster Care Teams were born last April, comprised of 12 Gwinnett communities, and have taken their first steps toward uniting sections of the county into neighborhoods.
>
> "The entire community needs to get involved," said Suzanne Brighton, coordinator for the teams. "We need to look at the environment we're raising our children in. Everybody has a responsibility to create a healthy environment where children can grow."
>
> Parents, teachers, senior citizens, clergy, business people, school officials and social service workers first met this new creation April 15 at a conference called "Together We Can," sponsored by the Gwinnett Coalition for Health and Human Services and BellSouth.
>
> The 200 participants split into 12 groups based on high school clusters and came up with particular ways to improve each cluster/community. But they did not stop at just a sketch.
>
> The 12 teams continued meeting throughout the year, drawing more community members and resources into their group, and creating strategic plans to accomplish their goals and shrink scary statistics that show children finding their way into drugs, pregnancy and violence.
>
> This fall, their imperative to heal and unite their neighborhoods took shape as tree plantings, youth dialogues, new youth basketball teams, grandparent adoptions and bilingual services.
>
> Metro United Way's vice president of community investments, Geralyn Sheehan, calls the teams a pilot program for the entire nation, teaching residents throughout America how to reconnect with others to build a healthier community.

[Ed. Note: To further illustrate what the U.S. Department of Education and U.S. Department of Health and Human Services book *Together We Can: A Guide for Crafting a Profamily System of Education and Human Services* (Contract #RP912060001: PrismDAE, a division of DAE Corporation: Chevy Chase, Maryland, 1993) outlined as a blueprint to follow for "local systems change," the writer will offer some excerpts from this publication. Jointly signed by Secretary of Education Richard W. Riley and Secretary of Health and Human Services Donna E. Shalala, the foreword to this book reads:

> This book was developed jointly... to help communities improve coordination of education, health and human services for at-risk children and families. *Together We Can: A Guide for Crafting a Profamily System of Education and*

Human Services reflects the work and experience of a study group of researchers and front-line administrators and practitioners working with promising programs that link education and human services. *Together We Can* leads the reader through a five-stage collaborative process with milestones and landmines portrayed through vignettes and case studies describing the personal experiences of the study group members.

Together We Can is a practical guide that can assist local communites in the difficult process of creating a more responsive education and human service delivery system. The guidebook emphasizes the effective delivery of supports for families, a crucial step toward assuring the future success of America's children. Recognizing that the current system of programs serving children is fragmented, confusing and inefficient, the guidebook advocates a radical change in the service delivery system. It encourages a holistic approach in treating the problems of children and families; easy access to comprehensive services; early detection of problems and preventive health care services; and flexibility for education, health and human services.

We believe this guide is a practical tool for the many communities that are working to create more comprehensive, family-focused service delivery systems for children and their families.

[Ed. Note: This is pure, unadulterated "communitarianism," which is defined as: "communitarian—a member or advocate of a communistic community" (p. 288) and "ism"—a doctrine, theory, system" (p. 474) in *Webster's New World Dictionary of the American Language* (William Colliers—World Publishing Co., Inc.: New York, 1976.), the system we have been told is "dead." The reader may want to refer to the 1997 entry dealing with the National Commission on Civic Renewal and its proposals for a fuller understanding of the implications of *Together We Can.*]

In the preface to *Together We Can* we find the following:

Across America, people are recognizing that all of the institutions and agencies whose mission is to nurture and strengthen children and families must collaborate....

The U.S. Department of Education and the U.S. Department of Health and Human Services charged the School-Linked Integrated Services Study Group with capturing the experiences of collaborative endeavors across the country and creating a guide for integrating services....

Basic to the guide is the concept of *systems change* [emphasis in original]. We define systems change as a revision of the ways that people and institutions think, behave, and use their resources.... The Study Group believes *collaborative strategies* [emphasis in original] are the key to systems change.... Collaborative strategies, in which partners share a vision, establish common goals, and agree to use their power to achieve them are necessary; commitment of resources and willingness to alter existing policies are a vital part of such strategies.

Most importantly, the children and families who participate in our education and human service systems are essential to its reinvention. They are indispensable partners with educators, human service professionals, business leaders, civic and religious leaders, leaders of community-based organizations, and other citizens in creating the profamily system that the guide envisions.

The School-Linked Integrated Services Study Group consisted of representatives of: "Institute for Educational Leadership, Washington, D.C.; Florida International University Human Resource Service Professional Development Center, Miami, Florida; Walbridge Elementary School, St. Louis, Missouri; National Center on Adult Literacy, Philadelphia, Pennsylvania; Center for Collaboration for Children of California State University, Fullerton, California; Prince Georges County Public Schools, Suitland, Maryland; San Diego City Schools, San Diego, California; Public School 146M, New York City; Savannah-Chatham County Youth Futures Authority, Savannah, Georgia [Anna Casey grant recipient which promoted school-based clinics]; School of Education at Stanford University, Stanford, California; Early Childhood and Family Education division of North Central Regional Educational Laboratory, Oak Brook, Illinois; Danforth Foundation, St. Louis, Missouri; Cities in Schools, Charlotte, North Carolina; Community Education Leadership Project of the Institute for Educational Leadership, Washington, D.C.; Better Boys Foundation, Chicago, Illinois; National Center for Services Integration of Mathtech, Inc., Falls Church, Virginia; Community Schools of Rochester City School District, Rochester, New York; Clinic Services/Family Counseling Center of the Massachusetts Society for Prevention of Cruelty to Children, Boston, Massachusetts; Lansing School District, Lansing, Michigan; Parent Action, Baltimore, Maryland; New Jersey Department of Human Services, Trenton, New Jersey; School of the Future of El Centro Familiar Office of the Family Service Center, Houston, Texas; New York State Department of Education, Brooklyn, New York; Walbridge Caring Communities Program, St. Louis, Missouri; and a practicing psychologist."

In the interest of fully informing the reader of just exactly what these projects are about and hope to accomplish, the writer is including highlights of a two-part appendix which are so totally invasive and frightening in their implications that they should relegate George Orwell's *1984* to the "light reading" stacks!

Appendix A
Checklist 1
Process for Crafting a Profamily System of Education and Human Services

Stage One: Getting Together
- Has a small group decided to act?
- Do the players meet the following criteria for membership in the collaborative:
    ___clout;
    ___commitment; and
    ___diversity?
- Are the right people involved...
- Have partners reflected on their work and celebrated their accomplishments?

Stage Two: Building Trust and Ownership
- Has the collaborative conducted a comprehensive community assessment that...

___produces a profile of child and family well-being in the community; ...
- Have partners defined a shared vision and goals for changing education and human services?...

Stage Three: Developing a Strategic Plan
- Has the collaborative narrowed its focus to a specific neighborhood for launching a service delivery prototype?
- Has the collaborative conducted a neighborhood analysis...
- Has the collaborative defined the target outcomes?...
- Is a mechanism in place for using program-level intelligence to suggest system-level changes?...

Stage Four: Taking Action
- Is the collaborative evaluating progress by:
    ___using process evaluation techniques; and
    ___measuring outcomes?
- Have partners reflected on their work and celebrated their accomplishments?

Stage Five: Going to Scale
- Has the collaborative built a formal governance structure?...
- Is the collaborative promoting change in the federal government's role in delivering services for children and families?
- Is the collaborative continuing to reflect and celebrate as it "climbs the mountain" of systems change?

Checklist 2
Indicators of Systems Change

Are agency agreements in place?...

Do program-level information and intelligence trigger policy-level changes across multiple systems?...

Have partners developed shared information systems?
- Is there ready access to each other's records? ...
- Have agencies replaced separate in-house forms to gather the same kind of information with a common form used by all members or other organizations to establish program eligibility? Assess case management needs? Develop case plans?

Have partner agencies incorporated the vision and values of the collaborative at their administrative and staff levels?
- Have partners altered their hiring criteria, job descriptions, and preservice or inservice training to conform to a vision of comprehensive, accessible, culturally appropriate, family-centered, and outcome-oriented services? ...
- Are outcome goals clearly established?
- Has the collaborative used its data collection capacity to document how well children and families are faring in their communities and how well agencies and child-serving institutions are meeting their mandates? ...

- Are outcomes measurable? Do they specify what degree of change is expected to occur in the lives of children and families during what period of time?
- Is shared accountability a part of outcomes that reflect education, human service, and community goals and objectives?

Has the collaborative devised a financing strategy to ensure long-term funding?

Has the collaborative gained legitimacy in the community as a key vehicle for addressing and resolving community issues regarding children and families?

- Are the collaborative's positions on community issues supported by commitments from public and private service providers, the business community, and the church- and neighborhood-based organizations whose members are often most directly affected by collaborative decisionmaking?

The above activities are advocated and coordinated through a center which was established with taxpayers' money and is described in the following explanation of its activities:

National Center for Services Integration

The National Center for Services Integration (NCSI) was established in late 1991 with funds from the U.S. Department of Health and Human Services and private foundations to improve life outcomes for children and families through the creative integration of education, health and human services. The center itself is a collaboration of six organizations: Mathtech, Inc.; the Child and Family Policy Center; National Center for Children in Poverty; National Governors' Association, Policy Studies Associates; and the Yale Bush Center. It also receives guidance from distinguished advisors knowledgeable about the issues and institutions concerned with service integration.

The primary purpose of NCSI is to stimulate, guide, and actively support service integration efforts throughout the entire country. To accomplish its mission, NCSI has undertaken a variety of activities through its Information Clearinghouse on Service Integration and a Technical Assistance Network.

The Clearinghouse, which is operated by the National Center on Children in Poverty at Columbia University, collects and disseminates information and materials on service integration issues and related topics. They have developed a computer directory of service integration programs, a separate directory of organizations, and an extensive research library collection that can provide information and support to community-based programs. Individuals, organizations, and localities can access any of the Clearinghouse services....

The Technical Assistance Network, which is operated by Charles Bruner of the Child and Family Policy Center [Kids Count, ed.] and Mathtech [government contractor for the evaluation of sex education programs, ed.], brings together leading service integration planners, practitioners, administrators, and experts to exchange ideas and information, to develop written resource materials for communities and practitioners and to convene working groups composed of persons in the forefront of particular issues to develop strategies for successfully resolving some of the challenges facing communities and governmental entities involved in service integration efforts.

[Ed. Note: If the reader has any questions about why school-based clinics, school-to-work, community education programs, year-round schools, one-stop training centers, and all of the other "locally conceived" programs have come into their communities with such force and fundamental support, the above federally funded and conceived plans should answer them. *Together We Can* brings together national and international plans for socializing all services to our citizenry. One example is the International Year of the Child proposals which originated in 1979 and are hereby funded, formatted, and fulfilled in *Together We Can*'s "how-to" instruction manual. These are the processes necessary to create the "perfect human resource"—the global worker. President Nixon vetoed the child and family legislation encompassing all of the above activities (the *Humphrey-Hawkins Child and Family Services Act*) in the mid–1970s, calling it the most socialistic legislation he had ever seen. *The New York Times* carried an article by Edward B. Fiske entitled "Early Schooling Is Now the Rage" in its April 13, 1986 issue which explained:

> Mr. Nixon not only vetoed the bill (Humphrey-Hawkins] but also fired off a scathing message to Congress, proclaiming that he would have no part in the "Sovietizing" of American Society. "Good public policy requires that we enhance rather than diminish both parental authority and parental involvement with children."

This comprehensive program links almost every entry in this book, from cradle to grave. None of this could have been accomplished without the use of behaviorist methods and change agent tactics carefully documented in this book. Americans would not have willingly turned over decision making in these areas unless manipulated into doing so; no one ever voted to conduct our government in this manner. *The Montgomery County Blueprint* of 1946—fifty-plus years ago—spelled out this approach. In the *Blueprint* Paul Mort pointed out that it takes fifty years to accomplish "systems change." He was right on target.]

[ddd]

"**STATE OF EDUCATION CRITICIZED—NONPROFIT ORGANIZATION HIRED AT** Former Governor's Urging Pinpoints Weaknesses Within Ohio's Academic System" is published in the March 24, 1999 issue of the *Akron* [Ohio] *Beacon Journal*. Excerpts from this article follow:

> COLUMBUS—A national organization, hired to look at Ohio's education system, issued a report card yesterday and the results were not good.
> The critical assessment, presented to the state's educational policy leaders, was surprising because the nonprofit organization, Achieve Inc., was hired at the urging of former Gov. George Voinovich, who helped devise the funding system.
> The organization is made up of executives from some of the nation's largest corporations—IBM, Boeing and Procter & Gamble—and governors from North Carolina, Michigan, Nevada and Wisconsin. [The National Governor's Association set up this organization to "manage" reform, ed.]...
> Among the findings:

- Ohio's academic goals are not clearly defined. Accountability standards are ineffective because there are no rewards or punishments associated with failure or success. The emphasis is on holding kids, not adults, accountable.
- If the state is serious about improving academics and holding schools accountable, it must provide districts with the resources and tools—that is, more money—to do the job.
- The state should provide assistance in districts that are performing poorly, close schools if no improvements are made and re-open them with new leaders....
- Fred Blosser, superintendent of Canton schools, agreed with Achieve's assessment.

"The state's academic goals are not defined," he said. While Canton has adopted its own goals—graduating every child with the ability to think and reason, to have concern for others and to have a desire to continue to learn—the state's only concern is getting children to a minimum level of knowledge, he said.

"All I am hearing is 'proficiency, proficiency, proficiency—and attendance.' There is more to educating a child than meeting minimum proficiency," Blosser said.

[Ed. Note: Note that the emphasis is placed on only attaining a "minimum" level of proficiency. If anyone still has any doubts by now what the full implementation of education reform will mean for the children, teachers and schools of America, read the article again carefully. Reformer (change agent) David Hornbeck's original recommendations for rewarding or penalizing schools, depending on the results of individual children's proficiency test scores, is now being widely implemented across America. Children will pass or fail based upon these test scores. Teachers will be rewarded or penalized based on the test scores of children in their classrooms. Schools which do not function up to par will be shut down or "managed." Under increasing pressure, teachers will be devoting massive amounts of time to "teach to the test." And the teaching method of choice will be direct instruction/mastery learning which drills the students like robots until they can spout out the correct answer without thinking.

One might wonder how Ohio students and schools fared with their first run-through of these new tests. *The Akron Beacon Journal*, in a follow-up article "State Ranking of Schools Sure to Rankle: Many Area Districts Are Scoring Very Poorly in Statewide Evaluation (April 6, 1999) reported:

About 1.8 million report cards went into the mail yesterday to the parents of each of Ohio's public school children....

While showing that students in general are doing better, especially on the state's ninth-grade proficiency tests, math continues to be a weak spot.

And many schools in the area are falling short of academic goals, according to the reports.

This year, only 15 of Ohio's 611 school districts achieved the highest rating of "effective." Not one of the 62 school districts in Summit, Stark, Portage, Medina or Wayne counties was in that elite group....

Akron Superintendent Brian Williams—whose district met only one of the 18 criteria—prepared the parents of his district for bad news by sending a letter home last week.]

THE CONFERENCE BOARD (ONE OF THE MOST INFLUENTIAL INTERNATIONAL groups promoting the world management/control system and workforce training in the schools) advertised its "1999 Strategic Learning Conference: A Tool Kit to Power Business Performance" to be held March 29–30, 1999 at the Marriott World Trade Center, New York City. On the front of the brochure at the very bottom it states, "The collective wisdom of executives worldwide." In regard to the subject of the conference, it states:

> The Strategic Learning Model was developed by Professor William Pietersen at Columbia Business School. At this conference, he and other leading-edge thinkers and corporate practitioners will walk you through a framework—from beginning to end—that will demonstrate how to create systematic learning initiatives that can result in better business strategy and bottom-line results.

"Dry stuff, that," you say. Not at all. Under the "Making or Breaking Strategy through Culture" one reads: "Culture is the key to success. This fundamental dimension of your strategic development can determine success or failure. Find out how to ensure you create a strong culture of success." Carlos Rivero, Ph.D., director of research, Delta Consulting, and Robert Bontempo, professor of executive education at Columbia Business School, are the presenters. The last two highlighted comments in this particular section state in distinctly Skinnerian terms the following:

What Gets Measured Gets Done

and

What Gets Rewarded Gets Done Repeatedly

[Ed. Note: This entry demonstrates how every facet of our lives will, in the future, be based on Professor B.F. Skinner's scientific and manipulative philosophy extensively discussed in this book.]

U.S. SECRETARY OF EDUCATION RICHARD RILEY DELIVERED THE SIXTH STATE of American Education speech early in 1999 in Long Beach, California. For the reader who has arrived at this point in this book, Riley's recommendations will come as no surprise. The reader could probably have written Riley's speech, since it covers everything painstakingly and consistently initiated over time using the Hegelian Dialectic, semantic deception and gradualism. Riley's proposals—including the "communitarian" *Together We Can* "systems change" in the January, 1999 entry—could have been lifted out of the 1946 *Montgomery County Blueprint* discussed in this book.

In his February 16 speech Riley called for: Community Partnerships, charter schools, schools open year-round/morning-to-night, "Schools [of the future] serving as centers of communities"; focus on reading [referring to the "landmark study by the Academy of Science"]; "Democracy of Excellence"; early childhood initiatives [Parents as Teachers, etc.]; school uniforms; violence-prevention programs; "sustained progress" [North Carolina, Maryland, Texas and Kentucky as "successes"—those states which have been struggling to keep their heads above water during the past twenty-five years, ed.]; teacher "quality"; "option schools"; "magnet schools"; school-to-work "opportunities"; and more choices. Obviously, the interpretation of this information depends on one's definition of Riley's words! Astoundingly, based on no supportive evidence, Riley said:

> We know a good deal more about how to turn around low-performing schools: from giving teachers more time for training and collaboration; to redesigning the curriculum; to removing a principal who doesn't provide leadership; to issuing school report cards that measure real achievement over time; to enforcing effective discipline policies.

[ddd]

Only a dumbed-down, brainwashed, conditioned citizenry could willingly accept what is being offered Americans under the guise of "remaining competitive in an increasingly global economy," and relinquishing our sovereignty in the name of "global understanding and peace." The following quotations from Edward Hunter, the man who coined the term "brainwashing" and author of *Brainwashing: The Men Who Defied It*,[60] speak to what we as Americans can still do to reverse the process:

> Surely there can no longer be a trace of doubt that brainwashing is sheer evil. The fight against it is the culminating issue of all time, in which every human being is protagonist. There can be neither escape nor neutrality where such responsibilities lie.
>
> There can be neither front nor rear, for the great lesson that came from the brainwashing chambers was that while every man has a cracking point, every man's cracking point can be immensely strengthened. That is the job of home, school, and church. The mother, teacher, and pastor are in the front lines in this ideological conflict, and every word they say to their sons and daughters is important to the struggle, for character more than anything else will determine the outcome.
>
> Truth is the most important serum and integrity the most devastating weapon that can be used against the totalitarian concept.... Nothing should be allowed to interfere with the task of getting those facts across to the people who need and can use them.
>
> Only an informed people can shoulder their responsibility effectively. When free men know both what they are fighting against and what they are fighting to preserve and enhance, they are unbeatable, stronger than any strategy.
>
> What is absolutely essential is that the full facts be given to all our people, for mind warfare is total war. This approach can make our struggle for the mind the crusade it should be. Never since man received reason beyond the instincts of animal kind has there been a more important issue. In the fight to give man forever the opportunity to develop, every possible weapon must be utilized on the field of battle, which is everywhere. There is no "behind the lines" any longer.

Endnotes:

1 The foregoing information was taken from Appendix A–1 of the SCANS publication *What Work Requires of Schools* (U.S. Department of Labor: Washington, D.C., 1991).

2 For those interested in seeing how Skinner's animal training works with teachers, Madeline Hunter's "Instructional Theory into Practice: ITIP" is a collection of Hunter's instructional materials which she developed and taught throughout her career. This material may be purchased from: Association for Supervision and Curriculum Development, 1703 North Beauregard St., Alexandria, VA 22311–1714, Ph: 1-800-933-2723.

3 World Education for All Forum Secretariat is located at: United Nations Educational, Scientific, and Cultural Organization, 7 Place de Fonteroy, 75352 Paris O75P, France.

4 *Polytechnical Education: A Step* by Robert H. Beck available by calling 1-800-637-7651.

5 Glavin, Matthew J., *Reach for the Stars: A Proposal for Education Reform in Georgia.* (Georgia Public Policy Foundation: Atlanta, GA, 1991)

6 In 1997 Michigan Governor John Engler funded and supported a report prepared by an appointed commission which recommended that Michigan's schools—as an example to the nation—be divested of public control and turned into "corporations." These "corporations" would give stock to families with children in the communities in which the schools were located and to employees of the schools—the employees would receive larger shares than the parent/citizen stockholders—and to other "interested entities" which could include business and corporate interests. Because of the structure of "corporations," the question was and could be asked concerning the possibility of investment by foreign, or certainly interstate, interests. This certainly raises the spectre of "corporate academies" being created out of our public schools.

7 Those interested in obtaining a copy of the Carnegie Corporation's report *A Nation Prepared: Teachers for the 21st Century*, published in the May 21, 1986 issue of *Education Week*, can do so by writing to: *Education Week*, Suite 775, 1255 23rd Street, N.W., Washington, D.C. 20003.

8 The Russian Deputy Minister of Education Elena Lenskaya was also a presenter at Willard Daggett's International Center for Leadership in Education, Inc., Second Annual Model Schools Conference in Atlanta, Georgia in the summer of 1994. She made a return appearance in the summer of 1998 at the Sixth Annual Model Schools Conference.

9 The USCEFA's definition for "basic learning needs," as put forth in their literature, is "the essential learning tools—such as literacy, oral expression, numeracy, problem-solving and basic learning content—required by all people to develop their full capacities to live and work in dignity, to participate fully in development, to improve the quality of their lives, to make informed decisions."

10 Education Development Center, Inc. in Newton, Massachusetts was the developer of the controversial social studies program *Man: A Course of Study* or *M:ACOS*, based on the work of B.F. Skinner and Jerome Bruner.

11 See 1991 New American Schools Development Corporation entry.

12 British Columbia Teachers' Federation, 100–550 West 6th Avenue, Vancouver, BC V5Z 4P2.

13 For more information regarding Community Learning Information Network, write CLIN, 1776 K St., N.W., Fifth Floor, Washington, D.C. 20006, Office: 202–857–2330.

14 The writer considers this publication a "Must Read"! It may be ordered by sending $12.00 to: Billy Lyon, Route #1, Box 37, Edgewood, TX 75117.

15 The reader may wish to order Ms. Rogers's first article, "In Loco Parentis: The Brave New Family in Missouri," as well as a complete copy of the excerpted article from: *Chronicles*, 934 N. Main Street, Rockford, IL 61103.

16 From personal collection of this writer, provided by a fellow researcher.

17 See previous reference to this conference in the 1981 entry of this book dealing with comments by Malcolm Davis.

18 See 1993 entry for M. Donald Thomas's "A Plan for Action," which contains proposals from Dr. Don Thomas concerning $50 fines for parents who refuse to volunteer.

19 For further information on this subject, the NAEP, and violation of privacy, go to www.deliberatedumbingdown.com for "When Johnny Takes the Test: How Your Child Is Identified and Tracked to the National Data Bank—and Beyond" by Melanie Fields, Anita Hoge and Sarah Leslie published by *The Christian Conscience*.

20 Florida and Texas were specifically selected because of their use in the data collection project for migratory children and their families.
21 Videotape from private collection.
22 For more information about the NTL Institute services, or its approach to change, contact: Russell Bong, Marketing Manager, NTL Institute for Applied Behavioral Science, 1240 North Pitt St., Suite 100, Alexandria, VA 22314–1403. Phone: 1–800–777–5227; FAX: 703–684–1256.
23 See entry for 1983 quote from book by Eugene Maxwell Boyce, *The Coming Revolution in Education and the New Theory of Schooling*.
24 "The Truth Behind Outcome-Based Education" was produced and distributed by Compass and can be ordered by calling: 1–800–977–2177.
25 William E. Brock has also served as a former U.S. Secretary of Labor and as chairman of the Labor Secretary's Commission on Achieving Necessary Skills (SCANS), appointed by then-Secretary of Labor Elizabeth Dole.
26 National Center for Education Statistics. *Financial Accounting: Classifications and Standard Terminology for Local and State School Systems*. (U.S. Government Printing Office: Washington, D.C., 1973) DHEW Publication No. (OE) 73–11800.
27 The Commission on Skills of the American Workforce produced this 1990 report. The commission included Marc Tucker, who wrote the now-famous letter to Hillary Clinton following the election of Bill Clinton as President. It should be noted that Hillary Clinton was appointed to the commission by William Bennett, then-secretary of education. (See 1986 entry dealing with this story.)
28 Please see the Internet version for Appendix XI "When Is Assessment Really Assessment?" and index references for Sticht and Oettinger.
29 *America 2000* eventually became *Goals 2000*.
30 The report from the Second Annual Conference on Model Schools was written by Cynthia Weatherly and published in the Jan. 1995 issue of *The Christian Conscience* (Vol. 1, No. 1).
31 "Voluntary," for the time being.
32 The words "forgotten half" are taken from the 1988 W.T. Grant Co.'s landmark report entitled *The Forgotten Half: Pathways to Success for America's Youth and Young Families*. (See 1988 entry for more about this report.)
33 Susan Kovalik formed her ITI company in 1982 and has now moved to the state of Washington. If the reader is interested in accessing Kovalik's materials, her Internet site address is: http://www.kovalik.com. This writer in no way endorses the work of Susan Kovalik, but is merely making this information available to provide the reader with original research.
34 Challengers for Insight's address is: 520 N. State Road 135, Suite M–125, Greenwood, IN 46142.
35 *Fire in the Minds of Men: Origins of the Revolutionary Faith* (Basic Books, Inc.: New York, 1980) was written by James H. Billington, librarian of the U.S. Congress in which he wrote in chapter 4, "The Occult Origins of Organization," the following: "The story of the secret societies can never be fully reconstructed, but it has been badly neglected—even avoided, one suspects—because the evidence that is available repeatedly leads us into territory equally uncongenial to modern historians in the East and the West.... In what follows I shall attempt to show that modern revolutionary tradition as it came to be internationalized under Napoleon and the Restoration grew out of occult Freemasonry; that early organizational ideas originated more from Pythagorean mysticism than from practical experience; and that the real innovators were not so much political activists as literary intellectuals, on whom German romantic thought in general—and Baviarian Illuminism in particular—exerted great influence...." (p. 87) It is helpful for serious education researchers who have uncovered evidence similar to that of Billington's to have an historian of his caliber confirming the influence of these occultic societies on the stability of society in general, and education in particular, over the ages.
36 For more background on the history of the "common ground movement" in education reform, see "Separation of School and State: Why We Cannot Sign," by Lynn and Sarah Leslie, published in the December 1997 issue of *The Christian Conscience*, which can be accessed at deliberatedumbingdown.com.
37 Educational Testing Service was created in 1946 and was launched by an initial endowment of $750,000 from the Carnegie Corporation.
38 For a summary report of the *Former Pasco Teacher Survey*, send a self-addressed stamped

envelope to: TFAE, 2527 W. Kennewick Avenue, #350, Kennewick, Washington 99336.

39 Ms. Kosiec can be reached by writing: Barbara McFarlin-Kosiec, 635 N. Fisher, Kennewick, Washington 99336. She is also available for speaking engagements/interviews.

40 Order *National Issues in Education* by calling 1–800–766–1156.

41 A note at the bottom of the article states: "The article was approved by the ACSI Executive Board."

42 If the reader is interested in reading this article in its entirety, please write: Association of Christian Schools International, P.O. Box 35097, Colorado Springs, Colorado 80935–3509, or call 1–800–367–0798.

43 Los Horcones's e-mail address is: walden@imparcial.comm.mx.

44 John Naisbitt is the author of *Megatrends* and *Megatrends 2000*, required reading for former Speaker of the House Newt Gingrich's seminars.

45 This is wording found in PPBS/MBO material.

46 Esther Dyson was also a speaker and active participant in the Progress and Freedom Foundation's meeting in Atlanta in 1994, "Cyberspace and the American Dream."

47 Refer to the 1984 National Council for Educational Research entry for the history of the *Reading Excellence Act*.

48 Private conversation with teacher who wishes to remain anonymous due to the political heat generated by these reading discussions.

49 Those interested in the activities of the Frank Porter Graham Child Development Center can access its website at: http://www.fpg.unc.edu.

50 George Soros is chairman of the Soros Fund Management. Born in Budapest, Hungary, Soros received his B.S. degree from the London School of Economics in 1952. Married for the second time to Susan Weber Soros, they have raised five children, two born of his first wife. Maintaining homes in Manhattan, London, and Southampton and Bedford, New York, he describes himself as a "financial, philanthropic, and philosophical speculator." Investment funds bearing his name have earned him a fortune estimated at $2.5 billion. He has now become more well known for giving money away than for amassing it, and has established a global network of philanthropic organizations. In the early 1980s he used his wealth to foster political and philosophical freedom in Eastern Europe. To overcome censorship in his native Hungary, Soros distributed photocopiers throughout the country. After building a record of worldwide giving which tops over $350 million annually, Soros has turned his focus on the United States, sponsoring controversial projects dealing with social programs—including drug policy reform and poverty (*Vanity Fair*, November, 1997). The August 14, 1998 issue of *USA Today* carried an article entitled "Soros Stirs Ruble Debate" which states: "But few people knowledgeable of financial markets—even those outside financial circles who dislike Soros for his donations to assisted suicide and the legalization of marijuana—are prepared to accuse him of a conspiracy to cause a Russian panic."

51 Refer to the 1993 entry dealing with H.R. 6.

52 Ms. Fessler can be reached at: 7530 Ross Road, New Carlisle, OH 45344, 937–845–8428, diana@fessler.com or http://www.fessler.com.

53 Formerly known as the *Drug Free Schools Act*.

54 National Center for Educational Statistics within the Office of Educational Research and Improvement of the U.S. Department of Education produced these handbooks for use by state and local education agencies in collecting data on all aspects of school- and community-related activities, arranged in detailed collection codes.

55 These handbooks are a central part of the Planning, Programming, Budgeting and Management System (PPBS) extensively documented in this book.

56 "Early Warning Family Response," the government's "Action Plan to Deal with Violence," which illustrates the oppressive hand of government at work, can be obtained by calling: 1–800–4ED–PUBS (1–800–433–7827) or by e-mail at edpuborders@aspersys.com.

57 National School Conference Institute (NSCI), P.O. Box 37527, Phoenix, AZ 85069–7527, Toll free: 888–399–8745, http://www.nscinet.com.

58 For more information on this project, contact L. Allen Phelps, Center on Education and Work: 608–263–3696 (Ph.) or 608–262–3063 (Fax) or aphelps@soemadison.wisc.edu.

59 For more information about Michael Farris and HSLDA, visit deliberatedumbingdown.com.

60 Edward Hunter. *Brainwashing: The Men Who Defied It* (Vanguard Press, Inc.: New York, New York, 1956), chapter 11, "A Matter of Integrity."

– Notes –

CONSOLIDATION

©'83 PETT   KAPPAN